The Government and Politics
of the Middle East
and North Africa

FOURTH EDITION

The Government and Politics of the Middle East and North Africa

edited by

David E. Long
Bernard Reich

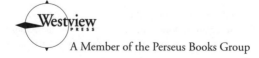

Westview
PRESS

A Member of the Perseus Books Group

All rights reserved. Printed in the United States of America. No part of this publication may be reproduced or transmitted in any form or by any means, electronic or mechanical, including photocopy, recording, or any information storage and retrieval system, without permission in writing from the publisher.

Copyright © 2002 by Westview Press, a Member of the Perseus Books Group

Westview Press books are available at special discounts for bulk purchases in the United States by corporations, institutions, and other organizations. For more information, please contact the Special Markets Department at the Perseus Books Group, 11 Cambridge Center, Cambridge MA 02142, or call (617) 252-5298.

Published in 2002 in the United States of America by Westview Press, 5500 Central Avenue, Boulder, Colorado 80301–2877, and in the United Kingdom by Westview Press, 12 Hid's Copse Road, Cumnor Hill, Oxford OX2 9JJ

Find us on the World Wide Web at www.westviewpress.com

A cataloging-in-publication data record for this book is available from the Library of Congress.

ISBN 0-8133-3972-3 (HC) 0-8133-3899-9 (Pbk.)
The paper used in this publication meets the requirements of the American National Standard for Permanence of Paper for Printed Library Materials Z39.48–1984.

10   9   8   7   6   5   4   3   2   1

Contents

List of Tables

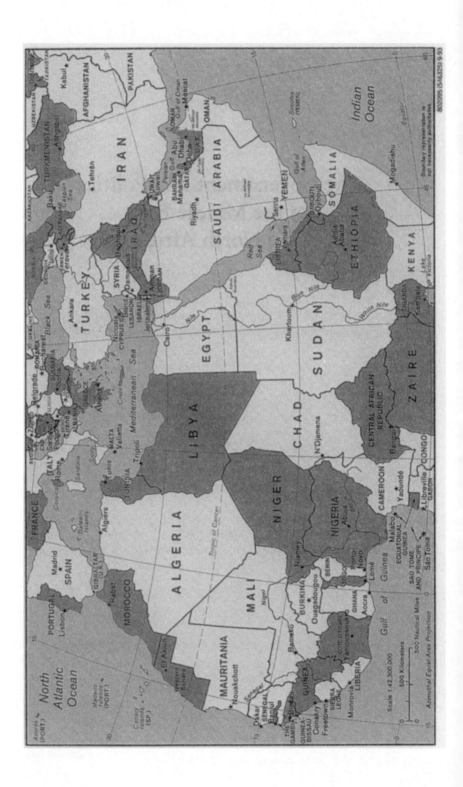

Preface

This fourth edition of *The Government and Politics of the Middle East and North Africa* not only represents an effort to update the earlier editions but also seeks to introduce to the reader the challenges facing the countries of the region in the twenty-first century. Substantial political and social changes have occurred since the last edition in 1995—including a succession of new leaders, important alterations in regional alignments, and efforts to achieve peace and to stabilize the region. There has also been significant technological change, in the electronic, telecommunications, and computer sectors, with far-reaching impact on the politics and economics of the region. Our authors were asked to consider all these factors, as well as to take into account the latest themes and methods of the disciplines on which this book is based.

In this edition, as in previous versions, we have gathered leading scholars on the respective countries and their politics. In most instances the authors of the previous edition revise their own work; in several cases we have added new authors to the team.

In recent decades considerable attention has been devoted to the Middle East and North Africa by people in all walks of life, from the layman to the student to the policymaker. Books and articles by serious scholars exist in large number and cover many aspects of the region, especially its history, politics, and economics. Despite this increased attention and interest, the present volume is still (as we noted in the preface to the previous edition) the only introductory work on the politics of the states of the region that is both comprehensive and up-to-date. This was the idea that generated the first edition, which appeared in 1980, and it inspired this fourth edition. Therefore, we sought the assistance of a diverse group of Middle East specialists with both policy and academic experience to produce a current, comprehensive, and general book that focuses on the politics (and especially the political dynamics) of the Middle East and North Africa. This book is also unique in that it includes North Africa in the area it defines as the Middle East.

Multiple authorship has the additional advantage of providing greater depth of expertise on the individual countries and political systems than can be provided by any single author. All the authors have followed a common outline, but each chapter differs according to the peculiarities of the particular political system being examined and the style of the particular author or authors.

In any work of this type it is impossible to capture all the details of continuing changes in the governmental systems and the political process and dynamics of the states and the region as they remain constantly in flux. However, the method employed since the initial edition permits the scholars to deal with eternal verities and broad concepts rather than relying on daily current events. The latter events provided the examples that are readily explained and analyzed within the political framework provided in the several chapters.

With a multiauthored book of this type, there are of course scores of people to whom we are indebted. As we do not want to leave anyone out inadvertently, we would like to acknowledge them all collectively. And most of all, we wish to acknowledge that without the assistance and understanding of our wives, Barbara and Madelyn, this volume would not have been possible.

David E. Long
Bernard Reich

1

Introduction

David E. Long
Bernard Reich

The Middle East as it enters the twenty-first century is a far different place than the one familiar to many students and observers of an earlier generation. The last half of the twentieth century saw monumental and dramatic change in a region beset by wars and revolutions, military coups and turmoil. But the region is also one of great accomplishment. There have been numerous changes of government and regime throughout the region and in many instances there has been a generational change in leadership. In some cases we have seen long-term leaders—King Hussein of Jordan, King Hassan of Morocco, and President Hafez al-Asad of Syria—replaced by members of a younger generation. Other long-term leaders remain with us, such as Muammar Qaddafi of Libya and Saddam Hussein of Iraq.

Developments within the region have gone in several directions since our last edition. The Israeli-Palestinian negotiations that were moving ahead in a limited positive way as we published the last edition are increasingly marked by an Israeli and Palestinian retreat from negotiations to tension and clashes (some would even call it "war"). The diminished centrality of the oil-rich Gulf region has come full circle as the world oil market has finally recovered from a twenty-year glut.

A decade after the implosion of the Soviet Union, Russia continues to play a significant, though diminished, role in the area, primarily with Iran and Iraq. China has become more dependent on the oil of the Middle East, and the European powers have sought to remain engaged in the region's international relations at a level they had not done in decades. The United States continues as a dominant external power with substantial interests and involvement in the region.

Despite these changes, however, the Middle East of the twenty-first century retains many of the attributes that the region possessed throughout most of the

previous century. Most, if not all, of its component states have acquired the characteristics that have increasingly become commonplace worldwide. The Middle East
and North Africa continue to be a region of great strategic significance owing to
their geographic location and their possession of most of the world's identified oil
reserves. But it is a region that has also been affected by generational changes in
leadership, by the impact of globalization, and by the impact of the Internet. Increasingly developments elsewhere readily crossed national boundaries even as
each state retained its individual identity.

The term *Middle East* was coined at the turn of the twentieth century to refer
to the Gulf area lying between the Near East and the Far East. Since then, *Middle
East* has come to incorporate the older term, *Near East,* and *North Africa* as well.
Politics has led to the inclusion and exclusion of various countries over time.
Egypt, Israel, the Arab states of the Fertile Crescent (and the Palestinians), and the
Arabian Peninsula constitute the core area. The remainder of North Africa, particularly the Magrib (Tunisia, Algeria, and Morocco), is sometimes considered sepa-
rately. Because of their close Arab ties, however, we have chosen to include those
countries in this volume. Turkey lies in both Europe and Asia, but it is an integral
part of the Middle East. For example, it has been a member of North Atlantic
Treaty Organization (NATO) for five decades but also has close ties with neighboring Arab states and shares an ethnic Kurdish problem with Iraq, Iran, and Syria.
Similarly, Iran is sometimes grouped with Afghanistan and Pakistan as an extension of South Asia, but its location in the Gulf area and its identity as a major Middle East oil producer dictate its inclusion in the Middle East.

In the recent past, especially since the implosion of the Soviet Union, the region has often been extended to include the states of central Asia and the Caspian
region. We have chosen the more traditional approach, in part to ensure continuity with previous volumes but also because historical and political factors suggest
the logic of our approach. We realize that our choice of countries is somewhat arbitrary, but we feel that it best represents the broadest group of countries exhibit-
ing sufficient commonality to constitute a single region.

For centuries the Middle East has fascinated scholars and observers and has
been the focal point of great-power attention. The region's strategic significance
and the variety and importance of its political, social, and cultural heritage have
generated this concern. Through the centuries the Middle East has had intense religious meaning for the peoples of the Western world. Judaism, Christianity, and
Islam all originated in the area, and the most sacred holy places of these three
monotheistic faiths are located there. In the latter half of the twentieth century
occasional wars and superpower rivalry added to the region's strategic dimension.
The overall importance of the region, however, is broader; that importance is tied
to the region's location and to its primary resource—oil.

Situated at the hub of Europe, Asia, and Africa, the Middle East is a crossroads
and a bridge. Historically it linked the trade routes connecting Europe with Asia

and Africa. Today its location makes the Middle East a critical link in the communications network joining Western and Eastern Europe with Eastern Africa, the Indian subcontinent, Southeast Asia, the Far East, and Australasia. The Middle East's military importance is a direct result of its location; the region has long fascinated the powers interested in greater control of that portion of the world and the adjacent areas.

Oil is the major resource of the Middle East. It is abundant, of unusually high quality, and exported in huge quantities. It is an essential energy source for the industrialized states and for many of the developing states. The export and sale of Middle Eastern oil, at high prices, has generated a surplus of "petro-dollars" in many of the oil-producing states, has contributed to area-wide economic growth, and has provided the leading producers with increased potential in the international financial community. The importance of Middle Eastern oil and the oil-producing countries' economic potential have combined to increase the concern shown for the Middle East by outside commercial and strategic-political interests.

This interest in the Middle East seems unlikely to abate. The ongoing efforts to achieve a settlement of the Arab-Israeli conflict continue to involve the major powers and numerous others in the Middle East. Furthermore, it seems likely that the dependence of both the industrializing and the industrialized world on Middle Eastern oil (and, increasingly, natural gas) will persist for the foreseeable future.

The states of the Middle East have a variety of political systems, each one reflecting its state's historical background, colonial experience (or lack of it), social and economic conditions, religions, geographical setting, climate, and population pressures. There is no single category that includes all these systems, which run the gamut of political structures and dynamics. Personalized one-man authoritarian regimes have coexisted in the region with Marxist regimes, monarchies, religiously oriented systems, and democratic regimes. However, the Middle Eastern governments perform the various functions of the standard political system, albeit with varying degrees of ability or success and in numerous and diverse ways. These differences in background and in existing conditions provide for variations in political life, structure, and style.

The very real differences that exist among the states of the Middle East should not obscure their similarities, such as the heritage of Islam, the presence of foreign influences, the concentration of leadership in the urban upper and middle classes, and the rise of new elites of technocrats and military officers. Throughout the Middle East, political life in the past few decades has been characterized by the shift from traditional to modern activity. The traditional family-based elites are either declining in power or have already been replaced in many of the political units in the area. A new salaried middle class is emerging as the most active political, social, and economic force, and leadership is increasingly passing into its hands. This group is made up of government and private-sector technocrats, university students, and middle-grade military officers. In many of the states the military forms the core of this new politically conscious middle class that is striving to modernize the state. Members of the military have assumed a modernizing role as a result of their training, skills, and motivation. The great majority of the population—the peasants and the workers—are only now beginning to enter the realm of politics.

Pan-Arabism and Islamism (commonly referred to as Islamic fundamentalism and/or political Islam) are integral parts of contemporary activity in the Middle East. In a sense they are complementary movements that have rekindled an Arab and Muslim identity among the diverse peoples of the area, which has affected both the foreign and the domestic policies of the Middle Eastern states. In the post–World War II era, for instance, pan-Arabism helped to determine the Arab response to Israel. It has also led to attempts at federation and economic cooperation among several of the Arab states. The Islamic heritage and revival have acted simultaneously as a revolutionary and a conservative force. In such countries as Saudi Arabia this force has helped to shape the response to modernization and Westernization by advocating an Islamic way of life in the face of change. At the same time, Islam has been a divisive force as differences between and among the various sects and traditions surface and intrude into politics.

This book has been planned in keeping with the general view of the Middle East just described. We provide not only a comprehensive discussion of the politics of the individual states, within the context of each system's unique characteristics, but also a view of the basic factors affecting politics so that comparisons across national boundaries can be made. The book reflects our view that certain commonalities exist in Middle Eastern political systems that can provide a basis for the comparison of their politics.

Understanding the politics of the Middle East requires more than an examination of the institutions of government. It is particularly important that the student of the Middle East understand the broader context in which the game of politics is played. Accordingly, this book examines the political systems in terms of their approach to the problems confronting them. The machinery of government is examined not only in terms of what it is but also in terms of why it is the way it is; why and how it works; and what it has done, or attempted to do, in confronting the state's problems.

Consideration of the legislative, executive, and judicial machinery of the state is thus complemented by study of the elements that affect the translation of goals and policy into action. To convey the full flavor of each individual system and its operation, we have examined its major components, including the historical setting, available resources, economic and social structure, and ideologies, as well as the more traditional topics: political parties and/or other instruments of mobilization, political elites, and leadership. Although these elements operate in each of the systems, they do so with differing results. Thus the factors are considered differently in each of the studies in this book. This, in itself, provides a useful means of evaluating systems and can be illuminating.

Obviously, a detailed investigation of all the influences on the politics of any country would require more space than can be allotted in one volume. Therefore, the scholar-authors have isolated the most important elements for examination and discussion. This system concept is reflected in the structure of the studies. Each country is examined in terms of its historical background, political environment, political structure, political dynamics, and foreign policy.

Historical Background

The Middle Eastern sense of history is strong, and comprehension of the political systems of the region is almost impossible without an understanding of the historical background of each of the states. Tangible evidence of ancient systems can be found not only in archaeological ruins and historical accounts and artifacts but also in functioning political systems. The origins of contemporary problems often can be traced to the ancient civilizations of the region. History in the Middle East tends to be of such importance that there is little attempt to divorce contemporary developments from historical events and little sense of time to suggest that they should be separated. Thus the origins of Judaism, Christianity, and Islam provide a working context for twentieth- and twenty-first-century politics. Specific historic events, such as the Jewish exodus from Egypt and the subsequent establishment of a Jewish state, the Ottoman Turkish conquests, and the European colonization and domination, continue to affect the political systems of the Middle East in profound ways.

The style of politics often emulates or responds to ancient methods and conflicts. In many of the countries, centuries of history have helped to determine the roles of the elites and the masses and the present-day interaction between them. The form and style of decisionmaking are also the result of historical development as well as of the modern demands placed upon the system. Nowhere is this more apparent than in the continued importance of the kinship group in the decision-making process. Ancient rivalries and boundary disputes also still affect the relations among the states of the region. In the Middle East the past tends to provide the parameters for the systems that operate today.

Political Environment

Despite history's crucial role in the development of the modern Middle East, it alone cannot completely explain modern politics. Geography, demography, climate, and economics have all contributed to the emergence of the Middle East as we know it. The individual political environment of each state provides further insight into the unique forces operating in it. Environment can help to explain the diversity of politics that exists in the face of shared historical background. The geopolitical uniqueness of the region and of its component states is essential in any explanation of political behavior. Geography partially determines the wealth or poverty of a nation and indicates its potential for development. Geography can also point to a nation's strategic value and to the problems it may face. Such problems, and the means and the methods used to deal with them, provide much of the substance of modern politics and policy.

Demography, too, must be considered. Wars, famines, and religious and national upheaval have led to large-scale immigration and migrations throughout the region. These migrations have left many of the states with substantial ethnic minorities as well as chronic problems of overpopulation or underpopulation. Regional, national, and religious minorities abound. In most areas these minorities have been relegated to second-class status, but in some they have become the ruling elite. In either case, the social structure that determines the weight and merit of minority groups as well as the problems that result from over- or underpopulation can tell us much about the nature of politics.

Economics also plays a key role in determining the political environment of the Middle East. All the states are undergoing economic and social development, and the governments are very much involved in the process by which development will be achieved. Here, too, however, there is diversity, for the states of the Middle East range from extremely wealthy to extremely poor; oil is a prime factor in explaining this disparity, but other conditions are involved as well. The population size, education, the human-resource endowment, and the state's success in modernization all affect the context in which policy is made. The different states have adopted different methods to meet the challenge presented by economic and social development. These methods reflect their own economic needs, resources, and capabilities.

Political Structure

The description and analysis of the formal governmental institutions, their powers, and their decisionmaking processes traditionally have been the initial focus in the study of a state's politics. The Middle East is characterized by a wide range of diverse political institutions—some of which have no match anywhere in the world.

The systems of the Middle East can be examined in terms of the presence, or absence, of such political institutions as constitutions, political parties, judicial systems, and modern bureaucracies. Examination of these institutions helps to provide insight into the decisionmaking process and to identify both the decisionmakers themselves and the locus of power within the system. This insight, in turn, yields a framework for making comparisons between and among the states of the region. It should also provide the ability to assess the differences and similarities among the systems and to understand the nature, extent, and direction of political development and modernization.

Political Dynamics

Identifying the institutions of politics and the constitutional frameworks, if any, by which they are supposed to work renders only a partial picture of a political system. Political theories, ideas, and ideologies all play a role—sometimes central—to how a system works. In any state there is a dichotomy between theory and practice. To appreciate the methods by which a state actually operates and the interaction among its institutions, one must assess its political dynamics. Essentially this involves an attempt to view the government in action. To the Western student (especially the American), who resides in a country where political systems operate relatively openly and in an orderly and systematic fashion, the methods of the Middle Eastern systems may seem unduly complicated and Byzantine. Those systems have their own dynamics conditioned by history and environment. To know only the institutions of government, without understanding the political dynamics involved, is to know only how the system ought to work—not how it does work. To understand Middle Eastern politics, one must keep in mind the particular viewpoint of the Middle East when one examines its political dynamics.

Foreign Policy

To help the reader understand the interaction of the history, environment, structure, and dynamics in the states, each study includes a review of foreign policy. Examination of the totality of international relationships for each state is impossible, but the main directions of that policy are examined to develop a picture both of the concept of politics at work in each system and of its methods of operation. These overviews of foreign policy provide insight into the decisionmaking process and into the views of those who craft the decisions and policies of the state. Foreign policy thus acts as something of a summary of state concerns, capabilities, and actions, as well as of the political processes within the system.

Ultimately, this multifaceted examination of the more than twenty independent states of the Middle East and North Africa reveals a good deal not only about the politics of the individual states but also about the region as a whole and about developing states in general. Because of their diversity and the wide range of patterns and approaches they represent, the states of the Middle East provide useful case studies of politics. By studying the basic factors affecting politics, the organization of the political system, and its dynamics and foreign policy, we will come to understand more about the complex and important part of the world known as the *Middle East.*

Finally, because this is the first edition to come out in the new millennium, we would be remiss if we did not briefly address the future. At the close of the twentieth century, several "revolutions" were under way that could have profound influence on the government and politics of the region in the twenty-first century. Foremost is the technological revolution, which has manifested itself in tremendous strides in communications, transportation, information, and military technology. Closely related to this is the globalization of the world economy, with major implications for domestic and regional economic developments throughout the region. It is still far too early to tell how all this will play out in the years to come, but one event, the terrorist attacks in New York and Washington on September 11, 2001, has underscored how interrelated local, regional, and global politics have become. It is possible that the worldwide trauma fueled by the instant, global media coverage of the attacks will abate and life will go back to "business as usual." After all, most domestic and regional relationships in the Middle East and North Africa are based on long-standing political and economic interests. On the other hand, some changes are probably inevitable. One cause for concern in the years to come is whether and to what degree the attacks will raise the threshold of terrorist violence by subnational and transnational groups. Only time will tell how this will affect the political systems we have examined in this work.

Bibliography

Two articles have attempted to capture the elusive confines of the Middle East: Roderic H. Davison, "Where Is the Middle East?" *Foreign Affairs* 38 (July 1960), pp. 665–675; and Nikki Keddie, "Is There a Middle East?" *International Journal of Middle East Studies* 4 (1973), pp. 255–271. For longer works, see Geoffrey Kemp and Robert E. Harkavy, *Strategic Geography and the Changing Middle East* (Washington, D.C.: Carnegie Endowment for International Peace/Brookings Institution Press, 1997); Peter Beaumont, Gerald Blake, and J. Malcolm Wagstaff, *The Middle East: A Geographical Study* (New York: John Wiley, 1976), and W. B. Fisher, *The Middle East: A Physical, Social, and Regional Geography,* 7th ed. (London: Methuen, 1978), which offer excellent and comprehensive overviews of the region's geography.

2

Republic of Turkey

George S. Harris

Historical Background

Modern Turkey differs from most of the nations that have emerged in the past century as independent states. It inherited a broad panoply of institutions and traditions from its Ottoman forebears. Although Turkey was only one of the countries that came into being in the lands of the former Ottoman Empire, it took over almost the entire ruling class of the multiethnic and multireligious Ottoman state.

A flair for bureaucratic organization distinguished the Ottomans since their earliest days in the late fourteenth and early fifteenth centuries, even though the empire suffered from periods of misrule and insurrection. Initially, the government apparatus was dominated by the armed forces. But once the era of conquest ended, the problems of administering the huge Ottoman territories demanded increased attention. In response, the civilian hierarchy expanded in prestige, size, and complexity. Thus, though the army always played an important role, the Ottoman Empire was far more than a praetorian state run by a dominant military caste.

To meet Europe's challenge, by the end of the eighteenth century the Ottomans had turned toward state-directed reform. The top leadership sought to galvanize the populace in ways that on occasion violated popular custom. It was an elitist approach, predicated on the notion that the rulers know best, an approach that has only recently begun to be challenged.

At the same time, the effort to keep the Ottoman state competitive triggered severe intra-elite conflict. On the one hand, secular modernizers, who were ascendant in the nineteenth century, saw adoption of European technology as the way to cope with intrusions of the West. On the other hand, traditionalists looked toward return to religious purity and rejection of Western materialism as the recipe for staving off Europe.

By the time the empire collapsed after World War II, however, the religious class was in full retreat. The need to embrace European technology was generally accepted, but dispute centered on whether wholesale cultural borrowings from the West were essential to complement technology or whether science and hardware from Europe could be implanted without disturbing traditional patterns. This debate continued into the republican era.

Organization by religious community proved a cost–effective method of rule in the centuries before national consciousness was awakened among the subject peoples. But the persistence of communal identity, which the Ottoman way fostered, provided a fertile ground for separatist movements once nationalism's seeds had been planted. These ethnic separatists threatened to dismember the empire from within while the European powers were pressing from without.

Turkish nationalism did not emerge full-blown until the Ottoman Empire disintegrated. But as early as the Young Turk period, protagonists of Turkism were in evidence. After the 1908 revolution, in reaction to the financial controls imposed by European creditors, the Turkists turned to economic nationalism. Yet although Enver Pasha, one of Turkey's triumvirs in World War I, urged the assembling of the world's Turks in a single state, neither he nor his fellow Young Turks ever abandoned their hopes of maintaining the empire, especially its Arab and Islamic elements.

The political structure erected by the Young Turks formed the base for the organization of modern Turkey. The Ottoman parliament that had been restored in 1908 continued as the Grand National Assembly in Ankara, and the Committee of Union and Progress served as the model for Mustafa Kemal Ataturk's own political vehicle, the Republican People's Party. Likewise, some of the patterns of political controversy carried over into the republic.

The First Republic

Ataturk is rightly credited with having established Turkey out of the ruins of the Ottoman state. Yet he built on local "defense of rights" organizations in Anatolia and Thrace that the Committee of Union and Progress had set up to resist the European effort to carve up the Turkish heartland after World War I. Ataturk served as a critical rallying point against the invading Greeks, who landed in Izmir in May 1919. Under his charismatic leadership, Turkey regained its independence, expelled the Greek army, and convinced the Western powers to end their occupation.

Ataturk then began extensive modernization of Turkish society. One of his major contributions was to recognize the folly of trying to retain Arab dominions. But he insisted on keeping a Kurdish-inhabited segment of the Anatolian core area, which he considered essential for modern Turkey. To boost pride in being Turkish, he sought to translate attachment to religion into patriotic fervor for the new state.

His approach was evolutionary in significant respects. The reform movement was centered on the Ottoman elite, which he expanded through education and co-option. Social mores were adjusted by fiat at times. But in the matter of women's dress, for example, he sought change by persuasion rather than compulsion.

The new Turkish state was a parliamentary republic in form, though an autocracy in practice. The basic slogan of the republic was "Sovereignty Belongs to the People"—a sovereignty formally exercised by a single-house parliament. Ataturk, however, who chafed under opposition, used his Republic People's Party to dominate the political scene. Backed by a handpicked parliamentary majority, he closed rival political organizations, starting with supporters of the caliph in the 1923 elections, the Progressive Republican Party in 1925, and even his own tame "opposition" Free Party when it threatened to get out of hand in 1930. Thereafter, he attempted to fuse his single party with the government. This effort at a corporate state, however, led to the atrophy of the party and the clear dominance of the government organs.

The concentration of power in the hands of one man could not long survive Ataturk's death in 1938. In fact, his successor, Ismet Inonu, gave notice almost immediately on taking office that he would liberalize the regime. This development, however, had to await the end of World War II.

Four prominent defectors from the Republican People's Party formed the Democrat Party in 1946. Headed by Celal Bayar, Ataturk's last prime minister, this party scored creditably in the July 1946 general elections, although the date of these contests was deliberately advanced so that the Democrats would not have time to organize in every province. In 1950, the party won handily, capitalizing on widespread discontent generated by years of Republican People's Party rule. Inonu thereupon gracefully surrendered power.

The smoothness of the transition concealed deep flaws in Turkey's democratic practice. Lacking a tradition of tolerance of dissent, the Democrats soon began to retaliate against the opposition. In 1953, they sequestered the assets of the Republican People's Party, which they claimed had been founded with state funds, and in 1954, the Nation Party was shut down for exploiting religion. In 1957, as opposition mounted, election coalitions were banned to head off a combination of the Republican People's Party and the small Freedom Party, which together would have outpolled the Democrats.

These acts contributed to a climate of oppression. Clashing socioeconomic interests of the emerging entrepreneurs and large landholders, backing the Democrats, on the one hand, and the bureaucrats, favoring the Republican People's Party, on the other, added special bitterness to the political contest. The persistent efforts of the Democrat Party to use foreign aid for partisan purposes and to enlist those upset by Ataturkist zeal in religious and social reform also increased the fervor of the combat. Finally, at the end of the 1950s, the Democrat Party appeared to be moving to quash the opposition, in an attempt to return to a one-party system.

The Second Republic

Reacting against these political abuses, the middle levels of the officer corps led a revolt in 1960. But the officers did not stay in power long. What proved to be the dominant faction within the junta viewed its role as merely to put the political process "back on the tracks" and to return power to responsible politicians. The presence of former general Ismet Inonu (who had historic ties to Ataturk's revolution) as head of the opposition during the decade before the military revolt offered the officers an acceptable alternative to staying in power.

Thus, after dissolving the Democrat Party and holding a referendum ratifying extensive constitutional checks and balances (including creation of an upper house, a Senate, and a Constitutional Court) intended to prevent the excesses of the earlier concentration of power, the junta allowed elections. But because many voters backed parties that campaigned more or less openly as continuations of the former Democrat Party, Inonu's Republican People's Party received merely a plurality in the lower house. With the specter of the military in the background, Inonu formed a series of weak and unstable coalitions that nonetheless served to reassure the officers that there would be no retaliation for their coup.

After Inonu's last cabinet was brought down during the budget debate in 1965, the Turkish political spectrum shifted to the right. The Justice Party, whose name reflected demands for fairer treatment of the Democrat Party politicians, won a majority in elections later that year. Suleyman Demirel, representing the moderate wing of the party, took over as prime minister. His administration granted amnesty to the Democrat Party members sentenced after the military takeover. Although Demirel made few economic departures, a rapidly rising tide of remittances from workers in Europe assured unaccustomed prosperity. As a result, the Justice Party scored a second victory at the polls in 1969, although its proportion of the popular vote declined.

Demirel was challenged, however, by growing extremism. Government indecisiveness in regard to the mounting student and labor disorder led the senior military commanders in March 1971 to issue an extraordinary public demand for more effective rule. Otherwise, they warned, the armed forces would use their "legal rights and seize power directly."

Demirel resigned on the spot, and parliament voted into power a series of cabinets of technocrats under nonpartisan prime ministers. These governments imposed martial law, banned the Turkish Labor Party (Turkey's only legal Marxist party), and made widespread arrests to suppress terrorism. Intellectuals, journalists, and labor leaders, some charged with the most nebulous offenses, filled the jails.

Constitutional forms were preserved during the ensuing two years of nonparty governments. Moreover, controls were relaxed somewhat during the election campaign in 1973. That vote produced a standoff among the major parties, as the Justice Party's right-of-center constituency fragmented. A religious party (the National Salvation Party) wooed Islamic activists; a group of conservative nationalists also left the Justice Party. These splinters ended up in the swing position between the Justice Party and the Republican People's Party, the latter led by Bulent Ecevit, who had replaced the aging Ismet Inonu in a final showdown.

The next seven years were difficult ones of coalition government, with Ecevit and Demirel alternating as prime minister. Each in turn relied on support from the National Salvation party, which extracted concessions in policy and personnel placement as its price. Ecevit's first coalition sent Turkish troops into Cyprus in July 1974, following a Greek-inspired putsch against President Makarios. But when Ecevit resigned hoping to force early elections to cash in on the popularity of sending troops, he was stymied by parliamentary arithmetic. After half a year of caretaker government, Demirel took over.

Both major parties increased their share of the vote in the 1977 elections at the expense of the minor factions. But Turkey still could not escape the uncertainties of coalition government. Bitter personal rivalry between Ecevit and Demirel contributed to political paralysis, as nearly equal alignments faced each other in parliament.

Although in January 1980 a Justice Party minority government was able to take bold economic departures to satisfy the International Monetary Fund (IMF) and shore up Turkey's external creditworthiness, the parliamentarians remained deadlocked. They failed to elect a president, despite voting that extended through summer 1980. The opposition ignored repeated warnings from the ranking generals to cooperate with the government in granting additional authority to the military to impose order. Instead, the National Salvation Party demonstrated open disrespect for the constitutional provisions against exploiting religion, Kurdish dissidence began to mount in the east, and the government's existence was challenged by motions of no-confidence against cabinet ministers.

The Third Republic

The generals cut through the deepening political impasse on September 12, 1980, ousting the civilian government, shutting down parliament, and rounding up hordes of suspected terrorists. On the economic front, the generals initially co-opted Demirel's financial team, led by Turgut Ozal, who had served as undersecretary for state planning. Although General Kenan Evren, who was chief of staff and headed the new military junta, promised eventual elections, he proclaimed the need for extensive political changes to ensure more effective government before party politics could resume.

It would be three years before a new constitution, an election law, and a political parties act could be put in place and elections held. During the first two years of this period, party propaganda was prohibited, the old parties were abolished, and institutions such as the universities and unions were fundamentally restructured. The generals then banned all officials of the previously existing parties from political participation for ten years, before permitting new parties to be established. General Evren, whose seven-year term as president was ratified in the constitutional referendum, used his power to limit the parties eligible to run to three: the conservative Nationalist Democracy Party, headed by a retired general; the free-enterprise Motherland Party, under Ozal, who had broken with the junta; and the left-of-center Populist Party, led by a trusted functionary.

In a clear rebuff to the generals who had called for its defeat, the Motherland Party won a solid majority in parliament in the November 1983 elections. Ozal used his parliamentary majority to enhance economic liberalization. In the political realm, he challenged President Evren by opening nationwide municipal elections to parties banned from the general elections only months before. Ozal's resounding victory in these contests stilled complaints that the Motherland Party was not truly representative of popular desires. Thereafter Ozal moved slowly but steadily away from the restrictions imposed during the years of military rule.

Freer political choice in the municipal elections undermined the legitimacy of the Nationalist Democracy Party and the Populist Party. The former soon dissolved, far overshadowed by the True Path Party, which was widely regarded as a front for Demirel. When the Populists ran well behind the left-of-center Social Democracy Party of Ismet Inonu's son, Erdal, the two parties combined in 1985 to form the Social Democrat Populist Party, in effect re-creating the banned Republican People's Party. But this unity on the left was shattered almost immediately by the emergence of the splinter Democratic Left Party under Bulent Ecevit's wife, Rahsan Ecevit, who ceded her place to him after his ban from politics was rescinded in 1987.

The rise of major parties not represented in parliament fed agitation for early national elections. Confident of his electoral support, Ozal advanced these contests to 1987. Thanks to the skewed proportional representation system, he again gained a parliamentary majority, but this time with only 36 percent of the popular vote. Erdal Inonu's party and Demirel's True Path Party also garnered a significant share of the popular vote, presaging a continuing challenge to Ozal's domination of the center-right constituency.

In the ensuing four-year period, the country faced surging Kurdish violence in the southeast, renewed religious agitation, and difficult inflationary pressures. Moreover, the Motherland Party was subjected to continuing charges that it did not represent a majority of the population, particularly after it scored poorly in municipal elections held throughout Turkey. The party was also accused of corruption and nepotism, which were associated with Ozal's policies and were reflected in such issues as the controversy over the bid of Semra Ozal, Ozal's wife, to lead the Istanbul party organization in February 1991.

Recognizing the downward spiral in his party's popularity, in 1989 Prime Minister Ozal used his parliamentary majority to secure election as president of Turkey. Although he resigned from the Motherland Party, as called for by the constitution, he remained a power behind the scenes in both the party and the government. In April 1991, on Ozal's initiative, restrictions were eased on the use of the Kurdish language and prohibitions on the right to espouse class or religious ideologies were dropped from the penal code. That contributed to an atmosphere in which small parties sprang up overnight to exploit the new freedoms.

The Motherland Party hoped to benefit from its apparent upsurge in popularity attendant on the Gulf War and advanced the elections to October 1991. These contests, however, ended the party's tenure in power. It ran a close second behind Demirel's True Path and just ahead of Erdal Inonu's Social Democrat Populist Party. The narrow margin separating the first three parties meant that none of them had a parliamentary majority. Turkey again faced coalition politics in which personal rivalries would play the major role.

In this situation, Demirel reached across the philosophical divide to bring the Social Democrat Populist party into the cabinet rather than seek Ozal's support, despite the general consonance of their views on many issues. But a diminishing socialist slant in the approach of Erdal Inonu's party provided the base for a relatively harmonious coalition arrangement.

Yet Demirel's coalition faced almost immediate challenges from domestic insurrection and foreign pressures. The aftermath of the Gulf War inflamed Turkey's own deepening Kurdish violence. Forceful government retaliation, including thrusts into northern Iraq against Kurdish Labor Party (PKK) bases, led the Kurdish wing of the Social Democrat Populist Party to split off, narrowing the coalition's parliamentary majority. And the ending of bans on the pre-1980 parties, which allowed the revival of the traditional Ataturkist Republic People's Party in 1992, also promoted defections from Inonu's party. Assassinations of professors and journalists laid at the door of religious extremists strained the political fabric as well.

Against this background, the death of President Ozal in April 1993 posed a test of constitutional procedure. With no hint of military pressure, Demirel was elected president; he then named newly selected True Path Party leader Tansu Ciller as Turkey's first woman prime minister; she formed a government again based on coalition with the Social Democrat Populist Party. But Ciller, though she started well in dealing with the Kurdish issue, for example, soon disappointed many of her middle-class supporters amid accusations of corruption. By the time of the

December 1995 elections, the True Path Party had lost enough luster that it ran slightly behind the Welfare Party under Necmettin Erbakan, which had emerged as the successor to the National Salvation Party of the 1970s. Welfare's appeal as untainted by corruption apparently overcame previous reluctance to support a religiously oriented party.

The plurality gained by the Welfare Party shocked the overwhelming secularist majority of civilian politicians and it was particularly distasteful to the leaders of the military establishment. Thus, as an expedient, in early 1996 Motherland Party leader Mesut Yilmaz overcame his strong personal animus toward Tansu Ciller to form a coalition government to share power backed by their two parties. This artificial alliance collapsed after only a few months when in April 1996 a parliamentary majority voted to investigate charges that Ciller, while prime minister, had manipulated government contracts for personal gain. Faced with court proceedings, Ciller in May 1996 pulled her party out of the coalition and the following month aligned it with Erbakan's Welfare Party to form a government that for the first time since the founding of the republic would have a prime minister (Erbakan) who headed an avowedly Islamist party, with Ciller as foreign minister and deputy prime minister. As part of the bargain, the Welfare Party, which had sponsored the charges against Ciller, agreed to drop them and allow her eventually to take her turn as prime minister again.

This political maneuver so enraged the ranking generals that at the end of February 1997 they, through the National Security Council, issued demands for an extensive political agenda to preserve secularist institutions, directly contradicting the policies espoused by the Welfare Party. That began a period in which the military appeared to play a much more active role in politics than during the Ozal years.

In this atmosphere, the Welfare Party decided to turn the prime ministership over to Ciller. But when the coalition resigned to make this change, President Demirel, instead of handing the mandate to Ciller as she and Erbakan had agreed, turned to Mesut Yilmaz again. With the clear approval of the military establishment, Yilmaz lured enough deputies away from the Welfare–True Path to form a left-of-center/right-of-center coalition in mid-1997.

One of the major preoccupations of the Yilmaz government was to press charges against the Welfare Party for acting against the principles of the secular republic. In January 1998, the Constitutional Court decided to ban the Welfare Party and exclude Necmettin Erbakan and six others from political activity for five years, a ruling that at his age of seventy threatened to end his chances of again becoming prime minister. When the court's ruling was published in February 1998, the Welfare parliamentarians joined the newly established Virtue Party, which had been set up in anticipation that Welfare would be closed. The new party was somewhat more circumspect in its anti-secularist approach and perforce had a different leadership, though it was commonly held that Erbakan continued to pull its strings from behind the scenes.

The Yilmaz government was seen as an expedient to take Turkey eventually to new elections, due by the end of 1999. But after Yilmaz was accused of corruption, his government lost a vote of confidence in November 1998. Intense parliamentary maneuvering followed, and in early January 1999 President Demirel gave the mandate to Bulent Ecevit, whose party had run fourth in the 1995 elections, to form a minority government to hold elections in April. During the three months of this government's life, it mounted a successful operation that caught PKK leader Abdullah Ocalan in February 1999, setting the stage for a radical diminution of the Kurdish insurgency in eastern Turkey. Having merely a caretaker status, Ecevit's government also eschewed the usual violations of budgetary discipline that parties in power routinely attempted to secure votes by initiating liberal public works programs on the eve of elections.

Bulent Ecevit's personal probity and the accomplishments of his short tenure in office boosted his party's popularity to the point where it gained a plurality of the popular vote. Close behind it ran the National Movement Party of long-time extreme nationalist Alparslan Turkes, who had died shortly before the election. Turkes's successor, Devlet Bahceli, proved to be a moderate bent on legitimizing his party's image as a mainline institution. To the surprise of many, indeed over the opposition of Bulent Ecevit's wife, a right/left coalition was formed including Bahceli's party and Mesut Yilmaz's Motherland Party and headed by Ecevit's Democratic Left Party. Its policies seemed largely set by Ecevit who, over the objections of the National Movement Party, blocked the death penalty from being carried out against Ocalan. This coalition also appeared more serious than its predecessors in enforcing budgetary discipline, thus lowering the inflation rate significantly and starting the difficult course toward meeting the criteria for inclusion in the European Union after that body had reaffirmed its acceptance of Turkey as a candidate for full membership.

These promising developments were set back by a serious economic shock to the economy in February 2001, brought on by banking scandals that threw some of Turkey's larger banks into bankruptcy. Overnight the currency depreciated by half, inflation rose, and credit dried up. To deal with this crisis, Ecevit called in World Bank Vice President Kemal Dervis to apply a stabilization program arranged with the IMF. That move helped arrest the decline, but did not restore confidence to a high level, as the cooperation of the politicians in applying economic stringency was not assured. So Turkey entered the new millenium facing serious questions.

Political Environment

Turkey is a land of pronounced physical contrasts. Extending 780,576 square kilometers (301,380 square miles), or over 40 percent larger than France, it ranges from sea level to the 5,165-meter (16,945-foot) peak of Mount Ararat, higher than any European mountain. The western part of the country, bordering on the Aegean and Marmara Seas, is a region of developed communication and easy access to the inland plateau. Well-watered farming areas produce cash crops, such as cotton, tobacco, and raisins. Eastern Turkey, abutting the Caucasian republics, Iran, and Iraq, is mountainous, cut by rivers into more or less isolated valleys. Its thinly covered lava terrain, which produces sparse vegetation except in the river corridors, and the relatively severe climate encourage pastoral pursuits in much of the area. The semiarid central Anatolian region supports dry farming as well as sheep and cattle raising. Extensive dams, however, are allowing irrigation in large areas of the southeast where formerly little could be grown. From the Mediterranean in the south and the Black Sea in the north, the land rises sharply to the rim of the Anatolian plateau. As for the narrow coastal strips, tea and hazelnuts are grown in the north, and citrus fruit, though increasingly displaced by early market vegetables, in the south.

The population of Turkey, about 65 million in 2000, is now increasing at a rate of somewhat under 2 percent a year. That represents a significant decline in recent decades, as urbanization has skyrocketed. Demographers project that Turkey's population might stabilize at about 100 million by the middle of the twenty-first century.

Population density generally declines from west to east and from the coast to the interior. Istanbul, the former Ottoman capital on the Bosporus, remains Turkey's largest city, with a rapidly growing metropolitan population of over 10 million. Ankara, the capital, located in west-central Anatolia, is a magnet second only to Istanbul in drawing power; it boasts some 5 million inhabitants. Izmir, on the Aegean coast, and Adana, on the Mediterranean (some 2.5 million each), complete the roster of major urban foci. The east, on the other hand, has the sparsest population; moreover, its inhabitants lead in migration to other parts of the country or abroad.

Modern Turkey is far more homogeneous than the multiethnic Ottoman Empire was. Yet the population is still divided by significant religious and ethnic differences. Census records indicate that Turkey is currently about 99 percent Muslim. The Sunni version of Islam clearly predominates in the country as a whole; but especially in central and northeast Anatolia, the heterodox Shi'a interpretation finds many adherents. Although the census data do not distinguish between these two forms of Islam, some experts allege that Shi'a number up to 25 percent of the total population.

The bulk of the Shi'a in Turkey, generally called Alevis, favor a politically reformist, secular approach by the government. In the past, this group backed the left-of-center stand of Ataturk's Republican People's Party, except for a brief dalliance with the tiny left-leaning Turkish Unity Party. In 1983, the Alevi vote seems to have been split between the Motherland and the Populist Parties. In subsequent elections, it appeared more fragmented, with the Welfare Party gaining a sizable share of the Alevi vote in 1991 and 1995. In 1999 the Nationalist Movement Party also appeared to benefit from this vote.

Kurds also constitute a significant minority in Turkey. Precise data are lacking, but a reasonable estimate is that they make up between 15 and 20 percent of the population. Speakers of the Indo-European language Kurdish, they form the overwhelming majority in Turkey's southeast provinces; but thanks to their continuing out-migration, over half the total Kurdish population is now found in the west of the country. Indeed, the squatter settlements of Istanbul contain the largest urban concentration of Kurds in the world today. This broad geographic spread and somewhat higher birthrate than ethnic Turks complicate the cause of those who would seek to carve out a separate Kurdish state from Turkish territory. That may account for the abandonment of a territorial option by Ocalan and other Kurdish leaders in recent years.

Most Kurds in Turkey have tribal connections, although the influence of traditional leaders is waning. These chiefs frequently also head branches of dervish orders (Nakshibandi and Kadiri) or belong to religious sects (such as the Nurcular, to which Kurds seem particularly drawn). Especially in eastern Turkey, this social organization both perpetuates an identity separate from that of the rest of the Turkish population and divides the various tribes and clans into rival units. This fragmentation caused the three tribal uprisings in the 1920s and 1930s to remain limited in scope. Moreover, the split has always enabled the Turkish central government to find Kurdish loyalists to stand with it against Kurds bent on armed insurrection. The village guards, hired by the government to protect Kurdish settlements against the PKK, are the latest manifestation of this tendency. As a result, the PKK has killed more Kurds than Turks in its efforts to foment revolt in southeastern Turkey.

The PKK is a small, dedicated terrorist organization that in 1984 burst on the scene in eastern Turkey promoting separatism. The group's attacks against traditional tribal leadership practices were apparently also a factor in attracting sympathizers in southeast Turkey. But the strategy of violence did not find many protagonists in the urban areas of western Turkey.

The aims of the PKK were never entirely clear and with the incarceration of its leader it may now be attempting to turn itself into a political rather than a terrorist organization and to promote cultural autonomy rather than separatism. The general success of the Turkish military in defeating the insurrection after the end of the 1990s has begun to change the nature of the contest. While small bands still operate, sometimes from bases in neighboring Iran or Iraq, the level of fighting has diminished to the point where Kurds who had fled the battlefield are now beginning to return to their homes. But the political aspects of the contest remain unresolved.

Without endorsing Kurdish separatism, Turkey's political parties have tacitly exploited Kurdish ethnicity in the past to expand their bases of support in the southeast. A popular tactic has been to offer tribal leaders prominent places on the ticket to capitalize on the propensity of their followers to vote for their chiefs.

Another important cleavage is the sharp rural–urban divide. The cities are home to an expanding cosmopolitan, secular, modernizing elite. The rapid influx of traditionally oriented, religiously observant peasants has given the urban areas a bifurcated appearance. Demographers expect that within three generations these new urban dwellers will become assimilated into the value structure and lifestyle of the long-term residents. But in the process, the reformist edge of urban culture is likely to be softened. Living conditions and social customs are changing even in the more remote villages, which, particularly in eastern Turkey, lack the accoutrements of modern life. By contrast, rural settlements near urban centers are rapidly becoming modernized; many serve as bedroom communities for workers in the larger cities and are increasingly part of the market economy. As peasants become exposed to city values, their willingness to follow their traditional leaders in voting is eroding.

Turkish culture has been highly status conscious. Age and position elicit respect. Traditionally, government and the military were the most honored careers; education and the free professions ranked next. In recent years, however, business has increased in esteem as industry expanded and began to offer far better salaries and perquisites than did the traditionally favored occupations. University education is the dividing line between the elite and the rest of the population. But the expanding numbers of educated urban dwellers are fragmented in political allegiance. The elite no longer proceeds in lockstep along a commonly agreed path.

Turkey has brought urban women into the mainstream of political, professional, and cultural life. The educational level of women has risen steadily, and the literacy rate of school-age girls is approaching that of boys. As a result, in the future virtually the entire population will be able to read and write. Although informal barriers exist, especially in blue-collar occupations, females have not faced legal obstacles since the 1930s. In the villages, however, the traditional male-dominated pattern of life persists, as it does to some extent in the urban ghettos, where new migrants from the countryside have settled.

The government was the pacesetter in employing women, and many serve as senior officials. Although females are well represented in the free professions as well, their numbers in political life declined for many years after Ataturk sponsored them in the one-party era. Whereas he used parliament as a showcase of women's progress, assuring the election of sixteen women to the then 339-seat assembly in 1935, with the advent of competitive politics, the ranks of female deputies thinned to the point where only four females—all representing major urban constituencies—won election to the 450-seat lower house in 1977. Women's numbers have risen somewhat since then, especially after the election of Tansu Ciller as prime minister in 1993. Twenty-two women became deputies in the

550-seat parliament elected in 1999, many of whom were members of the Democratic Left Party.

Economic development is a major engine of transformation of Turkish life. Until recently the state led the economic advance; indeed, responsibility for national planning was assigned by constitutions since 1961 to the State Planning Organization. Yet Turkey has always had a mixed economy (even though the largest enterprises have been state or quasi-public enterprises). Current emphasis on market forces to allocate resources has set in motion efforts to privatize these state enterprises, whose inefficient operations have burdened the treasury with ballooning debt. These efforts may be speeded up as Kemal Dervis attempts to stem Turkey's economic crisis.

Since World War II, foreign aid—mostly from the United States—and, more recently, Turkey's domestic resources fueled great infrastructure expansion. The extensive development of communications has changed the daily lives of the populace. Greater mobility facilitated large-scale migration of laborers in quest of work, of the untutored in search of education, and of the ambitious seeking opportunity. In the 1960s, this migration extended outside Turkey as well; at present there are about 3 million Turks in Europe, over one-half of them in Germany. Their remittances have helped ease Turkey's at times difficult balance-of-payment deficits. On the other hand, the migrants' propensity to clump into more or less indigestible neighborhoods has generated political strains between European states and the Turkish government.

Turkey has undergone an agricultural revolution. With the introduction of new seeds and techniques, the country turned from being a net importer of large amounts of food in the 1960s to being a significant exporter. Wheat is the main export crop, but market vegetables, cotton, tobacco, and dried fruits find ready markets in Europe and the United States. The extensive dam system on the Euphrates River in particular has begun to allow a faster expansion of agricultural production.

Turkey has witnessed an increasingly successful effort to create a competitive sophisticated industrial base. A growing business orientation has helped boost the efficiency of the steel and aluminum mills, oil refineries, and other major facilities built in the era of protectionist policies. Some of these installations have been sold off to private investors and others will be in the near future. The industrial sector, however, cannot for the foreseeable future soak up the substantial unemployment.

Of great promise has been the rise of large Turkish contracting firms. Emerging in the 1970s, these concerns gained expertise by competing successfully in the oil-rich states of the Middle East. They skillfully exploited having a Muslim workforce to secure large contracts in Makkah (Mecca) and other sensitive areas. They are now extremely active in Russia and Central Asia as well.

Turkish development, however, was burdened by repeated surges of rapid inflation. These intense convulsions reflect perennial overexpansion of public-sector spending and excessive money creation by the Central Bank. This course often reflected partisan efforts to use state machinery to influence voters on the eve of elections. After the world oil crisis began in 1973, Turkey entered a period of wild domestic inflation, unmanageable balance-of-payments deficits, and a sharp fall in imports. As a result, the gross national product (GNP) was in decline at the end of the 1970s.

To cope with this challenge, the Turkish leaders in 1980 finally accepted IMF urging to liberalize the economic structure, dismantle the system of subsidies on energy and other basic commodities, maintain a realistic exchange rate, and stimulate exports.

In reducing the advantages enjoyed by the state economic enterprises over private firms, the stabilization plan reoriented the economic structure away from the state-directed approach that had prevailed for over fifty years. The electorate unmistakably approved this change by bringing its architect, Turgut Ozal, to power in the Third Republic. And this general prescription is now accepted by the major parties, as is a value-added tax that raises the bulk of tax revenue for the Turkish state.

Yet even this recipe has not been able to curb rampant inflation in the absence of monetary and fiscal restraint. Taxation falls inequitably on salaried workers of the larger concerns. Tax avoidance by others is reputedly widespread. The Turkish economy has been strained by the battle against Kurdish insurgents in the southeast. More recently, the aftermath of the Gulf War has proven costly. United Nations–imposed sanctions on Iraq have disrupted the formerly lucrative bilateral trade. The initial closure of the oil pipeline from northern Iraq to the Mediterranean through Turkey cut an important source of revenue; partial resumption of these shipments under U.N. auspices toward the end of the 1990s reduced, but did not eliminate, this shortfall. These problems have contributed to an annual inflation rate ranging between 80 and 100 percent, though the relative fiscal discipline of the Democratic Left Party, the Nationalist Movement Party, and the Motherland Party after the 1999 elections appeared to be bringing down that rate significantly until the banking scandal disrupted the economy. Under Kemal Dervis's leadership, Turkey has been trying to meet IMF terms for a multi-billion-dollar stabilization loan. But returning to impressive economic development will require stronger backing from the politicians than yet seems likely. Moreover, high unemployment remains one of Turkey's most stubborn problems.

Political Structure

Turkey's rich variety of political mechanisms has endowed its multiparty structure with vitality. Except when the whole system is overturned, Turkey follows its constitution with legalistic precision. Even during military interventions (to be discussed in a later section), Turks have demonstrated a strong commitment to restoring constitutional practices. Indeed, elected government is what almost all Turks clearly associate with Ataturk's reforms, and thus the parliamentary regime enjoys great political legitimacy.

The 1982 constitutional structure, as amended, is centered on a 550-seat unicameral legislature. The Senate of the Second Republic was abolished in an effort to improve the efficiency of government. Assembly members are elected for five-year terms, although elections are often held earlier by consent of parliament. The deputies can pass legislation over the veto of the president by a simple majority; the prime minister is responsible to this body.

Executive authority is traditionally subordinated to the legislative in the Turkish construct. The cabinet can issue decrees with the force of law only if explicitly authorized for a specific period by the assembly. Cabinet ministers are "jointly responsible" for the execution of the government's general policy as well as personally liable for their ministries' acts. The prime minister, however, can dismiss ministers at will.

A continuing political controversy of the Third Republic has been over whether the 1982 constitution accorded the presidency powers that were real or merely symbolic. When Ozal became president in 1989, he initially seemed to be taking advantage of his vague constitutional right to assure that the organs of state function smoothly, much to the discomfort of the opposition parties. As prime minister after Ozal moved to the presidency, Suleyman Demirel had vigorously objected to Ozal's propensity to commit Turkey in foreign affairs. After becoming president himself on Ozal's death in May 1993, Demirel indicated that he did not expect to be completely uninvolved in government operations. That led to some friction with his successor as prime minister, Tansu Ciller, who asserted her prerogatives to executive authority. Demirel, however, positioned himself as mediator between the military high command and the various civilian prime ministers in the ensuing seven years of his incumbency. By the end of his term he had assumed an important foreign policy role, defining Turkish relations with the Turkic states of the former Soviet Union. He was the point man in Turkey's efforts to start construction of the Baku-to-Ceyhan (on Turkey's Mediterranean coast) oil pipeline.

Demirel's successor, the jurist Ahmet Necdet Sezer, who took office in May 2000, from the first announced that he wanted to see the powers of the presidency reduced. But he was immediately thrust into the thick of Turkey's foreign affairs, and the interrelationship of president and prime minister cannot be considered entirely settled.

An independent judiciary is integral to the Turkish system. As an innovation, the 1982 constitution set up state security courts to handle offenses against the integrity of the state, the democratic order, and the international and external security of the country. Under prodding from Europeans, military representatives were removed from these courts during the trial of PKK leader Abdullah Ocalan in the spring of 1999. Although superior administrative and military courts have final jurisdiction over cases within their competencies, the system also provides for a constitutional court to rule on the constitutionality of laws and decrees. Charges against the president of the republic and other senior officials would be considered by the Constitutional Court in its capacity as the Supreme Court. The Constitutional Court also decides all cases relating to the shutting down of political parties.

Several additional administrative organs played significant roles in the government of the state. The State Planning Organization, inaugurated in 1961, fulfilled the desire for more regular economic projections and helped shape economic policy. This body has lost much of its role in recent years, inasmuch as the prime minister has kept basic economic responsibility in the cabinet, and parties philosophically opposed to central planning have dominated many of the governments of the Third Republic.

An interest in preventing social strife is reflected in the government provisions regulating labor activities. The right to form unions without prior permission is recognized, but labor groups were prohibited from political activity or from having ties with a political party until the 1990s. Although strikes are legal, the union shop is not, nor can labor action be carried on "to the detriment of society." Collective bargaining is also permitted, subject to extensive government supervision. Some restrictions on labor were eased, especially in 1987, and state control over labor was eroded by the decision in 1991 to rescind laws outlawing social class doctrines.

Formally organized political parties are the basic units of parliamentary activity. Ataturk's original single party spawned most of its multitude of competitors in the First and Second Republics. These, in turn, gave birth to successor organizations in the Third Republic that compete to represent the more or less coherent right-of-center and left-of-center constituencies that emerged by the end of the First Republic.

The Motherland and True Path parties have long been locked in a struggle of personalities that diminishes the chances of either to represent the bulk of the right-of-center voting bloc, which has almost always commanded over 60 percent of the vote. The bitter rivalry of Ozal and Demirel in the 1980s, which kept the two at sword's point, was followed in the 1990s by the personality conflict between Mesut Yilmaz, Ozal's successor as head of the Motherland Party, and Tansu Ciller, who followed Demirel as head of True Path. This contest went on against the backdrop of the emergence as major contenders for power of first the Welfare Party in the early 1990s and, after it was banned, its successor, the Virtue Party, at the end of the decade. Both parties appealed to religiously oriented and traditionalist voters. In 2000, however, the Virtue Party faced a court challenge that resulted in its closure. Two different wings of the party seem set to enter the competition to be its successor. The scene was further complicated at the end of the 1990s with the surge of the extremist Nationalist Movement Party. This party, after its controversial leader Alparslan Turkes died, vaulted from minor-party status to garner 18 percent of the vote in 1999, becoming the second largest party on the political scene. Thus it does not seem likely that any one party can command the bulk of the right-of-center constituency.

The left-of-center constituency also is split into factions with a history of bitter rivalry. Its main components are the Democratic Left Party of Bulent Ecevit and the reestablished Republican People's Party, which in 1995 took over the Social Democrat Populist Party, at the time the largest social democratic political formation. In the past, the left-of-center vote rarely exceeded 40 percent. It now seems to be shrinking further; its two major parts together received only some 31 percent of the vote in 1999. Thanks to Ecevit's personal reputation for probity, his party came in first in the 1999 elections, with just over 22 percent of the vote. But its rival Republican People's Party did not cross the 10 percent national barrier to be able to elect any deputies. Ecevit was thus obliged to approach two conservative parties to form a coalition to be able to govern. Two years later, however, Ecevit's health seemed increasingly questionable, and as his party is thought to be largely an emanation of his personality, its long-range future did not seem assured.

Beyond these liberal and conservative voting blocs, in the past decade ethnicity has become a basis for political organization. In the early 1990s a group of Kurdish deputies from the Social Democrat Populist Party split off to form the People's Labor Party to represent Kurdish interests. This party was banned in 1993. After a successor organization was also banned, the current Democratic People's Party was formed with a similar orientation. But outside of the southeast, the response to these parties has been tepid; none on its own has been able to cross the national threshold to elect deputies. Nonetheless, the Democratic People's Party mayoral candidates swept the cities of the southeast in 1999, despite opposition from the security forces and a rash of unexplained assassinations of its members. Four of these mayors were briefly arrested in 2000 for alleged separatist activity. Despite such harassment, parties representing Kurdish interests are likely to be a permanent feature of the Turkish political scene.

Turkey's electoral constituencies are based on provinces. As of 2002, Turkish election law provides that Turkey's three most populous provinces be broken into two election districts each for Ankara and Izmir and three for Istanbul. Political considerations also caused the creation of a number of new provinces split from older ones, so that in 1999 ten of the eighty provinces had but two deputies each; Istanbul, on the contrary, saw its seats rise from fifty in 1991 to sixty-nine in 1999. Thus a major-party candidate heading the list in Istanbul, Ankara, or Izmir was virtually guaranteed election.

A person not constitutionally barred from being a candidate may run for office either on a party ticket or as an independent. But electors who vote for an independent lose the right to vote for candidates for other seats on the ballot, thus encouraging straight party-ticket voting. That enhances party leaders' control of deputies, who are generally beholden to the national leadership for their places on the ticket. Only in those few instances (such as in the election of the president by the assembly, Art. 102) where secret ballot is mandated are the individual deputies able to vote their preferences without fear of retaliation. The normal recourse for those who fall out of favor with their leaders is to change parties. Hence most important votes are party-line affairs.

After 1961, Turkey's election law was based on a version of the d'Hondt system of proportional representation: To elect any deputies, a party must win more than the quotient of the number of valid votes in an electoral district divided by the number of seats to be awarded. This system was modified a number of times. In 1983 the provision was added that only those parties receiving 10 percent of the nationwide vote would qualify for any seats in a general election. The change was intended to increase the bias in favor of the larger parties. It applies, however, only in general elections; in by-elections there is no nationwide barrier.

In the 1980s, this system allowed the Motherland Party to win a parliamentary majority with only 45 and 36 percent of the vote in successive national elections, because several smaller parties could not exceed the threshold to elect deputies. But despite the effort to curb splinter parties, the narrow separation between the larger contenders prevented any one of them from gaining a majority of the seats in 1991 and succeeding elections.

The resulting turbulence of multiparty politics reflected to a degree the rise in turnover rates among deputies. In the Third Republic, reelection rates declined, as parties split and urbanization brought a marked population shift. In no election since 1980 have as many as one-half the deputies been reelected. This process reached its apex in 1991, when even in some of the less-developed areas of the east (for example, Van province), where traditions persist, there was a complete turnover in parliamentary representation. Thereafter the trend slowly began to reverse.

Interest groups play a significant role. For example, the Turkish Union of Chambers and Stock Exchanges is generally led by a figure close to the prime minister, and the union's reports are taken seriously by the government. Other groups, such as the Confederation of Revolutionary Trade Unions (DISK), whose roles were restricted after the 1980 military coup are again trying to flex their muscles. Both politicians and labor leaders are trying through legal changes to erode the ban on unions' engaging in political activity. But the constitution (Art. 52) still prohibits unions from running their own candidates.

Student organizations are also restricted in political activity, having been in the forefront of the disorders that produced both the military ultimatum of 1971 and the 1980 military takeover. Politicians are reluctant to ease the tight restrictions on the political activities of youth, although desire to win the allegiance of the younger population did lead to dropping the voting age from twenty-one to twenty in 1987.

The 1982 Constitution prohibits political parties from forming women's branches. To get around that ban, the Welfare Party established "women's commissions" as part of its public relations branch. Other parties have begun to emulate this organization in order to increase their appeal to women voters. And the importance of women on the political scene is gaining recognition.

Political Dynamics

Political patterns in Turkey show remarkable continuity in spite of military interventions. Conduct of party leaders, broad voting patterns, and issues of political debate all bespeak a large debt to the past. On the one hand, that continuity reflects the longevity of political figures in Turkey, where thirty or even forty years as a major political leader is not uncommon. On the other hand, it stems from the fact that politics since the Second Republic has revolved around the contest of like-minded individuals to represent the right-of-center and left-of-center constituencies rather than efforts to expand these voting blocs by winning adherents across constituency lines. Thus the voting blocs themselves have changed little in proportion over the years, giving the right of center a marked edge if it were not torn by such intense personal rivalries for the same voting constituency.

Another major aspect of continuity has been the tenacious commitment to elective parliamentary rule, which alone is seen by all political elements in Turkey as according legitimacy to government. The military as well as the civilian politicians accept this need, an orientation only strengthened by the recent acceptance of Turkey as a candidate for eventual full membership in the European Union.

The political parties operate with relative efficiency in mobilizing voters. Participation in elections has generally been high (ranging between 64 and 94 percent of the eligible voters). Starting from the tradition of universal voting in the one-party era, however, the percentage of those actually going to the polls declined until 1973. Turkey's experience was thus contrary to the expectation of those who theorize that greater education, involvement in the political process, and development should be accompanied by rising interest in voting. To account for this turn of events, Turkish political scientists ascribed the falling participation rate to a decline in bloc voting as Turkey became modern. They argued that as individuals became responsible for their own voting decisions, there would be a natural fall in the number going to the polls. The generally higher rate of voting in the 1960s in eastern Turkey, where clan and tribal ties were strongest, seemed additional substantiation of this hypothesis.

The rebound in the participation rate since 1973 called this explanation into question, suggesting that the process went far beyond a simple link to modernity and the breakdown of bloc voting. It seems that each military intervention (1960, 1971, and 1980) spurred participation. At the same time, coalition politics and the increasing urgency of the issues at stake in the 1970s had a clear impact on voting. Moreover, the lower turnout in 1965 and 1969 appears to have reflected the fears of the traditional rural notables in the Republican People's Party over the "left-of-center" stance that the party introduced in 1965 and the bitter internal dispute that introduction triggered. These voters seem to have stayed at home in protest on election day.

By the 1970s, more avenues had become available to Turkish voters, after a religiously oriented party and an extreme nationalist party emerged as significant actors on the political scene, energized in part by a perceived need to combat the remnants of the Marxist-oriented Turkish Labor Party. The challenge of these newer interest groups to the traditional mainline political formations made for more spirited debate than in the past. Coincidentally, radio and then television were bringing election activities more intimately into the lives of Turks. The confluence of these trends produced a steady upswing in voting starting in 1973. This rising tide was most apparent in western Turkey, where the population was the most open to new influences.

A further sharp upsurge in political mobilization took place in the 1980s, when for the first time those who did not vote paid a small fine and also lost their franchise for the subsequent election. In this situation, the percentage of those going to the polls leaped from 72.5 percent in 1977 to 92.3 percent in 1983; it hit its peak of 93.3 percent in 1987 before falling to 83.9 percent in the 1991 elections, as the fine for not voting (under $10 in 1991) was clearly not a major deterrent. In 1999 the voting rate overall was 87.1 percent, and it was generally higher in the developed western part of the country (except Istanbul, with its large proportion of migrants from the east) than in the more traditionally organized eastern provinces. Given the interest in ethnic and religious parties, the rate of voting participation in Turkey is almost certain to remain higher than in most countries with free elections.

Turkey's political system, however, is a case study to demonstrate the baleful effects of proportional representation. In the First Republic, with its majority voting system, one party usually (though not always) swept the entire slate in a province. Under these circumstances, the larger parties, with their nationwide organizations, took the lion's share of the seats; minor parties, unable to secure representation in parliament, found their future unpromising. As a result, it was always possible for one party to secure a clear majority in parliament and form a government without recourse to coalitions.

The introduction of proportional representation in 1961 had an immediate effect in encouraging the splintering of the two major parties. In fact, the first elections after the 1960 coup produced a parliament so divided that no single party could form a government on its own. Yet the specter of the military in the wings kept coherence in the political scene until new elections four years later brought the Justice Party a clear parliamentary majority. Some of the smaller political formations simply faded out once the electorate had a chance to judge their performance.

Yet this gave only a temporary reprieve to the two major parties. In the freer political climate of the Second Republic, personality conflicts, coupled with disputes over tactics and emphasis among rival aspirants to top leadership positions, contributed to the defection of parliamentary factions from both of the larger parties. These fissiparous tendencies went so far that in 1973 and 1977 neither of the major parties could muster a majority in parliament. Turkey entered a period of precarious coalition politics, in which political paralysis was a constant threat and parties on the extremes were able to exert outsize influence. These parties used their swing position between the relatively evenly matched majors to extract concessions and bolted whenever they could cut a better deal.

The performance of the parties in the Third Republic shows that the fragmentation process is accelerating (see Table 2.1). The loosening of restrictions on ideological parties and the ability to found ethnic parties brought a number of smaller organizations onto the scene. Whereas only three parties were allowed to contest the 1983 elections, this number had swelled to twenty parties as well as a number of independents by the time of the 1999 elections. In the latter contests, only eight of the parties got as much as 1 percent of the vote and only five were able to cross the threshold to elect deputies.

Turkish parties reflect a blend of national and local interests. In Turkey reformist politics have always been national; local groups, in contrast, have been opposed to far-reaching social and cultural reform. The accommodation of these conflicting approaches without losing the essence of Ataturk's pragmatic modernizing thrust is one of the major achievements of Turkey's political life. As a result, the political contest has focused especially on tactics to achieve development and on the issue of how much disruption of traditional social mores is required to accomplish this end.

The need to propitiate local interests accorded politics in the multiparty era a character increasingly divergent from Kemalist reform. A principal way in which localism has modified Turkey's course has been in policy toward Islam. Ataturk, like many of his generation, saw attachment to religion as the main impediment to westernizing Turkey. He therefore disestablished Islam as the state religion and imposed rigorous restrictions on its practice. He closed the dervish lay orders, which had formed a separate hierarchy outside the control or guidance of the orthodox religious establishment, a wing of the government. He also shut the religious schools and banned clerics from wearing religious garb outside of places of worship. In addition, he imposed Turkish in place of Arabic in religious services.

Table 2.1 Parliamentary Election Results in the Third Republic: 1983–1999 (in percentages)

Party	1983	1987	1991	1995	1999
Democratic Left Party (DSP)		8.53	10.75	14.64	22.19
Nationalist Movement Party (MHP)		2.93	*	8.18	17.98
Virtue Party (FP)					15.41
Welfare Party (RP)		7.16	*	21.38	
Motherland Party (ANAP)	45.14	36.31	24.01	19.65	13.22
True Path Party (DYP)		19.14	27.03	19.18	12.01
Republican People's Party (CHP)				10.71	8.71
Social Democratic Populist Party (SHP)		24.74	20.75		
Populist Party (HP)	30.46				
Nationalist Democracy Party (MDP)	23.27				
People's Democracy Party (HADEP)				4.17	4.76
Great Unity Party (BBP)					1.46
Freedom and Solidarity Party (ODP)					0.8
Reformist Democracy Party			*		
Democratic Turkey Party (DTP)					0.58
New Democracy Movement (YDH)				0.48	
Liberal Democratic Party (LDP)					0.41
Democrat Party (DP)					0.3
Nation Party (MP)				0.45	0.25
Labor (Isci) Party (IP)				0.22	0.18
Work Party (EMEP)					0.17
Democratic Peace Party (DBP)					0.08
Renaissance Party (YDP)				0.34	0.14
Socialist Power Party (SIP)					0.08
Changing Turkey Party (DEPAR)					0.12
New Party (YP)				0.13	
Independents	1.13	0.37	0.13	0.48	0.87

*The Nationalist Movement Party, the Welfare Party, and the Reformist Democracy Party formed an election coalition for the 1991 elections. The combination received 16.9 percent of the vote.

SOURCE: State Institute of Statistics, Prime Ministry, Republic of Turkey, Results of General Election of Representatives: 20.20.1991 (Ankara: Devlet Istatistik Enstitusu Matbaasi, 1992); www.turkey.org/start.html, "Results of the General Elections in Turkey which was held on April 18, 1999."

Multiparty competition worked to relax these restrictions. Optional courses on religion were added to the academic curriculum in the 1940s; a faculty of divinity was reopened; Arabic was restored in worship; and local training schools for religious leaders were eventually permitted and proliferated, offering a far-reaching alternative to the state secular institutions. Moreover, as local pressures mounted, the public observance of religious festivals increased. Construction began on a large number of mosques, and it became fashionable for officials to fast during Ramadan. Many educated people started attending Friday noon prayers—even before the rise in the 1970s of the National Salvation Party, which encouraged this trend.

The resurgence of Islamic practice gained so much momentum that it influenced even the strongly secular Kemalist revival of the generals after 1980. Chief of State General Kenan Evren saw state-sponsored religious classes as an antidote to Communism, which at that time was still a major bugbear for Turkey's ranking officers. But soon the military was concerned about the reach of Islam. In the 1990s, in reaction to the rise of the Welfare Party to power, the generals successfully pressed the civilian coalitions to reduce the scope of alternative religious schools, making attendance at secular state schools obligatory for the first eight years of education.

Turgut Ozal, who took power after Evren, was widely perceived as religiously observant; as prime minister in 1987 he presided over the opening of the Kocatepe Mosque, a huge and prominent structure dominating the skyline of new Ankara—a development inconceivable in Ataturk's lifetime. Ozal was said to have used Nakshibandi connections to woo votes, although his wife's activism in pursuit of women's rights appeared to alienate religiously inclined voters.

After Ozal died, the upsurge in vote for the religiously inclined Welfare Party, boosting it to be the largest party, posed a more direct challenge to the secular system. It is still not clear how much of the vote for Welfare was primarily motivated by religious considerations, for the party managed an active support mechanism for new arrivals in the big cities and for those seeking university education. It also had an economic approach that appeared to defend the interest of mom-and-pop stores and small businesses against the onslaught of multinational concerns, an orientation that undoubtedly earned it some support. Its successor Virtue Party got a smaller percentage of the vote in 1999. Nonetheless, it seems reasonable to conclude that primarily religious concerns probably motivate about 10 percent of the voters. Hence even though the Virtue Party was banned in 2001, efforts to fill this gap are already under way.

Localism has also fostered changes in the socioeconomic interests represented in parliament. Ataturk's one-party regime ran heavily to military and civilian officials in his handpicked, single-chamber assembly. Once the transition to multiparty competition began, the character of the assembly began to change. Professionals, especially lawyers, became deputies in rising numbers. They were joined by businessmen, who had been scarce in the Ataturk era. At the same time, the contingent of officials declined. This transformation, reflecting the emergence of a middle class, came slowly. At first, it affected the lowest levels of power, but gradually new elements infiltrated the higher ranks.

In the Third Republic, a wave of engineers and technicians of all sorts was swept into parliament, forming the bulk of the Motherland deputies. The number of lawyers declined steadily, whereas that of managers in the private sector and bankers swelled to a significant proportion of the assembly. Civil servants and teachers had prominent representation, but in 1999 only six men of military background managed to gain election to the 550-person parliament.

Entry of these new elements had an effect on deliberations, especially those concerning domestic policy. Economic approach, the role of central planning, and the place of private enterprise were debated with rising intensity as the new arrivals challenged the older notion of state-directed reform. Clustered first around the Democrat Party, later the Justice Party, and then the Motherland and True Path Parties, these deputies, with their nongovernmental focus, were once accused of seeking to dismantle the Ataturk reforms. But the economic disaster under the import-substitution regime in the 1970s and the improvement after the shift to an export economy in 1980 demonstrated the impossibility of opting out of the interdependent world economy, and this debate subsided. Currently only differences of nuance separate the major parties in the economic field.

Just as the rise of the center-right constituency was associated with the burgeoning of the middle class, some political observers saw the emergence of a sizable industrial labor force after 1960 as favoring the left of center. Indeed, the rebound of the Republican People's Party from its low point in 1969 was attributed to this cause. From just over 27 percent of the vote in that year, the party managed to rise to over 41 percent in the 1977 elections.

Some scholars saw in this surge a "critical realignment" of voter support away from territorial and cultural cleavages and toward voting along class lines. The socialist approach of the Republican People's Party, they believed, best represented the interests of the workers in urban areas. Although this theory was comforting to the reformist elite, it turned out to be wishful thinking. The evidence since is conclusive that sectional, ethnic, linguistic, religious, and cultural factors are more important determinants of voting patterns in Turkey.

Indeed, the predominance of right-of-center votes in the Third Republic convincingly shows that Turks do not cast ballots on a class basis. Rather the ups and downs in major party performance appear to confirm that Turkish voters are seeking successful leaders who keep their promises and avoid the appearance of corruption. This image has proven to be difficult to maintain for a lengthy period. Hence the desire to change the party in power seems to grow in Turkey after at most two terms. That pattern was visible in the multiparty era of the First Republic; it continued in the Second Republic and has repeated itself in the Third. In 1991 the Motherland Party was turned out after two successive wins. No party thereafter has managed to maintain its plurality position in back-to-back elections. There is no reason to doubt, therefore, that it is the ability of the ruling party to govern effectively and find solutions to major problems that ultimately determines its staying power.

The Role of the Military

The armed forces have a special position in Turkey. Their political weight enters into a broad range of government calculations. This influence comes partly from their monopoly of legal force and their status as the last recourse in domestic conflict and partly from the peculiar history of the military in the Turkish reform movement and its centrality in the creation of the republic.

At the end of the Ottoman Empire, the armed forces, with their secular schools, were the main window on the West. As a result, officers were the reformists par excellence. Ataturk and his chief lieutenants were career officers when they launched the struggle for independence. Indeed, the fact that Ataturk's outlook was archetypal of the army's approach helped him rally military support for the cause.

Not until the political system began to jell early in the republic did the problem of mixing politicians and military officers became acute. When some of Ataturk's closest collaborators defected to the mounting civilian opposition in 1924, the threat of army disloyalty imparted urgency to a separation of the military and political tracks. In 1927, when the dissident generals sought to return to active army commands, Ataturk retired his military opponents. To parry accusations of partisanship, he and his loyal associates gave up their own active-duty status.

Yet Ataturk and Ismet Inonu maintained close ties with the armed forces, even after retirement. Marshal Fevzi Cakmak ran the military establishment on their behalf, keeping the forces out of day-to-day politics. Nonetheless, Ataturk continually cited the army as the ultimate guardian of the republic, making clear that its role was to defend the reform effort as well as to protect against foreign foes.

As part of the move to expand democratic practice, the armed forces were removed from the president's purview in 1944 and put under the direct control of the prime minister. Five years later, the general staff was placed under the Ministry of National Defense. The top generals, however, remained loyal to President Inonu. There are credible reports that senior commanders sounded him out on whether they should prevent the Democrat Party from taking over after it won the 1950 elections. But Ismet Inonu was adamant in opposing a military move.

Complex pressures led the armed forces to overturn the Democrat Party in 1960. The military officers, who had lost status and prestige during that party's decade in power, saw Prime Minister Adnan Menderes as deliberately denying the military its position as the ultimate guarantor of the state. Nonetheless, the officer corps might have remained loyal if the party had not threatened the parliamentary system. Even the Republican People's Party did not want the military to obey partisan commands of the Democrat Party administration. Of course, the line of disobedience was hard to draw. In the end, a group of colonels and younger officers led a revolt that brought the entire military apparatus along.

The military move was readily accepted in Turkey as necessary to prevent perversion of the political process. Trials of the Democrat leaders helped discredit Menderes. The execution of the three main defendants and the incarceration of many others were harder for the body politic to swallow, and decades later those executed would be reburied with pomp and ceremony in a gesture of rehabilitation. Nevertheless, although civilian politicians sought amnesty for the jailed Democrat Party members, there was no serious effort to deny the legality of the Second Republic or to seek punishment for the military junta, whose members were accorded ex-officio membership in the Senate.

Thanks to the general acceptance of the legitimacy of the military move, the junta could arrange to surrender the reins of government to a civilian regime after only sixteen months. But the military's stint in power had disrupted the chain of command, damaged discipline, and deeply politicized the officer corps. It took two abortive coups in 1962 and 1963 to teach officers that plotting carried severe risks. Colonel Talat Aydemir's execution for leading the 1963 putsch virtually ended efforts by those below the level of the senior commanders to overturn civilian government.

In the 1960s, the National Security Council, presided over by the president of the republic, provided a legal forum for the armed services to convey political messages. That meant that even the "coup by memorandum" that brought down the government of Suleyman Demirel in March 1971 was never subjected to legal challenge.

Demirel's downfall, however, lent the armed forces an aura of threatening the normal operation of the political process. Parliament continued to function, but the deputies formed cabinets of technocrats in order not to offend the generals. Yet there was a limit to this deference. In a rare show of unanimity, the party leaders rejected the candidacy of Chief of the General Staff Faruk Gurler for the presidency in the spring of 1973. Then the otherwise divided parliament settled on a long-retired admiral, Fahri Koruturk.

This outcome marked an apparent turning point in the relations between the military and civilians. It was widely read as a retreat of the armed forces before determined civilian opposition. It thus sent the misleading message that the military establishment was a "paper tiger," lacking the will to enforce its demands. That set the stage for trouble when the civilians could not elect a successor to President Koruturk at the end of his term in March 1980. Even retired officers proposed by the Republican People's Party were rejected by the Justice Party. This parliamentary paralysis was compounded by the injection of religion into politics by the National Salvation Party—a move that particularly alienated the secularist generals. Disrespect for the state shown at a party rally in Konya in September 1980 was the final straw in bringing the senior generals under Chief of the General Staff Kenan Evren to take power in a bloodless coup in September 1980.

The new military regime, with General Evren as chief of state, set up a government of technocrats, drawn mainly from civilian experts but headed by a recently retired admiral, Bulend Ulusu. The National Security Council became the organ for policy decisions and issuance of laws. The cabinet was reduced to merely administering the country under the guidelines of the security council.

General Evren recognized Turkey's constitutional inadequacies as well as its partisan failings. Yet with urging from the United States, he was willing to return to an elected democratic system after Turkey had a breathing spell, free of violence, in which to make necessary changes. Evren soon announced a six-point program to preserve national unity, restore security, reinvigorate state authority, ensure social peace, apply social justice, and reinstate civilian rule within a "reasonable" time. In short, Turkey was to be saved through institutional reform.

The commanders concluded that in addition to constitutional adjustments, new parties, new leaders, and new rules for political behavior were needed. Thus, in the process of banning old political organizations and ruling the former political leaders out of politics for ten years, the generals sought to ensure the dominance of elements committed to a return to Kemalist principles. To this end, they encouraged Turgut Sunalp, a former general, to form the Nationalist Democracy Party. And General Evren sought to assist this organization by appealing—albeit largely in vain—to voters to favor it in the 1983 general elections.

Concern over the legitimacy of the 1980 move was integral to the transition to civilian politics. The new constitution affirmed the legitimacy of the takeover and banned legal questioning of the acts of the military rulers. Popular acceptance of the intervention was high in any event, as the populace welcomed the respite from violence. There was wide agreement in Turkey that the political process had broken down, so the military had to move. What was less accepted was the abolition of the parties of the old regime. Efforts to re-create the old parties or to take over the new formed the leitmotiv of the political struggle of the 1980s.

With the civilians back in office after 1983, the role of the military reverted to that of an influential pressure group. Until 1989 President Evren defended its interests, although he no longer had active-duty status as a general. Thereafter, in a major change, three people of civilian background succeeded each other as president, without any sign that the armed forces were smarting from their loss of control of this prominent post. Civilian presidents presided over a revamped National Security Council, which acts as a watchdog over security and especially over the operation of emergency rule in force in the southeastern provinces challenged by Kurdish insurgents.

The extent of influence of the National Security Council and the scope of its interests remain live questions. Chief of the General Staff General Necip Torumtay, for example, resigned when he disagreed with the civilian leadership on Turkey's role in Operation Desert Storm during the Gulf War in 1990. During Operation Provide Comfort to furnish relief to the Kurds of northern Iraq, the Turkish General Staff fell into line on extending the effort until 1997, despite reservations about the effect autonomy for Iraq's Kurds would have on the Kurds in Turkey. But the military helped persuade Prime Minister Erbakan to reduce the operation's scope and rename it Northern Watch. The famous National Security Council meeting of February 28, 1997, which laid out extensive military desiderata for legal changes to promote secularism as well as security—pressure that ended up bringing down the Welfare/True Path Party coalition—also indicated that military activism continued to influence civilian politicians.

Growing interest in preparing Turkey to meet the criteria for membership in the European Union will also impact the role that the Turkish military will play. It will mean a less forward role for the National Security Council. Yet the military establishment is not likely soon to give up its strong role in setting policy toward the Kurdish question, its interest in the nature of military contracts to be awarded, and ultimately policy toward any threats to change the secular nature of the Turkish state. Now taken seriously by the civilian establishment, it seems unlikely that the military will again judge it desirable to take over the government. Days of outright military rule would appear to be over for good.

Foreign Policy

Ataturk set the basic goals for Turkish international relations. The corollary of his determination that Turkey be accepted as a powerful modern state was Western orientation. To the Kemalists, and soon to virtually all of Turkey, therefore, the foremost design of the republic was to become identified as European. This state of affairs, in turn, implied close ties with Britain and France in the interwar years and with the United States in the era after World War II. Thus there were deep roots in Turkish thinking that caused membership in NATO to be seen as confirmation of the Kemalist dream. Similarly, although joining the European Union has occasioned debate over timing and conditions, it is a goal that Turkish leaders and the population at large generally accept. In short, even after the demise of the Soviet Union, Turkey's Western alliance has a solid foundation in the modern Turkish state.

For Ankara there was, moreover, little alternative to grasping the West as tightly as possible after the end of World War II. Defense against Russia was a deeply felt need in Turkey, despite the earlier revolutionary cooperation between the new Turkey and the Soviet state in the 1920s and 1930s. It was a cardinal tenet of the Kemalist regime not to be caught in a position that would give Moscow either the opportunity or the provocation to confront Turkey. Turkish neutralism during World War II spared it the burdens of active military operations or military destruction. It also seemed to offer a way to prevent being forced into the embrace of the Soviet Union. Yet with the defeat of the Nazis, Turkey was left highly exposed to pressure from Moscow. Thus the Turks celebrated the Truman Doctrine of 1947 as a key element of support.

Once NATO came into being, first a Republican People's Party government and then a Democrat Party regime worked earnestly to gain Turkey's admission. In those days of cold war intensity, foreign policy was bipartisan in Turkey, and the U.S. connection was welcomed by all but a few leftists.

The Turks entered the Atlantic Alliance without reservations. The Democrat Party regime was willing to make whatever diplomatic moves (such as setting up the Baghdad pact, a defense alliance of Turkey, Iraq, Pakistan, Iran, and Great Britain) it judged pleasing to Washington. Military cooperation between the United States and Turkey was highly successful. Ankara's creaky armed forces were revitalized and upgraded. U.S. strategic interests were well served by a number of bilateral endeavors conducted with the Turks under the NATO umbrella. More difficult, however, were efforts to mesh Democrat insistence on using aid for partisan purposes with the desire of the World Bank and Washington to structure assistance on reasonable economic criteria.

The military rulers who overthrew the Democrat Party regime in 1960 were too preoccupied with domestic problems to devise major foreign initiatives. In any case, because they came out of Turkey's military tradition, they were for the most part satisfied with U.S. performance. Yet they did reflect greater national sensitivity than their predecessors. Moreover, the broader political debate permitted in the Second Republic, especially the rise of the socialist movement in the early 1960s, set the stage for problems in Turkey's Western orientation.

Cyprus was the main foreign issue to confront Turkey in the mid-1960s. In December 1963, violence between the small Turkish and much larger Greek Cypriot communities led Ankara to send planes over the island to demonstrate its commitment to the Turkish minority. Continuing communal troubles caused the Turkish Cypriots to group themselves in enclaves and the Turkish government to consider landing troops to protect Turkish Cypriot rights, a remedy provided in the Treaty of Guarantee that had established the Cypriot state in 1960. But in June 1964, before the Turks could dispatch forces, President Lyndon Johnson sent Prime Minister Inonu a harsh letter warning that NATO might not protect

Turkey from Soviet intervention if the Turks took military action on Cyprus. He categorically forbade Turkey to use American weapons for Cyprus operations. Turkey desisted under this pressure. However, public resentment against the United States was intense. The incident marked the end of the era of unquestioning diplomatic cooperation with Washington.

Under pressure from leftist extremists—who took up the cry of moving Turkey out of NATO—the Turkish authorities began to reinspect the alliance. A new agreement restricting the scope of U.S. privileges and activities was hammered out in 1969 after several years of negotiation. That stabilized relations for a time. But the new pattern of cooperation had more limited bounds, reflecting the somewhat divergent interests of Turkey and the United States.

Coincidentally, Turkey's position in the East-West confrontation had changed. In the aftermath of the Cuban missile crisis of 1962, medium-range surface-to-surface missiles had been removed from Turkish soil. This move significantly diminished the likelihood that Moscow would make a first strike on Turkey in the event of war with NATO. At the same time, the Turks became drawn into the process of East-West detente, with a noticeable increase in diplomatic exchanges with the USSR. Against this backdrop, the failure of the Western allies to support Turkey on Cyprus spurred normalization of Ankara's relations with the Soviet Union. In the mid-1960s, the Soviets and Turks concluded a program of major economic projects, including an aluminum plant and a steel mill. But the Turks refrained from seeking arms from the USSR so as not to risk disrupting NATO ties.

Turkey's foreign position faced an even greater challenge from events in Cyprus in July 1974. At this time, the military rulers in Athens mounted an initially successful coup against Archbishop Makarios. Although this action was not directed against the Turkish community in the first instance, the man who seized power in Nicosia, Nicos Sampson, was known as a longtime advocate of joining Cyprus with Greece and as a dedicated foe of the Turks. In response, Ankara landed troops on Cyprus, claiming that it was exercising its treaty rights to repair a clear violation of the Cypriot constitution. Under strong international pressure, however, the Turks halted their military action after two days, having secured merely a foothold in the Kyrenia region, north of Nicosia. During the ensuing peace talks, when the Turks thought the new regime in Athens was stalling, Turkey resumed military operations and speedily secured control over slightly more than the northern one-third of the island.

Although Ankara insisted that its actions were sanctioned by the Treaty of Guarantee, Turkey found itself largely isolated in the international community. The U.S. Congress imposed a complete embargo on all deliveries of arms to Turkey in February 1975, a ban that lasted until September. It was then partially lifted after the Turks closed all U.S. installations (leaving the NATO airbase in Incirlik open, however) and abrogated the 1969 Defense Cooperation Agreement. A continuing limited embargo also impeded the ability of other allies to supply Turkey's military requirements. Moreover, the European powers lent their combined influence to urging Turkey to offer concessions to the Greek side with respect to Cyprus.

In this context, Turkey's relations with Greece took a decided turn for the worse. Tensions generated by Cyprus were further inflamed by an emerging dispute over the continental shelf and air rights in the Aegean Sea. The geography of this body of water, with numerous Greek islands hugging the Turkish coast, presented complex problems in apportioning the seabed. Following discovery of oil in commercial quantities in Greek waters in 1973, the Turks issued licenses for exploration in international waters on their side of the median line, but in areas that Athens claimed were above the continental shelf of its islands.

Neither Turkey nor Greece, however, wished to see the dispute escalate into war. After Turkish seismic exploration in the Aegean raised tensions even more, both sides agreed to avoid inflammatory tactics and to pursue active negotiations. But the death of Archbishop Makarios in August 1977 set back progress on Cyprus. Neither side was prepared to make sufficient concessions to allow a settlement. After Andreas Papandreou's Socialist Party came to power in Athens in 1981 on a platform of intense suspicion of Turkey, relations with Greece deteriorated anew.

Behind the difficulties in dealing with Greece and Cyprus in the 1970s lay a new and painful fact for Turkey: The U.S. Congress, and not the executive branch, had become the articulator of Turkish-U.S. problems. Whereas American presidents were understanding of the compulsions that led Turkey to act in Cyprus, Congress was far less willing to credit Turkish arguments. This contest of wills in Washington slowed renegotiation of defense cooperation arrangements. But after Congress finally lifted the remaining limitations on arms to Turkey in September 1978, U.S. facilities were reopened and hard bargaining began on a new Cooperation on Defense and Economy Agreement. This accord was signed in March 1980.

It was in this context that the generals took over in September 1980. Their arrival immediately added new complexities to relations with Europe, for most Europeans were critical of military rule as well as of the treatment of former Turkish politicians. Rejection by some of Turkey's European allies pushed the Turks again toward the Middle East, and this time they succeeded in establishing commercial relations and winning lucrative contracts. Trade with Iraq and Iran spurted after the two became involved in prolonged conflict in the fall of 1980. To cement these favorable trade trends, Turkey deepened its involvement in the politics of the Islamic world and for a while lowered the level of its diplomatic ties with Israel.

Difficulties with allies were further inflamed by the unilateral declaration of independence of the Turkish Cypriot legislature in November 1983. This so-called Turkish Republic of Northern Cyprus was recognized by Turkey alone of all nations of the world. Sharp criticisms came from the United States, which had otherwise shown understanding of the period of military rule. Although the failure of congressional critics to prevent a sizable increase in aid to Turkey in 1984 limited Turkish unhappiness, grievances against the United States remained close to the surface. This bitterness was clearly visible in the Turkish anger at congressional interest in commemorating "genocide" against Armenians during World War I.

Over the next ten years, Turkey was also periodically torn by desire to renegotiate the Cooperation on Defense and Economy Agreement. But it faced the reality that in a climate of shrinking U.S. foreign aid, merely keeping what Turkey had was likely to be all that was possible. Thus the end of the cold war found Turkey with occasional strains in its relations with the United States, yet still with an overwhelming interest in not letting the comfortable bonds of the past snap.

Troubles with Washington also impelled the Turks to redouble efforts to smooth out tangled relations with Europe. After municipal elections in March 1984 revalidated the genuineness of Turkey's return to democratic procedure, European criticism abated. Turkey was allowed to resume its seat in the Council of Europe, though by the end of the 1980s Western accusations of serious human rights abuses against the Kurds in Turkey again soured relations. That, coupled with intransigent Greek opposition, doomed Ozal's continuing demands to enter the European Union and set the stage for the rejection Turkey faced toward the end of the 1990s, when the European Union countries left Turkey off the list of future members. It was an uphill struggle to get Turkey's bid for full membership put back on the agenda in 1999.

The disintegration of the Soviet Union at the end of 1991 capped a process of increasing strategic irrelevance of cold war politics. Turkey faced a need to develop a new rationale for alliance arrangements with its Western partners; at the same time it was freed from constraints in dealing with the Muslims and Turkic peoples of the former USSR. Turkish companies were sought after for joint ventures in Russia and the other successor states. Indeed, Turkey's efforts to establish links with Azerbaijan and the Central Asian states were seen by some as a race with Iran. That seemed a considerable distortion of reality, as Turkey's rhetoric belied the relatively small economic and cultural commitment it actually made to Central Asia. Economic concerns, not political rivalry, best explain Turkish activity in this field.

Oil diplomacy became the heart and soul of Turkish policy toward the Caucasus and Central Asia in the latter 1990s. Oil exploration in the Caspian basin produced substantial finds, impelling the major international oil companies to seek a route to get this oil to market. Russia wanted these routes to pass through its territory to assure sustained financial and diplomatic importance in this region. Turkey equally desired pipeline routes through its territory to the Mediterranean and also adamantly opposed increasing Bosphorus traffic, especially by loaded oil tankers whose passage through the tortuous straits posed a safety threat to Istanbul. With American help, Turkey has in the last years of the twentieth and the early years of the twenty-first century pressed Azerbaijan and Georgia to smooth the way for a pipeline from Baku to the Turkish port of Ceyhan on the Mediterranean. The countries agreed in principle in 2000, and engineering studies were begun.

The 1990s confirmed an increasing focus on regional problems in Turkish foreign policy. After the end of the Iran-Iraq war in 1988, it became increasingly difficult to maintain the important trade relationships with both these rival states that had bolstered Turkey's economy during the 1980s. Iraq's pressure on its Kurdish population led to a large outflow of refugees across the Turkish border. Before that could be fully resolved, Iraq's invasion of Kuwait in 1990 and the resulting Desert Storm operation led by the United States changed Turkey's relations with its southeastern neighbor. In consonance with U.N. resolutions, Turkey closed the important oil pipeline to the Mediterranean from northern Iraq and fitfully shut off much cross-border commerce. At the same time, that left Turkey as one of the key protectors of the autonomous Kurdish entity in northern Iraq, a relationship that reversed long-standing Turkish opposition to anything that could possibly encourage Turkey's own Kurdish population. Turkey mounts occasional cross-border operations into northern Iraq against PKK camps near the border in its efforts to wind up the Kurdish insurgency at home. And Ankara clearly wants Baghdad eventually to resume control of this northern area, a desire that could one day conflict with American interest in continuing the isolation of Saddam Hussein's regime in Iraq.

As Turkey enters the new century, the panoply of problems with friends and former foes confirmed the difficulties of a relatively small state in following the self-reliant pattern that the Turks had desired since the start of the republic. Turkish insistence that its allies join it in intervening to help Muslims in Bosnia was symptomatic of Turkey's painful new challenges. Whereas the United States espoused policies there and in Kosovo closer to what Turkey desired, the Europeans dragged their feet. It was a shock to Ankara to learn that as the international environment became more complex and the cold war receded, the levers that had worked so successfully for the Turks in the immediate postwar era no longer yielded fully satisfactory results. Its efforts to establish a multidimensional foreign policy with greatly expanded trade with the Third World proved difficult to accomplish. Turkey's reliance on the United States remained the principal prop of its foreign relationships and its course into the European Union posed difficult challenges, despite the recognition that it one day could be a full EU member.

Political Prospects

Turkey has impressive strengths in facing the future. Its political system has come a long way back from the 1980 military incursion toward full civilian control. Given the changes in Turkish political awareness and the increasing complexity of the problems the government confronts, as well as the international climate of the post–cold war world, the country is not likely to experience another interlude of military rule. The officers subscribe to the legitimacy of democratic procedure and recognize that popular tolerance for another military incursion would not be forthcoming. They then will probably be content to operate as a pressure group, indeed one with diminishing clout. Thus parliamentary democracy seems secure.

What contributes uncertainty to just how the parliamentary system will function, however, is the generational shift from leaders now in their seventies to men and women in their forties and fifties. In general, the younger would-be leaders are likely to have a more relaxed view of Kemalism; economic development rather than reform is their watchword. Often their tolerance for religious observance is greater than that of the intensely secular generation that preceded them. They also passed their formative years in the multiparty atmosphere of the 1970s and after, where political alignments were fluid and coalition building the order of the day.

Unfortunately some of the younger generation have already been brushed by accusations of corruption. Tansu Ciller, born in 1948, acceded to power in 1993 with the high hopes of many modern middle-class Turks, who were impressed with her dynamism and professional accomplishments. That view has been tarnished by parliamentary votes to refer her to the courts on charges that she tampered with the sale of state assets and used covert funds from the government for illicit purposes. Her rival Mesut Yilmaz, head of the Motherland Party, was also the subject of parliamentary accusations that he personally gained in the letting of state contracts while he was in charge of the government. Though parliament voted to exonerate Yilmaz, the general aura of suspicion of corruption surrounding these leaders contrasts sharply with the general sense that Bulent Ecevit and Suleyman Demirel, who have been leaders on the Turkish political scene for many decades, have not been tainted by such activities.

All the new figures who will take leadership roles in Turkey over the next few years are likely to accord high priority to seeking to remain at the top for a lengthy period whatever their electoral success. Retirement from politics is unusual in Turkey. The only recent example is in the reestablished Republican People's Party, where Deniz Baykal resigned a few days after the party failed to elect any deputies in the 1999 elections. But subsequently Baykal resumed his leadership position. Other leaders have preferred to ride out failure, depending on their autocratic control of party mechanisms to remain at the head. Thus on both the right and the left, the leaders who emerge in the present period of fluidity may emulate their predecessors in trying to entrench themselves in every way against rivals.

This generational shift is taking place when the system is facing a need to come to terms with what were seen in the past as fringe elements. Devlet Bahceli, the new leader of the Nationalist Movement Party, whose roots are in the ultra-nationalist wing of the political spectrum, has confounded those who expected that he would exemplify the radicalism of Alparslan Turkes, the long-time leader of this point of view. Instead Bahceli has conducted himself with great moderation, despite pressures from elements in his party to insist on positions that are dear to the party but would threaten the unity of the government coalition. It remains to be seen how these intraparty tensions will be resolved.

The place of religion in politics is also an open question. The Welfare Party exploited the disillusionment of the voters with old-line politicians to argue "You have voted for the rest, now vote for the best!" But the party lost luster during its year at the head of government, after it withdrew its corruption charges against Ciller when she agreed to enter a coalition with Welfare as a junior partner. Religiously oriented politics also suffered from the obvious disapproval of the military. Those factors help account for the Virtue Party's failure to keep the votes that had flowed to Welfare in 1995. It seems unlikely that any successor to the Virtue Party will be able to enter a government coalition in the near future, even though a religiously oriented party is almost certain to remain on the scene for some time to come.

Political activity on behalf of Kurdish issues forms another area where the Turkish scene is changing. Particularly now that the insurrection phase of Kurdish activity is winding down, efforts to find legal ways to advance Kurdish interests are likely to intensify. Even as Kurdish mayors of the larger cities in eastern Turkey are being arrested and the Democratic People's Party still faces court action that could close it, pressures to bring Kurdish life back to normal are rising. The United States has lent its support to political progress on this issue. In mid-2000, the U.S. Embassy urged the opening of a business center in Diyarbakir in the heart of the area inhabited by Kurds, a move that was blocked by the Ankara government.

Intertwined with the Kurdish issue is the matter of human rights. Turkey has been subjected to intense criticism from many quarters in recent years over the treatment of political as well as criminal prisoners. Although the notorious Diyarbakir prison was closed, there is little chance that politicians will depend on more than resolute police action to deal with the root causes of violence in Turkish society. Torture continues to be applied in all too many cases where the authorities see threats to the state. Even so-called "thought crimes" may land victims at least in solitary confinement. The international community is watchful of the treatment of Kurdish dissidents. It was reliably reported that Washington, as the price of its cooperation in the arrest of PKK leader Ocalan, insisted that he not only be taken alive, but be tried fairly. Most foreign observers feel that his trial was fair, though there is strong international pressure against his execution. And the Turkish human rights community itself is gaining strength, with moves to ban the death penalty and liberalize laws on dissent.

Although politics is the national pastime, Turkish leaders have all come to recognize that the economy is important not only to their chances for reelection, but
also to Turkey's larger position in the post–cold war world. Much work remains to
be done on that account, despite Turkey's success in joining the European Customs Union in December 1995. Such innovations as creating a capital market
through the Istanbul stock exchange do help to attract foreign capital, but all these
gains were jeopardized by the looting of Turkey's largest banks, which brought
crisis in 2001. In addition, considerable stabilization of the exchange rate will be
necessary for the Turkish economy to reach its full potential. Even though the underground economy appears vibrant—some say it represents about 40 percent of
the total economic activity—Turkish per capita GNP still lags far behind that of
European states. Until that gap is closed at least in part and until steps to combat
inflation become more effective, Turkey will not be ready to meet the requirements for full membership in the European Union.

Defense matters also pose questions for Turkey. Global threats have given way
to regional challenges. Ozal seized the opportunity to stress Turkey's continuing
role as a bridge to the Third World and an asset to NATO in out-of-area operations. Thus he did not hesitate to demonstrate that Turkey could be relied on to
cooperate in the Gulf War and humanitarian operations in the Balkans and Iraq.
His successors have followed along this path, although Bulent Ecevit initially expressed reservations about American policy toward Iraq. The American role in
helping capture Ocalan seems to have changed his mind. And the joint emphasis
on combating terrorism after the September 11, 2001, terrorist attacks in New
York and Washington seems likely to solidify the trend toward warming relations
between Turkey and the United States in the new millennium.

As in the past, the unresolved Cyprus issue poses complications with Turkey's
allies in general and the United States in particular. U.N. proposals for confidence-
building measures on the island have not paved the way for progress. Nor has
American involvement in recent years led to advances. European pressures to resolve this issue before Turkey is admitted to the European Union are likely to generate friction. The legacy of distrust between the communities on the island remains all but unbridgeable. Turkey thus seems unlikely to be able to get off the
defensive in dealing with this issue and it will burden Turkish foreign relations for
a long time to come.

When dealing with these challenging problems, Turkey must also cope with
rising social dynamism. Migrants to the city are not able to find the economic satisfaction they crave. Politicians are under increasing pressure to meet the expanding needs of the rural sector and hence come up with spending projects like the
massive Ataturk Dam complex on the Euphrates with its attendant irrigation
works. Yet over time, rural-urban differences will narrow, and eventually, a truly
national Turkish culture will come into being.

In sum, Turkey faces manifold difficulties, but its past performance gives reason for guarded optimism. The Turks have shown themselves to be flexible in their approaches and do not hesitate to try new ways when the old are blocked. They have the resources in talent and material to succeed in the challenging business of modernizing their society and polity. They now have to demonstrate the political will.

Bibliography

Feroz Ahmad, *The Making of Modern Turkey* (London: Routledge, 1993), presents a wide-ranging essay, bringing the modern Turkish scene up to the 1990s, with an emphasis on politics. Erik J. Zurcher, *Turkey: A Modern History* (New York: Tauris, 1994), gives a good overview of developments in Turkey. Stanford J. Shaw's two-volume *History of the Ottoman Empire and Modern Turkey* (London: Cambridge University Press, 1976–1977) contains a mine of data on the events it chronicles. Andrew Mango, *Ataturk: The Biography of the Founder of Modern Turkey* (Woodstock, N.Y.: Overlook Press, 2000), gives a somewhat more reliable account of Turkey's great leader than Lord Kinross (Patrick Balfour) did in *Ataturk: A Biography of Mustafa Kemal, Father of Modern Turkey* (New York: William Morrow, 1965).

The political system of the Third Republic is analyzed in Ergun Ozbudun, *Contemporary Turkish Politics: Challenges to Democratic Consolidation* (Boulder: Lynne Riener Publishers, 2000). For an earlier view, see George S. Harris, *Turkey: Coping with Crisis* (Boulder: Westview Press, 1985). Cigdem Balim et al., *Turkey: Political, Social and Economic Challenges in the 1990s* (Leiden: E. J. Brill, 1995), address specialized segments of the problem. For the evolution of political parties up to 1989, consult Metin Heper and Jacob M. Landau, eds., *Political Parties and Democracy in Turkey* (London: I. B. Tauris, 1991). Andrew Finkel and Nukhet Sirman, eds., *Turkish State, Turkish Society* (London: Routledge, 1990), contains a broad analysis of political trends as well as ethnicity in the Third Republic.

Peter A. Andrews edited a magisterial treatment of Turkey's cultural geography, *Ethnic Groups in the Republic of Turkey* (Wiesbaden: Dr. Ludwig Teichert Verlag, 1989). Useful as well are Helen C. Metz, ed., *Turkey: A Country Study* (Washington, D.C.: Library of Congress, Federal Research Division, 1996), and John C. Dewdney, *Turkey: An Introductory Geography* (New York: Praeger Publishers, 1971).

Z.Y. Herslag carried the story of the Turkish economy into the post-1980 period of export orientation. See his *The Contemporary Turkish Economy* (New York: Routledge, 1988). His treatment is complemented by Henri J. Barkey's coverage of the important question of Turkey's political economy in *The State and the Industrialization Crisis in Turkey* (Boulder: Westview Press, 1990). The multiauthored volume, edited by Tevfik F. Nas and Mehmet Odekon, *Economics and Politics of Turkish Liberalization* (Bethlehem, Pa.: Lehigh University Press, 1992), also delves deeply into aspects of this subject.

The role of the military in politics is well depicted by William M. Hale, *Turkish Politics and the Military* (London: Routledge, 1995). This subject is also extensively analyzed in the earlier volume by Metin Heper and Ahmet Evin, eds., *State, Democracy and the Military: Turkey in the 1980s* (Berlin: Walter de Gruyter, 1988).

Yasemin Celik's *Contemporary Turkish Foreign Policy* (Westport, Conn.: Praeger, 1999) is a workmanlike account of Turkey's foreign relations at the end of the twentieth century.

Canan Balkir and Allan M. Williams, eds., *Turkey and Europe* (London: Pinter, 1993), provide background on some of the difficulties attendant on this Western relationship. Alvin Z. Rubinstein and Oles M. Smolansky, eds., *Regional Power Rivalries in the New Eurasia: Russia, Turkey, and Iran* (Armonk, N.Y.: M. E. Sharpe, 1995), cover the early stages of Turkey's relationship with the newly independent states of the former Soviet Union. For the Cyprus issue, see Suha Bolukbasi, *The Superpowers and the Third World: Turkish-American Relations and Cyprus* (Lanham, Md.: University Press, 1990), and Tozun Bahcheli, *Greek-Turkish Relations Since 1955* (Boulder: Westview Press, 1990).

Richard Tapper, ed., *Islam in Modern Turkey: Religion, Politics, and Literature in a Secular State* (London: I. B. Tauris, 1991), gives the background to recent religious developments. A more specialized treatment is in Julie Marcus, *A World of Difference: Islam and Gender Hierarchy in Turkey* (London: Zed, 1992). Other women's issues are treated in Sirin Tekeli, ed., *Women in Modern Turkish Society: A Reader* (London: Zed, 1995). The Kurdish challenge is covered in David McDowall, A *Modern History of the Kurds* (New York: I. B. Tauris, 1996). See also Robert Olson, *The Kurdish Nationalist Movement in the 1990s* (Lexington, Ky.: University Press of Kentucky, 1996). For the background of the issue, see Ismet G. Imset, *The PKK: A Report on Separatist Violence in Turkey (1973–1992)* (Ankara: Turkish Daily News, 1992).

The latest twists and turns of Turkish developments are well reported by the *Turkish Daily News* (Ankara). See http://www.TurkishDailyNews.com/FrTDN/latest/heads.htm for a daily Internet edition.

3

Islamic Republic of Iran

John W. Limbert
Mark J. Gasiorowski

Iran is the only Middle Eastern state that has preserved its identity for more than two millennia through the upheavals of Arab, Turkish, and Mongol invasions. It is heir to one of the richest cultures in the Middle East—a culture that extends far beyond the current political boundaries of the Islamic Republic into Anatolia, Central Asia, the Caucasus, and the Indian subcontinent. The latest chapter in Iran's turbulent history began in April 1979 when Ayatollah Rouhullah Khomeini announced the formation of an Islamic Republic, an entirely new entity in the region. He told the Iranian people to turn their backs on their centuries-old tradition of kingship and reorganize their political system on the basis of Shi'a Islam.

The events of 1978–1979 broke tradition in another way. Changes of government in Iran had usually come through foreign invasion, a struggle among tribes, or a coup at the center of power. The movement that brought the Islamic Republic to power, however, combined ancient Iranian traditions of religious heterodoxy, clandestine organization, and assertion of national pride with a newer, populist strain of political action drawing support from almost the entire Iranian population. The triumphant revolutionaries went far beyond replacing one elite with another. They built an Islamic Republic that deliberately rejected much of Iran's long and tragic history.

Historical Background

Iran's written history and vast body of legends stretch over twenty-five centuries and record the tenacious survival of certain characteristically Iranian historical traditions. Despite centuries of political and social upheaval, four basic historical patterns have endured to preserve the Iranians' sense of national identity: charismatic leadership, a profound religious impulse (combined with affection for the unorthodox), concern with justice, and acceptance of foreign customs embellished and adapted in accordance with Iranian tastes. These traditions have survived whether Iran's rulers have been Sassanian emperors, Arab chieftains, Turkish warlords, Pahlavi modernizers, or religious visionaries. Their survival has meant that after the latest political upheaval has run its course, an underlying Iranian identity has reemerged in an altered, but unmistakably Iranian, shape.

The Great Persian Empires

Iranian peoples were latecomers to the Middle East. When they first arrived on the Iranian plateau and in the Zagros Mountains (in the eleventh and tenth centuries B.C.), other kingdoms, notably Egypt and Babylonia, were already of great antiquity. Non-Iranian peoples—Assyrians, Elamites, and Urartians—had dominated the Iranian plateau until the seventh and sixth centuries B.C. In the middle of the sixth century B.C., Cyrus the Great united two Iranian tribes—the Medes and the Persians—to form the first great Persian Empire. Cyrus and his descendants, called the Achaemenians after an eponymous ancestor, established a world empire that ruled Mesopotamia, Syria, Palestine, Egypt, Anatolia, and Central Asia. Achaemenian campaigns in Greece met defeat at Marathon (490 B.C.) and at Salamis ten years later.

This first Persian Empire fell in 330 B.C. to the Macedonian forces of Alexander the Great. But the Achaemenians bequeathed to the world a rich legacy. Their tombs and ruined buildings at Persepolis and Naqsh-e Rostam, although modern Iranians ascribe them to mythical heroes, are visible reminders of Iran's antiquity, power, and wealth. The ancient world viewed the Achaemenian Empire as the model world state: The Persian Empire was *the* empire; its king was *the* king; and its laws ("the laws of the Medes and Persians which changeth not") were ideals of permanence. The Achaemenian tradition of co-equal tribal leadership (among Medes and Persians), of allowing diversity in religion and social customs, and of adopting the practices of subject peoples provided the ancient world its best example of how to rule a large, multiethnic empire effectively.

After the civil wars that followed the death of Alexander in 323 B.C., one of his generals, Seleucus, became ruler of Babylon in 312. Seleucus and his descendants ruled the eastern portion of Alexander's empire until, in the mid-second century B.C., the Seleucids lost control of the Iranian plateau and Mesopotamia to the Parthians, Iranian nomads originating east of the Caspian Sea. The Parthians formed a decentralized empire that at its height extended from India to Armenia. Western sources consider the Parthians the great rivals of Rome: Parthian mounted archers destroyed the armies of Crassus at Carrhae in 53 B.C.

The next great Persian Empire began in the third century A.D. when Ardashir Babakan, a local king in southern Fars Province, led a coalition that defeated the Parthians in A.D. 224. Ardashir and his son Shahpur (ruled 240–272) established the Sassanian dynasty, which ruled Iran until the Arab invasion of the seventh century. Shahpur renewed the war against Rome and scored remarkable successes: In 256 he captured and devastated Syrian Antioch, and in 260 he defeated and captured the Roman emperor, Valerian. Shahpur commemorated the latter event in inscriptions and massive rock carvings throughout southern Iran.

Sassanian wealth and power reached its apogee during the reign of Khosrow I Anushiravan (531–579). According to Iranian national tradition, as recorded by later Islamic writers, Khosrow I, "the Just," provided the model of kingship. His reforms of taxation, administration, landholding, and military organization survived into the Islamic period.

The later Sassanians exhausted themselves in wars against Rome and its successor, the Byzantine Empire. The wars that pitted Byzantine Christianity against Iranian Zoroastrianism were especially intense. In the early seventh century Sassanian forces captured Jerusalem, occupied Egypt, and laid siege to Constantinople itself. The tide turned against the Iranians, and the Byzantine emperor Heraclius forced them to make a humiliating peace in A.D. 628. The battered Sassanian Empire fell into anarchy just as the Muslim Arabs were beginning their triumphant parade of conquests, which was to change the face of the Middle East.

Islamic Iran: Arabs, Turks, and Mongols

The Sassanian Empire collapsed quickly after the Arabs defeated the Iranian armies at Qadisiya in Iraq (637) and at Nahavand in central Iran (641). Attracted by fertile land and opportunities for booty, large numbers of Arab tribesmen settled in Iran in the first centuries after the Muslim invasion. At first the Arab conquerors controlled only towns, the major agricultural centers, and the communications routes. Unprepared to govern a large, heterogeneous empire, the new rulers adopted the administrative and taxation systems they found in conquered Sassanian territory. From the earliest days of the Arab conquests, the Iranians were receptive to Islam. At first, Iranian converts were second-class citizens compared to the Arab settlers, but gradually, by sheer force of numbers, the distinction between Arab and non-Arab Muslim became unimportant, as most Iranians accepted the new religion.

The Iranians became enthusiastic adherents of Islam and turned their considerable talents in art, architecture, government, military affairs, music, and poetry to serving their new faith. What emerged from the fusion of Islam and Iran was remarkable: an Iranian-Islamic civilization that broke the earlier limits of both the Iranian and the Arab cultures and that spread its religious and cultural message into North Africa, India, Central Asia, and Southeast Asia.

Iranian Muslims, unlike the native peoples of Egypt, North Africa, and Syria, did not adopt Arabic as a spoken language. Arabic remained the only written language of the new Islamic empire until the tenth century, when modern Persian, written in the Arabic script, emerged as a mature literary language at the capital of the Samanid dynasty, in Bokhara. The poet Ferdowsi composed much of his Persian-language national epic masterpiece, the *Shahnameh,* during the time the Samanids ruled in northeastern Iran and Central Asia.

From the seventh to the eleventh century, Iran was ruled either as part of the Arab caliphate or by local dynasties. Beginning in the eleventh century, rule shifted to Turkish military commanders whom local rulers and caliphs had recruited into service. Thus began a thousand years of almost uninterrupted political and military supremacy by Altaic-speaking peoples as well as the Turkification of about one-fourth of the Iranian population. The eleventh to thirteenth centuries also marked the zenith of Iranian cultural life, as Turkish sultans fostered the new Persian language, patronized Persian poets, followed Iranian models of administration (as interpreted by Iranian scholars), and endowed Iranian cities with some of their most magnificent monuments.

Civil strife among the Turkish rulers and the horrific Mongol invasions of the thirteenth century brought this golden age to an end. Flourishing centers of Iranian civilization at Nishapour, Marv, Balkh, and Herat never recovered from the Mongol destruction. Unlike the Turks, who were Muslims when they reached Iran, the Mongols remained faithful to their original nomadic customs and despised the settled traditions of Iranian life. Taking only a predatory interest in their subjects, they destroyed agriculture and trade by squeezing the last drop of revenue from the country. Although the last Mongol rulers converted to Islam, in the early fourteenth century the country disintegrated rapidly into anarchy and civil war among rival Turco-Mongol chieftains.

A Shi'a State

Modern Iran originated with the rise of the Safavid dynasty in the sixteenth century. Shah Ismail, the first Safavid ruler (ruled 1501–1524), laid the foundations of modern Iran by making Twelver Shi'ism, until then a minority faith, the state religion and by uniting territory within roughly the same boundaries that exist today. For the first time in centuries, most of Iran was neither ruled from outside as part of a larger empire nor divided among local warlords.

Shah Abbas I, "the Great" (ruled 1587–1628), brought Safavid power to its height. His empire equaled those of his contemporaries in both Asia and Europe: Queen Elizabeth I in England, Philip II in Spain, and Akbar the Great in Moghul India. Abbas enjoyed military successes against the Ottomans to the west and the Uzbeks to the east. In 1598 he moved his capital to Isfahan, where he and his successors built superb bridges, markets, palaces, and mosques. Thanks to Safavid town planning, Isfahan today is still the finest city in Iran.

After a long decline hidden by a facade of prosperity, the Safavids fell to Afghan invaders in 1722. There followed more than seventy years of anarchy and strife among local rulers and Ottoman and Russian invaders. Finally, in the late nineteenth century, the Turkish-speaking Qajar tribe, led by the eunuch Agha Mohammad Khan, defeated rival warlords (chiefly the Zands of Shiraz and Kerman) and reunited most of what the Safavids had ruled. Agha Mohammad Khan established his capital at Tehran, until then an insignificant village south of the Alborz Mountains, and proclaimed himself *shahanshah* (king of kings) of Iran in 1796.

Agha Mohammad's Qajar dynasty ruled Iran until 1925. These years were not fortunate for Iran, which deteriorated from a world-class empire under the Safavids to a bankrupt de facto colony of Britain and Russia, kept nominally independent only by their competing ambitions. Under the Qajars Iran somehow lost its energy and creativity and was unable to resist the encroachments of foreign powers, particularly Czarist Russia. In the early twentieth century, the Russians defeated the Iranians in two disastrous wars, and the outcome was not only the loss of Iranian territory in the Caucasus but the virtual loss of national independence. By the provisions of the Treaty of Turkmanchai (1828), Iran abandoned its right to maintain a navy on the Caspian Sea, paid a heavy indemnity to Russia, limited duty on Russian goods to 5 percent, and granted extensive extraterritorial privileges (or "capitulations") to Russian merchants.

On the eastern side of the Caspian Sea, the Iranians could do nothing but watch as the independent khanates of Central Asia fell one after another to the advancing Russians. Iran's current northeastern frontier was finally established following the Russian defeat of the Turkoman tribes at Geok-Tappeh (1881) and the czar's annexation of Marv (1884).

Internally, Qajar Iran was shaken by the Babi movement in the 1840s and 1850s, by the tobacco boycott of 1891-1892, and by the constitutional revolution of 1906-1911. Babism originated in a belief that a living "gate" (*bab*) could communicate with the Shi'a hidden imam. (The various Shi'a sects believe that a designated imam, or leader of the Muslim community descended from Imam Ali, miraculously disappeared and is in a state of occultation until he returns to the world on the Day of Judgment. "Twelvers," the predominant Shi'a sect and the sect of Iran, believe this occurred to the twelfth imam.) When a Shiraz preacher claimed to be this gate, his followers (called "Babis") came into open conflict with the authorities. The Qajars suppressed the Babis with great difficulty, and the movement's exiled leaders transformed its radical, messianic message into the universal, pacifist doctrines of the modern Baha'i faith. But the Shi'a clergy feared the pacifist Baha'is no less than the militant Babis, and persecutions have continued.

The later Qajars were constantly strapped for cash and paid their bills by selling concessions such as customs collection, port operation, and road construction to foreign adventurers. In 1891–1892, the sale of a fifty-year monopoly on tobacco distribution and export to an Englishman provoked a general strike in the major urban bazaars and a well-organized consumer boycott. United resistance (encouraged by the Russians) forced the Qajars to cancel the concession and pay heavy compensation to the concessionaires. In paying this compensation, the Iranians incurred their first foreign debt, and the memory of that burden and its indignities still echoes in today's debates over foreign loans and financing for development projects.

Iran's entry into the oil age passed almost unnoticed. In 1901, Shah Mozaffar al-Din signed an oil concession agreement with the Australian financier William Knox D'Arcy. Following the discovery of oil in 1908, D'Arcy's interests were reorganized into the Anglo-Persian Oil Company (APOC). On the eve of World War I, the British government bought a 51 percent share of the company, but oil income did not become a significant factor in Iran's economy until the 1930s.

The Pahlavi Dynasty

Although officially neutral, Iran became a battleground for competing armies during World War I. At the end of the war the country was in chaos, with an impotent central government beset by separatist and tribal uprisings from within and foreign pressures from without. In 1921 Reza Khan Pahlavi, commander of the Persian Cossack Brigade—one of the few cohesive military forces left in the country—engineered a bloodless coup in alliance with the pro-British journalist Zia al-Din Tabataba'i. Four years later, Reza Khan had suppressed tribal rebellions, forced Zia al-Din to leave the country, and made himself monarch after deposing Ahmad Shah, the last Qajar ruler.

A direct, brutal, and uneducated man, Reza Shah despised the debates and compromises of politics, the refinements of high Persian culture, and the social and religious traditions that he felt had kept Iran permanently backward and subservient to foreigners. During his sixteen-year reign (1925–1941) he undertook a radical transformation of Iranian society in imitation of Kemal Ataturk in neighboring Turkey. With the military as his base, he sought to (1) create an Iranian nationalism distinct from Islam and based on pre-Islamic, imperial glory; (2) weaken the power of the clergy in law, education, and family life; and (3) establish a centralized, industrial state and administration backed by a large, modern military.

Reza Shah admired efficient government administered from the top and had no patience with anyone who questioned his vision. His greed and brutality made him increasingly unpopular at home, but it was his affinity for the Germans that ultimately brought his downfall. For the Allies, Iran could be a major resupply route to the Soviet Union during World War II. In August 1941, when Reza Shah rejected British and Soviet demands to expel German expatriates and allow transit routes across Iran for supplies, the Allies invaded and forced Reza Shah to abdicate in favor of his son, Mohammad Reza Pahlavi. Shattered by his beloved army's rapid collapse, Reza Shah went into exile, first in Mauritius and then in South Africa, where he died in 1944.

The young Mohammad Reza Shah, twenty-two at the time of his father's abdication, remained a minor political figure during the war years and for the next decade. Center stage belonged to the occupying armies, the tribes, regional separatist movements, and strong-willed and ambitious Iranian politicians. Many of the last, such as Mohammad Mossadegh, Ahmad Qavam, and Zia al-Din, had been veterans of the pre-1925 political struggles. When the Allied occupation ended Reza Shah's restrictions on political life, these old warriors emerged from retirement and entered a boisterous and lively political arena.

In 1946, thanks to adroit Iranian diplomacy and Western support, major separatist movements in Azerbaijan and Kurdistan collapsed. The restoration of central government control in northwestern Iran, however, did not end the political clashes in Tehran, where colorful figures such as Mossadegh, Ali Razmara, Mozaffar Baqa'i, and Ayatollah Abu al-Ghassem Kashani contended for power. In 1949, under Mossadegh's leadership, four parties formed the National Front. The Front gradually focused its efforts on the questions of royal prerogatives and the struggle with the British government over the nationalization of the Anglo-Persian Oil Company.

Mossadegh became prime minister in 1951, but his coalition split apart when he was unable to resolve either the oil dispute with Britain or his political struggle with the shah. In August 1953 he fell victim to a pro-shah coup engineered by an alliance of royalist military officers (notably General Fazlollah Zahedi), hired street mobs (led by the notorious Sha'ban, "the Brainless"), and U.S. and British intelligence agencies. The shah and the empress, who had fled Iran when the coup appeared to have failed, returned in triumph, and National Front supporters were imprisoned, exiled, or executed. Mossadegh himself spent three years in prison and died while still under house arrest in 1967.

During the 1950s, the shah built the system of personal control that would characterize his rule until its collapse in the late 1970s. Although he put the coup leaders in key positions (and had his daughter marry General Zahedi's son), he made certain that none of them became serious rivals. In 1955 he removed the strong-willed Zahedi from the prime ministership and replaced him with the first of many nonentities. The stagnant economy revived, thanks to new oil revenues and financial aid from the United States. With this new money the shah bought loyalty from the army, the newly established security organization (SAVAK), and the technocrats who ran development projects.

A brief and modest liberalization in 1961–1962 ended when the shah removed Prime Minister Ali Amini from office. A financial crisis and pressure from the administration of U.S. President John F. Kennedy had forced the shah to appoint Amini, an ambitious and independent-minded Qajar aristocrat, to the prime ministership. When Amini was unable to work with either the shah or the National Front, he resigned and was replaced by Asadollah Alam, the shah's close ally.

In order to forestall criticism from the Americans and preempt the National Front's agenda, in 1963 the shah announced his own reform program, which he called the "white revolution of the shah and people." That same year he faced a serious challenge to his rule when the sixty-four-year-old Ayatollah Rouhullah Khomeini, from his teaching post in the holy city of Qom, launched direct, explicit attacks on the financial and moral corruption of the shah's regime. Although Khomeini's attacks contained heavy doses of clerical obscurantism (his attacks on coeducation, for example), many nationalists and liberals were impressed by Khomeini's refusal to be silent or to moderate his statements, when the slightest public criticism of the shah was unheard of. Excited by Khomeini's daring, they were willing to put aside their traditional anticlericalism and ignore much of the objectionable content of his message.

In June 1963 Khomeini's outspoken criticisms led to his arrest at the height of the mourning month of Moharram. The response to his arrest was three days of bloody rioting in the Tehran bazaars—the most serious challenge to the shah since the 1953 struggles with Mossadegh. But the military held firm, and the universities, for the most part, remained quiet. As for Khomeini himself, he spent a few months in prison and then resumed his outspoken attacks, this time choosing as his target fraud in the parliamentary elections of 1963 and provisions of a law drafted to grant immunities to U.S. military advisers and their families. In response, the government arrested and exiled Khomeini. He first went to Turkey and then settled in Iraq, in the Shi'a holy city of Najaf, where he continued to speak and write against the shah's rule until the dramatic events of 1978–1979 took him first to Paris and then triumphantly back to Iran.

The shah was at the height of his power between 1963 and 1978. He silenced public criticism, and his security forces suppressed weak and divided opposition groups. He surrounded himself with sycophants who fed his need for flattery and enriched themselves from Iran's oil income, which became a cascade after 1973. Masking a deep insecurity that originated in the events of 1941–1953, the shah showed the world a facade of self-confidence in extravaganzas such as his coronation in 1967 and the celebration of 2,500 years of Iranian monarchy in 1971.

The sharp rise of crude oil prices in 1973 and the enormous wealth that flowed into Iran put new strains on the country's delicate social and political fabric. The figures were spectacular. Between early 1971 and late 1973 the average posted price for a barrel of crude rose from $1.79 to $11.65, and the government's oil revenues rose from $2.3 billion in 1972 to $18.5 billion in 1974. The fifth development plan (1973–1978) provided for expenditures of $69 billion, compared to $8.3 billion in the fourth plan (1968–1972).

Inundated by this huge inflow of money, Iranian society lost its moorings. Although almost everyone benefited to some extent from the new riches, which paid for roads, electric plants, schools, hospitals, and power supplies, a visible minority gained far more than most of the population. The poor were better off in absolute terms, but their relative economic position deteriorated as they watched contractors, middlemen, and land speculators outdistance them in the economic race. The oil bonanza exacerbated existing divisions within Iranian society. There was a surplus of luxury villas and apartments and a shortage of affordable housing for middle- and lower-class families; students in government schools sat in overcrowded classrooms, whereas students from newly wealthy families flocked to booming private schools; some Iranians made monthly shopping trips to Europe, whereas others stood in line for onions and milk.

The government was never able to fulfill the promises it made in 1973, when the new oil wealth began to flow. Within a few years the private and public spending spree—and the accompanying mismanagement and corruption—had consumed even the quadrupled oil income, and Iran was again in economic crisis. At the same time, the shah could not maintain the harsh authoritarian control of political life that he had established in the late 1960s and early 1970s. His loss of control seems to have been due to a combination of factors, including the new economic strength and independence of Iran's middle and lower-middle classes, the talk of human rights by U.S. President Jimmy Carter and his administration, the shah's own desire for greater acceptance on the international scene, and his fatal illness, cancer, which was first diagnosed in 1974.

Islamic Revolution

Riots broke out in Qom in January 1978 and in Tabriz the following month. In spring 1978, rioting broke out in many Iranian cities, often on the fortieth day after previous rioting, when demonstrators, in accordance with Shi'a custom, held mourning ceremonies for victims of earlier disturbances. Following a summer lull in demonstrations, the regime and the revolutionaries began their final struggle in August–September 1978. In August several hundred died in the southern town of Abadan after arsonists (whose identity remained unknown) burned a cinema; and in September hundreds more died after troops fired on demonstrators in Tehran's Zhaleh Square. These events left little possibility of compromise. While the government was vacillating between repression and accommodation, larger and more strident crowds were calling for the end of the monarchy and the establishment of an Islamic Republic.

As the shah's government staggered under the blows of continuing strikes and demonstrations, it found itself in a death struggle with a coalition led by Ayatollah Khomeini and his close associates among the radical clergy. Based in the bazaars and in some mosques and theological schools (especially the Qom Center of Religious Scholarship), this group was uncompromising in its opposition to the shah and his programs. Fundamentally opposed to the idea of monarchy, it attacked the shah where he was most vulnerable: for corruption, destruction of Islamic values, and plundering the country on behalf of foreigners. The radical views and uncompromising stance of Khomeini and his associates attracted many radical lay Islamists to them, giving them a strong base of support among students and other sectors of society.

Groups with other programs—nationalists, Marxists, religious conservatives, and so forth—joined the opposition, but the radical clergy held important advantages that enabled it to dominate the revolution. During the years of royal dictatorship, while the shah's security apparatus was suppressing labor unions, professional associations, and political parties, the clergy had preserved its organizational bases in mosques, bazaars, Hoseiniyehs, and religious schools. Khomeini's record of uncompromising opposition to the shah, his incorruptibility, and his immense personal magnetism gave him and his associates, including politically astute clerics like Mohammad Beheshti and Ali Akbar Hashemi-Rafsanjani, an overwhelming political advantage over their coalition partners. Secular politicians, for example, had difficulty speaking to the urban masses and had little taste or talent for the street and neighborhood politics of revolution.

Despite the radical clergy's strong populist base, it was the middle-class constituency of the old National Front—professionals, civil servants, students, and teachers—who ensured the victory of the revolution. These groups added to the disorder in the streets by paralyzing Iran's modern sectors and shutting down banks, newspapers, oil production, schools, factories, and government offices. The paralysis did much to undermine the regime by convincing many Iranians that the shah was losing his grip and that they could safely air their long pent-up grievances. Those who had been politically apathetic became openly hostile to the government; those who had supported the monarchy became neutral, awaiting the outcome of the crisis. Some wealthy Iranians moved their money out of the country and decided to wait out the crisis from the safety of Europe or the United States. Others were said to have joined the *hezb-e-baad* (party of the wind), waiting to see which way the political wind would blow before committing themselves to the winning side.

In December 1978 the once powerful Iranian army stood aside and did nothing to prevent enormous opposition marches and rallies on the ninth and tenth days of Moharram. After this symbolic defeat, soldiers began massive desertions and mutinies, turning against their officers rather than firing on demonstrators. In

provincial towns first, government authority melted away, replaced by local neighborhood committees (*komitehs*) under clerical leadership. In many towns the army
and the revolutionaries tacitly agreed to avoid confrontations while awaiting the
final outcome in Tehran.

The end was not long in coming. In late December 1978 Shahpur Bakhtiyar, a
former National Front politician, agreed to become prime minister when the
shah promised to leave the country. The shah left on January 16, 1979; Khomeini
returned to a triumphant reception in Tehran on February 1 and appointed
Mehdi Bazargan to lead a provisional government. Army and police units disappeared from the streets, and on February 9 fighting broke out between armed revolutionaries and the forces that had remained loyal to the government. By the
evening of February 11 the revolutionaries had won control of Tehran and announced their victory over the state radio. Bakhtiyar went into hiding, and
Bazargan became prime minister of the new provisional government. In late
March a popular referendum overwhelmingly approved the establishment of an
Islamic republic, bringing the Pahlavi dynasty formally to an end.

Islamic Republic

Within a year of the actual revolution, the radical clerics and lay Islamists who had
been the core of the revolutionary coalition defeated their former allies and consolidated power in their own hands. From the first they prevented Bazargan from
forming an orderly government—which would, in their view, limit populist fervor and keep true revolutionaries out of power. Although during the revolution
the radical Islamists accepted support from secular nationalists, Marxists, and others whose views they did not share, they were not prepared to allow these groups
any voice in running the Islamic Republic. In November 1979, as the revolution
was disintegrating into political, local, and tribal squabbles, radical Islamist students
seized the U.S. embassy in Tehran and held its personnel hostage until January
1981, launching a so-called "second revolution" that brought down Bazargan's
provisional government. A powerful network of Friday preachers, neighborhood
vigilantes, well-organized street mobs, and leaders of the Islamic Republican Party
(IRP) took advantage of the embassy seizure and the subsequent "revelations" of
embassy documents to launch an all-out assault on their rivals. Their victory in
this power struggle enabled them to move from clandestine control of shadowy
"revolutionary institutions" into open mastery of the Iranian state.

Bazargan was replaced by a Revolutionary Council consisting mainly of radical clerics, which had been established by Khomeini shortly before the revolution. The Revolutionary Council oversaw the completion of a constitution for
the Islamic republic and its ratification in a December 1979 popular referendum.
With the foundations of the Islamic republic now in place, elections for the new

president and parliament could be held. The January 1980 presidential election was won decisively by Abu al-Hasan Bani Sadr, a relatively moderate lay intellectual who had been a key aid to Khomeini since the summer of 1978. Parliamentary elections were held in March and May 1980. The IRP swept these elections, giving the radical clergy and lay Islamists who dominated this party control over the new parliament and setting the stage for a confrontation between Bani Sadr and these radicals.

Bani Sadr and the radicals in parliament clashed for several months over appointments to the premiership and other cabinet positions. The radicals, led by Beheshti and Speaker of Parliament Rafsanjani, eventually forced Bani Sadr to accept Mohammad Ali Raja'i as prime minister. Bani Sadr and the radicals then haggled over the other cabinet appointments, leaving six vacant for several months and the position of foreign minister vacant for a year. During this period the beleaguered Bani Sadr became increasingly dependent on the Islamic leftist *Mujahedin-e-Khalq*, whose large cadre of urban guerrillas posed a serious threat to the radical Islamists.

Following more than a year of clashes along their common border, Iraq invaded Iran in September 1980. Iraqi forces seized some 4,000 square miles of Iranian territory during the first few months of the war, including much of the oil-producing territory in southwestern Iran. The Iranian government immediately began a massive effort to mobilize resistance to the invasion, producing a huge outpouring of volunteer fighters and a groundswell of popular support for the Islamic regime. Bani Sadr and his radical opponents both tried to take advantage of the situation by identifying themselves with the war effort. By early 1981 they had begun to use the war as a pretext to attack one another. When the U.S. embassy hostages were released in January 1981, the two sides attacked each other bitterly over the terms of the release.

The clashes between Bani Sadr and the radical Islamists grew increasingly tense in the first half of 1981. Bani Sadr's moderate backers and the Mujahedin organized a series of rallies that were attacked by radical vigilantes. The radicals held rallies of their own, which were generally much larger than the pro–Bani Sadr rallies. By April violent clashes were occurring almost daily. The parliament and other institutions controlled by the radicals began to strip Bani Sadr's powers and close down moderate newspapers, leading Bani Sadr to call for a popular referendum to resolve the confrontation. Frustrated by the factional infighting, in late May Ayatollah Khomeini began publicly criticizing Bani Sadr. With Khomeini apparently on their side, the radicals moved to eliminate Bani Sadr, filing legal charges against him, arresting many of his associates, assaulting his supporters, and calling for his execution. Khomeini dismissed Bani Sadr on June 22, leading him to flee underground with help from the Mujahedin.

With the radical Islamists now poised to consolidate control, the Mujahedin tried to initiate a counterrevolutionary uprising. They organized a huge rally on

June 20 that was brutally attacked by the radicals, leaving dozens dead, hundreds injured, and over 1,000 arrested. Arrests continued on the following days, and large numbers of Mujahedin and secular leftist guerrillas were executed. The Mujahedin then initiated a series of bombings and assassinations aimed at killing off the radical Islamist leadership and bringing down the Islamic regime. The most dramatic was a June 28 bombing that killed seventy-four top IRP leaders, including Beheshti, four cabinet ministers, and twenty-seven members of parliament. The radicals reacted with fury, arresting thousands of people and executing hundreds. Additional bombings and assassinations occurred in the following months. After Raja'i was elected president in late July, he and the newly appointed prime minister, Muhammad Javad Bahonar, were killed in another bombing. The arrests and executions continued for many months, leaving thousands dead and breaking the back of the Mujahedin. Most of the surviving members of the Mujahedin eventually fled to Iraq, where they were armed by the Iraqi government and permitted to carry out sporadic cross-border attacks. They continue to operate from bases in Iraq today.

In October 1981, Ali Khamene'i, a radical cleric, was elected president and Mir Hossein Musavi, a radical lay Islamist, was appointed prime minister. These men, together with Speaker of Parliament Rafsanjani, worked under the general guidance of Ayatollah Khomeini to consolidate the radical Islamists' control and bring order and stability to Iran. After defeating the Mujahedin, the most urgent priority was to drive Iraqi forces out of Iran, which was accomplished in May 1982. Iran then carried the war into Iraqi territory, hoping to bring down the government of Saddam Hussein and establish an Islamic state in Iraq. Iranian forces initially made some gains but soon became bogged down, producing a brutal war of attrition that lasted until 1988. Khamene'i was reelected in August 1985 and Musavi was reappointed in October 1985.

Having defeated their various opponents, the radical Islamists began to feud among themselves in the mid-1980s. The most important dispute was between the Islamic leftists associated with Prime Minister Musavi, who favored a radical redistribution of wealth and statist economic policies, and the Islamic conservatives associated with the traditional clerical elite and the bazaar, who favored laissez-faire economic policies. This dispute persisted throughout the mid- and late 1980s, preventing the government from carrying out effective economic policies.

Another dispute began in November 1986, when it emerged that the United States had been selling arms to Iran in exchange for the release of U.S. hostages held in Lebanon by Iran-backed guerrillas. This information was revealed by Mehdi Hashemi, a radical cleric and son-in-law of Ayatollah Hossein Ali Montazari, Khomeini's designated successor. Hashemi was later executed, apparently because the arms-for-hostages deal had been engineered by Rafsanjani. A third dispute emerged in the late 1980s, when Montazari and others began to call for greater liberalization. Khomeini tried to stop this trend in early 1989 by issuing a death sentence for British author Salman Rushdie, whose book *The Satanic Verses* was called offensive to Islam and by forcing Montazari to resign as his designated successor.

The Era of Moderation

Several key changes occurred in 1988 and 1989 that initiated a trend toward moderation in Iran. In July 1988, after most of its ground forces had been driven out of Iraq and much of its navy had been destroyed in clashes with the United States, Iran finally agreed to a U.N. proposal to end the Iran-Iraq war. In June 1989, after a long illness, Ayatollah Khomeini died. In July, Rafsanjani, who had emerged as a leading advocate of moderation, was elected president. At the same time, Iran's voters approved a package of constitutional reforms designed to reduce the gridlock that had largely paralyzed the political system since the mid-1980s. The most important of these reforms was a measure to eliminate the position of prime minister and thus concentrate executive power in the hands of the president.

President Rafsanjani assembled a government dominated by centrist technocrats. His highest priority was to reform the economy, which had deteriorated sharply as a result of the war and years of inept, ideologically driven policymaking. Rafsanjani's economic reforms met strong opposition in parliament, which was dominated by Islamic leftists. Accordingly, he drew closer to the conservatives, who vetoed many leftist candidates for the 1992 parliamentary elections. Most of the remaining leftists were defeated at the polls, giving the conservatives a majority in parliament, which they retained in the 1996 elections. The conservative-controlled parliament soon turned against Rafsanjani and the centrists, however, blocking most of the reforms they sought to implement.

The 1992 elections demonstrated to the leftists that they had lost most of their popular support, leading them to become much more moderate. Prior to the May 1997 presidential election, the leftists therefore established a pro-reform coalition with the centrists, who were disillusioned with the conservatives' opposition to their economic reforms. This reformist coalition backed Mohammad Khatami, a moderate leftist, in the presidential election. Khatami won a landslide victory, demonstrating that the reformists' views were much more popular than those of the conservatives.

Khatami's election temporarily threw the conservatives off balance and gave the reformists an opportunity to begin carrying out reforms. The reformists' highest priority was to promote democracy, since the conservatives' control over parliament and most other state institutions would prevent them from implementing other reforms. They therefore began to pursue political reform, liberalizing the press, loosening restrictions on political activity, and challenging the conservatives' control over state institutions. The conservatives soon responded, assaulting and arresting reformist leaders, closing their newspapers, and attacking them with demagogic rhetoric. Ayatollah Khamene'i largely backed the conservatives, using the broad powers of his office to block many reformist initiatives. By the summer of 1998 the two factions were locked in a bitter power struggle, bringing the reform process largely to an end.

The reformists won another landslide victory in the February 1999 nationwide municipal council elections. The conservatives continued their attacks, however, focusing especially on the reformist press. In July 1999 the parliament passed a bill sharply limiting press freedom, triggering six days of severe rioting that shook the foundations of the Islamic regime. The reformists then won yet another landslide victory in the February 2000 parliamentary elections, gaining control over this important body. The conservatives reacted bitterly, closing down almost all reformist newspapers, arresting many reformist leaders, and vetoing much of the legislation passed by the new parliament. By the end of 2000 the reformist movement had been stopped, and popular frustrations were very high. Iran's future was quite uncertain.

Political Environment

Population and Social Structure

Iran still has the characteristics of a multiethnic empire in which the Persian language and Shi'a Islam are the dominant cultural strains. Just as the Achaemenian state was the empire "of the Medes and the Persians," modern Iran is a country dominated by two major ethnic groups—Persians and Azerbaijani Turks—who share the Shi'a faith and a love of Iranian nationhood. These two groups constitute about 70 percent of Iran's 65 million people.

The rest of Iran's population includes smaller ethnic and religious groups such as Kurds, Gilakis, Mazandaranis, Baluchis, Lors, Turkomans, Arabs, Armenians, Assyrians, Jews, Zoroastrians, and Baha'is. Many of the ethnic minorities have links to communities in neighboring countries, and the Turkomans, Armenians, and Azerbaijanis in the former Soviet Union have recently established independent countries. About 10 percent of Iran's population, mostly ethnic minorities living in remote border regions adjoining Afghanistan, Pakistan, Turkey, Iraq, the Persian Gulf, and Turkmenistan, follow Sunni Islam. Iran's non-Muslim population is about 1 percent and includes both "recognized" minorities—Jews, Christians, and Zoroastrians—and Baha'is, who lack official status as a minority and who have suffered periodic waves of persecution.

Iran's deserts, mountains, and forests have created inaccessible refuges where the inhabitants have preserved unique languages, religions, and customs. Inhabitants of the fertile Caspian coastal plains and mountains have costumes, folklore, and a cuisine unlike anything else within the country. The remote desert towns of Yazd and Kerman still shelter small Zoroastrian communities, the remaining followers of Iran's pre-Islamic state religion. Kurds, Azerbaijani Turks, and Christian Assyrians intermingle near the remote northwestern town of Urumiyeh. The mountains of Kurdistan shelter followers of the Ali-Elahi and the Yazidi (called "devil worshippers" in Persian) sects. In the poor, inaccessible region between Lar and the Persian Gulf, Sunni Islam remains strong among people speaking obscure southern Iranian languages. Dotting the Turkish-speaking northwest are isolated villages where inhabitants still speak Tati, the original Iranian language of Azerbaijan.

Whoever rules Iran must control a vast territory with a mixed population. Until the early twentieth century, the government of such an area included little except an army and a treasury, the existence of each depending on the other. Effective rule meant controlling the major towns and the main communication routes. Dynasties were usually tribal, coming to power after either a successful uprising inside Iran or an invasion from outside. Although Iran has seen many religion-based rebellions, rarely have its dynastic struggles had any ideological component. Two exceptions were the Safavids, who began as a militant Sufi order supported by Anatolian tribesmen, and the Islamic Republic. Although Khomeini's followers explicitly denounced the Safavids, his revolutionary movement followed many of their successful tactics—charismatic leadership, an underground propaganda network, and a mix of religion and politics. For their shock troops, the Islamic revolutionaries just substituted well-organized urban demonstrators for the Safavids' Turkish tribesmen.

Until the twentieth century much of the country's population lived in remote villages or as nomads unaffected by the political struggles that swept across the Iranian plateau. Population pressures and the oil boom meant that by the mid-1970s, the majority of Iran's population was urban, with 15 to 20 percent living in and around Tehran, the capital. Although urban mobs have always been a factor in Iranian politics, the increasing concentration of population in the cities shifted the centers of power from tribe-based or even "modern" armies to the streets of Iran's major cities. The Islamic revolutionaries, whether by accident or by design, owed their victory and their survival to their control of the streets in the large cities—particularly Tehran.

Iran's birth rate increased dramatically in the 1970s and 1980s, producing a large "baby boom" generation that began to come of age in the early 1990s. Sharp increases in education levels for both men and women meant that this generation was also more sophisticated than its predecessors. These changes produced a huge base of support among the Iranian youth and women for the reformist movement that emerged in the late 1990s. Indeed, these two groups formed the core of Khatami's supporters.

No matter who rules Iran, the family remains the fundamental building block of society. Although governments have imposed, with varying success, their own ideologies on the population, a network of kinship alliances shapes and controls much individual behavior. Attempts to apply other standards—such as ideology or merit—have conflicted with primary family loyalties. These loyalties confer both benefits and obligations. At its best, the Iranian extended family—including parents, children, in-laws, siblings, and cousins—supports an individual throughout his or her lifetime and provides the combined services of employment agency, educational adviser, marriage counselor, health and old age insurance, ward boss, and marriage broker. In return, the same kinship network puts strict limitations on individual freedom. All must pay visible respect to family elders; males must protect the honor of the family's women; all must defer to family wishes in questions of marriage, career, residence, child raising, and so on. All must be especially careful to avoid some ill-considered action that would bring shame or disgrace on the family.

Beyond the family, religious and professional associations are powerful forces in Iranian society. These associations, which often operate parallel to "official" societies, can organize elaborate ceremonies on religious holidays; they may control enough funds to operate welfare and education more efficiently than the government. Typically members of such associations are linked through a neighborhood, a mosque, or a religious leader. Senior members of such associations have ties to both the national or local political leadership and members of the lower and lower-middle class. Within these associations, marriage ties may reinforce other links, so individuals become not only colleagues within a neighborhood religious association but also relatives by blood and marriage.

Although not all Iranians are religious, a distinct strain of religiosity runs through their society. Religion shapes not only much of the politics of the current government but also more intimate details, such as speech patterns, personal relations, and family life. Communal prayer, pilgrimages to large and small shrines, and visits to the graves of deceased relatives are all popular activities. The major shrines at Mashhad, Qom, and Shiraz are not centers of dry piety but tourist centers, where pilgrims can shop, sightsee, trade, and meet visitors from other parts of the Shi'a world.

This same religiosity has often led Iranians in unexpected directions. As a people, Iranians have been as prolific in creating and refining religions as they are in creating beautiful objects of cloth, metal, wood, and stone. Their religious impulses have often led Iranians to reject accepted wisdom and follow mysticism, heresy, and heterodoxy in the search for divine truth. Even Iran's orthodoxy is different from the Sunni orthodoxy of 90 percent of the world's Muslims. Whatever its roots, the revolutionary, activist Islam that overthrew the Pahlavis in 1979 is a radical departure from the religion practiced elsewhere in the Islamic world.

Under the Pahlavis, and for the first time in its history, Iran's middle- and upper-middle-class elite openly separated itself from the traditions of Shi'a Islam. Although members of this new elite might have been individually religious, they followed an outwardly Western way of life. In so doing, they were encouraged by an official ideology hostile to those traditions that governed the lives of most Iranians. Members of this new elite knew little (and often cared less) about the beliefs and lives of the majority of their countrymen. They had cast their lot with a secular vision of Iran—a vision that Khomeini and his followers saw as an abomination.

The Islamic revolution decimated this class, not by eliminating it, but by making it irrelevant. Although many "modern" Iranians, repelled by the corruption and excesses of the Pahlavis, had enthusiastically supported the revolution, they found that Khomeini's version of an Islamic Republic had no place for them or their values. Their values were no longer those of the society at large, and if they wanted to stay in Iran, they would have to conform outwardly to the new order. Khomeini's message was clear: "You may stay if you like; you may go if you like. But Iran is no longer your country with your values." Khomeini never worried about an Iranian brain drain. The more potential opponents who left, the better. If Iran lost its computer specialists, its petroleum engineers, its pediatricians, that was too bad. But he was not going to compromise his beloved revolution for their sake. From the earliest days he told them, "The exits are open for those who cannot live in the new Iran."

Over one million Iranians accepted this offer, producing an unprecedented wave of emigration. As a result, there is now a large Iranian diaspora in Europe and the United States, especially in southern California, where Iranian immigrants have reconstructed the society of north Tehran middle-class neighborhoods. This emigration has also shaken family structures, with young people fleeing military service, economic failure, political and religious persecution, and social pressures while their parents and grandparents remain behind to face a lonely old age. As the Islamic regime moderated in the 1990s, the government made repeated efforts to persuade Iranian emigrés to return to Iran. Many of these emigrés strongly support Khatami and the reformist movement, but few have been willing to return home so far.

Economic Conditions

The traditional economy of Iran was based on agriculture, trade, and crafts such as textiles, medicinal oils, carpets, and tile making. Iran's nomadic population produced much of the country's meat and dairy products on land unsuitable for farming. Income from the sale of crude oil changed this economy in the twentieth century, when Reza Shah Pahlavi used oil revenues and taxes to build roads, construct the trans-Iranian railroad, and set up industrial plants, especially plants to produce import substitutes such as textiles, refined sugar, shoes, cosmetics, and cement.

Iran began earning significant revenues from crude oil sales in the 1950s, following agreements with foreign companies to divide revenues fifty-fifty. With growing world demand and the quadrupling of oil prices in 1973, crude oil sales overshadowed all other sources of government income. Oil money went into new industries, particularly steel, oil refineries, and petrochemicals, and into education, roads, and arms purchases. Neglect and mismanagement of agriculture, combined with an overvalued Iranian currency, undermined the agricultural sector and led to massive imports of cheap food and a large-scale movement of farmers to the cities to work in the construction and industrial boom. In the mid-1970s, for the first time in its history, the majority of Iran's population was urban.

The Islamic revolution and the war with Iraq set Iran's economic development back two generations. The lack of imported spare parts and raw materials led to rationing, shortages, and black markets. Many engineers and other specialists emigrated, producing shortages of skilled manpower. The war severely damaged Iran's oil production facilities and soaked up much of its foreign exchange, leaving little for new investment. Oil production fell from 5 million to 6 million barrels per day before the revolution to 2 million to 4 million after it, and domestic oil consumption increased substantially. Oil revenue therefore fell sharply, especially after oil prices collapsed in the mid-1980s. High population growth put severe pressure on jobs, education, and housing. Despite efforts to encourage agriculture, Iran became increasingly dependent on food imports, further depleting its foreign exchange earnings. Real incomes fell sharply as a result of inflation and depreciation of the *rial*, which fell by 99 percent against the dollar in 1978–2000. Twenty years after the revolution, real income per capita was still 40 percent below its prerevolution peak.

Since the late 1980s, Iran's leaders have carried out a series of five-year development plans aimed at reforming the economy. The first two plans failed to reach their goals, due to overly optimistic objectives, domestic opposition, and unforeseeable circumstances. The first plan faced strong opposition from Islamic leftists in parliament, who feared that privatization, subsidy cuts, exchange rate liberalization, and tight monetary policy would hurt the poor. The Islamic leftists lost control of parliament in 1992, raising hopes that economic reform might move forward. However, the conservatives who replaced them soon moved in a populist direction, gutting the second plan. Moreover, a series of riots rooted in poor economic conditions occurred throughout the country in the 1990s, leading Rafsanjani's government to back away from some of its more painful reforms. Low oil prices and U.S. economic sanctions also undermined the economy.

President Khatami initially focused on political rather than economic reform. However, in the summer of 1999 his government began a much-needed effort to unify the exchange rate. Khatami then unveiled the third development plan, which called for further privatization, subsidy cuts, increased foreign investment and non-oil exports, and efforts to increase tax collection and reduce bureaucracy. Khatami's conservative opponents then blocked key elements of the plan. The reformist-dominated parliament elected in February 2000 also initially focused on political reform, and higher oil prices made economic reform less urgent. In late 2000, Iran's long-term economic prospects therefore did not look good.

Political Structure

In late 1978 Ayatollah Khomeini created the Revolutionary Council to oversee the transition to an Islamic regime. He then asked Mehdi Bazargan to serve as prime minister and assemble a provisional government, pending the establishment of the new regime. During the next few months the radical Islamists created a series of revolutionary institutions that operated parallel to Bazargan's government and increasingly undermined it. These included a series of ad hoc revolutionary courts and paramilitary *komitehs* (committees), which administered "revolutionary justice" in an arbitrary and often brutal manner.

The radical Islamists then began the process of creating permanent political institutions that would embody Ayatollah Khomeini's views of Islamic government. Khomeini's vision called for building a *nezam-e Mohammadi,* the political system of the Prophet Muhammad. In this system the supreme religious leader ruled from his mosque, administering the finances, justice, and military affairs of a far-flung empire. Khomeini's ideal, which he applied in his private life, was to imitate both the simplicity and the incorruptibility of the early Islamic state. Although his original vision was not entirely complete, it was far more specific than any alternative. Khomeini's single-minded pursuit of a simple political ideal, his enormous popularity, and the powerful example of his honesty and austere personal life made short shrift of any political groups with competing visions of a new political system.

The political system Khomeini envisioned was based on the principle of *velayat-e faqih* (guardianship of the supreme jurist-theologian), which was embodied in the constitution that was drafted and ratified in 1979. Under this principle, supreme authority was placed in the hands of the Leader (*Rahbar*)—a position created for Khomeini—who serves as trustee for the Shi'a hidden iman until his reappearance on the Day of Judgment. The Leader is selected (and can be removed) by a directly elected body of clerics called the Assembly of Experts. The constitution also called for a directly elected president and parliament and a prime minister and cabinet selected by the parliament. In addition, a body called the Council of Guardians was created and given the power to veto parliamentary legislation and all candidates for elected office. The Leader directly or indirectly chooses members of the Council of Guardians; he can remove the president from office; he controls the security forces, the judiciary system, and the radio and television media; and he has extensive informal influence as well.

After the constitution was ratified in December 1979, Bani Sadr was elected president and the Revolutionary Council was dissolved. The revolutionary courts were then integrated into the judiciary system and the komitehs were integrated into the Islamic Revolutionary Guard Corps (IRGC), whose primary responsibility was to protect the Islamic regime from the many threats it faced. Intense rivalry soon emerged between the IRGC and the regular armed forces, especially during the Iran-Iraq war. In 1988 Ayatollah Khomeini created a body called the

Expediency Council to mediate disputes between the parliament and Council of Guardians, and the constitution was amended in 1989 to eliminate the position of prime minister.

Iran has a broad spectrum of civil society institutions. The radical Islamist Militant Clergy Association and Coalition of Islamic Associations and Bazargan's Liberation Movement of Iran were created before the revolution and have served as key organizational vehicles for the Islamic conservatives and Islamic modernist opposition, respectively. The radical Islamist Islamic Student Association also predates the revolution and, together with several offshoots, remains an important vehicle for students. In early 1979 the radical Islamists established the IRP, which disbanded in 1987, and the Islamic leftists established the Mujahedin of the Islamic Revolution, which, together with the Militant Clerics' Society (an offshoot of the Militant Clergy Association) remains an important vehicle for this faction. The Labor House was created in the 1980s to represent workers. The vigilante group Supporters of the Party of God was created in the early 1990s by conservative hardliners. Several centrist or leftist reformist parties were created in the mid- or late 1990s, including the pro-Rafsanjani Servants of Construction and the pro-Khatami Islamic Iran Participation Front.

Political Dynamics

Iran has changed substantially since the Islamic regime was established. The early 1980s was a period of revolutionary social transformation. The radical Islamist leadership undertook a comprehensive effort to "Islamicize" Iranian society in this period, restructuring the country's laws and political institutions; turning schools, religious institutions, and the media into instruments of indoctrination; and forcing all Iranians to observe strict Islamic standards of behavior. To accomplish this transformation the radicals sought to mobilize their supporters with inflammatory rhetoric and with dramatic actions such as the U.S. embassy hostage crisis and the war with Iraq. They also had to neutralize not only their political opponents but also the Westernized segment of society, which strongly opposed their efforts. As a result, repression was fairly high during this period, though it did not approach the levels reached in Russia and China after those countries' revolutions. Although many Iranians opposed the new Islamic regime, many others supported it, giving it a populist character.

By the late 1980s, much of the revolutionary fervor that animated this period had been extinguished and popular unrest had grown considerably as a result of the war with Iraq, continuing repression, and economic deterioration. Rafsanjani responded to these changes by initiating a period of moderation when he became president in 1989. His basic strategy was to reduce unrest by revitalizing the economy and loosening sociocultural restrictions, while keeping the political system established in the early 1980s largely intact. As discussed above, opposition first from Islamic leftists and then from Islamic conservatives blocked Rafsanjani's economic reforms, producing anemic growth in the early and mid-1990s.

Rafsanjani's failure to revitalize the economy led many Iranians to conclude that much more extensive change was needed, though relatively few advocated eliminating the Islamic regime altogether. In addition, two important generational changes had occurred by the mid-1990s. First, the "baby boom" generation mentioned above had come of age, producing a large cohort of young people who were more sophisticated than their elders and had not developed a personal attachment to the Islamic regime by participating in the revolutionary upheaval or the war with Iraq. Second, the older generation of hardened revolutionary leaders who had been active in the 1960s and 1970s had begun to disappear, with many key figures retiring from politics, becoming less active, or dying. These forces were largely responsible for Khatami's landslide electoral victory in May 1997.

Khatami's victory demonstrated that the reformists were much more popular than the conservatives, but it did not fundamentally change the balance of power between these two factions. While the reformists now could win elections and, if necessary, organize large popular protests, the conservatives still controlled key institutions such as the Leader's office, the Assembly of Experts, the Council of Guardians, the security forces, the judiciary apparatus, the radio and television media, and the parliament (until 2000). Once the conservatives regained their balance, they used these institutions to stop the reformists from carrying out extensive reform. The reformists did gain control over the municipal councils and the parliament in the elections of 1999 and 2000, but the conservatives' entrenched institutional power has prevented them from using these bodies very effectively. Although it is difficult to say where Iran will go in the coming years, the close balance of power between these two factions suggests that the most likely scenario is a continuation of the current factional stalemate.

Foreign Policy

The Islamic Republic's foreign policy was born out of Iran's internal power struggles and the competing demands of national interest, ideological purity, economic pressure, and national survival. Competing visions within the revolutionary coalition drove Iran's foreign policy in conflicting and erratic directions. In 1979–1980, an unlikely alliance of leftist and conservative Islamists initiated a confrontation with the United States in order to undermine their secularist opponents, who favored normal, though distant, relations with the West. Young radical Islamists, including some who participated in the November 1979 U.S. embassy seizure, were able to gain control over Iran's foreign policy.

The new Islamic Republic put the world on notice that it intended not only to carry out revolutionary change inside Iran but also to export its revolution abroad. It launched a steady stream of harsh verbal attacks on the superpowers, the

European Union (EU) countries, and many of its neighbors, and it began to support radical Islamist forces and carry out terrorist attacks in some of these countries. In taking these hostile actions, the Islamic Republic deliberately sought confrontation and alienated itself from potential friends and supporters. Consequently, when Iraq invaded Iran in September 1980, these countries were indifferent to Iran's plight, and some openly backed Iraq. Only international pariahs such as Syria, Libya, and North Korea supported Iran.

When Iranian forces drove Iraq back across the border in 1982, Iran's leaders decided to carry the war into Iraq, hoping to establish a radical Islamic regime there and then spread their revolution elsewhere. Iran also became deeply involved in Lebanon in this period, creating the radical Islamist guerrilla group Hezbollah and encouraging it to carry out a series of bloody terrorist attacks on U.S. forces and to seize dozens of American and European hostages. Iran continued to support radical Islamist opposition groups in the Persian Gulf Arab countries in the 1980s and had a series of confrontations with Saudi Arabia during the annual pilgrimages to Mecca. It also began to attack oil tankers in the Gulf in the mid-1980s and clashed with U.S. forces there, threatening to spread the war more broadly.

Iran's foreign policy began to moderate after the war ended and Rafsanjani came to power. Rafsanjani's economic reconstruction efforts required foreign economic cooperation, a less-threatening security environment, and lower military expenditures. Accordingly, he took a series of steps aimed at improving relations with the conservative Arab states and the West, including the United States. However, Iran continued to support Hezbollah and other radical groups in this period, and it assassinated a number of Iranian exile figures. It also undertook a substantial rearmament program, focusing especially on weapons of mass destruction. These actions hindered Rafsanjani's efforts to achieve rapprochement with the conservative Arabs and the West.

During the last year of Rafsanjani's presidency, Iran's leaders apparently decided to moderate their foreign policy further in order to normalize relations with the Arab states and the EU countries. There were no reports of Iranian-supported terrorism or subversion in the Persian Gulf Arab countries from mid-1996 through 2000, and no moderate Iranian exiles were assassinated in this period. Iran also signed several important international arms control agreements in the mid-1990s and moderated its foreign policy in other ways. Khatami continued and extended the foreign-policy moderation initiated by Rafsanjani. As a result, most of the Gulf Arab and EU countries normalized their relations with Iran in 1997 and 1998.

Iran also made several overtures toward the United States in the 1990s. Rafsanjani helped arrange the release of the remaining U.S. hostages in Lebanon in 1990 and 1991, but the United States failed to respond. In 1995 he approved a major investment project by the U.S. oil company Conoco, in what was apparently a signal that Iran wanted better relations. The U.S. government forced Conoco to drop the project and then imposed a series of harsh economic sanctions on Iran, leaving

U.S. policy much tougher on Iran than it had been since the late 1980s, despite the moderation that was occurring there.

After Khatami was inaugurated he made a series of additional overtures toward the United States. This provoked strong opposition from the Islamic conservatives, leaving the issue of rapprochement with the United States increasingly tied up in Iran's domestic power struggle. The U.S. government responded positively but cautiously to Khatami's overtures, making a series of small concessions that were not enough to overcome the Iranian conservatives' opposition. Little progress toward rapprochement had occurred by early 2002, and it was not clear when relations between the United States and Iran would be normalized.

Bibliography

Standard reference works on Iran are the multivolume *Cambridge History of Iran* (Cambridge: Cambridge University Press, 1968–) and the still-unfinished *Encyclopedia Iranica* (Costa Mesa, Calif.: Mazda Publications, 1992). One-volume surveys for the general reader include John Limbert, *Iran: At War with History* (Boulder: Westview Press, 1987), and Sandra Mackey, *The Iranians* (New York: Dutton, 1996). Two books that illuminate the richness and complexity of Iranian social life are Terence O'Donnell, *Garden of the Brave in War* (New Haven: Ticknor and Fields, 1980), and William O. Beeman, *Language, Status, and Power in Iran* (Bloomington, Ind.: Indiana University Press, 1986).

On Iranian politics before the revolution see James A. Bill, *The Politics of Iran* (Columbus, Ohio: Merrill, 1972); Donald Wilber, *Riza Shah Pahlavi* (Hicksville, N.Y.: Exposition Press, 1975); Rouhollah K. Ramazani, *Iran's Foreign Policy, 1941–1973* (Charlottesville, Va.: University of Virginia Press, 1975); Richard Cottam, *Nationalism in Iran* (Pittsburgh: University of Pittsburgh Press, 1979); Shahrough Akhavi, *Religion and Politics in Contemporary Iran* (Albany: State University of New York Press, 1980); Homa Katouzian, *The Political Economy of Modern Iran* (New York: New York University Press, 1981); Ervand Abrahamian, *Iran Between Two Revolutions* (Princeton: Princeton University Press, 1982); Asadollah Alam, *The Shah and I* (London: I. B. Tauris, 1991); Mark J. Gasiorowski, *U.S. Foreign Policy and the Shah* (Ithaca: Cornell University Press, 1991); and Janet Afary, *The Iranian Constitutional Revolution, 1906–1911* (New York: Columbia University Press, 1996).

For books on the revolution and its aftermath, see Nikki Keddie, *Roots of Revolution* (New Haven: Yale University Press, 1981); Shaul Bakhash, *The Reign of the Ayatollahs* (New York: Basic Books, 1984); Rouhollah K. Ramazani, *Revolutionary Iran* (Baltimore: Johns Hopkins University Press, 1986); Said Amir Arjomand, *The Turban for the Crown* (New York: Oxford University Press, 1988); David Menashri, *Iran: A Decade of War and Revolution* (New York: Holmes and Meier, 1990); Mansoor Moaddel, *Class, Politics, and Ideology in the Iranian Revolution* (New York: Columbia University Press, 1993); Ervand Abrahamian, *Khomeinism* (Berkeley: University of California Press, 1993); Hamid Dabashi, *Theology of Discontent* (New York: New York University Press, 1993); and Mehrzad Boroujerdi, *Iranian Intellectuals and the West* (Syracuse: Syracuse University Press, 1996).

On recent Iranian politics, society, and foreign policy, see Samih K. Farsoun and Mehrdad Mashayekhi, *Iran: Political Culture in the Islamic Republic* (London: Routledge,

1992); Bahman Baktiari, *Parliamentary Politics in Revolutionary Iran* (Gainesville, Fla.: University Press of Florida, 1996); Asghar Schirazi, *The Constitution of Iran* (London: I. B. Tauris, 1997); Haleh Esfandiari, *Reconstructed Lives* (Washington: Woodrow Wilson Center Press, 1997); Jahangir Amuzegar, *Iran's Economy Under the Islamic Republic* (London: Tauris, 1997); Haleh Afshar, *Islam and Feminisms: An Iranian Case-Study* (New York: St. Martin's, 1998); Anthony H. Cordesman, *Iran's Military Forces in Transition* (Westport, Conn.: Praeger, 1999); Fariba Adelkhah, *Being Modern in Iran* (New York: Columbia University Press, 2000); Eliz Sanasarian, *Religious Minorities in Iran* (Cambridge: Cambridge University Press, 2000); Robin Wright, *The Last Great Revolution* (New York: Knopf, 2000); Elaine Sciolino, *Persian Mirrors* (New York: Free Press, 2000); Mark J. Gasiorowski, "The Power Struggle in Iran," *Middle East Policy* 7(4), October 2000; and Wilfried Buchta, *Who Rules Iran?* (Washington: Washington Institute for Near East Policy, 2000).

4

Kingdom of Saudi Arabia

David E. Long

Historical Background

Early History

In 1932, King Abd al-Aziz ibn Abd al-Rahman Al Saud formally united the Hijaz and Najd to form the Kingdom of Saudi Arabia. Saudi rule, however, dates back long before that. It is the history of the Al Saud (House of Saud), which has ruled over the vast desert reaches of Najd, as central Arabia is called, for over 250 years. It is the story of the evolution of a small oasis principality into the mighty oil kingdom of today.[1]

The founder of the Al Saud dynasty was Muhammad ibn Saud (c. A.D. 1703/4–1792), amir (ruler) of Dar'iyyah, a small oasis town located on the Wadi Hanifah, a usually dry streambed in central Najd. In 1744/5, Amir Muhammad became the patron of Muhammad ibn Abd al-Wahhab, a zealous religious revivalist who had been driven from his home, the neighboring town of Uyainah, because of his strict, puritan religious beliefs. The religious leader and the temporal leader formed a bond that has provided ideological cohesion for the Saudi state to this day.

Muhammad ibn Abd al-Wahhab's revival movement was based on the Hanbali school of Islamic jurisprudence, the most conservative of the four recognized schools of Sunni Islam, and many of its teachings were drawn from the writings of an early Hanbali jurist, Taqi al-Din Ahmad Ibn Taymiyyah (c. A.D. 1262–1328). The revival stressed strict adherence to the doctrine of *tawhid* (monotheism) and a return to the fundamentals of Islam. It condemned many of the religious practices that had cropped up since the time of the Prophet as heretical and accused those who followed them of idolatry and polytheism.

Outside detractors called followers of the revival "Wahhabis," after Abd al-Wahhab. The followers themselves rejected the term as implying worship of the founder rather than God and preferred to be called Muwahhidin (Unitarians or Monotheists). Muhammad ibn Abd al-Wahhab was known as the teacher, or "the Shaykh." His descendants are still called Al al-Shaykh (House of the Shaykh), and because they still provide religious leadership for the country, they are second in prestige only to the Al Saud.

By the end of the eighteenth century, the Al Saud had subdued nearly all of Najd and was preparing to expand even farther. Saudi control of Najd was accomplished almost without notice by the outside world, but in 1801, when the Saudis sacked the Shi'a holy city of Karbala in what is now southern Iraq, they came to the attention of the world, particularly the Islamic world. Convinced that pilgrimages to tombs of holy men was idolatry, the Al Saud destroyed the tombs of a number of revered Shi'a "saints," including that of Husayn, the grandson of the Prophet Muhammad. Husayn's tomb had been venerated by the Shi'a as a site for pilgrimages second in importance only to Makkah and al-Madinah.[2]

In 1806, Muwahhidin forces defeated the Ottoman garrisons in the Hijaz and seized Makkah and al-Madinah. In the east, another Saudi force pushed into Oman, forcing the sultan at Muscat to pay annual tribute. Persian Gulf mariners, newly converted to the religious revival movement, sent privateers against British and local merchant vessels, deeming the former to be nonbelievers and the latter to be heretics. Thus, in a few short years, Saudi domains had expanded from a small oasis principality to most of the Arabian Peninsula, and Saudi influence extended to the Gulf and the Arabian Sea.

One can speculate how far the forces of the Al Saud might have gone had they not encountered vastly superior military technology from the Ottomans. The capture of the holy places of Makkah and al-Madinah roused the sultan in Constantinople to action. He bade his viceroy in Egypt, Muhammad Ali, to send an army against the invaders. In 1811, Muhammad Ali sent his son Tusun to retake the holy places and invade Najd. Tusun was able to recapture most of the Hijaz but could not defeat the Muwahhidin. In 1816, Tusun's brother Ibrahim Pasha arrived with a well-equipped army and finally captured the Saudi capital at Dar'iyyah in 1818. Ibrahim's forces laid waste to the city, whose ruins can still be seen today, and cut down its date groves; they took the Saudi amir, Abdallah ibn Saud Al Saud, fourth in the line, into exile back to Cairo, along with other members of the Al Saud and Al al-Shaykh. Abdallah was later sent to Constantinople, where he was eventually beheaded.

During the next four years, the Ottoman-Egyptian occupiers set out to destroy the Al Saud base of power so that it could no longer threaten the holy cities of the Hijaz. They installed Abdallah's brother Mishari as amir, but he was fully under their control. The Egyptians finally withdrew from the Arabian Peninsula in 1822, after concluding that the Muwahhidin were no longer a threat to Makkah and al-Madinah. Najd was again freed of foreign control.

In 1823–1824, Turki ibn Abdallah, a son of Amir Abdallah's great uncle, reestablished Saudi rule. He also moved the capital twenty kilometers down the Wadi Hanifah to Riyadh, where it has remained to this day. Amir Turki was assassinated in 1834 and was succeeded by his son Faysal. In 1837, Faysal was ousted by a cousin, Khalid, with the help of Egyptian troops. Khalid ruled as an Egyptian puppet until he was in turn ousted by another cousin, Abdallah ibn Thunayan. In 1843, Faysal escaped from exile in Cairo, ousted Abdallah ibn Thunayan, and again became undisputed ruler of Najd. During Faysal's second reign (1843–1865), Saudi leadership reached the apex of its power and influence in the nineteenth century. Faysal restored peace, extended his rule to Jabal Shammar in the north, and laid claim to Buraymi Oasis on the Omani frontier. This claim was the basis of a territorial dispute between the kingdom, Oman, and Abu Dhabi that lasted until the 1970s.

Faysal's death in 1865 signaled another eclipse in the fortunes of the Al Saud. He was succeeded by his son Abdallah, but Abdallah's leadership was almost immediately challenged by a second son, Saud, who became amir in 1871. After Saud's death in 1875, Abdallah again became amir, but by this time, the Al Saud's grip on Najd was slipping. The Eastern Province (al-Hasa) was recaptured by the Ottomans in 1871; Buraymi Oasis was lost; and the Jabal Shammar tribes were rising in revolt. In 1887, the Saudi state again collapsed. This time, Muhammad ibn Rashid, amir of the Shammar, seized Najd and ruled it from the Shammari capital at al-Hail. Abd al-Rahman, a younger brother of Abdallah and Saud, served briefly as the Rashidi governor in Riyadh, but in 1891, after failing in an abortive revolt, he and his family were forced to flee to Kuwait, where they lived off the hospitality of the ruler, Mubarrak the Great.

From Desert Principality to Modern Oil Kingdom

The rise of the Al Saud from humiliating exile in Kuwait to leadership of the world's foremost oil state was due primarily to the accomplishments of Abd al-Rahman's son Abd al-Aziz ibn Abd al-Rahman Al Saud, known in the West as "Ibn Saud." Abd al-Aziz was an imposing figure. Well over six feet tall and handsome, he had the natural grace and poise of a true desert aristocrat, which enabled him to deal effectively with tribal shaykhs, oil executives, and heads of Western states alike. From his mother's family, the Al al-Shaykhs, he was well grounded in Islam. His famed prowess with the opposite sex was also in the best desert tradition. The true measure of his greatness, however, was in his breadth of vision. Even though he did not fully comprehend the revolutionary changes that his acts would ultimately produce, he brought his country from centuries of desert isolation to a place in regional and world political and economic councils.

The first step was the recapture of Riyadh in 1902. The nearly legendary tale of how Abd al-Aziz and his band of forty men retook Riyadh sounds like a plot for a Hollywood thriller. Having left Kuwait the previous year, and gathered tribal support on the way, the young prince and his followers stole over the city walls. Once inside the city, they lay alternately sleeping and praying all night long while waiting for the Rashidi governor, Ajlan, to emerge from the Mismak Fortress, where he slept as a security precaution. The next morning, as Ajlan set off for home, he was attacked by Abd al-Aziz and his men. Ajlan ran with his retinue back to the fortress, where a tussle occurred as each group tried to pull him through to its side of the postern gate. During the melee, Abd al-Aziz's cousin Abdallah ibn Jaluwi threw a spear into the gate; it broke off and the spear tip remained in place for many years. Ajlan was finally pulled through the gate into the fortress, but before the gate could be closed, Abdallah ibn Jaluwi forced his way in also and slew the governor. All resistance then ended.

It took two decades from that January morning for Abd al-Aziz to complete the conquest of the Ibn Rashids. His success was greatly facilitated by the fratricidal rivalries that split the Ibn Rashids, much as the Sauds had been split just a generation before. Nevertheless, Saudi control continued to expand. In 1912, Abd al-Aziz raised his Najdi state from an amirate to a sultanate, as befitted his growing status. By the time he captured the Rashidi capital of al-Hail in 1922, he had also recaptured eastern Arabia from the Ottomans. He named Abdallah ibn Jaluwi the amir of the Eastern Province, a position passed on to Abdallah's two sons, Saud and Abd al-Muhsin, before being assumed by a son of King Fahd, Prince Muhammad ibn Fahd Al Saud.

Abd al-Aziz's bedouin warriors, the Ikhwan (the Brethren), fighting under the banner of Tawhid, might have defeated the Ibn Rashids sooner had not World War I intervened. The war temporarily brought the Arabian Peninsula into the arena of great-power politics, with the British and the Turks in competition for the support of the peninsula's three major rulers, Abd al-Aziz of Najd, Saud ibn Rashid of Jabal Shammar, and Sharif Husayn of Makkah. Ibn Rashid sided with the Turks (and the Germans); the other two chose the British.

During the war period, three Britons came to fame in Arabia: Captain W. H. I. Shakespear, Colonel T. E. Lawrence (Lawrence of Arabia), and H. St. John B. Philby. Shakespear, as British political agent in Kuwait, had informally contacted Abd al-Aziz in 1910 and, while on a trek through Arabia in 1913, had visited him in Riyadh. With quickening British interest in central Arabia on the eve of the war, Shakespear was sent back to Riyadh in 1914 as the British political representative to Abd al-Aziz and was with him the following January when he attacked the Rashidis at Jarab. After initial success, the Saudis were pushed back in disorder. Shakespear, dressed in a British uniform and directing the fire of a single artillery piece, was killed.

In 1916, the British sent Colonel T. E. Lawrence to the Hijaz to encourage Sharif Husayn to revolt against the Ottomans. Lawrence subsequently won a place in history by leading Arab raiding parties against Turkish supply routes along the Hijaz Railroad. The following year, the British sent another mission to Abd al-Aziz to persuade him to side with Sharif Husayn and the Allies and to attack the Ibn Rashids. The mission included Philby, who remained in Arabia as an explorer and confidant of Abd al-Aziz.

With the war's end, Abd al-Aziz finally conquered the Ibn Rashids, but in the meantime, the Al Saud's relations with King (formerly Sharif) Husayn of the Hijaz had begun to deteriorate. Husayn proclaimed himself "King of the Arabs" and claimed precedence over the Al Saud, whom he regarded as mere desert chieftains. Husayn had seized Abd al-Aziz's brother Sa'd in 1912 and released him only after Abd al-Aziz accepted humiliating terms. In 1919, Abd al-Aziz's son (and later king) Faysal stopped by Paris on his way home from a visit to England and was snubbed by King Husayn's son Faysal, who was attending the Paris Peace Conference.

The tide was turning, however. The same year, Abdallah, another of Husayn's sons, set out east of Taif to claim the Oasis of Kurmah for the Hijaz. While encamped at nearby Turabah, his army was wiped out by the Ikhwan. Only men with horses (including Abdallah) escaped. Abd al-Aziz did not press his advantage until 1924, when the Ottoman caliphate was dissolved and King Husayn proclaimed himself the new caliph. This was more than the devout Abd al-Aziz could accept, and he set out to invade the Hijaz. Taif surrendered without resistance, but for a still unexplained reason, a shot rang out and the zealous Ikhwan sacked the city. When the rest of the Hijaz learned of the fate of Taif, they panicked and forced King Husayn to abdicate in favor of his son, Ali. Ali fared no better, however, and in January 1926, he too set sail from Jiddah to follow Husayn into exile.

In a quarter century, Abd al-Aziz, who had started with forty men, had regained the Saudi patrimony. In 1934, he acquired the Wadi Najran after a brief war with the Yemen, completing the present frontiers, pending settlement of remaining boundary disputes. After Abd al-Aziz conquered the Hijaz, he ruled the two countries as the Kingdom of the Hijaz and Sultanate of Najd, then the Kingdom of the Hijaz and Najd. In 1932, the two countries were consolidated as the Kingdom of Saudi Arabia.

With the restoration and consolidation of the kingdom, peace came to Saudi Arabia for one of the few times in recorded history. With no more wars to fight, the Ikhwan became restless, and the king had to put down a bedouin uprising at al-Sibilah in 1929, perhaps the last great bedouin battle in history. The Ikhwan were subsequently disbanded (except for the brief Yemen campaign), and on the eve of World War II, Saudi Arabia was one of the few countries in the world with no standing army. It did declare war on Germany, however, and became a charter member of the United Nations.

The Postwar Era

The history of Saudi Arabia since World War II has been one of unprecedented economic and social development. The enabling factor has been oil, first found in commercial quantities in 1938, but not exported in quantity until after the war. King Abd al-Aziz, by the time of his death in 1953, had constructed a firm foundation on which his successors could build a modern oil state.

King Abd al-Aziz was succeeded by his eldest surviving son, Saud (his eldest son, Turki, had died in the influenza pandemic of 1919). Saud had been groomed for rulership as viceroy of Najd under his father. More at home with tribal politics, however, he lacked the breadth of vision to propel Saudi Arabia from a desert kingdom to a major oil power. His reign was characterized by intrigue and lavish spending. Despite growing oil revenues, the treasury was often virtually empty. In 1962, Saud was obliged to turn government operations over to his half-brother Faysal; and in 1964, the royal family withdrew its support entirely, forcing him to abdicate. Saud left Saudi Arabia, choosing to remain in exile until his death in Athens in 1969.

King Faysal began his reign with nearly a half-century's experience in public affairs. In 1919, at the age of fourteen, he represented his father on an official visit to England. After his father conquered the Hijaz, Faysal was made its viceroy in 1926, and when the Ministry of Foreign Affairs was created in 1930, he became foreign minister, a position he held for the rest of his life, with the exception of a short period during the reign of his half-brother Saud, when Faysal retired to private life.

King Faysal was dedicated to the preservation of a conservative Islamic way of life both in Saudi Arabia and throughout the Muslim world, while at the same time encouraging material and technological modernization. These goals, which built upon foundations laid by his father, were articulated in a ten-point reform program, which Faysal announced in 1962 while he was still heir apparent and prime minister. The measure of his success in developing the kingdom can be explained in large part by his capacity to be ahead of his people, introducing economic and social development programs, but to never be so far out in front that the essentially conservative, Islamic Saudi public would not follow. By proceeding with care and deliberation, Faysal was able to win over even the most conservative segments of the population to such innovations as public radio and television and education for women. To dispel religious opposition to radio and television, for example, Faysal ordered large portions of programming time be devoted to religious instruction and readings from the Quran.

Faysal's greatest interest, however, was foreign affairs. As foreign minister, he became one of the most widely traveled Saudi officials of his time. For example, he attended the 1945 San Francisco conference that established the United Nations.

Faysal's primary focus was on the Muslim world and the preservation of its values. Because of Saudi Arabia's position as a key oil exporter, his ability to act as a moderating force in both the Arab world and the world at large was greatly enhanced by the dramatic increase in oil prices in the 1970s.

King Faysal was assassinated by a deranged nephew on March 25, 1975, and was succeeded by his half-brother Khalid. Another half-brother, Fahd, became heir apparent and attended to much of the day-to-day administration of the government. Because of Fahd's visibility, many considered Khalid a figurehead king, but such was not the case. Quiet, retiring, and pious, he was a very popular ruler in the kingdom. Khalid died of a heart attack in June 1982 and was succeeded in a smooth transition by Fahd, who also became prime minister. Prince Abdallah became the new heir apparent and first-deputy prime minister, also retaining command of the Saudi National Guard, to which he had been appointed by Faysal in 1962. Fahd's full brother Sultan, the minister of defense, became second-deputy prime minister and was widely assumed to be the next heir apparent.

As the twentieth century came to an end, King Fahd's increasingly bad health necessitated his turning over a large part of day-to-day government operations to Prince Abdallah, the heir apparent. As king, Abdallah will establish his own personal style of government, but based on precedent, Saudi domestic and foreign policies will likely continue to follow the lead of Kings Abd al-Aziz and Faysal, emphasizing economic development and social welfare within the framework of Islam and pan-Arabism.

Political Environment

The Land and People

Saudi Arabia occupies about 2 million square kilometers (772,000 square miles), between one-fourth and one-third the size of the continental United States. Occupying about 80 percent of the Arabian Peninsula, the country lies along the Red Sea in the southwest and the Gulf in the northeast; it is bounded by Jordan to the northwest and Iraq and Kuwait to the north. To the east are Bahrain (offshore), Qatar, the United Arab Emirates, and Oman, and to the south is Yemen.[3]

Traditionally, land borders were relatively meaningless to Saudi rulers, who looked on sovereignty more in terms of tribal allegiance. Tribal areas were huge and only vaguely demarcated, as the tribes themselves followed the rains from water hole to water hole and wandered over broad areas. Later, when oil became so important in the region, fixed borders were to acquire much more importance. A deviation of a few centimeters from a common point could translate into hundreds of square kilometers when projected for long distances over the desert.

The same can be said for offshore territorial limits. Saudi Arabia claims a twelve-nautical-mile limit offshore, as well as a number of islands in the Gulf and the Red Sea. With extensive oil discoveries in the Gulf, establishing an offshore median line dividing underwater oil and gas fields between Saudi Arabia and Iran became imperative. Nevertheless, it was not until the 1970s that the median line could finally be negotiated.

Because of Saudi Arabia's predominantly desert terrain, a shortage of water is one of its main resource problems. In the interior are nonrenewable aquifers, which are being tapped at an unprecedented rate, particularly as urbanization and population growth expand and as irrigated agricultural development projects have been created in the interior. To augment water supplies, the kingdom has created a massive desalination system.

Despite the arid climate, sporadic rains do fall in Saudi Arabia, and there is occasional snow in the mountains. This water has to run off somewhere, and as a result, there are numerous drainage systems made up of intersecting wadis, which are usually dry riverbeds and valleys. After local, and occasionally heavy, rains, the wadis can become rushing torrents. Among the major wadi drainage systems in the kingdom are Wadi Sirhan, located on the Saudi-Jordanian frontier; Wadi al-Batin, which flows northeast toward Kuwait; Wadi Rimah, which flows eastward from the northern Hijaz mountains; and Wadi Dawasir, Wadi Bishah, and Wadi Najran, which flow eastward from the southern Hijaz and Yemeni mountains.

Although nearly all of Saudi Arabia is arid, only a part of it consists of real sand desert. There are three such deserts in the kingdom: the Great Nafud, located in the north (*nafud* is one of several Arabic words meaning desert); the Rub'al-Khali (literally, "the Empty Quarter"), stretching along the entire southern frontier; and the Dahna, a narrow strip that forms a great arc from the Nafud westward and then south to the Rub'al-Khali. The sand in all three bears iron oxide, giving it a pink color that can turn to deep red in the setting sun.

The Rub'al-Khali, covering more than 550,000 square kilometers (over 250,000 square miles), is the largest quartz sand desert in the world. (The few local tribes call the area *al-rumal,* "the sands.") It is also one of the most forbidding and was virtually unexplored until the 1950s, when Arabian American Oil Company (Aramco) teams began searching for oil in the region.[4] Much of the Rub'al-Khali is hard-packed sand and salt flats, from which sand mountains rise more than 300 meters (1,000 feet). In places, these giant dunes form long, parallel ridges that extend for up to 40 kilometers (25 miles). Most of the area is uninhabited, and the dialects of the few who live there are barely intelligible to those from outside the area.

Excluding the Empty Quarter, the kingdom is divided into four geographical regions: central, western, eastern, and northern. Central Arabia, or Najd, is both the geographical and the political heartland of the country. Najd, Arabic for "highlands," is predominantly an arid plateau interspersed with oases.

Many cities and towns are scattered throughout Najd, the largest being the national capital, al-Riyadh. The name means "gardens": The city was so named for the number of vegetable gardens and date groves located there. From a small oasis town of about 7,500 in 1900, it grew to a major metropolis with a population over 3.5 million a century later. One of the world's fastest-growing cities, it is expected to approach 4.4 million by 2006.[5]

Riyadh remained generally closed to Westerners until the 1970s, when the Saudis opened it up to Western development. Between 1969 and 1975, the number of Western expatriates living in the capital rose from fewer than three hundred to hundreds of thousands. Just a few kilometers north, the ruins of Dar'iyyah, ancestral home of the Al Saud, have become a virtual suburb of the capital. Northeast of Riyadh is the district of al-Qasim, with its neighboring and rival cities of Unayzah and Buraydah. The inhabitants of al-Qasim are among the most conservative in the kingdom. Further north is Jabal Shammar and the former Rashidi capital of Hail on the edge of the Great Nafud.

Western Saudi Arabia is divided into two areas, the Hijaz in the north and Asir in the south. The Hijaz extends from the Jordanian border to just south of Jiddah, the kingdom's second largest city. The economic and social life of the Hijaz has traditionally revolved around the annual Hajj, or "great pilgrimage" to Makkah. With so much attention given to Saudi oil and Middle East politics, few Westerners are aware that to the Muslim world—one-fifth of the world's population—the kingdom is even more important as the location of the two holiest cities in Islam, Makkah and al-Madinah. Performing the Hajj once in their lifetimes is an obligation for all Muslims who are physically and financially able. Observed each year by roughly 2 million of the faithful, the Hajj is not only one of the world's greatest religious celebrations but also one of the greatest exercises in public administration. The Saudi government seeks to ensure that all those who attend do so without serious injury and with a minimum of discomfort.

Over the centuries since the beginning of Islam in the seventh century A.D., an extensive service industry has grown up to cater to Hajjis (pilgrims). With the discovery of oil, the Hajj has lost the economic importance it once had, but with 2 million Hajjis, many staying three to five weeks, it is still a major commercial season, somewhat analogous to the Christmas season in Western countries. Physical infrastructure to accommodate the Hajj is extensive, including one of the largest commercial airports in the world at Jiddah, the traditional port of entry, a modern commercial hub of over 3 million on the Red Sea. The Saudi government has also spent billions of riyals upgrading the Haram Mosque in Makkah and the Prophet's Mosque in al-Madinah, the two holiest sites in Islam.

Asir was quasi-independent until the Saudi conquest in the 1920s and 1930s, and it remained relatively isolated until modern roads were built in the 1970s. Its main cities are Jizan, a modest city on the coast; Abha, the provincial capital, atop the escarpment; and Najran, inland on the Saudi-Yemeni border. Not far from

Abha is Khamis Mushayt, site of a major Saudi military cantonment area. The capital of Asir is Abha and its major seaport is Jizan.

Eastern Saudi Arabia is a mixture of old and new. Now called the Eastern Province, it includes al-Hasa, the largest oasis in the world, and al-Qatif Oasis on the coast. The primary significance of the region is that underneath it lies the bulk of Saudi Arabia's huge oil reserves. The Ghawar field, which stretches for over 200 kilometers north to south, is the largest single field in the world. The economy of the Eastern Province is predominantly based on oil, and even recent efforts to diversify focus on petrochemical industries.

The capital and principal city of the province is Dammam, just south of al-Qatif. Once a small pearling and privateering port, it is now a bustling metropolis. South of Dammam is Dhahran, whose name is far more familiar in the West. It is actually not a city but the location of Saudi Aramco headquarters, King Faysal University, the U.S. Consulate General, and Dhahran International Airport. Nearby, on the coast, is al-Khubar, which grew from virtually nothing into a major industrial service town.

North of Dammam to the Kuwaiti border are located a number of oil towns and facilities, including Ras Tanura, the principal Saudi Aramco oil terminal, and farther north, Khafji, in what was part of the Saudi-Kuwaiti Neutral Zone until that zone was abolished in 1966. Just north of Ras Tanura is Jubayl, a tiny village when the first American oil men landed there in 1933 and now a major city and site of much of Saudi Arabia's petrochemical industry. The largest town in al-Hasa is Hufuf, now home to many Saudi Aramco workers.

The area extending along the kingdom's northern frontiers with Jordan and Iraq is physically isolated from the rest of the country by the Great Nafud. It is geographically a part of the Syrian Desert, and tribesmen in the area claim kinship with fellow tribesmen in neighboring Jordan, Iraq, and Syria as well as Saudi Arabia, occasionally possessing passports from all four countries. This area was the traditional caravan route for traders from the Fertile Crescent traveling to central and eastern Arabia.

There are no cities in the region. The two principal towns are Domat al-Jandal (al-Jawf) and Sakaka, located in oases just north of the Nafud. Prior to the 1967 Arab-Israeli war, the most important installation in the region economically was the Trans-Arabian Pipeline (TAPLINE), which carried crude oil from the Eastern Province to the Lebanese port of Sidon. With access to Lebanon now closed, TAPLINE has lost much of its economic importance, although oil is still sent through the pipeline to Jordan.

Saudi Arabia has a harsh, hot climate that one would associate with a desert area. There are variations, however. In the interior, the lack of humidity causes daytime temperatures to rise sharply. In the summer, daytime readings can register over 54° C (130° F), and then drop precipitously after the sun goes down, sometimes as much as 20° C (70° F) in less than three hours. In the winter, subfreezing temperatures are not uncommon, and the ever-present winds create a windchill that can be very cold for those not properly dressed.

The coastal areas combine heat and high humidity. The humidity usually keeps the temperature from exceeding around 40° C (around 105° F) in the summer but likewise prevents it from dropping more than a few degrees at night. Winter temperatures, in contrast, are more balmy and warmer at night than those in the interior, particularly the farther south one goes. Both along the coasts and in the interior, rainfall is very sporadic. Torrential rains can flood one area and entirely miss areas a few kilometers away. At other times, the same area can go without rain for five to ten years. The sporadic nature of the rains is the main reason desert pastoralists must cover wide areas in search for pasturage for their livestock.

The mountain areas are cooler, particularly in the Asir, where it can get quite cold at night. The Asir also gets the moisture-laden monsoon winds from the south in the winter, when most of its annual rainfall of around 500 millimeters (20 inches) occurs.

Saudi Arabia has an estimated population of 20 million, of which roughly 5 million are expatriates.[6] Though the country's population is relatively small in comparison to its great wealth, it has experienced a population explosion in the past quarter century that has radically changed the demography. There are some indications that the birth rate is stabilizing, declining from over 3.5 percent a year to around 3.2 percent, but with a median age of around eighteen years and a rapidly expanding life expectancy due to vastly improved health care, the kingdom still faces major socioeconomic problems far into the twenty-first century. Every year more and more young Saudis compete for a finite number of jobs and more and more of the aged must be supported by their children, both groups increasingly living off their families' income.

The indigenous Saudi population is among the most homogeneous in the entire Middle East. Virtually all Saudis are Arab and Muslim. Bloodlines, not geography, determine nationality, and being born in Saudi Arabia does not automatically entitle a person to citizenship. The importance of bloodlines is a manifestation of the basically tribal nature of Saudi society. (*Tribal* in this context refers to social organization, not occupation or politics.) The extended family is the most important social institution in Saudi Arabia. If put to the test, loyalty to one's family would probably exceed loyalty to the state. The state has been in existence for a few decades, but most Saudis trace their families back for centuries.

With genealogy so important, there is relatively little social mobility in Saudi Arabia. Najd is not only the center of Saudi political power; its tribal affiliations are among the most aristocratic in the Arabian Peninsula. Members of the leading tribal families of Najd are at the top of the social order, and nontribal families are near the bottom.

The Hijazi population is far more cosmopolitan than that of Najd because of centuries of immigration connected with the Hajj. The leading families constituted a merchant class that grew up in the Hijaz to serve the Hajj. The Eastern Province, with its concentration of the oil industry, also has a polyglot population. Many of the pre-oil families of the Eastern Province have close ties in other Gulf states. The Qusaybi (Gosaibi) family, for example, has a large branch in Bahrain.

The Eastern Province is the home of the only significant minority in the kingdom, the Shi'a community, which numbers between 500,000 and 600,000. The Shi'a live mainly in al-Qatif and Hasa Oases. Unlike much of the rest of the population, the Shi'a are willing to work with their hands and over the years have become the backbone of the skilled and semiskilled oil workforce.

A few families of non-Arabian origin have also become Saudi nationals. Most of them are found in the Hijaz and are descended from Hajjis who never returned to their homelands after the pilgrimage. Some of these families have lived in Jiddah and Makkah for centuries and have attained stature in society and high rank in government, mainly associated with the Hajj. Another group of Hijazis, Hadhramis, originally came from the Wadi Hadhramut in what is now western Yemen, particularly in the nineteenth century, and number among the leading merchant families of Jiddah.

A group of non-Arabs that have become Saudi nationals more recently are the Central Asian community, locally often collectively called "Tashkandis," "Turkistanis," or "Bukharis," after areas and cities in former Soviet Central Asia. They are descendants of a group of political refugees who escaped overland from the Soviet Union in the 1920s. Fiercely anti-Communist and devoutly Muslim, members of the community took refuge in several countries before finally ending up in Saudi Arabia. Because of their faith, loyalty, and lack of interest in inter-Arab politics, many of them were accepted into the Saudi military services.

Another group of naturalized citizens descends from a remarkable group of non-Saudi Arabs who came to the kingdom in the 1930s and stayed on as senior advisers. These included Rashad Pharaoun, a Syrian who originally came to serve as the personal physician to King Abd al-Aziz and remained to become a senior adviser; Yusif Yassin, a Syrian who became deputy foreign minister under Prince (later King) Faysal; and Hafiz al-Wahba, an Egyptian who also became a senior adviser.

The distinction between "foreigners" and "natives" breaks down somewhat when one looks at neighboring states. Many of the old Sunni families of Kuwait and Bahrain migrated from Najd some 300 years ago. Northern Saudis have close tribal ties in Jordan, Syria, and Iraq. Gulf ties are reflected during the Hajj, when members of the Gulf Cooperation Council (GCC) states are not required to obtain Saudi visas. No matter how long a person's family has resided in the country, however, he is still identified by his family's original place of origin.

The foreign community constitutes about one-fourth of the total population. Before the 1970s, most foreigners were concentrated in the Eastern Province where, before Saudization, Aramco employed thousands of foreigners. Most of the rest of them were traditionally located in the Hijaz, drawn there by the Hajj. The original function of foreign diplomats was to look after Hajjis from their home countries. Although the diplomatic community has now moved to Riyadh, many countries still maintain consulates in Jiddah, and caring for pilgrims is still a major task for Muslim countries. In summer, when the king and most of the senior government officials move to nearby Taif, Jiddah again becomes a diplomatic center.

In the 1970s, the oil boom spurred unprecedented economic development throughout the kingdom, and Najd was opened up to Westerners for the first time in a major way. A new diplomatic enclave, separate from the rest of the city, was created in Riyadh by the Saudi government, and many foreign and local businesses moved their headquarters to Riyadh as well. Thus, the capital is not only the largest city in the kingdom, it now probably contains most of the kingdom's foreigners. The largest number of foreign residents are from nearby Middle Eastern countries and South Asia and are preponderantly manual laborers. They include a large Yemeni community that, until the government reduced it for security reasons following Desert Storm, numbered as many as one million.

Although the status of foreign workers varies from skilled and menial laborers to highly paid executives, all are generally in Saudi Arabia for one primary thing—to make as much money as possible and return to their homelands. That, plus the closed nature of Saudi society, has greatly limited social intercourse between Saudi nationals and the foreign communities. Thus, despite the huge number of foreigners, their social impact on Saudi society has been relatively slight.

With the breathtaking pace of modernization in the past few decades, the miracle of Saudi society is not how it has changed, but how resilient the society has been in the face of change. The family system is still intact and, indeed, is probably the most stabilizing force in the country. Whatever Saudi Arabia's political or economic future, it is difficult to visualize it without the paramount importance of family ties.

Economic Conditions

The Hanbali school of Islam, ultraconservative on social and political issues, is one of the most liberal schools of Islamic jurisprudence on economic and commercial matters (though not on banking, for it proscribes charging interest). It is no accident that Saudi Arabia has one of the most wide-open free-market economies in the world. Islam places no stigma on amassing wealth, which is seen as God's bounty. At the same time, Islam teaches that it is incumbent on the rich to meet the needs of the poor, not as generosity but as a moral obligation. The backbone of the economy is oil, accounting for 75 percent of revenues and 90 percent of export earnings. Saudi Arabia has 26 percent of the world's proved oil reserves, the largest reserves in the world.

When one looks at Saudi Arabia's huge oil wealth, it is difficult to imagine that prior to World War II, the country was one of the poorest on earth. Following the incorporation of the Hijaz into the Saudi realm in the 1920s, revenues generated from the Hajj became the major source of foreign exchange. When the world economic depression and political disorders greatly reduced the number of Hajjis in the 1930s, the Saudi economy was badly hit, and although oil had been discovered, revenues were insufficient to fill the gap.

The first Saudi oil concession was sold to an entrepreneur from New Zealand, Major Frank Holmes, in the 1920s, but he allowed it to lapse. In 1933, Standard Oil of California (Socal) obtained a new concession in 1933 through the good offices of St. John Philby and Karl Twitchell, an American geologist who had explored for water in the kingdom.

Oil was first discovered in 1935 and discovered in commercial quantities in 1938, but international political and economic conditions prevented its being sold in significant quantities until after the war. For a while, Saudi Arabia lived off advances on future royalties provided by the oil companies. By the 1940s, however, the companies felt they could no longer do so and petitioned the United States and Britain to help fill the gap. In 1943, the United States signed a lend-lease agreement with Saudi Arabia, primarily as a means of keeping the Saudi economy afloat during the war.

In 1936, Socal had invited Texaco to help market Saudi oil by becoming a joint owner in its new Saudi production company, which ultimately became Aramco. In 1948, Mobil and Exxon also became Aramco partners. By that time, oil revenues were rapidly transforming the kingdom into a major oil state. For almost three decades, Aramco dominated Saudi oil production and set prices. The Organization of Petroleum Exporting Countries (OPEC) was established in the 1960s to try to exert pressure on the companies to maintain higher prices, but OPEC had little influence. In the 1970s, however, due to a major oil shortage, the oil-producing countries, including Saudi Arabia, were able to wrest control of pricing from the companies, and ultimately to get ownership of the oil itself.

Many OPEC countries simply nationalized the producing companies, but Saudi Arabia acquired ownership of Aramco in a gradual buyout called "participation," a concept developed in the late 1960s by Zaki Yamani, then Saudi oil minister. Yamani feared that without extended oil company participation, the oil-producing countries would engage in cutthroat competition that could collapse the entire oil market. By 1980, Saudi Arabia had acquired full ownership of Aramco, now known as Saudi Aramco.

Oil revenues skyrocketed in the 1970s, further accelerated by the Saudi-led Arab oil embargo of 1973–1974. The embargo actually ran counter to Saudi economic interests in maintaining stable, reasonable oil prices to maximize its long-term revenues. King Faysal initiated the embargo for political, not economic, reasons, in large part because he felt he had been betrayed by President Richard Nixon in the 1973 Arab-Israeli war. Having personally promised Faysal that the United States would remain evenhanded in the war, Nixon announced that it would extend $2.2 billion in military aid to Israel.

The high revenues of the 1970s led to a spending spree in Saudi Arabia, as the Saudis accelerated all their economic and social welfare programs. However, high oil prices also led to increased worldwide energy efficiency and a drop in per capita demand, and in 1980 the market entered a glut from which it had not yet fully recovered twenty years later. The recent economic history of Saudi Arabia is one of seeking to adjust to reduced (though still sizable) revenues.

The growth of oil wealth led to the development of modern Saudi financial institutions. Prior to World War II, both public and private financial institutions were rudimentary at best. Economic policy decisions were made according to the highly personalized system that had been in existence for centuries; paper money was distrusted and none was in circulation; banks were thought to be counter to the Islamic injunction on interest; and all financial transactions, including Aramco royalty payments, were made in specie, generally Saudi silver riyals and British gold sovereigns (although the bedouin often preferred Austrian Maria Theresa silver talers).

With technical assistance from the United States, France, and Britain, the Saudis created a monetary and banking system in the 1950s and 1960s. A central bank, the Saudi Arabian Monetary Agency (SAMA), was created in 1952. One of SAMA's first tasks was to introduce paper money, which it called "Hajj receipts" until the public became accustomed to it.

Paradoxically, while the kingdom was creating basic financial institutions, the economy itself was in shambles, largely due to mismanagement under King Saud. The situation improved in 1962 when Saud was forced to hand over operational control of the government to his half-brother Faysal, who succeeded him in 1964. King Faysal, following the direction set by his father, Abd al-Aziz, was really the author of economic development in Saudi Arabia. Heavily influenced by his mother's family, the Al al-Shaykhs, he placed Islam at the center of his development philosophy, which can be summarized in a single phrase, "modernization without secularization." As the two usually are interrelated, creating a development strategy that would accomplish Faysal's goal was a tall order, and it was a mark of his political skill as well as his foresight that he succeeded so well.

In contrast to the evolution of political institutions, Saudi economic development has been the result of a formal planning process, beginning with the first five-year plan adopted in 1970. The planning process bears no resemblance to the communist central planning process, however, and the plans could better be described as a combination of wish lists and statements of intent. They are not intended as detailed instructions for budgetary expenditures and should be viewed impressionistically rather than literally. They are nevertheless fairly accurate indicators of the direction in which the Saudis believe they should be heading and of what lessons they believe are to be learned from the previous five years.

Early plans concentrated on building economic and social infrastructure and on economic diversification, and because of the huge increase in oil revenues in the 1970s, they were very ambitious. With the oil glut of the 1980s and 1990s, revenues dropped drastically, creating deficit financing. Development plans were sharply reduced. The sixth plan (1995–2000) further reflected the need to restructure the economy, stressing human resource development, economic diversification, privatization, and liberalization of trade and investment. In 1998, a Supreme Economic Council was created to oversee these reforms.

No one foresaw that the oil glut would last so long or that the large Saudi foreign reserve holdings amassed in the 1970s would be drawn down so quickly. No one foresaw either that not even a fraction of the billions of dollars loaned by Gulf Cooperation Council countries to Iraq to shore up its economy during the Iran-Iraq war would be repaid, or that Iraq would turn on its former benefactors by invading Kuwait, precipitating the Gulf War, which cost the Saudis another $55 billion in payment to the United States. In addition, the continuing post–Gulf War military threats of Iran and Iraq prompted a higher level of Saudi defense spending.

In 1998, oil prices collapsed, creating another huge budget deficit and exacerbating the current-account crisis. Prices recovered the following year, and according to a December 19, 2000, press release, the ministry of finance and national economy reported a budget surplus of SR 45 billion ($12 billion) and a current-account surplus of SR 55.6 billion ($15.6 billion) for fiscal year 2000.

Non-oil exports were also up about 10 percent in FY 2000. Because of the oil-dominated public sector, the Saudi private sector has often been overlooked. The private sector is currently booming, albeit with generous subsidies from the government, and if the boom continues, as many Saudi businessmen believe it will, it is likely to gain a momentum all its own, significantly lessening the Saudi dependence on the oil-dominated public sector. The private sector represents about 35 percent of the gross domestic product (GDP), with the non-oil government sector making up 25 percent and the oil sector the remaining 40 percent. Non-oil industry is a mix of public and private enterprise and includes more than 2,000 factories, employing about 175,000 workers, most of them non-Saudis. The government is committed to privatization of many public enterprises, but progress has been slow.

Much external concern has been expressed about the linkage between Saudi deficit spending and political instability. There is certainly linkage between economics and politics, but Saudi political stability is not overly dependent on government welfare. The kingdom will not be so dependent as the West on a social security system so long as Saudi extended families, the main source of social stability, do not allow their members to be destitute when the families have the means to help them.

Even when the oil glut ends, however, it will be crucial for the kingdom to carry through its economic reforms. With oil exports dominating the Saudi economy for the foreseeable future and the cyclical nature of world oil prices, reforms are vital if the kingdom is to avoid future economic instability. With a median age of about 18 years, there are more young people entering the job market each year than there are acceptable jobs available, and with life expectancy increasing with improved health care, there will be more non-productive aged to care for.

In sum, although economic conditions do affect political stability in Saudi Arabia, the kingdom's tight-knit, family-based society is still strong insurance against the kind of political unrest found in many developing countries. But with the demographic problems the kingdom faces and inherent fluctuations in world oil prices, the end of the latest oil glut is no cause for complacency.

Saudi Political Dynamics

Three areas are particularly important to Saudi political dynamics: the country's political culture, its political ideology, and the Saudi decisionmaking process.

Saudi Political Culture

Saudi culture is overwhelmingly Islamic. More than a religion, Islam is a totally self-contained, cosmic system. In assessing the influence of Islam on Saudi political culture, one must emphasize cultural values rather than religious piety. There are several characteristics of Saudi culture that are basic to Saudi politics. Among the most salient are a heightened sense of inevitability, a compartmentalization of behavior, and a high degree of personalization of behavior.

The sense of inevitability is based on the Islamic emphasis on God's will, often expressed in the Arabic phrase *Insha'allah,* or "God willing." Nothing can happen unless God wills it. Thus, Saudis (and other Muslims) tend to accept situations as inevitable far more quickly than people from Western cultures. Conversely, if they are convinced that a situation is not God's will, they will persevere against it long after Westerners would give up.

Compartmentalization of behavior, common in non-Western societies, is a tendency to view events from a single context rather than to explore all the ramifications of how it might appear in another context. As a result, a single issue can elicit different, and occasionally incompatible, policy responses, depending on the context in which it is viewed. Because these overlap and cannot be neatly separated, tolerance of major policy inconsistencies is inherent in the Saudi decisionmaking process.

A third cultural characteristic is the personalization of behavior. In contrast to problem-oriented Western cultures, Saudis are mainly people oriented. Good interpersonal relations are the sine qua non of good political relations, and losing face is to be avoided at all costs.

One other cultural characteristic, not directly associated with Islam, is the high degree of ethnocentricity in Saudi Arabia, derived in large part from its historical isolation and geographical insularity. Saudis, particularly Najdis, tend to see themselves as the center of their universe. Personal status is conferred more by bloodlines than by money or achievement, and nearly all Saudis claim a proud Arabian ancestry. Having never been under European colonial rule, Saudis have not developed a national inferiority complex as have many colonialized peoples. They see themselves not merely as equals of the West but in fact believe their culture is vastly superior to secular Western culture. Close personal relationships aside, they tend to look on outsiders as people to be tolerated as long as they have something to contribute.

Saudi Political Ideology

For the past 250 years, the Islamic teachings of Muhammad ibn Abd al-Wahhab have constituted the political ideology of Saudi Arabia.[7] Those teachings have provided the Saudi regime an egalitarian, universal, and moral base that has served to bind the rulers and ruled together through many crises and troubles and has been a major factor in the survival of the Saudi state throughout its often turbulent history. One must use care, however, in looking at Abd al-Wahhab's revival movement as a political ideology. It has no ideology independent of Islam.

Saudi Decisionmaking

Islamic cultural traits have often made the Saudi political decisionmaking process appear highly arbitrary and capricious to the untrained eye. There is a systemic logic to the process, however. The creation of formal political institutions over the past sixty years has made government operations a great deal more orderly, but it has not fundamentally changed the system.

At the heart of the system are two fundamental concepts, *ijma'* (consensus) and *shura* (consultation). Consensus has been used to legitimize collective action in the Arab world for millennia and has been incorporated into Islam. Even the Saudi king, despite all the powers concentrated in him, cannot act without consensus. Thus, the chief task of the king is to create a consensus for action and then to implement it. Consensus is derived through *shura,* and those consulted actively participate in the decisionmaking process. Arabic has another word for consultation, *tashawir,* which is merely soliciting an opinion. *Tashawir* also takes place in Saudi Arabia, but it does not constitute participation in the political process.

In the oil age, the consultation-consensus system is under heavy pressure. Government operations are too large and too complicated for this traditional, personalized process always to work effectively or fairly. Nevertheless, for any sustained increase in political participation, it seems necessary for some form of the consultation–consensus process to be present.

Political Institutions

Saudi Arabia has always been ruled under Islamic law, the most recent reaffirmation being Article 1 of the Basic Law of Government, issued by King Fahd on March 1, 1992. It states, "The Saudi Arabian Kingdom is a sovereign Arab Islamic state with Islam as its religion; God's book and the Sunna [which together form the sources of Islamic law] are its constitution; Arabic is its language; and Riyadh is its capital."[8]

Unlike Christianity, which is largely a theological system, Islam is basically a system of divine law. Islamic theology is quite simple, consisting of five basic tenets, or "pillars" of the faith. They are profession of faith ("There is no god but God, and Muhammad is the messenger of God"), prayer (five times a day, facing Makkah), alms, fasting (during the Muslim lunar month of Ramadan), and performing the Hajj once during one's lifetime if one is physically and financially able to do so. Another tenet, sometimes called the sixth pillar, is *jihad*. Often translated "holy war," it is, in fact, a much broader concept, referring to both the private and the corporate obligation to encourage virtue and resist evil, by force if necessary.

Islamic law, or *Shari'a* (literally, "the Pathway"), is much more complex than Islamic theology and is the primary area of specialization of Islamic scholars. Despite theological differences among the various branches of Islam (for example, between Sunni and Shi'a), Islamic law is universally respected by all Muslims.[9] The sources of the law are the Quran and the Sunna ("Traditions" of the Prophet, Muhammad). The Sunna is composed of Hadiths, or sayings of the Prophet, which are considered divinely inspired.

The Saudi legal system is based on Sunni interpretations of Islamic law, principally but not exclusively according to the Hanbali school of Islamic jurisprudence.[10] Since Hanbali law is the most conservative of all the Sunni schools, particularly in family law, many of the conservative social practices observed in Saudi Arabia, such as veiling of women in public, although they may not be specifically required by *Shari'a* law, certainly have the backing of the religious establishment.

Islamic law is supreme in Saudi Arabia, even over the king. Thus, despite there being no formal separation of powers or democratically elected representatives of the people, Saudi Arabia is not an absolute monarchy in the historic European sense; the doctrine of "divine right of kings" would be considered heresy.

Since Islamic law is a self-contained system, there is no place for statutory law in the Western sense. To meet the need for modern legislation, royal decrees (called *nizams*) have been promulgated over the years. Thus, although there is no secular criminal, civil, or commercial code in Saudi Arabia, the *nizams* provide a basis for regulating commercial transactions. In addition, special administrative tribunals have been created to adjudicate labor and commercial disputes.

Other than the Islamic legal system, Saudi rulers had almost no formal political institutions until the capture of the Hijaz in 1925. Najd was ruled by Abd al-Aziz in a highly personalized way through *shura* (consultation) with leading members of the royal family, tribal and religious leaders, and an entourage of trusted lieutenants, all of whom were members of the royal *diwan,* or court. The Hijaz, in contrast, had a much more formal system of government, including cabinet ministers. When Abd al-Aziz conquered the Hijaz in 1926, he left its political institutions intact. The early development of Saudi national political institutions, therefore, can be seen as a process by which political institutions, initially found only in the Hijaz, were slowly and with little planning adapted and expanded to meet the political and bureaucratic needs of the whole country. A parallel trend was the evolution of public administration from a totally personalized system directly under the king to a more institutionalized system, still highly personalized, but having bureaucratic structure and more-standardized procedures.

Saudi government structure, therefore, can best be described as a work in progress, evolving over the past three quarters of a century from a loosely structured, paternalistic, and personalized rule under King Abd al-Aziz to a more institutionalized structure required of a major oil-producing country. Although still far more personalized than in the West, the institutional structure has greatly regularized government operations.

The first nationwide ministry to be created was the Ministry of Foreign Affairs, established in 1930. Of possibly more importance to the development of political institutions was the creation of the Ministry of Finance in 1932. Both ministries initially overlapped with separate Hijazi ministries, which continued to exist for a number of years. The Ministry of Finance was initially responsible not just for financial affairs but also for most of the administrative machinery of the entire kingdom, as its predecessor, the Hijazi Ministry of the Interior (abolished in 1934), had been.

Many of the subsequent national ministries thus began as departments under the Finance Ministry, some becoming independent agencies before being elevated to ministry level. In 1944, the Agency of Defense became the Ministry of Defense, and in the 1950s, several more ministries emerged—Interior, responsible for public security (1951), Health (1951), Communications (1953), Agriculture and Water (1953), Education (1953), and Commerce (1954). In the 1960s, Ministries of Petroleum (1960), Hajj (1962), Labor (1962), and Information (1963) were created. In 1970, the Ministry of Justice was created, and in 1975, Ministries of Posts, Telegraphs, and Telephones; Public Works; Planning; Municipal and Rural Affairs; Industry and Electricity; and Higher Education were added. The Ministry of Awqaf (religious endowments),[11] formerly a part of the Hajj Ministry, was created in 1993, and the Ministry of Civil Service was created in 1999, making a total of twenty-two ministries. One of Abd al-Aziz's final acts was to create a council of ministers, which he decreed in October 1953, just a month before his death.

Local government has been a source of considerable confusion in Saudi Arabia. Most national ministries have officials in the regional provinces (amirates) who report directly to the ministries in Riyadh, but who must also work closely under the regional amirs. The Regions Statute, issued by royal decree on March 1, 1992, did not greatly clarify the situation. Although the interior minister is directly in charge of regional and local government, the decree confers equal rank of minister on the regional amirs. According to the decree, each amir is responsible for subregional governorates, districts, and local government centers. The decree also stipulated that ten-man advisory councils be created for the regions.[12]

The most important political institution created recently is the Majlis al-Shura, or consultative council, decreed by King Fahd on March 1, 1992. In some respects, it completed the process of expanding Hijazi political institutions to the entire country, for the Hijaz had a similar institution in the early years of Abd al-Aziz's reign. One of King Fahd's first stated priorities when he became king in 1982 was to create a new, nationwide Majlis, but it took ten years for the idea to be given substance. The long delay was attributed in large part to objections by the religious leaders, many of whom argued that any institution that created statutory law was contrary to the *Shari'a* as a wholly self-contained system of revealed law.

A number of Western observers have assessed the Saudi Majlis al-Shura as an embryonic parliament in the Western sense and a possible precursor to democratic representative government. Whether or not such a democratic institution ever evolves in the kingdom, the Majlis was not modeled on a parliamentary concept. King Fahd undoubtedly saw the need to expand public participation in the political process, but he has publicly rejected a Western-style, democratic parliamentary system. Instead, he was drawing on the formal Islamic institution of *shura* to institutionalize what had been the informal means of political participation for centuries—consulting "people of knowledge and expertise and specialists" to come up with a consensus legitimizing public policy. With rapid modernization acquired with oil revenues, it was increasingly obvious that the informal system was no longer adequate to create a true consensus.

The Majlis al-Shura was inaugurated by King Fahd in December 1993. Originally made up of sixty members, it was expanded to ninety in 1997. They are appointed for four-year terms and meet in closed sessions at least every two weeks. The Majlis is charged with suggesting new decrees (regulatory law) and reviewing and evaluating foreign and domestic policies.[13] Among the members are businessmen, technocrats, diplomats, journalists, Islamic scholars, and professional soldiers, representing all regions of the country. Breaking with tradition, most of members are young by Saudi leadership standards—in their forties and fifties. Thus, although the majority come from well-known families, they tend not to be the family patriarchs that speculation had suggested would be appointed. Many have doctorates from the United States, Europe, or the Middle East. Similarly, the Islamic scholars are younger men with outside exposure, not the older generation of Islamic leaders. The real test for the Majlis will be the degree to which its members actually participate in the consultative process (*shura*), or whether they devolve into a mere sounding board or rubber stamp for government policies (which would amount to no more than *tashawir*). Whatever the future of the Majlis, it reflects remarkable vision as an adaptation of a classical Islamic concept to modern government,

Saudi Political Process

The Saudi political process basically works on three levels—royal family politics, national politics, and bureaucratic politics. All are separate but highly interrelated.

Royal Family Politics

The Al Saud family constitutes the main constituency of the kingdom, and without its support, no king can maintain power. Technically, this support is granted and withdrawn by an old Islamic institution, Ahl al-Hall wal-Aqd (The People Who Bind and Loosen), and requires a *fatwa,* or binding Islamic legal opinion, to give it legality, but in fact, the royal family dominates this institution. (Other members include religious leaders, technocrats, businessmen, and heads of important families not otherwise included above.)

Few outside the Al Sauds know how the royal family actually operates. It is large (an estimated 3,000 to 7,000 princes) and has historically been rife with rivalries and contention. Yet it assiduously shuns publicity and always seeks to maintain an outward appearance of unanimity. Consensus is key, but family, branch, generation, seniority, and sibling ties (being sons of the same mother—Abd al-Aziz had several wives) are very important. The ruling branch is composed of the surviving sons of Abd al-Aziz. Some grandsons have been appointed to senior positions, such as Foreign Minister Prince Saud Al Faysal, but they are generally less influential than their fathers' generation.

There are also collateral branches of the family, descended from brothers of former rulers. The two leading collateral branches are the Saud al-Kabirs, who descend from an older brother of Abd al-Rahman (Abd al-Aziz's father), and the Ibn Jaluwis, who descend from an uncle of Abd al-Rahman's, Jaluwi. Technically, the head of the Saud al-Kabir branch outranks all but the king, since the founder was an *older* brother of Abd al-Rahman's, but in fact, the ruling branch has a monopoly on influence. Another branch, the Thunayans, who descend from a brother of the founder of the dynasty, lived many years in Turkey. King Faysal's wife Iffat was descended from this branch. In time, the ruling branch will undoubtedly produce additional collateral branches.

Among the sons of Abd al-Aziz, seniority of birth is important but not absolute in determining political influence. Older princes not deemed capable of maintaining high government positions are excluded from the decisionmaking process except for purely royal family business.

National and Bureaucratic Politics

National politics is played out not in the royal family per se, but in the national ministries. The royal family has ensured that most senior national security-related cabinet posts are filled by family members, who can exercise their family positions to exert influence over political decisions. However, the regime has consistently named technocrats to ministerial positions not connected with national security. These posts deal mainly with economic and social welfare, and in those areas it may be said that a technocracy has developed.

As the government expanded rapidly over the years, the sheer size and complexity of its operations made it impossible for the king to be personally involved in all but the most pressing national issues. Thus, senior technocrats have considerable powers as principal advisers to the king on their areas of responsibility and as operational decisionmakers.

In recent years, an increasing number of the younger generation of Western-educated royal family members, including those from collateral branches, have entered government, creating a new category of "royal technocrats." However, because the more senior positions are occupied, the younger princes join the government in junior positions. It is too soon to see how they will ultimately affect the political equation, but so far the most successful have won respect on merit as much as rank.

On balance, the evolution of public administration in Saudi Arabia has consisted of a gradual shift from the traditional rule of King Abd al-Aziz to a more institutionalized, bureaucratized government. However, the creation of a government bureaucracy has not diminished the personalization of the policy process so much as rechanneled it, and it is within the present structure that bureaucratic politics has grown and flourished in Saudi Arabia.

Foreign and National Security Policies

Saudi foreign and national security policies revolve around three major goals: preservation of an Islamic way of life at home and abroad, protection of the territorial integrity and economic welfare of the country, and the survival of the regime.

How these are translated into relations with other states is largely a product of the Saudi view of the world. The Saudi worldview is influenced by two strong, though seemingly contradictory, themes. The first is an extraordinary cultural self-assurance based on a sense of Islamic heritage and tribe-based self-identity and on having never been under European colonial domination; the second is an "encirclement syndrome," a heightened sense of insecurity based on the historical experience of an insular people eternally surrounded by enemies.

Without the psychological baggage of a colonial past, Saudis never developed the same degree of anti-Western xenophobia as other Arab states and have consequently been far less reluctant to enter into close relations with the Western powers. The "rebirth" of secular Arab nationalism in the 1960s was largely a reaction to 200 years of Western political domination. The Saudis, who equate Arabness with the tribes of the Arabian Peninsula, had never lost their sense of Arab identity.

Likewise, pan-Islam is a relatively recent movement, originating in the nineteenth century as a spiritual and philosophical counter to Western secularism. The Saudi Islamic revival of Muhammad ibn Abd al-Wahhab emerged a full century earlier, and the Saudi worldview, uncluttered by Western perceptions, still conforms to the more classical bipolar Islamic view, which contrasts believers (monotheists) with unbelievers (atheists and polytheists). The believers (which also include Christians, Jews, and Zoroastrians)[14] inhabit Dar al-Islam, the Abode of Islam, and the unbelievers inhabit Dar al-Harb, the Abode of War.

The Saudi sense of their responsibility for the preservation of the Islamic way of life was substantially strengthened in the 1920s when Abd al-Aziz occupied the Hijaz, where the holy cities of Makkah and al-Madinah are. As guardians of these holy sites, the Saudis assumed the responsibility of defenders of the Islamic way of life throughout the Muslim world. It is in this context that one must view the title adopted by King Fahd in 1986, *Khatim al-Haramayn,* "Custodian of the Two Holy Places."

It is easy to see how the Islamic bipolar world coincided roughly with the bipolar world of the cold war, pitting the Muslim world and the nominally Christian West against atheistic communism. However, with the demise of the Soviet Union, the greatest ideological threat to the Islamic way of life in Saudi Arabia and the Muslim world in general, as Saudis see it, is secular materialism. A major foreign policy challenge in the twenty-first century will be to accommodate Saudi opposition to the secularism of the nominally Christian West with Saudi interdependence on Western powers, particularly the United States, for economic well-being and national security.

Saudi foreign policy horizons expanded slowly, and it was not until during and after World War II that they extended past the Arabian Peninsula. Perhaps the first, and certainly the most dramatic, instance of the king's expanded political horizons was the meeting between him and President Franklin D. Roosevelt aboard the USS *Quincy* in the Great Bitter Lake on February 14, 1945. That meeting cemented strong U.S.-Saudi relations, lasting to this day.

In the 1960s, secular Arab nationalism swept the Arab world. Radical Arab nationalists, personified by Egypt's President Gamal Abd al-Nasser, castigated both Israel and the West as enemies. The Saudis shared the Arab world's sense of injustice over the creation of Israel, but they did not share the secular socialist concept of Arabism. More importantly, the Saudis saw atheistic communism as an even greater threat to the Muslim way of life than Zionism and looked to the West as the last defense of the Muslim world. Though stridently anti-Zionist, particularly after Israel seized East Jerusalem and the Aqsa Mosque, the third-holiest site in Sunni Islam, Saudi Arabia maintained a low profile in Arab politics. During most of the decade, Faysal and Nasser engaged in a political confrontation that took on a military dimension in the Yemeni civil war (1962–1970), in which the Saudis supported the royalists against the republican government, which was propped up by 80,000 Egyptian troops.

Radical Arab nationalism declined in the 1970s, and the Saudis, enriched by the energy crisis, began to take a more active role both in regional politics and in international economic and petroleum affairs. Saudi Arabia also assumed an active role in the Arab-Israeli dispute. During the 1973 Arab-Israeli war, King Faysal led the Arab oil boycott against the United States and the Netherlands. It is problematic whether Faysal would have levied the embargo had he not been so angered at President Nixon's military aid package to Israel after Nixon promised Faysal in a personal communication that the United States would be "evenhanded" during the war.[15] The king felt that this was a personal betrayal, even as he believed earlier that President Harry Truman's support for partitioning Palestine broke the pledge made by Franklin Roosevelt to King Abd al-Aziz, Faysal's father, that the United States would not act on the issue without consulting him. In 1948, Faysal had wanted his father to break diplomatic relations with the United States; in 1973, he levied the Arab oil embargo.

The Camp David accords and the subsequent Egypt-Israel Peace Treaty of 1979 were considered a disaster by the Saudis. They believed that President Anwar Sadat not only had broken Arab consensus but also had been seduced into a separate peace for nothing more concrete than vague promises of Palestinian autonomy. The subsequent breakdown of the autonomy talks seemed to justify their fears. In 1981, Prince Fahd, who was then Saudi heir apparent, sought to restart the peace process outside the moribund Camp David formula by announcing an eight-point plan for a comprehensive peace. The "Fahd Plan" broke new ground by tacitly recognizing Israel through the affirmation of all states in the area to live in peace. The original plan was rejected by the Arabs at a foreign ministers' conference in 1981 but was adopted in modified form the following year at an Arab summit in Morocco. The opportunity to exploit Arab consensus was spurned by the United States and Israel, however, and the plan went nowhere. Thereafter, the Saudis disengaged from active participation in the peace process.

In the 1980s and 1990s, Saudi foreign policy was driven to a great degree by security concerns. The overthrow of the shah of Iran in 1979 led to a radical Islamic regime in Tehran, soon followed by the Iran-Iraq war, which lasted for most of the 1980s. For Saudi Arabia, Iran's revolutionary "Islamic" foreign policies represent a major security threat, only one part of which is military. Previously, the major security threat came from left-wing Arab states and underground groups. Now, the kingdom is threatened from the revolutionary religious right, not only directly by Iranian subversive activities, but also indirectly by Iran's support of Islamist subversive groups throughout the Muslim world.

Iran aspires to be the leader of the Islamic world and sees Saudi Arabia as a major competitor. Tehran has made a special effort to undermine Saudi claims to Islamic leadership, seeking to embarrass the regime each year by sending in provocateurs to disrupt the Hajj. One of the most egregious provocations occurred at the 1987 Hajj when Iran incited bloody riots in which over 400 Hajjis were killed. To the Saudis, the riots were not only a political provocation but also a religious desecration. Tehran, in addition to its challenge with respect to Islam, also pursues traditional Persian ambitions to hegemony in the Gulf, making it difficult to tell where Persian imperialism leaves off and spreading Islamic revolution begins.

Saudi relations with its southern neighbors have also been a problem area. The threat from the Yemen Arab Republic in the 1960s was replaced by the Marxist threat from South Yemen in the 1970s and 1980s. The two Yemens were reunited in 1990, eliminating the Marxist threat, but Saudi security concerns were revived when Yemen sided diplomatically with Iraq in Desert Storm in 1991, and these concerns grew after northern Yemeni troops crushed breakaway southern Yemeni troops in a civil war in 1994. The Iraqi invasion of Kuwait in 1990 also revived Saudi concern over the Iraqi threat, leading to unprecedented cooperation with the United States and other coalition partners during Desert Storm and, politically, to closer political cooperation with the Arab Gulf states in the Gulf Cooperation Council.

The development of Saudi military and security forces has been gradual. Having disbanded its tribal forces in the 1930s, Saudi Arabia was one of the few countries in the world not to have a standing army during World War II. Following the war, it sought to create a modern armed force, and asked help, primarily from the United States but also from Britain, France, Egypt, Pakistan, and other countries. Initially, a small population and financial constraints inhibited the pace of military development, but in addition, the Saudis have always been mindful of the predilection of Arab military forces to overthrow established regimes. As a security precaution and a counterforce, the tribe-based National Guard, loyal to the royal family and headed by the heir apparent, Prince Abdallah, was modernized.

Despite its military development, Saudi Arabia has long depended on the United States as its last line of defense in case of conventional military attack. Because of what the Saudis consider overweening U.S. support for Israel, however, they have always wanted to keep U.S. forces "over the horizon," and not stationed in the kingdom. However, Desert Storm convinced them of the need for closer cooperation with the United States, as well as the GCC and other allied Arab states, as long as Iran and Iraq remain potential military threats. The Iraqi invasion also convinced the Saudis of the need to continue to upgrade their own forces. Ironically, for the oil kingdom, the greatest constraint on military upgrading is financial, a result of a decade of deficit financing.

A final word should be should be said about the Saudi political system as the country enters the twenty-first century. The greatest challenge of the twentieth century was to adapt to the rapidly changing political, economic, social, and demographic environment through evolutionary rather than revolutionary change. The country met that challenge remarkably well. The Saudi political system of today is far from the 1920s when King Abd al-Aziz united Najd and the Hijaz to form a single kingdom.

The greatest challenge of the twenty-first century is likely to be adapting to the new global economy and the revolution in communications and information technology. Information can no longer be distributed on a "need to know basis," and policymaking can no longer be restricted to respected elders whose council and consensus is solicited. With a growing public demand for more transparency in government, neither foreign nor domestic policy decisionmaking can continue exclusively in quiet consultation. To avoid revolutionary change, the Saudi political system will have to continue to adapt to rapid but unstoppable economic and technological change.

Finally, in looking into the future, one needs to consider the possible long-term impacts of the September 11, 2001, terrorist attacks in New York city and Washington, D.C., on the government and politics of Saudi Arabia. In the immediate aftermath, a spate of heated criticism in the American media that the Saudi condemnation of the attacks was not vocal enough angered the Saudi Heir Apparent, Prince Abdallah, and strained Saudi Arabia's relations with the kingdom's most powerful ally, the United States. There have been such strains before, however, and given the two countries' strong mutual interest in the unimpeded flow of oil and in Gulf security, the relationship should weather this one as well.

Notes

1. Some of the materials in this chapter are developed from David E. Long, *The Kingdom of Saudi Arabia* (Gainesville, Fla.: University Press of Florida, 1997).

2. In Western literature, the cities are more commonly written *Mecca* and *Medina*. The official Saudi spelling, however, is *Makkah* and *al-Madinah,* which is a more accurate transliteration from the Arabic.

3. Saudi Arabia has agreed in principle to demarcated borders with Oman. A Saudi-Kuwaiti Neutral Zone and a Saudi-Iraqi Neutral Zone were created in 1922 to avoid tribal border hostilities. The first was abolished in 1966 and the second in 1975 and their territories divided among the parties. The decades-old Buraymi Oasis territorial dispute among Saudi Arabia, Oman, and Abu Dhabi was settled in 1974 when Saudi Arabia agreed to give up its claim to the oasis and adjacent territory in return for an outlet to the Gulf through Abu Dhabi. Since then, the kingdom has agreed in principle to demarcate the rest of its long border with Oman, and on June 12, 2000, Saudi Arabia and Yemen signed a treaty on their international land and sea borders, ending a dispute that went back to the Saudi invasion of Yemen in 1934.

4. One of the first outsiders to traverse the area was Wilfred Thesiger, a Briton who first came to the Arabian Peninsula with a locust control mission. See Wilfred Thesiger, *Arabian Sands* (New York: Dutton, 1959).

5. Based on a study by the Riyadh Development Authority reported in *al-Yamama* newspaper, September 27, 1999. See also Saudi Arabian Information Reserve, http://www.saudinf.com, update, June 29, 2001.

6. These estimates are based on a number of sources, including the Saudi Arabian Ministry of Information website, Saudi Arabian Information Reserve, and the CIA's *World Factbook, 2000* (Washington: GPO, 2000). Estimates can vary widely and those used here are on the conservative side.

7. Some of the ideas in the following section are drawn from my discussion of Saudi political ideology in "Saudi Arabia in the 1990s: Plus ça Change. . . ," Chapter 6 of Charles F. Doran and Stephen W. Buck, eds., *The Gulf, Energy, and Global Security: Political and Economic Issues* (Boulder: Lynne Rienner Publishers, 1991), pp. 91–92.

8. *The Basic Law of Government of the Kingdom of Saudi Arabia,* trans., Foreign Broadcast Information Service (FBIS), London, March 1, 1992.

9. The Shi'a also consider sayings of Ali and other Shi'a imams as divinely inspired.

10. Named after an early Islamic scholar, Ahmad ibn Hanbal (d. A.D. 855). The other recognized Sunni schools are Hanafi, Shafa'i, and Malaki. Ibn Taymiyyah, whose writings influenced Muhammad ibn Abd al-Wahhab, was a Hanbali. See John L. Esposito, *Islam: The Straight Path* (New York: Oxford University Press, 1988), p. 86.

11. *Awqaf* (sing., *waqf*) are Islamic religious charitable endowments. The practice of setting up such endowments dates to the early days of Islam.

12. Text of the *Royal Decree on the Regions Statute, Kingdom of Saudi Arabia,* trans., Foreign Broadcast Information Service (FBIS), London, March 1, 1992.

13. *Saudi Arabian Information Resource,* web site, http://www.saudinf.com/main/c52.htm. See also *Middle East Journal* 46, no. 3 (Summer 1992): 496.

14. Christians, Jews, and Zoroastrians (Parsees) are known as Ahl al-Kitab, or "People of the Book." Sura II, verse 62, of the Quran states, "Lo! Those who believe (in that which was revealed unto thee, Muhammad), and those who are Jews and Christians and Sabeans—

whoever believeth in God and the Last Day and doeth right—surely their regard is with their Lord, and there shall be no fear come upon them, neither shall they grieve."

15. An embargo had been levied in the 1967 war, but in a buyers' market, it had little effect. Moreover, King Faysal ensured that jet fuel continued to be shipped to U.S. forces in Vietnam, fighting against communism.

Bibliography

A great deal has been written about Saudi Arabia in recent years, much of it of very mixed quality. Definitive works are comparatively few. R. Bayly Winder's *Saudi Arabia in the Nineteenth Century* (New York: St. Martin's Press, 1985) is still the standard work in English on earlier history. Any of the several works by H. St. John B. Philby, though not scholarly, captures the feel of Saudi Arabia in the interwar and immediate post–World War II period. Two of his books, *Arabian Jubilee* (London: Robert Hale, 1952) and *Saudi Arabia* (London: Ernest Benn, 1955), written to commemorate the fiftieth year of Abd al-Aziz's reign, would be good places to begin. Another classic is T. E. Lawrence's *The Seven Pillars of Wisdom* (Garden City, N.Y.: Doubleday, 1935), about his exploits in the Hijaz during World War I. For a good study on the earlier history of the Hijaz, see William Ochsenwald's *Religion, Society and the State in Arabia: The Hijaz Under Ottoman Control, 1849–1908* (Columbus, Ohio: Ohio State University Press, 1984).

There are still relatively few good studies on Saudi society and internal political dynamics. John A. Shaw and David E. Long's *Saudi Arabian Modernization: The Impact of Change on Stability*, vol. 10, Washington Paper No. 89 (New York: Praeger, 1980), though dated, gives a good overview of the impact of social and economic development on the kingdom. A more recent work is Mordachai Abir's *Saudi Arabia: Government, Society and the Gulf Crisis* (London: Routledge, 1993). Mamoun Fandy's *Saudi Arabia and the Politics of Dissent* (New York: St. Martin's Press, 1999) is an analysis of Saudi dissidents in the 1990s, and Joseph Kechichian's *Succession in Saudi Arabia* (New York: I. B. Tauris, 2001) explores a subject that has generated much discussion in the West. Two studies concentrating on Saudi women are Lila Abu-Lughod, *Veiled Sentiments: Honored Poetry in a Bedouin Society* (Berkeley: University of California Press, 1986), and Mona Almunajjed, *Women in Saudi Arabia* (New York: St. Martin's Press, 1997). For readers interested in the modern Hajj, see David E. Long's *The Hajj Today: A Survey of the Contemporary Makkah Pilgrimage* (Albany: State University of New York Press, 1979). An interesting account of Makkah and the Hajj in the nineteenth century is C. Snouck-Hurgronje's *Mekka in the Latter Part of the Nineteenth Century*, translated by J. H. Monahan (Leiden: E. J. Brill, and London: Luzac and Co., 1931).

There are a number of good studies on the development of the Saudi oil industry. George W. Stocking's *Middle East Oil: A Study in Political and Economic Controversy* (Nashville: Vanderbilt University Press, 1970) is a classic. Daniel Yergin's exhaustively researched bestseller, *The Prize: The Epic Quest for Oil, Money and Power* (New York: Simon and Schuster, 1990), is must reading. The best scholarly treatment of U.S.-Saudi oil relations is David S. Painter's *Oil and the American Century* (Baltimore: Johns Hopkins University Press, 1986). A fascinating book on the Saudi Arabian Monetary Agency, the Saudi central bank, is *Saudi Arabia: The Making of a Financial Giant* (New York: New York University Press, 1983), by Arthur N. Young, who played a major role in the agency's creation.

Works on military and strategic issues are highly uneven. David E. Long's *The United States and Saudi Arabia: Ambivalent Allies* (Boulder: Westview Press, 1985) is a short but authoritative overview of U.S.-Saudi political, economic, oil, and military relations up to 1985. Two good, comprehensive studies on military and strategic issues, both predating the Kuwait invasion, are Anthony Cordesman's *The Gulf and the Search for Strategic Stability: Saudi Arabia, the Military Balance in the Gulf, and Trends in the Arab-Israeli Military Balance* (Boulder: Westview Press, and London: Mansell, 1984) and *The Gulf and the West* (Boulder: Westview Press, 1988).

Two nonscholarly books are worth looking into for their wealth of narrative, if not their interpretive analysis: Robert Lacey's *The Kingdom* (London: Hutcheson, 1981) and David Howarth and Richard Johns's *The House of Saud* (London: Sidgwick and Jackson, 1981). The most recent survey of Saudi Arabia is David E. Long's *The Kingdom of Saudi Arabia* (Gainesville, Fla.: University Press of Florida, 1997). Finally, those interested in the Rub' al-Khali should see Wilfred Thesiger's *Arabian Sands* (New York: Dutton, 1959).

5

Republic of Iraq

Phebe Marr

Historical Background

Between the Tigris and Euphrates Rivers lies a land rich in resources and history, Iraq. A major theme of Iraq's often turbulent history, stretching back to ancient times, has been the organization of the social and political environment to develop these resources, including the establishment of irrigation systems in the river valleys. Political failures have often led to factionalism, turbulence, and decay. Geography has also been a significant feature in Iraq's history. Known as Mesopotamia ("land between the rivers") until the twentieth century, Iraq has often been a battleground of strategic importance, a factor contributing to its frequent domestic strife. Bordered by deserts in the south and high mountains to the north, Iraq is virtually without natural defenses against invasion. The country has been occupied by Greeks, Romans, Persians, Arabs, Turks, and, in modern times, the British. All have left their mark on the people and culture, fashioning a society of considerable ethnic and cultural diversity.

Arab Conquests

The Arab–Islamic conquest of Iraq, begun in A.D. 633, was one of the most decisive events in Iraqi history. Arabic became the predominant language of Mesopotamia (except for Kurdish speakers in the highlands), and Islam became the religion of virtually all inhabitants. For over a century after the conquest, Iraq was governed as a province from the capital of the Islamic empire, located at first in al-Madinah and later in Damascus. Iraqis came to resent the power of Damascus (a theme that persisted until modern times) and often revolted against it. In the process, Iraq acquired a reputation, which it still has, of a territory difficult to govern.

Moving the Islamic capital to Damascus led to a religious schism that still cleaves the Islamic community. In 661, Ali, the fourth caliph and a son-in-law and cousin of Muhammad, was assassinated in Iraq. (Caliph is a corruption of the Arabic *khalifah,* meaning "successor"—the title was given to successors of Muhammad as leaders of the Muslim community.) Ali's rival, Muawiyah, established himself in Damascus as founder of the Umayyad caliphate. In 680, Ali's son Husayn challenged the Umayyads and he and a small band of men were killed by Umayyad forces in Karbala, in Iraq. Ali's followers, known as Shi'a (short for *Shi'at Ali,* the "Partisans of Ali"), went underground as opponents of the established regime. Followers of the Umayyads came to be known as Sunnis, those who adhere to the Prophet's traditions. Gradually, the Shi'a became a distinctive sect within Islam, with different leaders (called "imams" rather than caliphs) and some different doctrines. As a persecuted minority, the Shi'a acquired characteristics still evident among the community in Iraq today—a sense of alienation from society and feelings of oppression and injustice.

In A.D. 747, Abdul Abbas, a descendant of al-Abbas, Muhammad's uncle, revolted against the Umayyads, and in 750 Abdul Abbas established the Abbasid caliphate. In 762, the Abbasids founded a new city, Baghdad, to be their capital. The Abbasid period (750–1258) was a great era in Iraqi—indeed Islamic—history. Iraq came into its own as the center of a prosperous empire that stretched from southern France to the borders of China and a brilliant civilization in which science, architecture, and literature flourished.

The decline of the Abbasid caliphate was gradual, caused by factors that would be recognizable today. Prosperity was concentrated in the urban upper classes; little filtered down to the rural and urban poor, who often revolted. Turkish captives were used as warriors and administrators, and they gradually came to dominate the court. Factionalism within the ruling elite caused economic decline and neglect of the irrigation system. Weakness within encouraged incursion from without, including the intrusion of the Seljuq Turks, who governed Baghdad from 1055 on.

It was the Mongols, however, who caused the ultimate demise of the Abbasid caliphate. In 1258, Hulagu, the grandson of Genghis Khan, destroyed much of Baghdad and the irrigation system on which its prosperity depended. Even more devastating to Iraq was the invasion of Timur the Lame in 1401. He so devastated the country that it did not recover until the mid-twentieth century. In addition, Iraq's strategic location astride the major East-West trade routes was greatly undermined by the Portuguese when they discovered the sea route around the Cape of Good Hope. Thus, although Iraqis recall their glorious Abbasid past, their political and social environment—and much of their psychology—has been shaped mainly by the centuries of stagnation that followed.

Ottoman Rule

From 1258 until 1534, when Iraq was finally conquered by the Ottoman Empire, the country was divided into provinces, which were often ruled by Turkish tribal dynasties from capitals in Persian territory. Because of the lack of a central government, neither the irrigation systems nor the urban culture could be revived.

The Ottoman conquest of Iraq began in 1514 as an outgrowth of a religious and dynastic war between the Sunni Ottoman sultan and the Shi'a Safavid shah of Persia. Most of Iraq was incorporated into the Ottoman domain, and the country was divided into three provinces—Mosul, Baghdad, and Basra.

The Ottomans were unable to bring stability or prosperity to Iraq, primarily for two reasons. The first was a succession of Ottoman-Persian wars that continued until 1818. The wars not only ravaged the Iraqi countryside but also renewed Shi'a-Sunni distrust. Iraqi Shi'a sometimes sided with their coreligionaries in Persia, and the Ottomans came to regard them as a potential "fifth column." Eventually the Ottomans came to rely on Sunnis in the army and government, thus perpetuating Sunni political dominance. Second was the weakness of Ottoman power. As Ottoman society declined in the seventeenth and eighteenth centuries, direct administration ceased in Iraq and local tribal chiefs held sway in Arab and Kurdish areas. By the nineteenth century, fragmentation was complete. What little Ottoman control remained was inefficient and corrupt. The Ottoman Turks gradually came to be despised as aliens by most of the local population.

Ottoman administration revived for brief periods in the nineteenth century. In 1831, the Ottoman Sultan Mahmud II reasserted direct control over Iraq, though these gains were frittered away by subsequent rulers. Mihdat Pasha, Ottoman governor of Baghdad from 1869 to 1872, extended his authority into the countryside, brought secular education to the cities, and attempted land settlement among the tribes. His schools produced administrators and army officers who went on to become leaders of Iraq in the post–World War I period. Almost all these new leaders were Sunni Arabs. The Shi'a shunned the schools, since they were dominated by Turks.

During the nineteenth century, Iraq was also drawn into international politics and economics. The opening of the Suez Canal in 1869 increased Iraq's trade and, in the south, some landlords shifted from subsistence agriculture to cash crops. Printing presses and newspapers were introduced in the 1860s. Contacts with new ideas stirred a modest renaissance among religious leaders (Sunni and Shi'a) and Arabic scholars. Because of its strategic location astride overland routes to India, Iraq attracted increasing British concern. Meanwhile international commerce produced a small class of urban merchants and farmers tied to the new market economy. These benefits, however, could not overcome the centuries of indifferent and often corrupt Ottoman rule. Iraq entered the twentieth century a profoundly underdeveloped country, only marginally touched by the economic, scientific, and political developments that had transformed Europe in the nineteenth century.

British Mandate

The impact of the British in shaping modern Iraq has been second only to that of the Arab-Islamic conquest. The British created the state of Iraq and established its present boundaries, incorporating within them a diverse ethnic and sectarian population, a source of subsequent instability. The borders also caused disputes with neighbors, especially Iran, that would not accept the frontiers as demarcated.

Britain occupied Iraq in stages during World War I, starting with Basra (1914), then Baghdad (1917), and finally Mosul (1918). British control over Iraq was formalized at the San Remo Conference in April 1920, which granted Britain a mandate over the country, subject to supervision by the League of Nations. British control over the territory and its government was constrained by several factors. First, the mandate itself, since it was designed to prepare the country for independence, put legal limits on this control. Second, Great Britain faced a growing demand at the end of the war to cut back on financial commitments to Iraq, a sentiment hastened by the anti-British revolt of 1920, the suppression of which cost nearly 40 million pounds sterling—and many British lives. Third, a vigorous nationalist movement, which constantly agitated for the removal of British control, emerged.

As a result, the British sought a less expensive means of governing Iraq and found it in two instruments of indirect rule. First, they established a monarchy in Iraq in the person of Prince Faysal of the Hashimite house of Makkah, with which the British had cooperated during the war. In 1921, after a carefully controlled election, Faysal became the first of three Hashimite kings to rule Iraq. In the new constitutional system, the monarch was given considerable powers, including the right to appoint the prime minister and to dismiss parliament. It was through the monarchy and a network of British advisers in key ministries that Britain exercised its influence. Second, the British expressed their mandatory relationship with Iraq through a series of treaties, the first of which was signed in 1922. These provided the British with bases and other facilities in return for help, advice, and protection for the new state.

Although the British bequeathed to the new state Western-style democratic institutions, including parliament and indirect elections, responsibility for government was unclear. Ultimately the British came to rely not only on the king but also on a small group of Iraqi nationalists willing to work with them and on a parliament increasingly filled with tribal leaders and urban wealthy, willing to trade acquiescence to the mandate for privileges such as grants of land. The British also assisted in modernizing and restructuring the Iraqi army and bureaucracy inherited from the Ottomans; these became the backbone of the new state.

Several groups were not satisfied with the dispensation of power. The Kurds rebelled against accepting Arab rule and eventually were given special consideration, particularly in the use of their language in schools. Shi'a religious leaders led a rebellion against the mandate and ended up in exile in Iran. For much of the mandate period, Faysal was able to maintain the balance between the British interests and those of the nationalists. Finally, in 1929, the British negotiated a treaty that met most nationalist demands and the mandate formally ended. In October 1932, the League of Nations admitted Iraq as an independent member, and a new Anglo-Iraq treaty, providing Britain with bases and Iraq with military protection, went into effect.

Constitutional Monarchy

The end of the mandate and the reduction of British control ushered in a period of instability (1932–1945) that revealed the weakness of the constitutional structure and the fragility of Iraq's sense of nationhood. Several religious and ethnic groups asserted claims to a greater share of power.

In 1933 the Assyrian (Nestorian Christian) community demanded the right to self-government and was put down by the Iraqi army. In the process, a massacre of Assyrians, which besmirched the reputation of the new government, occurred in northern Iraq. In the mid-1930s a rash of rebellions broke out among the Shi'a tribes of southern Iraq. Shi'a religious leaders used this occasion to demand more Shi'a representation in government and more recognition of their religion and culture in the emerging state system. Little heed was given these requests, and both Shi'a and Kurds continued to be underrepresented in cabinets dominated by Arab Sunnis.

Another source of instability was the untimely death of King Faysal I in September 1933. Faysal was succeeded by his son Ghazi, a young man well liked by the army and the nationalists but too inexperienced to provide the leadership needed to balance Iraq's political and social groups. It was during Ghazi's reign (1933–1939) that the Iraqi army came to play an increasingly dominant role in political life. In 1936 the first of a series of military coups d'état took place. These were all aimed at replacing cabinets, not the monarchy, and were often led by civilian politicians desirous of holding office. The increased role of the military indicated the fragility of the constitutional system.

The monarchy was further weakened by the accidental death of King Ghazi in 1939. He was succeeded by his four-year-old son, Faysal II. Until his coming of age in 1953, the regency was assumed by Abd al-Ilah, a cousin of Ghazi and a pro-British politician, but a man unable to fill the shoes of Faysal I.

By 1939 the Iraqi political leadership was in disarray and unprepared to deal with the stresses of a war already on the horizon. The leading politician by this time was former general Nuri al-Said, who strongly favored the British connection as a means of protecting Iraq's security. However, the Iraqi political elite had split into two blocs, a pro-British group, led by Nuri, and a nationalist, anti-British contingent, supported by the army and led by Rashid Ali al-Gaylani, a civilian politician. The latter group looked to Germany for support, a position the British regarded as threatening to their interests. In 1941, the army and Rashid Ali led a coup that ousted Abd al-Ilah and the leading pro-British politicians, including Nuri. Fearful that this outcome would alter the balance of power in the Middle East in the Axis's favor, Britain reoccupied Iraq from 1941 to 1945. It restored Abd al-Ilah and the pro-British politicians to power and encouraged the removal of the anti-British elements in the army and the bureaucracy. This move restored stability to Iraq and placed the country firmly in the Western orbit, but it also created resentment inside Iraq toward the ruling group and its association with a foreign power. The 1941 coup can be interpreted as a forerunner to the 1958 revolution.

From 1945 to 1958 the power structure of Iraq remained relatively stable. The main hand at the helm was that of Nuri al-Said, who was prime minister thirteen times between 1941 and 1958. Stability was enhanced by the development of Iraq's oil resources and the expenditure of oil revenues on dams, roads, health, and education. As education spread to rural areas, more Shi'a and Kurds entered the political establishment, quieting ethnic and sectarian tensions. Between 1945 and 1958 there were two Kurdish and three Shi'a prime ministers.

Nuri was firmly convinced that foreign powers—especially Great Britain and the United States—had a role to play in Iraq's development and he cooperated closely with the West. In 1955, Iraq joined the Baghdad Pact, a Western-oriented defense alliance, with Turkey, Pakistan, Iran, and Great Britain, and with the United States as an observer.

However, the relative stability of the postwar period could not conceal the flaws of the political and social structure that eventually resulted in the regime's overthrow in a violent revolt. Behind a parliamentary facade, Nuri, an Ottoman-trained army officer, ruled with a heavy hand. Although elections were held periodically, he manipulated them to assure favorable results. Political parties were controlled and opposition leaders, especially Communists, were jailed and some were executed.

The regime's close ties with foreign powers were increasingly resented by the educated population. There were riots and demonstrations in 1948 (against a proposed new Anglo-Iraq treaty), in 1952 (against establishment of foreign bases, including an attack against a U.S. facility), and in 1956 (against the British, French, and Israeli invasion of Egypt). Nationalist sentiments were fanned by President Gamal Abd al-Nasser of Egypt, who attacked the Baghdad Pact and urged the people of Iraq to overthrow the regime. These antiforeign sentiments took root in the army, where younger officers formed a Free Officers group to plan the overthrow of the regime.

Social reformers also inveighed against the maldistribution of wealth and privilege in the country, pointing to an upper class of landlord-shaykhs and urban entrepreneurs who dominated parliament and blocked land-reform legislation. Rapid urban migration from the countryside created large slum areas in and around the capital, which accentuated class divisions.

Disaffection with the regime came to a head in 1958. On July 14, troops under the command of Brigadier Abd al-Karim Qasim and Colonel Abd al-Salam Arif, both Free Officers, moved on Baghdad and in a violent and bloody coup ended the monarchy, killing the royal family and Nuri al-Said and imprisoning many "old regime" leaders.

Republican Iraq

The overthrow of the monarchy ushered in a decade of political instability. Between 1958 and 1968 there were four changes of regime, several involving considerable bloodshed. Although a facade of civilian government was erected, the revolution placed the army in power, with officers assuming the most important political positions.

The republican period began with a regime headed by Abd al-Karim Qasim (1958–1963). The officers who assumed power replaced the monarchy with a three-man Council of Sovereignty, consisting of an Arab Sunni, an Arab Shi'a, and a Kurd. Within two weeks of the revolution, a provisional constitution was enacted, placing all executive and legislative authority in the Council of Ministers, with the approval of the Sovereignty Council. Parliament was abolished. Real power reposed in the hands of Abd al-Karim Qasim, who became prime minister and minister of defense, and Abd al-Salam Arif, who became deputy prime minister and minister of interior. In the initial euphoria of the revolution, the new government released political opponents jailed under the monarchy, including the Communists, and allowed Mustafa Barzani, the leader of a Kurdish rebellion in 1946, to return to Iraq.

The new government moved rapidly to institute social reforms and to change foreign policy. In September 1958 an agrarian reform law limiting the size of landholdings and placing a ceiling on rent was promulgated. Qasim also revised the personal status law, giving women more rights and security. Finally, in 1961, after a bitter dispute with the foreign-owned Iraq Petroleum Company (IPC), Qasim expropriated 99.5 percent of its concession area. These acts may have brought a measure of social justice, but they were poorly managed and began a process of economic decline.

In foreign policy the new regime abrogated the Baghdad Pact and recognized the Soviet Union and the People's Republic of China. In 1959 Iraq signed economic and arms supply agreements with Moscow. This orientation toward the Communist bloc and the break in treaty relations with the West began a period of isolation from and increasingly tense relations with the West, features that persist to the present day.

Unfortunately, the revolution failed to be institutionalized or to restrain the power struggle between the two main figures, Qasim and Arif, which began five days after the successful revolt. Their personal differences soon crystallized around a key policy issue—whether Iraq should move toward union with Egypt or remain independent and concentrate on reform at home. Arif, backed by Nasserites and the Ba'th Party, favored union. Qasim, supported by the Communist Party and the Kurds, opposed it.

In September 1958, Qasim dismissed Arif from office and imprisoned him on a charge of attempting to assassinate Qasim. This provoked the Arab nationalists, who precipitated a rebellion in Mosul in 1959. With the assistance of the Communists and the Kurds, Qasim suppressed the new rebellion, temporarily crushing the Arab nationalists. Their removal from the political scene allowed the ascendancy of the Communists and the Left. It was not long, however, before Qasim turned on these groups as well, removing leftist ministers from office and curtailing their influence. Although Qasim promised a new constitution and a legislature, none appeared. By 1961, Qasim had established a lackluster dictatorship, backed by his supporters in the army. Enemies of the regime were prosecuted in show trials, and dissidents were executed.

The Kurds also turned against the regime in 1961. Mustafa Barzani had gradually become disillusioned by Qasim's failure to fulfill his promises for Kurdish self-government, but Qasim was suspicious of Kurdish demands for autonomy. A series of tribal clashes in the north, manipulated by Qasim, soon degenerated into a full-scale guerrilla war, which did not come to an end until 1975. For the remainder of the Qasim era, the Kurds effectively engaged a large segment of the Iraqi army, intensifying the divisions within the country and eroding Qasim's dwindling support.

The final blow to the regime came with Qasim's inept claim to Kuwait. In June 1961, Qasim refused to recognize Kuwait's newly attained independence, claiming that Kuwait had been part of Iraq under the Ottoman Empire. His position alienated virtually every country in the Arab world and left Iraq hopelessly isolated. These events, together with underground opposition organization, finally precipitated his downfall.

On February 8, 1963, Qasim was overthrown in a coup led by the Iraqi Ba'th Party, together with sympathetic army officers and Arab nationalist groups. The overthrow was bloody, resulting in several days of street fighting between Ba'thists and Communists and the summary execution of Qasim and his followers. The Qasim era, which had begun with hope, left a legacy that remains today. The instability and violence that followed generated a fear of chaos on the part of successive governments that soon ended any hope of return to a democratic system. This fear polarized the ruling elite between nationalists and leftists and began an escalating cycle of violence and government ruthlessness. And it inaugurated a Kurdish revolt that destabilized successive regimes and strengthened Kurdish demands for self-determination.

The Ba'th regime that succeeded Qasim lasted only nine months. Abd al-Salam Arif, an Arab nationalist but not a Ba'thist, was appointed president, but Ba'thists, whether military or civilian, controlled all important positions. However, the new party leaders were young, inexperienced, and unready for governing. Moreover, they were split between moderates, who wanted to consolidate power in Iraq and move slowly on union with the United Arab Republic (UAR), and radicals, who favored closer unity with the new Ba'th government in Syria and wanted radical domestic reform. Attempts to unite with the UAR failed; so, too, did efforts to heal the breach with the Kurds, who would not countenance any Arab union. Finally, after severe internal power struggles, Arif succeeded in outmaneuvering the Ba'th leadership and, in a bloodless coup, wrested power from them in November 1963. Within a short period of time he had removed all Ba'th ministers from office.

Arif governed through a new National Revolutionary Council and a cabinet of military men and technocrats. The Arif regime went through several stages of development but in general was dominated by those elements supporting Nasser's brand of Arab socialism. In 1964 Iraq took several measures designed to bring Iraq's political and economic structure into line with that of Egypt. All political parties were asked to join an Arab Socialist Union on the Egyptian model. Even more significant, laws were passed nationalizing banks, insurance companies, and other key industries except for oil, moving the country in the direction of a socialist economy. These steps failed to produce union. Iraq had second thoughts on the desirability of sharing its oil wealth with a poorer Arab country, and in 1965, Arif appointed the first civilian prime minister since the monarchy, Abd al-Rahman al-Bazzaz, a respected lawyer, who moved the country in a more pragmatic direction, focusing on Iraq's domestic affairs.

These promising steps toward stability were abruptly halted in April 1966, when Arif was killed in a helicopter crash. The attempt to replace him with a new president generated a renewed struggle for power between the civilians, led by Bazzaz, and the military. The military won. Arif's brother General Abd al-Rahman Arif was promoted to the presidency, and power gravitated once again into the hands of a small coterie of army officers. However, these elements were unable to control factionalism in the military. In 1967 the military in Iraq, like its counterparts elsewhere in the Arab world, was humiliated by its defeat in the Six-Day War with Israel. This was the final blow. The enemies of the discredited regime sought an opportunity to move against it.

On July 17, 1968, the Abd al-Rahman Arif regime was overthrown in a bloodless coup by General Ahmad Hasan al-Bakr and a group of Ba'thist supporters, in collaboration with non-Ba'thist officers. This time, the Ba'thists were determined not to let power slip from their grasp, as they had in 1963. Two weeks after the coup, they removed all non-Ba'thist party members. Then, they inaugurated their rule with a series of secret trials and brutal executions designed to stamp out dissidents, terrorize the populace, and stabilize the country by force. This modus operandi succeeded in keeping them in power for the remainder of the century and beyond.

Ba'th Party Rule, 1968–Present

The government established by the new Ba'th regime was based on a Revolutionary Command Council (RCC), buttressed by the regional (Iraqi) command of the Ba'th Party and a cabinet. The two leading figures were Ahmad Hasan al-Bakr, RCC chairman, and Saddam Hussein, vice-chairman. In July 1970, an interim constitution, indicating that Iraq would follow a socialist economic path, was promulgated. This constitution, with a few modifications, still remains in effect. A new constitution, drafted in 1990, was not adopted. The RCC was given the authority to promulgate laws, to deal with defense and security, to declare war, and to approve the budget. The president (who was also the chairman of the RCC) was given the authority to appoint, promote, and dismiss judiciary, civil, and military personnel and members of the party's regional command, assuring party control of government. Cabinet ministers were reduced to executing RCC decisions. The constitution provided for the election of a national assembly, but this provision was not activated until 1980.

The first decade of Ba'th rule was notable for an increase in oil revenue, expanded economic and social development, and a period of sustained stability. Nationalization of oil resources and the oil price rise of 1973 greatly increased the revenue available to the government. As a consequence, the regime embarked on an ambitious economic and social program, mainly in the public sector. Programs to distribute land to the peasants were expanded, as were education and health services, especially in rural areas. Heavy industries—iron, steel, and petrochemicals—were established, mainly in the south. The regime also embarked on a military industrial program that included chemical and nuclear weapons.

In a further effort toward stability, the regime attempted to solve the festering Kurdish problem. In 1970, after two years of intermittent warfare, the Ba'th negotiated a settlement more comprehensive than any previous agreement. The Kurds were offered autonomy and an elected regional executive and legislative authority, a Kurdish vice president in Baghdad, and a larger share of oil revenues. However, there was to be a four-year delay for a census to determine the boundaries of the new autonomous zone. When it became clear that the Kurds would not receive the degree of autonomy or the extent of territory they desired, Barzani again revolted, this time with military aid from Iran and some financial help from the United States and Israel. The rebellion collapsed in March 1975 after Iran agreed to withdraw its support for the Kurds in return for Iraqi recognition of Iranian sovereignty over half of the Shatt al-Arab River. Barzani was forced into exile and later died in the United States.

In the aftermath of the agreement, Baghdad unilaterally established an autonomous region in the heavily Kurdish north with its own legislative and executive council and budget; however, real control over the region was kept in the hands of the central government. The government also instituted some land reforms and economic development in the north. To prevent renewed guerrilla activities, the government razed Kurdish villages along an 800-mile border with Iran, forcibly resettled Kurds in other regions, and encouraged Arabs to settle in the north. These activities stirred renewed hostility among the Kurds, and by 1979 the Kurdish opposition had once again begun guerrilla activities. In 1975, the Kurdish movement had split into two parties, the Kurdish Democratic Party (KDP), eventually led by Barzani's son, Mas'ud, and the Patriotic Union of Kurdistan (PUK), led by Jalal Talabani.

A Decade of War

The stability enforced by the Ba'th Party was not to survive into the decade of the 1980s. Saddam Hussein had been patient in sheltering his ambition behind the leadership of Bakr, but his desire to take charge finally won over patience. In July 1979, Saddam engineered the resignation of Bakr, who had been suffering from ill health, and assumed the presidency—and the full reins of power—himself. This act marked a transition from party rule to Saddam's personal dictatorship. Saddam's tenure as president has been marked by a ruthless suppression of all forms of organized activity not under his control, an extreme concentration of power in his person, and increased reliance on a coterie of family members and allies from his hometown of Tikrit (a city north of Baghdad) to maintain his power. The absence of checks on Saddam's power soon led to miscalculations in foreign affairs that plunged the country into two devastating wars in little more than a decade. The first was a war with Iran that lasted for eight years.

The Iran-Iraq war began on September 23, 1980, when Iraqi forces invaded Iran. Iraq had mixed motives for going to war. One was defensive. For over a year, the Islamic government in Iran had incited opposition elements (Shi'a and Kurd) to overthrow the regime. Iraq feared that if it did not move against the new regime, it would face a greater threat later. But Saddam also had more opportunistic motives. The collapse of the shah's regime provided an occasion for the Ba'th to reverse the 1975 decision on the Shatt al-Arab and possibly to "liberate" from Iran the oil-rich Khuzistan Province, inhabited largely by ethnic Arabs.

The war, which Iraq expected to be short, proved to be a profound strategic miscalculation and lasted eight years. After its thrust into Iranian territory, Iraq adopted a defensive strategy and soon lost the initiative. With the aid of "human waves" of suicide troops, Iranian forces counterattacked and by June 1982 had driven Iraq out of Iran. Iran then made the mistake of carrying the war to Iraq, hoping to unseat the regime in Baghdad. Iran was unable to marshal sufficient forces to win, and Iraqis, defending their homeland, fought hard; the situation settled into a long war of attrition. During the war Iraq made use of chemical weapons on the battlefield and on the Kurdish population in the north, bringing the regime an unsavory reputation. During the war Iraq got some support from the West and the USSR in the form of arms supplies, loans, and credits. It was also helped by a growing U.S. military presence in the Gulf to protect oil shipping. This force was eventually drawn into military actions against Iran. The tide of war turned in Iraq's favor in April 1988, when Iraq went on the offensive with intensive missile strikes on Iran's cities and a military thrust into Iran. Finally, in July 1988, Iran accepted a cease-fire, effectively ending the war.

The costs of the war were high for Iraq. Iraq's offshore oil export facilities were destroyed and the Shatt al-Arab waterway was closed to traffic, filled with sunken ships, chemical weapons, and other ordnance, making Iraq almost a landlocked country. As a result, Iraq had to turn to the port of Umm Qasr, bordering Kuwait, as its main shipping terminal. Estimates placed Iraq's war casualties at 400,000, about 150,000 of them killed. To pay for the war, Iraq acquired a debt of at least $80 billion, half owed to the Gulf states and half to Europe. Nevertheless, Iraq emerged from the war with its territory and its military intact and with a sense of nationalist pride at its defense of the country.

It also emerged with a need to rebuild its economy and repay its debt, but the regime did not take the opportunity to do so. Instead, within a year and a half of the cease-fire, it was embroiled in regional conflict with Kuwait that would lead to a second Gulf War—this time against the United States and a coalition of more than thirty countries.

This remarkable turn of events is best explained as a result of Saddam Hussein's miscalculations and his distorted view of his own power and role in the Arab world. Unfettered by any domestic opposition and still largely isolated from the international community, Saddam attempted to flex his muscles in the region. He challenged the continued U.S. military presence in the Gulf and in April 1990 threatened to burn half of Israel with chemical weapons if Israel attacked Iraq. He then turned his attention to Kuwait, with which Iraq had multiple disputes, including border problems, claims to oil fields that spanned both borders, and, far more important, a sharp disagreement about oil pricing. Iraq accused Kuwait of pumping more oil than allowed by its OPEC quota, thereby depressing oil prices, a factor that had left Iraq unable to meet its debt payments. Personal mismanagement of the crisis on both sides also played a role in fueling the conflict. Iraq demanded large sums of money from Kuwait and the GCC states for war reconstruction. When Kuwait refused to accede to Saddam's demands, Iraq, in a dramatic and unexpected move, invaded Kuwait. The invasion began on August 2, 1990, and about a week later Saddam announced that Kuwait would become the nineteenth province of Iraq.

The Iraqi invasion of Kuwait provoked a major international crisis. The United States, operating through the United Nations, organized a coalition to reverse the action. The Security Council imposed an oil embargo on Iraq and sanctions against exports except for food and medical supplies, and the coalition sent ground troops to Saudi Arabia. Iraq demanded negotiations, which were refused. On January 16, 1991, the coalition forces began an air bombardment of critical elements of Iraq's infrastructure in Baghdad, Basra, and other locations, and destruction of Iraq's military forces in Kuwait. When this did not succeed in obtaining a withdrawal from Kuwait, on February 23 coalition forces began a ground war that lasted 100 hours and resulted in the retreat of the Iraqi army from Kuwait in disarray.

The war and the devastating defeat very nearly unseated Saddam Hussein and his regime. On March 1, retreating soldiers started a popular rebellion in Basra. Within days, most of the Shi'a-inhabited territory from the outskirts of Baghdad to Basra was under the control of rebels. In the Kurdish area of the north, a similar rebellion took place, incited by the traditional Kurdish parties—the KDP and the PUK—but the rebellion did not succeed. Saddam Hussein, using military loyalists and playing on popular fears of chaos, brutally put the revolt down. In the south, some Shi'a fled across the border to Iran and into Saudi Arabia. In the north, the Kurdish flight was massive. Fearing renewed use of chemical weapons, half the Kurdish population fled to the borders of Turkey and Iran. The Turks declined to give asylum to these Kurds; instead, a U.N.-sponsored safe haven was established in northern Iraq, and under the protection of Western forces, the Kurds were returned to their homes. To assure their continued protection, coalition forces prohibited Iraqi aircraft from flying north of the thirty-sixth parallel. Saddam withdrew his forces from much of the Kurdish territory in the north, with the exception of Kirkuk, and the Kurds established a genuinely autonomous government, free of control from Baghdad for the first time in their history.

The rebellion scarcely touched Baghdad and the Sunni-dominated center of the country. In the year following the war, much of the infrastructure in Baghdad and its environs was repaired, although its maintenance proved difficult under sanctions. In the south, a low-level insurgency continued in the marshlands north of Basra and in some other areas. To protect the population of the south, the coalition also instituted a no-fly zone south of the thirty-second parallel, later extended to the thirty-third parallel, but Saddam's troops kept control on the ground. Saddam's reluctance to adhere to the cease-fire provisions instituted through U.N. resolutions, particularly those requiring elimination of his weapons of mass destruction, resulted in a continuation of sanctions and the oil embargo in the postwar period.

The second Gulf War was even more devastating for Iraq than the first. The loss of life from war and rebellion was substantial, though undocumented. The economy, despite Iraq's rich resources, declined drastically because of continued sanctions. Iraq's isolation was intense, and its sovereignty was curtailed by intrusive international inspection of its weapons industry until 1998; no-fly zones over its northern and southern provinces; and the development of a separate Kurdish entity in the north. Over a period of a decade, the continued sanctions prevented full rehabilitation of the economy and greatly impacted Iraq's economic well-being and social structure. While isolation and sanctions had eroded by 2001, the long-term damage to the population was severe.

Political Environment

Although Iraq is a state, it is not yet a nation. All Iraqi governments since 1920 have attempted to create a single political community from a diverse medley of peoples. The process of integration and assimilation has gone on steadily, but it is by no means complete. A competing Arab-nationalist identity, fostered by some of Iraq's leaders, has undercut the development of a distinct Iraqi national identity, as have residual ethnic, sectarian, and even tribal loyalties. These factors have made Iraq difficult to govern, despite its rich resource base and periods of economic development.

People

The population of Iraq is 23 million, and the country has an annual growth rate of 2.8 percent. The capital, Baghdad, is the largest city, with 5 million, over one-quarter of the country's population. Other urban concentrations include Mosul, Iraq's second largest city; Basra, its port; Kirkuk, an oil center in the north; Irbil, a Kurdish city now under Kurdish control; and Najaf, a Shi'a religious center in the south.

The most serious demographic division is ethnic. The overwhelming majority of the population is Arab, about 75 to 80 percent; Kurds are the most important minority, estimated at 15 to 20 percent. The Arabs dominate the western steppe and the Tigris and Euphrates Valley, from Basra to the Mosul plain; the Kurds have their stronghold in the mountainous terrain of the north and east. Many Kurds have migrated to the foothills and plains, and about one-quarter of them live in Baghdad. Iraqi Kurds are a portion of the larger Kurdish population inhabiting adjoining regions in Turkey, Iran, and Syria.

A second major fault line in Iraq's population is sectarian; Iraqis are divided between the two major divisions in Islam—the Sunni and the Shi'a. Since the overwhelming majority of Kurds are Sunni, this division affects mainly the Arabs, creating three distinct communities: Arab Sunnis, Arab Shi'a, and Kurds. Arab Shi'a constitute the majority of the population, between 55 and 60 percent. They inhabit the area from Baghdad south to the Shatt al-Arab, the most densely populated section of the country. Baghdad now has a Shi'a majority, and Shi'a also live in towns and villages along the Tigris and Diyala Rivers north and east of Baghdad.

Since early Islamic times, Shi'ism has had a strong foothold in southern Iraq. The tombs of their martyrs, Ali and Husayn, are in Najaf and Karbala, the sites of

Shi'a pilgrimages. Since the 1930s a substantial urban Shi'a professional class has emerged. However, despite their numbers and their progress since mandate days, Shi'a have been outnumbered in the high posts of state, a factor that has increased their resentment of the power structure in Baghdad. In the Shi'a south, where much of the population is rural and agricultural, lower standards of living and of literacy prevail. This, too, has fed Shi'a alienation from the government and, since the 1970s, spawned an organized Shi'a opposition to the Ba'th. This opposition is now led mainly by religious leaders headquartered in Iran, where a large number of Iraqi Shi'a exiles and refugees reside, possibly as many as 500,000. However, most Shi'a are loyal to the Iraqi state. They have never desired self-determination but seek representation in government commensurate with their numbers.

The Sunni Arabs are found in all strata of Iraqi society, but they dominate the military and political life of the country. Arab Sunnis have controlled all Iraqi governments, and they constitute a majority in the officer corps and the upper echelons of the Ba'th Party. As an elite they have benefited disproportionately from modernization and education, and in occupation and lifestyles, they tend to be more secular than Arab Shi'a.

The Kurds have been the most difficult group to assimilate. In the twentieth century, a sense of Kurdish identity based on language, close tribal ties, and a shared history has inspired demands for self-determination. Many Kurds are still engaged in agriculture, but a growing number form an urban, educated middle class. Traditionally, Kurdish tribal ties have been strong; many lived under the control of aghas (tribal chiefs and landholders), but modernization and land reforms have eroded their position. Much of the economy and society of the Kurdish north was drastically disrupted by the razing of over 4,000 villages by the Ba'th; the death and disappearance of many thousands of Kurds during a concerted campaign against them after the Iran-Iraq war; and the displacement of large numbers of Kurds as a result of the 1991 rebellion. By 2001 considerable progress had been made in resettling these Kurds in their native villages and in reviving agriculture. However, tens of thousands still remained in refugee settlements in and around urban areas. As a second generation grows up in these locations, they will probably become a permanent part of the urban population.

Iraq has a number of smaller minority groups, many with bonds to similar peoples across Iraqi borders. In northern cities and towns along the old trade routes from Turkey to Baghdad are Turkish speakers, known as Turkomen. Making up 2 to 3 percent of the population, they are mainly Sunni, middle class, and urban. Turkomen have strong ties with Turkey. Until the onset of the Iran-Iraq war, Iraq had a substantial group of Persian speakers, 1 to 2 percent of the population, inhabiting parts of Baghdad and some southern cities, especially Karbala. This group, because of its presumed ties to Iran, was largely expelled from Iraq during the Iran-Iraq war. In the south, inhabiting the marshes between the Tigris and Euphrates Rivers, are several hundred thousand Arab Shi'a known as marsh Arabs, who adapt to their environment by dwelling in reed huts, raising water buffalo, and fishing. Their way of life may be disappearing. In the aftermath of the 1991 rebellion, their environment was dramatically changed by the Ba'th regime, which has drained much of their marsh territory in an effort to eliminate a refuge for dissidents.

Finally, about 5 percent of the population is non-Muslim. Iraq has a variety of indigenous Christian sects, including Chaldeans (Nestorian Christians who re-united with Rome), Assyrians (Nestorians who remained independent), Armeni-ans, Jacobites, and Greek Orthodox communities. Yazidis, a Kurdish-speaking group with an eclectic religion drawn in part from Zoroastrianism, live in areas around Mosul, and Sabeans, a pre-Christian group, live in the south. Under the British mandate, Iraq had a large and flourishing Jewish community, but in the early 1950s most Jews migrated to Israel. Today they probably number only a few hundred.

Social Structure

Traditionally, Iraqi society was characterized by a pronounced dichotomy between rural society, for the most part organized by tribe, and urban life. Since 1950, the rural-urban gap has been greatly narrowed by massive rural-to-urban migration; by the spread of education and health services to rural areas; and by the emer-gence of a sizable middle class, possibly 15 to 20 percent of the population. At the end of the monarchy, about 70 percent of the population lived in rural communi-ties; in 2000, 70 percent lived in cities, although many of these people were recent migrants who had not been thoroughly urbanized, a factor that has sharpened class distinctions.

Rural agricultural areas remain much poorer than most cities, but conditions have improved since mandate times, when a few landlords and tribal leaders con-trolled large portions of the farmland and the peasants were virtual serfs. Succes-sive land-reform measures have eliminated most of this landlord class and gradu-ally extended landownership to a class of small and middle-level farmers. But under revolutionary regimes, agriculture has been neglected, leaving rural sectors poorer than urban areas.

The growth of education has had a significant impact on Iraq's social structure. Until the Iran-Iraq war, elementary schools were available to virtually all Iraqi children. High schools graduated students in the hundreds of thousands; colleges and universities in the tens of thousands. Over time, Iraq has produced one of the Arab world's largest professional classes, including a scientific and technocratic elite. Along with a middle class has come an urban working class, particularly in the oil and industrial sectors located in Baghdad and Basra. Under the Ba'th, much of Iraq's urban middle and lower classes work for the government as indus-trial employees, teachers, bureaucrats, or army officers. The impact of wars and sanctions, however, has impoverished and reduced Iraq's middle class as hundreds of thousands have emigrated.

Changing social structure has also improved the status of women, a trend encouraged by government legislation. In 1978 a law was passed restricting polygamy, granting women more freedom in the choice of a marriage partner, and in general giving women more control over their lives. By the mid-1980s, 50 percent of the students in elementary schools, 35 percent in high school, and 30 percent in universities were women.

Although religion still plays a very important role in traditional rural society and among recent urban migrants, secularism is strong in Iraq's middle class. In Iraq's larger cities, social and economic mobility have eroded traditional lifestyles and the role of traditional religious leaders. The Ba'th regime has strongly discouraged religious politics, but in the 1990s, under the impact of adverse conditions, there was a modest revival of religion among both Sunnis and Shi'a.

Despite the growth of modern institutions and the ubiquitous presence of the Ba'th government, however, family, clan, and tribal ties remain strong. In the 1980s and 1990s, as bureaucratic structures eroded under the impact of war and sanctions, there was renewed reliance on tribal and family ties in governance. Saddam Hussein governs by placing his kin in key political and security posts. In the countryside, he has called on tribal leaders to keep law and order and to maintain loyalty to the regime. Sons of former tribal leaders now hold important positions in the military and retain tribal loyalties. Kurdish leaders also rely on tribal followers for support. Beneath the facade of modern political parties and bureaucratic and military structures, the system functions through use of traditional patronage and kinship links.

Economic Conditions

Iraq is one of the few Middle Eastern countries with the potential for a balanced economy, but its political system has been so mismanaged that it has rarely achieved its potential. Since the 1950s, the Iraqi economy has been characterized by two dominant features: the preeminence of oil and increased government economic control.

Under the Ba'th, with its socialist philosophy, the economy has been dominated by the state, although that domination lessened after the onset of the Iran-Iraq war. According to government statistics, the share of the public sector in domestic production rose from 31 percent in 1968 to 80 percent a decade later. Government planning originated during the monarchy when long-range development plans were created to utilize oil revenues. Under revolutionary regimes after 1958, development plans followed Soviet philosophy, with emphasis on heavy industry, collective farming, and state management of the economy. This changed under the impetus of the Iran-Iraq war, when more efficiency was required. Iraq abolished collective farms, loosened government control, and encouraged the private sector in agriculture, services, commerce, and light industry. The conversion to a market economy was only partial, however. The government has refused to allow foreign private investment, preferring to hire foreign firms to undertake turnkey projects, which are turned over to the Iraqi government on completion.

Since mandate days, oil has played an increasingly dominant role in the economy, but the development of oil resources got off to a slow start in Iraq. Although the Iraq Petroleum Company began commercial export of oil from the Kirkuk field in 1934, it was not until the 1950s that Iraq earned substantial oil revenues. In the mid-1950s the rich Rumailah field was discovered in the south, near the Kuwaiti border, but it was not fully developed until the 1970s. In the early 1960s, Qasim's acrimonious dispute with the IPC and his expropriation of 99.5 percent of the IPC concession initiated a long, protracted struggle with the oil companies that resulted in neglect of Iraqi production in favor of its competitors in the Arab Gulf states. Finally, in 1972, the Ba'th regime nationalized oil resources, putting all oil revenue in government hands. The following year saw a fourfold increase in oil prices, which continued to climb for most of the decade. By 1980, Iraq was exporting 3.2 million barrels a day and earning revenues of $26 billion. Oil revenues at that time constituted over 60 percent of the gross domestic product (GDP). Iraq used much of this revenue to expand its oil facilities, building a new "strategic" pipeline from Kirkuk to the Persian Gulf and additional lines through Turkey to the Mediterranean and through Saudi Arabia to the Red Sea, along with two off-shore oil terminals in the Persian Gulf, numerous refineries, and a sophisticated petrochemical industry. Many of these oil facilities, damaged or shut down as a result of the two Gulf wars, were only slowly being repaired by 2001. By 2000, the U.N. oil embargo had reduced Iraq's exports to three-quarters of pre-1990 levels.

Iraq's oil potential is excellent. If facilities are repaired and expanded, Iraqi production could reach 6 million barrels per day (mbd). Iraq has at least 112 billion barrels of proven reserves, second only to Saudi Arabia, and possibly as much or more in unexplored areas of the Western desert. Realization of this potential, however, will require outside investment and a political climate greatly improved over the one that has prevailed in the aftermath of the 1991 Gulf War.

Non-oil industry has not played a major role in Iraq's economy. Under the monarchy, indigenous industries consisted almost wholly of food processing, textiles, and cement production. In the 1960s and 1970s, some progress was made in light and intermediate industry. After the oil price rise in the 1970s, there was rapid economic and social modernization, including expansion in heavy industry—petrochemicals, iron, steel and aluminum plants—as well as intermediate industries like metal working, machine tools, and car and truck assembly. Roads, communications, and other infrastructure increased, as did construction of homes, schools, and health facilities. Iraq's average growth rate between 1973 and 1981 was 10 percent. The spread of education and industry gave rise to a small but growing cadre of engineers and scientists. An expanding urban middle class achieved a comfortable standard of living, but most of this class was employed in government and services. In the late 1980s, the industrial sector produced only 10 percent of GDP and employed about 8 percent of the labor force. One area in which the Ba'th invested heavily was military industry, especially chemical weapons, missiles, and nuclear weapons.

Under the monarchy, agriculture had received the lion's share of the regime's attention. Development programs expanded dams and barrages and private entrepreneurs introduced pumps to expand production. The land under cultivation, in both the irrigated areas of the south and the rain-fed territory in the north, increased. In the 1950s, Iraq was able not only to feed itself but also to export wheat and barley. Unfortunately, most of the surplus profits went to wealthy landlords rather than to cultivators.

Despite attempts under revolutionary regimes to improve the land-tenure situation, agriculture has suffered since 1958. Early land-reform efforts took much of the land away from large landholders but failed to redistribute it in a timely fashion. Farming in the riverain tracts of the south requires intensive investment in drainage, small-scale irrigation systems, and agricultural extension programs to help the farmers. These have never been forthcoming. The Kurdish area, one of the most fertile in Iraq, has been thoroughly disrupted by war and the destruction of villages.

These difficulties have been responsible for a rather poor agricultural showing. The agricultural share of GDP dropped from 17 percent in 1960 to 8 percent in the 1980s. Meanwhile, food imports increased until they constituted nearly one-quarter of all imports. In the 1980s, agriculture employed only about 30 percent of the population.

Iraq also faces another difficulty in the agrarian sector. All its water sources lie outside Iraq's boundaries. The Tigris and Euphrates Rivers rise in Turkey, and Tigris tributaries flow from Iran. The Euphrates passes through both Turkey and Syria before reaching Iraq. Poor political relations with Syria in the mid-1970s resulted in that country's cutting Iraq's water flow, an act that dried up Iraqi irrigation and caused severe crop damage. Even more significant is a major dam project initiated by Turkey on the headwaters of the Tigris and Euphrates that will affect the flow downstream in both rivers in the future.

Iraq's economy and society have sharply deteriorated since the Gulf War of 1991 and the imposition of the oil embargo and sanctions on the country. Although war damage was partially repaired within two years, the sanctions have taken a major toll on Iraq's economic development and its once-prosperous middle class. Massive inflation, which reduced the Iraqi dinar to worthless currency, had depleted savings and reserves, of both government and population, leaving GDP at a third of what it was in 1989 and drastically reducing per capita income and living standards. The salaried population—most of the middle and lower-middle class—

must work several jobs to make ends meet. A decline in industrial and agricultural production, due to lack of inputs and investment, has resulted in high unemployment. Erosion of the infrastructure in health, education, electricity, and water supplies has led to a serious decline in health standards. The rise in infant mortality is estimated to be twofold; in mortality under the age of five as high as fivefold. Meanwhile a class of urban rich and well-to-do, dependent on government connections, has grown up. By 2001, sanctions had eased, providing more food and imported goods for those who could afford them, but the effects of sanctions after a decade were devastating. The consequences of Saddam Hussein's miscalculations on Iraq's economy will take years to repair.

Political Structure

Iraq is a republic dominated by the Arab Ba'th Socialist Party. Behind the party structure, however, power has been concentrated in the hands of the president, Saddam Hussein, who governs through the Revolutionary Command Council, with the aid of a network of intelligence and secret police services.

Technically, the Ba'th is a pan-Arab party, with supreme authority resting in a Ba'th National Command, a group headquartered in Baghdad and consisting of representatives from various Arab countries. In theory, the national command has authority over Ba'th Parties throughout the Arab world, but in practice it is not recognized outside Iraq. Although the Iraqi Ba'th Party is a branch of the same party that rules Syria, there has been little or no cooperation between the two parties because the two regimes have been on uneasy terms, mainly due to party disagreements.

Within Iraq, the party's Regional Command, headed by President Saddam Hussein, is the pinnacle of party power. This body formulates the ideology and policy of the party, which is then supposed to be translated into action by the government. The party maintains an identity and structure separate from the government, but personnel are intertwined at all levels, making it difficult to distinguish between the two in practice. Below the Regional Command level are province-based unit commands that are further subdivided into branches (*fars*); sections (*shubahs*); divisions (*firqahs*); and circles, or cells (*halaqahs*). Party units also exist in the military and the bureaucracy. Party members are carefully vetted and are promoted (or demoted) through party ranks based on service and loyalty to party goals. Since 1979, the role of the party has been greatly reduced, with infrequent party meetings and elections.

In 1973 a Progressive National Front was created to include other parties, notably the Communist Party of Iraq, the Kurdish Democratic Party, and some smaller groups. But these parties were given no real participation in the political system and the front did not survive the onset of the Iran-Iraq war. Non-Ba'thist representatives serve in the assembly and the cabinet.

Since the 1958 revolution, Iraq has been ruled under several constitutions. The most recent, an interim constitution promulgated in July 1970, has been modified several times, but is still in effect. Since 1980, an elected national assembly with 250 members has been in existence, but its powers are fairly limited. The most recent election was held in 2000. In 1990 modifications to the constitution permitted independent political parties to operate as long as they forswore separatism and confessionalism and remained loyal to the principles of the 1968 Ba'th revolution.

Executive powers are vested in the RCC and the presidency. The RCC issues laws and decrees, oversees all foreign and domestic policies, and chooses (by two-thirds vote) the president and vice president of the republic.

According to the constitution, the president is the chief executive and commander in chief of the armed forces. He is empowered to nominate the vice president and chooses his own council of ministers; he is also responsible for naming and dismissing judges. Under his direction, the government prepares the annual budget for presentation to the RCC and the National Assembly. The ministers under the direction of the president function only as executors. In 1995, Saddam Hussein was reelected president in a national vote.

The 1970 constitution also provides for a judiciary. Above the courts of first instance are five courts of appeal and, at the top, a court of cassation. The judiciary also includes religious courts and revolutionary courts. The latter are convened at the behest of the president or the RCC to hear political cases or cases involving state security and they often deliver summary verdicts, including execution. The legal system of Iraq is based primarily on the French code.

At the local level, Iraq has eighteen provinces administered by governors appointed by the president and responsible to the minister of interior. Because Iraq is a highly centralized system with all powers reserved at the national level, the governors' powers are very limited.

Prior to the Persian Gulf War of 1991, the three Kurdish provinces in the north—Dohuk, Sulaimaniyyah, and Irbil—formed a regional authority with a measure of self-government over local affairs. Following that war, and the upheaval of the Kurdish rebellion, the Iraqi government withdrew its forces and its administration from these three provinces. Under the protection of U.N. forces, the Kurds then established a Kurdish Regional Government independent of Baghdad. Elections held in 1992 provided representatives to a regional assembly and a cabinet, chosen mainly from the two Kurdish parties, the KDP and the PUK. However, the two parties could not maintain unity. In a power struggle, military clashes ensued in 1994 and 1995. Since then fighting has ceased but there are two de facto Kurdish administrations dividing the north, one with its capital in Irbil under the control of the KDP; the other with its capital in Sulaimaniyyah under the PUK.

Political Dynamics

The formal dominance of the RCC and the Ba'th Party in Iraq masks the true locus of power. In fact, the system is overwhelmingly dominated by President Saddam Hussein, who exercises control through a circle composed of his immediate family and through a network of collaborators, most of whom originate from his clan and from his hometown of Tikrit. This small coterie controls the RCC and has a monopoly on the key offices in the Ba'th Party, the intelligence apparatus, and the armed forces. By skillful manipulation of these groups, Saddam Hussein has maintained himself and his regime in power for over three decades despite a narrow power base.

This domination is reinforced by systematic use of domestic terror; under Saddam Hussein, Iraq has become a classic example of the *mukhabarat* (secret police) state. Several intelligence units embedded within the party, the Ministry of the Interior, and the military watch one another as well as the population, reporting on the slightest sign of antiregime activity. Punishments are swift and severe. Iraq has a well-documented record of human rights abuses, including the use of torture, extrajudicial executions, mass deportations, and the use of chemical weapons against its own citizens. The military itself has been compartmentalized, with several elite units maintaining regime security.

In addition to providing ideological direction, the Ba'th Party acts as the "eyes and ears" of the regime throughout Iraq. The party professes to be socialist and pan-Arab, but its ideology is not clearly defined and in the course of time has undergone modifications. It includes an amalgam of anti-imperialist sentiment, bordering on xenophobia; nostalgia for the glory of past Arab empires; and a commitment to modernization and to redistribution of wealth to benefit the poorer classes. Under Saddam's leadership, integral unity of the Arab world has been supplanted by a doctrine that stresses the independence of the Iraqi state and its leadership of the Arab world. The party acknowledges the important role of Islam in Arab society—an emphasis that increased in the 1990s—but stresses the secular nature of the state, a key point in Iraq's conflict with Iran. The ideology of the party is far less important, however, than the role the party plays in organizing and controlling society and providing a channel of upward mobility to less-privileged classes.

The size of the party is not known. Full party members, those who have reached the top of the hierarchy, probably number about 25,000. Since party membership is almost a necessity for career advancement, nominal membership is large, but the ideological commitment of this membership is probably weak. Since the Gulf War, the role of the party in the political process has declined. Policy is made in the presidential palace, mainly by Saddam Hussein. Family and clan ties have become increasingly important, with Hussein relying on his sons and relations from his Albu Nasir tribe. His youngest son, Qusayy, is in charge of the security apparatus; his oldest son, Udayy, is a member of the National Assembly and in charge of portions of the media and youth affairs. Key clan relations have been put in charge of important security and military functions. In areas where party control has loosened, the regime relies on tribal leadership to keep law and order.

A decade of war and the 1991 rebellion have greatly eroded support for the regime. Its position is strongest in the center of the country, where Arab Sunni elements that might lose their dominance in any change of regime are located. Even there, however, the regime's support has eroded under the weight of the Gulf War defeat and continued sanctions. And of course the Kurdish regions in the north, now under U.N. mandate, remain antagonistic toward Baghdad.

While dissent is not tolerated inside Iraq, a vigorous opposition has emerged outside. One group, with roots in the Shi'a community, the Supreme Council for the Islamic Revolution in Iraq (SCIRI) has its headquarters in Iran. Another, the Iraq National Congress, consisting of the major Kurdish parties as well as groups ranging from liberals to ex-Ba'thists and including Arab Sunnis and Shi'a, has called for the regime's overthrow and the establishment of a democratic government in Baghdad. It functions mainly in Europe and the United States. By 2001, none of these groups had made much headway in displacing the regime in Baghdad. Nonetheless, continued isolation, sanctions, and erosion of support inside Iraq have made the regime's future uncertain.

Foreign Policy

Under the monarchy, Iraq played an important role in regional and international affairs. It was a founding member of the Arab League in 1945, and in 1955 it joined the Baghdad Pact, a security arrangement linking Iraq with Great Britain, Turkey, Iran, and Pakistan. Until 1958, Iraq's foreign and security policy and its economy were tied to the West; diplomatic relations with the Soviet Union were shunned.

This foreign orientation changed with the revolution of 1958. Under republican regimes, Iraq gradually became more isolated and anti-Western. As nationalist ideologies, whether Iraqi or pan-Arab, took hold, Iraqis became unwilling to entertain foreign influence in their country. This was particularly true of the Ba'th regime. This trend meant that Iraqi leaders had progressively less experience of the outside world, and fewer Westerners had intimate dealings with Iraq, leading to intelligence failures and miscalculations on both sides. These failures account in large part for Iraq's stumbling into two unwinnable wars within a decade.

After 1958, Iraq turned toward the Soviet Union for most—though not all—of its arms supplies and technical assistance. After Iraq nationalized its oil, the USSR provided Iraq with help in developing its southern oil fields, and in 1972 Iraq signed a Friendship Treaty with the USSR. However, Iraq never allowed the

Soviet Union to establish bases on its soil, and when oil prices rose in the mid-1970s, Iraq shifted its purchases to higher-quality Western technology. During the Iran-Iraq war, Iraq sought some of its weapons in the West as well.

Despite its pan-Arab ideology, the post-1968 Ba'th regime had uneasy relations with its Arab neighbors, who feared its attempts to dominate the region and to unseat rival regimes. Since its advent to power, Ba'thist Iraq has been involved in a serious feud with Ba'thist Syria, which reached a peak when Syria supported Iran in the Iran-Iraq war and joined the coalition that fought Iraq in the Gulf. Iraq's relations with the GCC states have varied from hostile to uneasy. Iraq's 1990 invasion of Kuwait and the 1991 Gulf War left a legacy of fear and distrust of Iraq in most Gulf states, especially Kuwait. Some of this feeling had gradually dissipated after a decade of sanctions and popular sympathy for the plight of the Iraqi people, but wariness toward the regime remained. Iraq's relations with Jordan have been much better, however. Jordan's port of Aqaba served as Iraq's outlet to the sea when the Shatt al-Arab was closed by the Iran-Iraq war; and since the imposition of sanctions on Iraq in 1990, Jordan has become one of Iraq's main commercial lifelines to the outside world.

Iraq has been one of the most strident enemies of Israel in its rhetoric, but Iraqi forces made little more than perfunctory contributions to Arab military action against Israel in the wars of 1948–1949, 1967, and 1973. In 1978, Iraq hosted an Arab summit conference to impose sanctions against Egypt for its conclusion of a peace treaty with Israel at Camp David. However, during the Iran-Iraq war, when Iraq needed Western and regional support, it reversed its stand on Egypt and modified its position on Israel, claiming that any Arab-Israeli solution acceptable to the Palestinians would be acceptable to Baghdad. By 2001, Baghdad was taking a more militant view toward Israel and financially supporting the Palestinian uprising of that year.

Iraq's international fortunes began their dramatic descent with the country's initiation of the Iran-Iraq war. The invasion of Iran and the eight-year war that drained Iraq's resources shifted Iraq's foreign policy, of necessity, in a more pragmatic and pro-Western direction. In 1984 Iraq renewed diplomatic relations with the United States, cut since the 1967 Arab-Israeli war, and warmed up to Egypt, previously ostracized. At the same time, the war made Iraq dependent on its Arab Gulf neighbors for financial and moral support.

The trend toward pragmatism did not survive the end of the Iran-Iraq war. Misreading the international climate of détente in the aftermath of the cold war, Saddam Hussein saw a political vacuum developing in the Arab world and sought to fill it. He renewed hostile statements against the United States and Israel, and this rhetoric, together with his poor human rights record and his suspected nuclear program, cooled U.S. and Western relations with Iraq. His miscalculation in invading Kuwait on August 2, 1990, Iraq's defeat in the Gulf War, and the continued sanctions enforced by the West after the war left the Iraqi regime too weak to play a significant regional or international role. But sanctions and no-fly zones over the north and south of the country, although still in effect in 2001, failed to dislodge the regime. While sanctions and Iraq's regional and international isolation eroded in the late 1990s, the Ba'th regime under Saddam Hussein retained its strong sense of nationalism and its strident anti-Western rhetoric. Indeed, this militancy increased as Iraq attempted to free itself of international (mainly U.S. and United Kingdom) constraints. Despite its oil resources—possibly because of them—Iraq remained a destabilizing force in the region as the new millennium began.

Bibliography

The three books written over a period of years by Majid Khadduri are among the better studies of modern Iraq in English: *Independent Iraq: A Study in Iraqi Politics from 1932 to 1958* (New York: Oxford University Press, 1961); *Republican Iraq: A Study in Iraqi Politics Since the Revolution of 1958* (New York: Oxford University Press, 1969); and *Socialist Iraq: A Study in Iraqi Politics Since 1968* (Washington, D.C.: Middle East Institute, 1978). Khadduri's approach is historical, and the chief value of his work lies in the firsthand interviews he conducted with leading Iraqi politicians. The most comprehensive study of Iraq's modern history in one volume is Phebe Marr, *The Modern History of Iraq* (Boulder: Westview Press, 1985), which analyzes Iraq's political, social, and economic structure under various regimes. A good history of Ziraq, mainly from the perspective of those "out of power," is found in Charles Tripp, *A History of Iraq* (Cambridge: Cambridge University Press, 2000). A sharply critical study of Iraq under the Ba'th is found in Marion Farouk-Sluglett and Peter Sluglett, *Iraq Since 1958: From Revolution to Dictatorship* (London: KPI, 1987); Christine Moss Helms, *Iraq: Eastern Flank of the Arab World* (Washington, D.C.: Brookings Institution, 1984), takes an insider's view of the Ba'th Party and its political dynamics; and Amatzia Baram, *Culture, History and Ideology in the Formation of Ba'thist Iraq, 1968–1989* (Oxford: Macmillan, 1991), deals with Ba'thist ideology. Baram has also written the most authoritative study of Iraq's political elite: "The Ruling Political Elite in Ba'thi Iraq, 1968–1986," *International Journal of Middle East Studies* 21:4 (1989). A brilliant but polemical depiction of Iraqi society under the Ba'th is to be found in Samir al-Khalil (pseudonym for Kanan Makiya), *Republic of Fear* (Berkeley: University of California Press, 1989). There are two good biographies of Saddam Hussein: Said K. Aburish, *Saddam Hussein, the Politics of Revenge* (New York: Bloomsbury, 2000), and Efraim Karsh and Inari Rautsi, *Saddam Hussein, a Political Biography* (New York: Free Press, 1991).

On Iraq's pre-Ba'th economy, the most analytical study is Edith Penrose and E. F. Penrose, *Iraq: International Relations and National Development* (London: Ernest Benn, and Boulder: Westview Press, 1978). On Iraq's social and political structure there is no work comparable to Hanna Batatu's monumental study, *The Old Social Classes and the Revolutionary Movements of Iraq* (Princeton: Princeton University Press, 1978), probably the single best book on Iraq, but one that only introduces the Ba'th regime. On the Kurds, two good studies are to be found in Edmond Ghareeb, *The Kurdish Question in Iraq* (Syracuse, N.Y.: Syracuse University Press, 1981), and David McDowall, *The Modern History of the Kurds* (London: I.B. Tauris, 1997), both of which take a historical approach. The Shi'a are dealt with in a thoroughly scholarly work by Yitzhak Nakash, *The Shi'is of Iraq* (Princeton: Princeton

University Press, 1994), and in a work that deals with modern Shiʻa movements: Joyce Wiley, *The Islamic Movement of Iraqi Shiʻa* (Boulder: Lynne Rienner, 1992).

The two Gulf Wars have spawned a huge number of books on Iraq, many of uneven quality. On the Iran-Iraq war the best are Shahram Chubin and Charles Tripp, *Iran and Iraq at War* (Boulder: Westview Press, 1988), which relates the war to domestic society in both countries; Jasim Abdulghani's *Iran and Iraq* (Baltimore: Johns Hopkins University Press, 1984), which examines the origins of the conflict; and Dilip Hiro, *The Longest War: The Iran-Iraq Military Conflict* (New York: Routledge, 1991), a very good narrative of the conflict. Among the best of the many studies on the second Gulf War are Elaine Sciolino, *The Outlaw State, Saddam Hussein's Quest for Power and the Gulf Crisis* (New York: John Wiley, 1991), which gives a Western point of view, and Ibrahim Ibrahim, ed., *The Gulf Crisis, Background and Consequences* (Washington, D.C.: Georgetown University Center for Contemporary Arab Studies, 1992), which presents a more Middle Eastern perspective. David Long presents a brief discussion of Iraq's domestic and foreign policies in *The Persian Gulf: An Introduction to Its People, Politics, and Economics,* rev. ed. (Boulder: Westview Press, 1978).

Several good books have appeared on Iraq since the Gulf War. Sarah Graham Brown, *Sanctioning Saddam: the Politics of Intervention in Iraq* (London: I.B. Tauris, 1999), examines the impact of sanctions. Anthony Cordesman and Ahmed Hashim, *Iraq, Sanctions and Beyond* (Boulder: Westview Press, 1997), look at the security situation. Amatzia Baram, *Building toward Crisis: Saddam Husain's Strategy for Survival* (Washington, D.C.: Washington Institute for Near East Policy, 1998), looks at the relations of family, clan, and power in Iraq.

6

Eastern Arabian States: Kuwait, Bahrain, Qatar, United Arab Emirates, and Oman

Malcolm C. Peck

Before the discovery of oil, residents of the eastern Arabian states eked out a subsistence-level existence from pearling, fishing, sea-borne commerce, limited agriculture, and, among the nomads, animal husbandry. A dramatic transformation from austerity to oil-generated affluence has characterized each of them, with variations in speed and extent from one to the next. All display new international airports, luxury hotels, and the other obvious symbols of rapid economic growth. Beneath the glitter, however, each state is caught in an ongoing struggle with the daunting tasks of economic, social, and political development. This struggle has been made all the more difficult by dramatic regional changes in political, economic, and military conditions. The fall of the shah of Iran in 1979 led to a hostile clerical regime there. In 1980 war broke out between Iraq and Iran and continued for eight years, casting a threatening shadow over the small states of the Gulf. At the same time the oil glut of the 1980s significantly lowered the income of the Gulf states, confronting them with the challenge of budget deficits. The Iraqi invasion of Kuwait on August 2, 1990, and its aftermath will continue for some time to affect basic domestic and external realities for these states. Finally, the terrorist attacks of September 11, 2001, on the United States and the events that followed exposed them to new uncertainties and dangers, although it appeared that they would weather this storm as well.

Historical Background

Dramatic archaeological discoveries over the past four decades have revealed much about eastern Arabia's past. An early Gulf trading culture, dating back to the fourth millennium B.C., was linked with the ancient civilizations of Mesopotamia to the north and the Indus Valley to the southeast. Centered on the Bahrain archipelago, it came to be known as the Dilmun culture after the name of its principal urban settlement, the remains of which were discovered in 1953 just outside modern Manama. The Dilmun civilization extended from Kuwait to Qatar, with a related culture dominating what are now the United Arab Emirates and Oman. The fabled kingdom of Magan (or Makan), a somewhat later culture whose wealth derived from its control of copper sources, has been definitively placed in Oman.

After about 3000 B.C. increasing climatic desiccation greatly reduced the population in the interior of eastern Arabia, except in the oases, where date cultivation, beginning around 4000 B.C., provided a vital food source. Dates, which were highly nutritious and easily transported, were of central importance in nomad life. The indispensable factor for bedouin existence in the desert interior was the domestication of the camel, generally thought to have occurred in Oman around 1500 B.C.

Some of the population migrated outside the Arabian Peninsula, with profound consequences for the history of the Middle East and the world. Those migrants helped bring the ancient Mesopotamian and Egyptian cultures to full flower; a later migration helped to form the Canaanite and Phoenician cultures. Indeed, the Phoenicians may have inherited their maritime skills from their Gulf ancestors. Most of the people of Eastern Arabia turned to the sea for their livelihood. Fishing, pearling, and maritime trade reached their apogee in the early Islamic era—eighth and ninth centuries A.D.—when Arab seafarers (in ships very much like the dhows that still ply Gulf waters) created a maritime network that reached East Africa, India, and even the coast of China. Arab maritime trade was not superseded until the maritime ascendancy of Spain and Portugal in the fifteenth and sixteenth centuries.

In 1497 the Portuguese explorer Vasco da Gama sailed into the Persian Gulf, followed a few years later by a brilliant Portuguese general, Alfonso de Albuquerque, who seized the island of Hormuz and subsequently took and reinforced other strategic sites along the Gulf littoral and along the Gulf of Oman. This ensured Portuguese domination of the area's trade for the next century.

In the early seventeenth century the Portuguese yielded maritime primacy to the Dutch and English, whose commercial ambitions were reflected in the establishment of the English and Dutch East India companies, in 1600 and 1602 respectively. In 1622 the Persians and the English East India Company combined their forces to compel the Portuguese stronghold on Hormuz to capitulate.

The Dutch initially gained the upper hand over the British, but by 1765, the British had become the dominant external power in the region and they remained so up to the modern era. The British interest in the Gulf was initially commercial. Later, as India grew in importance, strategic concerns for maintaining imperial communications between London and India loomed large.

To protect their commercial interests, the British, like the Portuguese and the Dutch, adopted a policy of indirect rule, with a minimum of interference in local affairs. At the end of the eighteenth century, however, three factors interfered with British trade in the area—local privateering, civil war, and French designs in the Middle East under Napoleon. These impediments to British interests motivated the British government to enter into a number of special treaties with the littoral states. The first such treaty was concluded with Oman and coincided with the French invasion of Egypt in 1798. The pact was designed to deny the Gulf to the French and to improve the system for protecting Britain's lines of communication with its increasingly important Indian possessions. As the Napoleonic challenge in the Middle East rapidly evaporated, another challenge presented itself in the form of Arab privateers. Sailing especially from the shaykhdoms of Sharjah and Ras al-Khaymah, Gulf mariners would strike at commercial shipping, including that of Britain and other European states. Several Anglo-Indian expeditions were unable to halt such attacks until 1819 when, after heavy fighting, they decisively defeated the Arab fleet based in Ras al-Khaymah. A treaty signed the following year with the local shaykhs became the cornerstone of Britain's political, strategic, military, diplomatic, commercial, and administrative presence in the Gulf area for the next 150 years.

Although Arab harassment of British shipping in the Gulf and Indian Ocean ceased thereafter, a major problem remained in that the shaykhdoms continued to engage in war with one another, an issue not addressed in the treaty of 1820. Hence, in 1835, the British prevailed upon all the ruling shaykhs to sign a second agreement. This treaty prohibited the tribes under the rulers' jurisdiction from raiding each other during the fishing and pearling seasons, which in time came to be called the "trucial period." In 1838 the treaty was made to apply throughout the year, and in 1853 the trucial regime was made permanent in the Treaty of Maritime Peace in Perpetuity. These treaties formed the basis for the British imperium. Subsequently, treaties of 1861 and 1880 committed the British to protect the Al Khalifah rulers of Bahrain, and by the early twentieth century a British political agent resided in that shaykhdom. In 1892 Britain concluded "exclusive agreements" with the Trucial States, assuming responsibility for their foreign affairs and their defense. In 1899 a similar relationship, though not then made public, was established with Kuwait and in 1916 with Qatar. In addition to its direct control of these states' external relations, Britain assumed indirect control over their domestic affairs. Oman remained outside this treaty system, but the British retained a close relationship with that state, or, more precisely, with the state of Muscat, which was under the Al Bu Said sultans. In the nineteenth century Muscat lost effective control over the interior of Oman. Most rulers acceded to official British "advice." Those who refused or resisted risked almost certain exile, ouster, or British naval bombardment of their principalities. In this manner Britain introduced an unprecedented degree of stability to the region.

After World War II, especially following the granting of independence to India and Pakistan in 1947, British interest in the Gulf area changed significantly. Although the strategic need to protect India had ceased, the importance of oil interests in Iran, Iraq, Kuwait, and other states had grown enormously. In the minds of British policymakers, the British stake in the Gulf region's petroleum resources was sufficient to warrant the continued stationing of military forces in Oman, Sharjah, and Bahrain. In time, however, the costs to British taxpayers of maintaining a military presence in the Gulf area became an issue of increasing controversy in British politics. In response to growing disenchantment at home with the country's imperial policies, the British decided three years after the 1958 coup in Iraq to grant full independence to Kuwait, a decision echoed ten years later when the protected-state treaties with the nine remaining Gulf shaykhdoms were terminated.

The British left a lasting impact on the Gulf area in several ways. Their treaty system essentially froze the political power relationships as they were at the time and led to the establishment of European-style boundaries to define the shaykhdoms of the area as the territorially delimited states that exist today. In addition, the British introduced and developed modern administrative and legal practices, as reflected in the establishment of municipal councils and the application of Western-style legal codes. In at least a modest way the British launched economic and social development schemes that pointed the way to the much more ambitious projects that came after independence. An important consequence of the British imperium in the Gulf was the establishment of English as the area's language of international trade, defense, and diplomacy. Rooted in generations of cooperation between individual British officers and the indigenous inhabitants, Great Britain's mark upon the area is deeply graven and gives every indication of remaining so for many years to come.

Modern Gulf States

There are ten Gulf principalities and one sultanate, which together constitute five states: Kuwait, Bahrain, Qatar, the seven-member United Arab Emirates (UAE), and Oman. The governments of these states are all conservative politically, and each, save the UAE, which is a federation headed by a president, has a dynastic form of rule. Even in the UAE the local administrations have a greater impact on the daily lives of the citizens than does the federal government. The relatively stable political conditions that prevailed in the Gulf throughout most of the 1970s stood in marked contrast to the previous, often violent histories of a number of these states and to the tumultuous events of the 1980s and 1990s.

From 1980 to 1988 the eastern Arabian states faced the threat of Islamic revolution in Iran and Iran's rhetorical and other efforts to overthrow their rulers as well as the danger that the Iran-Iraq war, which broke out in September 1980, would spill over onto them. These challenges waxed and waned, according to the tide of battle and other factors, and varied from state to state in the intensity with which their impact was felt.

In 1981, Saudi Arabia, Kuwait, Bahrain, Qatar, the UAE, and Oman founded the Gulf Cooperation Council (GCC). There had been discussion of the creation of such an organization to enhance regional security since the departure of the British a decade before, but the idea never materialized, largely because of pressure from Iran and Iraq to be included. The Iran-Iraq war provided the incentive and also the opportunity to exclude those two states, which were preoccupied with each other. Although the main factor in the creation of the GCC was regional security, which appeared to be entirely justified by the Iran-Iraq war and subsequently by the Gulf War of 1990–1991, economic and political cooperation were also considered important. The GCC has grown into a significant forum for cooperation in all three areas.

Kuwait was the most severely endangered of the Gulf states because of its proximity to the warring parties in the Iran-Iraq war. In 1987 Iran initiated regular attacks on Kuwaiti oil tankers in retaliation for Iraqi assaults on Iran's tankers and loading facilities. This led to a Kuwaiti request for U.S. "reflagging" of a number of its tankers, a dramatic departure from the Kuwaiti and general eastern Arabian states' policy of maintaining their security through nonmilitary means, backed by an "over-the-horizon" U.S. military presence in the Indian Ocean. The United States provided naval escorts and Bahrain, where the U.S. Navy has access to facilities at Jufair, served as the main operations center. In a sense this was a prelude to the Desert Shield and Desert Storm operations, following the Iraqi August 2, 1990, invasion of Kuwait, when over a half million U.S., European, Arab, and other military personnel and their air, naval, and land weapons and equipment were based in the eastern Arabian states.

The Iraqi invasion of Kuwait and the Gulf War that followed have continued to shape and color the relations of the Gulf Arab states with each other and with the rest of the Arab world. They have restored normal relations with Yemen, Jordan, and the other Arab states that opposed Operation Desert Storm. They have resumed economic assistance to those states and to the Palestinians (although the demonstrated corruption of Yasir Arafat's Palestinian National Authority has limited the delivery of pledged aid to the latter). The painful breach that split the wider Arab world has been largely closed.

The Gulf Arab states' positions toward Iraq and Iran differ. Popular sympathy for the suffering of the Iraqi people led the states to call for a lifting of the U.N. economic sanctions imposed on Iraq after Desert Storm. However, ten years after its liberation, Kuwait continued to insist that the GCC support its opposition to normalization of relations with Iraq, as long as Saddam Hussein remained in power, and accept its views of Iran as a counter to the continuing threat of Saddam's Iraq. The UAE, in contrast, emphasized the need to relieve the hardships of the Iraqi population, and insisted that its GCC partners back fully its efforts to regain the three islands in the lower Gulf that Iran seized in 1971 on the eve of the UAE's independence.

A basic change has occurred in the way the Gulf states seek to ensure their physical security. The shift is most pronounced in Kuwait, which until the late 1980s had pursued a neutralist policy that aimed at balancing diplomatic and military ties with the United States and the Soviet Union and on keeping U.S. as well as Soviet forces out of the Gulf. Since the events of 1990–1991 Kuwait looks to a close military relationship with the United States as well as bilateral defense pacts with Britain, France, and Russia as the principal source of security. Kuwait and the other eastern Arabian states rejected a scheme put forward with U.S. support in 1991 for stationing Egyptian and Syrian troops on their soil. By mid-1992 Qatar and Bahrain had signed pacts similar to the Kuwaiti one with the United States, Britain, and France; the UAE signed one with the United States in mid-1994; and Oman reaffirmed and updated earlier understandings with the United States as a basis for a continuing close security relationship. In 2001 all of these states were maintaining close ties with the United States, and there were 11,000 U.S. military personnel on land throughout the region, as well as 15,000 regularly at sea. At the same time, the continued, visible, large-scale U.S. military presence, perceived U.S. bias toward Israel, and U.S. insistence on continuing economic sanctions against Iraq have created increased anti-American antagonism in the Arab Gulf states, even in Kuwait.

The eastern Arabian states, despite their small populations, also began to emphasize the buildup of their own military forces. Notwithstanding considerable U.S. and other rhetorical support for the application of an arms control regime in the Gulf, the pace of weapons acquisition accelerated. Between the 1990–1991 Gulf crisis and the end of 1996, the Arab Gulf states (Saudi Arabia and the countries considered here) contracted for $36 billion in arms purchases from the United States, a third of U.S. sales worldwide. After that, these purchases declined, though remaining significant, reflecting a need to rein in expenditures and a sense that the supplies of weaponry acquired for small armed forces were close to the saturation point.

The pattern of purchases from a variety of sources, however, militates against interoperability of these states' weapons systems, especially in the case of air defense, the most crucial component of their overall defense. This, in turn, creates a major impediment to meaningful joint military planning and cooperation. Nevertheless, there has been some movement toward more effective cooperative self-defense by the Arab Gulf states. The administration of U.S. President George W. Bush is likely to continue to promote former Defense Secretary William Cohen's idea of the Gulf states' link to an early warning network as part of a cooperative defense initiative (CDI). CDI, launched in 1998, aims to provide the Gulf states with sophisticated intelligence and to help them develop indigenous responses to attacks with weapons of mass destruction. The GCC contemplates a more than fourfold expansion of its 5,000-man Peninsula Shield force that was created in 1986, although differing threat perceptions, especially toward Iran and Iraq, continue to compromise efforts at meaningful joint action through this or other mechanisms. Nevertheless, at their December 2000 annual summit, the GCC heads of state signed a long-pending common defense pact, committing each to support any member state facing an external threat. Moreover, a positive step toward regional interoperability is the development of a GCC-wide early warning and communications network. Much of the Arab Gulf states' military defense policy consists of upgrades of systems installed just after the 1991 Gulf War. These bring new potential problems such as digital dependence and the vulnerability of computer systems to cyber attacks.

The 1990–1991 Gulf crisis helped to set in motion significant changes in the political systems of the eastern Arabian states, which continue. The Kuwaiti election of October 5, 1992, confirmed the survival of parliamentary government in that state. The most dramatic changes occurred in Qatar, following Crown Prince Hamad's peaceful overthrow of his father, Emir Khalifa Al Thani, in June 1995. As emir, Hamad has dramatically opened the country's political system to the electoral participation of male and female citizens. His Bahraini counterpart, Hamad bin Isa Al Khalifa, who became emir upon the death of his father in March 1999, has taken initial steps to liberalize Bahrain's government, including issuance of a charter that would reinstate the short-lived elected assembly dissolved in 1975. In Oman, Sultan Qabus has presided over the evolution of an entirely male council of royal appointees to one for which men and women are both eligible for selection by a limited franchise.

In fall 2001, following the September 11 terrorist attack on the United States, the eastern Arabian states joined the U.S.-led coalition against the alleged terrorist mastermind behind those operations, Osama bin Laden, and the Al-Qaeda terrorist network that he was believed to direct. The states' support was cautious, because public opinion in those countries, reacting to the suffering of Iraqi and Palestinian civilians, widely attributed to U.S. policy, and the U.S. bombing in Afghanistan, was in degree anti-American. In late November 2001, the collapse of the Taliban regime, which had protected bin Laden, seemed likely to make cooperation with the coalition easier. In any event, those states appeared certain to weather the crisis and maintain a resilient stability, their hallmark since independence.

Kuwait

Historical Background

The Kuwaitis trace their history to the late seventeenth and early eighteenth centuries, when several tribes of the great Unayzah confederation emigrated from their famine-stricken homeland in central Arabia. Calling themselves the Bani Utub (the people who wandered), roughly half of the emigrants settled in Bahrain. In 1716 the remainder founded present-day Kuwait. Over the years, several leading clans of the original settlers—the Al Sabahs, the Al Ghanims, the Al Khalids, the Al Janaats, and the Al Salihs, among others—combined to create an oligarchic merchant principality presided over by the Al Sabahs.

In 1899 Mubarak Al Sabah, known as "Mubarak the Great" (ruled 1896–1915), who had expanded Kuwaiti influence along with Al Sabah preeminence, entered into a protected-state relationship with the British. Mubarak feared that the Ottomans, who claimed nominal suzerainty over the shaykhdom, might try to implement political control. At his death, Mubarak's rule extended over a territory about twice the present size of Kuwait. In 1922 the British protectors negotiated away half of Kuwait's enlarged territory to the Saudis and to Iraq in the Treaty of Uqair. The treaty also created the Saudi-Kuwaiti Neutral Zone, which was split equally between the two parties in 1970.

The British allowed the bulk of domestic administration to remain in Kuwaiti hands, though in time the British would provide advisers to help create and staff the beginnings of a modern bureaucracy. As would occur elsewhere in the Gulf, British interests in Kuwait underwent a dramatic transformation following the discovery of oil. The Kuwait Oil Company, jointly owned by the Gulf Oil Company and British Petroleum (formerly the Anglo-Iranian Oil Company), received a concession in 1934 and discovered oil in 1938. The first commercial quantities, however, were not exported until after World War II.

In 1961 Kuwait gained full independence from Britain. At the time, Iraq made threatening gestures and claimed sovereignty over the state, basing its action on old Ottoman claims. Britain, under treaty provisions, sent troops to Kuwait, who were replaced shortly by Arab League troops, and the crisis subsided. In 1963 Kuwait became a member of the United Nations, and later the same year Iraq recognized Kuwait's independence, following a generous Kuwaiti financial arrangement with Iraq.

Even so, in 1973 Iraq laid claim to the Kuwaiti islands of Warbah and Bubiyan, which command the approaches to Iraq's naval base at Umm Qasr. In May of that year Iraq occupied the Kuwaiti border post of Samitah on the mainland, and a military clash ensued. Even during the Iran-Iraq war, when Kuwait was supplying crucial financial, logistical, and other support to Iraq, Iraq brought pressure on its neighbor to yield on the issue of the islands. It was certainly a factor, if not the central one, in precipitating the Iraqi invasion of Kuwait on August 2, 1990.

In the 1980s three factors threatened Kuwait's stability: the Iran-Iraq war, terrorism, and economic problems, especially the oil glut. In the early phases of the war Iranian aircraft attacked Kuwaiti oil facilities in an effort to frighten Kuwait into lessening or terminating its support for Iraq. Terrorist attacks, a spin-off of the war inspired, if not directed, by the revolutionary government of Iran, produced bomb attacks in December 1983 against the U.S. Embassy and other targets; a December 1984 Kuwaiti airliner hijacking that killed two Americans; a May 1985 attempt on the emir's life; and an April 1988 Air Kuwait hijacking that sought to force release of those captured, tried, and imprisoned after the 1983 violence. Eschewing its earlier diplomacy of purchasing security through economic development assistance or outright payoffs, Kuwait stood fast in the wake of these threats, tightening security measures, especially against its Shi'a population.

Falling oil prices reduced Kuwait's oil revenues from almost $18 billion in 1980 to $4.3 billion in 1984. Though Kuwait's financial reserves remained enormous, the drop in revenue compelled austerity measures, creating a certain hardship for many resident aliens. A crucial consequence of the oil glut was Kuwait's decision to produce above its OPEC quota to maximize revenues in a depressed market and to guarantee its market share in the future. Of all the OPEC members, this angered Saddam Hussein the most. Faced with the massive task of recovering financially from his costly war with Iran, Saddam desperately needed all the oil export revenues he could earn. Thus Kuwait's oil policies were probably a major factor in prompting him to accept the risks of invading Kuwait.

Political Environment

Population and Social Conditions

Kuwait lies at the northwest end of the Persian Gulf and occupies around 16,000 square kilometers (6,200 square miles) of land. Its land borders are with Iraq to the north and Saudi Arabia to the south. In addition, Kuwait shares a de facto marine boundary (as do all the other Gulf Arab states) with Iran. The terrain is mostly flat, sandy desert with occasional ridges and rock outcroppings, particularly to the west.

The population of Kuwait before the Iraqi invasion was 1.9 million, most of whom lived in the capital city, which, as in most of the other Gulf emirates, bears the same name as the state itself. Kuwait's estimated population in 1999 was 1,990,000, with Kuwaitis accounting for 45 percent of the total. The entire native Kuwaiti population is Muslim, of which 85 percent are Sunni and the balance Shi'a. The foreign and immigrant population had been a majority in Kuwait as a result of the need for skilled labor in the oil industry and ancillary enterprises as well as for staffing the government bureaucracy and schools. By far the largest nonindigenous group until 1990 was the Palestinian community, numbering as many as

400,000 people. The Palestinians, who began to arrive in significant numbers after the 1948 Arab-Israeli war, played a central role in developing both the private and public sectors of the country. From both conviction and the need for self-protection, Kuwait adopted a strongly supportive stance on Palestinian rights. Yasir Arafat worked as an engineer in Kuwait, and both Fatah, which he established, and the Palestine Liberation Organization (PLO), of which he has been president since 1967, were founded in Kuwait. Palestinians achieved considerable affluence and remitted large amounts of money to relatives, especially in the West Bank and Gaza. Despite their economic success and their attainment of high positions in business and government, only tiny numbers of Palestinians were granted Kuwaiti citizenship. In the rancorous atmosphere following the Iraqi invasion and occupation, when Arafat supported Saddam Hussein and some Palestinians collaborated with the Iraqi occupiers (though others heroically worked to protect endangered Kuwaitis), Kuwait was determined to reduce severely the number of resident Palestinians, by some accounts to no more than 40,000. It has increased the number of Egyptians and South Asians in the workforce, but Palestinian skills have been hard to replace, especially as promised Kuwaiti achievement of greater self-reliance has not been realized.

Kuwait's "cradle-to-grave" welfare system, supported by oil revenues, is one of the most extensive in the world. In the day-to-day administration of the system, little distinction has been made between resident aliens and native Kuwaitis, though this is changing. The government provides medical, educational, and welfare services for its citizens. Kuwait's educational establishment is comprehensive, compulsory for all children, and modern. It includes a tuition-free university and numerous vocational schools, all of which are subsidized by the state. The generous welfare program has been credited with reducing substantially the basis for social and economic unrest.

Economic Conditions

Prior to the production of oil most Kuwaitis engaged in traditional economic activities of the Gulf region, such as pearling and fishing on the coast and pastoral nomadism in the interior. Before the introduction of Japanese cultured pearls, Kuwait had a fleet of over 800 pearl boats and some 30,000 divers. Kuwaiti trading dhows also sailed annually to Africa and India carrying cargoes of limes, dates, and other exports from Iraq, returning with timber, textiles, and other essential items not readily available locally.

Since World War II, however, oil revenues have allowed Kuwait to develop its advanced welfare system, as well as to provide jobs for well over one-half million foreigners before the Iraqi invasion. In the 1970s, Kuwait acquired 100 percent equity in the Kuwait Oil Company (KOC) and nationalized its smaller concessionaires, becoming the first Arab Gulf state to achieve total ownership of its oil industry.

Concern about the depletion of oil reserves has resulted in accelerated attempts to modernize and diversify the economy, particularly in the fields of petrochemicals, fertilizer production, and shrimping. Agriculture remains practically nonexistent because of a lack of suitable soil and sufficient quantities of potable water. Indeed, Kuwait's chronic water shortage was not resolved until the 1950s when costly desalinization plants were installed. Before that most of Kuwait's fresh water was brought from Iraq in barges.

The state's success in diversifying its economy has been limited, owing to the paucity of non-petroleum resources, the small size of the domestic market, and the duplication of industries and projects by other Gulf states. Thus far most industrial enterprise is in state-owned corporations, with the private sector active mainly in retail marketing and investment banking. By the early 1980s Kuwait had become a textbook example of an advanced rentier state, earning as much income from its investments as from its oil exports. In 1976 it established the Reserve Fund for Future Generations to ensure that in the years ahead Kuwaitis would continue to receive the benefits enjoyed by the present population. Gifts and loans, the latter channeled primarily through the Kuwait Fund for Arab Economic Development, have benefited both Arab and non-Arab developing countries. Most of the fund's investments, however, are in Europe and the United States. Examples are its acquisition of Santa Fe International (a U.S. oil-drilling company) and the purchase of several thousand gasoline service stations (renamed Q8) in Europe.

The oil glut of the mid-1980s brought economic problems that were, as noted above, manageable, because of Kuwait's large financial reserves. One nettlesome result of the lowered oil production was the reduction in the production of the associated gas that Kuwait had contracted to supply to various overseas customers. This factor was significant in compelling Kuwait to pump oil beyond the reduced quota agreed to in OPEC. Another economic problem with major social and political implications was the 1982 collapse of the Souq al-Manakh, an unofficial stock market, whose bubble burst after massive, speculative stock purchases with postdated checks. The government vacillated in dealing with the problem, and the Al Sabahs drew fire when reports suggested that members of the ruling family who had lost investments would receive bailouts not available to others. The reverberations of the collapse of the Souq al-Manakh continued to be felt until 1998, when the parliament reluctantly approved legislation to settle remaining liabilities on terms thought to be excessively favorable to debtors, many of whom were members of the ruling family.

In economic terms the Iraqi occupation and the Desert Storm operation that ended it were extremely costly for Kuwait, primarily because of its major financial contribution to covering the cost of the coalition military operations against Iraq.

The cost of massive infrastructure replacement, though less than originally predicted, was the other major factor in reducing Kuwait's foreign exchange reserves from around $100 billion to perhaps less than $30 billion. The pace of physical recovery was remarkable. The hundreds of blazing oil wells, the most dramatically visible aspect of Iraq's sabotage, were extinguished in only eight months; key reconstruction was completed by late 1991; and by February 1993 Kuwait was pumping 2 million barrels per day (bpd) of oil, exceeding its prewar production level. At the same time, a less financially costly but more traumatic development was the loss of several billion dollars of overseas investments under the aegis of the Kuwait Investments Office (KIO). For years a leading symbol of Kuwait's astute management of its wealth, the KIO in the months after liberation was revealed to have been guilty of gross mismanagement and possibly of malfeasance. Combined with the still-unresolved fallout of the Souq al-Manakh scandal, this provoked calls for greater government financial accountability. In January 1993, the majlis passed legislation that enabled it to examine the financial records of all state-owned companies and investment organizations.

Kuwaitis have received several billion dollars in war reparations from Iraq, paid from Iraqi oil income through the U.N. Compensation Commission. Kuwaiti and other claims amounting to more than $250 billion remained to be compensated. The upsurge in oil prices, resulting from OPEC production cuts in 1999 and other factors, has eased the financial situation of Kuwait and the other eastern Arabian states. In 2001 the government was expecting to achieve its first budget surplus in many years.

Political Structure and Dynamics

The Al Sabah ruling family has exercised power through a patriarchal, dynastic regime since the early eighteenth century. In previous times power was closely shared with other leading families in an oligarchic arrangement. Oil wealth freed the rulers of financial dependence on the merchants and enabled them to create a strong and wealthy ruling house. In this century succession has been confined to the descendants of two sons of Mubarak the Great, the Al Salims and the Al Jabirs, and traditionally alternated between the two branches of the Al Sabah. This sequence was disrupted in 1965 when Shaykh Sabah Al Salim Al Sabah followed another Al Salim as emir, but it was restored when the present ruler, Shaykh Jabir al-Ahmad Al Sabah, an Al Jabir, chose an Al Salim, Shaykh Sa'd bin Abdullah, as heir apparent.

The judiciary is based on the Egyptian model and is an amalgam of Islamic law, English common law, and the Ottoman civil code. The highest court is the Supreme Court of Appeal, though the emir himself can act as a final court of appeal. There are also lesser appellate courts and courts of first instance that hear such cases as those involving divorce or inheritance. In 1975 a State Security

Court was established to handle political cases involving cases of violations of specific Kuwaiti laws.

Kuwait is divided into three administrative districts (Kuwait City, Al-Ahmadi, and Hawalli), each headed by a governor appointed by the emir. The governor (*wali*) is charged with maintaining and supervising the work of the municipalities and is himself responsible to the Ministry of the Interior.

Members of the military have been prohibited from participating in the governing process per se, and the armed forces have remained essentially depoliticized. Before the Iraqi invasion Kuwait's armed forces had a paper strength of 20,000 men. The Kuwaiti land forces do not have significantly greater military capability than before the Gulf War and still depend on foreign civilian support in field operations. With U.S. assistance the military is being restructured. Nevertheless, its small size will keep it from being an effective deterrent against the armies of its larger neighbors, even if the Kuwaiti military is better prepared and led than it was during the Iraqi invasion in 1990. In April 2001, Kuwait and the U.S. agreed to renew for another ten years the 1991 pact permitting U.S. forces to use Kuwaiti facilities and to station troops and equipment there. There are also a National Guard and a National Security Force under the direction of the Ministries of Defense and the Interior respectively.

In 1962, the year after gaining independence from Great Britain, Kuwait adopted a constitution that confirmed the Al Sabahs as hereditary rulers but placed some limitations on their power through the creation of a National Assembly. The emir and cabinet of ministers hold executive power and the emir shares legislative power with the assembly, which can override his veto with a two-thirds vote. The emir has twice suspended the assembly, in 1976 and 1986, when attacks on the ruling family became acute at times of strong political contention. Political parties are not permitted, though various political factions are clearly evident in elections and assembly deliberations. The electoral franchise is severely limited, as it is restricted to Kuwaiti citizens with family residence established in the state in 1920 or earlier, and women may not vote. Thus only about 15 percent of the Kuwaiti population has the franchise. This and the lengthy suspensions of the assembly, totaling almost one-third of the period since its establishment, have generated a degree of cynicism about the effectiveness of Kuwait's venture in parliamentary government. In 1990 it appeared that the experiment might have been sidetracked when a national council lacking legislative powers was elected in place of the assembly.

The experience of the Iraqi occupation, when those Kuwaitis who remained behind (about one-third of the 600,000 total) struggled to maintain as much order and self-governance as they could under the most difficult of situations, helped to fuel postwar determination to reestablish and, if possible, expand parliamentary government. In January 1992 the government lifted prepublication censorship of Kuwait's newspapers, allowing for vigorous coverage of the assembly election, which the emir had set for October 5, 1992. The election marked a watershed in

Kuwait's political history. Candidates identifying themselves with antigovernment factions won thirty-five of the fifty seats, with nineteen antigovernment winners running on religious platforms. The parliament elected in October 1996 contained a majority of pro-government members. Following a confrontation between the government and legislature over errors in copies of the Quran printed by the Ministry of Justice, *Awqaf* (religious endowments), and Religious Affairs, the parliament was dissolved in 1999. New elections were held within the constitutionally prescribed sixty days of suspension, in contrast to earlier suspensions. The 1999 elections confirmed the strength of the Islamists in parliament, which drew on their prominent role in the resistance to Iraqi occupation. However, liberals supporting greater political democratization have also gained strength. In May 1997, a new political organization of secular liberals from government, academia, and the professions was established under the name National Democratic Rally. Liberal support for the political rights of women led to the presentation of a proposal in the parliament in November 1999 to give the vote to women. The proposal lost by only two votes. In April 2001, the Constitutional Court ruled that the current electoral law denying women the political franchise was constitutional. It is likely, however, that pressure for women's participation in the political process, already granted in Bahrain, Qatar, and Oman, will continue.

Mistrust of other Arabs had led Kuwaiti leaders to declare that Kuwaitis would never again be a minority in their own land. They are now less than half the total, as noted above. However, Indians and other South Asians are increasingly relied upon in the place of Palestinians and other Arab expatriates. Moreover, over 100,000 *bidouns* (short for *bidoun jinsiyya,* "without nationality"), Arabs who have, in many cases, lived for generations in Kuwait but lack citizenship papers, remain in Kuwait, but have been denied most of the rights and benefits they previously received. It is estimated that twice as many more bidouns are living outside Kuwait.

Foreign Policy

For most of the first three decades of its independent existence, Kuwait compensated for its small size and weak military by using its oil revenues as the principal instrument of its foreign policy. It deflected threats through the disbursement of generous financial aid to potential enemies, such as Iraq in its war with Iran. A careful, accommodationist policy of trying to please every side was the other main principle of Kuwaiti foreign policy, evident in its scrupulously neutral policy with reference to the U.S. and Soviet superpowers. The nature of the terrorist threat in the mid- and late 1980s and of the Iranian threat persuaded Kuwait that not all external dangers could be bought off at a tolerable price. The demise of the Soviet Union helped pave the way to a close and explicit identification with the United States for security. In less than a decade Kuwait went from being the eastern Arabian state least disposed openly to acknowledge dependence on Western military forces for its security to the point of eschewing the assistance of other Arab states in favor of intimate alliance with the United States and other Western powers. At the same time, Kuwait looks inward to development of increased military, especially air defense, capability to preserve its security.

These dramatic shifts of position are, of course, a measure of the trauma that the events of 1990–1991 inflicted on Kuwaitis. Kuwait has haltingly, grudgingly, and incompletely made its peace with those in the Arab world who applauded Iraq's invasion or failed to support the efforts for Kuwait's liberation. Kuwait has indicated that a mending of ties with the Palestinians is predicated, among other things, on Palestinian efforts to persuade Baghdad to implement the U.N. Security Council resolutions imposed on Iraq after the Gulf War. In the decade since the war, tensions have erupted between Iraq and Kuwait on several occasions. In January 1993, Iraq made incursions into Kuwaiti territory following U.N. demarcation of the border, and in October of the following year Iraq deployed 70,000 troops at the border to try to force an easing of U.N. economic sanctions. In each case, the United States responded with the dispatch of troops, and in the first instance with air attacks on Iraq. By November 1994, Iraq had reversed course to recognize Kuwait's sovereignty, territorial integrity, political independence, and U.N.-defined borders. Tensions rose again over mutual accusations of territorial violations and over United Nations Special Commission (UNSCOM) inspections. In late 1998 and early 1999, a series of U.S.-led air strikes against Iraq raised tensions again. Iraq then threatened to rescind its recognition of Kuwait's sovereignty and borders. As long as Iraq blocks efforts to release or account for several hundred Kuwaitis abducted by Iraqi forces in their retreat from Kuwait in 1991, and does not unequivocally recognize Kuwait and its borders as codified by the United Nations after the Gulf War, no normalization of relations is possible. Kuwait and the other Arab Gulf states did not object to Iraq's inclusion in an Arab League summit in October 2000, and a month later at a meeting of the Organization of the Islamic Conference, Kuwait acceded to Qatar's attempt to reduce the level of its tensions with Iraq. At the February 2001 Arab League summit, however, Kuwait stated clearly that it would go no further toward rapprochement with Iraq.

Kuwait faces most acutely a dilemma that all the Arab Gulf states share—continued overwhelming dependence for external security on the United States at a time when popular resentment of the United States is growing in these states. If the Arab-Israeli peace process fails to resume forward movement, the dilemma will grow more acute and more dangerous.

Bahrain

The state of Bahrain consists of an archipelago of about thirty islands located between Saudi Arabia and the Qatar peninsula. The largest island, Bahrain (al-

Bahrayn), is forty-eight kilometers (thirty miles) long and fifteen and a half kilometers (nine and six-tenths) miles wide and contains the capital, Manama, with a population of 151,000 (1988 estimate). The second largest island is Muharraq, accessible by a four-mile causeway from Manama. It contains the state's second-largest city, also called Muharraq, and the international airport. The total land area is 662 square kilometers (c. 256 square miles), about the same size as New York City, and the population is 630,000 (1998 est.).

Historical Background

In the mid-eighteenth century the Al Khalifah, a branch of the Bani Utub tribe, which had settled Kuwait, moved to the northwestern tip of the Qatar peninsula and established a fishing and pearling settlement at Zubarah. In 1782 the Al Khalifah, with the assistance of the Al Sabah rulers of Kuwait, occupied Bahrain, driving out the previous Persian-backed rulers and ending Persia's exercise of political influence along the Arab side of the Gulf. At the end of the eighteenth century the Al Khalifah clan moved permanently to Bahrain, continuing to rule its Qatari territories until the Al Thani clan asserted its claim there in the latter part of the nineteenth century. A legacy of the contest between the two was the territorial disputes between Bahrain and Qatar, settled only in March 2001. The Iranian claim to Bahrain was renewed periodically in the nineteenth and twentieth centuries, especially during the Pahlavi dynasty, which revived the claim in 1968 when the British announced their intention of withdrawing from the Gulf by 1971. In 1970, however, Iran accepted the report of a special U.N. fact-finding mission sent to Bahrain and formally recognized Bahrain's independence.

Bahrain came under the same treaty system as the Trucial States. From 1902 on, a British official was resident in Manama. British influence was more systematically applied in Bahrain than elsewhere in the Gulf emirates and was personified by Sir Charles Belgrave, who was "adviser" and later "secretary" to the ruler for over three decades, starting in 1926. In 1946 the British resident, the senior British official in the Gulf, moved from Bushire, Iran, to Bahrain. Until their independence in 1971 Bahrain, Qatar, and the Trucial States (now the United Arab Emirates) all came under the purview of the resident.

Political Environment

Population and Social Conditions

The population of Bahrain is primarily Arab, though a great many of the local inhabitants are of Iranian origin. Native Bahrainis account for about 65 percent of the total population, in contrast to the situation in the other Gulf states (except

Oman), where foreigners have outnumbered natives. All Bahrainis and most foreigners are Muslim, but there are significant sectarian and other divisions within the indigenous population. The ruling Al Khalifah clan is Sunni, but as many as 70 percent of Bahrainis are Shi'a. Sunnis are divided between those of Arabian tribal origin and the *hawwalah* (or *muhawwalah*) Arabs, descendants of Arabs who migrated to Iran and later returned to Bahrain. The Shi'a are either *baharna*, indigenous to Bahrain, or *ajam*, a smaller group of Iranian origin.

By Gulf standards Bahrain has a sophisticated and well-educated society. Its oil industry dates from the early 1930s and is the oldest on the Arab side of the Gulf. Bahrain has an articulate labor force and has experienced labor unrest in the past. Bahrainis, who are noted for their intellectual and artistic traditions, boast some of the region's leading poets, artists, and writers.

The Bahraini system of modern schools dates back well over a half century, making it the oldest in the Gulf. School attendance is compulsory for children between the ages of six and sixteen. This has helped to create a highly capable workforce of native Bahrainis with technical skills. There are also free health and social services.

Economic Conditions

Before oil, Bahrain was largely dependent on pearling. In 1932, when Japanese cultured pearls undermined this source of wealth, oil was struck, and it was exported two years later. As the first of the eastern Arabian states to enjoy oil-based wealth, Bahrain was the first to develop a modern economy. At the same time, the modest scope of its oil reserves has also made it the first to make serious efforts to diversify its economy.

Oil production peaked at 76,000 bpd in 1970 and has been declining since. New recovery methods and the revenues shared with Saudi Arabia from a common offshore field will ensure at least modest continuing revenues, and offshore exploration holds promise for future natural gas production. Bahrain's large oil refinery has, since 1945, processed Saudi oil as well as its own, and the former now accounts for 80 percent of the throughput. In 1980 the government acquired 100 percent of the Bahrain Petroleum Company (BAPCO), a subsidiary of Caltex.

In the late 1960s Bahrain undertook several industrial projects in a serious effort to diversify its economy. The largest of these is Aluminum Bahrain (ALBA), which imports alumina from Australia and other raw materials from the United States and elsewhere, using natural gas for the smelting process. In general it has been a success, currently producing over 500,000 tons of aluminum annually. Among other projects are the Arab Shipbuilding and Repair Yard (ASRY), designed to accommodate ships of up to 400,000 tons, and the Arab Iron and Steel Company (AISCO), an ore pelletizing plant. Another effort at economic diversification is the establishment of offshore banking units (OBUs), which began as an attempt to capture some of the financial business that had fled Beirut with the outbreak of Lebanon's civil war in 1975. These institutions helped to finance imports into the Gulf area and generated significant income for Bahrain. The Iran-Iraq conflict and the Gulf War damaged Bahrain's position as an offshore banking center, but it has since largely recovered. Banking and tourism are a major part of a services sector that contributes 42 percent to the country's GDP, while manufacturing is responsible for 21 percent, indicating the degree of diversity achieved. Despite a generally positive economic outlook, young Shi'a men have experienced high unemployment, which has created political discontent.

Political Structure

Bahrain has developed a constitutional form of government that administers the country under the emir, a member of the Al Khalifah family. The constitution provides for separate executive, legislative, and judicial branches of government. Parliamentary elections were held in December 1973, shortly after the constitution had been ratified by popular referendum. The National Assembly was composed of thirty elected and fourteen appointed cabinet members. Although the assembly had fewer powers than that of Kuwait, its electorate was more widely based. The cabinet resigned in 1975 over the issue of alleged assembly interference in the administrative affairs of the government. In response to the resignations, the ruler dissolved the legislature indefinitely.

The executive branch of government is headed by the prime minister, Shaykh Khalifah bin Salman Al Khalifah, the uncle of the ruler. Shaykh Khalifah, prime minister since 1973, is charged with managing the fifteen-member cabinet. Since the adjournment of the legislature, the cabinet has performed both legislative and executive functions. The ruler, Shaykh Hamad bin Isa Al Khalifah, is advised by the cabinet but is energetically active in tending to the day-to-day affairs of state. He is also assisted by other members of the ruling family, who hold most of the key cabinet portfolios. Before succeeding his father, Shaykh Isa bin Salman Al Khalifah, on the latter's death in March 1999, Shaykh Hamad had long served as minister of defense. The new ruler, forty-nine years old when he became emir, had, unlike his father, a modern Western education. He studied at a "public school" in Cambridge, in the United Kingdom, at Mons Officer Cadet School in Aldershot, UK, and at the U.S. Army Command and Staff College at Fort Leavenworth, Kansas. Bahrain's constitution, unique among those of the Gulf states, stipulates that succession is through the ruler's eldest son.

Political Dynamics

The ruling family wields paramount influence within the Bahraini power structure despite the constitutional form of government. This pattern has at times enhanced and at times endangered the political stability of the country, where relatively sophisticated labor and leftist intellectual groups exist. Such groups have provided part of the impetus for many of the government's political and social reforms but have also spearheaded much of the country's labor unrest. After the dissolution of the National Assembly, however, the leftist reform movement was weakened. The ruling family relied increasingly on the state security forces to maintain internal security. At the same time it established joint labor-management consultative committees in major state-run enterprises to help resolve disputes peacefully.

In keeping with the general post–Desert Storm tendency toward greater political participation for the citizens of the Gulf Arab states, Bahrain's ruler and prime minister expressed support for the "reintroduction of democracy." In December 1992 Shaykh Isa announced plans for a consultative council whose members would be drawn from business, professional, religious, and academic backgrounds, with a number having served in the earlier assembly. This did little to assuage popular demands, and a 1994 petition calling for restoration of the National Assembly, signed by 20,000 Sunni and Shi'a professionals, prompted Shaykh Isa to increase the size and power of the Consultative Council. Shi'a protests over high unemployment and lack of political representation continued until Shaykh Hamad's accession. In March–April 1995, and again in December 1995 and January 1996, large Shi'a demonstrations brought harsh government response, including the arrest and detention of several hundred oppositionist activists. In 1997 and 1998, various government actions, including lenient sentences for several exiled oppositionists, reduced tensions somewhat. After coming to power in March 1999, the new ruler moved quickly to draft a National Charter that called for reinstatement of an elected legislature of both men and women, guarantee of freedom of the press and religious belief, establishment of universal suffrage, and assurance of private economic rights. The charter also called for codification of Bahrain's status as a hereditary emirate. The February 2001 referendum on the charter won the support of the Shi'a opposition, when the emir agreed to their demand for amnesty of 400 political prisoners and repatriation of over a hundred exiles. Although the referendum overwhelmingly endorsed the charter, the prime minister, who was a key architect of the previous crackdown against the opposition, remained the head of the government. Moreover, the new parliament's establishment was in the indefinite future, and its exact authority and relationship with the ruling family have yet to be determined. As of late 2001, the popular mood was optimistic, but the promise of a more open political system had yet to be realized.

The Bahraini armed forces, consisting of about 7,000 men, and the public security forces, 9,000 men, are headed by the emir. Both have been loyal to the government. The public security forces, under the direction of British and Pakistani personnel, are charged with maintaining internal order, which has been a greater problem in Bahrain than in any other emirate in the Gulf region. These forces are primarily responsible for controlling demonstrations and collecting intelligence on anti-regime activities within Bahrain. As the Gulf environment of the 1980s grew increasingly dangerous, Bahrain began to acquire significant new weaponry, including, for the first time, fixed-wing military aircraft. F-5 and, later, F-16 fighters were ordered from the United States, together with Stinger surface-to-air missiles and Sidewinder air-to-air missiles. Bahrain continues to look principally to the United States for its military arms requirements.

Foreign Policy

In keeping with its status as a small, militarily weak state, Bahrain has taken care to remain on good terms with its immediate neighbors. A long-standing territorial dispute with Qatar over the Hawar Islands, located just off the west coast of Qatar, flared up in 1982 when Bahrain named a naval vessel *Hawar,* but Saudi Arabia negotiated a "freeze" of the situation. In 1985 and 1986 Bahrain undertook construction of a coast guard station on the disputed reef of Fasht-e-Dibal, provoking Qatar to send troops and arrest the workers there.

Finally, in March 2001, all territorial disputes between Bahrain and Qatar were settled through a judgment of the International Court of Justice (ICJ). The settlement of a dispute that had roiled relations between the two states was possible because Bahrain's new ruler, after initially taking a hard line, agreed to let the ICJ decide the case. The court's decision, which equitably divided the disputed territories, met an enthusiastic reception on each side. It gave Qatar sovereignty over Zubarah, the Al Khalifah's former capital on the Qatari mainland, as well as Fasht al-Dibal. Bahrain was given the Hawar Islands, where there is a prospect of finding oil and gas. Other small islands were divided between Bahrain and Qatar, and a border dividing the two states' maritime zones was established. This settlement of the last major territorial conflict between Arab Gulf states is significant both for the states immediately concerned and for regional dynamics. Within days of the ICJ decision, Bahrain and Qatar were discussing new cooperative ventures, including a possible causeway between them.

In general the nature and orientation of Bahrain's external policies are conservative. In regional matters the country usually follows the lead of Saudi Arabia. Like the latter country, and indeed like all the countries of eastern Arabia, Bahrain has close ties with the West. Until Bahrain's independence in 1971 the British maintained a naval base at Jufair (near Manama). The United States, which had rented space from the British since 1949 for a headquarters for its Middle East Force (MIDEASTFOR), leased much of the former British facility directly from Bahrain from 1971 to 1977. MIDEASTFOR was essentially a naval command headquarters to which ships were to be assigned during times of crisis.

The Bahraini government was generally pleased to have the U.S. facility as an overt, official symbol of U.S. support for the regime. At the same time, a growing number of Bahraini officials began to view the U.S. presence as a potential liability because of the opposition it could attract from local and regional radical groups. Primarily for this reason, Bahrain decided to terminate the lease. In 1977 MIDEASTFOR technically ceased to use Jufair as its homeport, though the U.S. admiral who commanded MIDEASTFOR's flagship continued to make frequent use of the local facilities. In the late 1980s MIDEASTFOR was absorbed by a new U.S. unified command, Central Command (CENTCOM), with geographical responsibility for Southwest Asia.

In 1987–1988 the close U.S. security relationship with Bahrain was cemented when Bahrain provided vital assistance in serving U.S. warships during the "reflagging" of Kuwaiti tankers in the face of Iranian attacks. Again, in 1990–1991, during the military operations that followed Iraq's invasion of Kuwait, Bahrain played a key role in providing support services for coalition naval vessels. After the liberation of Kuwait, Bahrain soon followed Kuwait's lead in signing a bilateral defense pact with the United States. The defense pact has been renewed, and significant elements of the U.S. Navy's Fifth Fleet are based in Bahrain. The security relationship has become broader and deeper, and the deployment of forces, as elsewhere in the Gulf, is acquiring a permanent look and feel. In late 1995, Bahrain agreed to the temporary deployment of U.S. aircraft on its territory to deter a possible military threat from Iraq. But in February 1998 it refused to allow U.S. aircraft to attack Iraq from Bahraini bases, and in June 1998 U.S. aircraft were withdrawn from Bahrain. The presence of large American military forces has created tensions, and popular sympathy with the suffering of the Iraqi population has generated some anti-American sentiment. Further exacerbation of such feelings followed the collapse of the Israeli-Palestinian peace process and the perception of a pro-Israeli U.S. stance during the Israeli-Palestinian clashes that followed the collapse in September 2000.

Bahrain's positions toward its two large, dangerous Gulf neighbors reflect in part its geographic position and its majority Shi'a population. It has attempted to develop correct relations with Iran. Official ties were upgraded to the ambassadorial level in 1990. In the mid-1990s, however, relations deteriorated, because the Bahraini government suspected Iranian complicity in Bahrain's domestic Shi'a disturbances. Tensions had ceased by late 1997, with an agreement to exchange ambassadors again. As in most other states, the plight of the Iraqi population has generated much sympathy, and the United States has received much of the blame for it. However, the government is still fearful and distrustful of Saddam Hussein and unwilling to reestablish a full, normal relationship with Iraq.

Qatar

The state of Qatar occupies a mitten-shaped peninsula that extends for about 170 kilometers (105 miles) northward into the Gulf and measures eighty kilometers (fifty miles) at its point of greatest width. The territory of Qatar encompasses approximately 10,360 square kilometers (4,000 square miles). Approximately two-thirds of its population of about 600,000 lives in the capital of Doha, on the east coast of the peninsula. The land is mostly low lying and consists largely of sandy or stony desert, with limestone outcroppings and salt flats.

Historical Background

Like Bahrain and the United Arab Emirates, Qatar was under British protection until independence in 1971. The protective status was based on treaties signed in 1869, 1913, and 1916. Apart from its having been admitted to the Arab League, the Organization of Arab Petroleum Exporting Countries (OAPEC), OPEC, and the United Nations, the principal political development in the period just after independence was a nonviolent palace coup in 1972. On that occasion Shaykh Khalifah bin Hamad Al Thani, long known as one of the most forceful and development-oriented personalities in the Gulf area, ousted his cousin, Shaykh Ahmad, as ruler. Twenty-three years later, in June 1995, Khalifa's son, Hamad, overthrew him, because Khalifa had opposed the more liberal domestic and foreign policies that Hamad favored. The first six years of Hamad's rule witnessed a dramatic opening up of Qatar's political system.

Political Environment

Population and Social Conditions

Prior to the production of oil in 1949, the population of Qatar was one of the poorest of any in Eastern Arabia. The great majority of the inhabitants lived at subsistence level, with most of their income derived from fishing and pearling. Most of the indigenous population is Arab, and a large percentage of this group was made up of *muhawwalah* Arabs with ties of varying strength and duration to their kinfolk along the south Iranian coast. The Arabs of Qatar are largely Sunni Muslims and generally subscribe to the conservative teachings of the same Hanbali school of Islamic jurisprudence as practiced in Saudi Arabia. Qataris, however, tend to be a bit less austere than their Saudi counterparts.

There is also a large foreign population of Iranians, Pakistanis, Indians, and Palestinians. Native Qataris account for only about 30 percent of the total population. The Iranians constitute the majority of the small merchant class; many Indians and Pakistanis are employed as manual laborers, artisans, and clerical staff in local banks and businesses. Palestinians occupy the lower and middle levels of the bureaucracy and equivalent white-collar positions in the private sector.

Before oil production became a factor, Qatar lacked even the remotest semblance of a modern school system, hospitals, clinics, electricity, piped water, and many other government services. Great strides have been made in all these services in recent

years, however. Public education for both boys and girls began in a major way in the
1950s and is free but not compulsory. All primary-school teachers must be Qataris,
and the country, like its neighbors, now has its own national university. Free health
services are provided to both Qatari and non-Qatari residents.

Economic Conditions

Petroleum production and export, together with the leadership of reform-ori-
ented members of the ruling family, have been responsible for much of the dramatic transformation that has taken place in the country's social and economic
life. In 1975 the two major oil-producing companies, Qatar Petroleum Company
and Shell Oil of Qatar, were nationalized by the government. Qatar's petroleum
reserves of about 4 billion barrels are modest by Gulf standards and will sustain
production only a few more years into the twenty-first century. However, in the
North Dome field, Qatar possesses the world's largest deposit of unassociated natural gas (gas not mixed with oil). Qatar's proven gas reserves, conservatively estimated at 4.62 trillion cubic meters (163 trillion cubic feet), place it fourth or fifth
in the world. Exploitation of this field began in 1991, and in 1997 the second
phase of its development, construction of facilities for production and export of
liquified natural gas (LNG), was completed. Thus, Qatar is positioned for the time,
perhaps twenty years from now, when gas production will have entirely displaced
that of oil. The government has made considerable investments in infrastructure,
including an excellent road system connecting Qatar to adjacent states, an international airport, and a large modernized port.

Qatar is attempting to modernize and diversify its economy as rapidly and efficiently as possible to lessen its dependence on hydrocarbon production. In 1973 it
began to manufacture fertilizer. The country has also built cement and steel plants
as well as flour mills and has expanded its shrimping industry. Qatar's per capita
income of $17,000.00 (1998 est.) is one of the world's highest.

Political Structure

In 1970, a year before independence, Qatar became the first of the lower Gulf
states to promulgate a written constitution. It provided for a council of ministers
and an advisory council, stipulating that the former was to be appointed by the
ruler and that the majority of the latter was to be elected by the general population. The constitution also provides for a judicial system that includes five secular
and religious courts. A court of appeals also exists, but the function of a supreme
court is vested in the ruler, who has the power to waive or reduce penalties. Finally, although Qatar is a unitary state, progress has been made toward decentraliz-
ing the administration. Nevertheless, because half or more of the population lives

in Doha, the government has met with only limited success in its efforts to allocate political authority to the state's component political units.

The council of ministers (or cabinet) is led by the prime minister, who is theoretically appointed by the ruler, though in practice the ruler himself has served in that post. Members of the ruling family dominate the cabinet, which is responsible for proposing laws, which must be submitted to the ruler for ratification, and is also technically accountable for supervising the state bureaucracy and the financial affairs of the state.

The advisory council, established in 1972 after the coup, consisted exclusively of members appointed by the ruler. The council has been extended at four-year intervals since 1978. Although it is designed to represent major social and economic interest groups in Qatar, the council has little authority other than to make recommendations and, by itself, is not empowered to initiate legislation. In January 1992, fifty leading Qataris petitioned the emir to establish an assembly with legislative powers and to institute economic and educational reforms. His response was only to broaden modestly the advisory council's membership.

Political Dynamics

The 1992 petition foreshadowed a series of developments that have led Qatar from quiet political conservatism to dramatic liberal reform. In 1992, Emir Khalifah had granted his son Hamad, a graduate of Britain's Sandhurst Military Academy, effective control of Qatar's affairs, apart from financial matters. In 1995, a power struggle between father and son led to a coup on June 27. Shaykh Hamad's domestic reforms helped confirm his support in Qatar, and Saudi Arabia, the United States, and other countries promptly recognized him as ruler. He retained the posts of minister of defense and commander in chief of the armed forces. While he initially appointed himself prime minister, in October 1996 he relinquished that office to his younger brother, Shaykh Abdullah. At the same time, he appointed the third of his four sons, Shaykh Jasim, as heir apparent. Hamad's most significant domestic political action was the decision to create, through a new permanent constitution, a national assembly whose members would be directly elected. Formation of the assembly was to follow elections to Qatar's new central municipal council. On March 8, 1999, these elections were held, the first in Qatar's history and the first direct elections in any Arab Gulf state in which women could vote and run for office.

Shortly after taking power, Hamad revoked censorship of the news media, and abolished the post of minister of information and culture, later dissolving the ministry as well. As part of this move to liberalize Qatar's media and the image they project, the new emir established the Al-Jazeera television station, an all-news station independent of the government, which broadcasts by satellite to the whole

Arab world. Al-Jazeera is revolutionary, because it has introduced programs, including frank and provocative news reports and commentaries that are new to the Arab viewing public, long accustomed to vapid stories on state visits and broadcasts of official speeches. Several Arab governments have complained about programs that offered frank criticism of them, but, while several Arab governments have boycotted the station, its power and influence are such that the boycotts have not lasted. Although the station is a non-government entity, it is not yet able to survive financially without government subventions, and, despite critical commentary on the actions of its own government, there appear to be lines that may not be crossed with commentary on the Al Thani. Al-Jazeera gained instant international visibility when CNN broadcast the station's exclusive interview with alleged terrorist mastermind Osama bin Laden in Afghanistan, following the September 11, 2001, terrorist attacks on the World Trade Center in New York and on the Pentagon. It remains to be seen if Hamad's bold experiment will increase news media freedom and improve the quality of news reporting elsewhere in the Arab World.

These dramatic developments have not yet altered the centrality of the Al Thani in Qatar's government and the family's essential monopoly of political power. The establishment of a national assembly with legislative powers may have a significant impact on the ruling family's position, but it is reasonable to assume that the Al Thani will remain dominant. The Al Thani are the largest ruling family in the region, numbering, by some accounts, as many as 20,000. To a much greater extent than any of its counterparts in the region, the Al Thani has dominated most of the important functions of government. The primary constraints on the ruler remain Islamic law and the influence of what is undoubtedly the most conservative religious establishment of any of the emirates. The Al Thani, although close-knit and secretive like all the other ruling families of the area, harbors in its midst a great many factions and rivalries. This was evident in the bloodless coup that brought the present emir to power and in a reported counter-coup in which the former minister of economy, a member of the family, was involved.

The family generally holds around ten of the fifteen cabinet portfolios, including all the vital ones such as interior, defense, finance, and foreign affairs. Shaykh Hamad Al Thani maintains close control over the country's affairs, granting to select, trusted members of the family governmental positions to reinforce his position and to assuage their political ambitions. Qatar has an effective security force of more than 5,000 men, including a large number of expatriates.

The merchant class has traditionally exerted less influence on government affairs than its larger and older counterparts in Kuwait, Bahrain, Dubai, or Oman. The power of the merchants is primarily exerted on the commercial aspects of the state's developmental projects. However, as revenues have accumulated and as many members of the ruling family have become more interested and involved in business themselves, the traditional separation of Al Thani–dominated government and merchant class–dominated business has begun to disappear. The Al Thani and the business community, through a symbiotic process, have increased their collaboration in many areas relating to Qatar's economic growth.

Foreign Policy

Before the early 1990s, Qatar's foreign policy had been consistently conservative. Indeed, on many external policy matters Qatar had been apt to follow the lead of its large neighbor, Saudi Arabia. It was a dispute largely over the direction of foreign policy between the former ruler, Emir Khalifah, and his son, Hamad, that led to the coup in 1995. Changes in Qatar's foreign policy since then have been as dramatic as those in its domestic policy. A hallmark of Al Thani policy had been an effort to remain on friendly terms with all of the Gulf littoral states as a principal means of preserving the independence of a small, weak state. The principal exception was Bahrain, with which territorial disputes had soured relations since 1939. Qatar supported Iraq in its 1980–88 war with Iran, but it has sought tolerable relations with Iran, because of its own Shi'a community and a sensitive maritime border with Iran that impinges on the vast gas reserves of the North Dome field. Under Khalifah, Qatar was careful never to take positions at odds with mainstream Arab policies. In contrast, Hamad, as crown prince, had already pursued a foreign policy that departed markedly from Qatar's cautious external relations before 1992. He had begun to strengthen ties with both Iran and Iraq and moved boldly to establish links with Israel. In 1995, Qatar took a forward position among the GCC states by supporting the ending of U.N. sanctions against Iraq. Most dramatically, Hamad sought to establish economic ties with Israel. Discussions over possible export of Qatari liquefied natural gas (LNG) to Israel were pursued from 1994 to 1998, with an April 1996 visit to Qatar by Israeli Prime Minister Shimon Peres. However, by early 1998 the faltering of the Arab-Israeli peace process had caused Qatar to review its relations with Israel, leading to the abandonment of the LNG deal. With the collapse of the peace process in September 2000 and the Israeli-Palestinian violence that followed, Qatar finally yielded to Arab and Iranian pressure to cut its ties with Israel by closing the Israeli trade office in Doha in November. Even then, Israeli office staffers remained, and in June 2001 the Arab press carried allegations of continuing secret, high-level contacts between Israeli and Qatari officials.

Under Emir Hamad, Qatar has also begun to play a much more prominent international role. It hosted the fourth Middle East and North Africa (MENA) summit in November 1997, downgraded, however, to the status of a conference, when most of the Arab League states withdrew in protest over Israel's perceived failure to meet its obligations under the Middle East peace process. In November 2000, Qatar hosted the Organization of the Islamic Conference summit.

However, the most significant recent development in Qatar's external affairs was the settlement with its immediate neighbor, Bahrain, of territorial disputes that had festered for sixty-two years, poisoning their bilateral relations and compromising the capacity of the GCC to function effectively. As noted in the section on Bahrain, efforts to settle the dispute, including mediation by Saudi Arabia and other GCC states, were for long unavailing. Tensions were dangerously high in 1986, when Bahrain tried to build an artificial island on a disputed reef, and in 1995, when Bahrain announced a decision to build a tourist resort on the Hawar Islands. In 1991, Qatar had unilaterally instituted proceedings at the International Court of Justice and rejected Bahrain's demand that the two countries seek joint recourse to the ICJ. Later in the decade, relations improved to the point where diplomatic relations at the ambassadorial level were established and Qatar agreed to withdraw a number of challenged documents that it had submitted to the ICJ. Although the new ruler of Bahrain, Emir Hamad bin Isa Al Khalifah, initially took a tough line on the disputed territory, the pragmatic outlook of the two rulers made possible agreement to accept the ICJ's decision in March 2001. As previously noted, the judgment satisfied both states and seemed certain to prefigure cordial and close relations between them. Just as the Bahrain-Qatar dispute achieved resolution, the Qatar–Saudi Arabia border dispute, essentially resolved in 1996, was concluded with final demarcation of the border. These events, together with the settlement of Saudi Arabia's long-contested border with Yemen, mark the virtual end of the numerous territorial and border disputes that have complicated relations and threatened conflict among the Arab Gulf states.

In the decade following Qatar's participation in the coalition to liberate Kuwait from Iraqi occupation, it has maintained close military cooperation with the United States. In June 1992, the two nations signed a security pact, and in March 1995 Qatar signed an agreement giving the United States permission to preposition military equipment on its territory. A U.S. armored brigade was stationed there in 2001.

United Arab Emirates

Historical Background

In 1820, to protect maritime trading routes from privateers operating from ports in the lower Gulf, Great Britain devised and, in rapid succession, imposed by force on the littoral shaykhdoms the first of what would be a series of truces designed to put an end to practically incessant naval warfare. As a result, the area, formerly known as the Pirate Coast, came in time to be called the Trucial Coast, and the seven small principalities that dotted its shores were called the Trucial States.

The international status of these principalities as British-protected states continued until 1971, when Great Britain terminated its special treaty relationships with Bahrain, Qatar, and the Trucial States. For the previous three years, following the announcement of its intention to withdraw from the Gulf, Britain tried to promote creation of a federation that would include all seven of the Trucial States plus Bahrain and Qatar. Until 1970 Iran's claim to Bahrain prevented these efforts from bearing fruit. Subsequently Bahrain took the initiative and lobbied for inclusion in the new federation, with political power to be apportioned among the federation's members on the basis of population (Bahrain then had the largest population). When rebuffed, Bahrain opted to stay out of the federation. Qatar, which not only contested Bahrain's attempt to dominate the projected federation politically but also continued to dispute with its neighbor various territorial claims, then also withdrew, leaving only the Trucial States to form the new United Arab Emirates (UAE) federation. On December 2, 1971, the new state was declared, with Abu Dhabi, Dubai, Sharjah, Ajman, Umm al-Qaywayn, and Fujayrah as its members. Ras al-Khaymah joined in March 1972.

At the outset the UAE faced numerous difficulties. Abu Dhabi had an unresolved dispute with Saudi Arabia and Oman over the Buraymi Oasis in the eastern region of the shaykhdom. There were, moreover, strong traditional rivalries among the rulers that dampened an atmosphere otherwise conducive to achieving a measure of functional integration among the member states. Finally, on the eve of independence, Iran occupied the three islands of Greater and Lesser Tunbs and Abu Musa, long ruled by Ras al-Khaymah and Sharjah, respectively. The occupation of Abu Musa was in accordance with an eleventh-hour agreement arrived at between the shah and the ruler of Sharjah; but the ruler of Ras al-Khaymah defied Iran, and his troops forcibly resisted the Iranian seizure, resulting in loss of life on both sides. The Abu Musa situation contributed directly to a coup attempt in February 1972 that cost the life of the ruler of Sharjah. A settlement of the Buraymi dispute was negotiated in 1974, when an agreement between Abu Dhabi and Saudi Arabia paved the way to the establishment of diplomatic relations between Saudi Arabia and the UAE. More than twenty years later, the dispute over the islands continues to sour relations not only between the UAE and Iran but also between the latter and almost all the Arab Gulf states.

Political Environment

Population and Social Conditions

The UAE is a federation of seven shaykhdoms extending for some 692 kilometers (430 miles) along the southern coast of the Gulf and another 97 kilometers (60 miles) on the Gulf of Oman. Occupying approximately 83,300 square kilometers (32,050 square miles), the country has a population of approximately 3 million (2000 estimate). Abu Dhabi occupies almost 87 percent of the total land area and has nearly 42 percent of the federation's population. Six of the shaykhdoms—Abu Dhabi, Dubai, Sharjah, Ajman, Umm al-Qaywayn, and Ras al-Khaymah—have territory on the Persian/Arab Gulf, with Sharjah having additional, noncontiguous territory along the coast of the Gulf of Oman. Only Fujayrah is located wholly on the Gulf of Oman coast.

The most distinctive characteristic of the various shaykhdoms is tribal affiliation. Six principal tribal groups inhabit the country: the Bani Yas, a confederation of nearly a dozen different tribes, two branches of which (the Al Bu Falah and the Al Bu Falasah, respectively) provide the ruling families of Abu Dhabi and Dubai; the Manasir (singular, Mansuri), who range from the western reaches of the UAE to Saudi Arabia and Qatar; the Qawasim (singular, Qasimi), two branches of which rule Sharjah and Ras al-Khaymah; the Al Ali (also Al Mualla) of Umm al-Qaywayn; the Sharqiyin in Fujairah; and the Nu'aim in Ajman. All the tribes are Arab and Sunni Muslims.

Less than 15 percent of the local population can still be classified as bedouin. They usually live around oases and for some years have been migrating to and settling in urban areas. Because of their loyalty to the rulers, many of bedouin stock are found in the police and military forces.

A highly sophisticated merchant class has developed, particularly in Dubai. It has maintained and, where possible, expanded what for several decades has been a rather extensive relationship with the Indian subcontinent and, until the Iran-Iraq war, with Iran. Allied with Sunni Arab merchant families are numerous Persian and Indian families resident in the lower Gulf for generations. Among the most colorful merchants, after World War II and before the emergence of oil as the dominant factor in the region's economies, were those "free traders" in gold and other luxury items whose picturesque dhows concealed powerful engines capable of outrunning curious coast guard vessels of a half dozen countries.

The indigenous inhabitants of the UAE account for less than one-fifth of the total population, with that percentage lower still in the wealthy emirates. The desire for rapid economic development meant bringing in other Arabs, Asians, and Europeans in large numbers to provide the skills needed. Mirroring patterns established elsewhere in the wealthy Arab oil states, Palestinians worked as business managers, filled mid-level positions in the bureaucracy, and were prominent in the nation's press; Egyptians filled teaching positions; and Jordanians served as advisers in the military. Since the 1990–1991 Gulf crisis, the number of Palestinians and Jordanians has been reduced. South Asians form the largest expatriate community, with Indians, Pakistanis, and Sri Lankans accounting for at least half of the total population, most of them performing skilled or semiskilled tasks or managing small retail enterprises.

Medical care is free to UAE nationals, and the government operates a system of extensive social welfare benefits. Primary education is compulsory and enrollment of boys and girls at primary and secondary schools is about 90 percent of all school-age children. The National University at al-Ain in Abu Dhabi has an enrollment of about 15,000 men and women. Other institutions of higher education include the all-female Zayed University, which has campuses in Abu Dahbi and Dubai, and eleven Higher Colleges of Technology in five of the seven emirates. The HCTs provide three years of technical training in business administration, computers, engineering, health sciences, and other fields. Several internationally accredited private institutions have been established, including the American University in Dubai, catering to non-Emirians.

Economic Conditions

Even more dramatically than its neighbors, the UAE has made the transition from a largely subsistence economy to a highly developed economy that provides one of the world's highest standards of living. Per capita income in 1999 was $17,651. The UAE enjoys the highest rate of economic growth among the GCC countries. The principal engine of its economy is the oil and gas sector, drawing on 100 billion barrels of recoverable oil reserves (10 percent of the world total) and six billion cubic meters (212 billion cubic feet) of gas reserves (4 percent of the world total). Significant diversification of the economy and resourceful innovation have fueled the country's strong performance.

Before the discovery of oil in Abu Dhabi in 1958, only Dubai and Sharjah had developed an extensive entrepôt trade. The oft-reported rivalry between these two shaykhdoms stems in part from the fact that Dubai began to eclipse Sharjah both politically and commercially when Sharjah's harbor began to silt up in the 1940s. The conditions for perpetuating the former's economic edge over the latter were practically ensured when Dubai succeeded in dredging its own inlet (or "creek," as it is called locally).

Abu Dhabi Town, by contrast, was situated on an island and was little more than a mud-brick village before the discovery of oil. Today, however, it is the largest city in the UAE and by far the most advanced in terms of administrative and social welfare services. Dubai and Sharjah have also undertaken extensive development projects. The contrast between these three affluent shaykhdoms and the other four remains substantial, though the gap has been lessened somewhat in recent years, as the federal government, largely using Abu Dhabi money, has funded numerous development projects in the poorer states. The abundance of new income; the lack, to date, of a strong centralized planning authority with the power to veto or modify individual shaykhdoms' development ventures; and, most important, the continuation of intense competition among the various rulers for prestige inevitably have resulted in the duplication of many facilities, such as the five "international" airports—in Abu Dhabi, Dubai, Sharjah, Ras al-Khaymah, and Fujayrah.

The recovery of oil prices in 1999 boosted the performance of the country's hydrocarbon sector. Abu Dhabi accounts for more than 85 percent of the UAE's oil output and more than 90 percent of its reserves. Over the past decade, Dubai's oil production has declined from a peak of 410,000 bpd to 170,000 bpd (1999), while Sharjah produces modest quantities of gas and condensate and Ras al-Khaymah has small reserves of oil and condensate. While oil continues to underpin the UAE's economic development, a much enlarged role for natural gas is anticipated. Abu Dhabi, which has 90 percent of the UAE's gas reserves, will use its gas for domestic needs such as desalination, electricity generation, power for new industries, and feedstock for petrochemical projects and to meet oil field reinjection needs. Moreover, Abu Dhabi is creating a hub for a Gulf-wide gas network. Part of this is the Dolphin Project, scheduled for completion in 2002 or 2003, which entails construction of an 800-kilometer (500-mile) pipeline from Qatar's North Dome field to Dubai, which needs new sources of gas. The pipeline is projected to extend to Oman.

For the past two decades, the UAE has worked to diversify its economy so as to avoid excessive dependence on oil production. The non-oil sector now generates about three quarters of GDP. This strategy has largely taken the form of industrialization, composed of light industry, such as food processing, and heavy industry, such as cement production. The most impressive single example of a non-oil industry is the Dubai Aluminum Smelter (DUBAL), which started production in 1979. An integrated smelter, power plant, and desalination complex, DUBAL, one of the largest facilities of its kind, typifies the spirit of bold enterprise long associated with Dubai.

In 1991 the UAE experienced a major financial scandal when regulatory authorities in seven countries terminated, without warning, the operations of the Bank of Commerce and Credit (BCCI), in which the ruling family of Abu Dhabi held a controlling interest. The bank had been closed when it was discovered that BCCI authorities had committed major fraud, prior to the Al Nahyan purchase of the bank's shares. It was not until 1998 that the affair was settled, with the Abu Dhabi authorities making payments of $1.8 billion to compensate the bank's creditors. The BCCI scandal prompted a strengthening of the UAE Central Bank and stricter regulation of the country's financial sector. The UAE's banking sector suffered a loss of profit in 1999, reflecting global conditions, but recovered in 2000.

Despite its extreme aridity, the UAE has applied technology to expand its agricultural sector so that it is self-sufficient in dates, nearly so in fresh milk, and produces the bulk of its vegetable consumption. The fishing industry employs 19,000 men, Emirians and others, and fully meets local demand for fish.

Several important new ventures mark the UAE's economic development in recent years. Tourism, although only recently introduced, has grown rapidly, so that its contribution to the country's non-oil income is estimated at 15 percent. In keeping with its reputation for bold innovative enterprise, Dubai opened the world's tallest hotel, the Burj al-Arab, in 1999, and it hosts international golf and tennis tournaments. Dubai has also embarked on a $1.6 billion shopping and entertainment project called Dubai Festival City and has announced plans to build a resort on what would be the two largest artificial islands in the world. The UAE has moved rapidly to realize the benefits of e-commerce. About two thirds of its population was projected to have Internet access by 2002. In January 2000, Shaykh Maktoum bin Rashid Al Maktoum, ruler of Dubai, issued a decree establishing Dubai Internet City, which aims to become a regional sales, distribution, and trading center for goods sold over the Internet. This, in effect, adds a third free trade zone to those already successfully operating at Jebel Ali Port and at Dubai's international airport. One of the most important innovations in the UAE's economy is the UAE Offsets Group, which mandates that foreign firms winning defense contracts must invest a percentage of the value of their contracts in joint ventures with local partners. In this way, a number of significant projects, ranging from a shipbuilding company to a healthcare center, have been undertaken.

Political Structure

The UAE's constitution, which dates from 1971 and was made permanent in 1996, provides for federal legislative, executive, and judicial bodies. The legislature, called the Federal National Council (FNC), is in reality a consultative assembly, in keeping with the norms of traditional tribal and Islamic rule in this part of Arabia. The FNC is composed of forty members nominated by the president and approved by the rulers of the seven member-states, who constitute the Federal Supreme Council (FSC). In accordance with the relative size of their constituent populations, eight seats are apportioned to Abu Dhabi and to Dubai, six each to Ras al-Khaymah and Sharjah; and four each to the remaining three members. The FNC's duties are limited mainly to discussion and approval of the budget, to its authority to draft legislation, and to its role as a forum for discussion and debate of policies and programs under consideration by the government. This last duty is of no small significance because of the absence of political parties, trade unions, and various other kinds of voluntary associations familiar to Westerners. Further, the constitution would permit the FNC's evolution into an elected body exercising real legislative functions.

The Council of Ministers has a dual executive-legislative function. Two of its primary responsibilities are to draft laws and to act as a legislative body when the

FNC is not in session. The greatest concentration of authority within the federal structure is in the FSC. The seven-member council is charged with formulating and supervising all federal policies, ratifying UAE laws, approving the country's annual budget, ratifying international treaties, and approving the nomination of the prime minister, the president, and the members of the supreme court. In procedural matters a simple majority vote is sufficient for passage of any resolution. However, on substantive issues Abu Dhabi and Dubai have veto power. Thus on any substantive vote, five member-states, including the two leading shaykhdoms, must approve a resolution in order for the motion to have the force of law. The constitutional allocation of a preponderance of political power to Abu Dhabi and Dubai has been a major point of contention among most of the other shaykhdoms.

Since independence Shaykh Zayid has been president of the UAE, a post to which he was reappointed in 1976, 1981, 1986, 1991, and 1996. Shaykh Rashid of Dubai served as the union's vice president at its inception and, in 1979, became its prime minister as well. Rashid suffered a stroke in 1981 and remained bedridden until his death in 1990. In 1986 his son and successor as ruler of Dubai, Shaykh Maktoum, was elected both vice president and prime minister of the UAE, and he continued to hold those posts as of late 2001. Although the powers of the presidency are in theory subordinate to those of the FSC, Shaykh Zayid has been relatively successful in keeping together what has been the Arab world's foremost example of regional political integration. His success has been due in part to Abu Dhabi's preeminence as the most pro-federation state in the union and his own strong personal dedication to the UAE's development. Many of the federation's operations are almost completely funded by Abu Dhabi.

Foreign policy decisionmaking is vested in the federal executive branch. However, although Articles 120 and 121 of the constitution stipulate that foreign affairs decisions are the responsibility of the union, Article 123 states that the individual shaykhdoms may conclude limited agreements concerning local matters, for example, the granting of concessions—including the right to explore for, produce, refine, and export oil—to foreign economic interests. Thus, the individual shaykhdoms have considerable latitude and power in the conduct of foreign affairs.

The UAE's federal judiciary is made up of a supreme court and courts of first instance. Judges serve indefinite terms and may be removed only in extraordinary circumstances. The country's legal system places special emphasis on Islamic law (*Shari'a*) but is drawn from several sources, including Western ones. In February 1994, Shaykh Zayid ordered that a number of serious crimes, including murder, theft, adultery, and drug offenses, be tried in Shari'a courts rather then civil courts. The supreme court adjudicates disputes between individual shaykhdoms as well as those between individual shaykhdoms and the federal government. It also determines the constitutionality of federal or emiral laws when challenged. Like the federal bureaucracy, the judiciary has been heavily dependent on foreign residents' expertise, especially from Egypt and the Palestinian community. Efforts to staff the courts with trained native UAE jurists have been partially successful. Most of the cases submitted for adjudication in the UAE are dealt with by the lower courts in each of the shaykhdoms.

The powers reserved to the individual shaykhdoms, as stated in Article 122, imply that they remain responsible for all matters that do not fall under the domain of the federal authorities. They also retain a few stated powers.

Political Dynamics

The UAE has enjoyed a remarkable degree of political stability, based on the development of an effective modern administrative structure and the continued viability of an essentially traditional mode of governance. Since the inception of the federation, the strongest cohesive force within it has been Shaykh Zayid of Abu Dhabi, followed by Shaykh Sultan of Sharjah. Shaykh Rashid of Dubai was in a position to play a role in federal affairs. However, at least from the perspective of his critics, he did not seriously begin to perform such a role until he became prime minister, in 1979, just two years before his incapacitating stroke, preferring to concentrate most of his attention and energies on Dubai.

Politics within the shaykhdoms traditionally have been tribe-based and autocratic, even if tempered by such age-old concepts as social democracy, consultation, consensus, and adherence to the principles and norms enshrined in Islamic law. The ruler, or shaykh, is usually the oldest son of the immediately preceding ruler, though there are instances in which an uncle, brother, nephew, or cousin has acceded to power. To remain in power the shaykh must maintain the support of the inner circles of the ruling family and several groups, most particularly religious leaders and merchants, within the shaykhdom.

The past history of internal politics of the ruling families has been replete with intrigue and jockeying among contenders for the limited positions of official power. Before the establishment of the UAE, many local rulers fell victim to assassination at the hands of brothers, cousins, or sons. As recently as 1966 a palace coup in Abu Dhabi brought a new ruler, Shaykh Zayid, to power, and in February 1972 the UAE's minister of education, Shaykh Sultan bin Muhammad Al Qasimi, assumed the position of ruler in Sharjah following an abortive palace coup in which his predecessor was murdered. In 1981, by contrast, there were peaceful successions in both Umm al-Qaywayn and Ajman, and in 1984 there was a peaceful transition of power from the stricken Shaykh Rashid in Dubai to his four sons. In 1987, however, Shaykh Abdul Aziz bin Muhammad Al Qasimi tried to seize power from his brother, the ruler of Sharjah, an event that threatened the union's integrity, both because it raised the question of the legitimacy of all the rulers in the UAE and because Abu Dhabi initially backed the usurper and Dubai the incumbent. The FSC defused the crisis by arranging a compromise sharing of power, with Shaykh Sultan still ruler. The arrangement later broke down. Although future coups in Sharjah or other states cannot be ruled out, the seven emiral governments as well as the federal government have enjoyed remarkable stability.

Popular participation in local government along lines familiar to Westerners is limited. There are no trade unions, political parties, or popularly elected bodies through which local demands can be articulated. Neither is there a free press as defined by Western standards, though the UAE press enjoys more freedom than most others in the Arab world. Nevertheless, in the generally more open atmosphere following the 1990–1991 Gulf crisis, there has been considerable debate over development of a more responsive participatory system of government. This has been vigorously and extensively covered in the press. The great majority of Emirians, however, seem content with their government, most having known only the rule of Shaykh Zayid, not merely an astute and farsighted leader, but a revered father figure.

Delegation of responsibility between the federal and the local levels, like that in the United States during the first decades after its birth, is not in every instance as well defined as modern practitioners of public administration would prefer. Theoretically the federal government has control over defense, finance, and foreign affairs. In practice, however, the dual power exercised by the rulers as both members of the federal government and rulers of member states yields additional opportunities for control of the various shaykhdoms. In recent years, the governments of the smaller emirates have been able to provide many services, as in the tourist sector, previously provided by the federal government, because they now have access to skilled personnel trained in vocational and other educational institutions. Moreover, there has been some devolution of power within emiral governments, with municipalities assuming greater responsibility for their affairs as urban populations have grown. Sharjah has devolved some additional powers to its three enclaves on the UAE's Gulf of Oman coast. The integration of the shaykhdoms into a federation remains a complex task and a challenge fraught with myriad difficulties for the representatives of UAE officialdom.

In 1976 a potentially important step was taken toward integration when several emiral military forces were formally united and placed under the single command of the Union Defense Force. However, the two principal shaykhdoms, Abu Dhabi and Dubai, have still not fully integrated their defense forces into the union force; indeed the latter has created its own central military region command. Moreover, Fujayrah, Ras al-Khaymah, Sharjah, and Umm al-Qaywayn maintain their own national guard forces. The failure to develop a unified military reflects the general failure of the unionists, led by Shaykh Zayid, to create a centralized nation-state of the seven shaykhdoms. Thus far it is the loose federal model favored by his old rival, Shaykh Rashid, that has prevailed, and though many younger Emirians share Zayid's vision, the forces militating against it remain formidable. Well into his eighties, Zayid was, in 2002, no longer disposed to champion the cause as energetically as he once did, and no charismatic successor who might realize his vision of a strong union was in evidence. At the same time, the kinds of economic and security concerns that helped bring the seven shaykhdoms into a federation are still present, the habits of working together are well established, and the advantages of doing so are demonstrable. It seems likely, therefore, that the UAE will continue to muddle through as a loose federation for the indefinite future.

Foreign Policy

In its external relations the UAE is conservative and strives to maintain friendly ties with its neighbors. It is sometimes difficult for the outsider to understand UAE foreign relations inasmuch as each shaykhdom has considerable latitude in conducting its own economic and, to a lesser extent, political relations with foreign states. During the Iran-Iraq conflict of 1980–88, Dubai and Sharjah worked to preserve their close commercial ties with Iran while Abu Dhabi was providing financial and diplomatic assistance to Iraq. Iran's subsequent extension of its control in Abu Musa Island in 1992, which had been divided with Sharjah in 1971, may have induced greater caution in these shaykhdoms toward Iran. In the realm of oil policy, Dubai's vigorous, independent approach to the development of its wealth led it to remain outside of OPEC, leaving Abu Dhabi to face OPEC demands for adherence to a UAE quota that includes Dubai's production. (The UAE as a whole is now a member of OPEC.)

The UAE's leading foreign policy priority is Gulf security, which gives emphasis to the importance of its relations with its GCC neighbors. These are generally close and supportive, and longstanding border issues with Saudi Arabia and Oman have been definitively settled. In August 1990, when Iraq invaded Kuwait, the UAE was among the first of the Arab states to support an international military response. In October 1994, when Iraq moved its troops toward the Kuwaiti border, the UAE sent ground forces to Kuwait as an earnest of its support. Nevertheless, the UAE's interests and views sometimes cause it to pursue a course at odds with GCC partners. Just a year after supporting Kuwait against Iraqi threats, Shaykh Zayid called for an easing of U.N. sanctions against Iraq to reduce the suffering of the Iraqi people. Continuing a policy that placed it at odds with most of its GCC partners, the UAE in June 1998 restated its support for ending the economic blockade of Iraq, and in early 2000 the UAE restored diplomatic relations with Baghdad. The UAE's relations with the other major Gulf power, Iran, also caused tensions within the GCC. In the face of Iran's continued occupation of the Gulf islands claimed by the UAE, Abu Musa and the Tunbs, the GCC has diplomatically supported the UAE. However, the efforts of Saudi Arabia to pursue a rapprochement with Iran have caused great unease in the UAE.

The UAE has espoused a moderate policy on the Arab-Israeli conflict, supporting the peace process that grew out of the Madrid Conference of October 1991.

Since the collapse of the peace process in 2000–2001 and the Israeli-Palestinian violence that resulted, the UAE has been strongly supportive of the Palestinians. Shaykh Zayid has repeatedly criticized the United States for what he perceives to be a failure to pursue an evenhanded approach in its efforts to promote a settlement. UAE foreign policy has also focused special attention on resolution of inter-Arab differences. In his efforts to promote Arab unity during the 1980–88 Iran-Iraq conflict and to bring Egypt back into the Arab fold, Shaykh Zayid emerged as a leading Arab elder statesman.

Political and economic relations with the West have been important and generally friendly, though strained at times by Washington's policy on the Arab-Israeli conflict. The United States, Japan, and the United Kingdom are the UAE's major trading partners. With the moderation of Soviet policies the UAE extended diplomatic recognition to the Soviet Union in 1985 and has since established relations with the newly independent states of the former Soviet Union. In 1987–1988 the United States and the UAE cooperated closely to counter the threat to oil tankers by Iran, thereby laying the groundwork for close military cooperation with the United States and other members of the anti-Iraq coalition in 1990–1991. The UAE signed a defense pact with the United States in mid-1994. The pact has permitted the stationing of U.S. airborne refueling tankers on UAE territory.

In January 1995, the UAE also signed a defense accord with France, long a leading source of arms purchases, which provided for consultations in the event of aggression against or threats to UAE territory. In 2000, the UAE made an $8 billion purchase of eighty F-16 fighters superior to those in the U.S. Air Force's inventory. Through this deal, the UAE acquired software codes to permit alteration of friend-or-foe designations on the jets' cockpit displays that had never before been shared with a non-NATO ally. Further, the UAE pressured the United States to sell it Advanced Medium Range Air-to-Air Missiles (AMRAAMs), at that point not yet sold to any Middle Eastern country, including Israel, as the F-16 deal was being negotiated. Thus, an extraordinarily intimate security relationship has evolved between the two countries. However, the collapse of the Arab-Israeli peace process and the prospect of an indefinite continuation of Palestinian-Israeli violence, together with the ongoing issue of the Iraqi sanctions, suggests that the U.S.-UAE relationship will experience increased tensions.

Oman

Historical Background

Oman has a proud history dating back many centuries. It has maintained its independence since the expulsion of Portuguese garrisons from its coastal towns in the seventeenth century. A Persian attempt at occupation was thwarted through the leadership of Ahmad bin Sa'id Al Bu Sa'id, who was subsequently elected imam. The imamate in Oman was an Ibadi institution that combined religious and political leadership in a unique way. The Ibadis, distinct from Sunni and Shi'a Muslims, are a moderate branch of the Kharijites (or "seceders"), who rejected the authority of the caliphs who succeeded Omar, the second successor to the Prophet Muhammad. Ibadis adhere to a strict form of Islam that rejects limiting the selection of a caliph or imam to a particular clan or family, instead maintaining that the leader should be chosen only for his moral virtue and leadership ability.

Ahmad's successors abandoned the claim to the imamate and, in time, became purely secular rulers with the title sultan. This development created a political schism between the coastal areas administered from Muscat and the more conservative interior ruled by the imam. The sultans in Oman, as a security measure, developed a close association with Great Britain that continues to the present. With the assistance of British forces, the country was reunified in the 1950s after the military defeat of the imam at his interior stronghold of Nizwa. Unification was completed under Sultan Qabus, who, in a nearly bloodless coup in 1970, replaced his father, Sa'id bin Taimur (ruler since 1932), and changed the name of the country from the Sultanate of Muscat and Oman to simply the Sultanate of Oman.

The southernmost province of Dhufar, annexed in the late nineteenth century after it had been quasi-autonomous for years, became the site of an insurrection in the early 1960s. By 1968 leadership of the rebellion had been seized by the Marxist-oriented Popular Front for the Liberation of the Occupied Arabian Gulf (PFLOAG), the same group that changed its name in 1971 to the Popular Front for the Liberation of Oman and the Arab Gulf (also PFLOAG) and in 1974 to the Popular Front for the Liberation of Oman (PFLO). Supported by Soviet and Chinese aid channeled through South Yemen, the insurrection occupied large areas of the province by the early 1970s. The rebellion was finally put down in 1975, with British advisers and Iranian troops playing key roles in assisting Omani light infantry and tribal militia forces. Sultan Qabus assured Dhufari loyalties through the dispensing of generous development funds to the province. Under his rule the whole country was opened to the outside world on a scale unprecedented in its history, and the government simultaneously embarked on an ambitious program of socioeconomic development. For the first time an impressive array of modern government services has been extended to even the most remote regions of the interior of the country.

Political Environment

Located on the eastern reaches of the Arabian Peninsula, the Sultanate of Oman has an area two or three times greater than Kuwait, Bahrain, Qatar, and the UAE combined—212,000 square kilometers (82,000 square miles). There are no large cities in Oman. The population is 2,533,389 (2000 estimate). As much as a fourth of Oman's population is in the Greater Capital Area, which includes Muscat, the capital; Matrah, a major port; and Ruhi, the commercial hub of Oman. The main city of Inner Oman is Nizwa, traditional religious center of interior Oman. Sur, south of Muscat, is an important fishing port, and Salalah is the largest city and principal port of Dhufar, the southernmost province. Dhufar consists of three ranges of low mountains surrounding a small coastal plain and is separated from the rest of Oman by several hundred miles of desert. Oman proper consists of inner Oman and the coastal plain, known as the Batinah. Inner Oman contains a fertile plateau and the oldest towns in Oman. Separating this region from the Batinah is the Hajar mountain range, stretching in an arc from northwest to southeast and reaching nearly 3,000 meters (9,800 feet) in height at the Jabal al-Akhdar (Green Mountain). The majority of Oman's population is found along the Batinah coast, which has the country's greatest agricultural potential.

Population and Social Conditions

Most Omanis are Arab, though many Baluchis, who were originally from the coastal area of Iran and Pakistan, live along the Batinah coast. Many merchants of the capital region and the coast are Indians, either Hindus or Khojas (a community of Shi'a Muslims). There are also Persians and other groups of Shi'a Muslims, including some originally from Iraq or Iran. Dhufar and the surrounding desert are the home of several groups whose primary language is South Arabian. Shihuh tribes inhabit the northern, strategically important exclave of the Musandam Peninsula at the Strait of Hormuz. For years their origins were the subject of wild speculation; recent research has shown them to be of mixed Arab–Persian ancestry, as reflected in the mixed elements of their dialects. In recent years Oman has experienced an influx of migrant labor, principally from other Arab states and the Indian subcontinent. Oman's modest level of wealth has, however, enabled it to avoid the situation of Kuwait, Qatar, and the UAE, where foreigners have come to outnumber the indigenous population. The native population is about three quarters of the total.

With the change in government in 1970, Oman entered a new era. The accumulation of oil revenues over several years of production (exports began in 1967) was quickly put to work in an effort to modernize the country. Within a few years the number of schools increased from 3 to 431. By 1997, there were 967 primary and secondary schools, with a half million students in state education and over 19,000 in private education. The number of government employees was several hundred in 1970, and is now more than 100,000. A national university, named for Sultan Qabus, opened in 1986; its enrollment grew to over 5,000, almost evenly divided between men and women. At the start of Sultan Qabus's rule, the country was able to rely on the manpower and expertise of a number of Omanis who had migrated to Saudi Arabia and various Gulf countries for work and education in the years before 1970. Another important source of manpower was the "Zanzibaris"—Arabs of Omani origin whose ancestors had migrated to the former Omani possession of Zanzibar over the past two centuries. With the Africanization of Zanzibar many of them returned to Oman.

Economic Conditions

Economic development was almost totally neglected in Oman until the accession of Sultan Qabus. Since that time it has progressed steadily. In the early 1980s construction was completed on copper mining and refining facilities, and in 1984 two cement plants began operations. Since the mid-1980s Omani development policies for diversifying the economy have taken shape, thus lending it further strength. Light industry, including food processing, is being promoted at industrial estates in Muscat, Sohar, and Salalah, and privatization of government utilities is under way. Moreover, Oman is developing commercial laws that will facilitate foreign investment. By liberalizing its markets, Oman was able in 2001 to join the other small Arab Gulf states as a member of the World Trade Organization (WTO), further integrating itself in the global economy.

Oil is Oman's most important natural resource. Although the country's oil reserves are modest by Gulf standards, exploration has steadily expanded them, so that by 1995, production rose to nearly 760,000 bpd and oil-export earnings to a little less than $5 billion. By 1997 GNP was estimated at $10.6 billion, the equivalent of just under $5,000 per person. The upturn in oil prices in mid-1999 significantly enhanced Oman's economic performance. Increasing attention has been devoted to agriculture, which generates less than 3 percent of the GNP but employs as much as half of the labor force, although officially the figures indicated are much lower. Light industry is being developed to promote import substitution. Natural gas production continues to increase to reduce domestic demand for oil. Continued discoveries of new gas reserves make this a viable strategy for the next several decades. Tourism is also being developed. Oman alone among its neighbors has a minister of environment, and all new economic projects must have his approval.

Political Structure

Sultan Qabus's father, Said bin Taimur, maintained a basically traditional, personalized rule. Modern political institutions in Oman are therefore quite new. In November 1996, the sultan issued a decree establishing a Basic Statute of the State, which defines the state and its system of government and is, in effect, the sultanate's constitution. There are no political parties. The judiciary comprises both civil courts, which handle criminal cases, and Shari'a courts, responsible for family law matters. Judges are appointed by the sultan, and he is the final court of appeal. In the most remote regions, tribal law still functions in a rough and ready manner.

Sultan Qabus is head of state and all authority emanates from him. Shortly after coming to power, however, he created a formal council of ministers to carry out the administrative and legal operations of the government. The council is headed by the prime minister, who is appointed by the sultan. Although every important decision must have the approval of the sultan, the ministers have a great deal of discretion in day-to-day policy.

In 1976 the sultan reorganized regional and local government by establishing thirty-seven (currently fifty-nine) districts (*wilayats*), one province, and a municipality that embraces the capital. The districts are administered by governors appointed by the sultan. They collect taxes, provide local security, settle disputes, and advise the sultan. The province of Dhufar was historically a separate sultanate and still has more local autonomy than other regions. The municipality of Muscat was also considered important enough to warrant special status.

Over the past twenty years, Oman's political structure has evolved in three stages toward increasing popular participation in government. In 1981, reflecting concern that Sultan Qabus was insufficiently aware of public opinion, Oman established a consultative assembly to advise the sultan on matters of social, educational, and economic policy (defense and foreign policy are excluded). The members were drawn from the tribal and merchant communities as well as from government and were appointed by the sultan. Initially forty-five members served on the council, but the total was raised to fifty-five in 1985. This first experiment in representative government lasted for a decade.

In November 1990 the sultan announced the establishment of a new Consultative Council (Majlis al-Shura) to be made up of members selected from the country's districts. The sultan's decree called for regional representatives of each of the fifty-nine districts to nominate three candidates and the deputy prime minister for legal affairs to select one of the candidates to serve from each district, subject to the sultan's approval. In 1994 the Consultative Council's membership was expanded from fifty-nine to eighty, and women candidates could for the first time be nominated. Two were in fact selected in 1995. Although lacking legislative powers, the council was empowered to review social and economic legislation, to help draft and implement development plans, and propose improvement in public sectors. Ministries are required to submit to the council annual reports on their performance and plans and to answer questions from council members. The council may summon ministers at any time to discuss any issue within the purview of the various ministries. Moreover, the council is required to refer to its appropriate committees questions and suggestions from citizens on public issues and subsequently to inform the correspondents as to what action was taken. Members of the council are elected to three-year terms and may serve successive terms.

The Basic Statute of State reorganized Oman's government by creating an Oman Council (Majlis Oman), combining the Consultative Council with a new Council of State (Majlis al-Dawla). The latter was to comprise prominent appointed Omanis and serve a liaison role between government and people. In October 1997, elections were held for the Consultative Council with over 50,000 Omani men and women (3 percent of the total Omani population) eligible to vote in caucuses. From a total of 736 candidates, 164 were chosen, and Sultan Qabus then selected half of those to serve in the council. In September 2000, another election was held, with the number of those eligible to vote and run for election to the council increased to 175,000.

Political Dynamics

There are four politically important groups in Oman: the ruling family, the tribes, the expatriate advisers, and the merchant class. In many respects the Al Bu Sa'ids constitute the most important group. Among the sultan's most influential advisers are his cousins and uncles. They occupy a number of key ministerial and other government posts.

Traditionally the tribes have also played a significant role in the Omani political process. Under Qabus's father, Sultan Sa'id bin Taimur, manipulation of tribal rivalries was a major element in ruling the country. Qabus, on the other hand, has tried to decrease the power of the tribes through development of local administration such as local government councils. Although the tribes' influence may be reflected in the election of council candidates, especially in rural areas, their power has declined considerably.

Because of long, close relations with Great Britain, many of the foreign advisers are British. In the past Britons held key posts in the government and especially in the military. From 1984, when the army came under an Omani rather than a British commander, the process of Omanization of the military accelerated. Today, British personnel still play significant advisory roles in the military and security forces, but their influence is much less than before. In general, Oman continues to rely on foreigners for significant assistance in developing the country and will continue to do so for the foreseeable future.

The merchant community has traditionally been the sultan's link to the outside world. In addition to old Omani trading families, there are still many non-Omani merchant families from India and Pakistan, reflecting Oman's traditionally strong ties with the Indian Ocean countries. In recent years, however, there has been a more Westward orientation. Oman has participated in both Arab and world politics and has strengthened ties with the Western industrial world to acquire goods and services for its development programs. With the growth of oil revenues, many less-established Omanis have been able to enter the field of commerce, once monopolized by the traditional merchant families. The process has begun to dilute the latter group's power. Sultan Qabus and the political elite maintain an overwhelming monopoly of political power. The executive, legislative, and judicial authorities overlap, so that there is no real separation of powers. The Consultative Council has little real power, serving more as a sounding board for public opinion than as a real legislature. Nevertheless, the sultan appears to have set Oman on a course of transition, measured and deliberate, toward the establishment of democratic political institutions that will eventually exercise real independent power.

Foreign Policy

Before the reign of Sultan Qabus, Oman was one of the most isolated countries anywhere. It relied on the British air and naval bases in Salalah and on Masirah Island in the Arabian Sea. Qabus brought Oman out of its isolation both by necessity and design. He was obliged to seek outside support against the Dhufar insurgency, and he also sought to gain international and Arab acceptance for the Omani regime. He succeeded in reestablishing relations with Saudi Arabia, ruptured since 1955 when the Saudis (and other Arabs) backed the challenge of the imam of Oman against the regime. Qabus also established a close relationship with the shah of Iran, who sent troops to help in the fight against the Dhufari rebels. After the fall of the shah, Oman's relations with Iraq, which had supported the insurgents, quickly improved. In addition, Oman joined the GCC and became a leading advocate of closer military cooperation among its members in the face of the Iran-Iraq war. The sultan also strengthened ties with the United States, particularly in defense. In 1980, he signed an agreement granting the United States access to Omani military facilities, and Oman has subsequently participated in joint U.S. military exercises.

Oman often adopts independent foreign policy positions. It was one of only three Arab League states not to break relations with Egypt after Camp David and the Egypt-Israel Peace Treaty. Its 1980 security agreement with the United States drew considerable Arab criticism. Although Oman supported Iraq in its conflict with Iran, it moved quickly to improve relations after the war and established a bilateral economic cooperation committee with Iran in March 1989. Relations with South Yemen (now unified with North Yemen as the Yemen Republic) improved after mutual diplomatic recognition in 1983. The borders with Yemen have been settled and demarcated.

In keeping with its independent stance, Oman made an attempt to mediate the Gulf crisis of 1990, following Iraq's invasion of Kuwait. However, once such efforts were seen to be fruitless, Oman joined the Allied coalition and made available its facilities for both British and U.S. military forces during Operation Desert Shield/ Desert Storm, as it had during Western intervention in the Gulf in 1987–1988.

By the mid-1990s, Oman had begun to question the continuation of U.N. sanctions against Iraq. In November 1997, it expressed opposition to possible military action to force Iraqi agreement to weapons inspections by UNSCOM. Oman has continued to urge an end to the sanctions. Because Oman shares control of the Strait of Hormuz with Iran, it has always been anxious to maintain good relations with whatever government is in power in Tehran. Thus, Oman today seeks to promote bilateral links with Iran, especially in the economic field. Oman's penchant for pursuing an independent foreign policy is perhaps most evident in its relations with Israel. When Israeli Deputy Minister of Foreign Affairs Yossi Beilin visited Oman in 1994, it was the first official visit by an Israeli government representative to an Arab Gulf state. In December 1994, Israeli Prime Minister Yitzhak Rabin made an official visit to Oman to discuss the Middle East peace process, and his successor as prime minister, Shimon Peres, also visited Oman. The two countries agreed in January 1996 to establish low-level diplomatic relations. Although Oman withdrew the director of its trade bureau in Israel, because of the interruption of the peace process, it continued to maintain official contacts. For example, in September 2000, Youssef bin Alawi bin Abdullah, Oman's minister of state for foreign affairs, met with Israeli Prime Minister Ehud Barak in New York to discuss the peace process.

Bibliography

In the past few years a fairly considerable literature on developments in the Persian/Arab Gulf region has appeared. While some of it is of dubious quality, there is now a significant body of serious scholarly work on the Gulf Arab states to recommend to students of the area.

A good recent overview is *The Persian Gulf at the Millennium: Essays in Politics, Economy, Security, and Religion*, edited by Gary G. Sick and Lawrence G. Potter (New York: St. Martin's Press, 1997). An overview that links economics and politics in an interesting way is Khaldun al-Naqeeb, *Society and States in the Gulf and Arab Peninsula: A Different Perspective* (London: Routledge, 1990). Rosemarie Said Zahlan's *The Making of the Modern Gulf States: Kuwait, Bahrain, Qatar, the United Arab Emirates, and Oman* (Ithaca, N.Y.: Garnet, 1999) and Liesl Graz's *The Turbulent Gulf: People, Politics and Power* (New York: I.B. Tauris, 1992) may be usefully consulted.

For more detailed treatment of the individual states, the relevant volumes in the Westview Press series *Nations of the Contemporary Middle East* provide excellent starting points. They are: Jill Crystal, *Kuwait: The Transformation of an Oil State* (1992); Fred H. Lawson, *Bahrain: The Modernization of Autocracy* (1989); Bernard Reich and Steven Dorr, *Qatar* (1996); Malcolm C. Peck, *The United Arab Emirates: A Venture in Unity* (1986); and Calvin H. Allen, Jr., *Oman: The Modernization of the Sultanate* (1987). Each volume provides succinct descriptions and analyses of

the land, people, history, society, culture, economics, politics, and external relations of its sub-
ject. Two recent volumes on the UAE provide thoughtful essays. They are Joseph A.
Kechichian, ed., *A Century in Thirty Years: Shaykh Zayed and the United Arab Emirates* (Washing-
ton, D.C.: Middle East Policy Council, 2000), and Edmund Ghareeb and Ibrahim Al Abed,
Perspectives on the United Arab Emirates (London: Trident Press, 1997). Joseph A. Kechichian's
Oman and the World: The Emergence of an Independent Foreign Policy (Santa Monica, Calif.:
RAND, 1995) adds usefully to the literature on that country.

John E. Peterson's *Defending Arabia* (New York: St. Martin's Press, 1986), although dated,
provides an excellent background and introduction to security issues in the Gulf. Anthony
H. Cordesman's The *Military Balance in the Gulf* (Washington, D.C.: Center for Strategic
and International Affairs, 2001) presents a detailed analysis of the military balance and force
trends in the five countries covered in this chapter, as well as Iran, Iraq, Saudi Arabia, and
Yemen. Security issues broadly defined are dealt with in David E. Long and Christian
Koch, eds., *Gulf Security in the Twenty-First Century* (Abu Dhabi, UAE: The Emirates Center
for Strategic Studies and Research, 1997).

There are several good treatments of the internal politics of the Gulf Arab states. Jill
Crystal's *Oil and Politics in the Gulf: Rulers and Merchants in Kuwait and Qatar*, rev. ed. (New
York: Cambridge University Press, 1994) examines the impact of oil on the process of state
building in two of the states covered in this chapter. Mary-Ann Tétreault's *Stories of Democracy: Politics and Society in Contemporary Kuwait* (New York: Columbia University, 2000) is
the thoughtful analysis of a leading scholar on contemporary Kuwait. In *Oil Monarchies: Domestic and Security Challenges in the Arab Gulf States* (New York: Council on Foreign Relations Press, 1994), F. Gregory Gause III surveys the Gulf states, including Saudi Arabia, focusing on issues arising from the Gulf War. Though dated and, regrettably, long out of
print, John Duke Anthony's *Arab States of the Lower Gulf: People, Politics, Petroleum* (Washington, D.C.: Middle East Institute, 1975) remains a valuable source. *From Trucial States to Emirates* (London: Longman, rev. ed., 1996), by Frauke Heard-Bey, is a detailed and deeply in-
formed account of the process by which the UAE emerged. Although obviously dated,
John E. Peterson's *The Gulf Arab States: Steps Toward Political Participation*, Washington Paper
No. 131 (New York: Praeger, with the Center for Strategic and International Studies, Washington, D.C., 1988), remains a very useful source on the Gulf states' political institutions.

Two very good analyses of the Gulf Cooperation Council, its objectives, and structure
are Erik R. Peterson, *The Gulf Cooperation Council: Search for Unity in a Dynamic Region*
(Boulder: Westview Press, 1988), and John Sandwick, ed., *The Gulf Cooperation Council:
Moderation and Stability in an Interdependent World* (Boulder: Westview Press, in association
with the American-Arab Affairs Council, Washington, D.C., 1987). Also recommended is
Joseph W. Twinam's *The Gulf, Cooperation and the Council: An American Perspective* (Washington, D.C.: Middle East Policy Council, 1992).

A spate of books appeared in the aftermath of the Gulf crisis of 1990–1991. *The Gulf War
Reader: History, Documents, Opinions*, ed. Micah L. Sifry and Christopher Cerf (New York:
Times Books of Random House, 1991), is an excellent collection of official speeches and
commentaries representing a wide variety of viewpoints. *Islamic Fundamentalism and the Gulf
Crisis*, ed. James Piscatori (Philadelphia: American Academy of Arts and Sciences for the
Fundamentalism Project, 1991), and Ghazi A. Algosaibi, *The Gulf Crisis: An Attempt to Under-*

stand (London: Kegan Paul International, 1993), look at the crisis from important angles generally overlooked. The first examines responses by a number of Islamic movements to the Gulf War and the latter offers the perspective of a thoughtful Saudi Arab diplomat-scholar.

Periodicals are an important source of information on the Arab Gulf states. The *Middle East Journal*, published by the Middle East Institute, Washington, D.C., is a quarterly that publishes a very wide selection of book reviews and a chronology of events, as well as articles on the contemporary Middle East. The *International Journal of Middle East Studies*, published quarterly by Cambridge University Press, is the principal academic periodical devoted to the Middle East. *Middle East Report* (quarterly), *Middle East Policy* (quarterly), and *Middle East Insight* (monthly), are Washington, D.C., publications that frequently include useful articles on current developments in the Arab Gulf states.

Among the many Internet web sites that provide helpful information on the states covered in this chapter, that of the Gulf/2000 Project at Columbia University is worthy of special mention (http://gulf 2000.columbia.edu).

7

Republic of Yemen

F. Gregory Gause III

On May 22, 1990, North Yemen, or the Yemen Arab Republic (YAR), and South Yemen, or the People's Democratic Republic of Yemen (PDRY), united in a single state, the Republic of Yemen. Unification had been a stated policy goal of both regimes since their inceptions—the YAR, which replaced the imamate in 1962, and the PDRY, following independence from Great Britain in 1967.

Popular support for unity had always been strong on both sides, but numerous problems had to be surmounted. There was little historical precedent for a unitary state. Political fragmentation had been the dominant theme of Yemeni history due to tribal and confessional differences, and with a Marxist cast to the PDRY, or Aden, regime, ideological differences divided the two states. Between 1970 and 1990 bilateral relations had been stormy and occasionally violent.

The rivalry between the two political leaderships did not abate with unity; it simply converted to a domestic arena. The rivalry culminated in the summer of 1994 with an armed secessionist uprising in the south led by former leaders of the PDRY. Victory over the secessionists by the central government under YAR President Ali Abdallah Salih and his supporters—including Yemeni Islamists and disaffected members of the former PDRY leadership—ended separatism in the south, but it did not end the unified country's problems. After that, the Yemeni government struggled, with only mixed success, with the daunting tasks of state building and economic development.

The Land and People

Occupying the southeastern corner of the Arabian Peninsula, Yemen can be roughly divided into five geographical areas. The hot, humid coastal plain extending inland from the Red Sea Coast is called Tihama. Much of the population there is descended from emigrants and slaves from Africa. Its major city is the country's major port of Hudayda. North of San'a are the northern highlands, reaching 12,000 feet in elevation. They are home to the largest Yemeni tribal confederations. The major city is Sa'da. From San'a south to Aden and somewhat east is an area of less precipitous highlands, plains, and valleys, the center of Yemeni agriculture. Aden is the best natural port on the southern end of the Arabian Peninsula. Between those cities is the important commercial city of Taiz. Between this area and the great Rub' al-Khali desert to the east is an arid region known as the Jawf. There are no major cities in the Jawf; Marib is the most important town. Tribal social organization predominates in the Jawf.

The fifth geographical area is the Wadi Hadramawt, an immense, seasonally dry river valley running parallel to the Arabian Sea coast about 150,200 kilometers (90,120 miles) inland, in the eastern section of Yemen. The valley, in which seasonal cultivation is possible, begins in the highlands north of the port city of Mukalla, running northeast through the towns of Shibam, Sayun, and Tarim before turning south and reaching the Arabian Sea coast at Sayhut. The Hadrami economy was always oriented more toward India and Southeast Asia than toward Aden and the Red Sea. Hadrami merchant communities were established in Indonesia centuries ago, and a small number of Hadramis still reside there. Many of the Muslim princes of India recruited Hadrami mercenaries for their armies.

Yemen has been a distinct cultural and civilizational unit for millennia. Both the Bible and the Quran refer to the thriving South Arabian city states of Sheba (Saba), and Marib, which developed an extraordinary irrigation system fed by a grand canal from a reservoir based on a large dam, remnants of which still stand. Through control of the supply of frankincense and myrrh, highly valued in the pagan Roman Empire, South Arabia enjoyed a high civilization, with its own language and alphabet, that flourished in the centuries immediately before and after the start of the Christian era. Because the area is the beneficiary of monsoon rains and thus could support agriculture, Roman geographers called it Arabia Felix, "happy Arabia," to contrast it to the rest of the peninsula which they named Arabia Deserta.

Yemen's distinct ethnic identity is based in large part on tribal roots. All peninsula Arabs (and many non–Arabian Arabs) claim descent from one of two ancestors, Adnan and Qahtan. Most Yemenis are Qahtanis, whereas most other peninsular Arabs, particularly farther north, are Adnanis.

Yemen was among the first regions to accept the preaching of Muhammad, and Yemenis were prominent in the Arab Islamic armies that swept out of Arabia in the seventh century. The most enduring division in Yemeni society is sectarian and had its beginnings in the invitation extended by the two leading clans of Sa'da in A.D. 893 to a respected arbitrator from al-Madina, Yahya ibn Husayn ibn Qasim al-Rassi, to come to regulate their city's affairs. Al-Rassi was a descendent of the Prophet Muhammad and an adherent of the Zaydi branch of Shi'a Islam. He established a

Zaydi state in northern Yemen and is recognized as the first Zaydi imam of Yemen. Although the imamate's fortunes waxed and waned, the institution endured in northern Yemen until it was replaced by a republic following the 1962 revolution. About one-third of the population of the Republic of Yemen are Zaydi Shi'a Muslims; the others are adherents of the Shafi'i school of jurisprudence of Sunni Islam.

There has been an indigenous Jewish community in Yemen for millennia, mostly in the northern highlands. Though not on fully equal terms with Muslims, they enjoyed a protected status under the imams and were an accepted segment of the society. Following the creation of Israel in 1948, however, most of the Jewish community left in an airlift, "Operation Magic Carpet," which the United States helped to organize. No one expected such large numbers to migrate and many from remote villages apparently viewed the airlift as a mystical experience far removed from contemporary politics.

The two great tribal confederations in northern Yemen, the Hashid and the Bakil, trace their lineages to pre-Islamic times. They were the principal supporters of the Yemeni states that periodically grew up around dynamic Zaydi imams, providing the military support for the extension of imamate rule into the Shafi'i areas to the south and east. The tribes of northern Yemen would frequently allow an imam to act as judge in their disputes and would answer his call to jihad against non-Zaydis; but his rule always depended upon his personal stature and his ability to persuade. The mountainous areas of northern Yemen made it difficult for any central authority to control the tribes for an extended period of time. The imams relied on their ability to play the tribes off against one another, to bargain and adjudicate, and to appeal to sectarian loyalty in order to rule. Despite the tenuous and personal nature of imamic rule, for centuries the imamate and the two great tribal confederations provided an institutional basis for organized political life in the northern part of Yemen.

In other areas the institutional bases of large-scale political organization have not historically been present. Village rather than tribe was the dominant form of social organization in Tihama and the southern highlands. Tribes in Hadramawt and the areas north and east of Aden tended to be much smaller and more fragmented than those of the northern highlands. The southern areas tended to be governed by small, localized political units and were frequently subjected to invasion and occupation both by powerful imams from the north and by foreign empires, though Hadramawt, because of its geographical isolation, was less subject to foreign rule than Tihama or the southern highlands.

Modern Political History

The two most important foreign conquests for modern Yemen occurred in the nineteenth century. In 1839 the British Indian government captured Aden, placing it under the direct rule of the British raj in Bombay. Aden's port became an important strategic link in Britain's line of sea communications to India, and the opening of the Suez Canal increased the port's strategic and commercial importance. In 1849, in response to the British capture of Aden and as part of a general policy of reasserting central control over the hinterlands of the empire, the Ottoman government in Istanbul sent troops to San'a to reassert its long-lapsed control over the northern areas of Yemen. In 1873, reacting to efforts by the Ottoman governor of Yemen to bring tribal leaders near Aden under his control, the British government notified Istanbul that it expected the independence of those tribes to be respected. Between 1886 and 1914, Britain concluded a number of protectorate treaties with local shaykhs and sultans, offering British recognition and a stipend in exchange for a pledge not to enter into relations with any other foreign power, particularly the Ottoman Empire. In 1904 London and Istanbul demarcated their Yemeni spheres of influence, drawing the border that would later become the international border between the YAR and the PDRY.

Ottoman control in North Yemen never effectively extended into the mountainous northern highlands, where forbidding geography, tribal autonomy, and imamic authority proved to be significant barriers. The Hamid al-Din dynasty, which assumed the Zaydi imamate in the mid-nineteenth century, revived that institution and rallied tribal support in opposition to the Ottomans. In 1911 Imam Yahya ended the revolt against the Ottomans in the Treaty of Da'an. The Ottomans recognized Yahya's temporal control over the northern highlands in exchange for his acceptance of their rule in Shafi'i areas. When the Ottoman Empire collapsed at the end of World War I and Yahya asserted his control over all of North Yemen, the imamate was perceived by most Shafi'is as a sectarian rather than a national institution. Although he made no effort to convert his newly acquired Shafi'i subjects, Yahya (and his son Ahmad, who succeeded him as imam in 1948) installed Zaydi administrators in Shafi'i areas. Their limited efforts to build a modern military were based on recruitment of Zaydis. The Shafi'is, living in the more prosperous areas and controlling what commerce there was in Yemen, felt the harshest burden of the imam's taxes.

The state apparatus built by the imams was rudimentary at best. Efforts were made to develop a modern army, but they were hampered by a severe lack of resources. When seriously challenged, Imam Ahmad relied on the support of tribal forces to quell his opposition, as the regular army was neither capable nor reliable. Bureaucratic administration was nearly nonexistent: The imams relied upon Zaydi notables and religious scholars to collect taxes and manage local affairs. Little if any effort was put into the development of physical infrastructure or investment in human capital through education. Imams Yahya and Ahmad deliberately kept the country isolated, in a futile effort to keep ideological influences that would threaten their regime out of Yemen. Thus, on the eve of the revolution of 1962, the North Yemeni state was a relatively weak institution, the Zaydi tribes of the northern highlands had substantial autonomy, and elites in the Shafi'i southern areas of the country were politically disaffected but had few organizational avenues through which to express their dissatisfaction.

In the south, British colonialism had very different but equally important consequences for Aden, where Britain ruled directly, and for the tribal areas, where British influence was exercised through local rulers. For roughly the first hundred years of their presence in Aden, the British maintained a conscious distance from the domestic politics of the hinterland. Aside from preventing the growth of Ottoman power, Britain had little interest in the protectorate states. In the mid-1930s, a combination of pressure from Imam Yahya, who pressed his claim to the protectorates, serious economic crises in South Yemen, and a desire on the part of some British colonial officials to bring "good government" to the tribes led Britain to take a more active role in protectorate politics. The vehicle for that involvement was a series of treaties negotiated with the various shaykhs and sultans between 1941 and 1952; the rulers agreed to accept British advice in the conduct of their governments in exchange for British financial and military support.

These new treaties had the effect of freezing the previously fluid political environment in the protectorates, as Britain was committed to supporting particular rulers. British-officered military formations were established, British administrative and tax-collecting institutions introduced, and direct financial support to the individual rulers provided. Although these moves had the short-term effect of consolidating the power of Britain's clients in the protectorate states, in the longer term the rulers were cut off from the historical sources of their power. With British military and financial support, the rulers no longer needed to be sensitive to the nuances of local and tribal politics that had previously been the basis of their rule. In the name of "good government," many of the tenuous ties that linked ruler to ruled in the protectorates were severed: Cash disbursements to tribal notables were pared, nepotism reduced, and weapons no longer distributed to tribesmen. Local leaders who proved to be too independent were removed by Britain, replaced by more pliant relatives.

Socioeconomic changes also disrupted political structures in the protectorates. The introduction of private property converted many rulers and tribal shaykhs into landlords and their tribesmen into landless laborers, weakening the bonds of loyalty that had been historically reinforced by collective tribal control of land. The growth of motorized transport, British road building, and the consolidation by British advisers of customs collection threatened the livelihood of camel breeders and caravan merchants and of tribes that relied on caravan tolls for income. They often reacted by rebelling against local leaders and blockading the roads, which, in the most serious cases, prompted the British authorities in Aden to turn to aerial bombardment and dispatch of ground forces.

The socioeconomic and political changes in Aden during this period were even more dramatic. In the 1950s and 1960s Aden had no peer as an urban center in Yemen, or in all of Arabia. It was a major commercial port, the second busiest in the world behind New York in port calls in 1958; it was a major headquarters of a major British military presence for the entire Indian ocean; and its polyglot population included a large number of Indians and Europeans. The only modern secondary school in all Yemen was located there, and Aden's exposure to the outside world made it a major spawning ground for modern secular political ideologies introduced into the Yemeni political environment: liberalism, communism, Arab nationalism, and socialism.

Many of the earlier adherents of these new ideologies were sent to Britain as students by the Aden Trade Union Congress (ATUC). The students were drawn from an urban proletariat, mostly from North Yemen and the protectorates, who found work at facilities like the British Petroleum refinery, the port, and the military installations. Trade unionism was encouraged by British colonial administrators and the British trade union movement alike.

Both North and South Yemen thus approached the 1960s having undergone important political and, in the south, social change. Those changes, augmented by the interference of external actors, erupted in sustained political conflicts that would consume the political energies of both countries for the better part of the decade.

Having survived a number of challenges to his rule, Imam Ahmad died in September 1962 and was succeeded by his son Muhammad al-Badr. The new imam had something of a progressive reputation, largely because he had encouraged his father to ally with Gamal Abd al-Nasser's Egypt in Yemen's efforts to assert its claims to South Yemen. While Nasser was opposing British rule in South Arabia, his intelligence services established contacts with dissident officers in the imam's army. With the ascension of the new imam, these officers solicited Egyptian support in a coup. The coup was executed on September 26, 1962. Colonel Abdallah al-Sallal, the coup leader, became president of the new Yemen Arab Republic. The first contingent of Egyptian troops arrived the next day, and ultimately they numbered as many as 60,000.

The republican regime relied on Egyptian military support to maintain itself in power, although there were three Yemeni factions that supported the coup. The first was the army itself, whose strength in society depended largely upon Egyptian support. The second was made up of disaffected Shafi'is from the southern part of the country, where opposition to the imamate had grown in the 1940s and 1950s. A number of their leaders returned from Aden to take up positions in the new government, where they organized anti-imamate activity. The third group was a collection of tribal leaders who had split from Imam Ahmad after an abortive 1959 revolt. In the revolt's aftermath Ahmad executed the paramount shaykh of the Hashid tribal confederation, Husayn al-Ahmar, whom he suspected of involvement. The shaykh's son Abdallah, who succeeded his father, was a stalwart supporter of the republic.

Opposition to the new regime was widespread in the Zaydi tribal areas. The young imam escaped during the coup and, with the support of Saudi Arabia, began rallying tribal forces to oppose the republic. The Saudis felt threatened by a republican military coup on the Arabian Peninsula and by the presence of Egyptian troops near the Saudi border. Members of the new republican government voiced Yemeni claims to the border areas of Najran, Jizan, and Asir, won by Saudi Arabia in its 1934 war with the imamate, and Egyptian jets bombed Saudi territory near the border, where supporters of the imamate, who became known as royalists, were organizing their efforts against the republic. Thus the Yemeni civil war immediately assumed an inter-Arab dimension, becoming caught up in the Egyptian-Saudi feud and in the larger tensions between "progressive" and "reactionary" regimes (in Nasser's terms) in the Arab world.

The major turning point in the conflict occurred with the defeat of Egypt in the 1967 Arab-Israeli war. At that time some 40,000 Egyptian troops were still in Yemen, and Abd al-Nasser's involvement in the Yemeni civil war was seen by many in Egypt as a contributing factor in the defeat. The Egyptians withdrew from Yemen by the end of 1967. Two years of desultory fighting finally led to the March 1970 reconciliation among the YAR, the royalists, and Saudi Arabia that ended the civil war. The republican form of government was maintained, and major figures from the royalist camp, excluding members of the Hamid al-Din family, were integrated into the weak and decentralized North Yemeni state.

The principal result of the civil war was the strengthening of the independent power of the tribal shaykhs who had been courted during the hostilities by republicans and royalists, Saudis, and Egyptians, all offering cash payments and small arms. Because the shaykhs controlled the flow of money and guns to tribesmen, their political position inside their tribal areas was vastly strengthened, and the tribes themselves emerged from the fighting well armed and battle tested. During the 1970s tribal forces were more than a match for the regular Yemeni army.

Conversely, the idea of a strong central government had been delegitimized for many Yemenis by the controlling role that the Egyptians had come to play in San'a. President al-Sallal was overthrown shortly after Egypt's defeat in the 1967 Arab-Israeli war, and was replaced by a four-member presidential council and a legislative assembly. The 1970 peace settlement added an extra member to the presidential council and ten extra members to the assembly and guaranteed a substantial amount of autonomy for regional officials, most of whom were tribal leaders or local notables. State power in North Yemen was fragmented at the center and weakly enforced in the countryside.

The 1960s were also a decisive and strife-torn decade in South Yemen. The North Yemeni revolution and Egyptian hegemony over the republican regime provided a strong base of support for South Yemeni dissidents.

Opposition to the British during the 1950s had been largely centered in Aden itself, based on the trade union movement. Sporadic tribal uprisings in the protectorates rarely if ever took on an overt political coloration. That changed in 1963, when a tribal revolt in Radfan, north of Aden, came under the control of the National Front for the Liberation of South Yemen. The National Liberation Front (NLF) was formed at a meeting in San'a in February 1963. The prime movers behind the organization were the Sha'bi clan of Lahaj, led by Qahtan al-Sha'biSha'bi and his cousin Faysal al-Sha'biSha'bi. Although a number of tribal figures and dissident officers from the British-led forces in South Arabia participated, the core of the NLF was made up of adherents of the Yemeni branch of the Arab Nationalists' Movement (ANM), a Marxist-leaning pan-Arab group founded at the American University of Beirut in 1948.

The NLF distinguished itself from the Aden-based opposition groups by advocating armed struggle against the British and by concentrating as much of its organizational efforts in the protectorates as in Aden. Egypt supported the NLF from its inception. Though British forces had restored at least nominal control over Radfan in June 1964, the NLF organized military activity throughout the countryside and undertook a series of violent attacks on British interests in Aden itself. By the end of 1965, the NLF had succeeded in wresting control of most of the unions from the ATUC, and ATUC leaders created a rival group, the Front for the Liberation of Occupied South Yemen (FLOSY), which took refuge in Cairo.

In February 1966 the British government announced its intention to withdraw from the area by early 1968 and to terminate its treaties of protection with the local states. Egypt, anxious to consolidate its influence in the area, pushed the NLF to merge with FLOSY and other Aden-based opposition groups. Local NLF leaders rejected this pressure and broke with Nasser, whereas FLOSY and NLF leaders in North Yemen and in Cairo continued to look to Egypt for support. Under Egyptian urging, the rivals agreed to a reconciliation in August 1966, but it quickly fell apart. By the eve of the British withdrawal, the NLF had become the unquestioned leader of the independence movement.

As British units withdrew from the protectorates, the regimes of the British-supported shaykhs and sultans fell to forces of the NLF. The front won a brief civil war in Aden in September–October 1967, and the army trained by Britain to defend what was to be the successor state in South Yemen instead declared its allegiance to the front. British forces evacuated Aden on November 30, 1967, ending 128 years of rule, and the NLF formed the first government of the newly declared People's Republic of South Yemen the same day, naming Qahtan al-Sha'biSha'bi both chairman of the presidential council and prime minister.

The collapse of the shaykhs and the sultans left the field open for an organized and disciplined political party like the National Front ("Liberation" was dropped soon after independence) to dominate the new state. The front had resisted all Arab pressures to form a coalition with other opposition groups and had defeated its rivals for control of the new state on the battlefield. Having attained that goal, it set out ruthlessly to strengthen its hold both on the institutions of the state and on South Yemeni society as a whole. Unlike in North Yemen, where the experience of civil war had strengthened tribal autonomy and led to the emergence of a weak and fragmented state, in South Yemen the independence struggle had seen the destruction of tribal political structures and the monopolization of state power by a single political party. The National Front was not successful in eliminating tribalism as a social reality in the South, but it was able to destroy the capacity of tribal groups to challenge its political control. Through its control over economic and social institutions it denied any group in South Yemen the autonomy and power to develop as a political rival. With the help of the Soviet Union, and despite serious factional infighting, the National Front in South Yemen was better able to impose control over politics and society than was the regime of North Yemen.

Thus the two Yemeni states that emerged in the late 1960s were very different entities despite their common Yemeni identity. The North, with a population between 4.5 and 6 million, about four times greater than that of the South, was essentially a place where society was largely autonomous and the state struggled to assert a role. In the South the state smothered and controlled society, encouraging large-scale population movements to the North among southerners looking for greater political and economic freedom. However, during the late 1960s and the 1970s the two states both experienced violent political factionalism. With the lifting of the siege of San'a in 1968, the North Yemeni republican forces split along ideological lines, a split reinforced by sectarian differences. More doctrinaire leftist elements, made up mostly of Shafi'is and supported by the new South Yemeni republic, had strengthened themselves during the siege. More conservative and tribal republican elements, mostly Zaydis, mobilized to oppose them. In a full-scale battle in and around San'a in August 1968 the "republican conservatives" defeated the leftists, ending the chances that North Yemen would follow the ideological path of the South and causing tensions that would characterize the relationship of the two Yemens for most of the 1960s and 1970s.

Though the events of 1968 established the ideological direction of the North, they did not end instability at the top levels of the state. The civilian government that had assumed power after the coup against al-Sallal in 1967 was overthrown by Colonel Ibrahim al-Hamdi in 1974, ushering in a new period of military rule. Al-Hamdi was a strong and popular leader who attempted to build state institutions and a political party and to bring tribal political power under state control by using the regular army to confront tribal forces. He was assassinated in October 1977. His successor, also a military man, was Ahmad al-Ghashmi, who died in June 1978 when an emissary from South Yemen brought a briefcase loaded with explosives into his office. Colonel Ali Abdallah Salih succeeded al-Ghashmi.

Shortly after taking office, Salih was subject to an assassination attempt and a serious coup plot. A substantial armed opposition supported by South Yemen, called the National Democratic Front, actively challenged the Salih regime for control of large areas of the southern part of North Yemen. Salih was able to suppress the National Democratic Front after three years of fighting, including a brief border war with South Yemen. This incoherence at the top, combined with the original weakness of the North Yemeni state, meant that serious efforts at state building in the North were limited and fragmented during the 1970s. A bureaucratic infrastructure was developed, but the North Yemeni state had little ability to extend itself effectively into society, particularly outside the major urban areas.

South Yemen also saw a large amount of political violence in the late 1960s and early 1970s, though that violence was the result of factional infighting within the National Front, not challenges from other groups to the front's rule. In June 1969 the president of South Yemen, Qahtan al-Sha'biSha'bi, was overthrown by a group of Marxist militants. Although al-Sha'biSha'bi had been titular leader of the National Front during the struggle against the British, he had spent most of that time outside the country, either in North Yemen or in Cairo. The Marxist faction of the front was dominated by leaders of the armed struggle who had stayed in the country during the independence fight. As a signal of their more doctrinaire inclinations, the new leadership changed the name of the country in 1970 to the People's Democratic Republic of Yemen.

The new president of South Yemen, Salim Rubayya' Ali, faced a challenge from the head of the National Front party apparatus, Abd al-Fattah Ismail. Some sources attributed their differences to ideological interpretations of Marxism, with Salim Rubayya' seen as more of a Maoist and Ismail as more Soviet-style. Salim Rubayya' made his name in the front by organizing in the tribal hinterland. Ismail was a front organizer in Aden. The latter built the ruling party apparatus, whereas the former relied on state institutions, funneling foreign aid to projects of people loyal to him. Salim Rubayya' in the mid-1970s explored the possibility of a rapprochement between South Yemen and Saudi Arabia, whereas Ismail was a strong supporter of the country's ties with the Soviet Union. Their conflict erupted into violence in June 1978, in the aftermath of South Yemeni involvement in the death of North Yemeni President al-Ghashmi. In a day of bloody fighting in Aden, Salim Rubayya' was killed. In 1980 Ismail, who had assumed the presidency, was forced out of office by a coalition with the National Front that opposed his efforts to monopolize power in his own hands. Ali Nasir Muhammad, who had been prime minister, was named president of the state and head of the Yemeni Socialist Party, the successor organization to the National Front. By 1986 many of Ali Nasir's allies in the removal of Ismail had turned against him, and in January of that year more than a week of heavy fighting among the party factions convulsed Aden and the surrounding area, resulting in over 4,000 deaths and untold damage to property. Ali Nasir was ousted from power and escaped to the North. Haydar Abu Bakr al-Attas, the prime minister, was made president of the state and Ali Salim al-Baydh, one of the few old National Front cadres to survive the fighting, became head of the Yemeni Socialist Party.

The turbulence of the domestic politics of the two Yemeni states, particularly during the early 1980s, was exacerbated by the tensions between them. Both were committed to the principle of Yemeni unity, but the leaders were unwilling to make the necessary compromises to achieve that goal. Their reluctance was understandable, given the ideological differences between the two states. Unity would inevitably have required the victory of one side over the other. But their inability to find a compromise road to unity did not remove the issue from the agenda. Rather, the cause of unity was invoked as a reason for each Yemeni state to meddle in the domestic politics of the other, supporting opposition groups and attempting to change the regime in the other state.

The deterioration of relations between North and South began in early 1968 with the successful campaign by republican conservatives in the North against Northern leftist elements who were aligned with the new South Yemeni regime. Many of the latter found refuge in Aden after their defeat. Likewise, supporters of both the British-backed rulers in the South and the ousted South Yemeni president, Qahtan al-Sha'biSha'bi, found their way to the North. With the strong support of Saudi Arabia and a number of North Yemeni tribal and political figures, opposition groups launched attacks across the South Yemeni border in 1971 and 1972. The PDRY army answered in kind. San'a could do little to control the military situation and was happy to begin negotiations when Aden called for a cease-fire. Those negotiations, conducted in Cairo in October 1972, yielded the first agreement to unify the two countries. The agreement was rejected by South Yemeni dissidents and by important tribal leaders in the North, who saw it as the first step toward Marxist infiltration into the YAR. Saudi Arabia also applied heavy pressure within North Yemen to encourage opposition to the agreement. North Yemeni Prime Minister Muhsin al-Ayni, who negotiated the unity deal, resigned in December 1972, and the agreement became a dead letter.

A similar scenario played itself out in 1978–79, though with the players reversed. This time it was South Yemen encouraging domestic opposition groups in the North to challenge militarily the regime in San'a, which had been weakened by the assassinations of al-Hamdi and al-Ghashmi in less than a year. In February 1979 regular army units from South Yemen crossed the border to support the military actions of their allies in the North. By mid-March they were in control of significant amounts of territory in the south and east of the YAR. With its own army performing poorly, the North Yemeni government mobilized tribal irregulars to confront the southern forces. Saudi Arabia called on the United States to come to North Yemen's aid. Washington, whose relationship with the Saudis had been shaken both by the fall of the shah of Iran and the Camp David accords, sent naval forces to the region, rushed through an arms deal for North Yemen, dispatched AWACS (airborne warning and control system) aircraft to Saudi Arabia, and pressed Moscow to restrain its South Yemeni ally. Into this atmosphere of crisis stepped Syria and Iraq, temporarily allied against Camp David, with a cease-fire proposal that was accepted by both Yemeni states. The fighting ended with an agreement to unify the two states; it was signed by Ali Abdallah Salih and Abd al-Fattah Ismail in Kuwait in March 1979. As in 1972, Saudi Arabia and its allies within North Yemen again mobilized to oppose the agreement, with the Saudis eventually suspending aid payments to San'a. By spring 1980 North Yemeni President Salih had reversed course, patching up relations with the Saudis and moving to combat the power of South Yemen's allies in the North.

By summer 1982 Salih had succeeded in ending the armed opposition to his regime in North Yemen. With the ouster of Abd al-Fattah Ismail from power in Aden in 1980, the South Yemeni government ceased its active support for the North Yemeni opposition, ushering in an unprecedented period of calm in the relations between the two states. Salih used this calm to consolidate his regime. The 1980s was a time of political stability in the North, allowing for the strengthening of state institutions and for greater concentration on economic development. Salih also launched a ruling political party, the General People's Congress, the first of its kind in the North. While the North was enjoying a respite from political turbulence, the South was experiencing the chaos occasioned by political infighting at the top levels of the leadership, culminating in the 1986 explosion in Aden. In 1986 North Yemen remained scrupulously uninvolved in the events in the South. It prevented South Yemeni exile leaders from organizing the new waves of refugees pouring into the North into a paramilitary opposition. This restraint helped set the tone for further improvement in the relationship between the two Yemeni states, an improvement that culminated in the May 1990 unity agreement.

Political Environment of the United Yemeni State

The history of Yemeni politics has been one of dichotomies: Zaydi versus Shafi'i, republican versus royalist, tribe versus state, North versus South. The sectarian division is a continuing factor in Yemeni political life. Tribal power in the northern highlands and the Jawf remains a significant element of the political equation, and there are signals that tribal structures in what was South Yemen are reviving their political influence. However, it would be a mistake to underestimate the factors in favor of social cohesion in Yemen. The common Yemeni identity is strong, made stronger by the country's bordering on Saudi Arabia to the north. Millions of Yemenis have worked as laborers in Saudi Arabia since the oil boom of the early 1970s, and that experience has tended to strengthen their Yemeni self-identification. There is no substantial ideological or theological barrier to cooperation between Zaydis and Shafi'is, and Yemenis regularly discount the significance of sectarian identities in discussing their own politics. The border between the two former states was nothing more than a line on paper, with no geographical, sectarian, or ethnic division giving it more than a superficial political reality. If there is one area in Yemen that is historically distinct from the rest of the country, it is Hadramawt, with its long history of isolation from the political orders in Aden and San'a and its past ties to South and Southeast Asia. However, it appears that Hadramawt, as a result of British and then South Yemeni policies, has been firmly integrated into the Yemeni state.

There are both centrifugal and centripetal pressures in the united Yemen. With the defeat of the southern sessionist attempt in the summer of 1994, however, the fact of political unity is no longer challenged.

Social Conditions

The population of the Republic of Yemen is approximately 17.5 million (2000 est.), most of whom live in the North. Nearly half the population is below fifteen years of age. Two-thirds of the population remains outside urban areas, though the urban population, particularly in San'a, is increasing substantially. Per capita gross national product (GNP) in Yemen is very low, around $350 by rough estimates, but that figure probably underestimates the living standards of Yemenis. Much of the Yemeni economy remains "off the books," both in terms of local subsistence agriculture and barter trade and in terms of underreporting of remittance income sent back to the country from Yemenis working abroad. Although great strides have been made since independence in both the North and the South in providing social services to the population, Yemen continues to rank near the bottom in the world tables on indices of public health and education.

There is a small but growing middle class in the major Yemeni cities. It can be broken down roughly into two groups: the bureaucrats and the traders. With the growth of government in both Yemeni states during the 1970s and 1980s, more urban Yemenis came to be employed in the state apparatus. Beginning from very modest bases, both Yemeni states worked to provide primary and secondary education throughout their countries. Both states also developed a national university. Over time more of the teachers in the two systems were Yemenis than Syrians or Egyptians hired by the education ministries. Teachers, army officers, and bureaucrats form the basis of one part of the Yemeni middle class. The other part of the middle class is the merchants, primarily located in the major urban centers like San'a and Taiz and the port cities of Aden and Hudayda. The state controlled all foreign trade in South Yemen, and upon independence much of the non-Arab mercantile community (Europeans and South Asians, mostly) left the country. However, small-scale retail trade remained in private hands even during the most "socialist" periods in the South. In the North trade remained largely in private hands, though it was heavily regulated by the government. The merchant communities in these cities predate the independence of the two Yemeni states and play a key role in the politics and economics of the country.

The migration phenomenon has been a major part of the Yemeni social landscape in recent decades. Hadramis for centuries have ventured to South and

Southeast Asia, establishing trading communities and offering their military services to local rulers. There are Yemeni communities in Detroit, Buffalo, and central California, where Yemenis have come since the 1950s seeking work in factories and in agriculture. In remote villages today Yemeni men who spent years working in the United States collect monthly Social Security checks. With the oil boom in the Arabian Peninsula in the 1970s, enormous numbers of Yemenis went to work in Saudi Arabia and the smaller oil-producing states. It is difficult to estimate how many Yemenis have worked in the neighboring states, but probably at any given time during the 1970s and 1980s between 1 and 2 million Yemenis were working abroad. At the height of the oil boom, remittances probably contributed more than $2 billion to the Yemeni economy yearly, allowing the country to run massive trade deficits. The remittances that these workers sent back to Yemen raised the standard of living throughout Yemen and provided, particularly in the North, capital for local investment in infrastructure development.

One consequence of the Gulf War of 1990–1991 was the effective expulsion of between 750,000 and 1 million Yemeni workers from Saudi Arabia and other Gulf states as a result of Yemen's political sympathies toward Iraq during the war. Despite the temporary infusion of capital that the returning migrants brought with them, the closing of Saudi Arabia to Yemeni labor caused a devastating blow to the structure of the Yemeni economy and created major social disruptions. The Saudis have subsequently allowed the return of some Yemeni workers, but not close to the numbers prior to the expulsion.

Given that the vast majority of Yemenis still reside outside the major cities, it is not surprising that the extended family, the village, and the tribe remain the bases of social identity, and that political action is frequently mobilized along those lines. The government in the South was able to suppress manifestations of political opposition along tribal lines, but it failed in its more ambitious task of effacing tribal identity as an important element of personal identity. During the fighting in 1986 the rival leaders of the Yemeni Socialist Party mobilized support largely, although not exclusively, along tribal lines. In the North, as a consequence of the compromise settlement to the civil war, tribalism has been an acknowledged part of the political system. Shaykh Abdallah al-Ahmar has been able to use his position as leader of the Hashid tribal confederation to play a major role in national politics since the civil war. He is now president of the Council of Deputies (Majlis al Nawwab), the Yemeni parliament. Leaders of the Bakil tribal confederation in late 1993 established a council to coordinate political positions among the Bakil tribes in an effort to play a greater role in national politics.

Economic Conditions

The vast majority of Yemenis continue to make their living from agriculture and, along the coasts, fishing—62.5 percent of the local workforce, according to government estimates in mid-1990. Most are involved in either subsistence farming or small-scale retail farming, as demonstrated by the fact that less than 20 percent of the GDP comes from the agricultural and fishing sector. A major agricultural crop in both the North and the South is *qat,* a mildly narcotic leaf that Yemenis are fond of chewing. Much of the agricultural land in the North that in previous times produced coffee beans for export (mocha coffee takes its name from the Yemeni Red Sea port of Mukha) has now been converted to *qat* production, depriving the country of what could be a profitable foreign exchange-earning crop. Many Yemenis decry the effect of *qat* consumption on their society, particularly in terms of the productivity lost during the long, leisurely afternoon chewing sessions that are among the most charming aspects of life in Yemen for foreign visitors. The government began a campaign in 1998 aimed at reducing *qat* consumption, but without much effect. In the agricultural areas north, east, and west of Aden, cotton is the major cash crop.

The most promising economic developments in recent years in Yemen have been in oil production. In 1984 Hunt Oil Company announced the discovery of oil in commercially viable quantities in the Jawf near the ancient town of Marib. By 1987 a pipeline had linked the area to the Red Sea port of Salif, and Yemen began exporting oil to the world. Exploration continues in other areas of Yemen, with some success in the Shabwah area northeast of Aden in what used to be South Yemen. Cooperative approaches to joint oil exploitation near the border by the leaderships of the North and the South in the late 1980s helped to pave the way for the 1990 unity agreement. Yemeni oil production in 2000 averaged almost 440,000 barrels per day. Oil production provides the Yemeni government for the first time with a steady revenue base, much more reliable than the foreign aid upon which both the northern and the southern governments had to rely during the 1970s and 1980s. In 1998, government revenues, mostly from oil, accounted for 37 percent of GDP. However, hopes voiced by Yemeni officials in the early 1990s that the country would be producing closer to 750,000 barrels of oil per day by the year 2000 were not realized.

The industrial sector of the Yemeni economy is relatively small in terms of total employment, but supplies nearly 50 percent of the country's GDP. The lion's share of that percentage derives from the oil industry; other parts of Yemen's industrial sector are much less developed. Manufacturing accounts for only 10 percent of the GDP. Though North and South Yemen espoused very different approaches to economic questions, their industrial development policies were in fact similar. In both countries the state played a major role in the development of whatever heavy and medium industry there was, and foreign aid was a major source of capital. The People's Republic of China (PRC) and the Soviet Union helped both the North and the South to establish cement and textile factories in the 1970s. Particularly in the North, the food processing industry remained largely in private hands. In the

South, the major industrial concern is the British Petroleum refinery, which was nationalized in 1977. The government of united Yemen has made the modernization of the refinery, along with the development of a free-port area in Aden, a major economic development goal. The information technology revolution has not yet reached Yemen. The World Bank reported that in 1999, there were no Internet hosts in the country.

Both North and South Yemen relied heavily upon foreign aid during the 1970s and 1980s to finance not only development projects but also regular day-to-day government operations. North Yemen was very successful in diversifying its sources of development aid, receiving aid from the Soviet Union, China, Germany, Italy, the United States, Arab oil donors, and the Scandinavian countries, as well as international agencies like the United Nations Development Program. Saudi Arabia, however, remained the major source of direct cash aid to the government, allowing it to maintain expenditures in substantial excess of its revenues.

The Soviet Union and its Eastern European allies were the primary donors of aid for both development and current expenditure in South Yemen, though in the early 1970s China and in the late 1970s and early 1980s Kuwait played significant roles in financing development projects. With the collapse of the Soviet Union and the tensions in relations with Saudi Arabia stemming from the Gulf War, the united Yemeni state lost its two most important sources of foreign aid. The loss of remittance income from Yemeni workers in Saudi Arabia and the Gulf states in the wake of the Gulf War also had a deleterious effect on the country's economy in the 1990s.

Oil revenues, which fluctuated dramatically during the 1990s, were insufficient to fill the gap created by lost foreign aid and remittance income. Faced with the prospect of financial crisis, the Yemeni government instituted a series of IMF-recommended austerity measurers in 1995 and 1998. The riyal was devalued, imports were discouraged, and subsidies on food and gasoline were reduced. Public reaction to these moves was predictably negative. Riots after the announcement of the 1998 price increases left tens of people dead and hundreds wounded. But these monetary measures, combined with higher oil prices, produced Yemen's first current-account surplus in years, reducing the severity of the country's economic crisis. Whether structural adjustments to the economy can lessen Yemen's vulnerability to sudden shifts in world oil prices remains to be seen, but at least for the near term, the rise in prices has helped to alleviate the crisis.

Political Structure

With unity in May 1990, Yemen came to be governed by a presidential council of five members, three from the former YAR in the north and two from the former PDRY in the south. Ali Abdallah Salih, former president of the YAR, became head of the presidential council and Ali Salim al–Baydh, former president of the PDRY, became its vice president. The cabinets of the two states were merged into a single large and unwieldy government. The legislative assemblies of the two states also merged into a single legislative body. The major task of this cobbled-together government was to devise a new constitution for the unified state. A number of controversial issues arose during the drafting of that document. Secularists from the South clashed with Islamists from the North over whether the Shari'a, Islamic law, would be the *main* source or the *only* source of legislation in the new constitution. A compromise wording was found. There were also questions about the division of responsibilities among the members of the presidential council, which was retained as the highest executive body in the country.

The most striking change about the new constitution was the large amount of political freedom it guaranteed. Political parties were legalized. Previously only the ruling parties, the General People's Congress (GPC) in the North and the Yemeni Socialist Party (YSP) in the South, had been legal. The state monopoly in each country over the print media was lifted, though state control over radio and television continued. The new constitution was ratified by public vote in May 1991.

With the new constitution in place, the political energies of the country were focused on the elections held in April 1993. A plethora of political parties appeared, many composed of no more than a few individuals. The most important group to emerge on the political scene to challenge the dominance of the GPC and the YSP was the Yemeni Reform Party (*al-tajammu al-yamani lil-islah*). This party is a coalition of tribal forces under the leadership of Shaykh Abdallah al-Ahmar, paramount shaykh of the Hashid tribal confederation, and Islamist political groups, particularly the Muslim Brotherhood. The Reform Party has added a third dimension to Yemeni politics. Its Islamist ideology transcends regional and sectarian divisions, whereas its Hashid connection (President Salih is also from the Hashid) adds another tribal element to already enormously complex Yemeni political dynamics. Other political parties that formed or emerged into the open in the new liberal climate include a number of Ba'thist and Nasserist parties and the South Arabian League (one of the first political groupings to develop in British-controlled South Yemen in the 1950s). All told, about forty parties announced their formation in the period prior to the April 1993 elections.

Those elections were held in an atmosphere of freedom and openness unprecedented not just in Yemen but in the Arabian Peninsula. Party newspapers conveyed candidates' platforms to the public. Political rallies were held by various parties throughout the country. International monitors pronounced the elections free and fair, though some of the Yemeni parties complained of intimidation, interference, and vote rigging by the two ruling parties. Of the 301 seats at stake in the legislature, the GPC won 124, the Reform Party won 62, and the YSP won 56. Independents took 47 seats, and many of those subsequently attached themselves to one of the three main blocs. The only other parties to gain seats were the pro-Iraqi Ba'th (7 seats), the Nasserist coalition (3 seats), and *hizb al-haqq* (2 seats), the party representing the *sayyid* class (descendants of the Prophet Muhammad). Ninety percent of the seats in what used to be South Yemen were won by the YSP. The GPC apparently agreed not to run candidates in those districts.

After the 1994 civil war, the Yemeni Socialist Party lost its major role in the political process. While not formally banned, it has been marginalized by the regime. It chose to boycott the April 1997 parliamentary elections in which the GPS won 189 seats, the Reform Party won 53 seats, and the Independents won 59. While the Reform Party became the formal parliamentary opposition, its relationship with the Salih government is a fluctuating mix of informal cooperation on many issues and occasional public opposition on others.

The defeat of the secessionists in 1994 led to important constitutional changes in the executive. The five-member Presidential Council was abolished, and the parliament elected Ali Abdallah Salih president. In September 1999, he was re-elected in the first direct presidential elections in Yemen's history, receiving 96 percent of the vote. His only opposition was a member of his own party, the GPC, whom Salih himself encouraged to run to preserve the illusion of democratic choice. The Reform Party formally endorsed Salih. The YSP proposed to run a candidate against him but could not obtain the constitutionally required number of parliamentarians to nominate one. In protest, it and other opposition parties called for a boycott of the election, but to little effect. Voter turnout was officially put at 66 percent, an impressive number for an essentially meaningless election.

In February 2001, the Yemenis went to the polls to approve constitutional amendments to lengthen the term of office of the president and members of parliament, an obvious ploy by Salih to perpetuate his rule. More distressing, however, is increasing limitations on the freedom of speech, press, and assembly that flourished at the time of unification. Yemenis still enjoy greater political freedoms than most of their neighbors on the Arabian Peninsula, but substantially fewer than they did in 1990.

Political Dynamics

Yemeni political dynamics in the 1990s revolved around the unification of North and South Yemen, the challenge raised in 1994 to unification, and the subsequent challenges to centralized authority that emerged from the 1994 fighting. The story begins with the unity agreement of 1990.

The bilateral issue that brought the two sides together was oil. Both North and South Yemen were encouraging foreign oil companies to explore in the areas around the border dividing them, creating tensions between the two states. These tensions were resolved in 1988 when they established a joint-venture oil company to solicit bids for exploration in the border area.

The progress on the oil front occurred just as the Soviet bloc was beginning to come apart. The rulers of South Yemen began to fear what the future would hold for them, the Soviet Union's closest allies in the Middle East. It is hard to discern any great domestic pressure on the southern leaders to give up their independence at that time. However, events on the international scene must have been weighing heavily on their minds, because the YSP leadership responded positively to propos- als from the North aimed at unifying the two countries. The final judgment on why the southerners agreed to accept what was generally seen as a subordinate po- sition in the newly unified state must await the publication of YSP documents and the memoirs of those involved, but a preliminary hypothesis can be advanced. Given the fate of other pro-Soviet regimes, the YSP leaders perhaps thought that unity with the North, in which they would receive a share of power disproportion- ate to the population of their country, was the best deal they could get.

As momentum for unity grew, the northern leadership pressed for its date to be pushed ahead. Thus, upon the proclamation of unity in May 1990, a large number of administrative and political issues had yet to be resolved. Although plans were laid for the merging of government institutions, little progress was made in that area. The Gulf crisis and war of August 1990 through February 1991 absorbed the energy of the Yemeni political elite almost immediately upon unity, and after that, attention was focused on the 1993 legislative elections. In important areas, partic- ularly the military, dual administrative structures answerable to the former north- ern and southern leaders remained. Failure to integrate northern and southern armies was a major factor in the fighting that was to come.

Equally troubling for the new state's prospects were the manifestations of vio- lence that emerged in 1991. A number of local YSP officials were assassinated, and beginning in late 1991, major figures in the party were subject to a series of at- tacks. In October 1991 there were two days of riots in San'a sparked by the shoot- ing of a traffic policeman by an army colonel; there was a general strike in Aden in March 1993 protesting deteriorating economic conditions. Meanwhile, a serious dispute had broken out between Ali Salim al-Baydh and Ali Abdallah Salih over the powers of the vice president. In summer 1993 al-Baydh removed himself from the capital of the new, united state, San'a, and refused to leave his political strong- hold in Aden. In 1994 a number of his fellow YSP members in the government joined him, including Prime Minister Haydar Abu Bakr al-Attas. Al-Baydh com- plained that the government could not ensure the safety of YSP members in the capital and that President Salih was monopolizing power. The regular workings of the government ground to a halt. Army units on both sides began to take up posi- tions against each other.

By May 1994, clashes between northern and southern army units escalated into full-scale fighting. President Salih dispatched northern troops to launch a full-scale attack on the South, and southern forces responded with missile and air attacks on the North. The southern position quickly devolved into a secessionist attempt under al-Baydh. Aden received political and limited military support from Gulf states, still angered by Yemen's pro-Iraq stance in the Gulf crisis, but did not receive formal diplomatic recognition. By early July, the key cities of Aden and Mukallah had fallen, al-Baydh had fled into exile in Oman, and the secessionist effort had collapsed. In the aftermath of the fighting, Salih quickly called for reconciliation, granting amnesty to all southerners abroad with the exception of the secessionist leaders. After 1994, there was no significant challenge to unity.

In the process of putting down the secessionist movement, the Salih government unleashed other forces that continue to undermine its authority. Fearing that his regular army would not be able to defeat the secessionists, Salih mobilized tribal irregulars and Islamists—some of whom had fought against the Soviets in Afghanistan. Since then, both groups have taken advantage of the central government's weakness by acting outside the law.

Tribesmen with grievances against the government regularly kidnap tourists, oil company workers, and even diplomats to use as bargaining chips in negotiations with San'a for more benefits. From January 1996 to March 2000 Yemen witnessed 38 kidnappings involving 147 foreigners. The kidnappers usually had no political demands; rather they typically demanded jobs and government services for their villages. However, the picture of chaos these kidnappings presented to the world discouraged tourism and investment at a time when Yemen greatly needs both.

The radical Islamist challenge is more directly political. With President Salih beholden to armed Islamists for their assistance in 1994, and the government generally unable to extend its control over more rural parts of the country, Yemen became a haven for violent, fringe Islamist groups. Osama bin Laden and members of the Egyptian "Islamic Gihad (Jihad)" organization, as well as other veterans of the Afghanistan jihad, spent time in the country. Under pressure from Western and other Arab governments, Salih began in the late 1990s to crack down. The Islamist reaction has been violent. In December 1998, a group calling itself the Aden-Abyan Islamic Army kidnapped sixteen tourists, killing four of them during a government rescue effort. In August 1999, during the trial of some of its members for kidnapping, the group took responsibility for terrorist acts in San'a that killed eight and wounded forty. In October 2000, Islamists bombed the American destroyer USS *Cole* in Aden harbor, killing seventeen U.S. sailors. The Salih government has vowed to continue its crackdown on these groups, a task for which the United States has promised assistance in the wake of the September 11, 2001, attacks on New York and Washington.

Foreign Policy

The new, united state of Yemen had the distinct misfortune of facing a major foreign crisis within months of its coming into existence. With the Iraqi invasion of

Kuwait in August 1990 every Arab state had to make a monumental decision. In Yemen that decision was particularly difficult. North Yemen had joined with Iraq (and Egypt and Jordan) in the Arab Cooperation Council (ACC) at its founding in 1989. The united Yemeni state assumed North Yemen's ACC membership. North Yemen had given unreserved support to Iraq in its war with Iran from 1980 to 1988, and relations between the two capitals were very close, whereas relations with Saudi Arabia were strained by what San'a considered Saudi insensitivity toward Yemeni sovereign interests. At the same time, San'a had to consider that Saudi Arabia had been the major aid donor to North Yemen since the end of the civil war in 1970 and that Kuwait had given a substantial amount of project aid to both North and South Yemen over the years. Moreover, financial remittances from Yemenis working in Saudi Arabia were a major source of Yemeni foreign exchange and were certain to be jeopardized if San'a did not unequivocally condemn the Iraqi invasion.

Yemen held the Arab seat on the U.N. Security Council during the crisis, magnifying the international visibility of its positions. Yemen took what it considered to be a pragmatic and evenhanded stand in the crisis, opposing the Iraqi invasion of Kuwait but also opposing the dispatch of foreign forces to Saudi Arabia to resist that invasion. Its equivocal position was greatly resented by Saudi Arabia and Kuwait, however, as well as by the United States. The Saudis forced hundreds of thousands of Yemeni workers to leave the kingdom, Kuwait broke diplomatic relations, and the United States cut off foreign aid. After one Security Council vote in which Yemen opposed the anti-Iraq coalition, the U.S. representative reportedly told his Yemeni counterpart that the vote "was the most expensive one Yemen will ever cast."

That Yemen would line up against both the United States and Saudi Arabia may have come as something of a surprise to observers but was not really out of character. Even though Saudi financial aid was crucial for the North Yemeni state in the 1970s and early 1980s, the Yemenis had long resented the patronizing manner in which the Saudis treated them and still smarted under what they saw as the loss of Yemeni territory around Najran to the Saudis in the Saudi-Yemeni war of 1934. Moreover, the Saudis, fearful that Yemen, with its greater population, had the potential to be a major national security threat, had consistently interfered in the internal affairs of Yemen and had tried to stymie all Yemeni efforts at unification. The Saudis even tried to aid the southern secessionists in 1994 in the misguided notion that the once-hated Marxists could counterbalance a strong, potentially hostile Yemen on their southern frontier.

Since the end of the 1990–1991 Gulf crisis, Yemen has taken steps to repair its relations with Saudi Arabia. The two countries signed a treaty in June 2000 reaffirming the 1934 boundary, delineating their offshore boundary in the Red Sea, and setting out the principles for demarcation of their desert frontiers. If this agreement holds up, it will bring to an end seventy years of border tensions between the two countries.

Yemen's relations with its other Arabian Peninsula neighbors have not been as problematic as those with Saudi Arabia. Kuwait reestablished diplomatic relations in 2000. Oman, which had strained relations with South Yemen in the 1970s over the latter's support of anti-regime rebels in Oman's Dhufar province, now has correct if not warm relations with San'a. In September 1992, agreement was reached between the two countries on the demarcation of their common border. Yemen's relations with the other Gulf Arab states are good, particularly with the UAE, whose ruler traces his family back to a village in Yemen. Yemen maintains good relations with other Arab states as well, and strongly supports the Palestinian cause and other pan-Arab issues.

In the mid-1990s, Yemen's claim to the Hanish Islands in the Red Sea was contested by the newly independent state of Eritrea on the opposite shore. In December 1995 and August 1996, Eritrean troops occupied several of the islands. In October 1998, an International Arbitration Court of the International Court of Justice awarded sovereignty of four of the islands to Yemen, but by that time Eritrea's interests had shifted to their confrontation with Ethiopia.

After unification, Yemen's relations with the United States started off poorly, due to the Gulf crisis, but the breach was soon healed. The modest U.S. aid program to Yemen, cut off during the crisis, was restored in 1993, and Washington expressed strong if optimistic support for Yemeni democratization in the elections of 1993 and 1997. Washington also worked to help overcome the 1993–1994 domestic crisis, expressing its belief that a united Yemen was a factor for stability in the region. With the involvement of Hunt Oil Company in the development of the Yemeni oil industry and the subsequent entry of other American oil companies into Yemen, the United States has for the first time developed a direct and tangible interest in Yemeni affairs. That direct interest took on a military component in the late 1990s as U.S. Navy ships began to use the port of Aden for refueling and repairs. The Yemeni government, anxious to promote both the port and better relations with Washington, welcomed the increased American presence. The October 2000 bombing of the USS *Cole* in Aden port, which killed seventeen American sailors, did not appear to have adversely affected the growing relationship between the two countries.

Bibliography

On the historical background see the author's *Saudi-Yemeni Relations: Domestic Structures and Foreign Influence* (New York: Columbia University Press, 1990). For background on North Yemen, see Robert W. Stookey, *Yemen: The Politics of the Yemen Arab Republic* (Boulder: Westview Press, 1978); J. E. Peterson, *Yemen: The Search for a Modern State* (Baltimore: Johns

Hopkins University Press, 1982); Manfred W. Wenner, *The Yemen Arab Republic: Development and Change in an Ancient Land* (Boulder: Westview Press, 1991); Mohammed Zabarah, *Yemen: Tradition vs. Modernity* (New York: Praeger, 1982); Paul Dresch, *Tribes, Government and History in Yemen* (Oxford: Oxford University Press, 1989), and Robert D. Burrowes, *The Yemen Arab Republic: The Politics of Development, 1962–1986* (Boulder: Westview Press, 1987). For background on South Yemen, see Robert W. Stookey, *South Yemen: A Marxist Republic in Arabia* (Boulder: Westview Press, 1982); Fred Halladay, *Revolution and Foreign Policy: The Case of South Yemen, 1967–1987* (Cambridge: Cambridge University Press, 1989); and Helen Lackner, *PDR Yemen* (London: Ithaca Press, 1985). On both countries, see Fred Halladay, *Arabia Without Sultans* (London: Penguin Books, 1974), and Robin Bidwell, *The Two Yemens* (Boulder: Westview Press, 1983). For developments since unity, see Sheila Carapico, *Civil Society in Yemen* (Cambridge: Cambridge University Press, 1998).

8

Republic of Lebanon

M. Graeme Bannerman

Historical Background

Although the modern state of Lebanon is a creation of the twentieth century, the people of Lebanon have had a long and distinctive history. The coastal plain was the home of the Phoenician merchants whose ships sailed throughout the Mediterranean world more than a millennium before Christ.

In the seventh century A.D., when Muslim armies swept out of the Arabian Peninsula, the rugged Lebanon Mountains gradually became a refuge for Levantine Christians, predominantly Maronites, and other dissident groups who opposed the Islamic establishment. Under both the Umayyad (660–750) and the Abbasid (750-1258) caliphates, the Lebanese mountaineers retained a degree of political autonomy. Although the Muslim rulers easily controlled the coastal cities, they never achieved total domination of the mountains. Nevertheless, the Muslim Arabs who surrounded the mountains had considerable impact on their inhabitants. Many customs and social values of the surrounding region penetrated the mountain fastness. Symbolic of these changes was the slow growth in the use of Arabic. By the thirteenth century, Arabic had replaced Aramaic as the dominant language, although Syriac, a branch of Aramaic, was spoken in some villages well into the seventeenth century and remains the liturgical language of the Syrian (Syrian Orthodox) church.

By the end of the eleventh century three groups of dissidents—Maronites, Shi'a, and Druze—dominated in the Lebanese Mountains. The Maronites were predominant in the northern districts of Jubayl, Batrun, and Bsharri. Shi'a Muslims formed the majority in the remainder of Lebanon. During the eleventh century, however, the followers of Egyptian Fatimid Caliph al-Hakim (985–1021) entered Lebanon. Led by the disciple Darazi, the followers joined the local Lebanese to form a distinctive community, which is widely known as the Druze.

The Crusaders overran Lebanon in the early twelfth century, capturing Tripoli in 1109, Beirut and Sidon in 1110, and Tyre in 1124. The Crusades had a profound effect on the Maronites, for it was at that time that they were brought into union with the Roman Catholic church, establishing a link that still endures. In addition, the large French component among the Crusaders established ties with the Maronites, which later generations would view as the basis of a special relationship between France and Lebanon. The Crusades also had a devastating impact on the Lebanese Shi'a. Before the Crusades, Muslim Lebanon was predominantly Shi'a. The growth of Shi'a influence was largely due to the Shi'a Fatimid caliphate in Cairo, which had successfully competed for control of Syria with the faltering Abbasid (Sunni) Caliphate in Baghdad. The failure of the Fatimids to adequately protect Muslims from the Christian invaders, however, contributed to the decline of Fatimid power and influence in Syria and Lebanon. Without the protection of the powerful Shi'a in Cairo, the fortunes of Lebanese Shi'a also declined. A succession of Sunni dynasties initiated the countercrusade that ultimately led to the defeat of the Crusaders and to the decline of Shi'a political influence in Lebanon. This persists to this day.

In Egypt, the Sunni Ayubids succeeded the Fatimids. They in turn were replaced by Sunni Mamluk dynasties, which dominated Egypt, Syria, and Lebanon until the sixteenth century. Under Mamluk domination, Sunni Islam became firmly entrenched along the eastern shore of the Mediterranean. Less tolerant than their predecessors, the Mamluks pressed their subjects to convert to Sunni Islam. In Lebanon, the Shi'a and the Druze suffered most. In general, however, the Mamluks were not intent on dominating Mount Lebanon directly but were content to rule indirectly through local leaders. Thus, Lebanese autonomy continued to be preserved.

In 1516 the Ottomans defeated the Mamluks in northern Syria, establishing Ottoman control over the Arab Levant. The Ottomans dominated this area for the next four centuries. They continued the Mamluk policy of recognizing a local Lebanese notable as ruler of a semiautonomous state. Two great dynasties, the Ma'an and the Shihabs, reigned in the mountains of Lebanon until 1843. The Druze house of Ma'an was paramount until 1697, reaching its zenith under Fakhr al-Din II (1586–1635). His efforts to obtain total independence for Lebanon led ultimately to his defeat and execution. Nevertheless, this Druze leader did much for Lebanon by reopening the country to the West, as it had not been since the time of the Crusades. Having once been exiled in Tuscany, Fakhr al-Din II, after returning to Lebanon, allied himself with the rulers of that Italian state. These ties extended beyond the political realm. The Druze leader emulated his allies in attempting to create a modern army. He also imported engineers and agricultural experts to promote better land use. These efforts, however, had only a minimal long-term impact on Lebanon. Of greater significance was Fakhr al-Din's encouragement of the Maronite peasantry to move south. Over the subsequent centuries, the Maronites migrated from their northern Lebanese strongholds and slowly expanded their number and influence throughout the Lebanon Mountains.

In 1697 the Ma'an family was replaced by the Shihabs as the amirs (princes) of Mount Lebanon. Under Bashir II (1788–1840), the Shihabs again pressed for full independence. The early nineteenth century was a time when the Ottoman state was being torn apart by local rulers who, playing upon the weakness of the central government, strove to break away from the authorities in Istanbul. Bashir made an unfortunate miscalculation, however, by supporting Muhammad Ali of Egypt against the Ottomans, who, in turn, were supported by the British. As a result, in 1840, after the Egyptian leader was obliged to give up his claims to sovereignty in the Levant, his ally Bashir was forced into exile.

The next twenty years were marked by strife and turmoil. Internal Lebanese rivalries were exacerbated by Ottoman weakness and European intervention. During the preceding two centuries, the fundamental economic and political balance of Mount Lebanon had been upset by the growth in the Maronite population and its gradual migration southward from traditional strongholds in north Lebanon. Druze preponderance had been seriously eroded. The Ottomans, in an attempt to ward off potential intercommunal difficulties, in 1843 divided Lebanon into two districts (*qaim maqaimyyah*). A northern district was placed under a Christian subgovernor and a southern district under a Druze.

This system proved unsatisfactory. The Druze and Christian populations were already too intermingled and antagonistic to permit such a simple solution. Despite Ottoman efforts, tensions between the communities increased. These tensions were made worse by French protection of the Maronites and British protection of the Druze. Moreover, the Ottomans were not satisfied with the status quo. Istanbul desired to limit the traditional autonomous status of the inhabitants of Mount Lebanon and resented European interference in Ottoman internal affairs. Another problem was the growing resentment of the industrious Maronite peasantry toward their oppressive feudal aristocracy. In 1858 a peasant revolt broke out. In the northern district, the Maronite peasantry rose against the aristocracy. Because the Druze peasantry in the south felt closer bonds with their coreligionists than with the Maronite peasants, the hostilities south and east of Beirut became more a religious war than a peasant revolt. Druze and other Muslims massacred thousands of Maronites. These massacres contributed to Christian and Muslim suspicion and animosities that have yet to be assuaged.

Following direct European intervention, Mount Lebanon was reunited and made a semiautonomous governorship (*mutasarrifyyah*). The governor was a non-Lebanese Ottoman Christian who was appointed by the Ottoman sultan with the consent of the five great European powers. He was aided by an elected administrative council, which ensured representation to each of the major sects, and a locally recruited police force. This system remained in force until World War I.

The period from 1860 to 1914 was marked by increasing contacts between the Lebanese and the West. Intellectual activity increased, largely through the efforts of foreign missionaries. Presbyterians from the United States founded the American University of Beirut in 1866, and French missionaries founded Saint Joseph University in 1875. Economically, however, Lebanon held little prospect of supporting its own growing population. The Maronites, who had been expanding their area of settlement for over two centuries as a way of providing a livelihood for their growing population, found further expansion in Lebanon limited for political reasons. Therefore, increasing numbers of Maronites moved to the cities, particularly Beirut.

Greater political and cultural pressure was also exerted upon Lebanese Christians. In the late nineteenth century, Ottoman attempts at reviving their state were often colored with Islamic overtones and political repression. The lack of economic opportunity, combined with greater religious and cultural pressure, resulted in thousands of Maronites and other Christians seeking their fortunes in the United States, South America, and other nations after 1880.

Four centuries of Ottoman rule came to an end in Lebanon with World War I. Through wartime agreements, Lebanon was mandated to the French, who created the political entity of Greater Lebanon. This area included not only Mount Lebanon but also Beirut, Sidon, Tyre, southern Lebanon, the Biqa Valley, and the Akkar plain in the north. The French hoped that a larger Lebanon would make the area economically viable and a more influential friend. This expansion, however, altered the demographic balance by including large numbers of Sunnis and Shi'a in the new state, thus reducing the Christian preponderance.

Under the French mandate, Lebanese nationalist sentiment began to grow and the Lebanese made slow progress toward full independence. In 1926 the French mandate authorities promulgated a constitution. The Lebanese nationalists were not satisfied with this document because the French commissioner retained final authority. For example, in 1932 and again in 1939 the French suspended the constitution. Despite the French hold, the Lebanese were permitted to choose their first president and to assume responsibility for their own political destiny. Differences with the French led many Lebanese to examine alternate political philosophies, including Arab and Syrian nationalism and socialism. Nevertheless, the French continued to receive significant support from large numbers of Lebanese, particularly the Maronites.

The French mandate authorities were also instrumental in building the economic and governing infrastructure of modern Lebanon. Roads were constructed, electricity was brought to numerous villages, and Beirut harbor was enlarged and repaired. A bureaucratic structure that continues to be the foundation of Lebanese public administration was established. In 1943, as a result of the reduction of French power following the German occupation of France, the mandate came to an end, and Lebanon was granted full independence.

Political Environment

Land

Lebanon has a total area of 10,400 square kilometers (4,015 square miles) and is divided into four major geographical regions: a coastal plain, the Lebanon mountain range, the Biqa Valley, and the Anti-Lebanon Mountains. The coastal plain varies in width from more than a dozen kilometers (about seven and a half miles) in the north to almost nothing at some points. Most of the major towns and cities of Lebanon are situated on this plain, including the three largest—Beirut, Tripoli, and Sidon.

Rising abruptly from the plain are the Lebanon Mountains. Their highest peaks are within twenty kilometers (twelve and four-tenths miles) of the coast, creating a situation whereby one can be skiing on their slopes and still see the Mediterranean Sea below. The mountains are highest in the north, where the tallest peak is more than 3,000 meters (9,842 feet), and lower to the south, although Jabal Sanin, which is east of Beirut, is still more than 2,600 meters (8,350 feet).

The fertile Biqa Valley lies between the Lebanon Mountains on the west and the Anti-Lebanon range on the east. To the north of Baalbek, where the valley is widest, it is watered by the Orontes River, which flows north into Syria. For most of the valley, however, the Litani River provides the main source of water. The Litani River flows north to south for most of its length, but about twenty kilometers (twelve and four-tenths miles) north of the Israeli border it makes a ninety-degree turn and flows westward to the Mediterranean.

The Anti-Lebanon Mountains form the eastern frontier with Syria. They are not generally as high as the Lebanon Mountains and receive considerably less rainfall. At more than 2,900 meters (9,232 feet), Mount Hermon, on the Syrian-Lebanese-Israeli border, is the highest peak. In south Lebanon, the geographical regions are less distinct, as the Lebanon mountain range degenerates into the undulating hills of northern Galilee. A small line of hills divides the Biqa Valley from the northern drainage of the Jordan River.

People

The mountains of Lebanon have provided refuge for threatened minorities throughout history. Fleeing from conquering invaders or religious persecution, minority communities have found relative security in the isolated valleys and mountain hillsides of Lebanon, making it a patchwork nation with a mosaic of various groups. Almost all Lebanese now speak Arabic, although some speak another language at home. The distinctions among the numerous factions within Lebanon remain great, however. The focus of these differences is religion. But religion in Lebanon is more than solely a belief system. It represents a major element of self- and family identity as well as of communal values.

The approximately 3.6 million Lebanese are divided into two major communities—Christian and Muslim. Historically, each constituted about half the population. During the last several decades, however, fertility variance among groups, emigration, and immigration have changed the balance. Muslims today far outnumber Christians.

The Christians are further fragmented into more than a dozen sects. The largest is the Maronites, a Catholic sect that constitutes more than half the total Christian community and has dominated Lebanon since the modern state was founded. For the past four centuries, the Maronite population has been growing faster than the ability of the mountainous area to provide a living for the people. As a result, migration occurred. During the eighteenth century and the first half of the nineteenth, the Maronites moved southward through the mountains, until their movement was blocked by the hostile reaction from the Druze community. With this avenue closed, many Maronites emigrated. With independence in 1943, however, the majority of those who previously might have left the country congregated in Lebanon's urban centers. Beirut and its eastern suburbs soon had the largest concentration of Maronites in Lebanon. The economic and political turmoil of the 1970s, 1980s, and 1990s led to renewed emigration.

The Greek Orthodox community forms the second-largest Christian sect. Unlike the Maronites, the Greek Orthodox for the most part remained in urban centers in Syria, Jordan, Israel, and Lebanon where they lived under benevolent Muslim rule. The largest rural concentrations of the Greek Orthodox in Lebanon are: in the Koura district, southeast of Tripoli, where they form the majority of the population; in the Marjayoun area in southern Lebanon; and in several villages in the upper Metn. The Greek Orthodox historically have had more contact with Muslims than the Maronites have had, owing not only to the daily commercial exchanges in urban centers but also to the wider distribution of the Orthodox throughout the Levant.

The differing experiences as minorities greatly influenced the political outlook of both communities. The Greek Orthodox rarely deny their Arab ethnicity, unlike many Maronites. On the contrary, the Orthodox were in the forefront of those who assert that being an Arab is quite different from being a Muslim. Many leading late-nineteenth-century Arab nationalists were Greek Orthodox. By asserting and stressing the non-Islamic cultural and political heritage of being an Arab, these Orthodox were establishing a basis for giving their community equal standing with their Muslim neighbors. For most Arabs, however, Islam is a vital element of Arab nationalism. Therefore, early Orthodox hopes of fostering Arab nationalism without a strong Islamic emphasis have proven fruitless.

For similar reasons, Greek Orthodox were active in ideological movements that transcended national and Islamic borders. The Syrian Nationalist Party, which promotes a greater Syrian state including Syria, Lebanon, Jordan, and Israel, was predominantly Orthodox. Similarly, intellectually active individuals who were drawn to Western ideologies such as socialism and communism were often from the Orthodox community.

In Lebanon, although many Greek Orthodox were active in such organizations, a majority appear to have been politically quiescent or to have chosen to ally themselves with the larger Maronite community. Even in the latter case, however, the Greek Orthodox generally exhibited greater willingness to reach an accommodation with the Muslims than have the Maronites.

Greek Catholics constitute the third-largest Christian community in Lebanon. They are generally inclined to follow the Maronite lead but, as a community, do so with little zeal. Greek Catholic villages are often found in areas that are considerably less defensible than those where Maronite villages are located. Moreover, Greek Catholics do not dominate any particular area, such as Mount Lebanon. Their villages are scattered from the Syrian border in the north to the Israeli border in the south. The only rural area with a concentrated Greek Catholic population is in the hills southeast of Sidon. With the urbanization of Lebanon since World War II, the Greek Catholics have increasingly concentrated in Maronite-dominated areas of East Beirut.

The largest numbers of Christians to immigrate to Lebanon in the twentieth century were Armenians. Fleeing the Turks during and after World War I, they were welcomed into Lebanon, mainly Beirut. Of all the non–Arab groups, the Armenians have most strongly maintained their cultural identity. At the same time, they were active participants in the Lebanese political scene. Today, six of the 108 members of Lebanon's parliament are Armenian. The Armenians generally avoided becoming overly identified with one political faction or another and usually supported the forces in power. In this manner, they ensured the maximum freedom to run their community with a minimum of government interference. During the civil war, 1975–1990, however, because their community was concentrated in Christian Beirut and its suburbs, the Armenians were pressured by various Christian political factions to take a more active role in Christian Lebanese affairs. During that difficult period, large numbers of Armenians left Lebanon.

Numerous other Christian sects are identifiable. None, however, has a large impact on the Lebanese political system.

On the Muslim side of the political ledger, there are three major groups: the Sunnis, Shi'a, and Druze. The Sunni community tends to dominate the political system to a greater degree than its population would merit. The Sunnis are highly urban, probably the most urbanized of any major Christian or Muslim sect. They are concentrated in the large coastal cites of Beirut, Tripoli, and Sidon. Sunni villages are scattered elsewhere in Lebanon—near Sidon, in the Biqa Valley, and northwest of Tripoli toward the Syrian border—but most Sunnis are urban dwellers and were more politically active than other Muslims.

The Sunnis also historically had closer ties to the Arab world at large than other Lebanese groups. They were more aware of and in tune with trends in the predominantly Sunni Arab world. The Sunnis traditionally desired that Lebanon play a greater role in Arab affairs, resulting in sharp differences with many Christians. The rapid growth of the Shi'a in number and influence challenges Sunni dominance of the Muslim community. In order to maintain their dominant role the Sunnis have relied on their ties to the larger Arab community.

The Shi'a, who are the single largest religious group in Lebanon, are the most economically disadvantaged and politically underrepresented. They are heavily rural and are concentrated in the hinterland—south Lebanon and the Biqa Valley. They lack the European connections of the Maronites and the Arab ties of the Sunnis. More recently, closer ties with Iran have given the Shi'a a strong external ally. The Shi'a have generally lacked political influence commensurate with their numbers. Their villages are isolated and poor, and those who migrated to Beirut tend to be laborers and poor. Moreover, they were generally ill served by their traditional leaders, who were more often concerned with self-advancement than with protecting the community's interest.

In recent years, young Shi'a have turned to radical ideology and arms to solve their problems. The growth of influence of the Shi'a since the 1979 Iranian Revolution, and even more since the Israeli invasion in 1982, is the most significant shift in the balance of power in Lebanon in more than a century. The Taif Agreement in 1989 gave Shi'as parity with the Sunnis in parliament and increased the power of the Shi'a speaker of the Chamber of Deputies. Despite these changes, the Shi'a are still the only group whose numerical strength is far greater than its political representation.

Where the Shi'a have been limited by the political system, they have enhanced their national influence through the force of arms. Shi'a militias, predominantly Hizballah and Amal, remain important powers long after other Lebanese militias were for the most part disarmed and dispersed. Hizballah, in particular, increased its national standing by actively opposing the Israeli presence in South Lebanon and is frequently credited for Israel's unilateral withdrawal and the collapse of Israel's ally, the South Lebanese Army, in June 2000. Whether this success will be translated into more permanent enhanced political influence will take time to determine.

Although the Druze are historically an offshoot of Shi'a Islam, their beliefs have evolved to the point where many Muslims do not consider them as Muslims. Nevertheless, in the political spectrum of Lebanon, the Druze are placed on the Muslim side of the equation. Despite their relatively small number—less than 6 percent of the population—the Druze have political influence. They are the Maronites' neighbors in Mount Lebanon, mainly living in scattered villages in the mountains to the east and southeast of Beirut. As a well-organized, tightly knit community and by dint of their reputation as fierce fighters, the Druze are able to retain considerable political influence despite the relative decline in their numbers.

Even before their religion, Lebanese traditionally consider their extended families and villages to be the principal sources of self-identity. Because one usually does not marry outside one's religion, family and religious identification are mutually reinforcing. The extended family in Lebanon imposes a sense of mutual obligation and commitment that embraces distant cousins. The family is vital to the success of the individual, giving protection and support to its members in return for loyalty. The success of one member reflects well on the family as a whole, just as disgrace reflects poorly. The family traditionally was the vehicle for political advancement. To achieve success, an individual must have the full backing of the family, and the family that can best muster its total resources is likely to be the most successful in the political arena. The family also provided many of the welfare functions that elsewhere are performed by the state. The civil war weakened the institution of the family, but it still retains great importance.

The most significant shift in population occurred in 1992 when hundreds of thousands of Syrians were naturalized, ending any future claims of a Maronite majority and thus altering Lebanon's sectarian political balance. The action was taken under pressure of the Syrian government, which has always claimed hegemony over Lebanon.

Economic Conditions

The Lebanese have a long tradition of being clever merchants and craftspeople. The entrepreneurial spirit, which some date to the Phoenicians, has thrived in the towns of Lebanon. Small shopkeepers, artisans, and the service industries flourished under Lebanon's free-enterprise economy. Despite the number of large firms, self-employed family enterprises or small business continue to be the rule.

After independence and before 1975, Lebanon's regional economic role was enhanced by the ability of the Lebanese to benefit from economic and political developments elsewhere in the area. The independence of Israel resulted in the cutting of economic ties between the Arab states and most of the former British mandate of Palestine, leaving a large gap that the Lebanese filled. For instance, the terminal for the Iraq Petroleum Pipeline was transferred from Haifa to Tripoli. More important, overland transport and communications that might have traversed Palestine were funneled into Beirut. This created a boom in the Lebanese economy. International corporations and banks established regional headquarters in the Lebanese capital.

The Lebanese took advantage of the growing wealth of the Arab oil states. Beirut supplied a source of entertainment and investment as well as a transit point for goods and services. Arabs from the Gulf states, Syria, Iraq, and Jordan flocked to Beirut and the neighboring mountain villages each summer to escape the heat. The Lebanese provided these visitors with entertainment and European shopping in an Arab environment. Many of these Arabs purchased homes in the mountains or invested in Beirut. Lebanon's schools and universities educated many of the children of Arab leaders.

In the decade before the 1975 civil war, Lebanon experienced a rapid growth of the industrial sector. The large oil refineries at Zahrani and Tripoli had been the primary industry. In the 1960s an industrial belt began to grow in the poor sub-urbs that surrounded Beirut. Most of the enterprises were small and engaged in the production of light consumer goods or textiles or in food processing. Nearly 10 percent of the population was involved in such industry by 1975.

During this period, the importance of the agricultural sector gradually declined, while the distinction between rural and urban living diminished. Most Lebanese have easy access to a large town or city. Nevertheless, many people continued to earn part or all of their incomes from the land. Apples, citrus fruit, olives, olive oil, and grapes remained major items of export. The Biqa Valley was a breadbasket that supplied the cities with much of their agricultural needs. Most Lebanese farmers are small landholders, although there are also many tenant farms.

One of the more interesting aspects of the Lebanese economy was its perennial trade deficit. Year after year imports were five times as great as exports. This deficit was offset in a variety of ways. Lebanese emigrants—both longtime emigrants to the West and temporary residents in the oil-producing states—remitted money. In addition, Lebanese service industries earned significant sums of hard currency hoping to offset the trade deficit.

The fifteen years of civil war, from 1975–1990, however, severely set back Lebanon's economy. The industrial and commercial sectors were devastated. Many industries were destroyed. Communications facilities were also damaged. Water supplies, roads, and electric generation and transmission facilities at best were maintained, but clearly declined in comparison to the rest of the region. The diffi-culty of maintaining and improving the basic infrastructure did not end with the civil war. Several Israeli air raids in the decade following the end of the civil con-flict did significant damage to electric facilities in particular.

A desire to revive the Lebanese economy was a significant factor in the elec-tion of Rafik Hariri as prime minister in 1992. Hariri, an extraordinarily success-ful Lebanese businessman, had amassed a fortune in Saudi Arabia. Lebanese and many international observers hoped that Hariri would apply his business skills and entice significant international investment in Lebanon and, thus, restore Lebanon to its former standing.

The Hariri government undertook a vigorous program of redevelopment and reconstruction with the hope that the Lebanese community at home and abroad, as well as the international financial markets, would support these endeavors. Large sums of money were spent to make up for years of neglect and destruction. The cost of these projects far exceeded Lebanon's capacity to pay. As a result, the Government of Lebanon borrowed very large sums of money. When Hariri came to office the national budget was about $900 million; six years later, it reached $18 billion and was increasing rapidly. Debt service exceeded more than half the national debt. Despite large government deficit spending, economic growth was only modest, unemployment was staggering, and the once robust middle class saw its economic status erode. As much as 60 percent of the population slipped below the poverty line. Hariri's development efforts focused on central Beirut, leaving much of the country untouched. Most worrisome was the large number of educated and skilled Lebanese workers who had emigrated during the civil war and did not return to help rebuild their nation.

By 1996, Hariri was discredited and voted out of office. Hariri's failure was due at least in part to events beyond his control. Peace in Lebanon and the region were essential for his plan to succeed. This did not occur. Sanctions against Iraq further disrupted regional trade patterns. Finally, the heavy hand of Syrian and Israeli occupation stifled freedom and destroyed confidence in Lebanon's ability to again become an economic center.

Hariri's successor inherited an impossible economic and political situation, although he did well to prevent the economy from becoming even worse. After four years, the Lebanese were again willing to trust their fate to Hariri and he was reelected prime minister in the fall of 2000.

Hariri, however, was unable to revive the economy. The outbreak of the Palestinian Intifada in September 2000 and Hizballah attacks on Israeli forces in the Golan Heights created international tensions, which added political instability as an impediment to economic recovery. A huge national debt left over from his first term in office drained the government of the few resources it had. The stalled economy remained the greatest long-term threat to the future of Lebanon.

Political Structure

The system of government bequeathed to the Lebanese by the French in 1943 was modeled after that of France but took into account the peculiarities of the Lebanese situation. The two principal pillars on which the Lebanese governing system is based are the constitution and the informal national covenant. The 1989 Taif Agreement modified these but the basic principles remained in place. Although the constitution generally establishes a three-branch governmental system, Article 95 gives it a peculiarly Lebanese flavor by providing that religious communities shall be equitably represented in government, employment, and key ruling bodies, including the cabinet and the Chamber of Deputies.

The unwritten national covenant of 1943, however, was the vehicle through which this idea was elaborated and the unique political system fashioned. The system was one in which each of Lebanon's independent-minded religious communities felt its interests were adequately defended and a fair share of government largesse—bureaucratic positions, public works projects, scholarships, and so on—was received. The impact of this confessional system was felt throughout society.

The unicameral legislature, the Chamber of Deputies, is the primary vehicle used for preserving communal interests. Deputies are elected to the chamber, with seats distributed on both a confessional and a geographical basis. Deputies are chosen from geographical districts. Each district has a specified number of seats allocated by religion. All citizens in the district vote for candidates for all seats. In some districts, however, a religious confession that exists there may not have representation. For example, in Bint Jubayl in south Lebanon, the representatives are Shi'a, despite the existence of a Christian minority. In other districts, Muslim minorities are similarly not represented by coreligionists. The question of minority representation has not been a serious problem because, as a rule, the various religious sects tend to be concentrated in specific areas. Tripoli, Sidon, and Akkar are overwhelmingly Sunni; Batrun, Bsharri, Zghorta, Kasrawan, and Jubayl are similarly Maronite; Tyre, Bint Jubayl, Nabatiya, and Baalbek have Shi'a majorities. The Koura is predominantly Greek Orthodox. Even in areas of mixed population, villages tend to be composed primarily of a single religious group. In towns, mixed villages, and cities in which more than one religious sect is present, each group tends to live in its own neighborhood or quarter. The representative system that was established under the departing French was thus an attempt to adapt democracy to Lebanese demography.

Distribution of higher offices in the government and much of the bureaucracy also reflects the religious balance. The presidency is the preserve of the Maronites. The Chamber of Deputies chooses the president for a six-year term. A Sunni Muslim is prime minister, who then forms a cabinet. The speaker of the Chamber of Deputies is a Shi'a. The ministerial portfolios, as well, are allocated along confessional lines. Senior and many minor governmental positions in the executive, legislative, and judicial branches are also distributed on a sectarian basis. Even judges and teachers in schools and universities are recruited with an eye on quotas for each sect.

In addition to confessionalism, the national covenant dealt with the issues of the conflicting political, economic, and social orientation of the diverse groups. On the whole, the Christians, particularly the Maronites, looked toward the Western nations as their protectors. They often considered themselves to be a part of the Mediterranean community rather than of the Arab world. This attitude was expressed in a vigorous form of "Lebanese" nationalism, in sharp contrast to

"Arab" nationalism. The Muslims, on the other hand, considered this Western orientation unnatural and often viewed "Lebanese" nationalism as a denial of Lebanese Arabness and Lebanon's rightful position in the Arab world. The Christian desire to be something other than Arab appeared to the Muslims to be harmful to long-term Lebanese interests. To the Christian, the pan-Arab orientation of the Muslims seemed to sacrifice Lebanese, and particularly Lebanese Christian, interests to broader Islamic and Arab goals.

The national covenant was designed to reach a compromise between the "Lebanese" and the "Arab" nationalists. The Christians committed themselves not to attempt to alienate Lebanon from the Arab world or to draw Lebanon too close to the West. At the same time, the Muslims recognized Lebanon's uniqueness and agreed not to pressure the government to become overly involved in the affairs of the Arab states. The Taif Agreement fundamentally altered this aspect of the national covenant. Lebanon was clearly placed in the Arab or Islamic world. The "Lebanese" nationalists clearly had lost the struggle over the international orientation of Lebanon.

On top of this peculiarly Lebanese system, the constitution provided the framework for the freest democracy in the Arab world. All Lebanese were guaranteed basic rights that included equality before the law, equal aid, and political rights. Personal liberty and freedom from arbitrary arrest were provided. Freedoms of press, association, speech, and assembly were also guaranteed.

The Lebanese central government was given only limited powers. The system of checks and balances whereby each of the religious communities was secure in the belief that its interests were protected also guaranteed a very weak central government. In contrast to most modern states, the central Lebanese government provided only a minimum of services. It was truly laissez-faire. Private organizations, mainly religious, provided welfare, health services, education, and to some extent internal security.

The Taif Agreement modified the system. Sixty-two members of the Lebanese parliament met in Taif, Saudi Arabia, from September 30 to October 22, 1989, to modify the existing Lebanese system of government. It was their hope that this modification would address some of the problems within Lebanese society that had contributed to nearly a decade and a half of civil war. The Taif Agreement was striking in its moderation. The principles upon which the Lebanese constitution and national pact had been established were left in place. The Taif Agreement attempted merely to modify the system of government to reflect changes in the balance of power.

The Taif Agreement gave greater influence to the Chamber of Deputies at the expense of the president and changed the chamber's composition. Prior to the Taif Agreement, ninety-nine members were allocated to the various religious communities. There were fifty-four Christians and forty-five Muslims. The Christian seats were allocated as follows: thirty Maronites, eleven Greek Orthodox, six

Greek Catholics, five Armenians, and the remaining two seats to other Christians. The Taif Agreement increased the number of Muslim deputies to parity with the Christians. The Muslim seats were distributed as follows: twenty-two Sunnis, twenty-two Shi'a, eight Druze, and two Alawites. The powers of the Sunni prime minister and the Shi'a speaker of the Chamber of Deputies were also enhanced.

In the post-Taif era, under Syrian influence, subtle but significant changes occurred in the political process. The constitution, which was adhered to faithfully throughout the crisis, was violated. President Ilyas Harawi was allowed to remain in power for more than six years almost without protest even though the legitimacy of the Lebanese government was weakened. In contrast, during the 1958 crisis the nation rose in opposition to extending Camille Chamoun's presidency.

The basis of elections was shifted from the district to region. Although protested by many and boycotted by even more, especially Christians, resulting in the lowest voter turnout in Lebanese history, the changes stayed. The consequence was to undermine traditional leaders in favor of political party leaders. The result was a significant increase in party representation and a decline in local leaders. The largest parties in the parliament were Hizballah and Amal. The Christian boycott and the ban on key Christian leader participation greatly diminished the influence of Christian representatives in parliament.

Political Dynamics

The Lebanese constitutional system was designed to preserve the existing social order, and initially it did so effectively. Political control was concentrated in the hands of traditional leaders of the various religious communities. The replacement of the mandatory regime by the Lebanese government reinforced the position of these traditional leaders. The electoral districts were generally small, permitting traditional leaders to call upon village and family loyalties to win elections. Local and personal ties, consequently, far outweighed national or foreign commitments. The key elements of a traditional leader's political strength were his ability to form a coalition with other traditional leaders that could draw the widest popular support and his ability to provide services to his constituency.

In each electoral district, parliamentary seats were divided by religious sects in a general way that approximated the religious makeup of the district's population. During an election, traditional leaders formed competing lists. Each list was composed of one candidate for each seat. In most cases, competition for political influence in a district was between coreligionists. In Zahlah, for example, historically the dominant local leaders had been two Greek Catholics. Each of these men headed competing electoral lists, pitting Maronite against Maronite and Sunni against Sunni. If the system had been designed so that Christian competed against Muslim, a district such as Zahlah would probably have elected five Christians. In several other districts, a large Muslim minority would also likely have been disenfranchised. Conversely, Christian minorities in other districts would probably also have been unrepresented.

Another consequence of the list system was that a minority candidate tended to reflect the views of his fellow list members to a greater extent than those of his coreligionists. For example, a Christian elected from a predominantly Muslim district was more likely to support Muslim pan-Arab aspirations than Christian aspirations for close ties with the West. On the other hand, Muslims elected from preponderantly Christian districts would be Lebanese nationalists. As a result, votes in parliament rarely broke purely along religious lines.

Although support for a candidate was in part due to political, religious, and historical considerations, another important factor was the services he could render. Because the central government was weak, the parliamentary deputy often became the vehicle through which public services were distributed. The local leader also provided direct assistance in the form of loans and subsidies to his constituents from his own personal funds. In this way, he could build up a solid base of support.

Deputies and party lists also maintained support by the direct distribution of funds at election time. Expenditures included payments to political agents, general expenses, buying bloc votes, occasional bribes, and the transportation to the polling places of supporters residing outside the district. The greatest single expense, however, was the purchase of individual votes. Since most of this money went to those who in all probability would vote for the list in any case, these payments were more in the nature of a subsidy. Few voters actually searched for the highest bidder.

Independent candidates rarely did well. An independent usually had neither the family ties nor the financial backing to challenge established lists. Another important result of the political system was the failure of truly national parties to take root. Politics remained local, not national. Those few parties with a truly national following, as a rule, were not so much national political parties as nationwide lists led by prominent politicians. For instance, in 1972 the National Liberal Party, founded by Camille Chamoun, tended to be a coalition of local leaders who were personally loyal to Chamoun. Rank-and-file members often had little contact with one another. Thus, a Shi'a supporting the National Liberal Party from Tyre was probably a follower of Shi'a leader Kazim Khalil, who was allied with Chamoun. The individual Shi'a would have little in common with a National Liberal from the Maronite area in the Shouf and even less contact with him.

A few parties were based on a definite political ideology. These included the Lebanese Communist Party, the Syrian Nationalist Party, and the pro-Iraqi and pro-Syrian factions of the Ba'th party. These parties had little electoral success. On the whole, traditional Lebanese leaders were successful in preventing ideological parties from establishing a strong regional base. The very few members of parliament who have represented these parties were elected because of family ties rather than party affiliation.

Some parties combined traditional leaders with a party organization. For instance, the Progressive Socialist Party had two very distinct elements: those who were moderately leftist in outlook and the traditional Druze following of party leader Walid Jumblatt. Whereas the former tended to dominate the party hierarchy and certainly had the most articulate spokesmen, the latter formed the backbone of support for the party. Similarly, the Phalange Party combined traditional loyalty to the Gemayel family with a virulent form of Lebanese nationalism. Prior to the civil war, the Phalange had reached out beyond its traditional base to include non-Maronite Christians and Muslims. The civil war reduced Phalange membership to its Christian base. The Phalange, however, unlike the Progressive Socialist Party, also lost much of its feudal structure. The Gemayels lost their dominant role, whereas Jumblatt actually was strengthened.

Even the most successful alignments and political parties could not come close to dominating the parliament. A bloc of fifteen members was considered very large. Perhaps one-third of the deputies did not consider themselves committed to any coalition or bloc affiliation whatsoever. Alliances were made and broken; a onetime ally could easily become a political foe. Before the civil war, the Lebanese political system generally worked. Most Lebanese were reasonably satisfied that their basic concerns—security and a fair share of government largesse—were addressed. Many younger Lebanese grumbled about the anachronistic system and felt that they were held back by the rigid quota system, but when the time came to vote or to alter significantly the system, most preferred the status quo.

The great crisis of the first twenty years of Lebanese independence occurred in 1958. In that year, Camille Chamoun was supposed to relinquish the presidency of the republic, because the constitution prohibits an individual from serving more than one six-year term. Chamoun, however, attempted to force a change in the constitution so that he could succeed himself. He appears to have been motivated mainly by personal ambition. Nevertheless, he was also greatly concerned about the growing influence of Nasserism throughout the Arab world and the strong influence of the Egyptian leader on Lebanese Sunni Muslims; he, therefore, wished to move Lebanon closer to the West to protect it from regional trends.

Despite Chamoun's attempt to focus on these latter concerns, the key issue in the 1958 crisis became his attempt to subvert the constitution and national covenant, in which the Christians had agreed not to disassociate Lebanon from the Arab world in favor of the West. In 1958, each community feared the other was breaking the agreement and intercommunal conflict erupted.

According to the compromise that ended the fighting, Chamoun agreed to step down when his term expired. The new president was General Fuad Chehab, Maronite commander in chief of the army. Chehab and his chosen successor,

Charles Helou, governed Lebanon for the next twelve years by upholding the constitution and abiding by the principles embodied in the national covenant. Despite the relative political calm and the economic prosperity of this period, the fatal flaw in the system began to emerge. Through carefully balancing the country's many factions to ensure security for all, the designers of the system made it too inflexible. Modification was nearly impossible. As a consequence, the political system became less and less responsive to the changing political needs of the country.

The 1960s were marked by a rapid acceleration of social change in Lebanon. This change occurred in three areas—population growth, urbanization, and the political awakening of the resident Palestinians. Lebanon's population was growing rapidly, with the number of members in some sects increasing faster than others. Nevertheless, political representation was based on the 1932 census. Because of the fear that the delicate sectarian balance would be upset, no agreement on how to conduct a new census could be reached. The Christians insisted that overseas (emigrant) Lebanese be included, since they were mostly Christians. Many Muslims also had doubts as to how their own community would fare. Thus, although nearly everyone agreed that a census was necessary, no one was anxious to press for one. As a result, parliamentary representation became less and less representative.

Urbanization and all its related problems brought major changes to Lebanon during the 1960s when Muslim and Christian villagers flocked to Beirut. The capital's metropolitan area expanded to include between one-third and one-half the country's population. A belt of poor suburbs soon ringed the prosperous core. In each suburb, one religious confession tended to predominate. For example, Ayn Rummanah, Hadath, and Furn al-Shebak were Christian strongholds. Others such as Shiyah and Naba were predominantly Shi'a. The poor workers and unemployed of these areas were courted by the ideologues—socialists, communists, and rightists. Most, nevertheless, retained traditional loyalties. They still returned to their villages whenever possible. Families continued to be an important source of support, and communal identification remained strong. Finally, what little influence these people had on the government depended on the traditional deputy who represented their home village. Each person, even a second-or-third generation resident in Beirut, voted in the village of his family's origin.

With the growing economic prosperity in Lebanon in the early 1960s, disparity in the distribution of income became more apparent, resulting in the alienation of many of the urban poor. The Shi'a, fearing Israeli raids and looking for work, became disaffected and fled in large numbers from the south to Beirut. They were greatly influenced by Palestinian neighbors in the crowded districts in which they lived. Indeed, the Palestinian community proved to be a catalyst for social change in Lebanese society. The more ideologically oriented and militarily powerful Palestinian commando groups provided an umbrella under which Lebanese leftist organizations received direct financial assistance and training.

The transformation of the Palestinian community in Lebanon was another development with which the Lebanese system was incapable of coping. Following the 1948 Arab-Israeli war, more than 100,000 Palestinian refugees fled to Lebanon. Relatively less constrained in Lebanon than in other Arab states, this community grew and to some extent prospered. By the late 1960s, the Palestinians numbered more than 300,000. The poorer Palestinians, however, never escaped the squalid refugee camps.

The majority of Palestinians—even those who were well-off—were never fully integrated into Lebanese society. Only a distinct minority took Lebanese citizenship. Most did not want to be Lebanese; nor did the Lebanese want the Palestinians to remain. Although they were welcome guests with whose plight the Lebanese sympathized, most Lebanese considered them aliens. Moreover, a wholesale granting of citizenship would have further upset the delicate confessional balance and created severe economic strains and the Lebanese were not prepared to do this. In addition, the absorption of the Palestinians into the Lebanese political system would have permitted the international community to forget its obligation to the Palestinians, leaving the burden of providing for them totally on the Lebanese.

For the most part, the Palestinian community in Lebanon caused little difficulty until the 1960s. Hope of returning to their homeland rested with the Arab states. The Palestinians were politically docile. But in the early 1960s, the realization began to grow among the Palestinians that the Arab states were not fully committed to assisting the Palestinians' return to their homeland. Increasingly, young Palestinians came to believe that if they were ever to see their homeland, they would have to rely on themselves and not the Arab states. These young men formed the backbone of the nascent commando movements. The form of Palestinian nationalism espoused by the commandos, however, did not attract large numbers of active supporters until after the 1967 Arab-Israeli war. The humiliation of the Arab armies at that time convinced even the doubters that the Palestinians had no one to rely on but themselves.

This transformation of attitudes radically changed the Lebanese-Palestinian relationship. The Palestinians armed themselves and exerted pressure on all Arabs for more active support. For the Palestinians, the liberation of Palestine became the central aim of the "Arab struggle." In their view, all Arabs had to direct their energies to this struggle, and any act designed to reach this goal was justifiable. For many Lebanese, particularly Christians and rightists, the Palestinians became overbearing. Armed Palestinians on the streets of Beirut became the symbol of Palestinian arrogance. The weak Lebanese government and undermanned army, itself made impotent by sectarian politics, were incapable of dealing with the Palestinian militants. The inability of the government to cope with the situation was underlined by the growing cycle of Palestinian attacks on Israel, followed by Israeli retaliations against Lebanon.

Palestinians were able to take advantage of the inflexible Lebanese political system to gain allies among the Lebanese. For many Muslim Lebanese, a political alliance with the Palestinians gave them not only the mantle of Arab nationalism but also the military support of the commandos. For Palestinians, an alliance with the Lebanese left gave them a foothold in the Lebanese political system without becoming part of it. Even a small Palestinian foothold was sufficient to prevent a concerted Lebanese effort to limit Palestinian autonomy in Lebanon. In 1969, following a series of inconclusive clashes between the Lebanese army and the Palestinians, the Lebanese government and the Palestinians reached an agreement in Cairo that regulated Palestinian-Lebanese relations. The Cairo Accord, in fact, recognized the Palestinians' right to operate outside Lebanese sovereignty in some areas of Lebanon.

Because of the failure of the government to assert Lebanon's interests over those of the Palestinians, Lebanese rightists built or expanded their own militia. Of all the Lebanese parties, the Phalange was the most determined to provide sufficient military force to counter the Palestinians. The rightists also moved to strengthen their influence in the parliament so they could force the government to take a firmer stand against the Palestinians. In August 1970, by a fifty to forty-nine vote, a hard-line Christian rightist, Sulayman Franjiyah, was elected president. The election was generally regarded as a victory for the pro-Western "little Lebanon" supporters of former President Chamoun and as a defeat for the coalition of General Chehab that had dominated Lebanon for the previous twelve years. The rightists counted on Franjiyah, who had the reputation of being very tough, to use the Lebanese army to control the Palestinians.

The Jordanian army crackdown on the Palestine Liberation Organization (PLO) in 1970–1971 had significant consequences for Lebanon. Following the defeat of the Palestinians in Jordan, Lebanon was the only Arab state in which the commandos could still organize and operate freely. Consequently, thousands of armed Palestinians fled Jordan to the relative security of Lebanon. This influx of armed Palestinians further upset the military and political balance.

Thus, by the early 1970s the stage was set for the Lebanese civil war. The rigid political structure that proved so effective at preserving the status quo was incapable of adjusting to changes that were caused by the maldistribution of wealth, uneven population growth, rapid urbanization, and the growing militancy of the Palestinians. Attempts to reconcile the differences failed because the consensus that was embodied in the constitution and the national covenant was no longer accepted by a sufficient number of Lebanese and Palestinians.

The fifteen years of fighting that devastated Lebanon from 1975 to 1990 further exacerbated political differences. Some of the old restraints that prevented society from disintegrating were ignored. Palestinian commandos became intimately involved in Lebanese politics and fought for one faction against another. Leftist Muslims openly demanded that the national covenant be dropped. The Lebanese army became involved in sectarian struggles and disintegrated. The Syrians, who many believed wanted to absorb Lebanon into Syria, were invited into Lebanon to bring order. Finally, many Lebanese Christians and rightists allied themselves with the Arabs' primary foe, the Israelis. All became entangled in intra-Arab conflicts.

The Israeli invasion of Lebanon in June 1982 shattered the relative balance of forces and perhaps provided a brief opportunity for the Lebanese to bring stability back to their state. This was not the case, however.

Quite surprisingly, the election of Phalange militia leader Bashir Gemayel to the presidency gave hope to many Lebanese. Christians obviously saw order being restored by a strong confident leader. Some Muslims and Palestinians, however, also welcomed the election. They saw in Bashir a person who could control the most extreme Christian elements. Immediately after his election, Bashir made several conciliatory gestures to the Muslims that raised hopes that Lebanon was finally ending its ordeal.

These hopes were an illusion. Bashir was seen as too close to the Israelis. Therefore, the Syrians and their allies vehemently opposed his being sworn in as president, and he was killed by an assassin's bomb before he took office. In response, some of Bashir's supporters massacred hundreds of Palestinians and other residents of the Israeli-controlled neighborhoods and camps of Sabra and Shatilla just outside of Beirut. Sectarian feelings were inflamed, and a brief opportunity to stabilize the situation was lost.

Bashir Gemayel's older brother Amine was elected president by an overwhelming majority of parliament. Amine Gemayel faced an impossible situation. Israeli forces occupied the southern third of his nation. Syrians occupied the eastern half and the north. His area of control was primarily in the Christian areas of East Beirut and the Christian-controlled enclave to the east and north of Beirut. Nevertheless, hope rested with the United States, who had supervised the withdrawal of more than 15,000 Palestinians, including most of their combatants, in August 1982, and who reintroduced troops into Beirut following the Palestinian camp massacres. Unfortunately, these hopes were also dashed. The Americans brokered an Israeli-Lebanese agreement signed on May 17, 1983. Protracted negotiation, combined with the concessions extracted from the Lebanese government by the Israelis, provided the Syrians the opportunity to regroup after combat losses and to reassert their influence over Lebanese factions, which were increasingly opposed to Gemayel. This Syrian-backed opposition prevented the Lebanese government from implementing the May 17 agreement. Israeli occupation turned many who had welcomed the Israelis into critics.

The Lebanese government was further weakened by the Israeli decision to withdraw southward, turning over their positions not to the Lebanese government but to Druze forces, which were allied with Syrians. This unilateral Israeli action altered the balance of forces. The Gemayel government clearly was on the defensive. Gemayel's opponents realized that the Israelis would not support him and that the international force was too weak to be effective. Therefore, few Lebanese factions dealt seriously with Gemayel, because they saw that his position was weakening and that they could extract greater concessions in the future.

Gemayel's only hope was to turn to the United States. The Americans, however, did not wish to take sides in internal political disputes. They believed the Maronites, as represented by Gemayel, had to be willing to give more real power to disadvantaged Lebanese, including the Shi'a.

The unilateral Israeli withdrawal from the Beirut area also changed the U.S. role in the view of many Lebanese, including the Shi'a, Druze, and other anti-Gemayel Lebanese. Until the withdrawal, the United States was seen as protecting West Beirut and its southern suburbs from the Israelis. After the Israeli withdrawal, the only logical U.S. purpose was to protect the Gemayel government from its Syrian and Lebanese opponents. Just as Gemayel realized his best hope of maintaining his influence was securing U.S. backing, his opponents determined for the same reason that the Americans had to leave. The United States, however, did not realize that its role had changed. Consequently, when U.S. forces in Lebanon came under military attack, the country was surprised.

The United States responded to these attacks with naval bombardment and air attacks but would not make a larger commitment or withdrawal. On October 23, 1983, a lone suicide truck bomber blew up the U.S. Marine barracks in Beirut, killing 241 U.S. military personnel and wounding many others. Simultaneously, a French barracks was bombed, and a few days later, the same method was used to destroy an Israeli barracks in south Lebanon. Unprepared to cope with such large losses of life, the United States withdrew in February 1984.

In June 1985, for much the same reasons, Israeli forces also withdrew to a security zone in Southern Lebanon. Israel strengthened its allies, the South Lebanon Army (SLA), in the security zone. As a consequence, Lebanon was effectively partitioned into zones of Syrian influence and Israeli influence, and a Christian-controlled government of Lebanon, which was located in a small enclave east of Beirut. Despite the apparent simplification of the situation by the partition of Lebanon into zones of influence, the underlying reality remained more complicated. Neither Israel nor Syria proved able to pacify its zone effectively. Continued Syrian and Iranian support enabled Lebanese Shi'a to sustain their resistance to Israeli hegemony in southern Lebanon. Differences between Hizballah and Amal resulted in internal Shi'a conflicts.

Hizballah wanted to carry attacks into Israel and believed Syrian occupation was also a concern. It welcomed returning PLO fighters and tried to assist them. Amal, on the other hand, countenanced attacks only on Israeli and SLA units within Lebanon. Amal allied with Syria and sought to restrict any organized PLO presence by besieging the Palestinian refugee camps. A strategy of kidnapping and holding hostages, including citizens of Western countries, by small militant groups introduced yet another element of chaos into the situation. Although it was generally believed that hostages were held for specific reasons, such as to secure the release of kinsmen held in foreign prisons because of involvement in terrorist activities or to secure funds through blackmail or bribery, the hostage phenomenon made Lebanon an unsafe place for many foreigners. Consequently, in the absence of a general settlement that would enable state authority to be renewed, it was virtually impossible for external powers either to secure the release of the hostages or to give assistance to the Lebanese government.

The Christian community similarly fragmented. The Christians had maintained the independence of their enclave by not allowing their internal rivalries to interfere with their resistance to outside domination. Although Gemayel, supported by the Lebanese army and Metn militia, strongly disagreed with the Maronite Lebanese Forces, Gemayel and the Maronite forces were united in their opposition to the Syrians and other threats to their community. They differed on how to resist the Syrians, however. Gemayel was willing to enter into a dialogue with the Syrians. The Lebanese Forces favored confrontation.

Following the withdrawal of U.S. and Israeli forces, the Christians looked elsewhere for assistance. During the Amal-Syrian siege of the Palestinian refugee camps, the Christians assisted the Palestinians in breaking the siege. Even more surprising, they facilitated the infiltration of PLO combatants into the camps in order to strengthen the anti-Syrian forces. Moreover, the Christians turned to Iraq, which, as the archrival of Syria, was a natural ally.

The Christian enclave, under the presidency of Amine Gemayel, was the core opposition to the establishment of Syrian hegemony in Lebanon. This opposition was based on the international recognition of the legitimacy of the Gemayel government and the unity of the Christian community. Both were shattered in fall 1988. President Gemayel's term was nearing its end in September 1988. Gemayel resisted calls to circumvent the constitution and extend his time in office. Constitutional legitimacy was vital to the Christians. Syria would not allow an independent Christian to be elected president. At the same time, the Christians were not prepared to allow a Syrian puppet to be chosen. An impasse resulted. Minutes before the expiration of his constitutional term of office, President Gemayel appointed the Maronite commander of the Lebanese armed forces, General Michel Aoun, as acting prime minister of a caretaker government. The previous Sunni prime minister, Salim al-Huss, and his government, however, refused to step down. As a result, Lebanon had two governments and international recognition of the Christian government in the enclave was lost.

In an effort to break the impasse, in early 1989 Aoun embarked on a campaign to assert the authority of his government over the various militia, including the Maronite Lebanese Forces, and to rally the country against the universally unpopular Syrian occupation. Aoun's forces were not up to the task. Christian unity was shattered, which ended years of Christian preeminence and allowed Syrian dominance of Lebanon to be complete.

The international community would not allow the chaotic situation to continue. Under Arab auspices, a meeting of sixty-two of the seventy-three surviving members of Lebanon's ninety-nine-man parliament, originally elected in 1972, was convened in Taif, Saudi Arabia. The resulting Taif Agreement of October 22, 1989, called for changes in the Lebanese constitution that balanced Christian-Muslim representation in the parliament and reduced the power of the Maronite president. The role of the Sunni prime minister was increased, but the Shi'a did not see their position enhanced sufficiently to reflect either their numbers or military strength. Many Lebanese were encouraged by the commitment of the Taif Agreement to the withdrawal of Syrian forces. The Taif Agreement was opposed by Shi'a militia leaders and also by General Aoun, who rejected the legitimacy of the Taif process. The international community welcomed the agreement.

The Lebanese parliament met on November 5, 1990, in northern Lebanon and elected Rene Mu'awad as the next president. Mu'awad was an independent Maronite who had been opposed by the Syrians the preceding year. Before Mu'awad could exert his authority, he was assassinated by a car bomb in a Muslim area of West Beirut. The Lebanese parliament was reconvened in the Syrian-controlled Biqa Valley town of Chtura, and Ilyas Hrawi was elected president. Hrawi, coming from the Biqa, was clearly seen as the Syrian candidate. His election brought Lebanese institutions clearly under Syrian control.

The last resister to Syrian hegemony was the politically naïve General Aoun. Holding fast to his opposition to the Taif Agreement, saying that it had to include a clear timetable for the withdrawal of Syrian forces, Aoun soon fell into conflict with nearly everyone else in Lebanon, including the Lebanese forces. Fierce and destructive, yet inconclusive, intra-Maronite fighting for control of the Maronite region erupted in February 1990. The general found few international supporters except the Iraqis, who had problems of their own after their August 2, 1990, invasion of Kuwait.

The changed political environment in the Middle East following Iraqi President Saddam Hussein's attempt to invade and annex Kuwait left Aoun isolated. Syrian President Assad found it in his interest to join the allied regional and international coalition that marshaled forces against Saddam Hussein. Caught up in the midst of a far larger regional crisis than that posed in Lebanon, many members of the allied coalition who might otherwise have resisted further Syrian efforts to consolidate control in Lebanon accepted the Syrian move against the forces of General Aoun in October 1990.

With the successful suppression of General Aoun, Syrian control was effectively established over most of Lebanon. The Syrian-dominated government of President Ilyas Hrawi and Prime Minister Omar Karami was able to begin implementing the various provisions of the Taif Agreement. Partial dismantling of the Lebanese militias began; the Lebanese army began deploying over more of the country; armed

PLO militiamen were confined to their camps; and the new fifty-fifty Muslim-Christian ratio in the Lebanese parliament was instituted, although new members of the parliament were at first appointed, rather than elected. Most important, peace, unknown for many years, settled over most of the country. Thousands of émigrés returned home in 1991 to assess the situation. Moreover, U.S.-fostered peace talks involving all parties of the Arab-Israeli conflict, including Lebanon, were convened. The hope was that these talks could lead to the withdrawal of Syrian and Israeli forces from Lebanon. Finally, most of the remaining (and all American) hostages held in Lebanon were released by the end of 1991. Indeed, Lebanon's many years of conflict were over.

Progress was also made on the political front. Elections for a new parliament were held in three stages in August 1992. The overwhelming majority of Christians boycotted the election, protesting Syrian domination of the process. Nevertheless, the first general election since 1972 brought new faces to the Lebanese political scene. On the Muslim side of the aisle, Amal, Hizballah, and traditional Sunni groups brought more-representative leadership to power. Amal leader Nabih Berri was elected speaker. In a move designed to breathe life into the Lebanese economy, wealthy Lebanese businessman Rafik Hariri became prime minister in October 1992.

There was room for skepticism. In the first place, although Syria was publicly committed to withdrawing from Lebanon, many feared Syria had no such intention. Moreover, the price of tranquillity was significant repression by Syria and its pervasive intelligence activities in Lebanon. What is more, occasional acts of terrorism, such as car bombings at the American University of Beirut and in Muslim West Beirut in late 1991, were reminders that even Syrian control was unable to guarantee complete security.

After years of struggle between the Israelis, their South Lebanon Army (SLA) allies, and the Hizballah-led resistance, the Israelis decided to withdraw from South Lebanon in the spring of 2000. Almost overnight, the SLA collapsed. Several thousand SLA members and their families fled to Israel. The majority of SLA members surrendered to Hizballah and the Lebanese Army.

Hizballah was given credit by most Lebanese for forcing the Israelis out. Nearly twenty-five years of Israeli direct intervention in South Lebanon ended. Even some of Hizballah's staunchest Lebanese critics commended Hizballah for its achievement in liberating Lebanon from Israeli occupation. Beyond its military role, Hizballah became a major actor in Lebanese domestic politics. For nearly two decades Hizballah had provided major social services for the Shi`ites. In the mid-1990s, Hizballah entered the political scene. They became the largest party in the Lebanese Parliament and most observers believe their representation would have been even greater in truly fair elections.

Foreign Policy

Lebanon's foreign policy is largely determined by geography. Bordering the Mediterranean, Lebanon is a meeting place for the East and the West. To play this role successfully, the Lebanese have traditionally maintained their neutrality. They avoided taking sides in the cold war or in the intra-Arab politics. As much as possible, they attempted to avoid becoming involved directly in the Arab-Israeli dispute. The Lebanese believed that in order to maintain their neutrality, they had to be either a powerful regional state, thereby discouraging neighbors from interfering in Lebanese neutrality, or so weak as to make any move against them a blatant act of aggression. The Lebanese chose the latter course.

Communal differences made it difficult to obtain a consensus in foreign policy as well as in domestic policy. Despite these difficulties, Lebanon played an active role in international affairs. It was a founding member of the Arab League and generally placed itself in the moderate range on the Arab political spectrum. The Lebanese supported anti-Israel measures by the Arab states but not quite as virulently as some of their neighbors. As Palestinian influence within Lebanon increased, however, the Lebanese attitude toward Israel hardened. In the early 1960s it was often said that Lebanon would be the second Arab state to recognize Israel; this is no longer the case. Jordan signed a peace treaty with Israel in October 1994, and the PLO signed a Declaration of Principles in September 1993 recognizing Israel. Lebanon has not and cannot until Syria reaches a settlement with Israel.

Lebanon also provided a key regional center for educational institutions, international organizations, and diplomatic activity. Given Lebanon's good relations with Central and Eastern Europe, the West, some Third World states, and the Arabs, Beirut was a center of international communication. The Lebanese took their international role very seriously. They are founding members of the United Nations and viewed themselves as a bridge between the East and the West. This role has been greatly reduced as a result of the civil war.

The formulation of Lebanese foreign policy was hindered by the same disagreements that have marked Lebanese domestic affairs. The Christian community tended to stress the non-Arab Lebanese ties and Lebanon's long-established relations with the West. Moreover, the Christians emphasized the enduring links that Lebanon maintains with its large emigrant communities in the United States, Canada, Australia, and Latin America. The Christians usually preferred to emphasize the differences between Lebanon and its Arab neighbors rather than the similarities. In contrast, the Muslims, as a rule, preferred to enhance their role and that of Lebanon in the Arab world. Lebanese foreign policy was therefore a compromise, as embodied in the 1943 national covenant. Neither the Christians nor the Muslims, however, have yet abandoned the hope of prevailing someday. The compromise was significantly altered as Syria increased its control over Lebanon. Today, on major regional and international issues, Beirut takes its lead from Damascus.

Foreigners were used, and continue to be used, by Lebanese factions to strengthen their own faction against the others. As circumstances and the balance of forces shift, so do Lebanese attitudes toward foreigners. Syrians can intervene to save the Christians at one moment only to find themselves being attacked by the Christians at another. Palestinians can be fighting the Syrians one day, only to be allied with them the next. Israelis were welcomed by Shi'a villagers one year, only to be the target of Shi'a attacks the next. Until Lebanon places national reconciliation above factional interests, any foreign intervention—no matter how noble the motive—is likely to have the enmity of one or more factions.

At the same time, Lebanon remains hostage to the larger regional arena. Domestic aspects of Lebanese politics cannot be separated from the larger regional and international environment in which Lebanon exists. The complex ethnic and sectarian composition of Lebanon's diverse population reflects every religious and political strain found in the region. The rivalries and conflicts of the larger Middle East and Mediterranean region, therefore, continue to resonate in Lebanon and fuel the domestic conflict, which, in turn, calls upon the support of kindred external actors to intervene. The result, of course, has been a tragedy for Lebanon: As the weakest state in its immediate region, it seems incapable of reasserting its legitimacy and sovereignty on its own. Conversely, many outside parties have been drawn into the Lebanese conflict to their own detriment.

This situation is not surprising, since Lebanon initially gained its status as an independent state by external support and intervention. As the capability of France, and later Britain and the United States, to help defend this legitimacy has diminished, other forces challenging the established order in Lebanon have emerged. The unresolved nature of the continuing disputes in Lebanon reflects the unresolved nature of continuing disputes in the region as a whole. Stability will be restored to Lebanon in one of two ways: (1) a satisfactorily negotiated settlement of regional as well as local domestic issues; or (2) a major geostrategic change in the structure of the Middle Eastern balance of forces. One such change would be the Syrians' imposing complete control over Lebanon. Clearly, the Syrians have become the dominant influence in Lebanese foreign policy as well as domestic policy. Only time will tell whether stability and sovereignty will be restored to Lebanon and whether the Lebanese will again assert their own national identity in domestic and international affairs.

When terrorists attacked the World Trade Center in New York and the Pentagon in Virginia on September 11, 2001, Lebanon's international situation became more precarious. The American war on international terrorism placed Hizballah high on the list of international terrorist organizations. United States demands that the government of Lebanon curtail Hizballah were rebuffed. Across the political spectrum Lebanese reject the American characterization of Hizballah as an international terrorist organization. Hizballah had become an integral part of the Lebanese political fabric. In addition, Hizballah had strong and influential regional allies. Few Lebanese were willing to threaten domestic stability and the ire of regional powers to accommodate the Americans. Not becoming a venue of the American war on terrorism became an additional foreign policy challenge for the Lebanese.

Bibliography

There are dozens of excellent works on Lebanon, and the number has increased significantly in recent years as international interest has grown during the decades of turmoil. For an understanding of Lebanese history, Kamal S. Salibi's *The Modern History of Lebanon* (New York: Praeger Publishers, 1965) should be the starting point. This modern history is concise, well written, and not overwhelming in detail, and Salibi is perhaps the finest historian of Lebanon. This should be read in conjunction with his *A House of Many Mansions: The History of Lebanon Reconsidered* (London: B. Tauris Press, 1988). Since the first publication of *The Precarious Republic* (New York: Random House, 1968), by Michael C. Hudson, it has become the measure by which other works are judged. See also Helena Cobban's *The Making of Modern Lebanon* (Boulder: Westview Press, 1985).

Lebanon's political and social development is analyzed in more specialized works. Samir G. Khalaf, in "Primordial Ties and Politics in Lebanon," *Middle Eastern Studies* 4 (April 1968): 243–269, discusses the basic personal, family, village, and religious identification of Lebanese and how this self-perception affects politics. A most sympathetic explanation of the traditional Lebanese political system is found in Elie Adib Salem, *Modernization Without Revolution: Lebanon's Experience* (Bloomington, Ind.: Indiana University Press, 1973). Halim Barakat offers the best short study of the Lebanese political and social system in "Social and Political Integration in Lebanon: A Case Study," *Middle East Journal* 27, no. 2 (1973): 301–318. A fine study of the functioning of the Lebanese political system at the village and district levels is presented by Peter Gubser in "The Zu'ama of Zahlah: The Current Situation in a Lebanese Town," *Middle East Journal* 27, no. 2 (1973): 173–189. John P. Entelis discusses the formation and growth of the Phalange (Al-Kata'ib) in *Pluralism and Party Transformation in Lebanon: Al-Kata'ib, 1936–1970* (Leiden: E. J. Brill, 1974).

The 1975–1976 period of the Lebanese civil war has generated considerable literature. Kamal Salibi's *Crossroads to Civil War, Lebanon 1958–1976* (Delmar, N.Y.: Caravan Books, 1976) provides an excellent study of the trends and events that led to the crisis. Michael Hudson's "The Palestinian Factor in the Lebanese Civil War," *Middle East Journal* 32, no. 3 (1978): 261–278, presents a concise and well-developed analysis of the Palestinian dilemma in Lebanon. See also P. Edward Haley and Lewis W. Snider's *Lebanon in Crisis* (Syracuse, N.Y.: Syracuse University Press, 1979) for an emphasis on the international aspect of the conflict and Walid Khalid's *Conflict and Violence in Lebanon: Confrontation in the Middle East* (Cambridge, Mass.: Center for International Affairs, Harvard University, 1979).

The War for Lebanon, 1970–1983 (Ithaca: Cornell University Press, 1984), by Itamar Rabinovitch, provides a scholarly presentation written with a high degree of objectivity. Elie

Salem gives a firsthand account of the difficult years of the Amine Gemayel presidency in *Violence and Diplomacy in Lebanon: The Troubled Years, 1982–1988* (London: I. B. Tauris; New York [Distributed by] St. Martin's, 1995).

Augustus Richard Norton has written extensively on the Shiʻa. Perhaps none is better than *Amal and the Shiʻa: Struggle for the Soul of Lebanon* (Austin: University of Texas Press, 1987). Norton advances his discussion of Shiʻa politics and the future role of Hizballah in his excellent article, "Hizballah: From Radicalism to Pragmatism," *Middle East Policy*, (January 1998) Vol. V, pp. 147.–158. More has been written about the Druze. One study of note is Robert Brenton Betts's *The Druze* (New Haven: Yale University Press, 1988).

For the post–civil war period a number of articles and books have addressed the political, economic, and international problems facing the Lebanese. Michael C. Hudson discusses the limited political change brought to Lebanon by the Taif Agreement in "Lebanon After Taif: Another Reform Opportunity Lost?" *Arab Studies Quarterly* (Winter 1999). The economic challenges are critically addressed by Robert Springborg and Guilain Denoeux in "Hariri's Lebanon: Singapore of the Middle East or Sanaa of the Levant," *Middle East Policy* (October 1998). The subordination of Lebanese politics to Syrian interest and the prospects for Lebanon's future depending upon the Arab-Israeli conflict are analyzed by Augustus Richard Norton in "Lebanon's Conundrum," *Arab Studies Quarterly* (Winter 1999).

9

Syrian Arab Republic

Curtis R. Ryan

Like many other countries in the Middle East, modern Syria was carved out of the collapsing Ottoman Empire by the victors in World War I. After independence in 1946, Syria politics went through a period of instability and repeated coups d'etat until 1970 when General Hafiz al-Asad took power. At the time, many Syrians saw Asad as simply the leader of the latest coup. But unlike all his predecessors, Asad was able to keep power. His regime lasted for thirty years, and his Baʻth Party continued to rule the country after his death in June 2000. The resulting political succession in Syria came just over a year after the succession in neighboring Jordan, following the death of another long-serving ruler, King Hussein.

Unlike Jordan, however, Syria is a republic, and an avowedly radical and revolutionary one at that. Yet here too a son had been designated successor to his long-serving father. And here too, the son, Bishar al-Asad, did indeed succeed his father as ruler of the nation. This apparently dynastic succession is certainly unusual for a republic. It is still more unusual when one considers that Syria's ruling Baʻth party has long been a vocal opponent of monarchy in general and has seen itself as the very heartbeat of radical Arab nationalism in the Middle East. As he established himself as his father's successor, Bishar al-Asad concentrated on consolidating his regime. But the main issues that confront the second Asad regime are actually the same as those that confronted the first: getting back the Golan territory that was lost to Israel in the 1967 Arab-Israeli War, and reforming the economic—and possibly the political—system.

Historical Background

The Syrian capital, Damascus, is one of the oldest continuously inhabited cities in the world. In its ancient history, the country was ruled during different periods by

Assyrians, Babylonians, Persians, Greeks, and Romans. In its modern history, Syria fell under the dominance of the Ottoman Turks and later the French.

Modern Syria traces its unique heritage as an independent state to the seventh century Umayyad caliphate. Two years after the death of the Prophet Muhammad in A.D. 632, his followers captured what is now Syria from the Byzantine Empire. Following the Muslim war over succession to Muhammad during the 660s, Muawiyah, the governor of Damascus, was recognized as the fifth caliph, or leader, of the Islamic community. He transferred the capital of the expanding empire from the Arabian Peninsula to Damascus. Syria thus became the hub of an empire stretching from Spain to India. But the Ummayad Empire remained rooted largely in an Arab and Muslim military elite, ruling over large numbers of non-Arabs and non-Muslims. The narrowness of the regime led to the emergence of a diverse coalition of opposition groups, which eventually succeeded in toppling the state. The Umayyad dynasty was overthrown in A.D. 750 and replaced by the Abbasids, who moved the imperial capital to Baghdad. Damascus, once the proud center of the empire, became a provincial capital—a status it continued to hold until modern times.

Following the Abbasid revolution, Syria became a political pawn of more powerful neighboring states. Invading armies entered from Mesopotamia, Anatolia, and Egypt. All left their imprint, but none more than the Shi'ite Fatimid dynasty of Egypt. Conquering the eastern Mediterranean shore in the tenth century, the Fatimids, more than any other Muslim rulers over Syria, actively pushed the spread of Islam. In response to their increasingly difficult position, many Syrian Christians assisted the invading European crusaders, thus contributing to confessional divisions and strife. By the mid-twelfth century, however, Saladin (Salah ad-Din) reconquered the area held by the Crusaders. In the years following the restoration of Islamic rule, tensions persisted between many of Syria's Muslims and Christians over the lingering wounds of the Crusader Wars.

Relative stability returned to Syria when it was conquered by the Ottoman Turks in 1516. During the four centuries of rule from Istanbul, the foundations of modern Syria were laid. The Ottomans ruled not only Syria but also most of the Arab world. They gave autonomy to local governors and the various religious groups. Under the *Millet* system, personal law and certain civil functions were placed under the purview of a hierarchy in each recognized religious community. In addition, governors of major provinces had great latitude of action as long as taxes were paid regularly to the Sublime Porte in Istanbul. What is today modern Syria was not one province but several. Aleppo and Damascus were competing regional centers. This regional and communal autonomy can be seen in Syria politics and society even today.

As the Ottoman state declined, Western economic, political, and military penetration increased. The growth of Western interests in Syria, however, served to exasperate social divisions. Christians and other minorities developed close associations with the Europeans and benefited greatly. The French established particularly close ties with the Catholics, while the Russians took a protective interest in the Orthodox. The British, for their part, were the protectors of Protestant converts and the Druze. By the middle of the nineteenth century, European interference in Ottoman affairs had become direct and persistent. French troops, for instance, landed in Lebanon in 1860 to protect the Christian Maronites. The European powers compelled the Ottomans to establish an autonomous Mount Lebanon to guarantee Maronite security.

The Arab Muslim majority in Syria supported the Ottoman sultans and resented the advantages enjoyed by Christian minorities. When, in the last decades of the nineteenth century, Sultan Abdul Hamid II called upon Muslim Ottomans to support the revitalization of the Ottoman state, most Syrians readily gave him their support. As Ottoman territories were lost in Europe, Syria became increasingly important to the Ottoman rulers. Thus, by the end of the nineteenth century much attention was being paid to the development of Syria's commercial and agricultural wealth. These interests offered added reasons for Syrians to remain loyal to Istanbul.

The key to Ottoman success at that time was the sultan's appeal for pan-Islamic solidarity. Islam as a political force was soon challenged, however, by the emergence of Arab nationalism. During the last decade of the nineteenth century, a few Arab intellectuals began to discuss what they called their Arab heritage. They did not deny the importance of Islam to the Arabs or that of the Arabs to Islam, but they emphasized that being an Arab was something more. Among this group were a considerable number of Christian Arabs who either consciously or subconsciously were striving to find a common identity with their fellow Arabs that transcended religious differences.

The Arab nationalists did not begin to gain widespread support until after the Ottoman revolution of 1908, when the "Young Turks" began to implement policies that discriminated against Arabs in favor of the Turks. Wider acceptance of Arab nationalism was, to a great extent, a reaction to the overzealous advocates of Turkish nationalism. Many Arabs, however, still clung to the hope that the Young Turk regime would be based upon Turkish and Arab cooperation. Despite their continued support in the Arab provinces, the Ottoman authorities feared that Arab nationalism in Syria, Lebanon, Iraq, and Palestine might lead to a revolt. Moreover, the Christians were notoriously pro-French. Thus, when World War I broke out, Jamal Pasha, a member of the ruling Ottoman triumvirate, was sent to Damascus to strengthen Ottoman control over Syria. His harsh policies, however, drove the population further into the anti-Ottoman camp. In the spring of 1916 the Syrian people were thus receptive to Sharif Husayn of the Hijaz—a Hashimite—who proclaimed himself king of the Arabs. This he did as a means to end Ottoman rule in Arab lands—an action few would have supported several years earlier.

Both the Arab nationalists in Syria and the Hashimites believed that if they rose against the Turks, the British would support the establishment of an independent Arab kingdom. When Amir Faysal, son of Sharif Husayn, led the triumphant Arab army into Damascus in 1918, he was greeted as the liberator of Syria. With the assistance of Syrian nationalists, many of whom had served in the Ottoman bureaucracy, Faysal established an Arab administration in the interior cities of Damascus, Homs, Hamah, and Aleppo. A French force controlled the coast, and the British were in Palestine.

What followed, however, was a bitter disappointment that few Syrians have forgotten to this day. The Arab nationalists believed that when the Western nations spoke of freedom, self-determination, and the will of the people, these ideas were meant for all people, including Arabs. Therefore, after the war, when wartime secret agreements dividing the Arab east into British and French spheres of influence were revealed, the Arabs felt betrayed. In a futile attempt to thwart the European plan, Faysal called a general Syrian congress in July 1919. The assembled delegation expressed its wish for a sovereign and free Syria with Faysal as king. However, in April 1920, at the San Remo Conference, the European powers, ignoring the wishes of the Syrians, placed Syria under French control. In July, after limited Arab resistance, French troops entered Damascus. Faysal and many Arab nationalists fled. Two years later the League of Nations recognized France as the mandatory power over Syria.

The hostility of the Syrian Sunni Muslim population to French rule led the mandatory authorities to adopt a policy that played upon the divisions within Syrian society. Of all the groups in the Syrian mandate, the Maronites in Lebanon were most friendly to France. Therefore, the French expanded the border of the Ottoman district of Mount Lebanon and administered the area as a separate entity, which ultimately became the core of modern Lebanon. The remainder of French-mandated Syria was then divided into five zones. Each division was chosen to play upon traditional rivalries. Latakia was carved out for the Alawites, Alexandretta for the Turks, and Jabal Druze for the Druze. The Sunni Muslims, the majority population, were divided between Aleppo and Damascus. Moreover, Circassians and Alawites were brought into the local military force in numbers far exceeding their percentage of the population. Thus the Sunni Arab nationalists, who were primarily members of the urban educated classes, were isolated from much of the country.

French rule was generally regarded by Syrians as oppressive. French was introduced in the schools at the expense of Arabic. Singing the French national anthem was required and the French franc became legal tender. Embittered Syrian nationalists played upon these obvious symbols of the French presence and won widespread support in their opposition to French rule.

It was not the nationalists who caused the most difficulty for the French. Traditional ethnic and religious leaders led a series of minor rebellions. The most serious rebellion began in the summer of 1925, when rebel Druze tribesmen drove the French out of the towns and villages in Jabal Druze. Ironically, the Druze were not motivated by Arab nationalism but rather by opposition to the intrusiveness of the French administration in governing their community. Under the Ottomans they had managed to maintain their communal autonomy. The Arab nationalists in Damascus, seeing an opportunity to rid themselves of the French, called upon the Druze to liberate Damascus and initiated their own demonstrations in the capital. Despite the alliance between the nationalists and the Druze, overwhelming French military superiority, symbolized by a bombardment of Damascus, extinguished the revolt by the end of the year.

Thereafter, Franco-Syrian relations remained tense, but differences were generally played out in the political arena rather than on the battlefield. The next decade and a half was marked by slow progress in Syria's attempts to establish a political framework under which it could move toward full independence. A constituent assembly was elected in 1928, but efforts to draft a constitution foundered over the French high commissioner's refusal to accept several proposals and the assembly's refusal to compromise. One area of controversy was the Syrian insistence that all territories controlled by the French be considered part of Syria, thus denying the autonomy of Lebanon, Alexandretta, and Jabal Druze. In 1930, the high commissioner dissolved the assembly and promulgated a constitution based on the constituent assembly's draft, but without the offending articles.

The evolution of Franco-Syrian relations took another major step in 1936, when a Treaty of Alliance was worked out. This agreement followed considerable unrest in 1935 and a general strike the following year. The assumption of power in France by Leon Blum's liberal-socialist government also facilitated movement toward the agreement. Although the French Parliament never ratified the treaty, it served as a basis from which future ties evolved.

Nevertheless, Franco-Syrian relations were continually soured by the issue of the autonomous government in Lebanon. A series of weak French governments also created difficulties. The cession of the province of Hatay (the Syrian province of Alexandretta) to Turkey in 1939 further incensed the Syrians. Nearly all Syrians believed that Turkish neutrality in World War II had been bought at Syrian expense.

The turmoil of World War II, however, provided the opportunity for the Syrians to gain full independence. Some progress toward independence was made with the Vichy government, which established partial self-government in 1941 after riots in Damascus. When the free French arrived in the summer of 1941, they promised full independence in order to win popular support. *De jure* independence was in fact granted that September, but the French still acted as a mandatory power. Although an elected nationalist government came to power in 1943 under President Shukri al-Kuwatly, full independence was not achieved until 1946, when the last French soldiers withdrew. Even then, the British had to prevail upon France to leave gracefully.

Political Environment

The Land

Syria in a geographical sense includes all the states of the eastern Mediterranean shore. Jordan, Lebanon, Israel, the West Bank, Gaza, and the Turkish province of Hatay (Alexandretta) are part of geographic Syria. To the Syrians, the modern state of Syria is the remnant of the geographical area that the Europeans left after carving out special-interest areas. Palestine and Jordan were first separated in order to form a British mandate. Lebanon was taken to protect its Christian minorities, and Hatay was turned over to the Turkish minority because of French political considerations.

The boundaries of the modern Syrian state, therefore, have been determined more by political expedience than by geography or by the wishes of the Syrian people. For the most part, Syria's southern and eastern borders are arbitrary lines in the desert. In the west, the Syrian frontier with Lebanon generally follows the Anti-Lebanon Mountains northward until it turns west to the sea. Syria's coastline marks its only true natural border. Most of the historical Syrian coast, however, has been given to Lebanon or to Turkey. Syria's northern border with Turkey was drawn at the end of World War I. A key consideration of the great powers at that time was that the only east-west railroad in the region was located mostly in Turkey.

The area of the Syrian republic is 185,180 square kilometers (c. 71,000 square miles). Syria can be subdivided into five geographical zones: a narrow coastal plain, a high mountain range, a deep flat-bottomed valley, another range of hills, and an eastward-sloping plain. The eastern four-fifths of Syria is a large plain that gradually declines from west to east. The Euphrates River valley, which diagonally crosses the plain from the northwest to the southeast, and the line of occasional mountain peaks running from the southwest to the northeast are the only distinctive features of the plain.

The presence (and absence) of water has been a key element in the economic development of Syria. Sixty percent of the country is desert or semi-arid steppe receiving less than 200 centimeters (eight inches) of rain a year. Heavier rainfall is concentrated in the west and north. This rain is seasonal, with nearly all falling in the winter. Nevertheless, Syria, by Middle Eastern standards, has an abundant supply of arable land and a considerable potential for dry-land and irrigated farming. This land is in the west and, to a lesser extent, in the Euphrates and Tigris river basins to the north and east. Nearly 80 percent of all Syrians live in the western 20 percent of the country.

All of Syria's largest cities—Damascus, Homs, Hamah, and Aleppo—are located on the inland side of the two coastal mountain ranges. The cities have been both regional agricultural and mercantile centers, situated on the traditional east-west and north-south trading routes. Historically, each has a special relationship with a Mediterranean coastal city. Each could reach the coast through passes in the two coastal mountain ranges. However, political divisions in the twentieth century created problems for the two largest Syrian cities. Aleppo has been cut off from its principal port, Alexandretta (now Iskenderun, Turkey); and Damascus, to a lesser extent, has been cut off from Beirut in Lebanon and Haifa in Israel.

The People

Ninety percent of all Syrians are Arabs, and most are Sunni Muslims. The Sunni Arabs have generally been most conscious of their Islamic-Arabic cultural heritage and are the dominant cultural group in Syria. Nonetheless, with large Christian, Alawite, and even Kurdish populations, Syria remains a diverse society.

The Alawites, an offshoot of Shi'ite Islam, constitute between 11 and 15 percent of the Syrian population. They form a majority in the coastal Syrian province of Latakia and have vigorously maintained their religious and cultural identity. Many Muslims believe that the Alawites have strayed so far from Sunni Islam that they are no longer truly Muslims. Since 1970, despite their small numbers overall, the Alawites have nonetheless played a disproportionately large role in Syrian politics and in the armed forces.

The Druze, an even more distinct religious sect, constitute perhaps 3 percent of the Syrian population. They make up a majority in the area in southwestern Syria known as Jabal Druze and are numerous on the Golan and in Damascus. They, too, have maintained their autonomy and independent outlook. In addition to the Druze and Alawites are other schismatic Muslim sects, including Shi'ites, Ismailis, and Yezidis, but their numbers and influence are limited.

Christian Arabs, who compose about 8 percent of the population, are themselves divided into several groups. Most are Greek Orthodox, but also present are Syrian Orthodox, Greek Catholics, Maronites, Syrian Catholics, and others. The Christians generally live in the urban centers of Damascus, Homs, Hamah, Aleppo, and the coastal area near Tartus. The Greek Orthodox have been particularly active in the development of Arab nationalism and have contributed much to the ideological development of several political parties, including the ruling Ba'th Party.

The non-Arab portion of the population includes Kurds, Armenians, and smaller numbers of Turkomens, Circassians, Assyrians, and Jews. Perhaps 5 percent of all Syrians are Kurds, who mainly inhabit the mountainous regions along the Turkish border. A significant number, however, live in the Kurdish quarter of Damascus. Like most Syrians, the Kurds are Sunni Muslims.

The Armenians are the next largest ethnic group and make up approximately 3 percent of the population, with a particularly large community concentrated in Aleppo. Most arrived in Syria in the early part of the twentieth century, having fled from maltreatment at the hands of the Turks. They had lived in neighboring Anatolia for centuries. Nearly all the Armenians have settled in Syrian cities, with nearly three-fourths of their number residing in Aleppo. The rest are scattered throughout

Syria—mainly in the small towns along the Turkish border. They are Christians, primarily Armenian Orthodox, but perhaps 15 percent of them are Catholics. The Armenians generally are merchants and craftspeople. They have resisted assimilation, holding strongly to their Armenian identity. Their roles as merchants and their reluctance to identify with Syria have often strained the community's relations with the Arab majority. Many Armenians have emigrated, frequently going to Beirut's large Armenian quarter.

The Turkomens, who number less than one hundred thousand, originally migrated to Syria from central Asia. They speak a Turkish language and are Sunni Muslims. The Turkomens live primarily in the eastern region of Syria, although some live in and around Aleppo.

The Circassians are Sunni Muslims who fled from the nineteenth-century Russian invasion of their traditional homeland in the Caucasus Mountains. The Ottomans offered them asylum in the Arab provinces. In Syria, most Circassians settled in the vicinity of Qunaytrah in the Hawran region, occupied in large part by the Israelis in 1967. In recent years, the Circassians have increasingly assimilated into Syrian Arab Sunni society.

The Assyrian Christians and the Jews are two additional minority communities in Syria, each of which is declining in population owing primarily to emigration. The Assyrians are Nestorian Christians from eastern Syria. They were settled there by the French in 1933 to help them escape persecution in Iraq. Since then, many have emigrated to Lebanon. Most of the Jewish community emigrated from Syria after 1948. The once-prosperous community of perhaps forty thousand has been reduced by emigration to less than one thousand.

As a modern nation-state, Syria has been plagued by competitive regionalism centered especially around the major cities. Homs, Hamah, Damascus, and Aleppo each serve as a commercial center and marketplace for their own hinterlands. Aleppo and Damascus, moreover, have engaged in an intense rivalry for centuries. At one time, Aleppo was the second most important city of the Ottoman state. Since Syria became independent, however, Damascus assumed increasing prominence as the capital of all of the country.

Since the period of the French mandate, pressure has grown on most Syrians to raise their national identity above traditional peculiarities. Family, ethnic, religious, and regional loyalties have been challenged by a wider identity. The concepts of Arabism, Islamism, Syrian nationalism, Ba'thism, and socialism have forced many Syrians to reevaluate their loyalties. Even more important than these ideological movements in breaking down the barriers among Syrians has been the functioning of a state government centered in Damascus. As greater numbers of Syrians are touched by the central government through conscription, taxes, the provision of services, and better communications, a sense of loyalty to Syria has begun to take root. Many Syrians are now focusing on their Syrian nationality more than they had done previously.

The growth of Syrian national identity, however, has created strains within Syrian society. All Syrians feel this new pressure, but the minorities seem to be under the greatest strain because the Syrian national identity has developed a strong Arab-Islamic tone. The emphasis on Islam is natural and has occurred throughout the Arab world. Some groups, such as the Circassians, the Kurds, and the Alawites, are not as threatened by this trend. Others have found it very threatening. Therefore, many Armenians, Assyrians, and some Catholics have emigrated, in many cases to Lebanon. Among the Christians, the Greek Orthodox as a group have had the least difficulty in adjusting.

The process of identifying oneself as a Syrian first is by no means complete. Even among some of the most fervent nationalists, traditional ties remain very strong. Many continue to fear that someday Syria could be torn apart by its religious and ethnic cleavages. During the Lebanese civil war, many were concerned that sectarian tensions in Lebanon could have spilled over into Syria. Others predict that the Sunni majority will someday turn against the dominant Alawite minority. The ruling Ba'th Party, while ideologically committed to Syria's pan-Arab identity, has provided an avenue for upward mobility for many minorities while also attempting to assuage and co-opt the Sunni Muslim majority.

Economic Conditions

With a population of nearly 13 million and with a great deal of arable land, Syria is fortunate among Middle Eastern states to have a strong agricultural sector. In addition, Syria has some oil and other natural resources. Given Syria's relatively well-educated population and a tradition of commerce, the relatively slow pace of economic development has been surprising. Government economic decisions and regional political instability appear to have been the two greatest impediments to Syrian economic growth. Some economic growth did occur between independence and 1970, especially in state-controlled industries, such as textiles, food processing, and tobacco. Nevertheless, the socialist state-controlled economy inhibited growth, as did the revolving door governments of the 1950s and 1960s.

When Hafiz al-Asad came to power in 1970, economic reform was a prime objective. Asad introduced a new and more open economy, allowing the traditional Syrian merchant class to have a more active role with fewer government restrictions. The change in political alignments following the 1973 war and the rapid rise in the international price of oil provided Syria with significant capital. Syria's own oil production at that time was modest. Nevertheless, oil became the most important Syrian export in the last half of the 1970s, providing between one-half and three-quarters of Syrian export earnings. In addition, assistance from the oil-producing Arab states also increased.

The objectives of the Asad government were to achieve rapid growth and structural modernization, decrease dependence on agriculture, and raise the

Syrian standard of living to that of Israel and Lebanon. Most important, the Asad government realized that in order to compete with the Israelis, Syria had to match Israel's economic growth. The results were impressive. The gross domestic product (GDP) increased by more than 150 percent, with significant growth in all sectors of the economy.

Problems, however, also existed. Industrial production was concentrated in those sectors that produced consumer goods. Investment was still dominated by the state. Private sector investment was heavily weighted in favor of traders and middlemen. The government invested more in basic infrastructure and productive capacity. State-controlled and operated industries, moreover, proved to be inefficient.

When the 1970s ended, so did the period of rapid economic growth. It was followed by a decade of economic stagnation and sometimes decline. Industrial production increased only slightly while Syria's population grew by 20 percent. Assistance from the Arab oil-producing states declined and foreign currency reserves all but disappeared. The lack of foreign currency limited industrial production as needed raw materials could not be purchased. Iron and steel production at the Hamah plant actually stopped for two years. The gross industrial output (GIO) would actually have declined if oil production had not increased after 1986. Agricultural production also fell far short of expectations and, as a result, already strained hard-currency reserves were needed to pay for food.

The government proved incapable of adequately addressing the problems. Attempts made to reduce government spending were hindered by the perceived necessity to make large arms purchases to compete with the Israelis. As a result, investment and the provision of social services were reduced. These actions contributed to the economic decline.

By the end of the 1980s, however, the Syrian economy once again began to grow significantly. From the mid-1980s onward, emphasis was placed on increasing exports, helped by the rapid development of oil resources. The government even began to encourage foreign investment after years of economic nationalism. Privatization of the Syrian economy was strenuously resisted by much of the bureaucracy, which remained committed to a state-controlled economy and close economic cooperation with the Soviet Union and the other Eastern European countries. With the collapse of the communist economic and political systems, resistance to privatization decreased within Syria. In addition, the loss of allies and economic support from the communist states in part led Syria to join the U.S.-led coalition in the 1991 Gulf War and to participate in the Arab-Israeli peace process later that same year. These political realignments resulted in a new era of linkages to the United States and the European Union, which reinforced Syria's shift toward economic liberalism.

In sum, in the late 1980s and early 1990s Syria responded to the collapse of statist economies and political systems in Eastern Europe and the Soviet Union (and hence also to the loss of substantial foreign aid) by initiating a carefully controlled liberalization program. This included more economic than political liberalization, particularly in the form of Investment Law Number 10, which allowed for foreign investment and more room for private enterprise within Syria's previously statist economy. The Syrian system, in short, has allowed for an increasingly mixed economy, thereby extending the regime's support base to some extent across the public and private sectors and in particular co-opting elements of the Sunni business elite in Damascus. In addition, the last several rounds of elections to the Peoples' Assembly have allowed for increasing numbers of independents and a resultant decline in the numbers of Ba'thist or National Progressive Front representatives in parliament (while maintaining a solid majority for the NPF nonetheless). Thus liberalization in the Syrian context has been limited indeed, but it has provided just enough change to prompt many Syrians to hope for greater reforms under the Bishar al-Asad presidency.

Political Structure

Modern Syrian history has been marked by considerable political turmoil, which has resulted in frequent changes in the Syrian system of government. After the collapse of Ottoman rule, the Arab nationalist regime made the first attempt at creating a modern republic during the brief rule of King Faysal. The nationalists wrestled with the same problems Syrian leaders still face today: the need to blend Western and Islamic legal systems in such a way that minorities are protected and the majority is not harmed and the need to have an executive branch with sufficient authority to maintain order without creating a dictatorship. These problems and others have yet to be solved, and Syria remains a strongly authoritarian state under control of the Ba'th party leadership.

In 1919 the first Syrian constitution created a limited monarchy. It was never fully implemented because of the almost immediate collapse of the Arab Kingdom. The next constitution was promulgated in 1930 by the French high commissioner. It created a form of government modeled on the French republic that remained in force with modifications until 1950. In that year, Syria elected a constituent assembly, which studied numerous Asian and European constitutions and drafted Syria's first indigenous constitution. It protected the rights of all citizens, although the president was required to be a Muslim and Islamic law was established as the law of the land. In the 1950s and 1960s, the many coups d'etat in Damascus led to the promulgation of a series of new constitutions and sometimes revived former ones. That period of reforms and coups came to an end, however, when General Hafiz al-Asad took power.

In January 1973 a draft constitution was approved by the People's Council, and it was confirmed by a referendum in March. Many Sunnis, however, objected to the exclusion of the traditional article making Islam the state religion. After some agitation, the critics were satisfied by an amendment that declared that the president must be a Muslim—a claim that President Asad, an Alawite, made for himself despite the uneasiness of many Sunnis. Islamic jurisprudence was retained as the primary source of legislation, and the Arab character of the state was confirmed. Freedom of religion was guaranteed for all groups, however.

The Arab socialist orientation of Syria is retained in the current constitution. The state retains a great role in the economy, as has been the case under previous constitutions. Nevertheless, in response to traditional Syrian reliance on the family and the individual, a non-socialist tradition has been maintained through the securing of inheritance rights, patents, and copyrights.

The role of the president remains dominant. Syria, however, has made the first tentative steps toward a more open political system. For example, in 1990 the government expanded the Assembly in size to 250 members and held more open elections, in which some independent merchants and representatives of several political parties other then the Ba'th were elected. This was in sharp contrast to a decade earlier when members were appointed with Ba'th party approval.

The People's Assembly, however, has limited powers. It is, at best, a watchdog that monitors the actions of the prime minister and his government. In theory, the assembly can withdraw its confidence from a minister or the entire cabinet. In practice, however, this is not done.

The constitution also theoretically established an independent judiciary. The appointment, transfer, and dismissal of judges are all determined by a higher judiciary council, which is composed of senior career civil judges. There are three tiers of courts, the highest being the supreme court in Damascus. On the whole, however, legislation concerning the judiciary passed by the various regimes since independence remains in effect. No attempt has been made to restructure the entire legal system. Therefore, law in Syria is based on a combination of Western (mostly French) and Islamic concepts. Many personal cases are still handled by the Shari'a (Islamic) courts.

At the local government level, Syria is divided into thirteen provinces. Damascus is an independent city that, in status, is the equivalent of a province. The provinces are divided into districts that, in turn, are subdivided into localities. In Syria's highly centralized system of government, appointment to the subdistrict level or even to village positions must be approved by the Ba'th Regional Command Council. Local administration, therefore, has become an instrument for the Ba'th party to maintain its control at the grassroots level. In the village, the headman (*mukhtar*) is usually the leading figure or is approved by the village leaders personally. In either case, the Ba'th party must approve the choice.

Political Dynamics

Syria has undergone a major political transformation since independence. The rapid turnover in regimes led to fundamental changes in the Syrian ruling elite.

The closely knit traditional leadership was replaced by the Ba'th party structure and the military. At independence, political power was monopolized by the traditional Sunni leaders of the major interior cities—Aleppo, Hamah, Homs, and particularly Damascus. These leaders were generally from traditional landholding or mercantile families. Many had reached political maturity at the time of King Faysal, and nearly all had been active in the struggle for independence.

These leaders were divided into two principal groups representing different wings of the elite. The National Party was heavily Damascene, with a substantial representation of lawyers and industrialists. This party traced its origins to the National bloc that formed a majority in the constitutional convention of 1928. In inter-Arab politics it favored maintaining Syrian autonomy and allied itself with more distant Egypt and Saudi Arabia. The People's party (originally the Constitutional bloc) formed the opposition. It represented the landed class and merchants of Aleppo. Because of trade ties with Iraq, its members favored a union with Hashimite Jordan and Iraq.

Following the first Syrian coup in 1949, Colonel Husni Zaim established a military dictatorship, disbanded Parliament, and banned political parties. Zaim's was the first in a long series of military coups that thoroughly enmeshed the Syrian armed forces in politics. A military career became the primary means for political advancement. The politicalization of the military has had several significant consequences for Syria. First, the Syrian armed forces became torn by competing political factions, thus greatly reducing the country's military effectiveness. This was particularly so in the 1950s and 1960s, when many qualified officers were sent into exile and others were promoted on the basis of political loyalty rather than competence. Second, the minorities have been heavily represented in the military. Consequently, minority groups—Alawites, Druze, and Christians—have had a disproportionate influence on government policy.

Zaim's coup was welcomed by most Syrians, and he was cheered in the streets of Damascus. Syria's poor showing in the Palestine War, quarreling among the political leaders, rising prices, and a general feeling of discontent all contributed to the popularity of the coup. The weakness of the military government, however, resulted from the fact that the army reflected all the divisiveness of Syrian society. After only four and one-half months, Zaim was overthrown by Colonel Sami Hinnawi, who appeared to be a proponent of the old order. Hinnawi, however, was quickly overthrown by another colonel, Adib Shishakli.

Shishakli managed to be either the head of state or the power behind the government for the next four years. His relative success was due in part to his association with one element of the old order—Akram Hourani and his Republican bloc, an offshoot of the old National bloc. Hourani not only gave legitimacy to the regime but also induced Shishakli to introduce a number of social reforms. Moreover, it was under Hourani's guidance that the relatively liberal constitution of 1950 was promulgated. The parliament created by the new constitution, however, gave the old-line politicians a forum from which they could undermine the colonel's authority. Sensing the rising tide of opposition, Shishakli staged a second coup in November 1951 and struck at his opponents. He dissolved parliament and outlawed all sources of opposition, including political parties, student organizations, and trade unions.

Even then, Shishakli felt a need to maintain at least a veneer of traditional legitimacy. He replaced the political parties with his own Arab Liberation Movement, replaced the liberal constitution with one putting more power in the hands of the president, and had himself elected president for a five-year term. Shishakli's heavy-handed rule, however, solidified all factions of Syrian society against him. A coalition of dissidents overthrew him in February 1954.

Although the "new" coalition was dominated by the old-line politicians, a new element had emerged on the Syrian political scene in the form of ideological political parties. Three were of particular note: the Ba'th Party, the Syrian Nationalist Party, and the Syrian Communist Party. Over the longer term, the most important was the Arab Socialist Renaissance Party, or the Ba'th, which was established in 1953 from the merger of Akram Hourani's Arab Socialist party and the Arab Renaissance (Ba'th) party, led by Michel Aflaq and Salah Bitar. Hourani's party began as a youth group in Hamah, and most of its members were personally loyal to him. During the early 1950s, however, Hourani began to espouse more socialist beliefs. He thus brought to the Ba'th a socialist commitment, experience as a political leader, and a committed following, particularly among the Sunnis in Hamah. Aflaq, the founder of the Ba'th, was strongly influenced by the French leftist philosophy to which he had been exposed as a student in Paris. He rejected Marxism, but hoped to adapt his leftist social doctrine to an Arab society. Aflaq, a Greek Orthodox, became close friends with Salah Bitar, a Sunni Muslim from Damascus. Together they had founded the Arab Resurrection party in 1940.

The Ba'th ideology was not geared solely to the intellectual elite. Three key elements had much broader appeal. First of all, its program of social reform and economic justice appealed to a wide spectrum of the lower classes. Second, the Ba'thists stressed the idea of a greater Arab unity by pressing for political mergers between Arab states. They opposed any form of regional unity that did not have as its ultimate goal a union of all Arabs. Finally, the Greek Orthodox Aflaq recognized the unique relationship between Islam and Arabism. Aflaq structured his ideas upon the common memory of all Arabs of the glory of the golden age of Islam. Nevertheless, the Ba'thists asserted that discrimination against other religions was unacceptable and thus promoted religious tolerance as a basic tenet.

The Ba'thists considered their party to be not merely a Syrian party but, rather, a pan-Arab party. Much of the leadership's effort was spent winning support elsewhere in the Arab world. They had large followings in Iraq, Jordan, and Lebanon. The strength of the Ba'th rested in its organization. Bitar was the specialist in administration. The Ba'th party in each Arab state was designated a "regional command."

Regional in this instance referred to each individual state within the larger Arab nation. The supreme body was the National (pan-Arab) Command.

In Syria, the Ba'thists took particular care to organize young military officers. They promoted revolution rather than evolution, and in Syria the army remained the key power. As the Ba'th grew in popularity and power, it did so largely at the expense of other ideological rivals. These included the Syrian Socialist Nationalist Party and the Syrian Communist Party. Many Syrians found the former to be too focused on Syrian—rather than pan-Arab—nationalism, and too pro-Western in orientation. Similarly, many saw the latter party, the Communists, to be too atheistic and too closely aligned with the Soviet Union and its allies.

In 1956 the Ba'th entered the government for the first time. Shortly thereafter, Akram Hourani became the speaker of the House. For the next several years, the Ba'thists, though outnumbered by the traditional Sunni ruling elite, dominated the government through party discipline and ideological commitment. The Ba'thists and the traditional leaders were united in their opposition to a shift in Syrian policy toward the Soviet Union and away from Arab nationalism. When, under the growing influence of the Communists and other leftist elements, Syrian policy moved sharply to the left, the Ba'thists and their allies among the traditional leadership appealed to Nasser to merge Syria with Egypt to forestall what they believed was a possible takeover by pro-Soviet elements. Reluctantly, Nasser agreed. In January 1958 Syria and Egypt formed the United Arab Republic (UAR).

The merger of the two states turned out to be very unpleasant for Syria, as Nasser sought to make Damascus subservient to Cairo. Both the Ba'thists and the Arab nationalists soon regretted their push toward union. The Ba'thists, who had been riding a wave of success, found their activities increasingly restricted. Political parties were replaced by the National Union, an instrument designed to promote the interests of Nasser. When, in 1959, elections were held for ten thousand local committee officers, the Ba'th party received less than 2.5 percent of the votes. In protest over Egyptian control of Syrian affairs, the five Ba'thist ministers resigned in December 1959. The traditional Arab nationalists of the ruling elite, who had been losing ground to the rising middle class, found the last remnants of their power base destroyed by Egyptian-sponsored policies, which included land reforms.

Elements of the traditional elite, however, managed to foster a coup in 1961 that threw out the Egyptians. In the Syrian nationalist fervor that followed, the traditional parties—the People's party and the Nationalist Party—won the two largest blocs in Parliament. The election, however, was an aberration. The leadership represented only a small element of society, and one that was of decreasing importance. As the anti-Egyptian feeling waned, political squabbling and governmental paralysis led to popular discontent. This brief interlude was the last hurrah for the traditional Syrian Sunni leadership.

In 1963 a Ba'thist-supported junta seized control, and the Ba'th party has dominated Syrian politics ever since. Initially broad-based, with a wide spectrum of political opinion and ideology, the party became increasingly dominated by military members of the Ba'thist National Command. One aspect of the Ba'th party that did not change was the disproportionate number of minority members. The Alawites have been particularly influential. For the most part, the struggle for power within Syria has become a struggle for control of the Ba'th party and the army. In 1970, Hafiz al-Asad, an Alawite military officer and then the defense minister in the government, staged an internal coup and took power.

From November 1970 to June 2000, Hafiz al-Asad dominated the Ba'th regime, bringing a high degree of political stability to Syria. Asad ruled with the pragmatism of the moderate wing of the party, dominating the Ba'thist Regional Command and the army. Indeed, Asad's authoritarian regime was based mainly on the strength of the twin pillars of the party and the armed forces. To broaden his political base, he established a National Front within the People's Council with a range of moderate leftist Syrians represented, including such organizations as the Arab Socialists, the Communists, trade unions, and others. In this way, Asad made his potential opponents on the left responsible for government actions without sacrificing Ba'thist dominance. His policies did much to transform the Ba'th from the small, ideological, and closely knit party of the 1950s to an instrument of mass political mobilization.

The most serious challenge to Ba'thist political dominance in recent years came from Islamic fundamentalists. Between 1976 and 1982, anti-Ba'thist sentiment was focused in a revolt of these fundamentalists. The heart of the movement was the urban Sunni population. Terrorist attacks were common in every major urban center. The movement failed, however, to win widespread support in the countryside. As a result, the Ba'thist-dominated military was able to suppress the revolt with considerable brutality. The last gasp was the violent confrontation between Islamists and the army following an uprising in the city of Hamah in February 1982. Since then, no serious challenge to the regime's authority has been mounted.

The Political Succession

Speculation over Syria's succession percolated for years, especially given the often weak health of President Hafiz Asad, including a heart attack in 1983. But for many years the speculation centered on alternative power centers to Asad (such as the Muslim Brotherhood and non-Alawite factions of officers or party members) or on various members of Asad's family. For many years the conventional wisdom had held that any familial succession would probably pass power on to the president's brother, Rifa'at. And in 1983, when Asad suffered his heart attack and temporarily disappeared from the political scene, Rifa'at did indeed act on those expectations and on his own ambitions. Despite his illness, Asad managed to appoint a temporary council to govern Syria—all of whom were Sunni Muslims. He had thus pointedly left Rifa'at out of the ruling council.

Rifa'at utilized his considerable domestic power base, particularly in the form of his armed "defense companies" (*saraya al-difa'*—basically paramilitary units under his personal command) to make his claim to succeed his brother. In the end no shots were fired. But for a time thousands of Rifa'at's troops, which had deployed to the capital, faced off against regular army units in Damascus. The crisis ended when Hafiz al-Asad re-emerged in public, literally from his sick bed, to retake control. Rifa'at was promptly "promoted" to a powerless vice presidential role, losing all power over his paramilitary forces. By 1985, he had been further pushed out of Syrian politics and indeed into exile in Europe. Rifa'at did make a claim to the succession once again in June 2000, but that remained a demand from exile, with no real power base on which to stake his claim.

Having curbed the power of his ambitious brother, Asad began systematically to groom his eldest son, Basil, for the succession, even while denying these intentions. In 1994, however, Basil was killed in an traffic accident in Damascus, shattering his father's hopes for the succession. But Asad immediately recalled his other son, Bishar, an ophthalmologist in London, to Damascus to receive, in effect, the military and political training required for succession.

Bishar was promptly put through the military academy and between 1994 and 2000 had skyrocketed up the ranks of the military to become an army colonel. At the time of his father's death in June 2000, Bishar was also being more gradually introduced into the party apparatus. Hafiz al-Asad had in fact died of a heart attack just one week before the June 2000 Ba'th Party Congress at which, it was widely assumed, he had intended to ensure that Bishar would be elevated to a top party post. With the president's death, however, the question remained whether Bishar could legally succeed his father, and whether the ruling elite, much less the general public, would let him. But in the six years between the deaths of Basil and Hafiz al-Asad, Bishar had taken on more important and more public political roles, including advising his father on key appointments such as the new chief of the armed forces, serving as lead Syrian official for affairs in Lebanon, and taking the lead role in the state's much-touted "anti-corruption campaign." It was in this latter role that Bishar and his allies were able to isolate key potential opponents within the "old guard." Furthermore, Asad loyalists had spent those six years in a concerted campaign to ensure the succession for Bishar.

Still, obstacles to Bishar's succession remained. When Hafiz al-Asad died Bishar had yet to assume a top party post. He was only thirty-four years old and the constitution stated one had to be at least forty years old to assume the presidency. Furthermore, he held insufficient military rank to assume command of the armed forces. What then followed was orchestrated not just by Bishar and his supporters, but also by his father's colleagues and loyalists. These officials formed a largely *ad hoc* council that openly endorsed Bishar and helped secure the logistical details for his succession. Within a mere forty-eight hours, the Peoples' Assembly convened and changed the constitutional age of succession to thirty-four, the ruling

Ba'th Party officially named Bishar the party's candidate for the presidency, and the army promoted him to lieutenant general and also named him commander in chief of the Syrian armed forces. When the mourning period ended, the regime held a presidential referendum in July 2000 in which Bishar secured 97.29 percent of the vote, marking the last formal and official act in the succession to the presidency of Bishar al-Asad.

Foreign Policy

Syrian foreign policy has been largely influenced by two philosophies—pan-Arab and Syrian nationalism. At times these two doctrines have been mutually supporting; at other times they have conflicted. Neither has been able to dominate totally. When Hafiz al-Asad took power in 1970, he attempted to combine pan-Arab nationalist goals with more specific Syrian interests.

No matter which philosophical tendency took precedence at a specific time, Syrian foreign policy has been dominated by three related issues—Israel, Syria's roles in Arab politics, and the question of the fate of the Palestinians. The future of Israel is of greater importance to the Syrians than to most other Arabs for several reasons. First, the peoples of Palestine and Syria share a common ancestry. Palestinian Arabs and Syrian Arabs have been buffeted throughout history by the same forces. Therefore, the plight of the Palestinians is deeply felt. Second, many Syrians feel that they are in competition with Israel for geographical Syria. The Arab-Israeli conflict is certainly a central issue in Syrian foreign policy—a point underscored by the direct military confrontations between Israel and Syria in the wars of 1948, 1967, 1973, and 1982.

During the many years of the cold war, Syria gravitated toward the Soviet Union and its allies, receiving extensive economic and military aid and providing a Mediterranean port for Soviet vessels. Soviet military backing was critical in President Hafiz al-Asad's attempts to achieve strategic parity with Israel.

In the 1980s, when Iraq and Iran plunged into an eight-year war of attrition, Syria was one of few Arab states to back Iran against Iraq, a fellow Arab state. But Saddam Hussein's regime in Baghdad was a rival in many respects, including representing an alternative wing of the Ba'th Party. Syrian-Iraq hostility was so great that Asad shut off the oil pipeline leading from Iraq across Syria to the Mediterranean. The Syrian-Iranian alliance was surely one of the strangest bedfellows of Middle East politics: an alliance of a secular socialist and Arab nationalist republic with a Islamic fundamentalist theocracy. The alliance ultimately proved strong enough that it managed to survive the end of the Iran-Iraq war, the cold war, and even the second Gulf War in 1991.

But perhaps no issue challenged Syrian foreign policy interests more than the Lebanon situation following the onset of the Lebanese civil war in 1975. Syrian leaders believed Lebanon was within their sphere of influence. While some Syrians in 1975 still hoped to have formal union, most understood that political domination would be sufficient to satisfy Syria's basic needs. Conversely, foreign political or military influence in Lebanon was seen as a direct threat to Syria. Damascus was prepared to work with any Lebanese faction as long as that faction acquiesced to Syrian leadership and did not allow Israeli dominance in Lebanon. As a result, no Lebanese force was a natural ally of Syria, nor was one an automatic opponent. Therefore, over the course of the Lebanese conflict, the Syrians found themselves allied with or opposed to each of the major Lebanese factions at one time or another. Similarly, excluding the Israelis, the Syrians found themselves working with or opposed to numerous international and regional powers.

In March 1976 Syrian troops entered Lebanon to restore the military balance between the Lebanese and the Palestinians. Syrian motives for intervening were conditioned by wider strategic considerations. Syria, at that time, was isolated from the American-Egyptian search for regional peace. As a result, the Syrians sought parity with Israel through: (1) a massive arms buildup; (2) increased reliance on the Soviet Union as a great power ally; and (3) increased military/political influence over the affairs of its immediate neighbors, including Jordan, Lebanon, and the PLO. Syria's policy toward Lebanon was one element of this wider policy.

During the next decade Syria defeated all international and regional forces that challenged Damascus's hegemony in Lebanon. The most serious challenge came from the Israelis. In the mid-1970s, the Israelis began to assist anti-Syrian elements in Lebanon—particularly the Maronite militia. One factor in Israel's decision was to prevent Syria from having a totally free hand in Lebanon. At the same time, Israel acquiesced to a prominent role for Syria in Lebanon as long as this role did not put Syrian or Syrian proxy forces on Israel's northern border or increase PLO influence at the expense of Lebanese nationalists.

Although Israel tacitly approved the Syrian intervention, Israel was concerned that Syrian occupation of Lebanon did not extend to its border and therefore declared the existence of a "red line" beyond which it would consider Syrian presence as threatening to Israel. Although the precise definition of this red line was never spelled out publicly, it precluded the presence of Syrian forces in Lebanon south of the Zahrani river.

A new factor was the new Israeli government of Menachem Begin, leader of the Likud coalition, that assumed power in June 1977. Unlike the previous Labor government, which had offered military assistance to Lebanon's militia out of geostrategic perceptions of Israel's interests, Begin tended to perceive the Christians as another oppressed Middle Eastern minority, much as he viewed the Jews of Israel. He proved vulnerable to the appeals of the youthful, emerging Maronite strongman, Bashir Gemayel, who actively courted higher degrees of Israeli support and intervention against Syria and the PLO. He argued that Lebanese, Israeli, and American interests converged in establishing a nationalist Lebanese government—

a government that could control the PLO and thwart Syrian domination. This led to direct confrontations between Gemayel's forces and the Syrian army.

For the Syrians, the close alliance between the Christian militia and Israel was unacceptable. For Gemayel, only the military might of Israel and the political support of the United States could free Lebanon from foreign—primarily Syrian and PLO—domination. In 1982, Israeli forces launched an invasion of Lebanon to aid Gemayel, counter Syria, and attempt to crush the guerrilla forces of the PLO. In a multi-pronged attack, Israeli forces proceeded north into Lebanon, driving PLO forces before them into Beirut and the upper Bekaa Valley. The Israelis came into direct conflict with the Syrians. Syrian missiles and more than ninety Syrian aircraft were destroyed. Syrian forces were bloodied but not crushed. The Syrian military managed to halt the Israeli advance short of the Beirut/Damascus highway both in the mountains and in the Bekaa Valley.

Although the Syrians were defeated militarily, they used the American intervention in the summer and fall of 1982 to regain their political equilibrium and to rebuild their military forces. With the assassination of President Gemayel in 1982, terrorist attacks against U.S. and French intervention forces in 1983 (leading to their withdrawal from Beirut), and finally Israeli withdrawal in 1985, Syria began to consolidate its hegemony in Lebanon. That process was largely completed in 1991, as regional and global attention was focused on the war in the Gulf between Iraq and the U.S.-led coalition.

Syria had surprised many in the Arab world and the West in 1991 by supporting the coalition against Iraq. The longstanding rivalry between Asad and Saddam Hussein obviously continued, but the policy choice was also strongly influenced by the collapsing Soviet Union (and with it, much of Syria's foreign aid). Syria needed economic support, and joining the coalition, and deploying Syrian troops to Saudi Arabia, helped Syria begin to establish warmer ties to the United States, the European Union states, and the oil-wealthy Arab monarchies of the Gulf. By the end of the war, President Asad had arranged for the "Damascus Declaration"—a new regional alignment bringing together Syria, Egypt, and the six Arab monarchies of the Gulf Cooperation Council (Bahrain, Kuwait, Oman, Qatar, Saudi Arabia, and the United Arab Emirates).

Following the 2000 political succession from Hafiz al-Asad to President Bishar al-Asad, Syrian foreign policy continued to focus on the standoff with Israel, further enhancing ties to the Gulf states, the United States, and the European Union, while still maintaining the alignment with Iran. Syrian foreign policy under Bishar also emphasized a warming trend in relations with Jordan, while trying to end some of the hostility with Iraq. Tensions remained, however, in Syria's relations with its northern neighbor, Turkey, regarding water resources issues and Kurdish nationalist unrest.

In the early twenty-first century, Syrian foreign relations were for the most part stable. In domestic politics, the dominant themes remained the consolidation of

Bishar al-Asad's regime and the central questions of economic and political liberalization. In foreign policy, however, the thorny issues continued to be the occupied Golan, the plight of the Palestinians, and the ever-present threat of war with Israel.

Bibliography

A good place to begin looking more deeply into politics and government of Syria is in one of several general studies. *Syria: Modern State in an Ancient Land* (Boulder: Westview Press, 1983), by John Devlin, is a perceptive analytical study of the general Syrian scene.

Several more scholarly specialized works delve into particular aspects of the Syrian experience. In *The Struggle for Syria* (New York: Oxford University Press, 1965), Patrick Seale analyzes the regional and internal factors leading to the union with Egypt in 1958. In *Syrian Under the Ba'th, 1963–66: The Army-Party Symbiosis* (New York: Halsted Press, 1972), Itamar Rabinovich analyzes the crucial period of Ba'thist rule following the 1963 coup and the very special relationship between the party organization and the military. Umar F. Abdallah, in *The Islamic Struggle in Syria* (Berkeley: Mizan Press, 1983), provides a valuable analysis of the Muslim fundamentalist movement in Syria. Two excellent detailed analyses of Syrian political dynamics are Nikolaos Van Dam's *The Struggle for Power in Syria: Politics and Society under Asad and the Ba'th Party* (London: I. B. Tauris, 1996) and Raymond Hinnebusch's *Authoritarian Power and State Formation in Ba'thist Syria* (Boulder: Westview Press, 1990).

On Syrian foreign policy, see Fred Lawson, *Why Syria Goes to War: Thirty Years of Confrontation* (Ithaca: Cornell University Press, 1996). Regarding Syria's policy toward Lebanon, see Adeed Dawisha's *Syria and the Lebanese Crisis* (New York: St. Martin's Press, 1980) or Naomi Weinberger's *Syrian Interventions In Lebanon* (New York: Oxford University Press, 1987).

Several books have been written about President Hafiz al-Asad in recent years. The differing approaches to Asad in *Asad: The Struggle For The Middle East* (Berkeley and Los Angeles: University of California Press, 1989) by Patrick Seale and by Moshe Maoz in *Asad: The Sphinx of Damascus* (New York: Weidenfeld and Nicholson, 1988) make very interesting reading.

On Syria's political and economic transitions, see Eberhard Kienle, ed., *Contemporary Syria: Liberalization between Cold War and Cold Peace* (London: I. B. Tauris, 1994), and Volker Perthes, *The Political Economy of Syria Under Asad* (London: I. B. Tauris, 1995).

10

Hashimite Kingdom of Jordan

Curtis R. Ryan

In February 1999, King Hussein of Jordan died after a long battle with cancer. Hussein was one of the longest-serving monarchs of the last century, having assumed the Jordanian throne in 1953. The king had served for so long, in fact, that his imprint is indelibly marked on the evolution of Jordan as a modern state. But the king's passing in 1999, and the assumption of power by his son, who became King Abdullah II, actually marked the last in a series of dramatic transitions in Jordanian politics in the last years of the twentieth century. These included a process of limited democratization (since 1989), several rounds of economic adjustment and restructuring as the kingdom came to terms with globalization (also since 1989), and the conclusion of a full and formal peace treaty with the State of Israel (in 1994). As the kingdom entered the twenty-first century under King Abdullah II, these three transitions remained the central and most controversial issues in Jordanian politics.

Historical Background

Despite its central role in the history of the Arab-Israeli conflict and peace process and its geopolitical importance to major powers from the cold war era to the present, Jordan remains in many ways a young state with ancient roots. The Kingdom of Jordan is one of the many successor states of the Ottoman Empire. The territory east of the Jordan River, however, has a history dating back several millennia of being the crossroads between the Mediterranean, the Orient, and Arabia. The ancient biblical kingdoms of Gilead, Moab, and Edom were largely located in present-day Jordan. Because of its relatively remote though strategically important location, the area was usually the last conquered and the first abandoned as the great ancient empires ebbed and flowed. At various times, Egyptian, Hittite, Assyrian, Persian, Greek, Roman, and Byzantine armies each occupied the region.

Of all the peoples of antiquity, the Nabatean Arabs were most likely the direct ancestors of modern Jordanians. Shortly after 800 B.C., the Aramaic-speaking inhabitants of Petra created their kingdom along the key north–south trading routes, maintaining their independence until they were conquered by the Romans under Pompey in 64 B.C.

In sociological terms, the Islamic conquest of the area had the greatest impact. The battle of Yarmuk in A.D. 636 expelled the Byzantine Christians and laid the groundwork for the establishment of Islam as the religious and cultural foundation for the majority of the people. At various times, the area was ruled from Damascus, Baghdad, Cairo, Jerusalem, and Istanbul. Under Ottoman rule, southern Jordan was governed as part of the Hijaz while the north was included in the Damascus governorate.

Similar to the countries of the rest of the Levant, the modern Jordanian state emerged following the collapse of the Ottoman Empire during World War I. Arab tribesmen led by Amir Faysal, son of Sharif Hussein (al-Hashim) of the Hijaz (now Saudi Arabia) and advised by the famous Lawrence of Arabia marched northward against the retreating Ottoman forces. When Faysal's army defeated the Ottoman Turks and conquered Aqaba and Amman, the tribes east of the Jordan quickly joined the Arab revolt against Istanbul. By the end of the war, nearly all of present-day Jordan was in Hashimite hands. Nevertheless, Jordan's destiny was determined by other forces. Under the terms of the secret Sykes–Picot Agreement of May 1916, the Levant was divided into British and French spheres. What is now Lebanon and Syria came under French control, whereas Palestine eastward to Iraq was given to the British. At that time, few considered the area east of Jordan to be a separate entity. To the Arabs it was a part of greater Syria, which included the present states of Israel, Jordan, Lebanon, and Syria; to the British and the European Zionists, it was a part of Palestine.

Amir Faysal, who attended the 1919 Paris Peace Conference, pressed for the complete independence of the Levantine Arabs, basing his arguments on President Woodrow Wilson's Fourteen Points promoting self-determination for all people. Arab leaders also contended that in wartime they had been promised an independent state that included Transjordan and Palestine. Faysal failed to win his point against British and French imperial aspirations and Zionist demands for a homeland. Nevertheless, the Arabs were prepared to assert their independence without European acquiescence. In March 1920, a group of Arab nationalists convened the General Syrian Congress in Damascus and declared the independence of Syria (including Jordan, Lebanon and Palestine) and Iraq. The decision was opposed by Britain and France. In April, at the San Remo Conference, the Levant was divided in accordance with the Sykes–Picot framework, ignoring both Arab declarations and British promises. Palestine, including what is now Jordan, was effectively separated from Syria. In July 1920, an Arab force was defeated by the French, destroying Arab hopes for political independence in the Levant.

The status of Jordan remained unclear at that time. The British felt some obligation to the Hashimites for unkept wartime promises and feared a possible worsening of Anglo-French relations if Arab attacks on Syria were launched from Jordan. Amir Abdallah, the brother of King Faysal of Syria, was in Jordan organizing the tribes to strike the French in Syria. The British, realizing such an attack was not in their best interest, offered Abdallah, who was very popular with the Jordanian tribes, the opportunity to be the amir of Jordan. In this way, Anglo-French difficulties were avoided and British promises to the Hashimites were partially met. Abdallah accepted the British offer because an emirate in Jordan was a tangible gain and he had little chance of displacing the French from Syria.

The establishment of a governmental system for the new emirate took much time and effort on the part of the British. Being politically cut off from Syria, with whose government its people had been traditionally associated, Jordan lacked a national identity and had practically no economic base. The few Arab administrators in Jordan were those who had fled from the French in Damascus and were generally more concerned with reasserting Arab control in Syria than with making Jordan an independent, self-sufficient state. On the economic side, less than 3 percent of the land was under cultivation, and, with virtually no other economic assets in the country, the new government was heavily dependent on British economic support.

Thus, when Britain recognized Jordan as a self-governing state on May 15, 1923, Amir Abdallah was in no position to run a country. National borders were ill-defined. His father's kingdom of Hijaz to the south was collapsing before the followers of Ibn Saud, and he lacked the resources to assist his father or to protect his own interests. His nation, moreover, was totally dependent on British subsidies. Therefore, though recognized as self-governing, Jordan was, in fact, governed by the British.

The British were primarily interested in maintaining stability. The prospect of chaos and anarchy—or worse, some rival power assuming control of Jordan—forced London to take a more active interest in the fledgling country than it might otherwise have done. The British goal was to establish an effective local administration and thus reduce what was considered a drain that the British treasury could ill afford. British policy, therefore, was to provide British officials to train a pro-British local administration and military force that would become financially and politically independent, while remaining friendly to London.

With the assistance of a small but devoted group of British officials, Jordan under Amir Abdallah made slow progress toward true independence. At first, the administration was simple. Abdallah ruled with the advice of a small executive council. British officials handled defense, foreign affairs, and finance. A major step toward real independence came with a new treaty in 1928 that gave greater authority to the amir and his officials. However, London retained the right to oversee finance and foreign policy and British officers still controlled the Arab Legion. The Organic Law of 1928 took the first move toward a representative government by providing for a legislative council to replace the old executive council.

In the early 1930s Jordan gained the right to send consular representatives to other Arab countries. In May 1939 the legislative council was converted to a council of ministers, or cabinet. Although actual rule continued to rest with the amir and the British, a loyal opposition composed of Arab nationalists evolved during the 1930s. Their most prominent vehicle for dissent was the Istiqlal (Independence) party, which was also active in Palestine and Syria.

Throughout the period, Amir Abdallah demonstrated ambitions greater than just ruling a small desert kingdom. He envisaged a broader role for his dynasty. His immediate ambitions were directed at regaining the Hijaz from the Saudis and at reestablishing the Arab kingdom of his brother Faysal in Syria. During World War II, Jordan played an influential role in inter-Arab affairs. The Arab Legion, as Jordan's British-led army was called, helped to suppress the pro-German revolt of Rashid Ali in Iraq. Moreover, Abdallah was instrumental in the formation of the Arab League, the first concrete step toward pan-Arab unity. His wholehearted cooperation with the British stemmed in part from the hope that his cooperation would help him become ruler of a larger independent Arab state.

Abdallah's ambitions proved unrealistic, for opponents included the Zionists, the Syrian nationalists, the Lebanese Christians, the Saudis, the Egyptians, and the French. Abdallah had to be satisfied with achieving independence for Jordan and his recognition as king. In 1946, Jordan and the United Kingdom reached a new agreement whereby the Organic Law of 1928 was replaced by a constitution and Abdallah was recognized as king of Jordan. Two years later, London agreed to continue paying a subsidy in return for British access to two military bases.

The rising crisis in Palestine became the dominant concern of the fledgling state. Abdallah's policy toward Palestine differed from that of other Arab states. In fact, he met secretly with Zionist leaders, including Golda Meir, in an attempt to work out some modus vivendi with the Jews in Palestine. His position appears to have been based on a sense of realism and on a deep commitment to Jordan's vital links with Palestine. Nevertheless, when Israel declared its independence, the Arab Legion occupied areas of Palestine adjacent to Jordan that had been allocated to the Arabs in the United Nations Partition Plan of 1947. Although some of this territory was lost, Abdallah's forces were the most successful of the Arab armies. When the fighting halted, the Arab Legion held perhaps 20 percent of Palestine, including the old city of Jerusalem.

On April 24, 1950, Abdallah unilaterally annexed the portion of Palestine called the West Bank. This action unequivocally altered not only the history of the country but its political, social, and economic structure as well. The total number of

Palestinians, including refugees from Israeli-held areas and the inhabitants of Jordan's newly acquired West Bank, outnumbered those from east of the Jordan river. More important, most other Arabs joined the Palestinians in believing that Abdallah had betrayed them by annexing part of Palestine. Indeed, only Pakistan and Britain ever formally acknowledged the annexation. Jordan became a pariah among the Arab states, with only the fellow Hashimite regime in Iraq offering support.

The annexation of the West Bank was for Abdallah the natural outgrowth of his concern for a united Arab nation under his leadership. In the same vein, he alone among the Arab rulers extended full citizenship rights to the Palestinians. Nevertheless, he was detested by many Palestinians for what they perceived to be his self-serving action and his betrayal of their desire to obtain Palestinian national rights. The other Arabs opposed him as much for intra-Arab competition as for his role in Palestine. The Arab League so vehemently opposed the annexation that Jordan was nearly expelled. A settlement was reached with the Arab League when Jordan agreed that it was merely holding the West Bank in trust, and Abdallah promised that he would forgo any separate nonaggression pact with Israel. Many Palestinians, however, never forgave him. While praying in Jerusalem on July 20, 1951, he was assassinated by a Palestinian nationalist.

The smooth transition of power from Abdallah to his oldest son, Talal, was a reflection of the stability of the Hashimite state, primarily based on the loyalty of the British officers and the Arab Legion. Under Talal, a new constitution was promulgated in January 1952. Talal, however, had a long history of mental illness and under his doctor's advice abdicated in favor of his son Hussein, who was still a minor. A regency council of three was formed to govern for several months until the young Hussein reached maturity and assumed the throne in May 1953.

Political Environment

The Land

The Hashimite Kingdom of Jordan sits on part of the north Arabian plateau that Jordan shares with Syria to the north, Iraq to the east, and Saudi Arabia to the south. No natural frontiers exist between Jordan and its Arab neighbors. The western border of Jordan is the Great Rift Valley, through which the Jordan River flows. From an average of 600 to 900 meters (2,000 to 3,000 feet) on the plateau, the landscape plummets to well below sea level in the valley. The Great Rift Valley also includes the Dead Sea and the Wadi Araba extending to the Gulf of Aqaba in the south. Jordan's only coastline is a nineteen-kilometer (twelve-mile) stretch on the Gulf, including the port of Aqaba. Beyond the Great Rift Valley lie Israel and the West Bank highlands.

More than four-fifths of Jordan is desert or semidesert receiving less than ten centimeters (four inches) of rain annually. Prevailing westerly winds draw winter rains to the northern areas of the country, but in the south, dry winds from the

Sahara are the rule. Consequently, Jordan's population is concentrated in the western part of the kingdom where rainfall, averaging thirty to forty-one centimeters (twelve to sixteen inches) annually, permits some farming. All of Jordan's major cities—Amman, Irbid, and Zarqah—are concentrated in this area. Some attempt has been made to expand the area of settlement and cultivation. Of particular note are reforestation projects north of Amman and the East Ghor irrigation canal project in the Jordan River Valley. Moreover, plans have been discussed for years to dam the Yarmuk River, which forms a portion of the borders between Jordan and Israel and between Jordan and Syria. These plans could enhance the supply of water available for irrigation, but political problems have blocked the project. Already, the smaller Zarqah River is being used to provide water. As part of the terms of its 1994 peace treaty, Jordan began importing water from Israel.

Jordan is poor in minerals and fuels. Small manganese ore and copper deposits are located near the Dead Sea. Phosphates at Wadi al-Hasa are the only large earners of foreign currency other than tourism and the remittances from Jordanians working abroad.

The People

Most Jordanians are of Arab heritage and may be roughly divided into two principal groups: Palestinians and East Bank Jordanians. Palestinians are those Arabs (and their descendants) who lived in the British mandate of Palestine and who have been under Jordanian sovereignty since 1948. These include the refugees who fled from Israel and Palestine in the wars of 1948 and 1967. Palestinians now constitute more than half of the total Jordanian population. Perhaps a third still live in the United Nations Relief and Works Agency (UNRWA) camps. The others are more assimilated into the general population.

Since 1948 Jordan alone among the Arab states has given full citizenship to all Palestinians and no official distinction is made between Palestinians and East Bank Jordanians. Palestinians are afforded the same political rights as all Jordanians. Grievances remain, however, particularly among Palestinians who often feel that theirs is a secondary status in Jordanian society. Others, both Palestinian and Jordanian, feel that these distinctions are no longer important. Generally speaking, while Palestinians are heavily represented in private sector businesses and in the various professions, East Bank Jordanians dominate much of the public sector and the upper echelons of the military.

Between 1948 and 1967 the Palestinians were gradually assimilated into Jordanian society. Even the Jordan Arab Army (as the Arab Legion was renamed), the backbone of support for the monarchy, witnessed a growing number of Palestinians in the officer corps. The 1967 Arab-Israeli war, resulting in Israeli occupation of the West Bank, slowed this trend but did not stop it entirely. Many of the present business and government leaders on the East Bank are of Palestinian origin.

The East Bank Jordanians are, nevertheless, the rock upon which the Hashimite monarchy has been built. Most East Bankers are Sunni Muslims, although a small Christian minority is also present. Among the Palestinians, the percentage of Christians is higher. Many East Bank Jordanians are members of one of several hundred Arab tribes. Even though bedouins are a small minority of the overall population, bedouin values and traditions continue to have an important influence on society. The few who continue to live a nomadic life, and those who have settled in towns, maintain these values. In Jordan, more than any other state of the Fertile Crescent, tribal elements provide a disproportionate number of recruits for the military and are guaranteed representation in government, thus influencing government policy.

Two minority elements—the Christians and the Circassians—have also provided backing for the Hashimites. Jordan's Christian population is urban and has lived in the area for centuries. Predominantly Greek Orthodox and Greek Catholic, most are the descendants of early converts to Christianity, whereas others have allegedly descended from the crusaders.

The Circassians settled in Jordan in the last decades of the nineteenth century. They were part of the approximately 1 million Muslims who fled the Caucasus region when the Russians captured it from the Ottomans, and they were given land by the Ottoman sultan in what is now Israel, Jordan, and Syria. The Circassians are Sunni Muslims and they have been traditionally loyal to the monarchy and have held very senior positions in the government. They are particularly numerous in the armed forces as well as in the police force. Jordanian Circassians are divided into two major groups—the Adigah and the Chechen. Both groups of Circassians, like the bedouins and Christians, are guaranteed representation in parliament.

Economic Conditions

Despite a harsh climate, Jordan historically was an agricultural country. Even as late as the 1960s, 40 percent of the workforce was engaged in agriculture, forestry, and herding. Agricultural production, however, was as erratic as the rainfall. Cereal production, for instance, was 297,000 tons in 1967 and 56,000 tons in 1973.

Prior to 1967, the fewer than two million Jordanians appeared to be well on their way to becoming economically self-sufficient. The loss of the West Bank was a harsh blow to Jordan's economy, however. Before 1967 the West Bank accounted for 60 to 80 percent of the country's agricultural land, 75 percent of the GNP, 40 percent of the government's revenue, and nearly 33 percent of its foreign currency income. With the loss of the West Bank, the hope for self-sufficiency all but vanished.

Nevertheless, the East Bank did have significant economic assets. For example, Jordan's small industrial and mining sector was not severely hurt by the loss of the West Bank. The national power plant and the important phosphate mines were in the East. In addition, most of the larger manufacturing facilities were located between Amman and Zarqa. These included textiles, leather, batteries, food processing, brewing and bottling, and cigarette manufacturing.

Although possessing no oil of its own, Jordan indirectly benefited from the rapid rise in the price of oil during the 1970s. Subsidies from Arab oil-producing states and remittances from Jordanians working in those states helped provide necessary capital. Real GDP rose at an average annual rate of 11.7 percent, industrial production increased by 16.6 percent, and construction increased 23.8 percent annually in the 1970s. This rapid growth transformed the economy. By 1991, the service sector accounted for 63.7 percent of the GDP, industry was 28.2 percent, and agriculture was only 7 percent.

With the economic slowdown in the oil industry during the 1980s, the Jordanians experienced a decline in their economic growth rates to less than 5 percent. Remittances from workers abroad, however, remained fairly constant, as Jordanian workers were not as heavily involved in construction and the other sectors of the Arab Gulf economies that were drastically reduced. Subsidies from the Arab states to the Jordanian government were cut in half, contributing to the difficulties. With steadily declining foreign aid, the kingdom faced a series of shortfalls in the government budget in the late 1980s. By 1988, Jordan's debt was twice its GDP.

By March 1989, the government felt it had no recourse but to turn to the International Monetary Fund (IMF) for financial help. That help was forthcoming, but only in return for a severe economic adjustment program. The IMF program included cutbacks in state subsidies of staple foods and other products, which led to skyrocketing prices and ultimately to political unrest. Riots broke out throughout the country against the economic measures and against government corruption. The regime, caught off guard by the intensity of the unrest, moved to stave it off by sacking the government, restoring some subsidies, and announcing the resumption of elections and of more meaningful parliamentary life in the kingdom. Thus a positive outcome emerged from decidedly negative circumstances, as the kingdom embarked on a program of limited democratization. That program was not even a year old, however, when another external shock jolted the Jordanian economy. On August 2, 1990, Iraqi forces invaded Kuwait, triggering a major regional and global crisis.

By the time the 1991 Gulf War was over, the crisis had created still more challenges for the Jordanian economy. Subsidies from the oil-producing states were eliminated; Iraq, Jordan's largest trading partner and source of petroleum, was in ruins and was boycotted by the international community; and, 300,000 Jordanian citizens were forced to leave the Gulf States, causing the loss of hundred of millions of dollars in remittances. Moreover, a social safety net had to be provided for those returning without any income.

Many observers predicted the collapse of the economy under such pressures. This did not occur. The loss of assistance from the Gulf States was partially offset with a $450 million Japanese concessionary loan. The loss of trade with Iraq and the Gulf States forced Jordanian merchants to find new markets in Europe, Russia, China, and elsewhere in the Arab world. They were so successful that exports reached pre-war levels by mid-1992. The return of refugees, moreover, caused a brief but significant stimulus to the economy. Many had significant savings, which increased foreign currency deposits from $1.4 billion in February 1991 to $3.2 billion in July 1992. Furthermore, demand created by the need to provide housing and other services to the former Gulf residents provided a significant stimulus to construction and other industries. Efforts to restore full economic ties with the Gulf states also produced some significant results. In October 1991, Saudi Arabia allowed Jordanian trucks to enter the kingdom and much, but not all, of the pre-war trade was restored.

Although the Jordanian economy exceeded expectations following the Gulf crisis, serious problems remain. Political estrangement from the Gulf States continued for almost a decade with significant economic repercussions. Iraq remained under the U.N. embargo, depriving Jordan of a primary market. Large numbers of returnees are unable to find work. The already unacceptably high unemployment rate, combined with the fact that half of Jordan's population is under sixteen years of age, leaves little prospect for improvement. By late 1999, however, Jordan had managed to restore diplomatic ties with all six Arab Gulf monarchies and had revived part of the earlier economic partnership between Jordan and the Gulf states. Under King Abdullah II, Jordan strengthened its economic and military ties to both the United States and the European Union and also joined the World Trade Organization.

King Abdullah's regime clearly sees Jordan's economic and political future as closely tied to these powerful Western states and organizations. Ultimately, the hopes for an improved economy will rest on these economic relationships, on peace in the region, and on maintaining and expanding the opportunities for Jordan's well-educated population to find employment throughout the region.

Political Structure

Jordan is a constitutional monarchy. The current constitution, promulgated in 1952 during the brief reign of King Talal, gave increased authority to parliament. Nevertheless, ultimate authority over the legislative, executive, and judicial branches is retained by the monarch.

Executive power is primarily vested in the king. He appoints the prime minister and members of the cabinet and has the power to dismiss members of the cabinet. Power to dismiss the prime minister is vested in the parliament. When the parliament is suspended, the king assumes this responsibility. The king's considerable powers include the right to sign and promulgate laws, veto legislation, issue royal decrees (with the consent of the prime minister and four cabinet members), approve amendments to the constitution, command the armed forces, and declare war. In addition, he appoints and dismisses judges. The question of royal succession is also addressed in the constitution. The throne is guaranteed through the eldest male in direct line from King Abdallah. Should there be no direct male heir, the eldest brother becomes king. On occasion, the king has altered this formula by decree. If a king is either a minor or incapacitated for more than four months, a regent or regency council is established.

The Council of Ministers is empowered to perform necessary operational matters in the absence of a royal decree. The council, which consists of the prime minister and a variable number of ministers, shares executive responsibilities with the monarch and attends all affairs of state in implementing the policies of the king and prime minister. Its members can be appointed and dismissed by the king and prime minister, but the entire cabinet can be brought down by a vote of no confidence in the lower house of the legislature.

Under the constitution, Jordan has a bicameral national assembly. The forty senators in the upper house (*majlis al-ayyan,* or Assembly of Notables) are appointed by the king while the eighty deputies in the lower house (*majlis al-nu'ab,* or Assembly of Deputies) are directly elected. The prime minister originates legislation and submits proposals to the lower house. The approval of the upper chamber is necessary only when the lower house accepts a proposal. Should only one of the houses of parliament pass a bill, the two meet together to resolve their differences. Jordan maintains full adult suffrage, and women have had the right to vote and to run for office since 1973.

Jordan is divided into five provinces or governates: Amman, Irbid, Balqa, Karak, and Ma'an. Each province is administered by a governor who is appointed by the king. Loyalty to the monarch is the key element in each appointment. The governors have extensive local powers, including the right to void the election of a village mayor. This is important, for despite the extensive power of the central government and the governors, the village is the basic political unit for most Jordanians or, in the case of the bedouin, the tribe.

There are three sources of Jordanian law: Shari'a (Islamic law), European codes, and tradition. The Jordanian constitution and the Court Establishment Act of 1951 created a judiciary to reflect these sources of law. Three categories of courts were outlined in the constitution: regular civil courts, religious courts, and the special courts. The civil courts system, which is heavily based on Western law, has jurisdiction in all cases not specifically granted to the others. The religious court system has responsibility for personal status and communal endowment. Shari'a courts have responsibility for the Muslims, whereas the various Christian sects have their own councils. The special courts have responsibility for tribal questions and land issues. The king retains the right to appoint and dismiss judges and to pardon offenders.

In the process of regaining control of his kingdom and reestablishing more traditional ties with the West, King Hussein dismissed or forced out those in parliament most critical of his policies, resulting in a very docile parliament. Subsequent elections were held in October 1961, November 1962, April 1963, July 1963, and in May 1967. Little real authority rested with these parliaments. Little, if any, progress was made in building national representative institutions.

The 1967 war radically transformed the Jordanian political landscape. Half of the elected representatives had come from the Israeli-occupied West Bank. For the next two decades, the question of the composition of the parliament and the nature of the Jordanian relationship with the West Bank colored all aspects of Jordanian political life. No true parliamentary development was possible without making a determination on the future of the Jordanian/West Bank relationship. As a consequence, decisions were not made and institutional development did not occur.

Changing attitudes toward the future of the West Bank altered Jordanian views on how the parliament should be organized and who should be represented. The decision of the Arab states at Rabat in 1974 giving the Palestine Liberation Organization sole responsibility for the destiny of the West Bank further clouded the issue of West Bank representation in parliament. Subsequently, King Hussein dissolved parliament. This action appears to have been, at least in part, a result of his inability to challenge the Rabat decision and his unwillingness to accept it by organizing a purely East Bank parliament. Instead, in 1978, King Hussein replaced the parliament with a sixty-member National Consultative Council. Members of the council were appointed by the king for two-year terms. Powers were limited to reviewing bills, and members' views were not binding. The council was reappointed in 1980 and 1982.

By January 1984, King Hussein had determined that circumstances had changed. It was again in Jordan's perceived interest to increase its influence on the West Bank, open the political system to the increasingly well educated and prosperous citizens, and renew the search for peace with Israel. In order to accomplish these objectives, the king recalled parliament, including representatives from the West Bank. As it was not possible to hold elections on the West Bank, the parliament amended the constitution to allow elections to be held on the East Bank, with West Bank deputies to be chosen by parliament. This flurry of activity, in fact, had less to do with parliamentary development and more to do with determining Jordan's future relationship with the West Bank and the Palestinians. In 1988, the question of West Bank representation was rendered moot when King Hussein and the Jordanian government formally renounced claims to the West Bank.

Within Jordan, however, the need to open the political system was made very clear by the widespread political unrest of April 1989. The first election for a purely East Bank parliament was held in November, 1989. These elections underlined the acceptance of the Jordanian leaders that East Bank Jordan was a separate political entity. A temporary election law promulgated in late 1988 allowed for the election of eighty deputies from the five governorates of the East Bank. Parties were not allowed to participate. Although all candidates were officially independent, many were known to be affiliated with one particular party or group.

The results of the election in November 1989 alarmed many regime loyalists, as opposition candidates fared very well. Thirty-four of the eighty seats in the chamber went to candidates identified with the Muslim Brotherhood and to independent Islamists. Together they formed the single largest bloc in parliament. Leftist and Arab nationalist candidates won another thirteen seats.

The Jordanian establishment had to adjust its policies to adapt to changes in popular opinion. As a means of establishing a national consensus, the king appointed a sixty-member commission that included leaders from all factions, from leftists to Islamic fundamentalists. The commission wrote a National Charter, which was a political compact having in many ways as much authority as the constitution. The charter addressed all aspects of state and society and stressed the importance of political pluralism, equality of women, and education, and advocated a social safety net and updated labor laws. In agreeing to the National Charter, the political opposition in Jordan endorsed increasing pluralism and political liberalization. In doing so, the opposition also accepted the legitimacy of the ruling Hashimite monarchy.

The king endorsed the charter in June 1991 and ended the remaining elements of martial law the following month. In the spirit of the National Charter, parliament drafted a law legalizing political parties as a preliminary step for national elections. Throughout the early months of 1993, the king called for a national dialogue about an electoral system, similar to the dialogue through which the National Charter was written. Subsequently, the king announced basic changes in the law and laid the groundwork for elections in November 1993.

The elections of 1993 resulted in the election of a more moderate parliament. Traditional elements were strengthened and the Islamic groups and the leftists were weakened, although Islamists and their allies continued to be the single largest bloc. The loss of seats for the opposition, however, was due in large part to the new and controversial electoral law, which limited voters to one vote each. The previous electoral law had allowed each voter to vote up to the number of representatives for their district. Thus voters in Irbid in 1989 could vote for up to nine representatives for their city to the national parliament. The Muslim Brotherhood utilized this system to run blocs of candidates up to the exact number of seats in a district. That way, they were able to exploit the plurality-based system to gain representation well above their percentage of the overall national vote. But the 1993 electoral law had virtually the reverse effect. The one-person one-vote restriction was coupled with adjusted new districts that tended to enhance representation in traditionally pro-Hashimite areas—such as rural rather than urban districts.

This electoral law remains a bone of contention between the regime and the opposition. The regime also imposed more restrictive media restrictions prior to the 1997 elections, cutting back on much of the openness that had been achieved since 1989. In the 1997 parliamentary elections, an eleven-party opposition bloc boycotted the elections to protest the electoral law, the media restrictions, the continuing economic adjustment policies, and the normalization of relations with Israel. The electoral boycott led, naturally, to a relatively pliant proregime parliament. In effect, the issues that prompted the 1997 electoral boycott remained the central points of contention in Jordanian politics and in the November 2001 parliamentary elections. In sum, since the initiation of the political liberalization process the Jordanian political system took major steps toward pluralism, but then reversed or stalled many of those steps, leaving full democracy an ideal but not a reality.

The Political Succession

As noted in the beginning of this chapter, in February 1999 King Hussein died after a long battle with cancer, but not before having abruptly returned to the kingdom merely days before to change the succession from his brother Crown Prince Hasan to Hussein's eldest son, Abdullah. The change was nothing short of shocking, since Hasan had served as crown prince and presumed successor, and indeed had been groomed to be king, for thirty-four years. Yet the succession in 1999 took place smoothly, with Abdullah II crowned king.

King Hussein first began receiving treatment for cancer in 1991. In late 1992, he returned triumphantly to Jordan, accompanied by a massive outpouring of public support, having apparently conquered his cancer. But the disease returned in the years that followed, prompting the king to resume more rigorous cancer treatments in the United States. During his six-month absence from Jordan in late 1998 Hussein had, as usual, appointed his brother Crown Prince Hasan regent of the kingdom. This was a routine role for Hasan, although the medical treatments made this by far the longest period in which the crown prince managed the kingdom's affairs in the absence of the king. Naturally, then, most observers were shocked when the king returned to Jordan in January 1999 to change the succession (as it turned out, merely weeks before his death).

In shifting the line of succession from his brother Hasan to his first-born son, Abdullah, King Hussein argued that he was returning to the provisions of the Jordanian constitution, which does indeed call for succession from father to eldest son. Abdullah had been appointed crown prince before, shortly after his birth in 1962. He had then remained officially in line for the throne until 1965, when domestic and regional political unrest prompted the king to shift to an adult successor. Various failed assassination attempts in particular had led Hussein to choose his brother Hasan as his most capable successor. But Hasan was nonetheless abruptly and none-to-politely forced aside in January 1999. At issue was not just the immediate succession itself, but the one to follow. In short, would the next succession go to the son of Hussein or Hasan? It appears that one main reason for changing the succession was to keep the Hashimite succession within Hussein's family line.

Political Dynamics

Despite the structure of the constitutional monarchy, political power in Jordan remains with the king. Nevertheless, the king is a politician who must have public support for his policies. Although there is little doubt that King Abdullah believes in the benefits of a more representative government, the legislature is only as powerful as the monarch allows it to be.

The Army

It would be difficult to overemphasize the importance of the Jordanian army in the establishment and maintenance of the state. Some authors have gone as far as to say that Jordan was created by the army. It was recruited primarily from the East Bank Jordanian population, whose loyalty to the king was beyond question. Only twice—in the mid-1950s confrontation with the Arab nationalists and in the 1970 clashes with the Palestinians—has the throne been seriously threatened. On each occasion, new and less-reliable elements had increased their influence within the army. The alteration in the composition of the armed forces made the army more susceptible to political pressures, which permitted antiregime elements to attempt to undermine the military's support for the king. Both attempts failed.

The Arab Legion, as created by the British, was a small elite corps composed primarily of tribal elements. These tribesmen were loyal to the king and supported Jordan's traditional close ties with the British. With the coming of the Palestine War of 1948, the narrowly recruited elite force had to be rapidly expanded. Increasingly large numbers of East Bank townspeople were brought into the army.

The changing composition of the armed forces was such that regional political influences came to have a significant impact on elements within the army. By the early 1950s, British power and influence were receding throughout the Middle East in the face of a rising tide of Arab nationalism. This nationalist sentiment, which developed a decidedly anti-Western cast following the overthrow of the Egyptian monarchy, found many sympathetic ears in the Jordanian army. Some even blamed the Hashimites' close ties with the West as a key factor behind Jordanian and Arab military setbacks. As relations soured between the United States and Egypt over Cairo's purchase of Czechoslovakian arms and the U.S. failure to build the Aswan Dam, President Nasser's brand of Arab nationalism gained influence in Jordan at the expense of the British and Hashimite loyalties.

Pressure on King Hussein to join the pro-Western, anticommunist Baghdad Pact came from London and Washington, and from his cousin, King Faysal, in Baghdad. Hussein was forced to determine whether his primary interest lay in allying more closely with the West or with the Arab nationalists and Nasser. Although the Baghdad Pact was widely denounced as a "tool of the West" and a form of "neocolonialism," Hussein, in late 1955, decided to maintain his ties with Britain and Iraq. Flying in the face of popular wishes and growing Arab nationalist influence in the army, Prime Minister Hazza al-Majali announced in early December that Jordan intended to enter the alliance. Riots broke out in Amman. After three days, order was restored by the Jordanian army, but the incident drove the young king into the arms of the nationalists.

Jordan did not join the Baghdad Pact. Al-Majali was replaced as prime minister, and on March 1, 1956, General John Bagot Glubb (Glubb Pasha), commander of the Arab Legion, and his British staff were dismissed. The king attempted to ameliorate a hostile British reaction by emphasizing that he had made the decision on his own without pressure from the other Arab states, but such assertions were not convincing. Al-Majali had visited Syria, Saudi Arabia, and Egypt in the month prior to the dismissals, and these governments had encouraged Jordan to stay out of the Baghdad Pact.

The king, for his part, had made a daring move by aligning himself with the Arab nationalists. He was greatly influenced by the rising tide of Arab nationalist sentiment in the armed forces. Following Hussein's dismissal of the British, his popularity at home and throughout the Arab world was never higher. His move also appears to have been calculated to use this popularity to solidify his political position. To draw on this strength within the army, Hussein appointed a nationalist officer, Ali Abu Nuwar, to command the army and to complete the transition. He officially changed the army's name to the Jordanian Arab Army.

Although the Arab nationalists at home and abroad were supportive of the king's action, many were never completely loyal to him. The tenuous nature of his alliance became evident the following year. Believing that his destiny was more closely tied with the other Arabs than with the West, Hussein attended an Arab solidarity conference in January 1957. By an agreement signed at the conference, Egypt, Syria, and Saudi Arabia guaranteed the payment of a subsidy if Jordan terminated its relations with the British. In March, the Jordanians abrogated their treaty with Britain, resulting in the withdrawal of the last British garrisons from Jordan and the end of the British subsidy. Hussein's Arab allies, however, failed to replace his losses.

By cutting his ties with the British, Hussein had left the monarchy open to a direct challenge from the Arab nationalists. In April 1957, Abu Nuwar and a group of nationalist officers attempted to control the political process by vetoing the king's choice of prime minister. Some have termed Abu Nuwar's action an attempted coup. Hussein met the challenge by addressing his bedouin troops directly. They sided with him against the nationalists, forcing Abu Nuwar into exile. Henceforth, the influence of the Arab nationalists in the army was curtailed.

The Palestinians

With army loyalty assured, the only internal group able to threaten the monarchy was the Palestinians. Until the mid-1960s, however, the Palestinians had almost no effective organization and little in the way of a political program. Convinced that they were powerless to regain their lost homeland by themselves, they were compelled to look to the Arab states as the only force capable of confronting Israel. As time went on without any apparent success, a few Palestinians began to assert that they must rely on themselves and that the struggle was theirs rather than that of the Arab states. In the early 1960s, some Palestinians began to organize into commando groups, such as al-Fatah and the Popular Front for the Liberation of Palestine (PFLP). The commandos launched a few generally ineffective raids into Israel and failed to persuade the majority of Palestinians that the Palestinian people could achieve their goals without relying on the Arab states.

This attitude changed dramatically after the June 1967 Arab-Israeli War. Israel's humiliation of the Egyptian, Syrian, and Jordanian armies convinced most Palestinians not only that the Arab states were inept but also that they did not care about the Palestinians. The popularity of the commandos soared, and groups like al-Fatah had to turn away recruits. This growth in commando strength provided the Palestinians with a military force capable of challenging the Jordanian army. In addition, the loyalty of some elements of the Jordanian army was questioned. After twenty years of Jordanian citizenship, many Palestinians had entered the military. The Palestinian percentage in the military did not equal their majority status in the general population and they did not hold key positions, but the Palestinians, nevertheless, played a significant role.

As a result of the new Palestinian influence, combined with the devastating economic impact created by the loss of the West Bank, King Hussein faced the most serious crisis of his reign. More than half the population of the truncated Jordanian state was Palestinian. The army was discredited. The prestige of the commandos, who were the heroes of most Palestinians, was high. Each raid from Jordanian territory into Israel enhanced the popular mystique of the guerrillas, while leaving the Jordanian army to absorb the retaliatory blows of the Israeli Defense Forces. The Palestinians adopted a no-compromise attitude toward the Israelis and the Jordanians. They demanded that Jordan not interfere in their raids. When Jordanian authorities arrested a Palestinian group who had launched rockets against the Israeli port of Eilat, a threatened confrontation with the commandos forced their release.

More than any other incident, the battle of Karameh illustrated the rising tide of fedayeen (commando) popularity. In March 1968, the Israelis struck at the Karameh refugee camp on the East Bank of Jordan, a key center for cross-river Palestinian raids. The Israelis severely damaged the village but did not intimidate the fedayeen. With the aid of the Jordanian army, the fedayeen stood and fought, inflicting numerous casualties upon the Israeli troops. Despite the crucial role of Jordanian artillery, the battle was widely viewed as a great victory for the commandos, in contrast with the previous failures of the army.

The overwhelming popularity of the fedayeen, particularly al-Fatah, enabled the guerrilla organizations to assume de facto control of Palestinian camps and neighborhoods throughout Jordan. With the military assistance and training provided by other Arab states, they virtually became a state within a state, challenging the sovereignty of the king. In November 1968, a three-day battle between the fedayeen and the army was the first in a series of clashes. Each concluded with some Jordanian concession to the Palestinians, because Hussein's greatest fear appeared to be that continued fighting would lead to civil war.

By the summer of 1970, an all-out confrontation between the monarchy (supported by the East Bank Jordanians) and the Palestinians seemed inevitable. The conflict came to head in September 1970. For the next ten months the Jordanian army chipped away at Palestinian strongholds, ultimately bringing them under Jordanian control. At times, such as in later September 1970, the fighting was very intense. Jordan's action alienated most of the other Arab states. Syria sent 200 tanks across the Jordanian border, but losses, logistical difficulties, and the threat of Israeli intervention forced the Syrians to withdraw. Interestingly, although Baghdad strongly condemned Hussein, Iraqi forces in Jordan did not intervene. Libya broke relations and transferred its annual subsidy from the Hashimite government to the commandos. Kuwait ended its economic assistance. Bitterness toward the Jordanians led Palestinian nationalists to sever their ties with the Hashimites, who were widely considered, next to the Israelis, the greatest enemies of Palestinian nationalism. Hussein's confrontation with the commandos ended in a victory for the Hashimite monarchy, but the costs were high indeed. Thousands of Palestinians were killed, while thousands more fled or were expelled from the kingdom, many to Lebanon. Today, most Jordanians were born after the 1970 civil war, or what Palestinians call "Black September." In the more than three decades since that time, the wounds of that confrontation have healed for many, but not all, Palestinians and Jordanians.

Political Parties

Political parties were formally legalized in September 1992, after having been banned for more than three decades. In the early 1950s, parties had functioned freely, with the hope that Jordan's government could develop into a constitutional monarchy. The Ba'th, Nationalist, Liberal, Communist, Muslim Brotherhood, and other parties were all active. The majority of these were ideological or sectarian, without a wide popular base. Many were antimonarchy and most had ties to parties with connections outside of Jordan.

As tensions rose in Jordan with the increasing influence of the Arab nationalists, the political parties criticized Jordan's pro-Western policies and, sometimes, the king. In nonparty 1956 elections the Arab nationalists won the parliamentary election. Their leader, Sulayman Nabulsi, a West Bank Palestinian, became prime minister. Nabulsi, who was closely associated with Abu Nuwar, pushed for greater ties with Nasser and other Arab nationalist states. When the nationalists overstepped the bounds of loyal opposition in 1957, conspiring with Abu Nuwar against the monarchy, the king exercised his power. He not only removed Nabulsi from power, but banned political parties as well.

In 1989, King Hussein began the process of democratic reform. As part of that effort, nonparty parliamentary elections were held in 1989. A subsequent step in that process was the legalization of political parties. By the time the next parliamentary elections were held on November 8, 1993, twenty legal political parties participated. A wide range of parties included Islamists, centrists, and leftists. The most influential parties were the Islamist parties, specifically the Islamic Action Front.

The 1993 elections, however, demonstrated the weaknesses of the parties and not their strength. Less than a third of the elected members were party members; the majority were independents who supported the king. Even those who were members of political parties often ran without party affiliation. Family membership and local influence remained far more important than party identification. In 1997, party representation within parliament declined still further when the eleven-party opposition bloc boycotted the elections. Whether the political parties will be able to establish themselves as a meaningful and sustainable influence on Jordanian politics remains to be seen.

Foreign Policy

In the more than forty years since independence, Jordan's relative influence in regional affairs has diminished. Whereas in 1950 Jordan was a regional power that could thwart the will of its fellow Arab states by annexing the West Bank, and the Hashimite monarchy could rival the Saudi monarchy, in 2001 this was no longer the case. The lessened role has been the result of the decline of the relative military strength of the Jordanian armed forces and of Jordan's economic base with the loss of the West Bank on the one hand, and the rise of other powers in Arab world on the other. Consequently, Jordan's regional influence is less than before, and its foreign policy objectives have become limited.

In formulating its foreign policy, Jordan now finds itself more watchful of the policies of others. The preservation of the monarchy and the status of East Bank Jordanians appear to be primary objectives. Until the 1974 Rabat summit meeting, in which the Arab states recognized the Palestinian Liberation Organization as the sole representative of the Palestinian people, regaining the West Bank was of great importance. After that, determining Jordan's role in the search for peace with Israel and its relationship with the West Bank Palestinians were the primary concerns. Despite renouncing claims to the West Bank in 1988, Jordan's leaders did not entirely abandon the belief that they had a responsibility for their former citizens as well as the territory, including Jerusalem.

To achieve even its limited goals, Jordan generally sought outside support from two principal sources—the West and other moderate Arabs. Jordan's Western connection originated in the mandate era and the close treaty ties between Britain and the kingdom following independence. As the British influence and ability to intercede in support of the monarchy declined, the United States replaced the United Kingdom as the principal Western ally. In spite of some differences with Washington and considerable criticism from other Arabs, King Hussein maintained this relationship because it was in Jordan's best interest. The West provided a needed subsidy, arms, and some political support. The relationship with the United States, however, became increasingly frustrating during the 1980s. The Jordanians believed the limit of their relationship with the United States was determined by Israel and its supporters in the U.S. Congress. No significant arms sales to Jordan could win congressional approval. Arms sales, moreover, were rejected or never submitted to the Congress after humiliating public debates. Furthermore, overall assistance levels from the United States declined significantly. Because the Jordanian army relied heavily on American assistance, its relative capability declined as well. The Jordanians were forced to look elsewhere for assistance.

The moderate Arabs provided an alternative source of support. Whereas in the early 1950s the Jordanians were rivals of the Saudis, in the 1980s Jordan became increasingly dependent on Saudi Arabia and the other Gulf states for economic and political support. The economic support kept the Jordanian economy afloat and helped purchase needed military equipment. The political support provided an umbrella from Jordan's sometimes tumultuous relations with its neighboring Ba'thist regimes in Syria and Iraq. In some respects, Jordan became a buffer that protected the Arabian peninsula monarchies from the turmoil of the Fertile Crescent.

The Iran-Iraq war, from 1980 to 1988, created a new set of challenging circumstances for Jordan. As the war dragged on, Jordan increased its support for Iraq. This policy coincided with the policies of the Gulf states and the U.S. administration. Jordan provided Iraq a safe port, strategic depth, and a good trading partner. But if Iraq was Jordan's strongest regional ally in the 1980s, it seemed to be more of a liability with the onset of the 1990s.

The most serious international challenge faced by Jordan in two decades resulted from the August 2, 1990, Iraqi occupation of Kuwait. The overwhelming majority of Jordanians supported Iraq against the allied coalition. Facing such strong domestic sentiments, the Hashimite regime attempted to bridge the divide between traditional Western allies and Iraq. King Hussein shuttled between various capitals in a failed effort to avert war. But Jordan's fence-straddling policy alienated virtually all of its local and global allies, at great cost to the kingdom. The United States, the Western allies, the Gulf Arabs, Egyptians, and Syrians sharply criticized Jordan's actions. Foreign assistance all but evaporated. Three hundred thousand Jordanians were expelled from the Gulf States, and an allied armada searched ships entering and leaving the port of Aqaba. Despite the international criticism, King Hussein's popularity soared at home.

Even after the military defeat of Iraq, international pressure on Jordan continued. A never-ending series of accusations of violations of the international boycott of Iraq were leveled against Jordan. In this hostile environment, the Jordanians worked to reestablish good relations with its traditional allies. Similar to his actions in the mid-1950s, King Hussein abandoned traditional international alliances in recognition of overwhelming domestic popular opinion.

In the immediate aftermath of the war, the Hashimite regime played on Jordan's vital role to any Arab-Israeli peace settlement by enthusiastically accepting terms for multilateral negotiations to begin in 1991 in Madrid. The peace process, in short, served to reestablish Jordanian ties with the United States and Europe. By 1994, these efforts had resulted in a peace treaty with Israel, and Jordan moved closer than ever to the United States and the European Union. By the late 1990s, Jordan had restored diplomatic relations and financial-aid ties with each of the Arab Gulf monarchies, including Kuwait. Under King Abdullah, Jordan maintained each of these political, economic, and military ties while also moving closer to Egypt and even to both Syria and Iraq. With its external relations stronger than perhaps ever before, Jordan's main political focus necessarily turned inward once again. The most important issues in Jordanian politics in the early twenty-first century remain those that dominated the previous decade: economic adjustment, peace with Israel, and whether political liberalization will be allowed to proceed toward more meaningful democratization.

Bibliography

Peter Gubser's *Jordan: Crossroads of Middle Eastern Events* (Boulder: Westview Press, 1983) and Arthur R. Day's, *East Bank/West Bank: Jordan and the Prospects for Peace* (New York: Council on Foreign Relations, 1986) both provide solid overviews of Jordanian society, economy, politics and history—although both are obviously dated on contemporary politics.

A good general history is Kamal Salibi's *The Modern History of Jordan* (London: I. B. Tauris, 1998). In *Politics and the Military in Jordan: A Study of the Arab Legion, 1921–1957* (New York: Praeger Publishers, 1977), P. J. Vatrikiotis analyzes the role of the military in creating and supporting the Hashimite regime. Robert Satloff's *From Abdullah to Hussein; Jordan in Transition* (New York: Oxford University Press, 1993) examines the emergence of the Hussein regime in the early 1950s. By far the most detailed analysis of the emergence of Jordan as a country is Mary C. Wilson's *King Abdullah, Britain and the Making of Jordan* (Cambridge: Cambridge University Press, 1987).

Several articles have examined various aspects of the democratization process in the kingdom, including Rex Brynen, "Economic Crisis and Post-Rentier Democratization in the Arab World: The Case of Jordan," *Canadian Journal of Political Science* 25 (1) 1992: 69–97 and Glenn E. Robinson, "Defensive Democratization in Jordan," *International Journal of Middle East Studies* 30 (3) 1998: 373–387. For an analysis of the 1989, 1993, and 1997 elections, see Curtis R. Ryan, "Elections and Parliamentary Democratization in Jordan," *Democratization* 5 (4) 1998: 176–196.

An interesting and challenging discussion of Palestinian-Jordanian relations within the kingdom can be found in Mustafa Hamarneh, Rosemary Hollis, and Khalil Shikaki, *Jordanian-Palestinian Relations: Where to?* (London: Royal Institute of International Affairs, 1997). On the Islamist movement, see the excellent book by Quintan Wiktorowicz, *The Management of Islamic Activism: Salafis, the Muslim Brotherhood, and State Power in Jordan* (Albany: SUNY Press, 2000).

Former Arab Legion Commander Frederick G. Peake's (Peake Pasha) *A History of Jordan and Its Tribes* (Coral Gables, Fla.: University of Miami Press, 1958) remains a classic discussion of the Jordanian tribes. See also *Jordan: The Impact of Social Change on the Role of the Tribes*, Washington Paper No. 108 (New York: Praeger Publishers, 1984) by Paul A. Jureidini and R. D. McLaurin. Detailed studies of social and political structure on the local level can be found in Richard T. Antoun's *Arab Village: A Social Structural Study of a Transjordan Peasant Community* (Bloomington, Ind.: Indiana University Press, 1972) and Peter Gubser's *Politics and Change in al-Karak, Jordan* (London: Oxford University Press, 1973).

On Jordan's international relations, see the excellent studies by Laurie A. Brand, *Jordan's Inter-Arab Relations: The Political Economy of Alliance Making* (New York: Columbia University Press, 1994) and Marc Lynch, *State Interests and Public Spheres: The International Politics of Jordan's Identity* (New York: Columbia University Press, 1999).

11

State of Israel

Bernard Reich

Israel is a product of Zionism (the Jewish national movement). Since biblical days, Jews of the Diaspora (Jewish communities outside Israel) have hoped that they would return to Zion, the "Promised Land." While some Jews always remained in the Holy Land, the overwhelming majority were located in the Diaspora. Over the centuries Zionism developed spiritual, religious, cultural, social, and historical concepts linking Jews to the land of the historical Jewish states in Israel. The political variant of Zionism that saw the establishment of a Jewish state as a logical consequence of its actions developed in the nineteenth century partly as a result of political currents then prevalent in Europe, especially nationalism and anti-Semitism. Groups such as the Lovers of Zion (*Hoveve Zion*) movement, whose goal was immigration and settlement, were established to alleviate the problems of the Jewish communities in Europe through the development of settlements in Palestine.

Historical Background

In 1897 Theodor Herzl, a Viennese journalist who had proposed establishing a self-governing community for the Jewish people in his book, *Der Judenstaat* (*The Jewish State*), organized a conference at Basel, Switzerland, to assemble prominent leaders from the major Jewish communities and organizations throughout the world. This assembly shaped a Zionist political movement and established the World Zionist Organization (WZO). The Basel Program, which became the cornerstone of Zionist ideology, enunciated the basic aim of Zionism: "to create for the Jewish people a home in Palestine secured by public law."

World War I enabled the Zionist movement to make important gains. As a consequence of the war, the Ottoman Empire, which had ruled Palestine since the sixteenth century, was forced to relinquish the territory. With the aid of Chaim Weizmann, a prominent Zionist leader and chemist who contributed to the British war effort, the Zionist organization secured from the British government the Balfour Declaration (1917), stating, inter alia, that "his Majesty's Government view with favour the establishment in Palestine of a national home for the Jewish people." By the end of the war, British control had replaced Ottoman rule in Palestine. The Palestine mandate was allocated to Great Britain, which controlled the area between 1920 and May 1948.

During the mandate period, the Jewish community in Palestine (the *Yishuv*) established institutions for self-government and procedures for implementing political decisions. By secret ballot the organized Jewish community chose the Assembly of the Elected (*Asefat Hanevcharim*) as its representative body. It met at least once a year, and between sessions its powers were exercised by the National Council (*Vaad Leumi*), which was elected by the assembly.

The mandatory government entrusted the National Council with the responsibility for Jewish communal affairs and granted it considerable autonomy. The executive committee of the National Council—through a number of self-created departments concerned with education, culture, health, social welfare, and religious affairs—acted as the administering power for the Jewish community. The council also controlled the clandestine recruitment and military training of Jewish youth in the defense force (*Hagana*), which after independence formed the core of Israel's defense forces. The General Federation of Labor (*Histadrut*), founded in 1920, coordinated labor-related matters and engaged in social welfare and economic endeavors. Political parties were established.

Prototypical political institutions, founded and developed by the Jewish community, laid the foundation for many of Israel's public bodies and political processes. Several of the semigovernmental organizations that were created (most notably the Histadrut and the Jewish Agency[1]) continued to play important roles after Israel's independence. These contributed to the growth of a highly developed system of Zionist political parties and the consequent prevalence of coalition executive bodies in the Zionist movement and the local organs of Palestine Jewry. Weizmann, as president of the WZO, negotiated with leading representatives of Jewish organizations and communities throughout the world for their participation in the work of the Jewish Agency. In August 1929 these negotiations culminated in the establishment of a new body, the Jewish Agency for Palestine, popularly referred to as "the Expanded Jewish Agency." The agency included Jews and Jewish organizations sympathetic to the idea of a Jewish national home but not ideologically committed to Zionism. It took over the activities—such as fundraising and maintaining liaison with foreign governments—designed to build a national home, activities in which concerned Jews everywhere could participate. The agency conducted negotiations with the Palestine mandatory government, the United Kingdom, and the League of Nations and sought accommodation with the Arabs.

Throughout the mandate period, the Jewish and Arab communities of Palestine were in conflict over the future of the territory. Arab opposition to Jewish immigration and land purchase was a constant theme and was manifested in such actions as the Arab revolts in the 1920s and 1930s. British policy vacillated, but restrictions on Jewish immigration (such as the White Paper of 1939) became central elements of the British response to intercommunal violence. Unable to find a solution to satisfy these conflicting views, and concerned about the heavy cost in men and money, the British eventually conceded that the mandate was unworkable and turned the problem over to the United Nations, which placed the Palestine issue before its General Assembly in the spring of 1947.

The United Nations Special Committee on Palestine (UNSCOP) studied the problem and recommended that the mandate be terminated and that the independence of Palestine be achieved without delay; however, it was divided over the future of the territory. The majority recommended partition into a Jewish state and an Arab state linked in an economic union, with Jerusalem and its environs established as an international enclave—a *corpus separatum* (separate body). The minority recommended that Palestine become a single federal state, with Jerusalem the capital and with Jews and Arabs enjoying autonomy in their respective areas. On November 29, 1947, the U.N. General Assembly, over Arab opposition, adopted the majority recommendation proposal by thirty-three votes to thirteen, with ten abstentions. The Zionists reluctantly accepted the decision as the best practical outcome. The Palestinians and other Arabs rejected the vote.

Thereafter the situation in Palestine deteriorated rapidly. Disorders reminiscent of those of the 1920s and 1930s broke out in all parts of the territory, and as the end of the mandate approached, these degenerated into a virtual civil war. Israel declared its independence as a Jewish and democratic state on May 14, 1948. General Sir Alan Gordon Cunningham, the last British high commissioner, departed. Armies of the Arab states entered Palestine and engaged in open warfare with the defense forces of the new state. The United Nations secured a truce, and the military situation was stabilized in the spring of 1949 by a series of armistice agreements between Israel and the neighboring Arab states, but no general peace settlement was achieved.

The provisional government of Israel, which was formed at the time of independence and recognized by the major powers, was new in name only. It had begun to function following adoption of the partition resolution in 1947, and it drew on the experience gained by the Yishuv. After proclaiming Israel's independence, the provisional government repealed the British mandatory restrictions on immigration and the sale of land and converted the Hagana into the Israel Defense Forces (IDF).

The provisional government had three elements: a state council that acted as parliament; a cabinet elected by the state council from among its members; and a president elected by the state council. David Ben-Gurion, chairman of the Jewish Agency and leader of the dominant political party, MAPAI (Israel Labor Party), was selected as prime minister and minister of defense, and Chaim Weizmann was elected president. The provisional government directed the war against the Arab states, levied taxes, established administrative agencies, and conducted essential public services. The state council, at its session just before the national elections of January 25, 1949, adopted a transition ordinance transferring its authority to a constituent assembly, which convened on February 14, 1949. That assembly, which later declared itself the First Knesset (parliament), was a unicameral chamber composed of 120 members, who represented twelve of the twenty-four parties that had contested the 1949 elections.

Political Environment

Israel's special role as the world's only Jewish state has had a manifold effect on its political system. Israel is interested in the well-being of Jews everywhere and is concerned that all Jews who wish to immigrate are free to do so. The encouragement of Jewish immigration has left its mark on every aspect of Israeli life. The commitment to unfettered Jewish immigration was articulated initially in Israel's Declaration of Independence, which proclaimed that "the State of Israel will be open to the immigration of Jews from all countries of their dispersion." It was reaffirmed in the Law of Return of July 5, 1950 (which provided that "every Jew has the right to come to this country as an 'oleh' [Jew immigrating to Israel]"), and has been reinforced by the programs and actions of successive Israeli governments. Encouraging the ingathering of exiles has received overwhelming support in parliament and from the Jewish population, and it has been implemented almost without regard to the economic costs and social dislocations caused by the rapid and massive influx of people. Immigration serves Israel's needs by providing the manpower necessary for Israel's security and development.

Several problems have resulted from this policy. Unlike the period of the mandate when immigration was selective and severely limited by British-imposed restrictions, Israel has admitted whole communities virtually without regard to their economic usefulness or its own absorptive capacity. Between 1919 and 1948, about 90 percent of the Jewish immigrants came from Europe or other Western countries. But during the nascent years of Israel's independence, the Jewish communities of Muslim states of the Middle East and North Africa arrived in large numbers. The Jews of Yemen (about 45,000) and Iraq (about 123,000) were brought to Israel by airlifts, popularly known as Operation Magic Carpet and Operation Ali Baba.

After the Six-Day War in 1967, immigrants again came mainly from the West and the Soviet Union. Jewish immigration declined between the early 1970s and the mid-1980s, when it exceeded emigration only slightly. Nevertheless, in late 1984 and early 1985 nearly 7,000 Falashas (Jews of Ethiopia) were airlifted to Israel in an effort known as Operation Moses. More arrived in Operation Sheba. In May 1991 Israel rescued an additional 14,000 Ethiopian Jews in a massive airlift (known as Operation Solomon) that took only twenty-six hours to complete. In 1989, Soviet authorities began to relax emigration restrictions on Jews, and by the turn of the twenty-first century more than one million immigrated to Israel from what was and, later, had been, the Soviet Union. Among other issues, the large Soviet migration raised questions about whether the newcomers were Jewish under traditional interpretation of Jewish law (*halacha*).

Geographically and demographically Israel is an Oriental country; culturally, socially, and politically it is Western in inclination. The early Zionists laid the foundations for an essentially European culture in Palestine, and subsequent immigration accelerated the trend of Westernization. The Occidental (overwhelmingly Ashkenazi) immigrants developed the Yishuv structure of land settlement, trade unions, political parties, and education in preparation for a Western-oriented Jewish national state. Future immigrants had to adapt themselves to a society that had formed these institutions, and this presented a problem for those who were part of the immigration from non-Western countries.

Numerous difficulties have beset efforts to settle and absorb the masses of immigrants. Economic, social, and cultural assimilation of the immigrants in a short span of time would have been a formidable undertaking for a small country even under the most favorable conditions. In Israel, this has been attempted despite the obstacles posed by limited resources, defense needs, and the composition and character of the new immigration. Israel has been obliged to undertake the training or retraining of the immigrants for gainful employment and to provide housing, schooling, and medical facilities.

The nonmaterial problems, which are essentially those of cultural and social acclimation, are more complex. Although the basic religious tradition of the Jewish population is an asset because it provides a common core of values and ideals, there are major differences in outlook, values, frames of reference, levels of aspiration, and various other social and cultural components. Army service, which emphasizes education as well as the experience of common living and working and of learning the Hebrew language, facilitates acculturation and encourages evolution in the direction of a unified, multicultural society. Despite these efforts, the full integration of immigrants into Israel's society remains a great social problem.

The Arabs of Israel (that is, those who have lived in Israel since its independence and their offspring, who are Israeli citizens, not the Arabs in those areas occupied by Israel during the Six-Day War)—some 18 percent of the population in

TABLE 11.1 Political Parties and Knesset Election Results, 1949–1961

Party	1949 %	1949 Seats	1951 %	1951 Seats	1955 %	1955 Seats	1959 %	1959 Seats	1961 %	1961 Seats
MAPAI (Israel Workers)	35.7	46	37.3	45	32.2	40	38.2	47	34.7	42
MAPAM (United Workers)[a]	14.7	19	12.5	15	7.3	9	7.2	9	7.5	9
Ahdut Haavoda (Unity of Labor)[b]	–	–	–	–	8.2	10	6.0	7	6.6	8
Herut (Freedom)	11.5	14	6.6	8	12.6	15	13.6	17	13.8	17
General Zionists	5.2	7	16.2	20	10.2	13	6.2	8	–	–
Progressives	4.1	5	3.2	4	4.4	5	4.6	6	–	–
Liberal[c]	–	–	–	–	–	–	–	–	13.6	17
United Religious Front[d]	12.2	16	–	–	–	–	–	–	–	–
Mizrahi (Merkaz Ruchani—Spiritual Center)	–	–	1.5	2	–	–	–	–	–	–
Hapoel Hamizrahi (Workers of the Spiritual Center)	–	–	6.7	8	–	–	–	–	–	–
National Religious (MAFDAL)[e]	–	–	–	–	9.1	11	9.9	12	9.8	12
Agudat Israel (Association of Israel)[f]	–	–	–	–	–	–	–	–	3.7	4
Poalei Agudat Israel (Workers of the Association of Israel)[f]	–	–	–	–	–	–	–	–	–	–
Torah Religious Front[g]	–	–	3.6	5	4.7	6	4.7	6	1.9	2
Arab Democratic List	1.7	2	2.4	3	1.8	2	–	–	–	–
Arab Progress and Work	–	–	1.2	1	1.5	2	1.3	2	1.6	2
Arab Farmers and Development	–	–	1.1	1	1.2	1	1.1	1	–	–
Arab Cooperation and Brotherhood	–	–	–	–	–	–	1.2	2	1.9	2
Communist	3.5	4	4.0	5	4.5	6	2.8	3	4.2	5
Sephardim	3.5	4	1.8	2	–	–	–	–	–	–
Fighters List	2.1	1	–	–	–	–	–	–	–	–
Women's International Zionist Organization (WIZO)	1.2	1	–	–	–	–	–	–	–	–
Yemenites	1.0	1	1.2	1	–	–	–	–	–	–

[a]Formed 1948—Hashomer Hatzair, Ahdut Haavoda, Poalei Zion.
[b]Formed by merger of Poalei Zion (Workers of Zion) and smaller socialist Zionist groups. Included in MAPAM 1949 and 1951.
[c]Formed 1961—merger of General Zionists and Progressives.
[d]Elected as follows: Hapoel Hamizrahi, 6; Mizrahi, 4; Agudat Israel, 3; Poalei Agudat Israel, 3.
[e]Merger—Mizrahi and Hapoel Hamizrahi.
[f]In Torah Religious Front until 1961 elections and again in 1973 elections.
[g]Joint list Agudat Israel and Poalei Agudat Israel.

SOURCE: Bernard Reich and Gershon R. Kieval, Israel: Land of Tradition and Conflict, 2d ed. (Boulder, Colo.: Westview Press, 1993), pp. 94–95.

2001—are confronted by problems qualitatively different from those facing Jewish immigrants. Following Israel's independence, and as a result of the ensuing war between Israel and the Arab states, a large number of Arabs who had lived in the part of Palestine that is now Israel fled and took up residence in Arab states, either as refugees or as members of their permanent populations.

After the 1949 armistice agreements, activities of the Arab community were regarded primarily as the concern of Israel's security system, and most of the areas inhabited by the Arabs were placed under military control. A military government was established in these districts, and special defense and security zones were created. Israel's Arabs were granted citizenship with full legal equality but were forbidden to travel into or out of security areas without permission from the military. Military courts, in which trials could be held in closed session, were established. With the consent of the minister of defense, the military commanders could limit individual movements, impose restrictions on employment and business, issue deportation orders, search and seize, and detain a person if it were deemed necessary for security purposes.

Those who argued in support of the military administration saw it as a means of controlling the Arab population and preventing infiltration, sabotage, and espionage. Furthermore, it was contended that the very existence of the military administration was an important deterrent measure. As evidence developed that the Israeli Arabs were not disloyal, pressure for relaxation and then for total abolition of military restrictions grew in the Knesset and in public debate. The restrictions were gradually modified, and on December 1, 1966, the military government was abolished. Functions that had been exercised by the military government were transferred to relevant civilian authorities.

The major long-term problem for Israel's Arab minority is its social integration. Although Israeli Arabs vote, sit in the Knesset, serve in government offices, have their own schools and courts, and prosper materially, they face difficulties in adjusting to Israel's modern Jewish- and Western-oriented society. Most of the major factors facilitating Jewish integration are not operative with regard to the Arab minority. The Arabs tend to live in separate villages and in separate sections of the major cities. They speak Arabic, attend a separate school system, and, with few exceptions, do not serve in the army.

The Arab and Jewish communities in Israel have few points of contact, and those that exist are not intimate; the societies are separate and generally continue to hold stereotypical images of each other, often reinforced by the schools, the media, social distance, and—most significantly—by the tensions and problems created by the larger Arab-Israeli conflict in its numerous dimensions. There is mutual suspicion and antagonism, and there is a prevalent Jewish fear of the Arabs—a result of wars and terrorism.

Over time the Arab community has become increasingly politicized. Despite formal legal equality and surface equanimity, Israeli Arabs have been discontented with a perceived second-class status resulting from various forms of unofficial discrimination. In the wake of the Yom Kippur War (1973) and with the increased international standing of the Palestine Liberation Organization (PLO), the Arabs of Israel seemed to become more restive and more politically aware. In spring 1976, Israel's Arabs participated in their first general protest and staged the most violent demonstrations to that date in Israel's history. The riots, whose extent and ferocity surprised both Israeli Arabs and Jews, grew out of a general strike, centered in Nazareth, that was organized to protest land expropriations in Israel's northern section. The expropriation served as a catalyst; the initial demonstrations escalated and eventually became broader and more general in their focus, incorporating complaints about Arab second-class status and adding other issues to the list of grievances. Israeli Arabs demonstrated greater political activism after the beginning of the Palestinian uprising (intifada) in the West Bank and Gaza Strip in December 1987. They began to identify more strongly with the Arabs in the occupied territories and showed signs of growing nationalism and greater militancy. In the fall of 2000 Israeli Arabs rioted and demonstrated both in support of the Palestinians and to express long-standing grievances. Twelve died in clashes with Israeli police.

There has been growing political action among Israel's Arabs. Despite the existence of a number of Arab political parties, Israeli Arabs have failed to form a significant independent Arab political party that could appeal to the Arab voter, represent the Arab minority in the quest for Arab rights, and express its opinions and views. In the absence of important Arab political parties, the Israel Communist Party in its various incarnations has played an important role in the articulation of the Arab perspective and in promoting Arab positions. Few Arab leaders of national stature appeared on the scene, although some local leaders are relatively well known nationally.

In the 1999 election for prime minister, Azmi Bishara, a member of the Knesset elected on the National Democratic Alliance-Balad Party list, became the first Arab citizen to run. He campaigned for the extension of full civil and political rights to the Arab community, demanding, among other things, that Israel be transformed from "a Jewish state" into "a state of all its citizens." He withdrew from the prime ministerial race on the eve of the May 17, 1999, elections. Bishara was elected to the Knesset, where he continued to express strong views about the second-class status of Israeli Arabs and about the overall nature of the Arab-Israeli conflict and Israel's relations with the Palestinians.

Religion and the State

Israel's Jewishness is a basic element underlying its political system. However, the overwhelmingly Jewish character of the state does not ensure agreement on the appropriate relationship between religion and the state, nor on that between the religious and secular authorities, nor on the methods and techniques to be employed by religious authorities. Since independence, Israel has had to come to terms with the concept of its "Jewishness" and the question of "Who is a Jew?" and thus it has had to address the meaning of a "Jewish state." The conflict between secular and religious perspectives on these and related matters has been a continuing characteristic of Israel. The question "Who is a Jew?" has been at the center of a religion-state controversy in Israel (and with Jewish communities abroad) and has theological, political, and ideological overtones with specific practical dimensions. Secular and religious authorities and ordinary citizens have faced the question in connection with issues of immigration, marriage, divorce, inheritance, and conversion as well as in matters related to registration to secure identity cards and in the official collection of data and information. The question relates to the application of laws such as the Law of Return, the Nationality Law, and others passed by parliament, as well as those relating to marriage and divorce and their interpretation by secular and religious authorities. As a result it is essential to determine who is a Jew and to decide who would make such a determination and what criteria would be used. Over time a number of controversies relating to the question of who is a Jew have become well known.

Although Israel's government is secular, it takes into account the requisites of that segment of the population that observes religious tradition. The Ministry of Religious Affairs is concerned with meeting Jewish religious requirements, such as the supply of ritually killed (kosher) meat, rabbinical courts, and religious schools (Yeshivot), as well as with meeting the religious needs of the non-Jewish communities that enjoy religious autonomy. These functions are noncontroversial; few dispute the duty of the government to meet the religious requirements of the people. Nevertheless, there is sharp and recurrent controversy concerning the extent to which religious observance or restriction is directly or indirectly imposed on the entire Jewish population. The observant community, through its own political parties and through its membership in government coalitions, has been able to secure government agreement to establish separate school systems, to exempt its young women from army service, and to curtail almost all business and public activity on the Sabbath. The less-observant Jews of Israel often argue that they do not have religious freedom because of governmental acquiescence to demands of the observant Jewish groups, such as restriction of public services on the Sabbath and the limitations placed on the role of non-Orthodox Judaism in Israel.

Israel utilizes a modified millet system derived from the period of Ottoman control for distributing authority among religious communities. The various religious communities and religious authorities exercise jurisdiction in litigation involving personal status and family law and apply religious codes and principles in their own judicial institutions. Matters that are secular concerns in other states often are within the purview of religious authorities in Israel; even though there is no established state religion, all religious institutions have a special status and authority granted by the state and are supported by state funds.

The political reality of Israel has required coalition governments from the out-set. That same reality has necessitated inclusion of political parties of the religious community in virtually all cabinets as coalition partners: They seek to control the Ministry of Religious Affairs and usually also the Ministry of the Interior and the Ministry of Education. This has given the religious parties substantial political power and thus an ability to enforce many of their demands and perspectives con-cerning the role of religion in the Jewish state. The religious parties became par-ticularly prominent following the accession to office of Menachem Begin and the Likud in 1977; the coalition agreements by which the 1977 and 1981 govern-ments were established reflected the desire and ability of the religious parties to press for substantial concessions. The role of religion in Israel's everyday life clearly remains a major social and political issue.

The role of religion and of the religious political parties has continued to grow in Israeli politics. Among these factors the rise of the SHAS (Sephardi Torah Guardians) party has been particularly interesting and significant. SHAS has Ova-dia Yosef, the former Sephardi chief rabbi of Israel, as its spiritual mentor. The party was led initially by Rabbi Aryeh Deri, who was jailed on corruption charges after a lengthy trial, and was replaced by Eli Yishai in 1999.

SHAS split from the ultra-Orthodox Agudat Yisrael and contested the 1984 Knesset election. While ideologically close to Agudat Yisrael, Ovadia Yosef and other Sephardi rabbis decided to leave the Ashkenazi-dominated Aguda and set up SHAS after Aguda leaders limited the number of Sephardi candidates on the party's list for the 1984 election. The founders of SHAS wished to get the funds, political jobs, and other forms of support of which they had felt deprived. Eliezer Schach, an Ashkenazi rabbi and leader of non-Hasidic elements within Aguda, helped in the creation of SHAS.

SHAS won four Knesset seats in 1984 and its strength increased to six Knesset seats in the 1988 election. The party's success was largely the result of its participa-tion in the previous government of national unity. SHAS controlled the Interior Ministry—traditionally the bastion of the National Religious Party (MAFDAL or NRP)—which enabled it to channel funds through local governments to provide services to its constituency of Sephardi Jews. SHAS also exploited the Sephardi-Ashkenazi tension among Israelis, stressing the restoration of Oriental culture to a position of prominence in Israeli society. Although SHAS gained some votes in the 1992 election and initially participated in the coalition formed by Yitzhak Ra-bin, it did not manage to increase its Knesset representation.

SHAS made significant gains in the 1996 election, increasing its seats in parlia-ment to ten. The party continued to stress a combination of ethnic pride and tra-ditional values to compensate for the sense of cultural alienation felt by many of its constituents. SHAS won seventeen seats in the May 1999 Knesset election, be-coming the third-largest party in the parliament and joined the government led by Ehud Barak with several ministerial positions. It remained in the 2001 government of Ariel Sharon with its significant power base in the Knesset.

Economic Conditions

Israel's economy has undergone substantial change since independence, and the economic well-being of its people has improved significantly. Israel remains something of an economic "miracle," belying the preindependence prophecies that its troubled economy could not long endure. Instead, a country virtually bereft of natural resources and faced with substantial burdens imposed by massive immigration and by Arab hostility achieved a relatively prosperous economic standard by the late 1980s. By the beginning of the twenty-first century it had become a large economy by regional standards (with a GDP of more than $100 billion) and its people generally had become prosperous (with more than $17,000 per capita GDP). The standard of living in Israel and the productivity of its labor force are comparable to those in West European countries; its life-expectancy levels are among the highest in the world; and it has maintained extensive social services for its population. These achievements are matched in other sectors.

Israel's small size and lack of mineral and water resources profoundly affect its economy. Israel's dearth of energy resources has made it virtually completely dependent on foreign supplies of oil, coal, and gas and it has sought to diversify its sources of supply. Attempts have been made to utilize alternative sources such as solar and wind energy, and Israel has become a leader in the solar-energy field and the world's largest user per capita of solar water heating. These efforts have, however, had only limited success in reducing the country's need for imported energy. Since the 1980s Israel's oil imports have contributed significantly to its large balance-of-payments deficit.

Extensive irrigation and intensive farming methods have dramatically increased agricultural production for both domestic consumption and export. The amount of irrigated land and of agricultural exports rose substantially between 1948 and the 1980s. Agricultural exports have accounted for a declining percentage of total exports as Israel has developed its industrial base.

Israel's industrial development can be traced to an investment program financed from outside sources, including U.S. government loans and grants, the sale of Israel bonds, investments, and German reparations and restitution payments. At the same time, charitable contributions from the world Jewish community helped reduce the government's burdens in the social-welfare sector, thereby permitting the use of scarce funds for economic projects. Israel's substantial human resources have been a major positive factor as well.

Israel has maintained growth rates in real gross national product (GNP) exceeding 9 percent for prolonged periods. From 1950 to 1972, real output grew at an average annual rate of nearly 10 percent, and output per worker more than tripled.

Government expenditures have consumed a large portion of the GNP. Israel had double-digit inflation in the 1970s, and triple-digit inflation began in 1979. At the time of the July 1984 Knesset elections, the inflation level was estimated at more than 400 percent. This hyperinflation was brought under control in the late 1980s; inflation was measured in single digits by the early 1990s.

During the Labor Party's domination of politics from before independence to 1977, socialist economic policies were pursued in a mixed economy adapted to the special circumstances of Israel. The government played a central and decisive role in the economy, aided by semigovernmental institutions such as the Jewish Agency, the United Israel Appeal, the Jewish National Fund, and the Histadrut. The government owned and operated the railroads, the postal service, and the telephone, telegraph, and broadcasting facilities, in addition to the usual government public works such as road and irrigation projects. There was also substantial government investment in public corporations in areas such as oil, electricity, and fertilizer.

In 1977 the system was altered when the Likud government came to power. The overall goal was to eliminate the government role in the economy and to apply free-market principles. Although there were important changes, the basic problems remained and, in some instances, grew.

The 1984 Knesset election campaign focused attention on Israel's economic situation, and the economy became an early priority for the national unity government installed in September 1984. After additional attempts at various arrangements, it was decided to formulate a new economic program. A team of professionals constructed an economic stabilization program that was approved by the government in July 1985.

This program relied on a broad national consensus to generate a reduction in public and private consumption; to halt the spiral of price rises, devaluations, and wage adjustments; and to reduce inflation from its high levels to as low a point as possible. The budget deficit was cut, the national currency (the shekel) was devalued, and export subsidies were reduced. Taxes were increased and the budget was cut. Domestic prices were allowed to rise and then were frozen with significant price controls. The cost-of-living adjustment was suspended, and this created an erosion in real wages. The United States granted a special aid package to help achieve the program.

The program was successful in arresting inflation and reducing the public sector's budget deficit, and the aid from the United States eased pressures on the balance of payments. Inflation was reduced. Government involvement in the economy continued at a high level.

The stabilization program began to have its effects, but the economy was soon buffeted by unanticipated political developments in the form of the Palestinian intifada that started in December 1987 and the immigration of Soviet Jews (which began in 1989), and later by the crisis resulting from the Iraqi invasion of Kuwait in 1990.

In recent years Israelis have become more aware of economic issues and more concerned about the failure of the government to deal effectively with them. The growing public awareness was reflected in the 1992 Knesset election campaign, which focused on the question of national priorities, with immigrant absorption and settlement construction in the occupied territories often posited as alternatives for government expenditure. Unemployment, especially among newly arrived Soviet immigrants, and the balance-of-payments deficit were among issues debated before the public. The government established in 1992 included economic issues in its formal government program and suggested that the struggle against unemployment would be at the top of its economic and social order of priorities.

In the first half of the 1990s the economy expanded rapidly. It grew by an average of 5.9 percent per year between 1990 and 1994. During this period the high-tech sector took off, there was a large influx of immigrants, and prospects for regional peace improved, all combining to fuel the economy's strong performance. High growth was sustained through 1995, when real GDP growth peaked at 6.8 percent, although the economy slowed temporarily in the second half of the 1990s, managing only 2.2 percent per year in 1998 and 1999. This reflects the combined effects of a slowdown in world growth, the negative impact of the domestic security situation on tourism, the delayed effect of a prolonged period of high interest rates, and the government's efforts to implement fiscal austerity. It also reflects a cyclical downturn in private consumption and residential construction as the immigration wave of the first half of the 1990s dwindled.

A recovery of economic activity started in the second half of 1999, taking the form of a rapid expansion of GDP driven by industrial exports. A sizeable share of the increase of industrial exports has been in high-tech sectors, mainly electronics.

Besides a booming high-technology sector, Israel had undertaken important structural reforms (such as privatization and reduced controls on foreign currency exchanges and profit remittances by foreign companies). Apparent progress in peace negotiations was helping to attract tourists and foreign investment. However, Israel's economic prospects became more murky as a result of the sharp decline in tourism resulting from the Palestinian disturbances and terrorism widely known as the "al-Aksa intifada," which began in September 2000 and extended throughout 2001. Slowdowns in the global high-technology sector and in the U.S. economy also had adverse effects that were magnified after the events of September 11, 2001.

Over the last decade, Israel has made some progress in the direction of a more open, competitive, market-oriented economy, although public spending still accounts for more than half of the country's GDP and the top marginal income tax rates exceed 60 percent. Israel continues to make slow moves towards privatizing government-owned companies, including banks, the state telecommunications company (Bezeq), and others. In general, supporters of economic liberalization believe that Israel's economy is strong enough to compete globally. Both privatization and spending cuts are opposed by Israel's powerful labor movement and others.

Political Structure

Constitutional Consensus

Unlike most countries, Israel's system of government is based on an unwritten constitution. The first legislative act of the Constituent Assembly in February 1949 was to enact a "Transition Law" (small constitution) that became the basis of constitutional life in the state.

The First Knesset devoted much time to a profound discussion of the constitutional issue. The discussion continued for over a year, and on June 13, 1950, the Knesset adopted a compromise that has indefinitely postponed the real issue. It was decided in principle that a written constitution would ultimately be adopted, but that for the time being there would not be a formal and comprehensive document. Instead, a number of fundamental or basic laws would be passed dealing with specific subjects, which might, in time, form chapters in a consolidated constitution. By 2001 Israel had adopted Basic Laws dealing with various subjects: The Knesset; The Lands of Israel; The President; The Government; The State Economy; The Army; Jerusalem, the Capital of Israel; The Judiciary; The State Comptroller; Freedom of Occupation; Human Dignity and Freedom. The Basic Laws articulate the formal requirements of the system in specific areas of activity, thereby providing a written framework for governmental action.

Several areas of consensus, together with the extant fundamental laws, define the parameters of Israel's political system. Those disavowing allegiance to these Jewish-Zionist ideals serve as little more than protest groups. Israel's self-definition as a Jewish state is perhaps the most significant area of agreement, although there is a divergence of views on some of its tenets, their interpretation, and their implementation. Accord centers on the goals or purposes of Israel, such as the "ingathering of the exiles." There is also consensus that Israel should be a social-welfare state in which all share in the benefits of society and have access to essential social, health, and similar services, although there are conflicting views regarding the scope and method of implementation of the principle. Foreign and security policy constitutes another area enjoying wide consensus because of its overriding importance in light of continuing Arab hostility and the resultant conflict, although there is discord concerning methods and techniques of implementation of agreed goals. The Israel Defense Forces enjoys an enviable reputation.

Political Institutions

The president, the government (cabinet), and the Knesset perform the basic political functions of the state within the framework provided by Israel's constitutional consensus. The president is elected by the Knesset for a seven-year term and may not be reelected. He is head of state, and his powers and functions are essentially representative. In the sphere of foreign affairs these include signing instruments that relate to treaties ratified by the Knesset, appointing diplomatic and consular representatives, receiving foreign diplomatic representatives, and issuing consular *exequaturs.* In the domestic sphere, he has the power to grant pardons and reprieves and to commute sentences. Subsequent to nomination by the appropriate body, he appoints judges, *dayanim* (judges of Jewish religious courts), *qadis* (judges of Muslim religious courts), the state comptroller, the president of the Magen David Adom Association (Red Shield of David—Israel's Red Cross), and the governor of the Bank of Israel, as well as other officials as determined by law. He signs all laws passed by the Knesset, with the exception of those relating to presidential powers, and all documents to which the state seal is affixed.

The president is generally a figure of considerable stature with popularity and support among the population. Until 2000 all presidents completed their terms or died in office. This changed in the summer of 2000 when President Ezer Weizman resigned after the attorney general issued a report that criticized him for financial improprieties. The Knesset chose Moshe Katzav (an immigrant to Israel from Iran) of Likud (over Shimon Peres of Labor) as president.

The president's powers and functions relating to the formation of the government fall into a different category. After consultation with representatives of the parties in the parliament, the president selects a member of the Knesset to form a government. Although anyone may be chosen, traditionally the member has been the leader of the largest party in the Knesset. The president also receives the resignation of the government.

Until 1996 the president's role was clear. In that year an electoral reform law that the Knesset had passed before the 1992 election took effect. Under the terms of the new law, the process changed and the prime minister, as well as the Knesset, was chosen by popular vote. This eliminated the president's function of providing the mandate to the individual who would become prime minister after successfully forming a government. The change was short-lived; in March 2001 the Knesset eliminated the direct election of the prime minister and restored the previous system.

Another aspect of the presidential role that could have considerable political significance is his public position—his visits throughout the country, his speeches, and his formal opening of the first session of each Knesset.

The member of parliament entrusted by the president (or, in 1996, 1999, and 2001, the individual chosen by direct election) with the task of forming the government establishes a cabinet, generally with himself (or herself) as prime minister and a number of ministers who are usually, but not necessarily, members of the Knesset.

The prime minister is the most powerful figure in the Israeli system. The 1992 decision to change the method of selecting the prime minister partly was designed to further strengthen the office; some likened the directly elected prime minister to the president of the United States in power and influence. The election of the prime minister under this arrangement followed a simple system. In 1996 and 1999, when elections for the Knesset and prime minister were held simultaneously, each voter received two ballots—one for prime minister and one for a party for the Knesset. In February 2001 there was a ballot only for prime minister, with a choice between Ehud Barak and Ariel Sharon. In the prime ministerial election the winning candidate had to secure an absolute majority (more than 50 percent) of the vote cast. Although there were provisions for a runoff should a candidate not receive the majority, this did not happen in the three elections before the law was changed back to the old system.

The government is formally instituted upon obtaining a vote of confidence from the parliament. The cabinet is collectively responsible to the Knesset, reports to it, and remains in office as long as it enjoys the confidence of that body. There has been only one successful vote of no-confidence by the Knesset—in March 1990—causing the ouster of a government. A government's tenure may also be terminated by ending the Knesset's tenure, by the resignation of the government on its own initiative, or by the resignation of the prime minister.

The Knesset is the supreme authority in the state. It is a unicameral body of 120 members elected by national, general, secret, direct, equal, and proportional suffrage for a term not to exceed four years. Voters cast their ballots for parties, rather than individual candidates, although each party presents the voter with a list of up to 120 names—its choices for Knesset seats. After ballots are cast, seats in the Knesset are determined. From 1949 to 1988, only those party lists that received at least 1 percent of the total number of valid votes cast in the election were represented in the Knesset. The threshold was raised in October 1991 to 1.5 percent, in a move aimed at reducing the number of parties contesting the 1992 and subsequent elections and being represented in parliament. Any list failing to obtain this minimum does not share in the distribution of mandates, and its votes are not taken into account when determining the composition of the Knesset. The distribution of seats among the party lists is determined by dividing the number of valid votes obtained by all the lists that secured the minimum percentage by the number of Knesset members (120), and the result is set as the quota for each Knesset seat. Each list receives the nearest whole number of seats thus determined, and the remaining seats are allocated by a complicated formula that generally benefits the larger parties.

The main functions of the Knesset are similar to those of most modern parliaments. They include expressing a vote of confidence or no-confidence in the government, legislating, participating in the formation of national policy, and supervising the activities of the governmental administration. The Knesset must also approve the budget and taxation, elect the president of the state, recommend the appointment of the state comptroller, and participate in the appointment of judges. It is divided into a number of committees, each responsible for a specific area of legislation. Many of the Knesset's activities are performed in these committees. With some minor exceptions the ratio of committee memberships is generally proportional to that of the party's representation in the Knesset as a whole.

Judicial authority is vested in religious as well as civil courts. The latter include municipal and magistrates' courts for civil and criminal actions, district courts for appeals from the lower tribunals and matters beyond the jurisdiction of a magistrate, and the Supreme Court. The Supreme Court does not formally have the power of judicial review of legislation passed by the Knesset, but it has the power to invalidate administrative actions and interpret statutes it regards contrary to the law. Each major community has its own religious courts, which deal with matters of personal status. Rabbinical courts have exclusive jurisdiction over Jews in marriage and divorce, and they may act on alimony, probate, succession, and other similar questions, with the parties' consent. The Christian ecclesiastical courts have exclusive authority over marriage, divorce, alimony, and confirmation of wills of Christians, and they may judge other similar matters if the parties agree. The Muslim courts have exclusive jurisdiction in all matters of personal status for Muslims. The judicial appointment procedure seeks to discourage political influence, and judges enjoy continuous tenure subject only to good behavior.

Two other institutions unique to the Israeli system are significant elements of the political structure. The Histadrut and the Jewish Agency, although technically extragovernmental, perform governmental functions, and their personnel often attain positions of responsibility within the government. The Histadrut is of greater significance than the usual trade union organization and is unique in that it combines trade unionism, economic enterprise, cultural and social activities, and social welfare. It is one of the largest employers in Israel and has engaged in overseas projects in support of Israel's foreign policy.

The Histadrut was founded before the state and performed many quasigovernmental functions then. These were modified when Israel achieved statehood. Since both the Histadrut and the early Israeli governments were controlled by the Labor Party, there was much overlap in ideology, personnel, and policies. When Likud came to power in 1977 this changed and much has been altered since. In the mid 1990s the Histadrut health care system came under significant government control. The Histadrut has lost membership and in 2001 represented fewer and fewer workers. At the same time the Histadrut and the Labor Party have had a growing parting of the ways.

The Jewish Agency for Israel represents the World Zionist Organization and acts on behalf of Jews throughout the world who are concerned with Israel's development, Jewish immigration and settlement, and the cultural and spiritual ties and cooperation among the Jewish people. The agency has been responsible for the organization of Jewish immigration to Israel; the reception, assistance, and settlement of these immigrants; care of children; and aid to cultural projects and institutions of higher learning. It fosters Hebrew education and culture in the Diaspora, guides and assists Zionist youth movements, and organizes the work of the Jewish people in support of Israel.

Political Dynamics

Political life is intense in Israel and political parties play a central role in the social and economic, as well as political, life of the country. Israel's political system is characterized by a wide range of political and social viewpoints that are given expression not only in political parties but also in newspapers and a host of social, religious, cultural, and other organizations. Numerous minority and splinter factions freely criticize the government. This diversity has been most apparent in the existence of multiple parties contesting parliamentary elections (and in the factions within most of the major parties) and in the various coalition governments that have been characteristic of Israel since its inception (see Tables 11.1, 11.2, and 11.3). Political parties are overwhelming in their presence—virtually all political life is organized in and through the parties—and they are crucial for the political socialization of Israelis as well as for the policymaking of the state. Because Israelis vote not for individuals but for parties in parliamentary elections, it is the party that determines where individuals will be placed on the electoral list and thus who will represent it in parliament and in government. Individuals or groups of individuals, no matter how prominent, have not fared well when divested of the support of the established parties. In the several instances in which there has been notable success (such as that of the Democratic Movement for Change [DMC] in 1977) and the Center Party in 1999), the success has tended to be ephemeral. Electoral campaigns are controlled by the parties, which make the decisions, wage the campaigns, and spend the money. In the final analysis the voter focuses on the party, the party member looks to it for fulfillment of his or her needs, and the politician needs its leaders and machinery to assure a political future.

Israel's political parties and the blocs they have formed have gone through a substantial number of mergers and splits and disagreements and reconciliations as a result of ideological differences, policy disagreements, and personality clashes. Numerous parties have contested the 120 seats in parliament, and many have been successful in winning representation in it. The large number of parties, reflecting Israel's political fragmentation, is a result of the proportional representation system, compounded by personal and ideological differences and the intensity of views held by segments of Israel's polity on many issues.

Israel's complex party structure demonstrates various dimensions of cleavage, but socioeconomic, religious-secular, and foreign policy–national security issue areas tend to be the most significant. Israel's parties have economic views ranging from Marxism through liberal socialism to free enterprise. There are also different views concerning the role of government in economic (and consequently social) policy. The role of religion has differentiated those who seek to make Jewish religious law (*halacha*) a central factor in state activity from those who have sought to enhance the secular nature of the system and those who have worked to eliminate virtually all vestiges of religious influence. Views of the ultimate extent of the state and the role of Zionism have divided groups (for example, the Communists) that oppose the concept of a Zionist state from groups that have supported the notion of a binational entity or a truncated Jewish state and from groups that favor an exclusively Jewish-Zionist state in the whole of historic Palestine—both east and west of the Jordan River. Foreign policy issues have been less divisive than in the early days of the state. When the Soviet Union was an ardent suitor of the new Jewish state, it facilitated the adoption of pro-Soviet foreign policy stances by political groups with a Marxist orientation, such as the United Workers Party (MAPAM). At the same time, parties of the Right (such as the General Zionists and Herut) advocated a Western orientation. Soon, however, the choice was unrealistic, and since the early 1950s a pro-Western orientation has dominated Israeli thinking.

Interest groups have created parties to represent their views and to secure their interests more effectively. These parties have reflected a wide spectrum of perspectives and concerns, ranging from the ethnic and social goals of the Arab parties and parties seeking to represent Yemenites and Sephardim to the more practical attempts of some groups to promote narrow goals such as revocation of the income tax. Individual and personal factors have also played a role in party formation. Individuals with ambitions or personal concerns, such as animosity to other political figures or a desire to achieve a particular status, have established their own parties to contest Knesset elections; this was the case with Shmuel Flatto-Sharon in 1977, who sought election and the accompanying parliamentary immunity as a means of avoiding extradition for trial in France. Historical developments, mostly during the preindependence period, and personal differences among the political elite have been important elements in fostering party proliferation.

The multiplicity of parties, the diversity of views they represent, and the proportional representation electoral system have resulted in the failure of any one party to win a majority of Knesset seats in any of the thirteen elections between 1949 and 1999, thus necessitating the formation of coalition governments. Prior to the national unity government formed in 1984, only twice have the coalitions been truly broad based. Those were established in times of national stress—the provisional government formed on independence and the government of national unity formed

TABLE 11.2 Political Parties and Knesset Election Results, 1965–1984

Party	1965 %	1965 Seats	1969 %	1969 Seats	1973 %	1973 Seats	1977 %	1977 Seats	1981 %	1981 Seats	1984 %	1984 Seats
MAPAI (Israel Workers)	IA										IA	–
MAPAM (United Workers)[a]	6.6	8	IA		IA		IA		IA		IA	
Ahdut Haavoda (Unity of Labor)[b]	IA		IA		IA		IA		IA		IA	
Alignment (MAPAI and Ahdut Haavoda)	36.7	45										
RAFI (Israel Labor List) (Reshimat Poalei Israel)[c]	7.9	10	IA		IA		IA		IA		IA	
Israel Labor[d]			IA		IA		IA		IA		IA	
Maarach (Alignment of Israel Labor and MAPAM)			46.2	56	39.7	51	24.6	32	36.6	47	34.9	44
State List[e]			3.1	4								–
GAHAL (Gush Herut Liberalim)[f]	21.3	26	21.7	26								–
Independent Liberals[g]	3.8	5	3.2	4	3.6	4	1.2	1				–
Shlomzion[h]							1.9	2				–
Free Center[i]			1.2	2								–
Likud[j]					30.2	39	33.4	43	37.1	48	31.9	41
National Religious (MAFDAL)[k]	9.0	11	9.7	12	8.3	10	9.2	12	4.9	6	3.5	4
Agudat Israel (Association of Israel)[l]	3.3	4	3.2	4			3.4	4	3.7	4	1.7	2
Poalei Agudat Israel (Workers of the Association of Israel)	1.8	2	1.8	2			1.4	1				–
Torah Religious Front[m]					3.8	5						–
TAMI									2.3	3	1.5	1
Morasha (Heritage)[n]											1.6	2
SHAS (Sephardi Torah Guardians)[o]											3.1	4
Arab Progress and Work	2.0	2										–
Arab Cooperation and Brotherhood	1.4	2										–
Alignment-affiliated Arab and Druze lists			3.5	4	2.4	3						–
United Arab List							1.4	1				–
New Communists (RAKAH) (Reshima Komunistit Hadasha)[p]	2.3	3	2.8	3	3.4	4						–
Israel Communists (MAKI) (Miflaga Komunistit Israeli)[p]	1.1	1	1.2	1								–
Democratic Front for Peace and Equality (Hadash)[q]							4.6	5	3.4	4	3.4	4
Moked[r]					1.4	1						–

Party												
Flatto-Sharon	—	—	—	—	—	—	2.0	1	—	—	—	—
Citizens' Rights Movement (RATZ)	—	—	—	—	2.2	3	1.2	1	1.4	1	2.4	3
Democratic Movement for Change (DMC) (DASH)[s]	—	—	—	—	—	—	11.6	15	—	—	—	—
Shinui	—	—	—	—	—	—	—	—	1.5	2	2.6	3
Haolam Hazeh	1.2	1	1.2	2	—	—	—	—	—	—	—	—
Shelli (Shalom Lemaan Israel—Peace for Israel)[t]	—	—	—	—	—	—	1.6	2	—	—	—	—
Progressive List for Peace	—	—	—	—	—	—	—	—	—	—	1.8	2
Telem	—	—	—	—	—	—	—	—	1.6	2	—	—
Ometz (Courage to Cure the Economy)	—	—	—	—	—	—	—	—	—	—	1.2	1
Yahad	—	—	—	—	—	—	—	—	—	—	2.2	3
Kach	—	—	—	—	—	—	—	—	—	—	1.2	1
Tehiya (in 1984 Tehiya-TZOMET)	—	—	—	—	—	—	—	—	2.3	3	4.0	5

IA: In Alignment

[a] Formed 1948—Hashomer Hatzair, Ahdut Haavoda, Poalei Zion.

[b] Formed by merger of Poalei Zion (Workers of Zion) and smaller socialist Zionist groups.

[c] Formed 1965—Ben-Gurion splinter group from MAPAI.

[d] Formed 1968—merger of MAPAI, RAFI, Ahdut Haavoda.

[e] Ben-Gurion splinter group from Israel Labor. Later part of Likud (in 1977 as part of La'am).

[f] Formed 1965—merger of Herut and majority of Liberal Party.

[g] Minority of Liberal Party not joining in merger with Herut.

[h] Joined Likud after 1977 election.

[i] Formed 1968—splinter group from Herut.

[j] Formed 1973 merger of GAHAL, State List, Free Center, Greater Israel Movement, La'am—formed within Likud 1976—part of Free Center (Merkaz Hofshi), State List (Reshima Mamlachtit), Greater Israel Movement (Hatnuah Leeretz Israel Hashlemah).

[k] Merger—Mizrahi and Hapoel Hamizrahi.

[l] In Torah Religious Front until 1961 elections and again in 1973 elections.

[m] Joint list Agudat Israel and Poalei Agudat Israel.

[n] Splinter from NRP and Poalei Agudat Israel.

[o] Sephardi split from Agudat Israel.

[p] Split of Communist Party in 1965 resulted in formation of RAKAH and MAKI.

[q] Formed 1977—RAKAH and some Israel Black Panthers.

[r] Israel Communist Party and Tchelet Adom (Blue-Red) Movement.

[s] Formed 1976—Shinui (Change), Democratic Movement, Free Center, Zionist Panthers, various individuals. Led by Yigael Yadin. Split September 1978.

[t] Formed 1977—merger of Moked, Haolam Hazeh, independent socialists, and some Black Panthers.

SOURCE: Bernard Reich and Gershon R. Kieval, *Israel: Land of Tradition and Conflict*, 2d ed. (Boulder, Colo.: Westview Press, 1993), pp. 96–98.

during the crisis preceding the 1967 war and maintained until summer 1970. The 1984 national unity government was unique in that it was based on a principle of power-sharing between Labor and Likud, the two major political blocs. This experiment was repeated after the 1988 election and lasted until spring 1990.

Notwithstanding these factors, the coalitions proved remarkably stable until the 1990s, when the Knesset was divided into numerous relatively small parties necessitating extensive government negotiations. Only once was a government brought down by a vote of no-confidence. Israel had only six prime ministers during its first three decades of independence: David Ben-Gurion (1948–1953, 1955–1963), Moshe Sharett (1954–1955), Levi Eshkol (1963–1969), Golda Meir (1969–1974), Yitzhak Rabin (1974–1977), and Menachem Begin (1977–1983). Yitzhak Shamir (1983–1984) and Shimon Peres (1984–1986) came to office following Begin's resignation and after the Knesset election of 1984, respectively. And Shamir served again from 1986 to 1992, and then Rabin returned to the premiership as head of the Labor Party and served until his assassination in 1995. Peres's interim stint was followed by Benjamin Netanyahu for three years before his defeat by Ehud Barak in 1999 and Barak's ouster by Ariel Sharon's victory in February 2001. The personal stabilizing influence of Ben-Gurion, Sharett, Eshkol, and Meir during their respective tenures as prime minister and the preponderant strength of MAPAI and the Labor Party were important factors in maintaining stability. After the 1977 election Menachem Begin played a similar stabilizing role in the governments he headed, until his resignation in 1983. The rigorous discipline of Israel's parties has curbed irresponsible action by individual Knesset members. Continuity of policy also has been enhanced by the reappointment of many ministers in reshuffled cabinets and the continuity of bureaucratic officeholders.

The requirements of coalition government have placed limitations on the prime minister's ability to control fully the cabinet and its actions. The prime minister does not appoint ministers; he or she reaches accord with the other parties, and together they select the individuals who hold the several portfolios and who share in the cabinet's collective responsibility for governing Israel. Similarly the prime minister does not have the power to dismiss the ministers, although Peres managed to force Yitzhak Moda'i out as minister of finance in 1985 after Moda'i attacked the prime minister personally. In early 1990 Shamir sought to dismiss Ezer Weizman from the cabinet because of his contacts with individuals associated with the Palestine Liberation Organization (PLO). The prime minister eventually settled for Weizman's removal from the smaller, policymaking, inner cabinet. The prime minister does, however, possess substantial powers that enable him or her to influence the process by which ministers are selected and removed. Cabinets often contain individuals selected because of party loyalty, not qualification, who may well be divided in regard to perspectives and quarrelsome in regard to procedures. The bargaining resulting from the coalition system has permitted the religious

TABLE 11.3 Political Parties and Knesset Election Results, 1988–1999

Party	1988 %	1988 Seats	1992 %	1992 Seats	1996 %	1996 Seats	1999 %	1999 Seats
One Israel[a]	–	–	–	–	–	–	20.2	26
Labor Party[b]	30.0	39	34.6	44	26.8	34	–	–
MAPAM	2.5	3	–	–	–	–	–	–
Shinui	1.7	2	–	–	–	–	5.0	6
Citizens' Rights Movement	4.3	5	–	–	–	–	–	–
MERETZ[c]	–	–	9.5	12	7.4	9	7.6	10
Likud	31.1	40	24.9	32	25.1	32	14.1	19
National Religious Party	3.9	5	4.9	6	7.8	9	4.2	5
Agudat Israel	4.5	5	–	–	–	–	–	–
Degel HaTorah[d]	1.5	2	–	–	–	–	–	–
United Torah Judaism[e]	–	–	3.2	4	3.2	4	3.7	5
SHAS	4.7	6	4.9	6	8.5	10	13.0	17
TZOMET[f]	2.0	2	6.3	8	–	–	–	–
Tehiya	3.1	3	1.2	–	–	–	–	–
Moledet[g]	1.9	2	2.3	3	2.3	2	–	–
Arab Democratic Party[h]	1.2	1	1.5	2	–	–	–	–
Progressive List for Peace	1.5	1	0.9	–	–	–	–	–
Democratic Front for Peace and Equality (Hadash)	3.7	4	2.3	3	4.4	5	2.6	3
Yisrael Ba'aliya	–	–	–	–	5.7	7	5.1	6
Third Way	–	–	–	–	3.1	4	–	–
United Arab List	–	–	–	–	2.9	4	3.4	5
Center Party	–	–	–	–	–	–	5.0	6
National Unity (Haichud HaLeumi)	–	–	–	–	–	–	3.0	4
Yisrael Beiteinu (Israel Our Home)	–	–	–	–	–	–	2.6	4
National Democratic Alliance (Balad)	–	–	–	–	–	–	1.9	2
One Nation for Israeli Workers and Pensioners	–	–	–	–	–	–	1.9	2

[a] Formed 1999 – electoral coalition of Labor, Gesher, and Meimad
[b] Formed 1988 – merger of Israel Labor and Yahad
[c] Formed 1992 – merger of MAPAM, Shinui, Citizens' Rights Movement
[d] Formed 1988 – splinter group from Agudat Israel
[e] Formed 1992 – merger of Agudat Israel, Degel HaTorah, Moriah
[f] Formed 1988 – splinter from Tehiya-TZOMET
[g] Led by Rehavam Zeevi
[h] Led by Abd el-Wahab Darawshe

parties—MAFDAL, Agudat Israel, Poalei Agudat Israel, TAMI, and more recently SHAS—to gain considerable policy concessions and to play strong roles in government decisionmaking because they were essential to secure a majority in the Knesset.

Coalition formation is one of the more interesting and arduous tasks of the prime minister. Each party and each political leader has a complex set of interests and concerns and seeks to maximize his gain from his participation in and support of the prime minister's government. Each party leader wants ministerial slots, concessions on policy matters, and funding for institutions, as well as patronage and positions for party loyalists. Parties traditionally sought control of certain ministries that focused on matters of their central interest—thus religious parties have focused on the Ministry of Religious affairs, the Ministry of Education, and the Ministry of the Interior. Similarly the left-of-center, civil-rights-focused parties such as Meretz have had a strong interest in the education ministry and its control of school curriculums. The Russian-based parties have sought the Ministry of the Interior because of its control over citizen registration and thus the matter of who is registered as a Jew.

Despite party proliferation and general political diversity, Israel's political life has been dominated by a relatively small and cohesive Jewish elite that has been mostly homogeneous in background. Most of its early leaders have been European in origin, arrived in Israel during the Second Aliyah (1904–1914), and were personally acquainted, if not intimate. The political elite has been predominantly civilian in character and background. Religious elements have had a somewhat similar position. They have exerted strong influence in the cabinet and Knesset as political parties because of their role in government formation. The rabbinate is not considered part of the political elite, and the religious establishment generally does not intervene directly in politics.

The Israel Defense Forces (IDF) is virtually unique in the Middle East in that it does not, as an entity, play a role in politics, despite its size, budget, and importance. Individual officers and senior commanders have secured important political positions, but they have done so as individuals, after retiring from active military service, and without the backing of the military as an institution. Only after their retirement did such military men as Generals Moshe Dayan, Yitzhak Rabin, Yigael Yadin, Ezer Weizman, Haim Bar Lev, Ehud Barak, Amnon Lipkin Shahak, Yitzhak Mordechai, Matan Vilnai, Rafael Eitan, Yigal Allon, and Ariel Sharon play key roles in political life. They have attained position and power by working within the bounds of the political system and by joining political parties, not by their utilization of the military in opposition to the system. Their military reputations and popular prestige enhanced their chances for, but did not ensure, significant political careers.

The officer corps has not, and probably could not, become closely aligned with one political faction or party. The criterion of loyalty to the regime or to the leader has not been central to the decisionmaking process by which senior military positions are filled or retained. Rather, competence and skill have been the major factors involved in the determination of senior positions in the IDF. Moreover, the highly developed and sophisticated nature of the political system and its institutions, and the complex and often bewildering array of political and quasi-political institutions, make it extremely difficult for the army to play an independent political role and to seek to seize power through political means. The close identification of Israel's leadership with the development of the state would significantly reduce the ability of the army, even if cohesive, to claim that the political leaders had betrayed the state and therefore had to be replaced by a military coup or a similar device.

New Dimensions in Politics

The turmoil in the political process and political life of Israel at the time of the Yom Kippur War (1973) set in motion forces that subsequently affected the political process. The change from euphoria before the war to uncertainty after it accelerated political change and facilitated the replacement of personalities and the alteration of policies. The effect was not obvious in the elections for the eighth Knesset and local authorities, held at the end of December 1973. Golda Meir was charged with creating a new government and did so in early 1974, only to resign a month later, primarily because of dissension within the Labor Party that centered on the question of political responsibility for serious lapses in decisionmaking at the outset of the war.

This situation set the stage for the selection of Yitzhak Rabin, a hero of the 1967 war, former chief of staff, and former ambassador to the United States, as well as a scion of a prominent labor-movement family, as Labor Party leader and prime minister. Rabin's government represented a departure from the past and ushered in a new era in which some of Israel's best-known names and personalities moved from the center of power. Leadership had begun to be transferred from the immigrant-founder generation to the native-born sons. Golda Meir's singular role gave way to the representation of diverse views in Israel's three-man shuttle-diplomacy negotiating team (Rabin, Yigal Allon, and Shimon Peres) and in their coterie of advisers.

In a more general sense, many of the forces set in motion by the Yom Kippur War and its aftermath seemed to coalesce in a tangible way when Israel's electorate went to the polls in May 1977. They gave the largest number of votes to the Likud, led by Menachem Begin, and Labor lost a substantial number of seats compared to its showing in 1973. Many of Labor's lost mandates went to the newly established Democratic Movement for Change (DMC), but Likud also gained additional members. This ended the Labor dominance of Israeli politics that had begun in the Yishuv period. The Likud, under Begin's leadership, emerged as the leading political force.

Israel's 1977 elections were seen as a political "earthquake" reflecting and fore-shadowing substantial change. Menachem Begin and the Likud formed the government and took control of Israel's bureaucracy. The parties constituting the Likud bloc (especially Begin's Herut) had been serving as the opposition since independence, with the exception of their joining the "wall-to-wall" government of national unity during the 1967 war crisis and remaining in it until their withdrawal in 1970, when they vocally opposed the government and criticized its programs, politics, and leadership. As a consequence of the 1977 election, Likud established the coalition responsible for establishing and implementing programs and policies for Israel. It sought to implement its own program within the broad ideology developed decades earlier by Vladimir Zeev Jabotinsky. Once in power as prime minister, Begin found in Jabotinsky a source of inspiration and a guide for concrete policy and worked toward the implementation of Jabotinsky's revisionist vision of a Jewish State in all of the Land of Israel.

The 1981 Knesset election was not conclusive in identifying a popular preference for Likud or Labor. The electorate virtually divided its votes between the two blocs but awarded neither a majority of votes or seats in parliament, and coalition politics continued to characterize the system. President Yitzhak Navon granted the mandate to form the new government to Begin, and the latter succeeded in forming a Likud-led coalition that subsequently received the endorsement of the Knesset. The election highlighted the political dimension of the ethnic issue: Likud secured the majority (probably some 70 percent) of the Oriental Jewish vote, following a pattern foreshadowed in the 1977 election. ("Oriental Jews" are non-Ashkenazi Jews, primarily of Afro-Asian origin. In Hebrew they are called collectively *Edot Hamizrach,* "Eastern, or Oriental communities." Generally the term refers to Jews whose origins are in Muslim lands.)

Extensive Oriental Jewish support for Begin and the Likud in 1981 must be seen as a desire to achieve change through support of a party and government perceived as sympathetic to the Oriental plight. Begin's popularity in the Oriental community was a direct result of previous Oriental failure to secure appropriate representation in the Knesset, his courting of the community even as opposition leader, and his responsiveness to their concerns during his first administration. This support of Begin and Likud, an apparent identification of a political home, to a significant degree came in lieu of an effective independent Oriental political organization. Such an organization did not exist at that time, although both TAMI (in 1981 and 1984) and SHAS (in 1984) were able to draw some voters to their Oriental-based political movements. Likud was widely seen as the party that would assist the Oriental community in emerging from its second-class status.

The second Begin government (1981–1983) came to office with a narrow margin in parliament, but the prime minister was able to maintain control despite the traumatic events associated with the war in Lebanon and major economic problems. Begin, personally, was a popular politician with strong charismatic appeal to broad sections of the populace, and he was an able and skilled political leader, in much the same manner as David Ben-Gurion and Golda Meir were. He remained popular and powerful until his resignation from office in fall 1983. His foreign minister, Yitzhak Shamir, a relative newcomer to politics, replaced him. The short-lived Shamir government, officially endorsed by the Knesset in October 1983, was virtually the same as its predecessor in personalities and policies. Shamir pursued a policy of continuity to the extent possible.

The 1984 election results seemed partly to reflect a small but perceptible shift to the right in the electorate as a whole. Fifteen of the twenty-six political parties that contested the 1984 election secured the necessary 1 percent of the valid votes cast to obtain a seat in parliament. The two major blocs were relatively close—the Labor Alignment secured 724,074 votes (forty-four seats), and the Likud secured 661,302 votes (forty-one seats). The Labor Alignment and its closest parliamentary allies together secured about the same number of seats they had held in the outgoing parliament. Likud lost some of its mandates, but the secular-nationalist Tehiya Party, to its right, gained seats. Meir Kahane's Kach Party, after failure in previous elections, gained nearly 26,000 votes, the minimum required for one mandate. In a major sense the results of the election were inconclusive.

This division in the Israeli body politic proved to be the main factor that contributed to, and complicated the formation of, a government of national unity that was approved by the Knesset in September 1984. The negotiations leading to the formation of the government were lengthy and complex, and the basis for the new government was a complicated series of compromises and concessions. The new government inaugurated an experiment in Israeli politics, at the basis of which was an agreement by the two dominant parties to share power, with the unusual proviso of a rotation of Shimon Peres and Yitzhak Shamir in the positions of prime minister and foreign minister. The national unity government, with the power-sharing and rotation concepts, lasted its full term despite numerous forces attempting to terminate its tenure and more numerous projections of its downfall. It survived largely because there was strong public support for its continuation and no politician wanted to be responsible for bringing it down and thereby to be seen as flouting the popular will.

The jockeying for power between the left portion of the center and the right portion of the center continued in the election campaign of 1988. The results of the election, however, were similar to the inconclusive outcome of the 1984 balloting. Likud emerged with only a slight edge over Labor, winning forty Knesset seats to Labor's thirty-nine. Likud's showing represented a loss of one seat from 1984 and eight seats from 1981. The Oriental Jewish community continued to vote for Likud in greater numbers than for Labor, although there were indications that Oriental support for Likud was weakening, that some Orientals no longer regarded Likud as the party most sensitive to their needs and were turning more to SHAS and other religious parties.

Labor's poor showing in the 1988 election underscored the power of the incumbency of Yitzhak Shamir and Likud. As prime minister during the national
unity government's first two years, Shimon Peres established himself as the dominant figure in Israeli politics, transforming his image from that of a widely dis-
liked, unscrupulous politician to that of a dignified, self-confident political figure
and statesman and an asset rather than a liability to the Labor Party. Peres's negative perceptions became a matter of public discussion once again in spring and
summer 1990 and contributed to his replacement as party leader in 1992 by his
longtime rival Yitzhak Rabin. During the latter half of the national unity government's term, however, Foreign Minister Peres struggled to pursue an activist foreign policy, trying to revitalize the Arab-Israeli peace process so that he would not
be overshadowed by Shamir, who was then prime minister. In the end, Peres's
diplomatic maneuvering did not enable him to escape the relative political obscu-
rity of the foreign ministry. Even within the Labor Party, Peres found himself at a
disadvantage compared to Rabin, who benefited from the importance and high
visibility of the defense portfolio, which Rabin retained throughout the government's term. This became especially important after the outbreak of the Palestinian intifada in December 1987.

A significant and unanticipated result of the voting in 1988 was the success of
the religious parties in capturing a total of eighteen seats, six more than they had
won in 1984. This success came despite the fragmentation of the three existing religious parties—NRP, SHAS, and Agudat Israel—so that six religious parties participated in the election. Another religious party, TAMI, which had had one seat
in the outgoing Knesset, was absorbed into Likud prior to the 1988 election. Its
leader, Aharon Abuhatzeira, was given a safe seat on the Likud list and put in
charge of attracting votes for Likud among Jews of North African origin. The
NRP, SHAS, Agudat Israel, and Degel HaTorah (which broke off from Agudat Israel on the eve of the election) won seats in the Knesset. MEIMAD (the Religious Center Camp), a dovish offshoot of the NRP, fell short of the minimum
proportion of votes needed to secure a Knesset mandate.

The establishment of a new and different national unity government in December 1988 under the leadership of Yitzhak Shamir was a complicated process.
After weeks of maneuvering, Shamir was able to establish a government in which
he would remain as prime minister throughout its tenure. Labor's Shimon Peres
was appointed finance minister, where he would have little international visibility
and little opportunity to generate popular support within Israel. Peres's chief Labor Party rival, Yitzhak Rabin, retained the post of defense minister. This government managed to survive until spring 1990.

In early 1990 there was a breakdown between the two main elements and the
various smaller components of the government. The Labor members' resignation
from the government and the subsequent vote of no-confidence in the Knesset
led to the fall of the government. Peres and Labor gained an opportunity to secure

a mandate to form a successor coalition. Peres tried but was involved in a number of episodes of political maneuvering and promises of patronage that further tarnished his image and raised serious doubts about his leadership qualities. He was unable to construct a viable government. Shamir ultimately succeeded in establishing a government supported by Likud and by parties and individuals from the political Right and from the religious bloc. Eliezer Mizrachi of Agudat Israel and Ephraim Gur of the Labor Party also voted for the government. The new government was relatively narrow and potentially fragile.

In the wake of the formation of the new Shamir government, there emerged within Labor new questions about Peres's role as party leader. A test of these views took place within the party hierarchy in July 1990, but Peres succeeded in retaining his position as party leader.

The Likud-led government, under Shamir's leadership, was soon tested by the Iraqi SCUD missile attack. The government showed remarkable restraint, in part in response to U.S. President George Bush's request. In October 1991, after the Iraq War, Israel entered peace negotiations with its Arab neighbors in Madrid, Spain. The opening plenary session soon gave way to separate bilateral meetings between Israel and several Arab delegations. In January 1992, after three rounds of bilateral talks, the right-wing Tehiya and Moledet Parties, which together held five parliamentary seats, resigned from the government over Shamir's willingness to discuss an interim agreement on Palestinian self-rule in the West Bank and Gaza Strip. The defection of the two parties deprived the coalition of a majority in parliament, and Likud and Labor subsequently agreed to schedule a national election on June 23, 1992.

The imminent election provided a new opportunity for Yitzhak Rabin to try to unseat Shimon Peres as Labor leader. Since Rabin's unsuccessful challenge in July 1990, the party had adopted a primary election system for choosing its leader. In a dramatic showdown in February 1992, Rabin won the primary election for party leader. The subsequent election to select the party's slate of Knesset candidates resulted in a list that included many new faces and was generally younger and more dovish than previous Labor Party electoral lists.

The election of June 1992 for the Thirteenth Knesset was contested by twenty-five political parties, representing virtually all points of the political spectrum. Five additional parties, including the two successor groups to the late Meir Kahane's political legacy, were banned from participation because the electoral commission determined that they advocated racist and antidemocratic programs. A number of new parties or coalitions were created, such as MERETZ, which was the union of Shinui, Citizens' Rights Movement, and MAPAM; and United Torah Judaism, a combination of Agudat Israel, Degel HaTorah, and Moriah. Some parties were constructed by individuals or groups that split from major parties, including the New Liberal Party, led by Yitzhak Moda'i. At the same time, a number of new parties formed to reflect specific concerns and interest groups.

Democracy and Aliyah (DA), for example, was created by and for immigrants from the former Soviet Union.

Political commentators called the outcome of the 1992 election another "earthquake," or *mahapach,* in the sense of revolutionary change, as in 1977. This time Labor was the victor, winning more than 900,000 votes and forty-four Knesset seats—an increase of more than 200,000 votes and five seats—and ending a decade and a half of Likud rule. Likud lost eight mandates, falling to thirty-two. MERETZ emerged as the third-largest political bloc, with twelve seats. The secular-nationalist TZOMET increased its parliamentary representation from two to eight seats. The religious parties fell from eighteen to sixteen seats, but more important, they lost their traditional role of kingmakers.

Ultimately, ten parties were able to secure the 1.5 percent of the valid vote necessary to secure a seat in parliament. The crucial element in the outcome was the creation of a blocking majority of sixty-one parliamentary seats composed of Labor, MERETZ, and the Arab parties, which meant that Yitzhak Shamir would not be able to reconstruct a Likud–right-wing religious party coalition. The election result was a classic case of voters punishing the incumbent party for years of bad or ineffectual government. It also reflected in part the impact on the electoral system of new immigrants from the former Soviet Union, who were voting for the first time. Israeli pollsters estimate that 47 percent of the new immigrants voted for Labor. Yitzhak Rabin moved quickly to forge a coalition that included MERETZ and SHAS, though his original plan was to form a broad-based coalition, balancing left and right, and secular and religious, with Labor at the center. The new government was presented to the Knesset on July 13, 1992, and won its approval by a vote of sixty-seven to fifty-three.

Labor's return to control of the Knesset and government meant there would be attendant changes for politics, policies, and patronage. While Labor's victory generated an initial euphoria among many in Israel, external observers, especially in the United States, were especially hopeful that the peace process might be reinvigorated. This soon proved to be the case.

In 1992 Rabin became prime minister at the head of a Labor-led coalition government. After his assassination in November 1995, Peres delayed and then called for elections in May 1996, which he then lost, by a margin of less than 1 percent, to Benjamin (Bibi) Netanyahu and a Likud-led coalition government.

The 1992 election was conducted under the old system, whereby each voter cast only one ballot, for the party of the voter's choice. The 1996 elections were held under a changed electoral process that allowed Israelis to cast two ballots—one for a party list for the Knesset and one for direct election of the prime minister.

The outcome of the 1996 elections was interesting in a number of ways. In the first direct election for prime minister, Shimon Peres, the incumbent, who campaigned on the theme of continuity and expansion of the peace process, was defeated by Benjamin Netanyahu, who focused on the need for security as the first imperative, with peace achievable at the same time. Labor employed the legacy of assassinated Prime Minister Yitzhak Rabin to evoke sympathy for its cause, while Likud used the memory of those killed in a wave of mass suicide bombings in February–March 1996 to inspire distrust of the Labor government's security and peace policies. The ultra-Orthodox camp supported Netanyahu. One reason was a shared hard-line view on the peace process. Perhaps more important, however, was the religious parties' loathing of the stridently secularist MERETZ party, which had been Labor's junior partner in the outgoing government, and of the secularists within Labor, who also were seen as threatening the Jewishness of the state.

The 1992 electoral law was intended to alter the process of politics and its dynamics. The prime minister and the larger political parties were to be strengthened. Although the prime minister's position was strengthened, he was still limited by the parliament's ability to cast a vote of no confidence and by the nature of the coalitions in the Knesset. At the same time, there was the assumption that the large parties would get larger and the smaller parties would get smaller, or lose their positions in parliament entirely, thus facilitating coalition formation and reducing the bargaining power of the small parties in the Knesset. The assessments proved to be inaccurate. In 1996 the voters split their ballots—choosing Peres or Netanyahu for prime minister but then splitting their ballots and voting for another party for parliament. Thus, rather than facilitating coalition formation and strengthening the prime minister, the result of the election-law changes was that more parties in parliament could hold out with the prime minister for their demands because the prime minister needed their votes to form a government.

The shift from Labor to Likud brought with it a change in the substance and style of Israel's peace process strategy and tactics towards peacemaking. Under the Labor government of Yitzhak Rabin and Shimon Peres, Israel made gains in its quest for peace and the normalization of relations with the Palestinians and neighboring Arab countries. Direct bilateral negotiations were held between Israel and its immediate Arab neighbors—Syria, Lebanon, Jordan, and the Palestinians. Agreements were concluded between Israel and the Palestinians and Israel and Jordan. Nevertheless, the outcome of the May 29, 1996, election, held against a background of terrorist bombings, indicated that the majority of Israelis perceived Labor's peace strategy as riskier than Likud's and, consequently, voted in favor of what was envisioned as a more controlled and balanced approach.

Netanyahu's rhetoric during the campaign and his record as Likud leader suggested that he would modify Israel's approach to the peace process. Netanyahu promised Israeli voters that he would achieve a "secure peace" and that while he accepted the reality of the Oslo framework for Israeli-Palestinian negotiations, he would never accept a Palestinian state. The prospects for peace with the Palestinians appeared bleak as Netanyahu assumed the premiership, and the Arab-Israeli conflict remained the country's most important problem.

Netanyahu's tenure in office was marked by an effort to govern based on the popular mandate as a prime minister chosen by the people, rather than as head of the coalition government required by the outcome of the Knesset elections. But the reality was that Netanyahu was dependent on a fractioned Knesset and a coalition government. He suffered from discord on both domestic and foreign policy issues, especially the latter. Foreign policy–especially the peace process—proved problematic. Although negotiations with the Palestinians moved slowly under Netanyahu, eventually there were the Hebron Agreement of January 1997 and the Wye accords of 1998, which were both approved by narrow margins in the Knesset. However, Netanyahu could not keep his restive coalition of Likud and secular-nationalist and religious parties together, and agreement was reached to hold new elections, for both the Knesset and prime minister, in the spring of 1999.

Ehud Barak—newly chosen leader of the One Israel bloc comprising Labor, Gesher, and Meimad—was elected prime minister in May 1999, defeating the incumbent, Benjamin Netanyahu. Barak gained 56 percent of the vote, compared with 44 percent for Netanyahu. However, One Israel was able to obtain only twenty-six seats in the parliamentary election, leading to a broad and disparate coalition. Despite his significant margin of victory over Netanyahu, Barak was faced with a very divided Knesset (the most fractioned in Israel's history). Labor (running as One Israel) and Likud together held fewer than half the seats in the parliament with thirteen parties initially sharing the remainder. And, they represented virtually all points on the political spectrum. Nevertheless, Barak succeeded in cobbling together a coalition of these diverse political units. Its longevity was questioned from the outset, but it seemed to hold together as Barak began his efforts to achieve peace and security.

After June 2000 the coalition unraveled. David Levy, the leader of Gesher and the minister of foreign affairs, left One Israel in protest of Barak's handling of the peace negotiations, and the National Religious and ultra-Orthodox parties also left the coalition. The most influential of the coalition defectors was the SHAS party, with seventeen Knesset seats. Barak's government was reduced from a total of seventy-five of the Knesset's 120 seats in July 1999 to only thirty seats as of August 2000, although the prime minister could rely on some support from outside the government for retention of power. Nevertheless he soon called for a new election. This time he faced Ariel Sharon, who replaced Netanyahu as Likud leader in the aftermath of the 1999 election.

Following Ariel Sharon's overwhelming victory in Israel's prime ministerial election in 2001, his first priority was to put together a governing coalition. His most urgent challenge was Palestinian violence. In the near term, it was certain that the intifada would continue in one form or another, and the standard by which Sharon's performance as prime minister would be judged would be his response to that challenge, since it was personal security (or insecurity) that was the pivotal election issue.

Sharon initially managed to hold together his diverse national unity government. The government, which controlled seventy-eight of the 120 seats in the Knesset, was comprised of Sharon's Likud party, the Labor Party, SHAS, and several smaller parties. The coalition included religious and immigrant parties. At the outset, the coalition parties set aside their differences and focused on the Palestinian-Israeli conflict, despite the breadth of views of the parties on security issues. Sustaining the coalition consensus on how to deal with the intifada and the Palestinian negotiations was Sharon's central task.

Foreign and Security Policies

The primary objectives of Israel's foreign and security policies are the quest for peace through negotiations with the Arab states and the assurance of security in a region of hostility through an effective defense capability. The goals of peace and security derive from the continuing conflict with the Arab states that remains the preeminent problem confronting Israel; it affects all of Israel's policies and activities—both domestic and foreign—in every area of concern and application. Israel recognizes that peace and cooperation with the neighboring Arab states is vital for the long-term survival and development of the Jewish state, and this remains the cornerstone of its foreign policy.

Israel's preoccupation and preeminent concern with peace, national survival, and security is a consequence of its geostrategic situation, particularly the conflict with its Arab neighbors. During its first thirty-four years of existence (between 1948 and 1982) Israel fought six wars with Arab states and the Palestine Liberation Organization. Wars, countless skirmishes and terrorist attacks, and incessant, vituperative rhetoric, combined with the Holocaust and with Arab hostility during the mandate period, all left their mark on Israel's national consciousness. Israel spends, on a continuing basis, a major portion of its budget and GNP/GDP on defense and defense-related items and has, by regional standards, a sizable standing army and reserve force widely considered to be of great quality and capability. Israel's military power is substantial but not unlimited, and constrained by its own demography and economy as well as by international factors.

Israel's quest for peace with its Arab neighbors dates from its establishment, when the Arabs opposed the partition of Palestine proposed by the United Nations and declared war in response to Israel's declaration of independence upon termination of the mandate. The armistice agreements of 1949 that followed the first Arab-Israeli war (1948–1949) were intended to facilitate a transition to "permanent peace in Palestine." Israelis tended to be hopeful, but negotiations were not begun, and Israel soon became preoccupied with the need for security. The Suez War of 1956 reinforced that concern.

The Six-Day War of 1967 generated dramatic change in Israel and in Israeli perceptions of their situation. The realities of Arab hostility, the nature of the Arab threat, and the difficulties of achieving a settlement became more obvious. At the same time, the dynamic of the conflict changed with the extent of the Israeli victory: Israel occupied the Sinai Peninsula, the Gaza Strip, the West Bank, East Jerusalem, and the Golan Heights. Israel adopted the position that it would not withdraw from those territories until negotiations with the Arab states had led to peace agreements that recognized Israel's right to exist and accepted Israel's permanent status and borders. The Arab view was articulated in the Palestine National Covenant of 1964, which called the creation of Israel "null and void," and in the resolutions of the Arab League summit meeting in Khartoum, Sudan in 1967, which spoke of "no peace with Israel, no recognition of Israel, no negotiations with it."

Throughout the period between the Six-Day War and the Yom Kippur War (1973), the focal point in the Middle East was the effort to achieve a settlement of the Arab-Israeli conflict and to secure a just and lasting peace. In these attempts, based on United Nations Security Council Resolution 242 of November 22, 1967, the regional states, the superpowers (and other powers), and the main instrumentalities of the international system were engaged. Israel focused its attention on peace and security objectives and developed positions concerning the occupied territories, the Palestinians, and related questions. Although some of the interwar efforts were promising, peace was not achieved.

The Yom Kippur War created a new environment for the quest for peace and the development of Israeli foreign policy. Israel's position deteriorated with the outbreak of the fighting, as the country was condemned by various states and some severed diplomatic relations. During the course of the war and immediately afterward, Israel's ties with most of the states of sub-Saharan Africa were broken. Except for South Africa, no major African state publicly backed Israel or offered assistance. To most Israelis this fact symbolized not only the injustice of the international community but also the success of the Arab oil weapon and the failure of Israel's program of international cooperation. Israel had provided many of these African states with technical assistance, which the Africans had lauded publicly, for promoting African development. Israel retained relations with only five African states: South Africa, Malawi, Lesotho, Botswana, and Swaziland.

The ruptures with Africa were a disappointment, but a shift in the attitudes and policies of the European states and Japan was more significant. Israel's international isolation was exemplified by the unwillingness of the European allies of the United States (with the exception of Portugal) to allow the use of their facilities or airspace for the shipment and transfer of supplies to Israel during the war. The Europeans were reluctant to be associated with the U.S. support for Israel and were concerned about the reduction of Arab oil shipments to them. Japan, heavily dependent on Middle Eastern oil, had hitherto maintained a posture of neutrality in the Arab-Israeli conflict; it now shifted to a more pronounced pro-Arab position. The war thus increased Israel's dependence on the United States. No other country could or was prepared to provide Israel with the vast quantities of modern and sophisticated arms required for war or the political and moral support necessary to negotiate peace. Nevertheless, there were questions about the U.S. role on such matters as the cease-fire, the peace negotiations, and the terms of a Middle East settlement.

In the wake of the Yom Kippur War, modifications of Israel's policy were relatively minor, and there were no dramatic shifts in objectives and content. The primary goals remained the achievement of an Arab-Israeli settlement and the assurance of security in the interim. This constancy resulted, in part, from Israel's collective conception of its fundamental international position—and the limited policy options that flowed therefrom—which was not substantially altered. Israel's view of itself as geographically isolated and lacking dependable allies, its geographical vulnerability, and its need to acquire and produce arms for self-defense were reaffirmed by the Yom Kippur War. Israel believed that it won a military victory and that its strategic concepts were vindicated.

After the 1977 elections, the Begin government maintained Israel's focus on the goal of establishing peace that would include the end of war, full reconciliation and normalization, and an open border over which people and goods could cross without hindrance. On the question of the occupied territories, the new government could rely on a consensus opposing a return to the armistice lines of 1949, thus ruling out total withdrawal, although there was disagreement concerning the final lines to be established and the extent of compromise. The focus of territorial disagreement was the West Bank. There was a substantial difference between the Begin-Likud view, which opposed relinquishing any territory, and the compromise views articulated by Labor and others to Likud's left. The Labor-led coalition governments between 1967 and 1977 had generally tried to limit Jewish settlements to those that could serve a security function and had sought to avoid conflict between the settlements and the local Arab populations. The Begin government elected in 1977 altered that policy. Rather than restricting settlements in Judea and Samaria to those that were primarily security oriented, it supported settlement in that area as a natural and inalienable Jewish right. The broadest and most articulate consensus continued to revolve around the question of a Palestinian state and the PLO—Israel's refusal to negotiate with the PLO and its opposition to the establishment of an independent Palestinian state on the West Bank and in the Gaza Strip were reaffirmed.

Israel's national consensus focused on the need for peace, and the main obstacle appeared to be the continuing Arab unwillingness to accept Israel and to negotiate with it. This was modified as a result of the November 1977 initiative of President Anwar Sadat of Egypt that led to his visit to Israel and to the inauguration of direct negotiations between Israel and Egypt. The negotiations culminated in the Camp David summit meeting of September 1978 at which Israel, Egypt, and the United States agreed to two frameworks for continued negotiations. The primary objective of post–Camp David negotiations was to convert the frameworks into peace treaties. Despite efforts to secure the involvement of other Arab states, none agreed to participate. The parties concentrated their initial efforts on the Egypt-Israel Peace Treaty, which was signed at the White House on March 26, 1979.

The Egypt-Israel Peace Treaty was a significant accomplishment that represented a first step toward a comprehensive Arab-Israeli settlement and regional stability. The process of normalization of relations between Egypt and Israel moved ahead on schedule and without major interruptions. Normal relations officially began in early 1980 after Israel had completed most of its withdrawal from the Sinai Peninsula and after the borders between the two states were opened and direct communications links were inaugurated. Peace was established, but it was often a "cold" peace, one in which long-standing mistrust had not been replaced by the warmth of friendly relations.

Begin also fulfilled his government's pledge regarding the Golan Heights. In December 1981, the Knesset adopted the Golan Heights Law, which extended Israel's "law, jurisdiction, and administration" to the area. Begin cited Syrian President Assad's refusal to negotiate a peace treaty with Israel as the main reason for the decision.

The peace process soon was overshadowed by the sixth Arab-Israeli war—the war in Lebanon in 1982. The continued presence in Lebanon of surface-to-air missiles that had been moved there by Syria in the spring of 1981 remained an Israeli concern. So were PLO incursions into northern Israel from bases in southern Lebanon and terrorist attacks against Israeli and Jewish targets worldwide, despite a U.S. arranged cease-fire in summer 1981. On June 6, 1982, Israel launched a major military action against the PLO in Lebanon (called "Operation Peace for Galilee"), which sought to remove the PLO's military and terrorist threat to Israel and to reduce the PLO's political capability. The military objectives were to assure security for northern Israel; to destroy the PLO infrastructure that had established a state within a state in southern Lebanon; to eliminate a center of international terrorism; and to eliminate the PLO from Lebanon so that its territory would not serve as a base of operations from which Israel could be threatened. The political objectives of Operation Peace for Galilee were not as precise—primarily there was the goal of weakening the PLO so that it would no longer be as significant politically, but there was also the hope that a new political order in Lebanon might lead it to consider becoming the second Arab state to make peace with Israel.

In many respects the results of the war in Lebanon were ambiguous. Israel's northern border was more secure, but Israeli troops who remained in Lebanon until summer 1985 became targets of terrorists and others, and numerous casualties resulted. The costs of the war were high. Externally, Israel's military actions caused concern and dismay in many quarters, including the United States, and its international isolation was increased. The achievements were primarily in the military realm—the PLO was defeated, and its military and terrorist infrastructure in

Lebanon was destroyed. The political achievements were less tangible. Despite some losses the PLO remained the primary spokesman for the Palestinians and Yasir Arafat, operating from Tunis, soon rebounded to his preeminent position in the organization. Although an agreement between Israel and Lebanon calling for Israeli withdrawal and for the normalization of relations between the two countries was concluded in May 1983, it was soon unilaterally abrogated by the government of Lebanon under Syrian pressure.

Menachem Begin's tenure as prime minister brought peace with Egypt and reduced, significantly, the military danger to the existence of Israel by neutralizing the largest Arab army, with which it had fought five wars. Operation Peace for Galilee led to debate and demonstration within Israel but did not expand the peace domain for the Jewish state. The government of Prime Minister Yitzhak Shamir, endorsed by the Knesset in October 1983, proposed continuity in principles and policy, but its brief tenure was not highlighted by major developments in the quest for peace.

As prime minister from 1984 to 1986, Shimon Peres set three major foreign policy objectives. The first was to withdraw Israeli forces from Lebanon as quickly as possible. Peres and Defense Minister Yitzhak Rabin also focused their efforts on the unilateral creation of a security zone along the border in southern Lebanon. The security zone would be policed by an Israeli-created and supported militia, the "South Lebanese Army" of General Antoine Lahad. By January 1985 the groundwork for Israel's withdrawal was in place. Peres's second objective was to improve relations with Egypt following the tensions caused by Israel's invasion of Lebanon. The third objective was to engage Jordan's King Hussein in direct peace talks.

Upon assuming the premiership in October 1986, Shamir pledged that he would continue the policies initiated by Peres. Nevertheless, it was evident that his approach would be different on the critical issues of Arab-Israeli peace. Shamir reaffirmed his adherence to the Camp David framework and made it clear that he would not deviate from that path as prime minister.

In December 1987, Palestinians in the Gaza Strip began a wave of violent protests and riots, which quickly spread to the West Bank and became a new feature of Palestinian life under Israeli occupation. The initial effect of the uprising (intifada) on Israel was to reinforce the sharp cleavages dividing the public between those who believed the Palestinian problem had to be resolved through territorial compromise and those who believed Israel could have both peace and the territories. To Israeli moderates, the uprising exposed the folly of their compatriots who insisted that the territorial status quo was tenable; the uprising reaffirmed the urgency of withdrawing from the bulk of the territories and returning them to Jordan. To Israeli hard-liners, the uprising underscored the dangers Israel would face if it relinquished control over the territories.

Dialogue was opened in December 1988 between the United States and the PLO, in the wake of Arafat's acceptance—to U.S. satisfaction—of United Nations

Security Council Resolutions 242 and 338, recognition of Israel and renunciation of terrorism. This development added to the growing internal and external pressures on Israel to work on a constructive policy to deal with the Palestinian intifada and to advance the peace process.

In January 1989, Defense Minister Rabin suggested publicly that the government should consider adopting Labor's idea that the Palestinians in the West Bank and Gaza Strip elect their own representatives to peace talks. On May 14, 1989, the Israeli cabinet adopted a similar Shamir proposal as its official policy. The election initiative became the focal point of efforts to advance the Arab-Israeli peace process, and the United States sought to build on it. Over the months, the United States worked to narrow the differences between Israel and the Palestinians and to start direct negotiations. The diplomatic maneuvering was carried out in the context of political differences in Likud and in the national unity government. And in March 1990, the national unity government fell in a Labor-sponsored vote of no-confidence over Likud's unwillingness to respond affirmatively to U.S. proposals.

Shamir formed a new Likud-led government in June 1990. In presenting the government to the Knesset, Shamir noted that it included "all the national forces which have fought and worked for the sake of Eretz Yisrael," and he pledged to continue working for peace on the basis of the Camp David Accords and his proposal for Palestinian elections.

When, in August 1990, Iraq invaded Kuwait, much of the world's attention was diverted from the Arab-Israeli conflict. After the Persian Gulf War ended, on March 6, 1991, President George Bush announced to Congress that "the time had come to put an end to Arab-Israel conflict," and he dispatched Secretary of State James Baker to the Middle East on a round of exploratory diplomacy. Over the ensuing months, Baker made several more trips to the region, seeking the consent of Israel and the Arabs to participate in an international peace conference. This conference convened on October 30, 1991, in Madrid, Spain.

The Madrid conference did not achieve a substantive breakthrough, although it broke the procedural and psychological barriers to direct bilateral negotiations between Israel and its immediate neighbors by having Israeli and Syrian, Egyptian, Lebanese, and Jordanian-Palestinian delegations meet at an opening public and official plenary session and deliver speeches and responses. Bilateral negotiations between Israel and each of the Arab delegations followed.

The Madrid meetings were followed by bilateral talks in Washington in December 1991 and in 1992, 1993, and 1994. Progress was measured chiefly by the continuation of the process rather than by the achievement of substantive accord on the issues in dispute. The wide gap between the Israeli and Arab positions was not meaningfully narrowed in these initial encounters, and it could not be bridged by the intervention of outside actors.

In the bilateral discussions, the Israeli-Palestinian and Israeli-Syrian negotiations proved to be both the most central and the most difficult. In the case of both

Jordan and Lebanon, the general perception was that agreements would be relatively easy to achieve, although they would have to await the resolution of the Syrian and Palestinian talks. In the case of Syria, the central issues were peace, security, and the future of the Golan Heights. In the Israeli-Palestinian discussions, the disagreement centered on the Palestinian desire for an independent state in the West Bank and Gaza Strip and the Israeli opposition to that goal.

The Madrid-inaugurated process included multilateral discussions on several broader regional issues—refugees, economic development, water resources, environment, and arms control. An initial organizing conference met in Moscow in January 1992. The goal was to achieve progress on these issues, even without a political solution, and to reinforce the bilateral negotiations.

Israel's Knesset election campaign in spring 1992 slowed the Arab-Israeli peace process. But the outcome of the election was widely heralded as a significant and positive factor that would alter the regional situation, the prospects for progress in the Arab-Israeli peace process, and the nature of the U.S.-Israeli relationship. Agreement was soon reached with the new Labor-led coalition government on the resumption of the bilateral process in Washington in late August 1992. The bilateral and multilateral negotiation processes continued over the ensuing months, albeit with little apparent progress. In part because of this lack of movement and related regional and international factors, secret negotiations between the PLO and Israel began in spring 1993.

The secret negotiations between representatives of Yasir Arafat's PLO and Israelis in Oslo, Norway, in spring and summer 1993 resulted in an exchange of mutual recognition in September 1993, soon followed by the formal signing on the White House lawn in Washington, D.C., on September 13, 1993, of a Declaration of Principles (DOP). The DOP was a first step on the long road to a comprehensive peace in the Arab-Israeli conflict, but it was a crucial and historic breakthrough. Further implementing agreements were signed in Paris and Cairo in spring 1994. Israel and Jordan began official, public, high-level negotiations in summer 1994. In late July 1994, Prime Minister Yitzhak Rabin and King Hussein of Jordan signed, on the White House lawn, the Washington Declaration, formally ending their state of belligerence. In October Israel and Jordan signed a formal peace treaty, which ushered in an era of peace and normalization of relations between the two states. The process begun at Madrid was thus overshadowed by this new bilateral and practical approach to a core set of problems in the Arab-Israeli conflict.

The Madrid process moved ahead, albeit in slow motion. When Barak assumed power in July 1999 great optimism followed that there could now be progress in the peace process. Barak transferred some territories in the West Bank to the Palestinian Authority. He also hinted that he might return virtually all of the Golan Heights to Syria in exchange for peace. This generated criticism and protest from settlers and from others who saw the need to keep the heights, given their security value for Israel. Negotiations brought the parties close together but summit talks in

Shepherdstown, West Virginia, with U.S. President Bill Clinton participating, and in Geneva, Switzerland, failed to bring an agreement. At the time of Syrian President Hafez Assad's death in June 2000 the process had reached a stalemate, despite substantial agreement between Assad and Barak negotiating through intermediaries.

On the Lebanon front, concurring with growing public sentiment, Barak brought about significant change. In May 2000, having failed to negotiate a comprehensive peace agreement with Syria and Lebanon, he unilaterally withdrew Israeli troops from Lebanon back to a U.N.-marked international border.

Despite some progress in other sectors, there was little to record on the Israeli-Palestinian front. Madrid opened the way for negotiations between Israel and the PLO in Washington, but it was the secret talks in Oslo, Norway, that led to the White House lawn signing ceremony and the transfer of territory from Israel to the PLO as a first part of the process of reaching an overall accord to achieve peace and security.

The process was slow and while some interim agreements were reached, the final status issues had not been considered by the time Barak took office after the 1999 Israeli elections. Barak's accession to power generated a euphoria about achievements but movement was slow.

A summit took place at Camp David in the summer 2000, at which President Clinton, Barak and Arafat focused on a comprehensive peace agreement. Despite intensive efforts and some areas of accord, no agreement was reached. The failure of the Camp David II summit and the ensuing violence brought the Oslo process to a halt. The Clinton administration was followed by that of George W. Bush; Ariel Sharon replaced Ehud Barak as Israel's prime minister. The peace process that had marked the decade of the 1990s was replaced by violence—the al-Aksa intifada broke out in September 2000 and continued unabated throughout 2001— and periodic talk of "war." The problem was further exacerbated in the wake of the terrorist attacks in New York and Washington, D.C., of September 11, 2001, when Palestinian terrorists escalated their attacks against Israeli civilians. The assassination of an Israeli cabinet minister and large-scale attacks against Israeli civilians in Jerusalem and Haifa in November 2001 that left dozens of Israelis killed and hundreds wounded elicited an Israeli response (recognized as legitimate self-defense by the United States) seeking to rout out the terrorists and forcing Arafat and the Palestinian Authority to arrest them and prevent the support of the terrorists by various Palestinian organizations.

Sharon made it clear in his election campaign that the Oslo process "was dead," and that the security of Israel (and Israelis) was the paramount concern and central objective of his administration. His demand was that the violence must stop before the negotiations could take place. Given continuous violence and the lack of confidence between Israel and the PLO, the peace process remained moribund.

The twenty-first century began with Israeli foreign policy continuing its quest for peace. Many Israelis questioned their situation more than a decade after the end of the Gulf War, the defeat of Saddam Hussein, and the subsequent Madrid conference that inaugurated the Middle East peace process. Despite the efforts of six prime ministers in the 1990s and the first years of the twenty-first century (Shamir, Rabin, Peres, Netanyahu, Barak, and Sharon) Israel's overall acceptance in the region was only marginally advanced (peace was achieved only with Jordan in 1994), security for Israel deteriorated (as evidenced in the al-Aksa intifada), and Israel was far from being accepted as an integral part of the Middle East region in which it was located.

The Search for Friends and Allies

Israel's broader approach to foreign policy began to take shape once it became clear that peace would not follow the 1949 armistice accords with the Arab states that marked the end of its War of Independence. The Arab threat and Israel's isolation suggested a need for positive relationships with other states, but from the outset, Israel's approach to alliances has been marked by ambivalence. Israel directed its attention beyond the circle of neighboring Arab states to the international community in an effort to establish friendly relations with the states of Europe and the developing world, especially Africa and Latin America, as well as the superpowers, and to gain their support in the international arena. These relationships were seen as having a positive effect on the Arab-Israeli conflict and bilateral political and economic advantages that would help to ensure Israel's deterrent strength through national armed power and through increased international support for its position.

At the outset Israel also held a positive view of the United Nations, fostered by that organization's role in the creation of the state. With the increasingly large anti-Israel majority in the United Nations and the resulting virtually automatic support for Palestinian and Arab perspectives, Israel's views changed markedly, and the United Nations was regarded as an unhelpful factor in the quest for peace and security. This changed after the Madrid peace conference and the consequent bilateral negotiations between Israel and its neighbors and the multilateral negotiations, which involved a large number of other powers. In addition, the collapse of the Soviet Union and the disintegration of the Soviet bloc led to the restoration of Israel's relations with a large number of states that previously had been hostile. All of this contributed to the alterations in the voting patterns and decisions of the United Nations that contributed to an improved relationship with Israel in the decade of the 1990s. But with the failure of the Oslo process and the resort to the United Nations by the Palestinians and the Arab states, this view was again altered. At the start of the twenty-first century Israel's perspective of the United Nations was marked by an ambivalence concerning the role the organization might play in Israel's foreign policy.

The developed and economically advanced, industrialized states of Europe plus Japan and Korea and Canada are, and have been, of great significance to Israel.

Primarily these are states of substantial economic development and long history as independent states and, some, as colonial powers. Most are middle and larger powers (including Britain, France, Germany, the Netherlands, and Italy) and also OECD and European Union members. Japan and Korea, while clearly important economic powers and, in the case of Japan, a significant political actor, differed from the other members of this group in history and background.

Europe posed an interesting challenge and presented a significant opportunity for Israeli policy makers. Israel has sought to maintain positive relations with Europe based on the commonality of the Judeo-Christian heritage (its biblical links to Christianity) and democratic tradition and the memories and "guilt complex" of the Holocaust. With Israel seeking links to significant powers for military (aid and arms acquisition) and economic (trade and economic aid) assistance, Europe seemed a logical choice. A tacit alliance with France was supplemented by links with Great Britain and Germany and a formalized relationship with the European Economic Community (EEC) and, now, the European Union (EU). The establishment of the EEC in 1957, and its evolution into the EU, opened a new and major area of concern for Israeli foreign policy. Israel embarked on a course of action designed to maximize the economic, and especially trade, opportunities presented by the increased economic potential of a Europe united economically. Over time Israel has been successful in establishing economic links with the EEC and EU, albeit within limitations, as a group but also with various European states (especially Germany and France) on a bilateral level. France proved a valuable supplier of military aid until the June 1967 Six-Day War while Germany, through its reparations, was an indispensable factor in Israel's economic development.

Israel's relations with the developing world, which began in earnest in the late 1950s, have focused on the country's ability to provide technical assistance in the development process.

The emergence of the new states of Africa and Asia in the 1950s and 1960s led Israel to pursue a policy in keeping with Afro-Asian aspirations for economic development and modernization. In an effort to befriend these states and to secure their support, Israel's multifaceted program focused on technical assistance, exchange and training programs, loans, joint economic enterprises, and trade. The program grew dramatically and remains an element of Israeli policy. It had successes in economic and social terms and proved politically beneficial in various international venues. Third World support helped to prevent the United Nations from adopting anti-Israel measures after the 1967 war, and in the early 1970s a committee of African presidents worked to achieve Arab-Israeli negotiations (albeit without success). The nadir of the policy was reached at the time of the 1973 war, when virtually all the African states with which Israel had established ties broke those relations in support of the Arab effort to regain the territories lost in the 1967 war. For some Israelis this reflected a policy failure although some African states have reestablished close links and some sustained informal but significant ties despite their official actions (for example, Kenya's link to Israel as demonstrated during Israel's Entebbe hostage rescue operation in 1976).

Despite substantial effort in these sectors, the centrality of the Arab-Israeli conflict has enlarged and enhanced the role of the superpowers, particularly the United States, in Israeli eyes.

Israel's leaders early recognized the crucial role that the great powers would play in ensuring the country's defense and integrity. In the euphoric days following independence it was believed that nonalignment in the cold war was possible and that Israel could establish and maintain friendly relations with, and secure support from, both East and West (the Soviet Union and the United States), although most realized that Israel's long-term interests lay in the West. Nonalignment was in accord with Israel's perception of its national interest and seemed to be a realistic assessment in light of the policies and activities of both powers in the period following World War II, when Soviet and U.S. support for Israel and the competition between them was seen as auguring well for the new state.

In keeping with that perception, Israel's government, upon attainment of statehood, proclaimed a policy of noncommitment (nonidentification) in the East-West conflict. Although Israel noted that in the ideological struggle between the democratic and communist social orders it had chosen democracy, it was nonaligned and not identified with any bloc in the cold war. This policy was made easier to adopt by Soviet actions in support of the new state when it voted for the partition plan of 1947; accorded de jure recognition to Israel shortly after its independence; supported its applications for membership in the United Nations; and gave it moral, political, and material support. However, soon after the end of the War of Independence, various factors, including ideological sympathies, the large size and importance of Western Jewry, and Soviet abandonment of support for Israel and denial of loan requests, coupled with a relatively constant flow of economic aid from the U.S. government and American Jewry, contributed to Israel's shift to a pro-Western orientation. Israel's support for the U.N. resolutions and actions concerning the invasion of Korea was seen in the Soviet bloc as an unfriendly act.

Relations between the Soviet Union and Israel deteriorated rapidly from 1949 to 1953, and Israel's foreign policy no longer reflected belief in Soviet friendship and support. Soviet support for, and expanded relations with, the Arab states by the mid–1950s tended to confirm this perspective. Soviet economic and military assistance to the Arab world, the Soviet bloc's rupture of relations with Israel in 1967, and the continuation of that break led Israel farther into the Western camp, although it continued to seek the restoration of ties to the Soviet Union and its allies and to promote the well-being and emigration of Soviet Jews. Emigration began to grow in 1989 and diplomatic relations were restored in October 1991, on the eve of the Madrid peace conference.

From World War II to the 1990s, the superpowers (the United States and the Soviet Union) were the encompassing major players of the international system.

In the case of the Soviet Union it was not simply the relationship with the superpower itself but also its bloc partners. From independence to the 1990s, Israel, like
all other states, had to operate within the confines of the cold war. But there were
multiple factors whose cumulative impact was greater on Israel than on most
other states. Both superpowers were also significant as the location/residence of
large segments of the world's Jewish population.

Israel was initially somewhat successful with its early policy of nonalignment.
While other states often tried to play the United States and the Soviet Union
against each other to secure from them the benefits of alliance, Israel was unable
to do so in its earliest days of independence. And, curiously, the United States and
the Soviet Union each sought Israel's allegiance when it became independent and
it joined the United Nations. But soon, Israel's nonidentification gave way to a
pro-Western orientation and later to a United States–Israel connection or alignment. The special relationship (or the "alliance" seen by some) between the
United States and Israel developed only later and remains unformalized in treaty
form even today.

The lens of Zionism and the associated "ingathering of the exiles" required Israel to be concerned for Jewish communities elsewhere and their well-being *and*
potential to emigrate from their (imperiled) locations to the haven of the Jewish
state. Thus in focusing on the superpowers an additional concern of Israel was for
what was then the world's two largest Jewish communities (in the United States—
still the world's largest—and in the Soviet Union, then the world's second, and today third, largest).

Anti-Semitism was (and arguably is) an endemic feature of Russian (and Soviet) society and history. Not only were Soviet Jews unable to assist the Jewish
state in its birth and consolidation, Israel (during the cold war) was unable to protect them and could not secure large-scale emigration of those at risk. This began
to change in the last years of the Gorbachev era, and immigration to Israel became
a continuous flow with the end of the Soviet Union and of the cold war.

The relationship between the Union of Soviet Socialist Republics and Israel
underwent substantial change over the years. The Soviet Union and the Communist Party were opposed ideologically to Zionism, but in 1947 the Soviet Union's
representative at the United Nations, Andrei Gromyko, supported the Palestine
Partition Plan, which led to the creation of Israel. In 1948 the Soviet Union became one of the first states to recognize the new state of Israel and it was instrumental in assuring arms from the Soviet bloc to Israel via Czechoslovakia during
Israel's War of Independence.

However, positive relations in the first years deteriorated in the early 1950s,
culminating in the Soviet arms supply to Egypt announced in 1955. A factor in
the relationship then, as later, was the relationship between Israel and the Soviet
Jewish population. Israel's desire to ensure the well-being internally of the Soviet
Jewish population and to ensure the right of emigration for those who wished to

leave the USSR led to conflicts with Soviet authorities and Moscow's official position. The relationship between the Soviet Union and the Arab states grew in the
decade following the Sinai War of 1956, although correct if cool relations were retained with Israel. In 1967, the Soviet Union contributed to the Six-Day War
through circulation of a fallacious rumor concerning Israeli military mobilization.
At this time the Soviet Union and its East European allies (except Romania)
broke diplomatic relations with Israel.

After the 1967 conflict the Soviet Union attempted to become a more significant factor in the peace process. At the same time, with the advent of the Gorbachev approach to foreign policy, the relationship of the two states improved.
Consular contacts and exchanges took place, Soviet Jewish emigration increased
substantially, and several East European states restored diplomatic relations with
Israel. Nevertheless, the Soviet Union maintained that it could not reestablish relations with Israel until there was substantial movement toward peace and the
withdrawal of Israel from the occupied territories. On October 18, 1991, the
USSR and Israel reestablished diplomatic relations. This was part of the process
of preparation for that month's Madrid conference to negotiate a solution to the
Arab-Israeli conflict.

Upon the collapse of the USSR in December 1991, Russia took over most of
the Soviet Union's functions in Middle East diplomacy, including cosponsoring
(with the United States) the Madrid process. In January 1992, Moscow hosted the
first session of the multilateral talks of the Madrid peace process. Beginning in
the early 1990s some 750,000 citizens of the former Soviet Union emigrated to
Israel, and there was significant growth in bilateral relations with Russia and several of the former Soviet republics in the cultural and commercial domains. Nevertheless Israel remained skeptical about Russia's ambitions in the Middle East, as
reflected in its relations with militant Arab regimes (including Syria, Libya, and
Iraq) and its transfer of military technology to Iran.

The United States has changed from a power providing limited direct support
for Israel to become the world's only superpower linked to Israel in a free trade
area and a crucial provider of political, diplomatic, and strategic (security) support
as well as economic aid.

The complex and multifaceted "special relationship" with the United States
that had its origins prior to the independence of Israel has been centered on the
continuing U.S. support for the survival, security, and well-being of Israel. During
the first decades after Israel's independence, the U.S.-Israeli relationship was
grounded primarily in humanitarian concerns, in religious and historical links,
and in a moral-emotional-political arena rather than a strategic-military one. The
United States declared an arms embargo on December 5, 1947; there was practically no U.S. military aid or sales of military equipment and no formal, or even informal, military agreement or strategic cooperation between the two states. Extensive dealings in the strategic realm became significant only in the 1970s and

1980s. The concept of Israel as a "strategic asset" was more an outcome of the developing relationship than a foundation for its establishment. U.S. policy on arms supply evolved from embargo to principal supplier, and arms became an important tool of U.S. policy to reassure Israel and to achieve policy modification.

The two states developed a diplomatic-political relationship that focused on the need to resolve the Arab-Israeli dispute, but although they agreed on the general concept, they often differed on the precise means for achieving the desired result. The relationship became especially close after the Six-Day War, when a congruence of policy prevailed on many of their salient concerns. Nevertheless, the two states often held differing perspectives on regional developments and on the dangers and opportunities they presented. No major ruptures took place, although significant tensions were generated at various junctures.

Israel's special relationship with the United States—which is based on substantial positive perception and sentiment evident in public opinion and official statements and manifest in political-diplomatic support and in military and economic assistance—has not been enshrined in a formal, legally binding document joining the two states in a formal alliance. Israel has no mutual security treaty with the United States, nor is it a member of any alliance system requiring the United States to take up arms automatically on its behalf. The U.S. commitment to Israel has taken the rather generalized form of presidential statements that have reaffirmed the U.S. interest in supporting the political independence and territorial integrity of all Middle Eastern states, including Israel.

Nevertheless, the United States is today an indispensable, if not fully dependable, ally. It provides Israel, through one form or another, with economic (governmental and private), technical, military, political, diplomatic, and moral support. It was seen as the ultimate resource against the Soviet Union; it is the source of Israel's sophisticated military hardware; it is central to the Arab-Israeli peace process.

The United States and Israel have established a special relationship replete with broad areas of agreement and numerous examples of discord. There was, is, and will be a divergence that derives from a difference of perspective and overall policy environment. Nevertheless, they maintain a remarkable degree of parallelism and congruence on broad policy goals. And Israel continues to focus on the centrality and significance of the ties.

Note

1. The term *Jewish Agency* first appeared in Article 4 of the Palestine mandate, which recognized the WZO as "an appropriate Jewish Agency . . . for the purpose of advising and cooperating with the administration of Palestine in such economic, social, and other matters as may affect the establishment of the Jewish National Home and the interests of the Jewish population in Palestine."

Bibliography

Bernard Reich, *Historical Dictionary of Israel* (Metuchen, N.J.: Scarecrow Press, 1992), and Bernard Reich and David H. Goldberg, *Political Dictionary of Israel* (Lanham, Md., and London: Scarecrow Press, 2000) are convenient reference works; and Bernard Reich and Gershon R. Kieval, *Israel: Land of Tradition and Conflict,* 3rd ed. (Boulder: Westview Press, 2002), is a description and analysis of all aspects of modern Israel, with an emphasis on politics. On the Arab-Israeli conflict the reader is referred to Bernard Reich, ed., *An Historical Encyclopedia of the Arab-Israeli Conflict* (Westport, Conn: Greenwood Press, 1996), and Bernard Reich, ed., *Arab-Israeli Conflict and Conciliation: A Documentary History* (Westport, Conn., and London: Praeger, 1995).

On the history of Israel consult Howard M. Sachar, *A History of Israel: From the Rise of Zionism to Our Time* (New York: Knopf, 1976) and *A History of Israel, II: From the Aftermath of the Yom Kippur War* (Oxford: Oxford University Press, 1987). The mandate period is discussed in J. C. Hurewitz's *The Struggle for Palestine* (New York: Norton, 1950) and Christopher Syke's *Crossroads to Israel* (Cleveland: World Publishing, 1965). Shlomo Avineri's *The Making of Modern Zionism: The Intellectual Origins of the Jewish State* (New York: Basic Books, 1981) and Walter Laqueur's *A History of Zionism* (New York: Holt, Rinehart and Winston, 1972) provide a comprehensive history and examination of the Zionist movement, its origins, and its diverse ideological trends.

Studies of Israel's parliament include Asher Zidon, *Knesset: The Parliament of Israel* (New York: Herzl Press, 1967); Eliahu S. Likhovski, *Israel's Parliament: The Law of the Knesset* (Oxford: Oxford University Press, 1971); Gregory S. Mahler, *The Knesset: Parliament in the Israeli Political System* (Rutherford, N.J.: Fairleigh Dickenson University Press, 1981); and Samuel Sager, *The Parliamentary System of Israel* (Syracuse, N.Y.: Syracuse University Press, 1985).

Various aspects of Israeli politics and policy have been the subject of specialized studies, including Myron J. Aronoff, *Israeli Visions and Divisions: Cultural Change and Political Conflict* (New Brunswick, N.J.: Transaction Books, 1989); Marcia Drezon-Tepler, *Interest Groups and Political Change in Israel* (Albany: State University of New York Press, 1990); Dan Horowitz and Moshe Lissak, *Trouble in Utopia: The Overburdened Polity of Israel* (Albany: State University of New York Press, 1989); Bernard Reich and Gershon R. Kieval, eds., *Israel Faces the Future* (New York: Praeger, 1986) and *Israeli Politics in the 1990s: Key Domestic and Foreign Policy Factors* (Westport, Conn.: Greenwood Press, 1991); and Ehud Sprinzak, *The Ascendance of Israel's Radical Right* (New York: Oxford University Press, 1991). Political parties are the particular focus of Peter Y. Medding, *Mapai in Israel: Political Organization and Government in a New Society* (Cambridge: Cambridge University Press, 1972); Peter Y. Medding, *The Founding of Israeli Democracy, 1948–1988* (London: Oxford University Press, 1989); and Yonathan Shapiro, *The Road to Power: Herut Party in Israel* (Albany: State University of New York Press, 1991).

Studies of the salient domestic, political, economic, and social issues include: S. N. Eisenstadt, *The Transformation of Israeli Society* (Boulder: Westview Press, 1985); Yair Aharoni, *The Israeli Economy: Dreams and Realities* (London: Routledge, 1991); and Yoram Ben-Porath, ed., *The Israeli Economy: Maturing Through Crises* (Cambridge, Mass.: Harvard University Press, 1986). The relationship of religion and the state is discussed in Charles S. Liebman and Eliezer Don-Yehiya, *Civil Religion in Israel: Traditional Judaism and Political Culture in the Jewish*

State (Berkeley: University of California Press, 1983). Jacob M. Landau, in *The Arabs in Israel: A Political Study* (London: Oxford University Press, 1969), presents a comprehensive survey and analysis of the role of the Arabs in Israel. An alternative perspective is provided by Sabri Jiryis, *The Arabs in Israel* (New York: Monthly Review Press, 1976).

For an overview of Israel's foreign policy, see Aaron S. Klieman, *Israel and the World After Forty Years* (Elmsford, N.Y.: Pergamon, 1989), *Israel's Global Reach: Arms Sales as Diplomacy* (Washington: Pergamon-Brassey's, 1985), and *Statecraft in the Dark: Israel's Practice of Quiet Diplomacy* (Boulder: Westview Press, 1988); Ilan Peleg, *Begin's Foreign Policy, 1977–1983: Israel's Move to the Right* (Westport, Conn.: Greenwood Press, 1987); Bernard Reich and Gershon R. Kieval, eds., *Israeli National Security Policy: Political Actors and Perspectives* (Westport, Conn.: Greenwood Press, 1988). *Israel's Foreign Relations, Selected Documents, 1947–1997,* sixteen volumes (Jerusalem: Ministry of Foreign Affairs, 1976–1999) provides the major documents of Israel's foreign policy from its inception through 1999. Gershon R. Kieval, *Party Politics in Israel and the Occupied Territories* (Westport, Conn.: Greenwood Press, 1983), provides a detailed analysis of Israel's policy. Bernard Reich, in *Quest for Peace: United States-Israel Relations and the Arab-Israeli Conflict* (New Brunswick, N.J.: Transaction Books, 1977), deals with Israel's relations with the United States in the context of the efforts to resolve the Arab–Israeli conflict. Bernard Reich, *The United States and Israel: Influence in the Special Relationship* (New York: Praeger, 1984), examines Israel's crucial links with the United States. Bernard Reich, *Securing the Covenant: United States-Israel Relations After the Cold War* (Westport, Conn.: Greenwood Press, 1995) examines the special relationship of these allies.

Yigal Allon, *The Making of Israel's Army* (New York: Bantam Books, 1971), and Amos Perlmutter, *Military and Politics in Israel: Nation-Building and Role Expansion* (London: Frank Cass, 1969), consider the role of the military. For a general overview of the IDF, its background and development, see Ze'ev Schiff, *A History of the Israeli Army (1870–1974)* (New York: Simon and Schuster, 1974).

The government of Israel is a prolific publisher of high-quality materials, such as the *Israel Government Year Book* and the *Statistical Abstract of Israel,* that would serve the interested reader well.

12

The Palestinians

Ann Mosely Lesch

The Palestinians are central players in the Arab–Israeli drama. The core issue involves the conflicting claims to the same piece of land made by Israeli Jews and Palestinian Arabs. Palestinians believe that the creation of a separate state for the Jewish minority at the expense of the Arab majority, the denial of Palestinians' right of self-determination, and the inability of Palestinian refugees to return to their homes or regain their personal assets following their vain attempt to recover their homeland in 1948 all constitute a grave injustice that must be assuaged for the conflict to be resolved.

The terms of assuagement have evolved since 1948 when Palestinians sought the restoration of all their land and properties. After the Israelis occupied the rest of Palestine in 1967, the consensus evolved that any restoration must at least include a sovereign Palestinian state on the West Bank and Gaza, and that Israel must at least recognize its responsibilities toward the refugees in a satisfactory way.

A second major factor in the Palestinian quest for statehood is its ambiguous relationship with neighboring Arab states. From the outset, the Palestinian cause has been espoused as a pan-Arab cause. Nevertheless, each Arab government necessarily gives priority to its own foreign policy interests in how it approaches the Arab–Israeli conflict. Arab states have collectively given political, economic, and military support to the Palestinians, but when Palestinian priorities clash with their own interests, Palestinian interests per force suffer. Moreover, Arab governments often seek to control the Palestinian national movement, and serious tension can arise when Palestinians' efforts to assert their independent political will do not conform to competing Arab state interests.

The Ottoman Period

The contest for control over the land of Palestine began long before the Israeli occupation of the West Bank and Gaza Strip in June 1967 and even before 1948,
when the Israeli war for independence resulted in the dispersion and exile of most
Arab residents. It can be traced to the late nineteenth century, when the area was
part of the Ottoman Empire. At that time, the concept of Zionism began to gain
support among European Jews, who suffered from discrimination. Some Jews
concluded that the only way to end this discrimination would be to establish an
independent Jewish state in their ancestral homeland. These Zionists organized
the World Zionist Organization (formed in 1897), the Jewish National Fund, and
offices in Jaffa and Jerusalem that aided immigrants.

As early as 1891, a group of Muslim and Christian notables in Palestine cabled
Istanbul to urge the government to prohibit immigration and land purchases by
European Jews, since the petitioners feared that large-scale immigration would
displace the Arab residents. After the Young Turk revolution of 1908, middle and
upper class Palestinians expressed their concerns through the parliament in Istanbul as well as through newly permitted political and cultural societies and newspapers. The experience that Arabs gained in municipalities, district councils, and religious institutions fueled their aspirations for self-rule. Elite families' authority
was buttressed by extensive landholdings and involvement in international trade.
The rural majority—illiterate and relatively isolated—shared the elite's unease at
the increasing number of Jewish agricultural villages. Palestinians successfully persuaded the Turks to curtail Jewish immigration and land buying.

By the time that World War I broke out in 1914, the Jewish community in
Palestine (Yishuv) comprised 11 percent of the total inhabitants (about 75,000 out
of 690,000). That was a visible change since 1880, when the Yishuv was 6 percent
of the population (35,000 out of 485,000). Nonetheless, the community's political
influence inside Palestine was limited.

The Mandate Period

The situation was transformed when the war ended. The British army and allied
Arab forces defeated and dismantled the Ottoman Empire; the British army occupied Palestine. Arab leaders thought that Palestine would be included in the area
promised independence by Sir Henry McMahon, the British high commissioner
for Egypt, in letters he wrote during 1915–1916 to Sharif Hussein of Makkah.
Hussein and McMahon had agreed that Arab independence would be recognized
by the British if the Arabs launched a revolt against the Ottoman Empire. Indeed,
young Palestinian men volunteered for the British and Arab forces on the assumption that this would hasten their liberation. The British, however, promised France
that Palestine would come under international (European) rule and, in the Balfour

Declaration, offered to support "the establishment in Palestine of a national home for the Jewish people."

That proclamation, issued on November 2, 1917, and later incorporated into the British Mandate for Palestine, transformed the balance of power between the Arab majority and the Jewish minority. The declaration gave the Zionist movement its long-sought legal status. Even though the declaration included the qualification that "nothing shall be done which may prejudice the civil and religious rights of the existing non-Jewish communities in Palestine," it was clearly incompatible with the McMahon correspondence.

The Arab politicians in Palestine had assumed that they would gain independence when Ottoman rule disintegrated, either by establishing a separate state or by merging with neighboring Arab lands. They felt betrayed when Britain imposed the mandate and they immediately objected to the Zionist organization's privileged status as well as to the alienation of the land. In the 1930s, with thousands of Jews fleeing Nazi Germany, their fear of Jewish immigration deepened. The Jewish population grew from 11 percent of the population in 1914 to 28 percent in 1936. Immigration reached a high in 1935, when 60,000 Jews came to Palestine.

During the 1920s, the nationalist movement was led by Palestinian elites who, for the most part, employed nonviolent tactics. During the 1930s, however, radicalized youth and labor activists goaded the leadership to use strikes and violence to confront the British and the Zionists. Palestinians launched a general strike in 1936 that they sustained for an unprecedented six months. The strike was followed by a widespread rural revolt that lasted nearly two years. The rebellion welled up from the depths of Palestinian society—unemployed urban workers, displaced peasants crowded into towns, debt-ridden villagers. Most merchants and professionals in the towns supported the uprising, and the elite formed an Arab Higher Committee, which presented Arab demands to the British administration.

The British responded by trying to crush the uprising. The Arab Higher Committee, which the British had never recognized, was banned in 1937. Its members were jailed or fled into exile, leaving the revolt without effective leadership. In July 1937, a Royal Commission proposed territorial partition, which would create a Jewish state in just under 30 percent of Palestine, leave Jerusalem under British control, and link the remainder to Transjordan. Most Palestinians rejected the partition plan, which would deny them independence and expel those living in Jewish-held territories. In May 1939, Britain did an about-face and proposed to place sharp limits on Jewish immigration and land purchases and create one state in which Arabs and Jews would share power. Palestinians were wary of this proposal, even though it would enable them to remain the majority in the entire territory. In any event, the power-sharing formula was unworkable at this late date, given the intensity of both peoples' nationalisms. The Yishuv, which had welcomed the prospect of statehood in 1937, was furious when it was withdrawn only two years later and became more militant in demanding independence, particularly with Nazi persecution expanded in Europe.

After the British decapitated the Palestinian national movement and forcibly suppressed the revolt, Palestinians had no coherent organizations or skilled leaders with which to press for self-determination, and Arab states, for the most part still in the last stages of gaining their own independence, were too involved in domestic issues to be of much support. Jewish violence against the British and Arabs, on the other hand, increased. Finally, in 1947, the British, forsaking any hope of a peaceful settlement, announced that they were ending the mandate and turning Palestine over to the United Nations.

In November 1947, the United Nations passed a partition plan of its own that created a Jewish state on 55 percent of Palestine, even though Jewish land holdings comprised less than 7 percent of the total land surface or 12 percent of arable land.[1] The Jewish state would have nearly as many Arab as Jewish residents. The Arab state would control only about 40 percent of Palestine; deprived of the best agricultural land and seaports, it would retain only Galilee, the central mountains, and the Gaza coast. The United Nations would administer Jerusalem, set aside as an international zone.

The Palestinians rejected the partition plan and tried to defend their homeland, but their village-based militias could not stand up to Jewish forces, who seized control of nearly all the areas assigned to the Jewish state during a five-week campaign in April and May, 1948. That campaign forced 300,000 Palestinians to flee from their homes in villages and cities such as Tiberias, Haifa, and Jaffa.

Following the British withdrawal on May 14 and the unilateral declaration of independence by Israel, Arab states sent in troops, and full-scale fighting erupted. They were no match for the better trained and better equipped Israeli forces, and when an armistice was signed ending the fighting in 1949, only 23 percent of Palestine remained in Arab hands, and an additional 400,000 had become refugees. The Egyptian army held the Gaza Strip, and Transjordanian forces held the West Bank, including East Jerusalem. Nazareth was the only important city in which the Israeli government let Arabs remain, due to its significance to European and American Christians.

From a humanitarian perspective, the worst result of the fighting was the uprooting of three quarters of a million Palestinians from the territory that became Israel. The Israelis refused to allow them to return to their homes, to offer any reparation for their belongings, or to accept any responsibility for their plight, thereby creating the Palestinian refugee problem that continues to be a major impediment to peace.

Fragmentation in Exile

In comprehending the Palestinian situation following 1948, three phenomena should be borne in mind. First, Palestinian society was changed profoundly by this trauma. The society was previously highly stratified and largely rural, with a powerful landed aristocracy and a substantial class of urban merchants. Overnight, Palestinian peasants were forced into wage labor, the elite lost the land that underpinned its power, and merchants lost their livelihoods. In time, dispersal transformed Palestinians into a mobile but highly insecure people among whom educational attainment and political activism ranked high as criteria for social standing.

Second, the physical dispersion made it difficult to reestablish a coherent political center. Living under different authoritarian regimes and subject to restrictions on political expression, the Palestinians suffered from constant pressure toward fragmentation.

Third, Palestinians' political aims evolved significantly. At first Palestinians were determined to regain all of their country, but starting in the 1970s an increasing number conceded that territorial partition—the establishment of a Palestinian state alongside Israel—was the most that could be achieved. The concept of partition remains controversial, but for many it seemed the only way to ensure their national survival.

The Palestinian community was shattered by the fighting and flight in 1948–1949, which they called *al-nakba* (the disaster). At least 750,000 Arabs fled from the area that became Israel. Fewer than half of the 1.2 million Palestinians remained in their own homes: 150,000 inside Israel and the rest on the West Bank (annexed by Jordan) and in the Gaza Strip (administered by Egypt). The situation facing the Palestinians in the countries to which they fled varied considerably. However, there were certain common elements in the political realm, in their psychological reactions, and in the attitudes of the host countries toward them.

At the political level, the landed and professional political elites lost credibility and legitimacy. Their disunity and ineffectiveness were blamed for *al-nakba*. Only the village-level structures remained somewhat intact, since family and local institutions helped to organize life in the refugee camps. Lacking agricultural land— and private ownership of homes—the village structure was severely distorted in the refugee camps.

The refugees underwent profound psychological transformations. At first they felt lost, disoriented, and disrupted from their familiar ways of life. The humiliation of being landless contributed to their sense of alienation. The older generation succumbed to an ever-lengthening wait for *al-awda* (the return).

The sense of alienation was increased by the ambivalence of host countries toward the refugees. Although the commercial and professional skills of the Palestinian middle class were initially welcomed by the Arab states, the mass of displaced farmers and laborers could not be absorbed. Moreover, politically active Palestinians resisted efforts to cancel their refugee status, since that could undermine their right to reclaim Palestine.

Controls imposed by the host countries took different forms. In Israel, Arabs gained citizenship but lived under strict military administration until 1966. The movement of Arab residents was closely regulated, access to education and employment was restricted, and political activities were curtailed. In the Gaza Strip, the Egyptian military government maintained tight control over the restive Palestinians, of whom 80 percent lived in refugee camps. Egypt did establish a largely elected national assembly in Gaza in the late 1950s as a political safety valve. Palestinians living in Syria had the same access to jobs and schools as Syrian citizens, but their ability to travel abroad was curtailed. The Lebanese authorities were especially restrictive, denying Palestinians the right to study in public schools or obtain permanent employment. Lebanese troops entered the refugee camps to arrest residents. Friction developed between the Palestinians, who were largely Sunni Muslim by religion, and those Lebanese politicians who sought to retain the special status of the Maronite Christian minority; granting political rights to the Palestinians could upset the confessional balance.

Life was least disrupted on the West Bank, where most people remained in their original homes and the residents gained Jordanian citizenship. Palestinians staffed the administrative and educational systems in Jordan and developed many of its commercial enterprises. But the regime never trusted them with senior posts in sensitive ministries and in the armed forces, and their loyalty to the monarchy remained tenuous. Moreover, the West Bank faced economic hardship as trade with Europe through Mediterranean ports was blocked, villages lost valuable agricultural land to Israel, and the Jordanian government favored the East Bank for industrial and agricultural development.

During the 1950s, Palestinians were attracted to the various forms of pan-Arabism that asserted that Palestine could only be regained if the Arab world were united politically. The idea of Arab unity received a blow in 1961 when the union between Egypt and Syria dissolved after less than three years. Moreover, the ideological cold war between Egypt and Saudi Arabia—played out on the battlefields of North Yemen—polarized the Arab world. The belief in Arab military strength was destroyed in June 1967 when the Israeli army defeated the combined Arab forces in a lightning strike and seized the Golan Heights from Syria, the West Bank from Jordan, and the Gaza Strip and Sinai peninsula from Egypt.

That disillusionment accelerated processes that were already under way among Palestinians. Their feeling that they were discriminated against by fellow Arabs and their disappointment with the rhetoric of Arab regimes led many Palestinians to set aside their own passivity and reject their dependence on Arab states. They sought to transform their situation through their own actions rather than wait for Arab governments to rescue them. Small underground guerrilla cells sprang up in the early 1960s. Al-Fatah, founded in Kuwait in 1959 by the prosperous engineer Yasir Arafat and several professional colleagues who had been student activists in Egypt in the early 1950s, launched its first raid into Israel on New Year's Eve 1965. The fedayeen (guerrillas) had a twofold strategy: They asserted that self-reliance was the route to liberation, as Algerians had just demonstrated in their successful eight-year war against France, and they sought to catalyze popular mobilization that would shame the Arab rulers into fighting Israel.

Evolution of the PLO

Arab governments, aware of the renewed discontent among Palestinians, tried to channel that discontent by forming the Palestine Liberation Organization (PLO) in 1964. Although its leadership was middle and upper class and closely circumscribed by Egypt and other Arab governments, the PLO nevertheless represented a critical step in the process of reestablishing the Palestinians' political center. The first Palestinian National Council (PNC), a kind of parliament in exile that convened in Jerusalem in May 1964, adopted an uncompromising political charter. Just as the Palestinians before 1948 had rejected partition, so too the Palestinians refused in 1964 to acknowledge the right of the state of Israel to exist. The charter called for a return to the status quo that existed before 1948 so that the refugees could reclaim their homes and knit back together the threads of their lives torn in *al-nakba*.

The June 1967 war, which pitted Israel against Egypt, Syria, and Jordan, once more transformed the Palestinians' situation. Israel gained control over all of pre-1948 Palestine and almost half of all the Palestinians when its armed forces seized the West Bank (including East Jerusalem) and the Gaza Strip. The occupation severed ties between the West Bank and Jordan, although limited trade and travel continued. Gaza became isolated from Egypt but was suddenly linked to the West Bank. The residents of those occupied territories could communicate with Palestinian citizens in Israel, enabling families to rediscover each other after nearly twenty years' separation.

The war discredited the Arab states and their armed forces. When guerrilla warfare escalated in its wake, Palestinians felt that the fedayeen defied Israeli power more bravely than the Arab states' heavily armed troops. Volunteers rushed to join the guerrillas, particularly after they withstood Israel's attack on Karameh (Jordan) in March 1968. During 1968–1969 the guerrilla organizations gained control over the PLO. Amendments to the PLO charter at the fourth PNC (1968) reflected the shift: They emphasized popular armed struggle, rejected Zionism and the partition of Palestine, termed Judaism "a religion . . . not an independent nationality" (Article 20), and called for "the total liberation of Palestine" (Article 21). The charter upheld Arab unity but emphasized that, just as the PLO would "not interfere in the internal affairs of any Arab state" (Article 27), it "reject[ed] all forms of intervention, trusteeship and subordination" (Article 28) by Arab governments. The charter could only be amended by a two-thirds vote of the more than 400 members of the PNC, at a special session.

At the fifth PNC in February 1969, the guerrilla groups ousted the old-guard politicians and selected Arafat to chair the PLO Executive Committee, since Fatah was the largest and politically most active guerrilla organization. Fatah called for the establishment of a "democratic, non-sectarian Palestine state in which all groups will have equal rights and obligations irrespective of race, color, and creed." As chair of the PLO, Arafat commanded the Palestine Liberation Army (PLA). PLA units had been adjuncts to the Egyptian, Jordanian, and Syrian armies, but Arafat tried to make them autonomous of the Arab regimes.

By June 1970 the Unified Command of the guerrilla groups included Fatah, the largest; the Popular Front for the Liberation of Palestine (PFLP), founded by Greek Orthodox physician George Habash in December 1967; the Popular Front for the Liberation of Palestine-General Command (PFLP-GC), founded at the end of 1968 by the former Syrian army captain, Ahmed Jibril, who broke away from the PFLP; the Democratic Front for the Liberation of Palestine (DFLP), founded in February 1969 when its Jordanian head, Naif Hawatmeh, left the PFLP; the Syrian-sponsored Saiqa, formed in 1968; and the Iraqi-sponsored Arab Liberation Front (ALF), formed in 1969. The PLO provided an umbrella for the diverse groups, but they often worked at cross-purposes. Fatah focused on freeing Palestine from Israeli rule and sought amicable relations with Arab governments. In contrast, the PFLP and the DFLP worked to overthrow conservative Arab regimes prior to liberating Palestine. Saiqa and ALF were controlled by rival branches of the Ba'th Party, which called for Arab unity rather than Palestinian nationalism. The groups also differed over tactics: Fatah, Saiqa, and DFLP denounced PFLP and PFLP-GC for hurting innocent third parties when they hijacked airplanes and launched other acts of terror against civilians.

Immediately after the 1967 war, Arab regimes felt compelled to support the rapidly growing Palestinian guerrilla movement. The Palestinian cause retained so much popular support that criticism was unthinkable. Nonetheless, Egypt and Jordan accepted U.N. Security Council Resolution 242 of November 1967, which accorded Israel the right to live in peace and security behind essentially its prewar borders. This appeared the only way to regain control over the territories they had lost in the June war. That resolution mentioned the Palestinians only as refugees, not as a people with political rights.

The contradiction between PLO aims and Arab governments' policies became clear in 1970. Washington proposed a negotiated settlement in which Jordan and Egypt would regain substantial land that was taken by Israel in 1967; once again, the Palestinians were ignored. When the PLO denounced the plan, it collided with the two Arab regimes on which Palestinians relied most heavily.

The PLO had become a state-within-a-state in Jordan and used its territory as the base from which to attack Israel. Its presence challenged the authority of King Hussein, particularly when radical Palestinian movements called for the overthrow of the monarchy. When Fatah organized demonstrations against the U.S. peace plan and the PFLP hijacked airplanes to an airfield in Jordan, the Jordanian armed forces forced the king to crush the Palestinian movement militarily. The Jordanian army defeated the PLO in a bloody showdown in September 1970, seized control over the refugee camps, and forced the guerrillas to flee to Lebanon in July 1971.

The civil war in Jordan revealed the fragility of the PLO's military structure and the incoherence of its political strategy. The PLO could not find a secure base from which to strike Israel. It could not stand up to the Arab regimes when their interests clashed. Its maximalist goals could not be sustained by its actual power.

Nonetheless, in the 1970s, the fedayeen reemerged in Lebanon, where the PLO developed a sophisticated organizational structure that extended far beyond guerrilla operations. PLO auxiliaries provided medical services in the refugee camps and created much-needed jobs by opening workshops and light industries. Affiliated federations of workers, engineers, writers, journalists, teachers, students, and women mobilized Palestinian communities throughout the Middle East. The Palestine National Fund handled fund-raising, although Arafat's insistence on retaining personal control over the disbursement of funds led to mounting criticism of corruption.

Palestinian despair was signaled by terrorism launched by Black September commandos—their name drawn from Jordan's September 1970 attack on the PLO. Operations included the assassination of the Jordanian prime minister in Cairo in November 1971 and the kidnapping and murder of eleven Israeli athletes at the Olympic games in Munich in September 1972. Guerrillas raided northern Israel from strongholds in south Lebanon, against which Israel retaliated with aerial and artillery bombardments of refugee camps and Lebanese villages.

The experiences of Palestinians living under Israeli military occupation differed significantly from those outside. The former had to face the harsh reality of living under military occupation that restricted movement and made major changes in the educational and judicial systems. Israelis confiscated nearly half the land and began constructing Jewish settlements, measures that violated international law regarding occupied territories. The Israelis attempted to obscure the violation by changing the nomenclature to "Judea and Samaria" or "the administered territories." East Jerusalem and extensive West Bank territory around it were unilaterally joined with Israeli-held West Jerusalem and proclaimed the united capital of Israel, an indication of the government's ultimate intention to annex large parts of what it considered its historic homeland.

The Israelis clamped down on both civil and violent resistance, deporting mayors, religious leaders, teachers, lawyers, and doctors who articulated residents' political grievances and organized boycotts and strikes. They banned political meetings and political parties and initiated heavy censorship of the press. Israeli military courts sentenced to lengthy prison terms Palestinians who joined political organizations or used violence. Despite these harsh punishments, a full-scale rebellion engulfed the Gaza Strip in the late 1960s.

In the wake of Black September, Palestinians living under the occupation were severely demoralized; political leaders began to reassess their political strategy and consider accepting a Palestinian state in the West Bank, Gaza, and East Jerusalem. A few were attracted by King Hussein's proposal to form a federation between the

East and West Banks, which would accord the West Bank Palestinians a higher political status within Jordan than they had held before 1967.

The PLO responded by revising its goals. The eleventh PNC (January 1973)
resolved in secret to form an umbrella political structure in the occupied territories, called the Palestine National Front (PNF), which would use political rather
than military means to end the Israeli occupation. The PNF sought to help residents overcome their demoralization and build a cohesive national political movement. The PNF encompassed all the political groups that opposed a return to Jordanian rule and that accepted the concept of a separate state alongside Israel. Its
principal components came from Fatah and the Communist Party (CP), the only
Palestinian political party that had supported a two-state solution, ever since 1947.

The Arab-Israeli war in October 1973 led to further shifts in Palestinian attitudes. Whereas the 1967 war altered the territorial map, the 1973 war began to alter the psychological map. Moreover, PLO leaders feared that Egypt and Syria
might sign peace accords with Israel that would ignore Palestinian rights, especially if the PLO failed to articulate a realistic program.

In June 1974 the twelfth PNC advocated the establishment of an "independent
combatant national authority for the people over every part of Palestinian territory that is liberated."[2] This somewhat bellicose language in fact represented a major shift toward accepting Israel's right to exist in return for statehood. Even
though the PNC did not formally accept a permanent peace with Israel, hard-line
groups such as the PFLP withdrew from the PLO's Executive Committee, accusing Arafat of recognizing Israel. For Israel, the statement did not go far enough.

It did legitimize the PLO internationally, however. The Arab summit in Rabat
in October confirmed the right of the Palestinian people to self-determination
and confirmed the PLO as the sole legitimate representative of the Palestinian
people. Two years later nationalist politicians swept the elections for municipal
councils on the West Bank, supporting the PNF and calling for the end to occupation. In November, the PLO's international stature was further enhanced when
Arafat addressed the U.N. General Assembly and the PLO obtained observer status at the United Nations.

The PLO took another step toward a negotiated peace settlement at the thirteenth PNC (March 1977), which stressed the Palestinians' "right to establish their
independent national state on their own land" alongside Israel.[3] The effort was rebuffed by Israel, however, and was sidetracked by Egyptian President Anwar Sadat's bilateral negotiations with Israel, by the civil war in Lebanon, and by the Israeli invasions of Lebanon in 1978 and 1982.

Camp David

After the 1973 war, Palestinians hoped that multilateral negotiations under U.N.
auspices would not only enable Egypt and Syria to regain land but also facilitate

their own effort to achieve statehood. That hope was dashed by the Egyptian-Israeli peace treaty in March 1979. Egypt removed itself from the military arena and regained Sinai in return for establishing diplomatic relations with Israel. Syria, Jordan, and the PLO were left isolated, their strategic posture severely compromised.

The Egyptian-Israeli treaty called for negotiations to establish a five-year transitional period of Palestinian self-rule in the territories.[4] However, the Israelis subsequently undercut the idea of self-rule by accelerating construction of Jewish settlements in the territories, declaring a unified Jerusalem to be Israel's eternal capital, annexing the Golan Heights, and launching an air raid that destroyed a partly built Iraqi nuclear reactor in June 1981.

The Camp David framework compelled the Israeli government to acknowledge both the applicability of U.N. Security Council Resolution 242 to the territories and "the legitimate rights of the Palestinian people." But the framework did not address the issue of Jerusalem, admit the unity of the Palestinian people, or mention the status of land and Israeli settlements. The framework also assumed that Jordan would help to implement the agreement; the PLO would not be included at any stage.

Subsequent U.S. and Egyptian statements stressed that autonomy provided an opportunity for Palestinians to end the political impasse, for trust to be built on both sides, and for a base to be laid for an eventual independent Palestinian state or at least confederation with Jordan. But the Israeli government made autonomy seem a trap, especially as it stressed that all state land and water resources would remain under Israeli control, settlement by Israelis would continue, the Palestinian council would administer but not legislate, and the military government would be withdrawn but not abolished. Israeli armed forces would patrol the territories and, in the final stage of negotiations, Israel would claim sovereignty.

Since Israel controlled the land and since Washington could not convince Israel to stop constructing settlements, Palestinians feared that accepting the plan would legitimize perpetual Israeli rule. Most West Bank residents also opposed renewing formal links with Jordan and argued that the PLO was their sole representative. They called for self-determination, national independence, and sovereignty, with complete Israeli withdrawal to the pre-1967 lines.

On October 6, 1981, Anwar Sadat was assassinated, and shortly after autonomy talks broke down. Israel and Egypt retained diplomatic relations, however, and in April 1982, Israel withdrew from Sinai, gaining a virtually demilitarized buffer zone while enabling Egypt to regain political sovereignty over the peninsula.

The new Likud-led government in Israel immediately launched an all-out campaign to crush the PLO in Lebanon and destroy its influence in the occupied territories. Military authorities closed nearly all the elected municipal councils on the West Bank and the appointed municipalities in the Gaza Strip. Israeli colonels ruled the towns, thereby removing an important buffer between the public and the military government. The change provoked heated Palestinian protests and caused a marked deterioration in services provided to urban residents.

The Expulsion from Beirut

No longer feeling vulnerable to Arab counterattack, Israel invaded Lebanon in June 1982. The backdrop of the invasion was the protracted Lebanese civil war, which erupted in 1975, and threatened to undermine the territorial base that the PLO had established there after its expulsion from Jordan. The PLO tried to avoid taking sides in the internal strife, but quickly found itself the target of the Phalange, a Maronite militia controlled by the Gemayel family. The Phalange argued that Lebanese independence was compromised by the PLO's state-within-a-state and charged the PLO with aiding radical, secular groups based in Muslim and Druze communities.

By 1982, Israel had already intervened directly in south Lebanon, where it had established a security zone jointly controlled by its army and the South Lebanese Army (SLA), a Lebanese militia that Israel fully funded and equipped. It had also provided arms and funds to the Phalange. The June invasion was partly designed to bring Israel's Phalange ally, Bashir Gemayel, to power as president of Lebanon. The principal aim of the invasion, however, was to destroy the PLO's military and political infrastructure.

During the sixty-seven-day Israeli siege of Beirut, Arafat negotiated the withdrawal of PLO forces from the Lebanese capital. In August, he transferred the PLO headquarters to Tunis; PLO troops were evacuated to several distant Arab countries. Some PLO forces remained in east and north Lebanon, but Palestinians living in refugee camps near Beirut were no longer guarded by the PLO. Phalangists, monitored by Israeli troops, attacked the defenseless refugees soon after, killing hundreds in the houses and streets of Sabra and Shatila refugee camps.

The PLO was severely divided and weakened by the Israeli invasion, especially when several Fatah officers, led by Abu Musa, blamed Arafat for the collapse of the Palestinian forces in southern Lebanon. The split in the PLO suited the interests of the Syrian government, which sought to dominate the PLO. Syria unleashed Abu Musa's forces against Arafat loyalists in bitter battles within refugee camps in north Lebanon during 1983. Damascus also hosted the PFLP, DFLP, and PFLP-GC, whose leaders denounced Arafat for being willing to negotiate with Israel.

Nonetheless, Arafat reinvigorated his diplomacy and formed a counterweight to Syria by aligning with his erstwhile antagonists, Egypt and Jordan. He made a dramatic visit to Egypt in December 1983 after he had fled the internecine fighting in Lebanon. Arafat also worked out a negotiating formula with King Hussein in February 1985, after he held the seventeenth PNC (November 1984) in Amman. The two leaders accepted the "land for peace" formula articulated in U.N. Resolution 242 and called for a confederation comprised of Jordan and a Palestinian state on the West Bank and Gaza Strip. The joint accord was intended to appeal to the United States, which insisted on Jordan's playing a major role in negotiations and rejected full independence for the Palestinians. Washington, however, was not willing to meet with Palestinian representatives, even jointly with Jordanians. This took the pressure off Israel to respond to the initiative.

Meanwhile, hard-liners in the PLO derided Arafat for believing that he could achieve results through diplomacy. Moreover, regional tensions escalated after the Israeli air raid on the PLO headquarters in Tunis on October 1, 1985, and the hijacking of the *Achille Lauro* cruise ship soon after by a member of Abu al-Abbas's Popular Liberation Front (PLF). Although the PLF was a member of the PLO's Executive Committee, the PLF operation was intended to undermine the possibility of negotiations and to damage Arafat's credibility. The multiple pressures meant that Arafat could not make further diplomatic concessions. Given the failure of Washington and Tel Aviv to accept the joint initiative and the intra-PLO pressure on Arafat to withdraw his support, King Hussein set the initiative aside in February 1986.

The divisions in Palestinian ranks and contradictory pressures placed on the PLO by Syria, Egypt, and Jordan were mirrored on the West Bank and Gaza. Given Israel's ban on political parties, the jockeying for influence was reflected in elections for student councils in local universities, trade union boards, and directors of chambers of commerce. When the military government seized control over most of the municipalities in 1982, Palestinians responded by developing myriad local-level institutions to provide rudimentary services and empower communities. Medical and agricultural committees became particularly active. They were initiated by political movements, notably the CP, PFLP, and DFLP. Medical programs focused on preventive measures, such as improving hygiene, education, and prenatal care. Agricultural committees, operating in the absence of an agricultural bank or effective government agricultural extension programs, provided seeds, seedlings, loans, and technical advice to individual farmers and cooperatives. Women's committees provided day care for children of working mothers as well as literacy programs; these were often coordinated with the medical and agricultural efforts. Associations of journalists, writers, and artists promoted exhibits, although the army often raided them and seized paintings and books. Theatrical troupes presented plays with veiled political messages, despite Israeli censorship and frequent disruptions of performances by Israeli security forces.

The military government tried to create or support alternative political structures, notably the village leagues and the Muslim Brotherhood. The Israeli-financed and armed village leagues claimed to represent the rural areas, but their credibility was undermined by their funding from Israel and by their members' actions as armed vigilantes who controlled and harassed fellow Palestinians. Moreover, the increase in land expropriation for Israeli settlements angered farm families and damaged the credibility of the leagues' claim that cooperation with Israel would benefit Palestinians. Indeed, by the late 1980s, Israel seized more than half of the West Bank lands and 40 percent of the Gaza Strip.

The Muslim Brotherhood, a long-established Islamist movement, viewed Israeli rule as a tribulation brought on the Palestinian Muslims for deviating from their religion. Islamists emphasized that Palestinians had to return to personal piety before political change could occur. They opposed the PLO's secular orientation and the prominent role played by Palestinian Communists in local political and cultural life. In the early 1980s, the military government tolerated the brotherhood's activities since their primary targets were leftist and nationalist Palestinians. The brotherhood even physically attacked voluntary organizations and student groups that represented nationalist or leftist trends. Israel also allowed the brotherhood to establish charities, clinics, and educational programs that broadened its public appeal.

The Intifada

Although Palestinians appeared divided and demoralized in the 1980s, a profound transformation was taking place at the grassroots level that reinvigorated the national movement. The committee networks that tried to solve economic and social problems brought urban professionals in contact with residents of refugee camps, villages, and poor quarters in the towns. Palestinians realized that even though they could not employ violence to expel the Israelis, they could exploit a mobilized public to shift the political advantage to their side.

During 1987 Palestinian strategy crystallized in a way that helped the Palestinian effort to mount focused protests against Israeli rule. The eighteenth PNC (April 1987) restored unity to the PLO. PFLP and DFLP, concerned that their boycott of PLO institutions had only resulted in isolating them from the people, resumed their seats on the Executive Committee. And for the first time, the dovish Communist Party gained a seat on the Executive Committee. Only the numerically insignificant Abu Musa dissidents and PFLP-GC remained outside the PLO, with the PFLP-GC launching a series of terrorist attacks in Europe to promote its militant agenda. Nevertheless, the enlarged PLO strengthened Arafat's hand in the Arab world and in the occupied territories.

Partly as a result of these developments, the various nationalist groups inside the occupied territories began to cooperate more effectively. Their social and cultural organizations and trade unions started to coordinate activities and regain a sense of common purpose. Moreover, Islamist-oriented groups began to alter their priorities. The Islamic Jihad, a new organization whose members were mostly former prisoners from Gaza, denounced the Muslim Brotherhood's political passivity. In the summer of 1987, Islamic Jihad militants killed a senior Israeli military officer in Gaza city and engaged in shoot-outs with Israeli troops that sparked demonstrations at the local Islamic university. Islamic Jihad's operations electrified the atmosphere in Gaza.

In contrast to the enhanced coordination among Palestinians, the preoccupation of the Arab states was with other issues. The Arab summit meeting in Amman in November 1987 focused on reinforcing Arab support for Iraq in the protracted

Iran-Iraq war. King Hussein feared that Iran might overwhelm Iraq and sought to rally Arab support, including persuading several countries to restore relations with Cairo despite its peace treaty with Israel.

Palestinians were shocked at the summit's apparent lack of urgency toward the Palestinian cause. Their internal cohesion and feeling of external isolation combined to produce the explosion known as the intifada (literally, "shaking off") that began in December 1987. Initiated spontaneously by young people who were born after 1967 and who had faced the Israeli armed forces all their lives, the uprising surmounted the barrier of fear that paralyzed their parents.

The intifada differed significantly from prior protests. In the past, mayors and intellectuals had led the political movements; the Israelis had forced them out of office, banned their coordinating bodies, and jailed or deported many of them. The intifada's leadership, on the other hand, was decentralized and loosely coordinated through the Unified National Leadership of the Uprising (UNLU). The UNLU members remained anonymous, in order to enable the activists to avoid being detained. Anonymity also emphasized the intifada's grassroots character.

The UNLU issued declarations that gave specific instructions: the days on which general strikes and demonstrations would be held; what hours shops and factories should open and close; and messages to particular towns, villages, and refugee camps that applauded their actions. UNLU was linked to committees in neighborhoods that helped residents survive the pressures of curfews, arrests, and diminished income. Medical, agricultural, educational, and women's committees provided services.

The intifada's goals evolved rapidly during the first year. Initially, activists talked about ameliorating the conditions under occupation, but they soon shifted to call for the end to the occupation and the creation of an independent state alongside Israel. That shift reflected the growing confidence that residents felt in their ability to sustain the intifada and to transform it into a strategic victory. Activists realized that the uprising had compelled Washington to turn its attention to the Middle East; they hoped to capitalize on that attention. They emphasized that the United States must not let King Hussein play the leading role in negotiations and they supported convening an international conference in which the PLO would represent Palestinian interests.

The PLO leadership sensed the shift in morale and strategy by the Palestinians on the West Bank and Gaza and sought to capitalize diplomatically on the intifada. A special meeting of the Arab League in June 1988 voiced support for the uprising and called for renewed diplomatic efforts. Local leaders on the West Bank formulated their own peace proposal that summer and issued a draft declaration of independence, shortly after King Hussein announced on July 31, 1988, that he would no longer bear legal responsibility for the West Bank.[5] The West Bank leaders called for a Palestinian state alongside Israel, not replacing the Jewish state. In November 1988, the PNC endorsed the establishment of an independent state on the West Bank and Gaza, with its capital in East Jerusalem. U.N. Resolutions 181 and 242 would be the state's legal underpinning. The PNC also renounced the use of terror. Moreover, in a press conference in December, Arafat explicitly affirmed the right of Israel to exist as a Jewish state. It took the intifada for the PLO to gain the confidence necessary to make that historic move. The administration of U.S. President Ronald Reagan responded by opening direct meetings with the PLO through the U.S. ambassador in Tunis. Israel, caught off guard by the shifts in the U.S. and Palestinian positions, insisted that the PLO was still not an acceptable interlocutor. But newly elected President George Bush urged Israel to formulate a realistic peace proposal.

The Gulf Crisis

The combined force of the intifada and the PNC resolutions proved insufficient to change the situation. The hard-line Israeli government that came to power on June 8, 1990, placed onerous conditions on negotiations and accelerated the construction of settlements. Some cabinet members advocated expelling Palestinians en masse from the territories. Palestinians were worried by a potential demographic transformation in Israel, as thousands of Russian Jews poured into the country. Palestinians were also angry that Congress supported Israel's moves to make united Jerusalem its capital and that the United States vetoed a U.N. resolution on the human rights situation in the territories. Then, the PLO suffered a diplomatic setback when the United States suspended the dialogue on June 20, 1990, in the wake of an aborted attack on Israel from the sea by Abu al-Abbas's PLF. In desperation, Palestinians turned to Iraqi President Saddam Hussein for strategic support. In April 1990 he had hinted that he would attack Israel with long-range chemical weapons if Israel attacked Jordan or deported Palestinians from the West Bank. Palestinians hoped that his threatened balance of terror would prevent Israel from expelling them.

Iraq's seizure of Kuwait on August 2, 1990, however, posed a dilemma for the PLO. Arafat could not condone that occupation without seeming to justify Israel's occupation of the West Bank and Gaza. Arafat stressed that Iraq and Kuwait should negotiate; he strongly opposed the presence of U.S. military forces in Saudi Arabia. When Saddam Hussein claimed on August 12 that Israel must withdraw from the occupied territories before he would consider leaving Kuwait, many Palestinians welcomed that linkage. Palestinian support for Iraq reached fever pitch in January 1991, when Iraq hit Israel with SCUD missiles during the U.N.-sanctioned war that forced Iraq out of Kuwait.[6]

In the aftermath of Iraq's defeat, Palestinians were traumatized and the PLO was isolated. Saudi Arabia and Kuwait cut off all financial aid to the PLO, Syria continued to disarm Palestinian enclaves in Lebanon, and the disintegration of the Soviet Union removed a diplomatic counterweight to the United States. Kuwaitis wreaked vengeance on Palestinians who had remained in Kuwait during the Iraqi occupation, arguing that they had collaborated with Iraq: Within a year, only 25,000 of the previously nearly 400,000 Palestinian residents remained in Kuwait.[7] Most fled to Jordan, which was already suffering heavy unemployment as a result of the trade dislocations caused by the Gulf crisis. In addition, Israel placed the Palestinians under total curfew during the war, followed by tight restrictions on their movement within the territories. Remittances from Palestinians living in the Gulf dried up and unemployment soared.

Despite those inauspicious circumstances, Palestinians agreed to the U.S. proposal to engage in negotiations. They were compelled to accept onerous conditions for participating in the multilateral talks that opened in Madrid in October 1991 and in the bilateral negotiations that began in Washington in December. Only Palestinians from the West Bank and Gaza Strip participated in the negotiating team, in tandem with Jordan. East Jerusalem residents were relegated to advisory status because Israel refused to negotiate if East Jerusalemites were members of the formal negotiating team. And Israel refused to let the PLO participate. (Nonetheless, the United States allowed a PLO official to come to Washington to advise the Palestinian negotiators.)

Negotiations focused on establishing a five-year period of self-rule, with the final status left for later negotiations. Palestinians feared that self-rule would be meaningless without control over land, particularly as Israel was accelerating the pace of building settlements. The Palestinians' self-rule plan stressed that "all these territories [occupied since June 1967], the land, natural resources, and water" and "all the Palestinian inhabitants" must come under the jurisdiction of the interim self-government, whose legislative assembly would be elected by the Palestinian residents.

The election of a Labor party government in Israel in the summer of 1992 gave hope for renewed vigor in the negotiations, but the new prime minister, Yitzhak Rabin, did not alter the content of the Israeli self-rule plan significantly. As talks dragged on, Palestinians became increasingly disillusioned, and violence escalated.

The level of violence had already increased significantly during and after the Gulf crisis. Palestinian militants attacked Israeli soldiers and settlers in the territories and also targeted other Israeli civilians. The killing of alleged collaborators by Palestinian groups intensified, despite efforts by Palestinian politicians to stem internecine bloodshed. Moreover, during the summer of 1992, the increasingly strong Islamist movement, led by Hamas, attacked Fatah supporters in the Gaza Strip. Hamas, formed by the Muslim Brotherhood in 1988, tried to outdo the Islamic Jihad in militancy: Renouncing the brotherhood's former passivity, Hamas called for an Islamic state in all of Palestine and denounced the PLO for seeking to negotiate with Israel. Israel tolerated Hamas attacks on Fatah activists, but cracked down when Hamas began to kill Israelis. In fact, in December 1992, Israel deported more than 400 activists connected with Hamas and Islamic Jihad, ostensibly to punish persons responsible for inciting violence but especially to remove opponents of negotiations.[8] The mass expulsion backfired when the Lebanese government refused to accept the deportees, the United Nations denounced the expulsions, and the PLO rallied behind the expellees. Palestinians feared this could lead to the expulsion of many more political activists.

The Oslo Accords

Just as negotiations were grinding to a halt, a secret track of PLO-Israeli talks reached a dramatic conclusion. Meeting under the auspices of the Norwegian foreign minister, the two sides hammered out a Declaration of Principles (DOP), which was signed in a formal ceremony in Washington, D.C., on September 13, 1993. Both parties realized that the failure to conclude an accord was rapidly undermining their own internal power and legitimacy. If Rabin could not build a more secure and prosperous Israel through negotiations, public support was likely to shift back to the Likud annexationists. If Arafat could not gain self-rule and recognition of the PLO, the uncompromising Islamists could overwhelm his movement. Moreover, Israeli politicians finally realized that excluding the PLO from negotiations meant that negotiations would fail; only the PLO could deliver.

The impetus was not merely negative. Both sides perceived the need to overcome animosity and mistrust and to place the relationship on a new basis. Israeli Foreign Minister Shimon Peres, in his speech on the White House lawn, called for a fundamental "reconciliation" and "healing" between the two peoples, with their "two parallel tragedies."[9] Arafat stated that his people hope "that this agreement . . . marks the beginning of the end of a chapter of pain and suffering . . . [and ushers] in an age of peace, coexistence, and equal rights." Indeed, the preamble of the accord stressed the importance of this "historic reconciliation."

The agreement provided for Palestinian self-rule in the Gaza Strip and Jericho, followed by Palestinian civil administration over the rest of the West Bank for a five-year interim period. The Palestinian Authority (PA) would control the police to maintain internal security, operate the educational, health, social welfare, and tax systems, and have considerable authority over the economy. Negotiations on final-status issues, including Jerusalem, settlements, statehood, and refugees were supposed to begin in December 1995.

An accord signed in May 1994 enabled Arafat and PLO officials to establish the PA and rule the town of Jericho and most of the Gaza Strip. But the PA did not gain control over other towns on the West Bank until another agreement signed in September 1995 (dubbed Oslo II). Oslo II also enabled the PA to hold elections in January 1996 for an eighty-eight-seat legislative council and for the presidency, which Arafat won handily.

Despite their general enthusiasm for the elections, Palestinians were disappointed that Arafat subsequently concentrated power in his hands and ignored the efforts by the legislative council to finalize a constitution and hold the executive accountable. Palestinian security courts replicated the interrogation techniques and rapid judgments that the hated Israeli military courts had used. Moreover, the frequent Israeli closure of its territory to passage by Palestinians caused severe damage to the Palestinian economy and made it difficult for the PA to collect taxes and operate the education, health, and social welfare systems effectively. According to the World Bank, as of December 1997, "Palestinian real per capita incomes have fallen by a quarter [since 1993] . . . . The number of Palestinians living in poverty . . . has risen to more than twenty-five percent of the population, and over a third in Gaza."[10]

In addition, Israel's redeployment remained limited under the terms of Oslo II. The area of the West Bank under exclusive Palestinian control—known as Area A—totaled only 3 percent. (According to a supplementary agreement in January 1997, the town of Hebron was divided between the PA and Israel: Israel remained in control of 20 percent of the city, where some 500 Jewish settlers and 20,000 Palestinians lived.) Another 20 percent—Area B—fell under Palestinian civil and administrative rule, but the Israeli army and security forces effectively controlled that zone. Taking into account modifications made in 1997–1998, areas A and B now comprise 40 percent of the West Bank. This leaves 60 percent of the West Bank and a third of the Gaza Strip—termed Area C—under exclusive Israeli control, including areas with Jewish settlements and military bases. Militant Israelis challenged even these limited changes; the religious Jew who assassinated Rabin in November 1995 denounced the prime minister as a traitor for signing the Oslo accords.

Arafat's authority was challenged by Hamas, which boycotted the legislative council elections and decried the meager results of negotiations. In the summer of 1995 and spring of 1996 Hamas and Islamic Jihad militants bombed buses and markets in Jerusalem and Tel Aviv; more than sixty Israeli civilians died in the bombings that spring. Arafat was unable to stem this violence, particularly as the perpetrators came from areas that were still under Israeli security control. But the violence undermined the Labor government and propelled the Likud back into power in May 1996. Tensions mounted as Israel continued to expropriate land and expand settlements in Area C and the army set up roadblocks in Areas B and C that blocked travel within the West Bank as well as to Jerusalem and Israel.

Ehud Barak's election as prime minister in May 1999 on a platform that called for accelerated peace talks offered some hope for an accord. However, Barak resisted signing additional interim agreements and reneged on his pledge to withdraw from two villages next to Jerusalem. Serious negotiations did not occur until July 2000 when President Clinton hosted two weeks of intensive talks with Barak and Arafat at Camp David. Although the leaders addressed previously taboo subjects, they could not bridge all the gaps. They came close to agreeing to a Palestinian state on most of the West Bank and Gaza and all of the Gaza Strip, but Israel insisted on controlling the borders, air space, and water resources as well as annexing the areas with

80 percent of the West Bank settlers and all the settlements in East Jerusalem. Barak agreed to accept a token number of Palestinian refugees into Israel on humanitarian grounds but not on the right of return.

In retrospect, the talks were too ambitious and too pressured by President Clinton's overriding desire to reach a settlement before his term of office expired the following January. The talks ended with both sides blaming the other for the failure to reach agreement. Israelis criticized Barak for conceding too much whereas Palestinians praised Arafat for not yielding to U.S. and Israeli pressure.

In the tense atmosphere that followed, Likud leader Ariel Sharon marched onto al-Haram al-Sharif (the site of the Temple Mount) on September 28, in a manner that clearly asserted Israel's claim to political sovereignty. His deliberately provocative action catalyzed months of spontaneous violence that swept across the West Bank and Gaza. This renewed intifada was fueled by rage and frustration over the failure of the Oslo accords to improve Palestinians' lives as well as fear that the terms proposed at Camp David would leave them far short of their goal of sovereignty and independence.

The Israeli government held Arafat responsible for this violence and retaliated by launching mortar barrages and systematic helicopter rocket attacks against alleged terrorist leaders in residential areas. The Israeli Defense Force closed off West Bank and Gaza towns and villages, causing serious human suffering and economic hardship. The result was an increasing cycle of violence that made further negotiations futile despite frantic attempts to narrow the differences before President Clinton's term expired. The resounding electoral defeat of Prime Minister Barak by Sharon on February 6, 2001, put an end to the Oslo peace process, at least for the near term.

Conclusion: The Past Is Prologue

The saga of the Palestinians could well be called "birth of a nation." Palestine as a political unit was a creation of the British after World War I and did not exist under the Ottomans. Yet a new sense of Palestinian national consciousness arose during the mandate years, in part as a reaction to Jewish immigration and political demands. Palestinians were fragmented by the creation of Israel in 1948, which forced half the Palestinians into exile, physically isolated a significant Arab minority that remained in Israel, placed Gazans under Egyptian administration, and enabled King Abdallah to absorb West Bankers into his newly formed Hashimite Kingdom of Jordan.

The fragmentation was reversed when Israel occupied the West Bank and Gaza in the 1967 war, which physically reunited West Bank and Gaza Palestinians with each other and with relatives living in Israel. Ironically, Palestinian nationalism was further boosted by Israel's efforts after 1967 to absorb the occupied territories economically and politically into the Jewish state. The West Bank and Gaza became dependent on Israel for jobs, but efforts to absorb them politically—for example, annexing East Jerusalem and surrounding areas and building Jewish set-tlements in Arab territory—had the opposite effect of reigniting Palestinian na-tionalism and the demand for self-determination.

It is equally ironic that years of Israeli occupation also helped the Palestinians prepare for statehood as local, sub-rosa groups sprang up to provide basic social services denied by the occupation government, and the PLO and Islamist groups provided an arena for consensual political activity. That experience has enabled the Palestinian Authority to maintain a degree of cohesion despite the constraints forced upon it by Israel, by the autocratic and personalized rule of Yasir Arafat, and by the United States. In sum, it could be argued that the Palestinians are bet-ter prepared for statehood than many of the former colonial states that received their independence following World War II.

For the Palestinians, independence has always been a question of when, not whether. Despite the return of violence following the collapse of the peace process in 2000, more progress has been made toward their goal of self-determination than one might think. Despite the fever pitch of mutual animosity engendered in the wake of the collapse of the Oslo peace process, five wars (1948, 1956, 1967, 1973, and 1982) still seem to have taught both sides that achievement of their national goals can not be attained by force of arms.

The Egyptian-Israeli peace process was a serious step toward an Arab settle-ment with Israel, but it did not adequately address Palestinian concerns for true territorial self-determination or a settlement of the refugee problem. The Madrid peace process, begun in 1991 under the aegis of the United States, represented mutual Palestinian-Israeli acceptance of the need for a negotiated settlement, but these core issues were still ignored and participation by the PLO was rejected de-spite the overwhelming consensus by Palestinians that the PLO represented the Palestinian people.

The first breakthrough was the Oslo Declaration of Principles in 1993, negoti-ated directly between the PLO and the Israelis without U.S. participation. While avoiding issues such as Jerusalem and the refugees that appeared still irreconcil-able, the declaration marked the first time that Israel recognized Palestinian rights, at least in principle.

Nevertheless, the failure to build on the promise of the Oslo DOP resulted in renewed violence, and there was a real danger that the bloodletting of 2001 could put back attempts at a negotiated settlement for decades. And the escalating strife following the September 11, 2001, attacks on the World Trade Center and the Pentagon exacerbated that danger. Many Palestinians remain skeptical that even their minimal aspirations can be achieved. They question whether the process ini-tiated in Oslo could ever lead to a sovereign Palestinian state, given the intractabil-ity of core issues such as Jerusalem, Jewish settlements, and Palestinian refugees.

But one could also make the counterargument that the two sides are too closely linked geographically, economically, and, in a perverse way, politically to escape the necessity for ultimately reaching a negotiated settlement. Now that the Palestinians have in fact recognized the right of Israel to exist, the harder task rests with the Israelis to accord the same right to the Palestinians in return for the security they seek. Even here, there is a chance for guarded optimism amid the gloom. The proposals put forward by President Clinton before he left office posited an independent Palestinian state, something Israelis have never had the will nor the Americans the courage to admit is a sine qua non to peace. But for the first time, at least, the idea has been placed on the negotiating table.

Notes

1. John Ruedy, "Dynamics of Land Alienation," in Ibrahim Abu Lughod, ed., *The Transformation of Palestine* (Evanston, Ill.: Northwestern University Press, 1971).

2. Quoted in *Journal of Palestine Studies*, III, no. 4 (summer 1974): 224. For a thorough analysis of the evolution of Palestinian thinking as expressed in the charter and PNC resolutions, see Muhammad Muslih, *Toward Coexistence: An Analysis of the Resolutions of the Palestine National Council* (Washington, D.C.: The Institute for Palestine Studies, 1990).

3. *Journal of Palestinian Studies,* VI, no. 3 (spring 1977): 189.

4. The text can be found in William B. Quandt, *Camp David: Peacemaking and Politics* (Washington, D.C.: The Brookings Institution, 1986), pp. 376–381.

5. The peace proposal was seized by security officers when they searched the office of Faisal Husseini, head of the Arab Studies Society. Palestinians then provided a translation to the *Jerusalem Post,* which published it in full on August 12, 1988.

6. For analysis of Palestinian views as of October 1990, see my "Contrasting Reactions to the Persian Gulf Crisis: Egypt, Syria, Jordan and the Palestinians," *Middle East Journal*, 45, no. 1 (winter 1991): 32, 46–48.

7. See my "Palestinians in Kuwait," *JPS*, XX, no. 4 (summer 1991): 42–54, and the follow-up article by Michael Dumper, "Letter from Kuwait City: End of an Era," *JPS*, XXI, no. 1 (autumn 1991): 120–123.

8. Israel was compelled to let all of the expellees return home, where they were viewed as heros by the Palestinian public. Many became even more active in organizing political resistance against Israeli control.

9. Texts of Peres's and Arafat's speeches in the *New York Times*, September 14, 1993; text of the draft agreement in the *New York Times*, September 1, 1993.

10. Statement by the World Bank at the Consultative Group meeting in Paris, December 14–15, 1997, cited in Rex Brynen, *A Very Political Economy* (Washington, D.C.: U. S. Institute of Peace Press, 2000), p. 5.

Bibliography

The Palestine problem has been studied exhaustively from different political and analytical perspectives. Charles D. Smith, *Palestine and the Arab-Israeli Conflict*, 2nd ed. (New York: St. Martin's Press, 1992), details historical trends and diplomatic issues. Baruch Kimmerling and Joel S. Migdal, in *Palestinians: The Making of a People* (New York: The Free Press, 1993), emphasize the interaction of socioeconomic changes and the growth of Palestinian nationalism. Philip Mattar's *Encyclopedia of the Palestinians* (New York: Facts on File, 2000) is an indispensable resource.

Among the few studies of pre–twentieth century Palestine, Beshara Doumani's *Rediscovering Palestine: Merchants and Peasants in Jabal Nablus, 1700–1900* (Berkeley: University of California Press, 1995) is outstanding for its insight into the political economy of an important town. Efforts to reconcile Arab nationalism and Zionism during the late Ottoman period are the focus of Neville Mandel, *The Arabs and Zionism before World War I* (Berkeley: University of California Press, 1976). The evolution of Palestinian nationalism before and after World War I is examined by Rashid Khalidi in *Palestinian Identity: The Construction of Modern National Consciousness* (New York: Columbia University Press, 1997) as well as Muhammad Muslih, *The Origins of Palestinian Nationalism* (New York: Columbia University Press, 1988). Edward W. Said's penetrating *The Question of Palestine* (New York: Times Books, 1979) reflects on this nationalism in its broad historical context.

For overviews of the British mandate period, the reader can study J. C. Hurewitz, *Struggle for Palestine* (New York: Norton, 1950), and my *Arab Politics in Palestine, 1917–1939* (Ithaca: Cornell University Press, 1979). Yehoshua Porath provides detailed chronicles in *The Emergence of the Palestinian-Arab National Movement, 1918–1929* (London: Frank Cass, 1974) and *The Palestinian Arab National Movement, 1929–1939* (London: Frank Cass, 1977). Philip Mattar focuses on the controversial al-Hajj Amin al-Husayni in *The Mufti of Jerusalem* (New York: Columbia University Press, 1988). *Before Their Diaspora: A Photographic History of the Palestinians, 1876–1948*, Walid Khalidi, ed. (Washington, D.C.: Institute for Palestine Studies, 1984), offers visual evidence of family life, culture, and customs in Palestine. Neil Caplan critiques diplomatic efforts during the 1930s in his two-volume *Futile Diplomacy* (London: Frank Cass, 1983, 1986) and Barry Rubin addresses Arab diplomacy in *The Arab States and the Palestine Conflict* (Syracuse, N.Y.: Syracuse University Press, 1981).

The centrality of land to the conflict is emphasized by Gershon Shafir in *Land, Labor and the Origins of the Israeli-Palestinian Conflict 1882–1914* (New York: Cambridge University Press, 1989); Kenneth W. Stein, *The Land Question in Palestine, 1917–1939* (Chapel Hill: University of North Carolina Press, 1984); and Benny Morris, *The Birth of the Palestinian Refugee Problem, 1947–1949* (New York: Cambridge University Press, 1987). *Jerusalem, 1948: The Arab Neighbourhoods and Their Fate in the War*, ed. Salim Tamari (Jerasulem: The Institute of Jerusalem Studies and Badil Resource Center, 1999), provides background on the city and details the fighting and flight of Palestinians in 1948. *All That Remains: The Palestinian Villages Occupied and Depopulated by Israel in 1948*, ed. Walid Khalidi (Washington, D.C.: Institute for Palestine Studies, 1992) lists more than four hundred villages destroyed during and after the 1948–1949 war. Susan Slyomovics sensitively analyzes the continuing interplay between displaced Palestinians and Israeli Jews who now inhabit their former homes, in *The Object of Memory* (Philadelphia: University of Pennsylvania Press, 1998). Benjamin N. Schiff examines the U.N. refugee programs in *Refugees Unto the Third Generation: UN Aid to Palestinians* (Syracuse, N.Y.: Syracuse University Press, 1995) and Donna E. Arzt assesses the prospects of their returning home in *Refugees into Citizens* (New York: Council on Foreign Relations 1996).

The Jordanian dimension of the Palestine problem is analyzed in Shaul Mishal, *West Bank/East Bank: The Palestinians in Jordan, 1949–1957* (New Haven: Yale University Press,

1978) and Amnon Cohen, *Political Parties in the West Bank Under the Jordanian Regime, 1949–1967* (Ithaca: Cornell University Press, 1982). Avi Shlaim emphasizes King Abdullah's crucial role in 1948 in *Collusion Across the Jordan: King Abdullah, the Zionist Movement, and the Partition of Palestine* (New York: Columbia University Press, 1988). Samir Mutawi discusses Jordan's loss of the West Bank in *Jordan in the 1967 War* (New York: Cambridge University Press, 1987).

The status of Palestinian citizens of Israel has been examined by Sammy Smooha in his two-volume *Arabs and Jews in Israel* (Boulder: Westview, 1989, 1992); Ian Lustick, *Arabs in the Jewish State* (Austin: University of Texas Press, 1980); and Elia T. Zureik, *The Palestinians in Israel* (London: Routledge and Kegan Paul, 1979). Former Palestinian citizens have reflected on their childhoods under Israeli control, notably Sabri Jiryis, in *The Arabs in Israel* (Beirut: Institute for Palestine Studies, 1968) and Fouzi El-Asmar, in *To Be an Arab in Israel* (London: Frances Pinter, 1975). Michael Gorkin's *Days of Honey, Days of Onion* (Berkeley: University of California Press, 1991) provides insight into the experiences of a Palestinian family in Israel. And Father Elias Chacour's autobiographical *Blood Brothers* (Old Tappan, N.J.: Chosen Books, 1984) details his painful experiences growing up as a Christian Palestinian in Israel.

The conditions and political struggles in the occupied territories have preoccupied many analysts. Details on these publications can be found in my chapter on the West Bank and Gaza Strip in the *Handbook of Political Science Research on the Middle East and North Africa*, ed. Bernard Reich (Westport, Conn.: Greenwood Press, 1998). Analyses highlighted include George Emile Bisharat, *Palestinian Lawyers and Israeli Rule: Law and Disorder in the West Bank* (Austin: University of Texas Press, 1989); Rita Giacaman, *Life and Health in Three Palestinian Villages* (London: Ithaca, 1988); and Kitty Warnock, *Land before Honour: Palestinian Women in the Occupied Territories* (New York: Monthly Review Press, 1990). Joost R. Hiltermann's *Behind the Intifada* (Princeton: Princeton University Press, 1991) examines the grassroots movements among women and workers that prefigured the intifada. Orayb Aref Najjar provides vivid images of women's lives in *Portraits of Palestinian Women* (Salt Lake City: University of Utah Press, 1992) and Ebba Augustin gives voice to women activists in *Palestinian Women: Identity and Experience* (London: Zed, 1993).

Moshe Ma'oz, in *Palestinian Leadership on the West Bank: The Changing Role of the Mayors under Jordan and Israel* (London: Frank Cass, 1984), and Emile Sahliyyeh, in *In Search of Leadership: West Bank Politics Since 1967* (Washington, D.C.: The Brookings Institution, 1988), offer insights into local politics. The first Israeli military governor, Shlomo Gazit, defends Israeli policies in *The Carrot and the Stick: Israel's Policy in Judaea and Samaria, 1967–68* (Washington, D.C.: B'nai B'rith Books, 1995). Fawzi A. Gharaibeh, *The Economics of the West Bank and Gaza Strip* (Boulder: Westview, 1985), reviews the major economic transformations in the first two decades of Israeli rule, and Sara Roy, *The Gaza Strip: The Political Economy of De-development* (Washington, D.C.: The Institute for Palestine Studies, 1995) provides a comprehensive analysis of Israeli policies that stifle Gaza's economy. Details on legal, socioeconomic, and political conditions are contained in Naseer H. Aruri, ed., *Occupation: Israel over Palestine*, 2nd ed. (Belmont, Mass.: Arab American University Graduates, 1989) and in my essays on the Gaza Strip, published in Ann Mosely Lesch and Mark Tessler, *Israel, Egypt and the Palestinians: From Camp David to Intifada* (Bloomington, Ind.: Indiana University Press, 1989). The complexities of life under Israeli occupation are depicted by novelist Sahar Khalifeh in *Wild Thorns* (New York: Olive Branch Press, 1989) and Raymonda Tawil in her autobiography, *My Home, My Prison* (New York: Holt, Rinehart, and Winston, 1979).

The intifada spawned many books, of which the reader might note Zachary Lockman and Joel Beinin, eds., *Intifada* (Boston: South End Press, 1989), Jamal R. Nassar and Roger Heacock, eds., *Intifada* (New York: Praeger, 1990), Zeev Schiff and Ehud Ya'ari, *Intifada* (New York: Simon and Schuster, 1990), and F. Robert Hunter, *The Palestinian Uprising* (Berkeley: University of California Press, 1993). Helen Winternitz illustrates the impact of the uprising on a West Bank village in *A Season of Stones: Living in a Palestinian Village* (New York: Atlantic Monthly Press, 1991), and Dick Doughty and Mohammed El Aydi focus on a refugee community in *Gaza: Legacy of Occupation—A Photographer's Journey* (West Hartford, Conn.: Kumarian Press, 1995).

Yezid Sayigh has written the most detailed history of the PLO, entitled *Armed Struggle and the Search for State* (Oxford: Clarendon Press, 1997). Shorter accounts of the Palestinian movement before 1982 can be found in Helena Cobban, *The Palestine Liberation Organization* (New York: Cambridge University Press, 1984), Abdallah Franji, *The PLO and Palestine* (London: Zed, 1982), Alain Gresh, *The PLO, The Struggle Within* (London: Zed, 1985), Bard E. O'Neill, *Armed Struggle in Palestine* (Boulder: Westview, 1978), and William Quandt et al., *The Politics of Palestinian Nationalism* (Berkeley: University of California Press, 1973). The late Salah Khalaf (Abu Iyad)'s *My Home, My Land* (New York: Times Books, 1981) describes his key role in the establishment and growth of the PLO. Rashid Khalidi details the PLO's withdrawal from Beirut in *Under Siege: PLO Decisionmaking During the 1982 War* (New York: Columbia University Press, 1986). Galia Golan unravels the evolving relationship with Moscow in *The Soviet Union and the Palestine Liberation Organization: An Uneasy Alliance* (New York: Praeger, 1980).

Laurie Brand considers the circumstances facing Palestinians in exile in *Palestinians in the Arab World: In Search of State* (New York: Columbia University Press, 1988). Shafeeq Ghabra focuses on *Palestinians in Kuwait: The Family and Politics of Survival* (Boulder: Westview, 1987). Julie Peteet addresses dilemmas faced by Palestinian women in *Gender in Crisis: Women and the Palestinian Resistance Movement* (New York: Columbia University Press, 1991). And Rosemary Sayigh, *Palestinians: From Peasants to Revolutionaries* (London: Zed, 1979), focuses on the political awakening of Palestinian refugees in Lebanon. Salma K. Jayyusi's comprehensive *Anthology of Modern Palestinian Literature* (New York: Columbia University Press, 1992) captures the spirit of Palestinians living in exile and under Israeli rule.

Several analysts address the possibility of Palestinian statehood. They include Mark A. Heller, *A Palestinian State* (Cambridge, Mass.: Harvard University Press, 1983), Mark A. Heller and Sari Nusseibeh, *No Trumpets, No Drums: A Two-State Settlement of the Israeli-Palestinian Conflict* (New York: Hill and Wang, 1991), Jerome M. Segal, *Creating a Palestinian State: A Strategy of Peace* (Chicago: Lawrence Hill, 1989), and my *Transition to Palestinian Self-Government: Practical Steps Toward Israeli-Palestinian Peace* (Cambridge, Mass.: American Academy of Arts and Sciences, 1992). Some of the problems and limitations of the interim period are spelled out by Glenn E. Robinson, in *Building a Palestinian State* (Bloomington, Ind.: Indiana University Press, 1997) and Rex Brynen, in *A Very Political Economy: Peacebuilding and Foreign Aid in the West Bank and Gaza* (Washington, D.C.: United States Institute of Peace Press, 2000). Edward W. Said pens a scathing critique of the underlying principles and implementation of the Oslo accord, in *The End of the Peace Process: Oslo and After* (New York: Pantheon, 2000).

13

Arab Republic of Egypt

Louis J. Cantori
Sally Ann Baynard

Historical Background

Throughout recorded history the civilization of the Nile Valley flourished as a result of a combination of plentiful water, good soil, and climatic conditions contributing to a long growing season. The Nile River also provided swift, efficient, and cheap transportation and became the focal point of both ancient and modern civilizations. In ancient days a series of great kingdoms ruled by pharaohs developed in the valley and made important and long-lasting contributions to civilization in the fields of science, architecture, politics, and economics. These ancient kingdoms provided a base for the development of the modern Egyptian political system. Throughout its history Egypt has remained essentially a united entity, ruled by a single government, in part because of its need for overall planning for irrigation and agricultural production.

After the sixth century B.C., Egypt fell under the influence of Persia, Greece, Rome, and the Byzantine Empire. Beginning with the Persian conquest in 525 B.C., Egypt was ruled for nearly 2,500 years by alien dynasties or as a part of a foreign empire. This foreign domination left its imprint. Christianity was brought to the Nile Valley, and in A.D. 639 Arab invaders from the east entered Egypt. They converted Egypt into the Arab and Islamic society that it has remained ever since. The period of Arab political domination, however, was broken by other powers, notably the Mamluks (1252–1517) and the Ottomans (1517–1882), with a monarchy of foreign origins ruling until 1952. This legacy of foreign control has been a significant factor in the Egyptian political culture and world outlook.

In some respects, the most significant external influence came after the Ottoman Turks gained control of Egypt and made it a province of the empire in 1517.

That initial Ottoman influence was modified by the Napoleonic invasion of 1798 and the developments that followed, which assisted the transition from the military feudalism of the past to a new system. The Western impact of the French intervention, the important reforms of Muhammad Ali (1805–1849), known as the founder of modern Egypt, and the construction of the Suez Canal in the mid-nineteenth century all contributed to the development of the modern Egyptian state.

Muhammad Ali was neither an Egyptian nor an Arab, but an Albanian who came to Egypt from Kavara (Macedonia) as an army commander in charge of a unit of the Ottoman army sent to deal with Napoleon. In 1805 the Ottoman sultan appointed him governor of Egypt with the title of pasha. Muhammad Ali brought significant change to the country and, to a large degree, established its independence from the Ottoman sultan. Under Muhammad Ali, Egypt began to develop the elements of a modern state and a more European cultural orientation. He launched a series of ambitious domestic projects designed to improve the economy and general condition of the state. Agricultural production was improved and reorganized, and a program of industrialization was inaugurated. He forced Egyptian products into the European market and encouraged the production of cotton. Turks were replaced with Egyptians in the administration. He stressed education and sought to improve its quality. He created a modern national army, organized on European lines, which gained substantial experience in various areas of the Middle East during his reign. He created the base for a modern political system and the conditions for the rise of Egyptian nationalism.

Although European powers had been interested in Egypt for some time, the opening of the Suez Canal to world navigation and commerce in 1869 vastly increased great-power interest in Egypt. England, the greatest sea power of the time, was particularly concerned with the canal because it provided a shorter and more efficient link to much of the British Empire, especially India. Problems associated with the operation of the canal and Egypt's financial mismanagement provided the framework for the British occupation in 1882, although other European powers had also been concerned about the financial situation of Egypt. Foreign creditors, anxious about the funds they had entrusted to Khedive Ismail, pressed their respective governments for relief and assistance. As a result, Egyptian finances were controlled by foreign creditors and Ismail was deposed in 1879. Popular opposition formed against the khedive, his court, and the foreign powers. Khedive Tawfiq, who succeeded Ismail, ruled a country that was heavily taxed and under British and French financial supervision and political control.

In response to this situation, Colonel Ahmed Arabi led a group of Egyptian nationalists who, scorning the weakness of the khedive, protested British and French interference in the sovereignty of Egypt and the lack of indigenous political participation. They sought constitutional reform, liberalization of Egyptian political participation, and an end to foreign interference in the affairs of Egypt. The

British and French supported the khedive. In July 1882 British forces landed in Egypt and crushed the Arabi revolt. Although they were originally supposed to leave after the restoration of order, British forces remained in Egypt until the 1950s, and real control over the affairs of state resided in British hands for seven decades, thereby giving Britain control over the canal. The khedive (and later king) remained the titular authority, but the British representatives (under various titles) were the final authorities on the affairs of state.

World War I added a new dimension to the commercial and strategic importance of the Suez Canal for Britain and the West. In December 1914 Britain proclaimed Egypt a British protectorate, and the title of khedive was changed to that of sultan.

Opposition among Egyptians to the British intensified during World War I. Exasperation and frustration characterized the Egyptian nationalist movement. There had been some hope engendered by such events as the Arab revolt against the Ottoman sultan and such declarations as Wilson's Fourteen Points. Within Egyptian society there emerged the beginnings of nationalistic ideas of a political nature that were to spearhead the movement to remove British control and establish indigenous Egyptian rule over the country. In this post–World War I context a new political organization was formed, *al-Wafd al-Misri* (the Egyptian Delegation), known as the Wafd. Under the leadership of Saad Zaghlul and later Nahas Pasha, the Wafd sought independence from the British and self-rule in Egypt. The Wafd hoped to present its position to the great powers at the postwar conferences—especially at the Paris Peace Conference, where the fate of the Ottoman territories was to be determined. British opposition to Egyptian independence prevented the Wafd from achieving its goal.

In the aftermath of World War I Egyptian opposition to British rule became increasingly hostile. In the face of such pressure, the protectorate was terminated and in February 1922 the British unilaterally proclaimed Egypt a constitutional monarchy. However, the British formally reserved their freedom of action on four matters: the Sudan, the defense of Egypt against foreign intervention, the security of the canal (which remained the communications link of the British Empire), and the protection of foreign interests and minorities. In March, Sultan Fuad became the king of Egypt. Thus, by 1922 Egypt had become technically an independent country with its own king, a country in alliance with Britain (which provided assistance in defense and related matters). The reality was continued British control.

A constitution was written and promulgated in April 1923; a parliament was elected, and a government was formed. Domestic politics began to operate, and rivalries between power blocs and political institutions began to develop. Local politics reflected the rivalry between the king on the one hand and the government and parliament on the other (both of the latter were generally dominated by the Wafd, which opposed both the king and the British). Many of the concerns of Egyptian society, especially of the vast majority of the population who were peasants, were not effectively dealt with because the main political forces devoted their energies to conflict with each other. Fortunately, there was more agreement on the question of the British position in Egypt. All elements of Egyptian society generally agreed that the British should leave and that full control should be vested in Egyptian authorities.

British influence, however, remained paramount. British troops and officials were stationed in Egypt, mostly but not solely concerned with the canal and the security of the imperial communications system. Through them, the British were able to influence political activity and policy decisions. British-Egyptian negotiations continued, on a somewhat sporadic basis, until 1936. At that time a new Anglo-Egyptian treaty was written that altered but did not terminate the British role. On many of the key issues little changed and British influence remained significant, although its formal trappings were modified.

World War II provided an important milestone in the political development of Egypt. Its territory was used as a base of Allied operations, but local sentiment was strongly against Britain as the hated occupier. Britain's straightforward use of force in February 1942, when the British high commissioner surrounded the palace and forced the king to appoint Nahas Pasha and a pro-British government, highlighted British control and infuriated young nationalists. Following this incident, many nationalists, including some young officers, began to turn against the Wafd as well as the king. The war, however, sapped British strength and financial resources, and Britain was soon forced to reconsider its position throughout the Middle East, setting the stage for a major political realignment throughout the area, especially in Egypt and Palestine.

After World War II Egypt became involved in two related matters that laid the foundation for the Egyptian revolution. The first was the creation of Israel—which Egypt opposed—following the British withdrawal from the Palestine mandate in 1948, which, in turn, led to the Arab-Israeli war of 1948–1949. With some individual exceptions, the armed forces of Egypt performed poorly. The corruption and inefficiency of the government of King Farouk (whose rule had begun in 1936) were later cited as major causes for the poor performance of Egyptian military forces against the new state of Israel. The war was probably the most important single event in Egypt's political development before the 1952 revolution. It helped to complete the rupture between the king and the army, many of whose officers believed they had been sent to battle poorly equipped and ill trained. Increasingly ruthless police actions were instituted by the government in response to the political turmoil that followed the war. Egypt's economic crisis also worsened as mismanagement and corruption became rampant.

The second issue was the continuing opposition by the nationalists to the British role in Egypt. Negotiations to revise the 1936 treaty, especially those aspects of the agreement relating to the questions of the Sudan and the canal, were unsuccessful. Throughout its existence, the Wafd opposed British imperialism and sought Nile unity, with the Sudan as a part of Egypt. Clashes between the British and Egyptian nationalists became increasingly frequent. On October 15, 1951, the government of Egypt, under Prime Minister Nahas Pasha, unilaterally abrogated the 1936 treaty and proclaimed Farouk king of Egypt and the Sudan.

By the beginning of 1952 the new government had become unable to govern. First, there was an impasse in the relations between King Farouk and politicians (especially the Wafd, the most important political party in Egypt until its abolition following the 1952 revolution) that deadlocked the processes of government. Political disturbances, which had been growing in number since 1949, broke out, and mobs attacked foreign establishments in Cairo. The British protested, and clashes between British troops and Egyptians intensified. January 26, 1952, a day of great violence, came to be known as "Black Saturday;" it was followed by the ouster of Nahas Pasha and the proclamation of martial law.

The Egyptian Revolution of 1952

On July 23, 1952, members of a small, clandestine military organization known as the Free Officers launched a coup d'état that established a new system of government. This group of officers, whose inner circle numbered about a dozen, had been meeting secretly since sometime in the late 1940s, in hopes of overthrowing the corrupt and unpopular monarchy. King Farouk was forced to abdicate and left the country on July 26, 1952.

The 1952 coup was swiftly and efficiently executed. The military controlled the major instruments of force, and there was no significant opposition to its actions. There were at least two other clandestine military groups operating at the time, but their numbers had been dwindling, and once the Free Officers had made their move, the threat of other groups receded dramatically. The guiding hand of the new system was the Revolutionary Command Council (RCC), whose titular head was a senior military officer, General Muhammad Naguib, one of the few successful Egyptian officers in the Arab-Israeli war of 1948. General Naguib had not been one of the inner circle of the young Free Officers, but he had been asked to join the conspiracy because of his rank and his fine reputation as an officer, and probably also because he was half-Sudanese by birth and the young officers still shared the dream of previous Egyptian governments: to bring the Sudan into union with Egypt.

The immediate concern of the RCC was to dismantle the corrupt structures of the monarchy and to create a new political order that would institute major social change. Since the ouster of Farouk was the major objective of the coup, the Free Officers did not have a specific and articulated plan for the ordering of Egyptian life after the coup. Their basic goal was to end political corruption and inefficiency and to prevent further humiliations such as the Arab-Israeli war of 1948–1949 and the British control of Egypt. Moreover, the Free Officers had not determined how to achieve their long-term goals of ousting the British from Egypt (especially the canal zone) and securing the linkage with the Sudan. A six-point statement of position, one that any nationalist could endorse, was proclaimed: The new regime declared its opposition to colonialism, imperialism, and monopolies and asserted its support for social justice, a strong military, and a democratic way of life.

Although Farouk was forced into exile, the constitutional monarchy was preserved at first, and a regency council was established to preside in the name of Farouk's infant son, Fuad II. A general purge of corrupt officials was instituted, and land reform was declared to be a major goal of the RCC. At this time, the RCC intended to return Egypt to a civilian government as soon as possible.

After a period of some uncertainty concerning the organization and structure of the government, the RCC decided that the changes envisaged were not possible within the existing political system. In December 1952 the constitution of 1923 and the parliamentary form of government were suspended. The following January General Naguib announced that all political parties had been banned and their funds confiscated and that constitutional government would not operate for a three-year transition period. In February 1953 an interim constitution was proclaimed that provided the terms for the operation of the government during this time. This constitution noted that the people were the source of all authority, but it vested all power in the RCC for the transition period. With the abolition of political parties, the RCC created a new political organization called the National Liberation Rally to help mobilize political support for the new regime.

In June 1953 the RCC moved to the next step in the conversion of the political system. The monarchy was abolished. A republic, with Naguib as both president and prime minister, was declared.

The Emergence of Nasser

The most crucial factor in the period immediately following the 1952 coup d'état (always called *the revolution* in Egypt) was the emergence of Gamal Abdul Nasser as the primary force in Egyptian national life. Although it became clear later that he had been the leader of the Free Officers movement—or at least first among equals—since its inception, Nasser appeared in the public view rather slowly. When the Free Officers overthrew Farouk, attention was focused on General Naguib as the titular and apparent head of the new regime. Nasser appeared to be no more than another colonel in the RCC. Slowly his role as the guiding force behind the revolution began to become clear as he emerged as the victor of a power struggle within the RCC. The struggle for control between Nasser and Naguib went through several stages, culminating in the ouster of Naguib on November 14, 1954, and in his being placed under house arrest. Thus Nasser's dominant position was secured within the system, allowing him to become the undisputed leader of Egypt and, later, of the Arab world.

Political Environment

Egypt's social and economic structure is closely linked to the Nile River, which has traditionally been an important source of revenue and a central factor in daily life. Even today wealth is still often measured in landownership and control of agricultural production. Despite the increasing urbanization that has made Cairo a city of over 16 million people, of whom perhaps half do not have permanent housing, the majority of the Egyptian population are the *fellahin*, the peasants. They are the backbone of the Egyptian system, even if they are relatively deprived economically and educationally, as well as in terms of life expectancy, wealth, health, literacy, and most of the other measures of well-being. Both Nasser and Anwar Sadat traced their roots and publicized their connection to this group. In addition to the *fellahin* there are the traditional wealthy, upper-class landowners, the middle-class city dwellers, and the growing numbers of urbanized poor. The traditional supporters of the king and members of the court came from the upper class. Since the 1952 revolution, however, young men from the lower and middle classes have moved up the social ladder through the huge and growing bureaucracy and the military officer corps.

At the time of the revolution Egypt was a poor country facing a host of social and economic problems: low per capita income, unequal income distribution, disease, low life expectancy, high infant mortality, and a low literacy rate. Agriculture was the dominant sector of the economy, and this required the use of Nile water for irrigation. Industry, which was significantly limited by poor natural and mineral resources and by the lack of sufficiently trained workers, was a minor factor.

The Egyptian revolution of 1952 was launched to deal with a political issue, but almost as crucial were the substantial economic and social problems of Egypt, which were among the earliest problems tackled by the regime. There was a two-class system—a very rich upper class and very poor lower class, with the latter vastly larger than the former. The upper class—bankers, businessmen, merchants, and landlords—controlled the wealth of the country and dominated its political institutions. It could and did prevent the adoption of reform measures that would diminish its economic and political control. Much of Egypt's land was concentrated in the hands of relatively few absentee landowners. The poor, mostly landless peasants constituted more than 75 percent of the population. They were illiterate and had little opportunity to improve their situation. Their health standards were deplorable. Education was severely limited. This disparity between the landowning rich and the poor peasantry was further compounded by overpopulation, exacerbated by the high birthrates of the poor. The population growth rate surpassed that of agricultural production increases. Moreover, the possibility of food production's keeping pace with population growth was limited by lack of control of the water resources of the Nile.

One of the goals of the revolution, announced shortly after the takeover by the Free Officers, was the achievement of social and economic justice through elimination of the corrupt system and the monopoly of wealth. Although lacking a specific ideology and well-developed programs for implementing these goals, the new government attempted to raise the standard of living of the average Egyptian, especially of the *fellahin* of the Nile Valley, and to reduce the poverty and disease that had permeated Egyptian society for so long.

Agriculture

Egypt, the "gift of the Nile," has been dependent on that single main source of fresh water for the thousands of years of its recorded existence. There is a narrow strip of poor land along the Mediterranean coast where some crops can be grown when there is minimal rainfall. Except for this area and a few small oases, all agriculture is dependent on irrigation from the Nile. The land made inhabitable and cultivable by the river constitutes a small portion of Egypt's overall land area (about 4 percent); therefore, agricultural production, despite the rich soil of the Nile Valley and the favorable climate, has been limited. Nevertheless, it is the main occupation of, and provides the livelihood for, most Egyptians.

The limited agricultural production does not provide sufficient food for Egypt's increasingly large population. Despite efforts at control, Egypt's population growth rate hovered at almost 3 percent per year up to the 1990s. At this rate of growth, Egypt's population will number between 65 and 70 million by the year 2002—a population beyond Egypt's projected capacity to feed, clothe, house, and employ.

Agrarian reform became the first and most significant domestic effort of the new regime, as demonstrated by the Agrarian Reform Law of September 1952. It limited individual landholdings to less than two hundred *feddans* (approximately two hundred acres), reduced the rents paid for lands, and increased agricultural wages. In an effort to redistribute existing agricultural land and to divide the wealth of the country more equitably, some lands were expropriated (with compensation) and redistributed.

Related to the Agrarian Reform Law were other measures of considerable importance, of which the Aswan High Dam was among the most significant. The purpose of the dam was to improve Egypt's economic system by increasing the already high productivity levels of the Nile Valley lands through an improved irrigation system. The dam was designed to increase water storage capacity, to prevent devastating floods, to add cultivable land, and to create substantial additional hydroelectric capacity. The dam also had symbolic value as an achievement of the revolution.

The Aswan High Dam, finally completed in 1971, has had mixed effects. Many of the anticipated benefits have been realized. There has been a significant increase in the cultivated area of Egypt and in net agricultural output; flood control has also fostered productivity gains; additional electrical power, primarily for industrial use, has been made available; navigation along the Nile, which is utilized as a major transportation artery in Egypt, has been improved; and a fishing industry has been developed in Lake Nasser. However, there are some problems. For example, the silt that fertilized the lands of the Nile Valley with the annual flood has been trapped behind the dam in Lake Nasser. This makes it necessary to use larger amounts of chemical fertilizer, which is imported and expensive. Salinity has increased in the northern portion of the river and in some of the land that was formerly drained by floods.

Other Economic Sectors

The 1952 revolution was of little immediate consequence to the Egyptian economy. The land reforms resulted in some redistribution of land and wealth, but the economy continued to be based on private enterprise. Although some restrictions were placed on the economy, they were directed mainly toward foreign trade and payments. By the end of the 1950s government attitudes had shifted to favor public participation in, and direct regulation of, the economy; in 1961 a series of decrees nationalized all large-scale industry, business, finance, and virtually all foreign trade. Private enterprise and free trade were replaced by Arab socialism, which was proclaimed the basis of the economic system. In practice, this meant establishing a mixed economy with a large public sector (including all foreign trade) and with the remaining private economic activities subject to various kinds of direct controls. Prices were regulated, and resource allocation was determined by administrative action and decision.

The system derived its socialist character mainly from the fact that all big business was controlled by the government. Modern manufacturing, mining, electricity and other public utilities, construction, transport and communication, finance, and wholesale trade were primarily owned by the government, whereas most retail trade, handicrafts and repair, housing, professional services, and agriculture were privately owned. The government imposed some controls on agricultural production through its control of the irrigation system and through compulsory participation in government-sponsored agricultural cooperatives. Control was also exercised over the distribution of capital goods, raw materials, and semi-manufactures as well as over prices and wages.

By 1962 the Egyptian economy and the context in which it functioned had changed considerably. Ownership of the main branches of the economy had been transferred to the government. The wealth remaining in private hands was essentially real estate and that, too, was carefully controlled. Government budgets accounted for about 60 percent of the gross national product. Inequality of wealth and income had been greatly reduced, largely through a process of agrarian reform, higher taxation, the extension of social services, and a series of national-izations and sequestrations. The role of foreigners in the economy had been sub-stantially reduced and, in some sectors, eliminated. Industry had made substantial progress—accounting for more than 20 percent of the GNP—and continued to increase its proportion.

Efforts to improve the economic system were severely hampered by the losses suffered in the 1967 Arab-Israeli war. As a consequence of that conflict, Egypt lost substantial revenues from the closure of the Suez Canal, the loss of some oil fields in the occupied Sinai Peninsula, and the loss of tourism. All three elements had been important to Egypt's earning of foreign exchange for its development and for the purchase of needed imports.

After the October 1973 Arab-Israeli war, President Sadat inaugurated the eco-nomic *infitah,* or open-door policy, to encourage foreign and domestic private in-vestment. The Suez Canal was reopened in 1975, and the Sinai oil fields were later returned to Egyptian control. Fueled less by these economic policies and more by external factors such as oil revenues, Suez Canal tolls, tourism revenues, and re-mittances from Egyptians working abroad, economic performance began to im-prove and the gross domestic product increased by an annual average of over 9 percent between 1974 and 1981. Major aid from Arab oil-producing states, which had been contributing huge amounts of money every year since 1967, ceased after Egypt signed the peace treaty with Israel in 1979, although U.S. aid increased greatly.

Although there had been some improvements during the Sadat era, Hosni Mubarak encountered chronic economic difficulties upon taking office in 1981: an expensive government welfare system, rising inflation, foreign exchange short-ages, balance-of-payments problems, and a foreign debt estimated at about $21 billion. Five years later the foreign debt had grown to more than $46 billion, mak-ing Egypt the region's greatest debtor nation. The debt had risen to about $51 bil-lion by 1989.

Three factors have combined to make Egypt's economic picture brighter. First, by 1987, thanks to Mubarak's low-key diplomacy, ties had been restored with the Arab world; aid and investment from the wealthy Arab states had begun to return. Second, Egypt's support of the Saudi-U.S. coalition in the 1990–1991 Gulf crisis brought huge infusions of cash and debt cancellation from the Arab oil producers ($2 billion in cash and $7 billion in debt cancellation in 1990–1991), reducing Egypt's external debt to $40 billion in 1990. New grants were made by the Euro-pean nations, and U.S. aid rose significantly. The third factor improving Egypt's economic situation was the decision by Mubarak in 1991 to begin a massive structural adjustment program in cooperation with the International Monetary Fund (IMF) and the World Bank. The program was designed to move Egypt to-ward a market economy; it included a wide range of monetary reforms, ending most subsidies on basic commodities (except bread). Progress has been made on this major program, though privatization (a sensitive political issue) is proceeding slowly.

By early 1994 Egypt's economy had shown distinct improvement. The country had a strong balance-of-payments position and was proceeding with debt reduction more or less according to its rescheduling agreements. Major government efforts at birth control had succeeded in lowering the rate of population increase from about 3 percent in 1985 to about 2.3 percent in 1993. Although cotton exports had declined, agricultural output rose by about 5 percent in 1992, with record harvests of wheat, rice, corn, and citrus fruits. Suez Canal revenues had risen. Egypt has sizable gas reserves as well as oil and is hoping to turn to gas for much of its energy requirements, given problems with hydroelectric power generation resulting from droughts upstream on the Nile. An estimated 2.5 million Egyptians working abroad continue to send remittances home, but this source of foreign exchange is vulnerable to a variety of changes in other nations and the international economy.

Serious economic problems—both long- and short-term—remain for Egypt. In late 1992 fundamentalist attacks on tourists resulted in a sharp drop in revenues from this important source of foreign exchange. Although the violence had subsided somewhat by early 1994, tourism levels were still below the years leading up to 1992. Population growth, though advancing at a lower rate, is still high; the population reached about 60 million in 1994. The same densely populated land must support increasing numbers of people every year. Furthermore, migration to the cities has created nightmarish housing shortages, especially in Cairo, where the population grew from about 7 million in 1976 to about 9 million in 1980 and to over 16 million in 1993. Life expectancy at birth has risen to about sixty, but this is still far below the figure for the developed countries. The most important single economic problem remains one that is itself a product of a host of complex economic factors: A large portion of the Egyptian people live at no more than the subsistence level.

Political Structure

There have been several variations in Egypt's basic political structure since the 1952 revolution. With Nasser at its head, the RCC held the reins of political power. During this transition period a number of outstanding problems, including the final removal of British forces from Egypt and the canal zone, were finally resolved. In 1956 Nasser formally inaugurated a new system that consolidated power in his own hands.

On January 16, 1956, a new constitution was proclaimed in which extensive powers were concentrated in the hands of the president. The constitution also established a single political party, the National Union, which replaced the National Liberation Rally. The party, the National Assembly, and the other organs of government and politics remained under the control of Nasser, who was elected president by more than 99 percent of the vote in a plebiscite in 1956. The inauguration of the new constitution, formally approved in a plebiscite, ushered in a number of changes in the political system: Martial law was terminated, political prisoners were released, the RCC members became civilians (with the exception of General Abdul Hakim Amer, who was minister of defense) and joined various agencies of the government. This new system was short-lived.

In February 1958 Nasser yielded to the demands of a new government in Syria that the two nations be joined to form the United Arab Republic (UAR). The union of these two dissimilar and geographically noncontiguous political units into a single state called for the creation of a new political structure with, at least theoretically, Nasser sharing power with the Syrian leadership. The provisional constitution of the new UAR was proclaimed, and Nasser became president. Nasser received nearly all the votes cast in the presidential election on February 21, 1958. Both Egyptians and Syrians were represented in the institutions of government, but most of the actual governing was by decree of Nasser and his chief advisers and aides—especially General Amer, who largely controlled the Syrian region. In September 1961, Syria, disenchanted with Egyptian domination and Nasser's growing socialism, severed ties with the UAR and reestablished its independence. Egypt continued to be known by the name "United Arab Republic" until it became the Arab Republic of Egypt (ARE) in 1971.

With the termination of the union of Egypt and Syria in 1961, there was an intensification of Nasser's socialist programs in Egypt. A new governmental system was again devised and implemented soon thereafter, with a clear socialistic focus. Socialist measures adopted in the early 1960s included further agrarian reform, progressive tax measures, nationalization of business enterprises, and, in general, increased governmental control over the economy. A new charter and constitution were created, and a new political organization, the Arab Socialist Union (ASU), was formed. Elections for parliament took place. A new constitution was adopted in 1964 that provided the framework for the remainder of the Nasser tenure.

A new phase in Egyptian politics began with the death of Nasser on September 29, 1970, and his replacement by Anwar Sadat. Sadat's consolidation of political control in May 1971 was followed by changes in the political structures and processes of politics. On September 11, 1971, the present constitution was approved by general referendum. It is similar to its predecessor in continuing the strong presidential system extant in Egypt since the revolution. According to the constitution, the president of the republic is head of state. He is empowered to declare a state of emergency in the case of national danger, subject to a referendum within sixty days. Legislative power is vested in the National Assembly, composed of 444 directly elected members and others nominated by the president; members of parliament serve a five-year term. The president may object to laws passed by the National Assembly within thirty days of their passage, but the assembly has the right to override his objection by a two-thirds vote. The president has the power to appoint vice presidents, the prime minister and his cabinet, High Court judges, provincial governors, university presidents, and even some religious leaders. He is the supreme commander of the armed forces. Although the constitution increased the powers of the National Assembly, dominant authority remained with the president, who has the right of temporary rule by decree. Presidential decrees have the power of law. The constitution includes guarantees of freedom of expression, as well as assurance of freedom from arbitrary arrest, seizure of property, and mail censorship. Press censorship is banned except in periods of war or emergency. At first, the Arab Socialist Union was declared the only authorized political party, but this was gradually modified, beginning in 1976. Islam was declared the state religion, although freedom of religion was guaranteed.

In 1976 Sadat initiated what appeared to be a move toward a multiparty system when he announced that three ideological "platforms" would be organized within the ASU. The centrist group—the Egyptian Arab Socialist Organization—had Sadat's personal support and won a vast majority of the seats in the 1976 parliamentary election. Sadat still refused to allow independent parties to be formed, and the three organizations never took root as genuine vehicles of political participation. Only after the violent clashes over increased prices of basic commodities in January 1977 did Sadat permit parties to be formed. The opposition from these parties was too much for Sadat to bear, however, and he soon clamped down on such groups as the New Wafd Party and the leftist National Progressive Unionist Party.

In July 1978 Sadat created the National Democratic Party (NDP) and later permitted a leftist party to organize as an official opposition. Both the Egyptian Arab Socialist Organization and the Arab Socialist Union were abolished in April 1980. An Advisory Council was established to serve the functions of the old ASU Central Committee, and in the September 1980 elections for that council, Sadat's new NDP won all 140 seats, with the seventy remaining posts being appointed directly by the president. Sadat, like Nasser before him, wanted to create a political organization but was unable to tolerate the loss of political control that would occur if these "parties" were to become genuine vehicles for mass participation.

Sadat's assassination in October 1981 by Islamic fundamentalists opposed to his peacemaking with Israel changed very little about Egyptian domestic politics. Sadat's successor, Hosni Mubarak, left the basic structure unaltered. He allowed the New Wafd to participate in the 1984 parliamentary elections, but the NDP won handily and some opposition parties failed to get sufficient votes to secure even one seat in the assembly. The NDP, still the party of the president, won 384 seats in the November 1990 election, with the main opposition parties boycotting the polls. Mubarak was elected to a third presidential term in October 1993 and a fourth in September 1999. Parliamentary elections were held in November 2000.

Despite all the changes, Egypt remained a strong presidential system with a facade of elections and party rule. The judiciary is independent, but the government can, and has, used military courts or the "state of emergency" (in force without interruption since 1981) regulations to ignore judicial decisions it does not favor. There are eleven legal political parties in addition to the NDP, the government party. Neither the other parties nor the NDP has much mass support. The greatest threat to the government is from the various Islamic fundamentalist groups. The largest, oldest, and best organized is the Muslim Brotherhood, founded in 1928 in Egypt. It was banned by Nasser in 1954 and is still technically illegal, but it is officially tolerated because its efforts to Islamize society are made from within the existing political system. This is not the case with the more radical Islamic groups that have resorted to violence to advance their cause. After the assassination of Sadat, there was a lull in these violent activities. They resumed in the 1990s, as the radical groups gained young recruits frustrated at unemployment and poverty. In October 1990 the speaker of the People's Assembly was killed. An anti-fundamentalist journalist was assassinated in June 1992, part of a dramatic upsurge in fundamentalist violence, often directed against Coptic Christians, government officials, and, starting in October 1992, against foreign tourists. Although the attacks on tourists abated somewhat by the late 1990s, it has only been at the cost of brutal government suppression.

Political Dynamics

Nasser ruled Egypt from 1954 until his death in 1970. He was the first Egyptian since the pharaohs to control Egypt for any long period. During his tenure he captured the attention and imagination not only of the Egyptian people but also of the Arab world, much of the Third World, and other portions of the international community. Egypt ended British control, established a republican form of government, and began extensive political change.

The 1950s were the heyday of Nasser's rule. He succeeded in nationalizing the Suez Canal. He thwarted the objectives of Israel, Britain, and France in the 1956 Sinai War and was able to turn military defeat into achievement—if not victory— with the aid of the United States and the Soviet Union, which both insisted on the removal of foreign troops from Egypt. He secured arms and aid for the Aswan High Dam from the Soviet Union and Soviet bloc allies after the United States and other lenders decided not to provide the necessary assistance. Nasser became a leader of the Nonaligned Movement, and despite the many difficulties in implementing any form of Arab unity, he mobilized people all over the Arab world to think of themselves as members of a group larger than their own state. Nasser symbolized renascent Arab strength for many of the ordinary citizens of the Arab world.

Nasser's accomplishments in the 1950s were soon followed by difficulties. The United Arab Republic dissolved acrimoniously in 1961, Egypt became involved in the civil war in Yemen in the early 1960s (which turned out to be a quagmire from which it would be difficult to withdraw), and there were feuds with other

Arab states and challenges to Nasser's role as Arab world leader. The 1967 Arab-Israeli war proved disastrous and resulted in the loss of the Sinai Peninsula (one-seventh of Egypt's land area), the closure of the Suez Canal, and the loss of a substantial portion of Egypt's military capability.

Despite these reverses, Nasser was still the preeminent Egyptian and Arab, the most influential figure in the Middle East, and a focal point of regional and international attention. Nasser's role extended beyond that designated in the constitution. He exercised unwritten powers by virtue of his unique standing in the system, his accomplishments, and his charismatic appeal to the peasantry that formed the backbone of the Egyptian polity. He controlled all the main instruments of power and coercion, including the army, the secret police and intelligence agencies, and the Arab Socialist Union. He dominated the cabinet and the National Assembly. Nasser's central role and his charismatic appeal to the overwhelming majority of Egyptians raised doubts, at the time of his death, about a successor's ability to replace him as the undisputed leader of Egypt and the Arab world. Nasser died of a heart attack on September 29, 1970, following intense negotiations he had brokered between King Hussein of Jordan and PLO Chairman Yasir Arafat, whose forces had been at war for that whole month in Jordan.

The constitution in force at that time called for Vice President Anwar Sadat to succeed Nasser in office, but there had been no indication that Nasser favored Sadat, or anyone else, as his ultimate successor. Sadat initially enjoyed the legitimacy of being the formal successor and of his long association with Nasser (he was virtually the only former Free Officer left in office by this time), but it was generally assumed that he would soon be replaced by one of the powerful rivals maneuvering behind the scene. Although Sadat was elected president in an October 1970 referendum (receiving only 85 percent of the vote, as opposed to Nasser's traditional 99 percent), the long-term stability of his regime was not yet assured.

Sadat sought to consolidate his position but did not make a major overt move until May 1971, when he suddenly purged the government of all senior officials who opposed him. This group included Vice President Ali Sabri, a prominent left-leaning figure who had headed the ASU and was regarded as Moscow's favorite candidate, as well as the minister of war, the head of intelligence, and other senior officials. These officials were later tried for high treason.

Sadat did not enjoy the widespread adulation Nasser had evoked from the masses and had even been derided as Nasser's yes-man. His declaration that 1971 would be a "year of decision" that would result in war or peace in the Arab-Israeli conflict did nothing to improve his popularity, as the year ended with no movement toward achievement of this objective. By 1972 Sadat had become an object of ridicule and cruel jokes, which raised doubts about his leadership. It was in partial response to domestic criticism and to the concerns and complaints of the military that he decided to terminate the role of the Soviet advisers in Egypt in 1972. Sadat soon began to prepare for the October War (the Arab-Israeli war of 1973) because he saw little progress toward a political settlement of the conflict with Israel. He achieved a formidable success in taking the Israelis by surprise and crossing the heavily fortified Suez Canal at the beginning of the war in October 1973. Although he ultimately lost the war in a military sense, with the Egyptian Third Army surrounded by Israeli troops, his initial success in the field and his mobilization of support from the conservative Arab oil producers (who, at his behest, used oil as a political weapon for the first time) made the war a political success. Sadat was able to place Israel on the defensive internationally, to secure further international support for the Egyptian and Arab positions, and to attract increased aid from the oil-rich Arab states. Of the many honorary titles he received, Sadat was said to have favored above all the phrase that came into use after Egyptian troops took the Suez Canal back from the Israeli forces that had held its eastern shore since 1967: "Hero of the Crossing."

In April 1974 Sadat produced a document called the October Working Paper, which discussed the new era ushered in by the October War. It called for extensive reform and change in Egypt and suggested that the lot of the average Egyptian would improve. It embodied his new approach to politics and economics, especially the liberalization of politics, the economic "opening" to Western aid and investment, and the restructuring of the Egyptian government toward decentralization and away from the centrally planned economy. Sadat's turn to the West, which actually began with the expulsion of Soviet advisers in 1972, accelerated during the period after the October 1973 war, and culminated with the Egypt-Israel Peace Treaty of 1979, may all have been part of a huge economic gamble: By turning to the West, could he attract substantial aid and investment and get rid of the heavy economic burden of the war with Israel (and regain the Sinai Peninsula), while at the same time not totally alienate the oil-rich Arab states that had supported Egypt since 1967 with aid and investment?

By 1980 domestic tension in Egypt had grown, although Sadat's grip on power was in no way diminished. Confessional conflict had occurred between the large Coptic Christian minority and the Islamic fundamentalists, and Sadat placed restrictions on both. In the years after 1979 it became clear that there remained serious opposition to Egypt's move toward the West and its peace with Israel, especially from Islamic fundamentalists. What may have been Sadat's economic gamble was not paying off as well as he might have hoped: There was some Western aid and investment, but it was not substantial, and Arab aid and investment dropped sharply. Egypt had been ejected from the Arab League for making peace with Israel and remained isolated in the Arab world. More pressing yet, there had been no significant economic progress, and the standard of living of the average Egyptian was very low and getting worse. Sadat held his course. The years 1980 and 1981 were marked by increasing political violence, including clashes between Coptic Christians and Islamic fundamentalists. The Sadat government reacted repressively.

Sadat initiated severe repression of his opposition in September 1980, beginning with the formerly tolerated leftist party, but the major move was made almost a year later, in September 1981, when more than 1,500 Egyptian political figures of all political persuasions were arrested. Certain religious groups were banned and their newspapers closed. A number of Muslim Brotherhood leaders were arrested, and Sadat dismissed the Coptic leader, Pope Shenuda III. Many fundamentalist mosques were taken over by the government, and the security apparatus began to clamp down on universities. Foreign journalists who had criticized Sadat were expelled, along with the Soviet ambassador and other Soviet diplomats.

On October 6, 1981, Sadat was assassinated by Muslim fundamentalists at a parade celebrating the eighth anniversary of his supreme military achievement: the crossing of the Suez Canal at the opening of the 1973 October War. A state of emergency was declared, and the National Assembly nominated Vice President Hosni Mubarak to succeed Sadat. Although the assassins were quickly arrested, conflict broke out in Asyut between the security forces and Muslim fundamentalists. The anti-Sadat demonstrations were limited in scope and were soon quelled. A presidential referendum was held, and Mubarak was sworn in as president on October 14, 1981.

Although Mubarak cracked down on the religious extremists associated with Sadat's assassination, he released many of the other political figures whom Sadat had had arrested a month before his death. The battle against corruption started from the top, and Sadat's brother and some of his closest associates were taken to court for corrupt practices. Unlike Sadat, Mubarak and his family maintain a low profile and live modestly.

Despite the release of many political detainees, Mubarak kept a tight rein on Egyptian politics. The state of emergency is likely to remain in force, even though the emergency following Sadat's death has long passed. Mubarak made substantial economic progress and managed to put Egypt back into the center of the Arab world without reneging on the Egypt-Israel Peace Treaty of 1979. He faced down serious challenges to his rule, such as the February 1986 uprising by 20,000 conscripts of the Security Force, and the challenges that the Islamic fundamentalists continued to pose, all of which were brutally suppressed. As long as Mubarak continues to retain the all-important confidence of the Egyptian military, his regime is stable. If the economy continues to improve, and the fundamentalist threat remains controllable (even with ruthless suppression), Hosni Mubarak may feel strong enough to try genuine political liberalization, which was clearly on a back burner in 2001.

The Political Structure

The idiom of expression of contemporary Egyptian politics has combined several political ideas—state nationalism of a Western type overlaying older ideas of pan-Arabism and pan-Islamism. Over the past fifty years, political expression by both those in power and by the organized politically disaffected has used various combinations of these ideas, beginning with Nasser's Arab socialism and, now, increasingly, contemporary militant political Islamism. The Egyptian political structure, on the other hand, has remained relatively constant. The principal elements of the Egyptian political structure are patrimonial leadership, a powerful political class, and influential corporatist groups.

The Patrimonial Leader: Nasser, Sadat, and Mubarak

Gamal Abd al-Nasser (1952–1970), Anwar al-Sadat (1970–1981) and Hosni Mubarak (1981–present) can all be characterized as patrimonial leaders. The principle of legitimacy of the patrimonial leader is an ascribed one; that is, it is a characteristic of both the leadership role itself and it is attributed to the leader by his followers. This principle, while strengthening the authority of the leader, also is not sufficient in itself. Each of these leaders was also operating as the leader of a regime that was legitimized by the dominant idea of its time. For all three this was pan-Arabism, although from Sadat onwards, pan-Arabism was dialectically challenged by the political Islamism of the Islamic religious revival.

In the case of patrimonialism, all three leaders when addressing the Egyptian people often used the vocabulary of the family. This was especially the case with Sadat, who, in 1978, when he was negotiating the Camp David peace agreement with Israel, began a radio address by saying, "My brothers and sisters, my sons and daughters, I have terrible news to relate to you tonight. Today our sons prevented their fathers from going to work [i.e. students on university campuses were engaging in a campus boycott by way of protest against the policy]." It was Nasser among the three leaders who was able to go beyond the inherited patrimonialism of the leadership role and connect himself with the ideological principal of Arabism. In so doing he exceeded patrimonialism and by a combination of personality and ideology, his leadership became charismatic and even exceeded the bounds of Egypt. His anti-colonialism not only helped force the British military to withdraw from the Suez Canal Zone in 1954, but led him to join the positive neutralism of the Bandung Conference of 1955 and become a leader of Third World international stature.

In 1956 Nasser engaged in a dispute with the United States and the West over funding for the construction of the high dam at Aswan and nationalized the Suez Canal, still owned by British and French capital. Although militarily defeated by a British, French, and Israeli invasion force, Nasser was to emerge as the political "victor" upon the force's evacuation and his ability to remain in power. It was the prestige of these accomplishments that led him to another blow for pan-Arabism when he engineered the union of not only Egypt and Syria but also briefly Yemen in the United Arab Republic (1958–1961).

This union did not last, however, and was followed by Egypt's military intervention in Yemen on the side of revolutionaries, which dragged on until 1967.

Earlier in that year, still within the framework of pan-Arabism, Nasser, as the pre-eminent Arab leader, rhetorically tested Israel, only to have the latter inflict a devastating defeat upon him in the 1967 war.

In November 1970 Nasser succumbed to heart failure and was succeeded by his vice president, Anwar Sadat. Sadat was the last of the Free Officers who had engineered the revolution of 1952. The manner in which he had survived was due to his near political invisibility. During the time until his ascension to power he was known in Egypt as Nasser's "lap dog" or alternatively as *Sayyid Na'm Na'm* (Mr. Yes Yes). Unlike the revolutionary Arab leader Nasser, Sadat had no ideological principle of legitimacy attached to him. In any case, the 1967 defeat had been the death knell of Arabism. In a remarkable fashion, Sadat quickly sensed that the next ideological stage in Egypt's political development was to be Islam. The 1967 war had triggered the beginning of the Islamic revival. Sadat moved to gain Islamic support by beginning to free from prison the thousands of Islamic radicals placed there by Nasser. In addition, Sadat became a conspicuous practitioner of Islam by ostentatiously acquiring the dark callus on the forehead called a *zabiba,* which results from repeated contact with the prayer rug. This permitted Sadat to not only play the role of father but also of a fatherlike *imam* or leader of prayer.

Sadat had to address the Israeli military occupation of the huge expanse of the Sinai peninsula as a consequence of the 1967 war. This occupation was not only humiliating to Egypt but also cost the country hundreds of millions of dollars annually in lost revenues from the closure of the Suez Canal and from seized oil fields.

Sadat began to boldly plot the military expulsion of the Israelis. Nasser had, after 1967, invited 15,000 Soviet military advisers into Egypt to reform his military. By July 1972 they were ordered out of the country. They had completed their mission and their arrogance and the fact they restricted the military planning of Egypt meant they had to go. Sadat shrewdly planned the limited war of October 1973. The Egyptian surprise assault caught the Israelis off guard and the first two weeks saw a limited territorial gain in Sinai, which was needed to bring about serious diplomatic negotiations. On the other hand, in the last two weeks of the war, the Israelis had surrounded an Egyptian army and in effect this restored lost dignity to the Israelis.

Sadat initiated the diplomacy that eventually led to the withdrawal of the Israelis in 1982, but his nation was economically impoverished. He therefore began a program of political and economic liberalization (called *infitah* or the "opening" after the military success in Sinai) designed to appeal to the United States. The combination of this policy plus his willingness to break ranks with the Arab states and negotiate with America's ally Israel resulted in at first small and then later larger U.S. economic assistance. The result was to be ultimately, after two preliminary agreements, the Egypt-Israel Peace Treaty (1979) in which Israel agreed to evacuate Sinai, and Egypt established diplomatic relations with Israel.

The Political Class

The political class provides the patrimonial leader with the support necessary to make him authoritative politically. The relationship is one of political support on the one hand and economic benefits on the other. The existence of such a class in Egypt over the last 200 years of modernization has been intensely investigated by three scholars in the three different time periods from the period of the great modernizer of Egypt, Muhammad Ali (1805–1849) onwards, the Revolution of 1919 against the British, and during the time of Nasser. This phenomenon has been the basis of political strength over this long period and at the same time it is the basis of the strategic weakness of the state in performance terms. The developmental potential of the state is traded off for enduring political loyalty and stability. The definition of ruling class (*ayyan khassa*) is that it consists of the top 20 percent of the population who receive 48 percent of the income of the country. Accompanying this concentration of wealth is the ruling class's ability through government and, increasingly, private-sector leadership to dominate the corporatist group structures of the society. This symbiotic relationship accounts for how in the pre-1991 period of Egyptian regional hegemonic leadership, domestic stability strengthened the leaders' foreign policy hand. On the other hand, in the post-1991 geoeconomic period, this relationship became one of a dysfunctional inability to develop and produce, thus weakening Egypt's ability to compete economically.

Informal Corporatist Groups

The corporatist group structure reflects the division of labor necessary for the maintenance of society. These groups consist of two categories. There are first informal family, peer group, and "old boy" networks, which provide the basic procreational and support functions of society. Second, there are the formal groups that carry out the labor of society, such as trade unions and bar associations. The Egyptian family (*a 'ila*) is classically Middle Eastern sedentary in character. It is patriarchical, extended, endogamous, and patrilocal. It is both the model of political authority as reflected in the concept of "patrimonialism" and the basic unit of allegiance in Egyptian society. Family loyalties and the authority of the father are primary. The extension of loyalty to a network of grandparents, aunts, uncles, cousins, and so on makes the range of the family extensive. The practice of arranged marriages and first cousin marriages increases family solidarity. So does the tendency of families to live concentrated in a single geographical area. At the age of puberty, the boy leaves the house of his closely knit family and forms a play and membership peer group called a *shilla*. The *shilla* is a lifetime membership group that has responsibilities for the security of the neighborhood. On occasion, such as the 1977 riots in Cairo over the raising of bread prices, the *shilla*s can become politically activated.

Those who graduate from high school, university, or military academy have alumni status as a *duffaa* known by the year of graduation. For example, it was the *duffaa* of 1938 from the Royal Military Academy that carried out the revolution of 1952. The class of 1938 served together and was promoted together on the principle of solidarity. It was they who went to fight in Palestine against the Zionist Jews in 1948. There they suffered the humiliating defeat that attributed to the corruption of their leaders. In the words of Nasser, "The Enemy was in Egypt!" This solidarity grouping provides a further potentially political membership group.

Formal Corporatist Groups

Corporatist groups are formal for at least two major reasons. The first is that they cannot exist at all except with the permission of the state by law. It is the need to formally apply for such approval that makes them corporatist groups and not civil society groups. The second reason is that in fact, once given approval to operate, they then have a familiar identity as trade unions, medical associations, engineering societies, and so on. With the granting of approval, an informal compact *(mithaq)* is entered into whereby the organization agrees that it will not engage in political activities and will support the state in exchange for a grant of a monopoly of its sector.

Illustrative of this point about licensing is the role of the army and that of the Islamic groups. The army is the keystone institution of Egyptian society. It is the arbiter of Egyptian politics and the guarantor of the "strong" state. Its "license," therefore, follows from the respect the state accords it. It does not, however, seek a political role for itself. Under Nasser it possessed this role and the result was the ignominious defeat of Egypt in 1967. Thus in the bread riots of 1976 in protest against the threatened end of food subsidies, the army intervened, restored order, and withdrew. It was to do this again in 1986 when paramilitary troops rebelled. The segment of the army prepared to carry out this support of the regime and the defense of the constitution has been the army of combat. There is also the army of production, which significantly makes Egypt self-reliant in arms production but also produces consumer goods. The army is free from budgetary accountability and the "production" army is especially free from scrutiny and is monopolistic in its activities.

Whereas the army has found its accommodation within the system, the Islamic groups have not. The mainstream of Islam would like to be licensed and included in the system but the regime refuses to do this. Instead it lumps such moderate groups together with the extreme and violent minority.

All these formal corporatist groups have the primary responsibility for their internal affairs, including the ability to benefit themselves economically. The internal affairs of such groups, with the exception of the professionalized army, are characterized by the presence of informal corporatist groups such as family, peer groups, and old boy networks that operate in elections to the presidencies and executive committees of the trade unions, bar associations, and similar units. The informal groups have acted as political parties or factions. More recently, Islamic groups, notably the moderate Muslim Brotherhood, have supplanted informal groups. This has prompted government interference in these internal group elections and even their cancellation.

The Dualism of Egyptian Society

The existence of a political class of great wealth and privilege suggests the possibility that Egyptian society might be interpreted in terms of class structure: for example, bourgeoisie, proletarian, and peasant classes. It is a further dimension of the politically strong and capability weak state that this is not the case. The ability of a strong executive and a cooperative political class to maintain themselves in power does not mean that they can organize the society for productive purposes or mobilize the masses of the population for greater productivity. In other words, the quietism of the politically strong state distances itself from the masses and the weakness of the economic state creates a gap and space and not the conditions of alienation and class-consciousness. It has been suggested that the informal sector is also Islamic. As a result, a political and economic distance exists between the political and economic capabilities of the state on the one hand and the masses on the other. It is estimated that 80 percent of small businesses are in the informal sector and free from the payment of taxes and 30 percent of the GDP is located there. This gap is reinforced by the 54 percent illiteracy rate that creates dialectical and regional differences.

As noted, a further gap is in law enforcement, where the most serious of criminal acts are sometimes dealt with informally by means of customary law.

The parliamentary elections in October and November 2000 were illustrative of these themes of the strong and the weak state. The elections were evidence of the relative strength of the state in that the state was able to manufacture a desired political outcome. The government's National Democratic Party (NDP) was finally able to cobble together a majority of 388 seats (87 percent) out of a total of 444 contested seats (ten can be appointed by the president). This percentage compared with 97 percent in 1995. But these figures do not show the government's declining ability to dictate the outcome by the forced mobilization of the voting population. In fact, in actual voting success the NDP won only about 175 seats outright and had to pressure/bargain with 213 "independents" to persuade them to switch to the government party.

The real electoral contest was not with the official opposition parties but rather with "independent" candidates who, in fact, were identified by the public as the illegal, politically moderate Muslim Brotherhood (MB). They ended up with a remarkable seventeen seats, gained despite beatings, intimidation, and occasional killings. What is further remarkable about this is that the perpetrators of the violence were not the usual state security forces but rather male and female toughs hired by NDP candidates intent upon gaining what they regarded as their due. In other words, even the classic exercise of coercion had slipped from the hands of the state into the hands of the state's underlings. The relative success of the Muslim Brotherhood was further evidence of the degree of the Islamization of the Egyptian state.

Foreign Policy

Overview

Napoleon once labeled Egypt "the most important country" because of its central location, which provided a key to Africa and the Middle East. In the post–World War II period Egypt has become even more significant. The Suez Canal, although it cannot accommodate the largest supertankers, is a prime artery for oil. Egypt is a leader among African, Islamic, Arab, and other developing nations. It is also the primary state for the establishment of peace or the waging of war in the Arab-Israeli conflict. It has been courted by both the United States and the Soviet Union, each in pursuit of its own interests in the region and in the broader international community.

Egypt is the leader of the Arab world in a number of other respects. Its population and military forces are the largest. It has led the Arab world in communications (publishing, arts, literature, films) and other spheres. In the nineteenth century and the early part of the twentieth century, Egypt spearheaded Arab contact with the Western world and helped to develop the intellectual bases for Arab, as well as Egyptian, nationalism. It was a leader in the establishment of the Arab League. Furthermore, its Suez Canal was an important strategic and economic asset.

After the 1952 revolution Egypt emerged as an important Third World neutralist and nonaligned power, and Egypt and Nasser were increasingly relied upon for leadership in the Arab world and beyond. Egypt's foreign policy was virtually nonexistent prior to the 1952 revolution, since Egypt was largely controlled by non-Egyptians. Major and assertive foreign policy positions developed only after the revolution and seemed to be reactive, responding to events as they developed. Nasser's foreign policy focused, in the first instance, on the need to eliminate the British colonial presence in the canal zone and in the Sudan. In the second instance, there was the problem of Israel. It is in these contexts that Egypt's relations with the United States and the Soviet Union emerged.

Initial successes included the agreement on the withdrawal of the British from their positions in Egypt and the resolution of the Sudan problem (although Sudan eventually chose independence rather than union with Egypt). On February 12, 1953, Britain and Egypt signed the Agreement on Self-Government and Self-

Determination for the Sudan, which provided for the latter's transition to self-government and its choice between linkage with Egypt or full independence. The Suez question was settled in an agreement of October 19, 1954. That agreement declared the 1936 treaty to be terminated and provided for the withdrawal of British forces from Egyptian territory within twenty months.

Relations with the superpowers were different. Although the United States was initially helpful to the new regime and provided technical and economic aid, as well as some assistance in the negotiations with the British, there were difficulties concerning Nasser's requests for arms. Moreover, U.S. Secretary of State John Foster Dulles viewed Egypt's increasingly close ties with Communist China and the Soviet Union with suspicion. The Baghdad Pact, a Western-oriented defense alliance, conceived and sponsored by the United States, was not viewed positively by Nasser, who saw it as a threat to Arab independence and autonomy. Raids on Israel by fedayeen and counterraids by Israel into Gaza sparked, in Nasser's view, a need for arms for defense, and his quest led him to closer links with the Soviet bloc, thus further straining ties with the United States. The Dulles decision that the United States would not fund the Aswan High Dam was a major blow to the plans of the new regime, which decided to continue building and to secure the necessary funding and assistance from alternative sources. The Soviet Union was prepared to assist in the construction and to provide some financial aid. But in Nasser's view a more demonstrable act was needed. Thus, in July 1956, he nationalized the Suez Canal and stated that the canal revenues would go to the construction of the dam.

While the U.S.-Egyptian relationship was deteriorating, the Soviet role in Egypt (and elsewhere in the Arab world) was improving. Soviet assistance for the Aswan Dam project and the supply of arms essential to the continued stature and satisfaction of the Egyptian military and, ostensibly, to the defense of Egypt against Israel were elements that helped to ensure the positive Soviet-Egyptian relationship.

Then came the Sinai-Suez war of 1956, when Israel, France, and Britain joined in an effort to unseat Nasser and restore the canal to Western control while destroying Egypt's military capability (especially its ability to use the newly acquired arms). The United States opposed the invasion and exerted considerable pressure on its three friends to withdraw from Egyptian territory. In assisting the Nasser regime, the United States won much goodwill in the Arab world, especially in Egypt. But this goodwill was soon dissipated when the United States became involved in the 1958 Lebanese crisis and opposed the Egyptian position.

The chill between the United States and Egypt thawed slightly during the Kennedy administration, but with the death of John Kennedy and the establishment of President Lyndon Johnson's position on foreign policy, the relationship began to deteriorate once again. By the time of the Six-Day War of June 1967, relations between the two states were poor, and the war itself precipitated the break of diplomatic relations. The relationship between the United States and Egypt remained antagonistic until the end of the October War, when President Richard Nixon and Secretary of State Henry Kissinger established the policy that led to a rapprochement. A cordial relationship grew in the mid-1970s in virtually all the bilateral spheres, demonstrated by state visits by Sadat to the United States in 1975 and 1977 and a 1974 state visit by Nixon to Egypt.

Relations with the Soviet Union were somewhat different. Beginning in the mid-1950s, Soviet economic and technical assistance were important elements in the Aswan Dam project and in Egypt's economic development. Military assistance was another element in the developing relations of the two states. Because Nasser felt that Egypt required arms to maintain the regime and to deal with Israel, the Soviet Union became a major factor inasmuch as it was prepared to provide arms under cost and with payment terms acceptable to the Egyptians. The Egyptian military soon had a Soviet arsenal. Soviet equipment provided the arms essential for the Egyptian armies in the 1956, 1967, 1969–1970, and 1973 wars. But despite the consummation of a treaty of friendship between the countries in 1971, the Soviets were never popular with senior members of the Egyptian military.

The rift between Egypt and the Soviet Union began when the Soviet Union attempted to influence the choice of Nasser's replacement after his sudden death in 1970. After Sadat's consolidation of his position following the arrest of his major opponents, Egypt's relationship with the Soviet Union deteriorated further, as the Soviet Union and its Egyptian clients began to differ on the type of equipment the Soviets were willing to provide and on Soviet attempts to constrain Egyptian military plans. This culminated in the expulsion of Soviet advisers in July 1972. Although Egyptian-Soviet relations improved somewhat during the months that followed, the relationship never returned to its former levels. After the October War Egypt complained that the Soviets were lax in resupplying the Egyptian military forces. Egypt increasingly turned to the West, especially the United States, and Sadat articulated the view that the United States held the crucial cards for peace in the region and could also become the source of essential economic and technical assistance for Egypt. The policy seemed to be a zero-sum game: Better relations with the United States spelled poorer relations with the Soviet Union.

Arab nationalism has always been a key concept in Egyptian foreign policy, although its passionate espousal during the Nasser period diminished to lip service under Sadat and Mubarak. In his *Philosophy of the Revolution,* Nasser argued that Arab unity had to be established, for it would provide strength for the Arab nation to deal with its other problems. Arab unity was a consistent theme during the period of his tenure. Sadat retained that general theme but focused much of his foreign policy on the Arab-Israeli conflict and the future of the Palestinians. His signing of the Camp David Accords and the Egypt-Israel Peace Treaty of 1979 left him open to charges that he had forgotten the Palestinians and the rest of the Arab world in his pursuit of Egyptian interests alone. The brotherhood of the Arab people has not disappeared from the political lexicon of the Egyptian leadership. Even during the early

1980s, when Egypt remained isolated from the Arab world, Mubarak did not disown the concept. The heyday of Arab nationalism, however, had clearly passed, for a number of reasons, including perhaps Sadat's willingness to go it alone with Israel and Mubarak's ability to survive the isolation from the Arab world that followed.

Another important theme of Egyptian policy has been its leadership role in the Arab world. Developed as a part of the pan-Arab or Arab nationalist approach, this theme acquired added dimensions with Nasser's increasing interests in the Arabian Peninsula and the Gulf region in the 1960s. Increasingly, Egypt became the Arab leader in the conflict with Israel. The Arab-Israeli conflict and the wars of 1956, 1967, and 1970 (the War of Attrition along the Suez Canal) consumed Nasser's attention in foreign policy, and Egypt played the leading role in most aspects of the Arab side of the conflict. After 1967 the radical/conservative split in the Arab world was more or less healed at the Khartoum Summit, and Egypt's leadership began to encompass even the more conservative Arab states.

Following the October War, Sadat initiated a dramatic transformation of Egyptian foreign policy. He began with the assumption that the key to both his domestic and his foreign policy problems lay in closer ties with the United States, for he felt that only the United States could push Israel to relinquish territories occupied in the 1967 war (most critical for Egypt, the Sinai) and provide the technical and economic assistance the Egyptian economy desperately needed. The U.S. option thus seemed logical for both political and economic reasons.

The postwar approach began in the months following the war. In January 1974, Kissinger achieved a first-stage disengagement agreement separating Israeli and Egyptian forces along the Suez Canal and in Sinai. Relations between Egypt and the United States began to improve dramatically, and relations with the Soviet Union continued to deteriorate. After further and substantial effort, a second-stage disengagement between Israel and Egypt, known as Sinai II, was signed in September 1975. It provided for further Israeli withdrawals and the return to Egypt of important oil fields in Sinai. Nixon visited Egypt in June 1974, with the Watergate scandal at its height, and Sadat later visited the United States (October-November 1975).

In the wake of the Sinai II agreement, Egyptian policy took on a new cast. Sadat seemed to be interested in maintaining the role of the United States as the power that would help attain peace by pressuring Israel to change its policies. Movement was slowed, however, by regional developments—especially the civil war in Lebanon—and by the U.S. presidential elections. The conclusion of the elections in November 1976 and the temporary winding down of the Lebanon conflict set a new process in motion. During the initial months of President Jimmy Carter's administration there was substantial movement toward the establishment of a process to lead toward peace or at least toward a Geneva conference designed to maintain the momentum toward a settlement. But the movement seemed to have slowed substantially by October 1977, thus leading to Sadat's decision to "go to Jerusalem" and to present his case and the Arab position directly to the Israeli parliament and people. In so doing he set in motion a new approach to the Arab-Israeli conflict in which direct Egyptian-Israeli negotiations became, for the first time, the means to peace in the Middle East. The direct negotiations were continued at the Cairo Conference and Ismailia Summit of December 1977 and in lower-level contacts over the ensuing months. Then, in September 1978, Sadat met with President Carter and Israeli Prime Minister Menachem Begin at the Camp David summit, which provided a framework for peace between Egypt and Israel and, ultimately, for a broader arrangement between Israel and the other Arab states. On March 26, 1979, Sadat signed the Egypt-Israel Peace Treaty in Washington. Implementation of the treaty, which normalized relations between the two states, proceeded as scheduled, and diplomatic relations were established. At the same time, various contacts were made, including tourist and communications links. These actions led to Egypt's expulsion from the Arab League and its isolation in the Arab world, which refused to accept Sadat's argument that the treaty and peace with Israel were in the best interests of the Palestinians and the other Arabs. Failure to achieve substantial progress toward implementation of the other Camp David framework, which provided for arrangements for the West Bank and Gaza, further complicated Egypt's and Sadat's position. Despite U.S. effort, the talks were suspended.

Sadat's assassination in October 1981 raised questions about Egypt's foreign policy direction, particularly its arrangements with Israel. President Mubarak reaffirmed and built upon the policies he inherited from Sadat, emphasizing negotiated solutions to the Arab-Israeli conflict, maintenance of the peace with Israel, and close and positive relations with the United States. The peace treaty's provisions were implemented on or ahead of schedule. Although Mubarak insisted on maintenance of the peace with Israel, he also has been critical of Israel at times. He sharply criticized Israel's June 1982 invasion of Lebanon and withdrew his ambassador from Israel following the Sabra and Shatilla refugee camp massacres in September 1982. (Egypt's embassy remained in Tel Aviv, however, just as Israel's embassy remained in Egypt, and the Egyptian ambassador later returned.) Nevertheless, Mubarak worked to reduce Egypt's Arab world isolation by gradually restoring and improving relations with the Arab states. He succeeded in improving ties with the moderate Arab states, and Egypt was readmitted to the Islamic Conference in early 1984. Mubarak also shrewdly utilized the opportunity presented by the Iran-Iraq war to improve his ties with several Arab moderate states, in part through offers of assistance to Iraq. By 1987 he had succeeded in returning Egypt to the mainstream of the Arab world without making a single concession, and in May 1989 Egypt rejoined the Arab League.

Another inter-Arab conflict gave Mubarak the chance to improve Egypt's situation. Egypt played a key role in pulling together the Arab states opposed to Iraq's invasion of Kuwait. With Saudi Arabia and Syria, Egypt provided the major Arab element of the coalition that joined with U.S. and European forces in the offensive against Iraq in January 1991. Egypt sent the second-largest foreign force in the Gulf after the United States: 27,000 men to Saudi Arabia and some 5,000 to the UAE.

After the Gulf war, Egypt's relations with several of the Arab states—Syria and Libya in particular—improved sharply. Libya invited Egypt to mediate in its conflict with the United States and the United Kingdom over the bombing of the Pan Am jetliner over Lockerbie, Scotland, in 1988. Conversely, Egypt's relations with the Arab supporters of Iraq—Jordan, Yemen, and Sudan—have remained poor. Relations with Sudan deteriorated not only because of a border quarrel but also because of Mubarak's fears that the Islamic fundamentalist government in Khartoum was sponsoring the training and infiltration of fundamentalist insurgents into Egypt and other moderate Arab states (such as Algeria).

Relations with Israel under Mubarak have been correct, if not warm, but Mubarak has played a strong role in supporting and sponsoring Israeli negotiations with other key players in the Arab-Israeli conflict, principally the PLO and Syria. In Cairo in February 1994 Israeli Foreign Minister Peres and PLO Chairman Arafat signed an agreement that recorded some progress in implementing the breakthrough agreement signed by the PLO and Israel in Washington in September 1993.

Relations with the United States have remained positive since their restoration in 1974. The personal chemistry between Sadat and Carter was an important factor in this development. Mubarak has been able to broaden and strengthen the relationship since his accession to office. Numerous exchanges of visits between U.S. and Egyptian officials (including regular trips by Mubarak to Washington) have allowed the dialogue on Middle Eastern and other issues to continue. U.S. economic and military assistance to Egypt rose to several billion dollars a year in the 1980s and to about $2.5 billion a year in the late 1980s and early 1990s and remained near that level into the twenty-first century. Mubarak obtained an unwritten agreement to have U.S. aid to Egypt tied to the level of aid to Israel, although at a slightly lower level.

Egyptian Foreign Policy: A Net Assessment

One way to look at Egyptian foreign policy is to assess its strengths and weaknesses. A major strength, at least from the viewpoint of the foreign policy decisionmakers, is the centralization of authority in a patrimonial executive supported by an acquiescent political class. On the other hand, Egypt's lack of economic resources severely limits its ability to influence other countries to adopt policies in furtherance of its national interests, either through diplomacy or, indirectly, through force of arms. As a result, Egypt has had to pursue a foreign policy of seeking infusions of foreign financial and military assistance to maintain internal stability and external security and to create economic growth.

During the cold war, Egypt's ability to play one superpower against the other facilitated this effort, and with tensions running high in the Middle East, it was successful in building up its military, first with Soviet and then, in the 1970s, with American arms. When President Sadat negotiated a peace treaty with Israel in 1979, Egypt exchanged peace for economic assistance, and since that time, Egypt has received the second-largest amount of economic assistance given by the U.S. worldwide, next to Israel itself.

The apex of Egyptian regional influence in the Arab world occurred in the 1960s under the charismatic Gamal Abd al-Nasser. Sadat became a pariah in the Arab world following his peace treaty with Israel, and though his successor, Hosni Mubarak, engineered Egypt's return to the Arab fold, his priorities have centered more on domestic problems than foreign policy.

Bibliography

A review of the background of modern Egypt and the nature of its people is essential to an understanding of its political culture. Two particularly important works in this regard are Henry A. Ayrout's *The Egyptian Peasant* (Boston: Beacon Press, 1963) and William Lane's *Manners and Customs of the Modern Egyptians* (New York: Dutton, 1923). The historical background of modern Egypt is considered in Robert O. Collins and Robert L. Tignor, *Egypt and the Sudan* (Englewood Cliffs, N.J.: Prentice-Hall, 1967); Peter Mansfield, *The British in Egypt* (New York: Holt, Rinehart & Winston, 1971); and Nadav Safran, *Egypt in Search of Political Community: An Analysis of the Intellectual and Political Evolution of Egypt, 1804–1952* (Cambridge, Mass.: Harvard University Press, 1961). Jamal Mohammed Ahmed, in *The Intellectual Origins of Egyptian Nationalism* (London: Oxford University Press, 1960), provides an introduction to nationalism as it developed in Egypt.

Among the many good studies of Egypt since the revolution are Anouar Abdel-Malek, *Egypt: Military Society—The Army Regime, the Left, and Social Change Under Nasser* (New York: Random House, 1968) (translated by Charles Lam Markmann); R. Hrair Dekmejian, *Egypt Under Nasir: A Study in Political Dynamics* (London: University of London Press; Albany: State University of New York Press, 1972); Peter Mansfield, *Nasser's Egypt*, rev. ed. (Baltimore: Penguin Books, 1969); Georgiana G. Stevens, *Egypt: Yesterday and Today* (New York: Holt, Rinehart & Winston, 1963); P. J.Vatikiotis, ed., *Egypt Since the Revolution* (New York: Praeger Publishers, 1968); Keith Wheelock, *Nasser's New Egypt: A Critical Analysis* (New York: Praeger Publishers, 1960); John Waterbury, *Egypt: Burdens of the Past, Options for the Future* (Bloomington, Ind.: Indiana University Press, 1978); John Waterbury, *The Egypt of Nasser and Sadat* (Princeton: Princeton University Press, 1983); Panayotis J.Vatikiotis, *Nasser and His Generation* (New York: St. Martin's Press, 1978); Mohamed Heikal, *Autumn of Fury: The Assassination of Sadat* (New York: Random House, 1983); Raymond Baker, *Egypt's Uncertain Revolution Under Nasser and Sadat* (Cambridge, Mass.: Harvard University Press, 1978); Elie Kedourie and Sylvia G. Haim, eds., *Modern Egypt: Studies in Politics and Society* (London: Frank Cass, 1980); and John Waterbury, *Hydropolitics of the Nile Valley* (Syracuse, New York: Syracuse University Press, 1979).

An understanding of revolutionary Egypt is facilitated by the works of three of its presidents: Mohammad Naguib's *Egypt's Destiny: A Personal Statement* (Garden City, N.Y: Doubleday, 1955); Gamal Abdul Nasser's *Egypt's Liberation: The Philosophy of the Revolution* (Washington, D.C.: Public Affairs Press, 1955); Anwar el-Sadat's *Revolt on the Nile* (New York: John Day, 1957); and Anwar el-Sadat's *In Search of Identity: An Autobiography* (New York: Harper & Row, 1978).

Studies of particular aspects of politics of Egypt include Iliya Hark, *The Political Mobilization of Peasants: A Study of an Egyptian Community* (Bloomington, Ind.: Indiana University Press, 1974); James B. Mayfield, *Rural Politics in Nasser's Egypt: A Quest for Legitimacy* (Austin: University of Texas Press, 1971); J. Vatikiotis, *The Egyptian Army in Politics: Pattern for New Nations?* (Bloomington, Ind.: Indiana University Press, 1961); and Malcolm Kerr and El Sayed Yassin, eds., *Rich and Poor States in the Middle East: Egypt and the New Arab Order* (Boulder: Westview Press, 1982).

Egyptian foreign policy has not engendered many full-length studies. Nevertheless, several works provide a useful beginning. They include Charles D. Cremeans, *The Arabs and the World: Nasser's Arab Nationalist Policy* (New York: Praeger Publishers, for the Council on Foreign Relations, 1963); and A. I. Dawisha, *Egypt in the Arab World: The Elements of Foreign Policy* (New York: John Wiley, 1976). More specific themes are considered in Karen Dawisha's *Soviet Foreign Policy Towards Egypt* (New York: St. Martin's Press, 1979); and Ismail Fahmy's *Negotiating for Peace in the Middle East* (Baltimore: Johns Hopkins University Press, 1983).

Valuable studies of Egypt's economy are provided in Bent Hansen and Karim Nashashibi, *Foreign Trade Regimes and Economic Development: Egypt* (New York: National Bureau of Economic Research); Charles Issawi, *Egypt in Revolution: An Economic Analysis* (London: Oxford University Press, for the Royal Institute of International Affairs, 1963); Robert Mabro, *The Egyptian Economy, 1952–1972* (London: Oxford University Press, 1974); Patrick O'Brien, *The Revolution in Egypt's Economic System: From Private Enterprise to Socialism, 1952–1965* (London: Oxford University Press, 1966, issued under the auspices of the Royal Institute of International Affairs); Khalid Ikram, ed., *Egypt: Economic Management in a Period of Transition* (Baltimore: Johns Hopkins University Press, for the International Bank for Reconstruction and Development, 1980); and Alan Richards, *Egypt's Agricultural Development, 1800–1980: Technical and Social Change* (Boulder: Westview Press, 1982).

Finally, more recent studies include Robert Springborg's *Mubarak's Egypt: Fragmentation of the Political Order* (Boulder: Westview Press, 1989); Anthony McDermott's *Egypt from Nasser to Mubarak: A Flawed Revolution* (London: Croom Helm, 1988); Raymond Baker's *Sadat and After: Struggles for Egypt's Soul* (Cambridge, Mass.: Harvard University Press, 1990); and Mary Morris's *New Political Realities and the Gulf: Egypt, Syria and Jordan* (Santa Monica, Calif.: Rand, 1993).

14

Socialist People's Libyan Arab Jamahiriya

Mary-Jane Deeb

Libya is situated in North Africa, bordered by the Mediterranean Sea in the north, the Arab Republic of Egypt and the Sudan in the east, Niger and Chad in the south, and Tunisia and Algeria in the west. It has an area of about 1,774,150 square kilometers (685,000 square miles), more than 90 percent of which is desert. Libya is composed of three distinct geographical units: Tripolitania in the west, with an area of about 248,640 square kilometers (96,000 square miles); Cyrenaica in the east, with an area of about 699,300 square kilometers (270,000 square miles); and Fezzan in the south and southwest, with an area of about 826,210 square kilometers (319,000 square miles).

Libya has a small population estimated at 6.2 million.[1] Ninety percent of the people live in less than 10 percent of the total area, primarily along the Mediterranean coast. About 70 percent of the population is urban, mostly concentrated in the two largest cities, Benghazi and Tripoli. The majority of the population is of Arab origin, descending from a number of Arab tribes, including the two powerful tribes of Beni Hilal and Beni Sulaiman, who came originally from the Arabian Peninsula. But Libya is also partly African (in the Fezzan region) and Berber (in the north and central regions). Berbers are descendants of the original inhabitants of North Africa. Virtually all Libyans are Sunni Muslims.

Historical Background

In the earliest days the area that is now Libya was visited by Phoenician sailors, who established trading posts along the coastline. Later the Greeks landed. Subsequently, the control of part of the area fell to Alexander the Great and later to the

Egyptian kingdom of the Ptolemies. Rome annexed Cyrenaica and Tripolitania, and both became part of the Roman Empire. Eventually Pax Romana prevailed, and Libya enjoyed a long period of prosperity and peace. A period of decline began in the middle of the fourth century. In the seventh century Arab invaders arrived from Egypt, and most of the Berber tribes embraced Islam. The Arabs who swept across North Africa in the seventh century ruled for 900 years, interrupted by the Normans, the Spaniards, and the Knights of St. John. They were finally replaced in 1551 by the Ottoman Turks, who ruled until 1911. Italy declared war on the Ottoman Empire in September 1911, and Italian troops landed in Tripoli in early October and later that month in Benghazi.

The Italian conquest was not accomplished without difficulty, despite a Turkish-Italian treaty in October 1912 by which sovereignty was conceded. The Italian conquest faced opposition from the powerful Sanusiya movement. During World War I, Muhammad Idris al-Mahdi al-Sanusi, the grandson of the movement's founder, with Turkish support, opposed the Italian conquest. The Sanusiya movement was a Muslim reformist movement that started in the Hijaz in 1837 and a few years later moved to Cyrenaica. It was primarily a missionary movement whose functions were to spread the call throughout North Africa and mediate intertribal conflicts. It became a powerful political movement in the last two decades of the nineteenth century when it sought to curb Ottoman power in the region and later when it tried to push the Italians out of Libya.

In 1929 Italy officially adopted the name "Libya" to refer to its colony consisting of Cyrenaica, Tripolitania, and Fezzan. Until then it had been known by the name of its capital, Tripoli, although the term *Libya* had been used in early times by the Greeks to denote a much larger area in Africa. Colonization along the coast included the settlement of Italian peasants and consolidation of Italian control. Resistance against Italian control continued until 1931, although by 1932, Fascist rule had subdued all opposition.

World War II interrupted Italy's plans: By the end of 1942 British and French forces had swept the Italians out of the country. The North African campaigns of World War II devastated the country, leaving Benghazi partly destroyed. The head of the Sanusiya, Sayyid Muhammad Idris I, who had gone into exile in Egypt in 1922 but continued to support resistance to the Italian occupation, had sided with the British during the war and had been promised, at minimum, freedom from Italy. Between 1943 and 1947 the British established a military administration in Tripolitania and Cyrenaica and the French set up one in the Fezzan on a caretaker basis until the final status of the territories could be settled.

The machinery for settling the country's future was contained in the Italian Peace Treaty of 1947, which provided that the future of Italy's former colonies should be decided by Britain, France, the Soviet Union, and the United States, with the stipulation that if no agreement were reached, the question would be taken to the United Nations. Each of the powers proposed a different plan (as did Egypt in 1945 and 1946), and it was decided that a four-power commission should ascertain the wishes of the Libyans. In 1947, after visiting Libya, the commission ended in disagreement on many of the specifics; however, the members reached accord on the view that the Libyans wanted independence but were not yet ready to rule themselves. By summer 1948, it was clear that the four powers were unable to agree and the matter went to the United Nations, where it was debated in the General Assembly in spring 1949. Initial sentiment seemed to favor the postponement of independence and the establishment of some form of trusteeship. But agreement could not be reached on this approach, and support for independence increased. On November 21, 1949, the General Assembly adopted a resolution that Libya (composed of three territories) should become an independent state no later than January 1, 1952.

The assembly resolution allowed approximately two years for Libya to be prepared for independence. British and French administration continued during much of the period, as Adrian Pelt, the U.N. commissioner appointed to assist in the transition to independence, helped to prepare the institutions of self-government. Pelt was assisted by an international advisory council composed of representatives of several U.N. member countries and a committee of twenty-one Libyans (seven from each region). A constituent assembly was convened in December 1950, but it encountered difficulties in its efforts to devise a constitution and establish institutions of government. Eventually, Libya was established as a federation in which substantial autonomy was given to each of the three component units. Libya became independent on December 24, 1951, as the United Kingdom of Libya, composed of Fezzan, Cyrenaica, and Tripolitania, and with Sayyid Muhammad Idris I as its monarch.

Political Environment

The main economic and social problems facing Libya are interrelated and tend to reinforce each other. Primarily, Libya faces a lack of both human and natural resources (except for oil). In the early days following independence, the problem was far more acute, for oil had not yet been discovered in commercial quantities. In addition the Italian legacy was of limited value and had an essentially negative effect. At the time of independence, at least 90 percent of the population was illiterate and no significant educated elite existed. With the best agricultural land held by Italian settlers, there was no indigenous economic infrastructure. Furthermore, the substantial amounts of capital required for development were not internally available. These deficiencies were partially overcome by outside assistance. The need for capital was met in part by grants from the United States and the United Kingdom, whereas large-scale technical aid was made available by the United States and the United Nations. Other countries, notably Italy, also provided some assistance. Although petroleum revenues became available as a source of development financing and foreign capital assistance became less necessary, the need for outside technical services continued because few Libyans had the education or skills essential to the management of the expanding economy. To overcome the shortage of qualified personnel, Libya recruited foreign experts in industry, agriculture, education, and planning and development through the United Nations and its specialized agencies and from various governments, most notably from Egypt. Libyans also studied abroad on government fellowships to acquire and refine their knowledge in technical and administrative fields.

The nature and prospects of the Libyan economy changed drastically with the discovery of important petroleum reserves at the end of the 1950s. Although small amounts of oil had been found as early as 1935 east of Tripoli and an Italian oil company, Azienda Generale Italiana Petroli (AGIP), had attempted to drill for oil in Sirtica in 1940, it was not until 1955 that the first major oil find was made at Edjeleh, on the border with Algeria. That year the Libyan government passed its first petroleum law, which was designed to encourage diversity among companies wishing to have oil concessions in Libya and to prevent any one country or company from being the sole concessionaire. That policy remained unchanged under the monarchy and under the Qaddafi regime.

Although the first major oil finds were in the western part of Libya (Esso drilled a well in January 1958 that began yielding 500 barrels per day [bpd]), most of the other major finds were further northeast, primarily in Sirtica. In 1959 Esso oil wells in the Zelten field in Sirtica yielded 17,500 bpd, and other major oil strikes were made in the same area that year and the following one. The discoveries in 1959–1960 thus revealed that Libya had important petroleum reserves and that very large supplies would soon become available. Libya's position was strengthened even further after the June 1967 Middle East war because, with the closing of the Suez Canal, Libyan petroleum exports to Europe had a significant comparative advantage over petroleum from the Gulf area, which had to be either transshipped or routed around Africa. Production and exports continued to increase very rapidly: Exports rose from 6 million barrels in 1961 to 40 million barrels in 1962 to 108 million barrels in 1963 to 621 million barrels in 1967 and peaked in 1970 at 1,209 million barrels a year.

Once Muammar Al-Qaddafi seized power in a coup in September 1969, he decided to have more control over oil production in Libya. In April 1970, serious negotiations began with the major oil companies operating in Libya over a reduction in production, an increase in prices, and control of the companies' operations in Libya. With expert legal advice, Libya put certain proposals on the table and then threatened the companies with nationalization if they did not agree to the Libyan terms. Several companies refused to give Libya 51 percent control of their operations and left Libya, but the majority agreed to renegotiate the terms of their concessions. The outcome was a decline in production and a tremendous increase in revenue for the Libyan government. Whereas in 1969 (the year of the coup) Libya was producing 1,120 million barrels of oil and its revenues from oil totaled $1,175 million, by 1973 production had declined to 794 million barrels and oil revenues had risen to $2.22 billion. In 1974, after the Arab oil embargo, Libya was producing 544 million barrels and its revenues had increased to $6 billion.

Throughout the 1980s Libyan production hovered around 1.1 million bpd, the quota limit set by OPEC, but it rose to 1.5 million bpd in the early 1990s, a time when the price of oil on the world market remained very low. Revenues from oil declined by half between 1980 and 1991, from $21 billion to $10.2 billion, and by 1998 had dropped to an estimated $5.7 billion.[2] However, in 1999 the price of oil began rising very significantly on the world market and Libya's revenues from oil grew commensurably. In the early 1990s Libya's proven reserves of crude oil were estimated at 22.8 billion barrels. Most of the oil wells are in the eastern part of the country in the Sirte basin in Cyrenaica, but Libya also has access to major offshore deposits, such as those from the continental shelf between Libya and Tunisia, which may contain as much as 7 billion barrels of oil, and those next to the Maltese coast.

Libya's major resource before the discovery of petroleum in the 1950s was agriculture. However, only 1.2 percent of Libya's land is arable and of that, less than 1 percent is irrigated. The agricultural sector still retains its importance and together with forestry and fishing represented 7 percent of the gross domestic product and employed 29 percent of the labor force at the end of the millennium. However, the country does not produce enough to feed its population: Libya imports 75 percent of its food requirements.[3]

Water is scarce, and in areas where the main source of water is rainfall, the supply is very irregular. Water for irrigation has been drawn from aquifers in the Jefara plain at a rate equivalent to six times the amount of rainfall that recharges those aquifers. In 1984 a massive water pipeline project, the Great Manmade River (GMR) was inaugurated at the Sarir Oasis. Seven years later, in 1991, the first phase of the project was partially completed and water was brought to Suluq near Benghazi through a 430-kilometer-long pipeline. Water was drawn from 225 underground wells at Tazerno and at Sarir in the east-central region of Libya. The second phase, which became operational in the late 1990s, linked new wells from the southern oasis of Kufra that parallel the first-stage line. The plan is to provide irrigation to 500,000 hectares, of which 40 percent will be for 37,000 farms in the Sirte region in the north-central plains of Libya. Part of the water is to be used for pastureland for sheep and cattle.

The problems surrounding the irrigation project, which may become one of the largest of its kind in the world, are many. The cost is estimated at over $25 billion. There have been major technical problems, including the malfunctioning of 126 wells drilled by a Brazilian company. Since only 29 percent of the Libyan workforce is employed in agriculture, Libya has had to depend on foreign workers to develop that sector. At one point an estimated one million Egyptians were invited to Libya to settle and work on the reclaimed land.

The non-oil manufacturing and construction sectors account for 15 percent of the gross national product. The manufacturing sector includes not only the processing of agricultural products but also more complex industries such as the manufacture of petrochemicals and of iron and steel. The only identified nonhydrocarbon deposit in Libya is the iron ore at Wadi Shatti, which has an estimated 2 to 3 billion tons, ranging from 25 to 50 percent iron content. The government plans to use it instead of the iron that is currently imported for the iron and steel complex in Misrata. A wide variety of other goods are also manufactured in Libya, such as cement for construction, textiles and clothing, leather goods and footwear, metal products, and paper and wood products.

After the 1969 revolution, the Revolutionary Command Council (RCC) redirected the economy toward rapid economic development, a more equal distribution of income and services, greater government economic control, and independence from foreign influence. Among the most important policies of the regime have been those designed to manage and deal with the problems attendant upon a lack of natural and human resources. Managing the petroleum resources of the state and the revenues to be derived therefrom became a major government strategy. The revenues, in turn, were to be used to effect some improvement in the human-resource base.

An increase in the literacy of the population was sought through compulsory and free elementary education. The literacy rate, which in 1973 was estimated at 40 percent for the Libyan population as a whole, with a much lower rate for women, rose to 76.2 percent in the late 1990s, with a literacy rate for males reaching 88.9 percent and for females 57.2 percent. This is considerably higher than any other North African country, including Egypt and Tunisia.[4] Secondary schools, universities, and adult and technical education also became more widely available. The two universities, Al-Fateh in Tripoli and Gar Yunis in Benghazi, have new campuses in Tobruk. A new university opened in Sebha in 1986, and there is a college of science and technology at Marsa Brega with additional facilities in Misrata. Until 1982 a large number of Libyan students were sent abroad to study. After that, deteriorating relations with the West, coupled with a decline in financial resources, resulted in a sharp decrease in the number of students studying abroad.

Upgrading of health standards and other elements designed to improve the personal situation of the population also contributed to the improved resource base. The number of medical doctors rose from 1 per 3,860 people in 1965 to 1 per 500 in 1990, and the ratio of Libyan nurses rose from 1 per 850 people to 1 per 320. It is important to note that medical personnel were brought in from around the world but primarily from Egypt, Sudan, Lebanon, and other countries in the region to staff hospitals and health-care centers. The infant mortality rate dropped from 160 per 1,000 live births in 1960 to 72 in 1991, and an estimated 30.8 in 2000, and life expectancy rose sharply from 46.7 years in 1960 to an estimated 75.45 years in 2000.[5]

Under the Qaddafi regime, the role of the government in the economy became predominant. Libya not only took majority control of the oil companies operating on its territory but also nationalized some companies completely, such as Shell in 1974. Starting in November 1969, it also nationalized all foreign banks, including the Arab Bank, Banco di Roma, and Barclay's Bank. By the end of 1970 the number of commercial banks had been reduced to five, three of which were state owned and two state controlled. Insurance companies had been completely nationalized by 1971 and were merged into two state-owned companies. Basic infrastructural facilities, including major airlines, electric power plants, communications, and others became state owned and state operated.

Large- and medium-sized industries with foreign proprietors—primarily Italians, who owned 75 to 80 percent of all industrial plants in Libya—were taken over by the state. Those included tobacco, tanning and leather, textile, lumber, and construction plants, as well as food industries, including canning sardines and tomatoes and bottling soft drinks. In the agricultural sector new policies were adopted: In 1972 agricultural cooperatives were established that gave financial, technical, and marketing assistance to the farmers who joined. The small-business sector prospered at first, as the government adopted a policy of giving contracts to Libyan firms and lending up to 95 percent of the capital to finance indigenous commercial enterprises. Between 1969 and 1976 the government issued 40,000 licenses to new grocery stores in the district of Tripoli alone. Starting in 1971 workers became part owners and were given a larger share of the economic profits made by the firms that employed them. Free housing was provided to some, and loans were given to others to buy suitable housing.

Although the aim of the government in implementing these policies had been to stimulate Libyan entrepreneurship and develop a strong indigenous middle class that would become a powerful political base for the regime, the policies had different outcomes. Local businesses that were assured of receiving government contracts or loans began to depend more and more on government subsidies and foreign labor and know-how, and many became mere fronts for non-Libyan interests. A number of the large agricultural projects that were meant to modernize and develop the rural sector foundered because of a shortage of water, poor planning and management, and the small size of the rural labor force. The settlement policy pursued by the government to induce farmers to remain in rural areas was by and large unsuccessful, as the rural population continued to migrate to cities seeking employment and a higher standard of living. In the industrial sector the policies of the government led to an increase in the importation of capital goods and raw materials. Because of shortages of skilled manpower and administrative personnel, labor had to be imported as well. In 1975, 58 percent of the managerial and professional manpower in Libya was foreign, as was 35 percent of the technical personnel, 27.5 percent of the skilled and semiskilled workforce, and 42.2 percent of the unskilled workers.

The attempt to develop an entrepreneurial middle class failed as well when the Libyan businessmen who had government contracts reaped huge profits and then invested them abroad. What was taking place was not so much the formation of a new middle class of small businessmen, supportive of the regime, as the consolidation of the economic power of the traditional urban notability, who had the skills, the practice, and the connections to take advantage of government-sponsored programs to enrich themselves. That process in turn frightened the Qaddafi regime because it perceived the notables as a major potential force of domestic opposition.

Consequently, the policies of the state became more radical in the period 1976–1980. Qaddafi's *Green Book,* expounding his political and economic philosophy, first appeared during that period. He called on workers to take over a large number of commercial and industrial enterprises from their Libyan owners. A law was promulgated in 1978 specifying that every family had the right to own a home of its own and that tenants, therefore, could take immediate possession of their rented homes. Those two injunctions dealt a very severe blow to the urban notables, who lost both their commercial establishments and their real estate investments. By some estimates the private sector had invested 41 percent of its capital in real estate. Furthermore, all foreign trade was to be conducted by the state, whereas until then the private sector had been allowed to import goods and sell them on the Libyan market.

In the 1980s the confrontation that pitted the United States against Libya because of the latter's support for terrorism resulted in the imposition of economic sanctions banning U.S. import of Libyan oil and export of high technology equipment to Libya. After 1985 the United States stopped importing products derived from Libyan crude, such as naphtha, methanol, and low-sulfur fuel oil. In 1986 Libyan assets in the United States, estimated at $1 billion to $2 billion, were frozen. The impact of those embargoes, bans, and freezes, coupled with a decline in the price of oil, resulted in a major decline in Libya's export revenues.

The outbreak of the Gulf crisis in 1990 led to windfall profits for several months, owing to an increase in crude output and prices. But Libya began facing economic difficulties after 1992, when the U.N. Security Council imposed major economic sanctions on Libya for its alleged role in the bombing of Pan Am Flight 103 over Lockerbie, Scotland, in 1988. U.N. Resolution 731 banned flights to and from Libya and prohibited the supply of aircraft or aircraft parts to Libya and the sale or transfer to Libya of military equipment of any kind. It also called on all U.N. member states to significantly reduce diplomatic personnel and staff in Libyan embassies on their territories. In 1999, the U.N. sanctions were lifted, although the U.S. unilateral sanctions remained in place. Since then Libya has attempted to attract European investments in various fields including energy, agriculture and tourism. Libya is also trying to upgrade its infrastructure, especially in the road and transport sectors.

Because of its dwindling resources, and its international trade problems in the early 1990s, Libya was unable to pay the salaries of government officials and the armed forces regularly or to maintain 1980s levels of expenditure on health and education. To reduce the deficit and deal with the economic crisis, Qaddafi called for privatization in September 1992 and passed Law No. 9 urging Libyans to form joint stock companies and to set up family firms, partnerships, and individual businesses. In March 1993, for the first time since the nationalizations of the 1970s, Libya allowed the establishment of private banks, and in July of that year the government permitted private-sector companies to engage in wholesale trade.

In the retail trade area, the process of economic liberalization had started even earlier. Beginning in 1987, the private sector was allowed to open stores and sell goods, replacing state cooperatives. In mid-1996, however, privatization and economic liberalization came to a halt. The reason given was the spread of corruption, and "purification committees" were set up to put an end to those practices. Shops that sold imported goods were closed down, and the shopkeepers imprisoned. Later, members of the purification committees themselves were accused of corruption and "volcano committees" were set up to purge them. Although many of the shops that were closed later reopened, the government continues to keep a strong hold on imports and retail trade and enforces strict regulations that hinder the free flow of commerce at all levels.[6]

Political Structure and Dynamics

Kingdom of Libya

The 1951 constitution established the United Kingdom of Libya as a constitutional monarchy under Muhammad Idris al-Mahdi al-Sanusi. Sovereignty was vested in the nation but entrusted by the people to Idris and his male heirs. Islam was declared the religion of the state and Arabic the official language. Executive power was granted to the king, whereas legislative power was shared by the king and parliament. King Idris was to exercise his executive power through an appointed prime minister and cabinet, or council of ministers, whereas legislative power was vested in a parliament, which he convened and could adjourn (for up to thirty days) or dissolve. The king sanctioned and promulgated all laws and made the necessary regulations through the relevant ministries for their implementation. In "exceptional and urgent circumstances" when parliament was not in session, the king was permitted to issue decrees, subject to confirmation by parliament when it convened. He could veto legislation, and his veto could be overridden only by a two-thirds vote of both the Senate and the House of Representatives. The king was supreme commander of the armed forces; he could proclaim a state of emergency and martial law, declare war, and conclude peace, with the approval of parliament. In addition, he appointed senators, judges, and senior public servants. The king was supreme head of state, "inviolable," and "exempt from all responsibility."

The cabinet was appointed and dismissed by royal decrees on the prime minister's recommendation. Although the cabinet was selected by the king, under Article 86, the cabinet members were collectively responsible to the lower house of parliament, and each was individually responsible for the activities of the ministry that he headed. A vote of no-confidence by parliament could force the resignation of any or all ministers. The cabinet was responsible for the direction of all internal and external affairs of the state.

Parliament consisted of two chambers. The Senate had twenty-four members (eight from each province), one-half of whom were appointed by the king. The others were elected by the legislative councils of the provinces. Each served for eight years and could be reappointed or reelected. The House of Representatives consisted of deputies elected by popular suffrage on the basis of one deputy for every 20,000 inhabitants or any fraction of that number exceeding half (although each province was required to have at least five members). The deputies served for a maximum of four years. Parliamentary sessions were called by the king in November. During sessions, a bill could be introduced by the king or by one of the chambers; it had to be adopted by both chambers and ratified by the king before becoming law. However, only the king and the House of Representatives could initiate bills involving the budget.

The federal government exercised legislative and executive powers as described in Article 36 of the constitution, which provided a detailed listing of areas for the exercise of its power. In other areas there were provisions for joint powers between the federal and provincial governments. The provinces were to exercise all powers not assigned to the federal government by the constitution. Each province was to have a governor (*wali*) appointed and removed by the king and representing the king in the province. An executive council and a legislative council would be established in each province.

The original adoption of the federal system was a necessary compromise in the drafting of the constitution. It allowed for a common political authority while preserving some autonomy for the three provinces of Cyrenaica, Fezzan, and Tripolitania. Local affairs were administered independently in each province, and certain powers were reserved for the federal government. Those included power over all matters relating to Libya's foreign relations, defense and security, international and interstate transport and communication; all matters relating to federal taxation, to customs and customs duties, to currency, the issuing of bank notes and the minting of coins; all matters relating to institutions of higher learning and issuance of degrees; and matters affecting the federal government, government employees, and government property.

The federal structure was abolished in 1963, when a new constitution established a unitary system that had jurisdiction over all matters within the state. The country's name was changed to the Kingdom of Libya (instead of the United Kingdom of Libya), with Idris I remaining the monarch. The provinces surrendered administrative and financial decisionmaking to the national government, whose authority was exercised through ten administrative districts, or *wilayas*.

The shift from the federal to a unitary system did not alter the government greatly because much of the structure established in 1951 remained intact at the national level. The major changes in the revised constitution related to the federal elements contained in the 1951 constitution. Each of the ten administrative districts was headed by a *wali* appointed by the council of ministers and empowered to execute the policies of the government in his district. The council also had the power to transfer or dismiss the *wali*. The powers of the *wali* were more limited than those of the governor of a province or state under the 1951 constitution. All matters except those dealing exclusively with local affairs were under the direction of the national government. Another significant change related to parliament. The 1963 constitution empowered the king to appoint all the senators, and he could increase their number. Elections for members of the lower house were opened to universal suffrage. Overall, the new constitution eliminated the fragmentation of power among the palace, the organs of the federal government, the organs of the provincial governments, and other centrifugal powers, including certain religious institutions.

King Idris was the strongest single source of power in the Libyan political system. He determined the policies, which were implemented by his ministers, whom he appointed and dismissed at will. Often he did not appear to be involved in the daily activity of the government and allowed the prime minister and cabinet to adopt policies they deemed appropriate as long as they had the confidence of parliament and stayed within the broad outlines established by the king. The king's dominant position in the political system was the result of many factors: his religious role as leader of the Sanusiya movement and the fact that he was the grandson of the founder of the movement; his political role in leading the resistance against Italian domination and achieving independence for Libya; his unique ability to keep the country together when regional forces sought to tear it apart; and his ability to preserve internal order and stability at a very difficult juncture in Libya's history.

The political circle Idris led was centered in the palace and in the special ties to Cyrenaica—not in the populace. Political expression was limited, and political parties were disbanded soon after independence. The ministers were close to and dependent on the monarchy, despite the provisions of the constitution that stated that they were collectively and individually responsible to the lower house of parliament. In the governmental structure the only significant potential alternative power center was the House of Representatives. It was the only place in which policies were publicly discussed, evaluated, and frequently criticized, and it provided a forum for the opposition to express its views.

In less than two decades King Idris achieved certain major successes. With no significant domestic strife, he was able to preserve the unity and integrity of the Libyan state. By means of political alliances and diplomacy he protected his very weak country from external aggression and intervention. He obtained the assistance Libya needed to feed the population as well as to build schools and hospitals at a time when Libya was one of the poorest countries in the world.

The discovery of oil transformed the Libyan political scene, as did the rise of Nasser as a major charismatic figure in the Arab world and in Libya. A younger, more aggressive leader could have been more effective in adapting the Libyan political system to the changing times. King Idris was old (he was eighty in 1969 when he was overthrown) and in poor health. He had lost interest in the day-to-day running of the affairs of his country. His entourage had become progressively more powerful and more wealthy and was creating a great deal of resentment among the Libyans. By the late 1960s significant opposition to the policies and programs of the state was coming from many quarters.

The Revolution of 1969

On September 1, 1969, a bloodless military coup d'état overthrew the government of King Idris (who was out of the country at the time). There was little resistance, even by elements loyal to the king, such as the police and the tribes of Cyrenaica. Although the king made an attempt to secure British assistance to restore him to power, he was unsuccessful and the monarchy was abolished. Little was known about the coup makers except that they called themselves the Free Unionist Officers and advocated "social justice, socialism and unity."

In the first few weeks a number of moderate civilians and army officers were appointed to the first post-coup cabinet. Although strongly nationalistic, these people were not antagonistic to the Western powers and were prepared to develop good relations with the West after the evacuation of the Western military bases. Regionally, they were more pro-Arab and spoke more openly of supporting Arab causes, such as Arab unity and the Palestinians. Although socialism and social justice were discussed, the first Libyan cabinet did not plan to nationalize any sector of the economy, and foreigners who lived in Libya were to be allowed to keep their property. The RCC, however, headed by a young army officer named Muammar Qaddafi, advocated radical economic, social, and political change.

The confrontation between the Free Unionist Officers and the cabinet took place in December 1969 when the prime minister and a number of his cabinet ministers were accused of attempting to overthrow the regime and were arrested. The next day all powers were transferred to the Revolutionary Command Council, which was made up of the Free Unionist Officers, and it was proclaimed the supreme authority in the land. The direction the political system was to take was decided then.

At the outset Qaddafi attempted to follow in the footsteps of Nasser of Egypt, going as far as to name a party that he created the Arab Socialist Union, like its Egyptian counterpart. In the mid-1970s, however, Qaddafi moved away from Nasserism and invented his own brand of socialism, which he called "natural socialism." He enunciated its principles in his *Green Book,* published in three volumes between 1976 and 1978. He preached complete egalitarianism, the abolition of wage labor, and private ownership of land. Trade was portrayed as exploitative and nonproductive and therefore had to be taken over by the state. He strongly upheld the principles of Arab nationalism and called for support of the Palestinians and the creation of a powerful bloc of Arab states to fight Israel.

Religious reform was a very important part of his ideology: He emphasized that the Quran was the only source of Islamic law, or *Shari'a.* He claimed that Muhammad, the Muslim prophet, was just an intermediary between God and man, and that since the Quran was in Arabic, anyone could read it and understand it and did not need a clergyman or imam to interpret it for him. From the mid-1980s on, he moved even further from the traditional Sunni Muslim position and claimed that religion had nothing to do with politics and that men of religion should focus on the spiritual rather than on the mundane in their Friday *khutba,* or sermon. He cracked down on Islamic militant groups inside Libya and shared intelligence with Egypt, Tunisia, and Algeria on the movements of those groups and their leaders in the region. In February 1994, however, Qaddafi appeared to change course, probably to undermine the rising tide of Islamic fundamentalism, by calling for the implementation of Islamic law in Libya primarily for criminal offenses but also for marriage and divorce. In the same vein, he called for the revival of the tradition of Sufi brotherhoods as a source of Islamic teachings.

Muammar Qaddafi was born in 1942 in the area of Sirte on the Mediterranean coast midway between Tripoli and Benghazi. He was the only surviving son of a poor Arabized Berber family belonging to the Qaddafi tribe. At the age of ten he was sent to elementary school in the town of Sirte, and in 1956 he moved with his family to Sebha, where he attended the Sebha Preparatory School until 1961. Those five years were his politically formative years. It was there that he created the first command committee with many of the people who would become his closest allies and members of the RCC after the revolution. It was during that period also that he learned about the events in Egypt: the 1956 Suez Canal crisis, the evacuation of the British forces, Nasser's agrarian reforms and nationalizations. But perhaps what would influence him most would be Nasser's call for a united Arab world.

Qaddafi and his family then moved to Misrata in Tripolitania, where he completed high school in 1963, and then entered the Military Academy in Benghazi. Three of his classmates from Sebha and Misrata joined him at the Military Academy, where they formed the nucleus of the Free Unionist Movement, which planned to overthrow the monarchy and take over power in Libya. After graduating from the academy in 1965, Qaddafi was sent to England to attend an army school at Bovington Hythe in Beaconsfield, where he took a six-month signal course. On his return to Libya he enrolled in the history department at the University of Benghazi, but was commissioned in 1966 to the signals corps of the Libyan army and never completed his university education. He remained in regular contact with the large network of fellow officers and friends he had developed over the years and built a secret organization that enabled him to carry out the coup in 1969.

Once firmly in control of the government in Libya, having jailed the leaders of a potential opposition to his policies, Qaddafi began to build his political power base. The first political organization he built in 1971 was the Arab Socialist Union (ASU), in name and in spirit very much along the lines of the sole party in the Egyptian system that he was emulating. The ASU was supposed to mobilize the population in support of the new regime and its policies. Half its members had to be farmers and workers, and its structure was to have local, regional, and national units and be headed by the RCC. It became apparent very soon that the ASU was an ineffectual political instrument that represented government policies but did not mobilize popular enthusiasm for the revolution. In 1976, at its Third Party Congress, the Arab Socialist Union ceased to exist as a political party.

Earlier, in 1973, Qaddafi had attempted to create a so-called cultural revolution, this time using the Chinese model, to mobilize popular support for the regime by criticizing the government bureaucracy, the bourgeoisie, the RCC, and the cabinet. He advocated the destruction of the bureaucracy, the suspension of all laws, the arming of the people, and a return to the principles of the Quran and he called on the people to take over the responsibilities of government. The outcome of this "cultural revolution" was a period of chaos during which were launched the first "popular committees," which were to involve people directly in the process of governing Libya. Qaddafi claimed that direct democracy was the only real democracy and, therefore, that it was only through such organizations that Libya could become really democratic.

Those popular committees were small units (sixteen to twenty people) of directly elected individuals representing people at the level of the workplace, school and university, village community, and city neighborhood. The popular committees selected some of their members to represent them at the district level. District committees sent representatives to the larger provincial committees. Once a year the provincial committees sent members to the General People's Congress. The decisions made at the congress were submitted to the participants so that they could be implemented by the popular committees. The General People's Congress was also a vehicle for informing the ruling junta of the basic problems and demands of the people at the grassroots level.

In the second half of the 1970s, when Qaddafi felt that the Libyans were again becoming apathetic about the political system, when they were not either trying to change it or to overthrow it, he came up with new ideas for political organization. In 1977, he formed the revolutionary committees (*lijan thawriya*), whose function was to act as watchdogs over the political activities of the popular committees and the secretariats of the popular congresses. These revolutionary committees became extremely powerful and quite unruly at times. They could arrest people arbitrarily on charges of subversive activities and thus were able to instill fear in people, to settle personal scores, and to act as spies for the government. The experiment with popular committees was reintroduced in the mid-1990s, when "purification committees" were set up to root out corruption in the private sector retail trade. These committees, in turn, suffered a similar fate, when "volcano committees" were organized to purge their members accused of corruption.

Until 1977 government activities were managed by a cabinet appointed by the RCC. The cabinet was composed mainly of civilian technocrats, but RCC members held such critical cabinet posts or secretariats as defense and interior. After the attempted coup against Qaddafi by members of the RCC in 1975, the RCC was reduced from the original twelve members to only five. In 1977, in a carefully orchestrated maneuver, a General People's Congress of elected representatives changed the country's name to the Socialist People's Libyan Arab Jamahiriya, proclaimed the establishment of people's power, and vested all official power in the General People's Congress, abolishing the RCC as the supreme authority, but naming the five remaining RCC officers as members of the congress's secretariat. Those five, with Qaddafi as the undisputed leader, continued to be the real power in Libya for the next two decades. The cabinet became the General People's Congress Committee.

In November 1988 Qaddafi announced the restructuring of the military and the creation of a new voluntary paramilitary organization under a separate command. He felt that the army that had tried to overthrow him on a number of occasions had become even more threatening after its defeat in Chad in 1987. Consequently, the restructuring of the traditional army was meant to purge its more dangerous elements. Paramilitary organizations such as the People's Militias and the Jamahiri Guards had been in existence since the late 1970s.

Opposition to the regime, however, continued unabated. There were reports of mutinies in the military throughout the 1980s, and one took place in 1993. The reaction was always swift and deadly. In the case of the 1993 mutiny the air force was used to bomb selected military targets. Monarchist organizations, such as the Libyan Constitutional Union, established in 1981, called for general elections and the return of the monarchy. The best-known organization opposing the Qaddafi regime is the National Front for the Liberation of Libya (NFSL), which was also founded in 1981 and which is headed by a former ambassador to India, Muhammad al-Maqaryaf. This organization succeeded in bringing together Islamists and secular prodemocracy opponents of the regime under one umbrella. Some members of the Muslim Brothers left the NFSL in 1982 and some secularists left in

March 1994 (forming a new opposition organization calling itself the Movement for Change and Reform). The principal organ of the NFSL is the *Inqadh* (*Salvation*), a publication that appears seven or eight times a year with articles condemning the regime, exposing human rights violations in Libya, and discussing the social, economic, and political conditions in the country. The NFSL also publishes a bimonthly newsletter and has a radio program, *Voice of Libya,* that has been broadcast daily from Cairo since 1982. The NFSL attempted to overthrow the regime in 1984 with a military attack against the barracks of Bab al-Aziziya. The attack failed, but the NFSL subsequently built a paramilitary wing to the party: the Libyan National Army.

In the 1990s the Islamists became another major opposition force in Libya. They have their roots in older movements such the *Ikhwan,* the Muslim Brothers, a movement that developed in Libya with the arrival of Egyptian school teachers in the 1950s. The *Hizb al-Tahrir* (the Liberation Party) and *Jabhat al-Tahrir al-Islami* (the Islamic Liberation Front) are examples of such offshoots. Other Islamic opposition groups include *Al-Jama'a al-Islamiyah 'Libya'* (the Islamic Group–Libya), *Al-Haraka al-Islamiya 'Libya'* (the Islamic Movement–Libya), and *Al-Takfir wa-al-Hijra* (Apostasy and Migration). Libya has responded to this opposition like other governments in the region, by cracking down on them, imprisoning their leaders, and censoring their publications.

Foreign Policy

King Idris followed a pro-Western foreign policy. Treaties signed with Britain in 1953 and the United States in 1954 provided for the maintenance of military bases and forces in Libya in exchange for ensuring Libyan security, and both Britain and the United States were the source of development grants and budgetary subventions. An agreement with France in 1955 provided for communications facilities in the southwestern desert areas. Close ties were also maintained with Turkey and Greece. Libya joined the Arab League in 1953 but remained basically neutral in inter-Arab and Arab-Western conflicts, following the theory that it was in Libya's security interest not to be involved. The king's decisions not to close the British military bases in 1956 during the Suez Canal crisis and not to participate in the 1967 Arab-Israeli war created resentment among young Libyans, who felt that the country was being kept out of Arab affairs and marginalized in the Arab world. Under internal and external pressure for the liquidation of foreign bases, the government, after 1964, publicly supported the early evacuation of these bases but took few practical steps in that direction. The issue was brought up again in 1967, and the process of liquidation began in earnest.

Qaddafi regarded the coup of September 1969 as the starting point of Libyan independence. In order to legitimize its power, the RCC gave priority to removing the foreign bases. It could then claim that it was the new regime that had liberated

Libya from foreign imperialism. Agreement was soon reached between the RCC and the U.S. and British governments to evacuate the Wheelus base and the British bases at Tobruk and al-Adam in spring 1970.

Libya's relations with its neighbors have been characterized by numerous attempts at unity. Those attempts, however, did not always come from Libya. The first took place in December 1969 when Libya, Sudan, and Egypt attempted to set up a federation. The new Libyan regime's goal was not merely to formalize its adherence to the principles of Arab unity but also to boost its questionable legitimacy domestically, by being associated with Nasser, the most important leader in the Arab world in the eyes of the Libyans. The Federation of Arab Republics (with Egypt and Syria), promulgated in September 1971, was a continued attempt by Libya to cement its alliance with Egypt, especially after Nasser's death. Although Qaddafi's position was somewhat weakened by Nasser's death, he attempted to take Nasser's place and consequently enhance his legitimacy at home by becoming the new ideologue of Arab nationalism and Arab unity. In January 1974, Libya and Tunisia announced the formation of a union following several months of talks between Tunisian President Habib Bourguiba and Qaddafi. The plan called for a single state, the Arab Islamic Republic, and the original offer came from Tunisia in an effort to wean Libya away from Egypt. When Libyan-Egyptian relations deteriorated after the October 1973 Arab-Israeli war, Libya pursued the merger with Tunisia to ensure itself a regional ally. Opposition within Tunisia as well as from Algeria aborted the merger plans. In 1975 Libya and Algeria signed a mutual defense pact, the Hassi Mas'ud Treaty, which ensured Libya a major regional ally. When Egypt attacked Libya in July 1977 and destroyed Soviet radar installations on the Libyan-Egyptian border, Algeria intervened on Libya's behalf and the bombing was stopped. In return Libya supported Algeria against Morocco on the Western Sahara issue and supplied the Polisario Front with both financial and military resources for the next six years. In 1981 Libya merged with Chad in an attempt to put an end to the war between the two countries. Libya also wanted to ensure its dominance of northern Chad. That merger worsened relations with Algeria, which turned toward Tunisia and then Mauritania and signed the Treaty of Brotherhood and Concord in 1983, which did not include Libya. The Arab-African Federation, set up between Libya and Morocco in August 1984, was in part a reaction to the renewed regional isolation of Libya and in part a reaction to King Hassan's concern with retaining control of the Western Sahara. The outcome was a significant decline of Libyan support for the Polisario, and the support was further eroded because of Libya's dwindling resources after the fall of oil prices in the mid-1980s.

In February 1989 Libya, Tunisia, Algeria, Morocco, and Mauritania announced the creation of the Arab Maghrib Union (UMA). The union is meant to foster economic integration on the model of the European Community. The countries of the Maghrib wanted to enlarge their markets and find an alternative outlet for their labor. Although they lack economic complementarity, they have set up joint companies and joint projects to increase efficiency and prevent duplication in the manufacturing sector, for instance. Libya has been the only country capable of absorbing some of the regional labor surplus. It has removed trade barriers with its neighbors, which has enhanced trade and allowed Libyans to go shopping in Tunisia for goods they could not find at home. Libya is a major partner in the Arab Maghribi Bank for Investment and Trade and has a large number of joint projects with its neighbors, including Egypt, in the agricultural, transport and communications, industrial, and petrochemical sectors.

Libya's relations to Egypt for the last quarter century have been turbulent. From the early closeness with Nasser of the first year of the Libyan revolution, the relations deteriorated progressively with Sadat, culminating in Egypt's bombing of Libya in 1977, partly in retaliation for Libya's subversive activities in Egypt and partly because Libya allowed the Soviets to survey Egypt's military installations by means of a radar based on the Libyan-Egyptian frontiers. In the 1980s, however, the relations with the Mubarak regime improved markedly. Tens of thousands of Egyptians live and work in Libya, and a large number of joint infrastructural, industrial, and agricultural projects were set up between the two countries. Mubarak and Qaddafi have shared intelligence on Islamic fundamentalists on both sides of the borders, and Mubarak has personally interceded on behalf of Libya for the lifting of the U.N. sanctions against that country.

Under Qaddafi, the Libyan government has been uncompromising in its stance toward Israel. Qaddafi has condemned Zionism as aggressive nationalism and supported the more radical groups among the Palestinians such as the PFLP-GC. Although he has provided financial, moral, and political support to the PLO, he has also had strong disagreements with its chairman, Yasir Arafat. After the Camp David Accords of 1978 and the Egypt-Israel Peace Treaty of 1979, Libya became a leader of the "rejection front," Arab states that denounced any political settlement with Israel. Qaddafi was against the 1993 peace initiative between the Palestinians and the Israelis, but in May 1993 he sent 200 Libyans on a pilgrimage to Jerusalem and invited Libyan Jews who lived abroad to come and visit Libya. Since the second Palestinian intifada (uprising) that began in the fall of 2000, Libya has again become very vocal in its criticism of Israel and of U.S. policy in the region. Qaddafi has also worked actively for over two decades to counter Israeli influence in sub-Saharan Africa.

Libya's relations with the United States deteriorated over the years. Until the 1973 Arab-Israeli war, Qaddafi had merely been critical of U.S. Middle East policy. After the war, when Sadat moved closer to the West and to the United States, the Libyan leader perceived that move as threatening Libya's security, and he moved closer to the Soviet bloc. His support for terrorist groups in various parts of the world caused the United States to stop selling arms or military hardware to Libya. In December 1979 the U.S. embassy in Tripoli was sacked and burned. The

Reagan administration then chose Qaddafi as the principal target of its antiterrorist policy and adopted further economic and political measures to isolate Libya regionally and internationally. This culminated in the bombing of Tripoli in 1986 in retaliation for a terrorist bombing that was later traced to the Abu Nidal Organization.

In 1991 the United States and the United Kingdom formally charged Libya with the bombing of Pan Am's Flight 103 over Lockerbie, Scotland, while France issued arrest warrants for four Libyans, accusing them of participating in a 1988 bombing of a French UTA airline that exploded over Niger. The Lockerbie and UTA charges led to the passing of the U.N. Resolutions 731 and 748 in 1992, which imposed sanctions on Libya, including a ban on all flights to and from Libya and a prohibition on the supply of aircraft, aircraft parts, or military equipment of any kind to Libya. The United States and Great Britain demanded that Libya extradite to either of these countries two Libyans who were accused of the bombing. Libya refused. In the mid-1990s the United States passed a law on secondary sanctions on non-U.S. firms that invested in the oil sectors in Libya and Iran. It became known as the Iran and Libya Sanctions Act, ILSA for short. The European Union, in turn, strongly objected and passed legislation to block the impact of ILSA, making it illegal for European firms to comply with it.

Due to many factors, including the very significant fall in the price of oil at the end of the 1990s, Qaddafi decided to turn in the two Libyan suspects. In April 1999 the men were sent to the Hague to a specially convened Scottish court where the trial opened a year later. At the end of the trial one of the men was found innocent of all charges, while the second was found guilty. Qaddafi promised to appeal the case. The United Nations sanctions against Libya were suspended the moment the two suspects were turned over to the Scottish court at the Hague, although the U.S. sanctions remained in place.

Libyan-Soviet relations became closer after the rapprochement between Egypt and the West that began in 1974. Relations were based primarily on mutual interest rather than on ideology, as Qaddafi had been consistently critical of communism. Libya needed a stable supplier of arms and a strong ally to balance U.S. influence in Egypt. The Soviet Union was assured of a client that could pay its bills and was located strategically, with the longest coastline on the southern Mediterranean. The sharp drop in oil prices and Libya's inability to pay its debts soured the relations between the two countries. For a time oil was used to pay some of Libya's debts, estimated at $4 billion. Russia respected the sanctions and refused to sell arms to Libya until Libya handed over the two Lockerbie bombing suspects. After that, Russian-Libyan relations improved significantly and trade between those two countries resumed.

Libya's relations with Western Europe—especially those with Germany, Italy, Austria, and France, with which Libya has extensive business dealings—have been better than its relations with the United States. Those countries were given major oil concessions and were making significant oil discoveries in the Sirte basin as late as 1993. Libya has also invested in Europe, buying, for example, 2,300 gas stations in Italy in 1993. Libya also exports its light, sweet crude to Western Europe, primarily to Germany and Italy, and imports foodstuffs, capital goods, medicine, and other commodities from those countries as well.

Two cases of state-sponsored terrorism, one in France and the other in England, were settled in 1999. Libyan suspects in the bombing of an UTA plane flying over Chad were found guilty in absentia by a French court, and Libya paid $33 million in compensation to the families. The family of a British policewoman shot in front of the Libyan embassy in London was also compensated by the Libyan government. In the aftermath of the suspension of the U.N. sanctions, a number of Western countries, including Great Britain and Italy, resumed diplomatic relations with Libya in 2000, in the hope of improving bilateral trade relations with that country.

Qaddafi has supported Muslims in Africa and Asia politically, financially, and culturally. He has aided Muslim insurgents in the Philippines, built mosques and schools in Niger and Mali, and given financial aid to a large number of states, including Uganda, Togo, Burundi, the Central African Republic, and Gabon in Africa, and to Indonesia, Malaysia, and Pakistan in Asia. The Organization of African Unity passed a resolution in June 1998 declaring that its member states would no longer recognize the U.N. embargo on flights to and from Libya, nor respect the U.N. sanctions against Libya unless the United States and the United Kingdom agreed to hold the trial of the Libyan bombing suspects in a neutral country. The OAU's action and Nelson Mandela's support for Libya were critical in the final negotiations to hold the trial at the Hague.

Since coming to power, Qaddafi sought to have Libya associated with "revolutionary" causes and movements. He has been active in various regions in support of coups and in the funding and training of guerrilla groups and opposition political movements. He has been implicated in efforts to assassinate rival leaders and opponents to his regime and in support of terrorist groups and movements. Moreover, he was involved in military ventures in Uganda in 1979 in support of Idi Amin and has occupied the Aouzou Strip in Chad since 1972–1973. In September 1988 Libya was accused of manufacturing chemical weapons at a plant in Rabta designed to produce poison gas. These and similar activities strained Libya's relations with many of the European states and the United States over the years. In 1993, in response to U.N. sanctions, Libya closed down the offices of the notorious terrorist Abu Nidal and his followers in Tripoli and, in May, issued a statement renouncing terrorism. Libyan officials also met with British officials in Geneva in June 1993 and gave them information about the Irish Republican Army, which had received Libyan assistance.

Libya today remains under the control of a small group of men led by Muammar Qaddafi. Economic liberalization is still limited and political liberalization has not taken place, nor is it likely to occur under the present regime.

Notes

1. *The Economist* Intelligence Unit, *Libya: Country Profile 2000–01* (London: EIU, 2000), p. 3.

2. Alistair Lyons, "Oil Price Rise Gives Libya Temporary Respite," Reuters from Tripoli, September 10, 1999.

3. *The World Factbook 2000–Libya,* CIA.

4. United Nations Development Program, *Human Development Report 1997* (New York: Oxford University Press), Table 2, p. 149, and Table 7, p. 164.

5. *The World Factbook–Libya,* CIA.

6. *The Economist* Intelligence Unit, *Libya: Country Profile 2000–01* (London: EIU, 2001), p. 23.

Bibliography

Historical works on Libya include John Wright, *Libya* (New York: Praeger Publishers, 1969), which provides a general history of Libya, especially of the period 1911 to 1951; Wright's second volume, *Libya: A Modern History* (Baltimore: Johns Hopkins University Press, 1982), covers the history of Libya briefly before 1951 and then until 1981. E. E. Evans-Pritchard, *The Sanusi of Cyrenaica* (London: Oxford University Press, 1949), provides an important study of Libya's main religious order and its role in the country's development, as does Nicola Ziadeh in *Sanusiyah: A Study of a Revivalist Movement in Islam* (Leiden: E. J. Brill, 1968). Henry Serrano Villard, the first U.S. minister to Libya after independence, gives a general overview in *Libya: The New Arab Kingdom of North Africa* (Ithaca: Cornell University Press, 1956). The U.N. commissioner in Libya, Adrian Pelt, describes the transformation of Libya from an Italian colony to an independent state in *Libyan Independence and the United Nations: A Case of Planned Decolonization* (New Haven: Yale University Press, for the Carnegie Endowment for International Peace, 1970). Lisa Anderson covers the social and political history of Libya for a century and a half in *The State and Social Transformation in Tunisia and Libya, 1830–1980* (Princeton: Princeton University Press, 1986). Majid Khadduri, in *Modern Libya: A Study in Political Development* (Baltimore: Johns Hopkins University Press, 1963), considers the monarchy in detail.

Studies of the Libyan political, social, and economic system since 1969 include J. A. Allan, *Libya Since Independence: Economic and Social Development* (London: Croom Helm, 1982); Omar L. Fathaly and Monte Palmer, *Political Development and Social Change in Libya* (Lexington, Mass.: Lexington Books, 1979); Harold D. Nelson, *Libya: A Country Study,* 3d ed. (Washington, D.C.: American University, Foreign Area Studies, 1979); John K. Cooley, *Libyan Sandstorm* (New York: Holt, Rinehart & Winston, 1982); Marius Deeb and Mary-Jane Deeb, *Libya Since the Revolution: Aspects of Social and Political Development* (New York: Praeger Publishers, 1982); Mary-Jane Deeb, *Libya's Foreign Policy in North Africa* (Boulder: Westview Press, 1991); Ruth First, *Libya: The Elusive Revolution* (Middlesex, England: Penguin Books, 1974); Ronald Bruce St. John, *Qaddafi's World Design: Libyan Foreign Policy 1969–1987* (London: Saqi Books, 1987); Lillian Craig Harris, *Qadhafi's Revolution and the Modern State* (Boulder: Westview/Croom Helm, 1986); E. G. H. Joffe and K. S. McLachlan,

Social and Economic Development of Libya (Cambridgeshire, England: MENAS Press, 1982); Jonathan Bearman, *Qadhdhafi's Libya* (London: Zed Books, 1986); J. A. Allan, *Libya: The Experience of Oil* (Boulder: Westview Press, 1981); Mirella Bianco, *Gadafi: Voice from the Desert* (London: Longman Group, 1975); David Blundy and Andrew Lycett, *Qaddafi and the Libyan Revolution* (Boston: Little, Brown, 1987); Edward Haley, *Qadhdhafi and the United States Since 1969* (New York: Praeger, 1984); Rene Lemarchand, *The Green and the Black: Qadhafi's Policies in Africa* (Bloomington, Ind.: Indiana University Press, 1988). Recent books include Tim Niblock, *"Pariah States" and Sanctions in the Middle East: Iraq, Libya, Sudan* (Boulder: Lynne Rienner Publishers, 2001); Dirk Vandewalle, *Libya Since Independence: Oil and State-Building* (Ithaca: Cornell University Press, 1998); J. Millard Burr and Robert O. Collins, *Africa's Thirty Years War: Libya, Chad, and the Sudan, 1963–1993* (Boulder: Westview Press, 1999); Judith Gurney, *Libya: The Political Economy of Oil* (Oxford, New York: Oxford University Press for the Oxford Institute for Energy Studies, 1996).

15

Kingdom of Morocco

Gregory W. White
Mark A. Tessler
John P. Entelis

Historical Background

From 1873 to 1894, Morocco experienced enlightened rule under a dynamic sultan, Mulay Hassan, who reestablished the authority of the Alawi Sharifian empire, founded in 1666. He restored the country's finances, thanks to a flourishing export trade, maintained internal order, built up an army, and obtained diplomatic assistance from Britain to impede the annexationist ambitions of France and Spain.

After his death, however, the country fell into immediate difficulties, largely owing to mismanagement by Hassan's son and heir, Abd al-Aziz (1894–1908). A young and weak ruler, Abd al-Aziz surrounded himself with venal foreign agents who advised him poorly on financial matters. He was forced to borrow heavily and soon incurred a large external debt. As the country was no longer able to resist European pressures and creditors, its internal sovereignty was quickly undermined. By 1908 Moroccans were in general revolt against Abd al-Aziz, accusing him of having abandoned the country to foreigners and foreign financial interests. His brother, Mulay Hafid, replaced him.

In a futile attempt to rid the country of its enormous financial obligations, Mulay Hafid further indebted Morocco. At the same time, dissident tribes in Fez besieged him, and he turned to France for military, political, and economic assistance. The conditions under which France agreed to intervene were set out in the Treaty of Fez, signed on March 30, 1912. Morocco became a French protectorate, ceding control of national defense, foreign policy, and economic and financial affairs.

The French retained the basic structure of the sultan's government. The sultan signed official decrees and legislation and promulgated them in his own name; thus he remained at the center of public life as the nominal source of authority in the country. Furthermore, extensive European colonization in Morocco came late, since actual pacification of the country was not achieved until the 1930s.

Unlike French colonialism in Algeria, colonialism in Morocco left domestic political and social institutions relatively intact. The traditionally privileged classes were preserved, especially the commercially and culturally dominant Arab bourgeoisie in the cities of Fez and Rabat and the Berber tribal notables of the countryside. Similarly, internal social evolution was modest. On the one hand, the traditional elite was not infused with fresh blood by upwardly mobile lower-status groups. On the other hand, few of these elites either received a French education or gained access to administrative and professional careers, as had, for example, some Tunisians.

It took nearly a quarter century for France to pacify Morocco, however, and of the three Maghribi states, only Morocco maintained a genuine "continuity of resistance." Early opposition centered among the tribes in the countryside, particularly the Anti-Atlas. The northern tier of Morocco, for its part, came under Spanish control, with the Spanish zone extending from the Algerian frontier to Tangier along the Mediterranean coast and including most of the mountainous Rif and Jabala areas. The Spanish did not pacify the region until 1925, when Rifian Berbers, under the leadership of Abd al-Krim al-Khattabi, were defeated by combined armies of both France and Spain. In 1921, the Spanish lost more than 20,000 men in the battle of Annual, a humiliating defeat for a European army proud of its abilities to subjugate colonial peoples.

Nationalists among the traditional elite of Morocco eventually capitulated to French demands and reluctantly accepted their status. They retained their national identity, however, and after 1926 their ranks were joined by a small group of populists—young, well-educated men from leading urban families, who were also embittered by the French presence. Disaffection emerged as well among skilled urban craftspeople who were beginning to suffer because of strong competition from manufactured goods introduced by the colonialists. The combination of disaffected traditional elites, radicalized younger elites, and lower-middle-class elements constituted a powerful nationalist front with an urbanized focus.

The national independence movement gained momentum on May 16, 1930, when the colonial authorities in Rabat issued a *dahir,* or Berber decree, establishing a separate system of customary-law tribunals in Berber-populated parts of the country. It was part of a French effort to isolate the rural areas from the growing nationalism of the cities. Empowered to deal with civil matters, these tribunals created an artificial division between the Arabs and the Berbers by removing the latter from the national system of Muslim jurisprudence on civil matters. The politics of

Berber identity remain salient until this day, with Berber identity reemerging with particular passion in the late 1990s.

Incipient nationalist elements representing traditionalists, such as Allal al-Fassi, as well as pro-French intellectuals, such as Ahmad Balafrej, immediately and vigorously protested the decree, and their protests soon attracted the skilled craftspeople and shopkeepers of the towns to their cause. Although French authorities sought to dilute the impact of the *dahir,* the damage had already been done. Nationalist consciousness quickly spread, especially among Morocco's youth.

In May 1932 the Kutla al-Amal al-Watani—the National Action Bloc—was formed as the first overtly nationalist party in the country. The bloc worked peacefully but in vain for reforms within the framework of the protectorate until the French dissolved the party in 1937. Thus, there was no effective political organization to lead the nationalist movement until the formation of the Istiqlal Party in 1943. *Istiqlal* is Arabic for independence. The Istiqlal demanded full freedom for Morocco and a constitutional monarchy under Sultan Muhammad Ben Yussuf (Muhammad V).

After World War II, the Istiqlal was joined by two other parties—a splinter party known as the Democratic Independence Party and the marginal Communist Party. The Istiqlal had strong support in the towns and a tacit alliance with the throne. It was challenged, however, by powerful rural chieftains allied with the French, by some traditionalist elements in the cities, and by the heads of some religious brotherhoods.

During the late 1940s, the Istiqlal transformed itself from an elite party into a broad-based independence movement. As the alliance between the Istiqlal and the monarch became more overt and began to challenge French hegemony in the country, colonial authorities took action. In August 1953, they sent Muhammad V and his family—including his son, Hassan II—into exile in Madagascar and replaced him with a more docile relative. Once again, however, the French had miscalculated. The deposed sultan became a martyr and saint in the eyes of the population, and the French action catalyzed the nationalist movement into an all-out fight for independence.

A relatively quick political settlement was achieved, which thereby prevented the occurrence of widespread violence; Muhammad V's return from exile in November 1954 marked the effective end of colonial rule in Morocco. On March 2, 1956, the formerly French-controlled regions of the west and south were joined with the Spanish-controlled areas of the north and east, and the French formally granted Morocco independence. In 1957, the country was proclaimed a kingdom and the sultan became king.

The monarch unexpectedly emerged as the major beneficiary of independence at the expense of the nationalist elite, which was relegated to a secondary role. Indeed, Morocco is virtually unique in the Arab world in that its struggle for independence revolved around the capture, revival, and renovation of a monarchy that had appeared rather ineffective and dissolute prior to colonial rule. The population revered Muhammad V for his *baraka,* or mystical religious qualities. In addition, the diverse forces of contemporary nationalism looked to him to satisfy their demands for a national government. The king was thus the one leader whose right to rule rested on sufficiently diverse grounds to satisfy virtually all sectors of Moroccan opinion.

Political Evolution Since Independence

Upon independence Morocco enjoyed a sufficient level of national unity, institutional stability, and effective political leadership to give it a promising future. The political parties, with the Istiqlal in the lead, provided necessary cadres for the new government. The urban resistance forces were incorporated into the police, and the Army of Liberation, one of the last groups to recognize the monarchy, was absorbed into the Royal Armed Forces (FAR). Civil servants were recruited from the former protectorate government and from newly trained Moroccan youth. Over this diverse and heterogeneous group King Muhammad V ruled as the arbiter and symbol of Moroccan unity.

Within five years, however, the working relationship between the king and the political parties broke down. Muhammad V was unwilling to become a constitutional figurehead, and the Istiqlal leadership was unwilling to accept the secondary role that the king envisioned for it. The Istiqlal also experienced internal strains that hampered its attempts to reduce the political predominance of the monarch. Tension between the conservative and radical wings of the party reached a breaking point in 1959, when Prime Minister Abdallah Ibrahim of the Istiqlal joined a group of young, secular intellectuals and trade unionists to form a new left-wing party, the National Union of Popular Forces (UNFP), closely allied with the large Moroccan Workers Union (UMT). The UNFP charged the traditional Istiqlal leadership with not standing up to the king sufficiently and with indifference to meaningful social and economic reform and called for a new constitution creating a democratic monarchy, with sharp limits on the palace's authority.

The fragmentation of the Istiqlal and the limited appeal of the UNFP outside urban areas, however, greatly facilitated the king's efforts to develop the institution of the monarchy. Muhammad V had already, in 1957, designated his son, Hassan II, to be crown prince and to act as head of state whenever Muhammad V was out of the country. Thus, Muhammad V established the principle of primogeniture, which Hassan later institutionalized formally. In turn, Hassan II's son, Muhammad VI, ascended to the throne in 1999 upon his father's death.

King Muhammad V dismissed the government of Prime Minister Ibrahim and his predominantly UNFP cabinet in May 1960, naming himself prime minister and making Crown Prince Hassan his deputy. Muhammad V died the following February after routine surgery and was succeeded by Hassan on March 3, 1961.

Hassan, who was educated in France, with a law degree from Bordeaux, quickly consolidated power in his own hands and further reduced the political role of the parties. He firmly believed that the role of political parties was to organize support for the monarchy, not to represent the electorate in the formulation of public policy. The young king lacked Muhammad V's charisma, however, as well as the advantage of being a nationalist hero. In the absence of genuine popular appeal and personal standing, Hassan's consolidation of royal authority led to serious political conflicts.

With a minimum of consultation, but in keeping with his father's public promise, King Hassan introduced a constitution, which was approved in a national referendum in December 1962. Largely inspired by Charles de Gaulle's Fifth Republic constitution, this new document formally established a constitutional monarchy with guaranteed personal and political freedoms. Yet the constitution's principal provisions solidified the king's power at the expense of the legislative branch—the lower house of representatives and the upper chamber of counselors. The king was also given the authority to dissolve the legislature and exercise unlimited emergency powers.

In the first national elections under the new constitution, in May 1963, Hassan encouraged the creation of parties loyal to the throne, including the Constitutional Institutions Defense Front (FDIC) and a conservative Berber party, the Popular Movement (MP). The FDIC, a hastily formed coalition of non- or anti-Istiqlal participants in the nationalist movement, was unable to win the majority the king hoped for, and the next two years witnessed a succession of cabinets, none of which commanded strong support in the parliament, or Majlis. The loyalist FDIC itself underwent an internal split, further diminishing the king's political standing. Finally, on June 7, 1965, following a series of demonstrations, strikes, and bloody riots in Casablanca, Hassan invoked the emergency powers granted to him under Article 35 of the constitution and personally assumed full legislative and executive power.

This nonetheless failed to end the political and social unrest that had existed since the death of Muhammad V. The gulf between the throne and the opposition parties, principally the Istiqlal and the UNFP, widened even more with the abduction in Paris of the popular UNFP leader, Mehdi Ben Barka, in 1965. Ben Barka had been sentenced to death in absentia by a Moroccan court because of his criticism of Hassan's rule and he was living in exile when Moroccan agents seized him in a Paris café in broad daylight. Although his fate was the subject of speculation for years—with Hassan claiming in interviews that he was not involved—revelations and the release of official documents in 2001 indicate that Ben Barka was tortured to death in France, with French connivance. In turn, Ben Barka's body was flown to Rabat, where it was dissolved in a vat of acid.

Throughout the late 1960s, the police seized newspapers and made many arrests, and sanctioned political activity in Morocco virtually disappeared. In July

1970, the king unexpectedly announced that a new constitution would be submitted for a national referendum. It had become increasingly apparent that the monarchy, relying principally on security forces and the army for support, had isolated itself and jeopardized its legitimacy. Thus the king, taking advantage of a period of relative calm, sought to open a new era of cooperation with the political parties. Critics complained that they had not been consulted about the new constitution and charged that it merely legalized the king's excessive powers. Nevertheless, despite opposition from the main political parties, trade unions, and major student organizations, the national referendum approved the new constitution.

Elections for a new single-chamber Majlis were held immediately after the July referendum, in August. The Istiqlal and the UNFP—which had joined together in a *Kutla Wataniya*, or National Front, to oppose ratification of the new constitution—tried to organize a boycott of elections for the Majlis. In both instances, the Kutla's efforts were futile in the face of the regime's campaign to arouse popular support. Nevertheless, by opposing the constitution and the elections, the Kutla did deprive the king of a meaningful popular mandate. In the end, the regime was forced to continue its reliance on loyal "independent" politicians, the internal security forces, and, ultimately, the army.

The elimination of effective political opposition failed to prevent—or perhaps prompted—two attempts by army and air force officers to assassinate the king: one in July 1971 at Skhirat and the other in August 1972 in Rabat. Discontent over Hassan's autocratic rule and over corruption among many of his associates helped to bring on the attempted coups. Hassan emerged uninjured in both instances, more determined than ever to suppress those elements he perceived to be dangerous.

The August 1972 coup attempt provided the country with one of its most renowned political episodes: the death of General Mohammed Oufkir. Oufkir was a former defense minister and a longtime ally of Hassan—now known to be present at Ben Barka's torture and murder. Nevertheless, Oufkir conspired to overthrow the king, ordering air force fighters to strafe the royal jet on August 16, 1972. Hassan survived the attack, and by evening the general was dead. According to official accounts, Oufkir confessed to the plot and promptly committed suicide. Yet bullet holes were found in the back of his head. Security forces sympathetic to the king arrested the general's family and imprisoned them for nearly twenty years. They were released in 1991 and finally allowed to leave the country in 1996.

In 1972, the king announced a third constitution. Executive power was to be vested in the government and a new chamber of representatives. Two-thirds of the chamber's membership was to be elected by universal suffrage, compared with one-half under the 1970 constitution. The Kutla, caught unprepared, again urged a boycott of the constitutional referendum and again accused the government of rigging the balloting, which had registered overwhelming support for the new constitution. With the split between the palace and opposition elements as wide as ever, the cabinet appointed in April was substantially similar to its predecessor. Elections for the new Majlis were postponed indefinitely.

Once the king felt confident that he had reestablished control of the military, he ignored the demands for more political freedom by the opposition parties, which were in disarray. Differences between the Istiqlal and the UNFP had reemerged, ending the Kutla coalition. Moreover, differences within the UNFP—between a wing headed by Ibrahim Ben-Siddiq (Casablanca) and Abderrahim Bouabid (Rabat)—led to a formal rupture in July 1972. The Bouabid faction, which became dominant, reconstituted itself as the Union Socialiste des Forces Populaires (USFP), while the Casablanca group retained the old name and gradually declined in influence.

At the same time, Hassan slowly began to liberalize foreign trade relations with Europe. In this way, he combined his ability to outmaneuver the squabbling opposition parties with economic liberalization measures that created the impression of change and progress. This combination of savvy maneuvering and control of Morocco's foreign policy—along with a willingness to suppress dissent when necessary—helped the king to maintain his monopoly of power throughout his reign.

In 1973, King Hassan undertook additional economic programs designed to increase support for the monarchy, including the distribution of nationalized foreign-owned land (mostly French) among the peasantry. In addition, he introduced an ambitious five-year development plan (1973–1977) that called for an annual economic growth rate of 7.5 percent.

Hassan also launched several foreign policy initiatives designed, perhaps, to defuse domestic unrest, including a strong stand in a fishing dispute with Spain in 1973. Conflict with Spain and, in turn, the European Union over access to Morocco's Atlantic fisheries persists to this day as Morocco has sought to develop its deep-sea fishing sector. The king also scored a major political victory in 1974 and 1975 by reasserting his country's historic claim to the former Spanish Sahara. This move mobilized popular support from all segments of society and raised Hassan's political fortunes enormously. Moreover, both the Istiqlal and the USFP, which supported "reintegration" of the Western Sahara, were placed on the defensive. Spanish withdrawal from the territory also set the stage for a major public relations coup. In November 1975, Hassan organized the *massira*, or "Green March," in which approximately 350,000 civilians assembled on Morocco's border with the Western Sahara and staged a short symbolic walk into the disputed territory. The event is celebrated annually as a major national holiday. Since the northern two-thirds of the territory obtained by Morocco contained large deposits of phosphate as well as oil and uranium, the victory seemed to portend economic and political gains. Morocco was already the world's largest exporter of phosphates, and a rise in the price on the international market in 1974 had relieved some of the financial pressure on the kingdom.

In the late 1970s, Hassan, with his political circumstances improved, permitted the resuscitation of political life. In 1976, the security apparatus eased press restrictions and released political detainees, and the government held elections for provincial assemblies and municipal councils. A year later, the long-postponed parliamentary elections took place as well. After nearly seven years of royal dictatorship, these moves were received with enthusiasm in Morocco, but they were not associated with a reduction in monarchical authority. Hassan sought to create a state of political normality in which opponents could be either co-opted or contained and in which his own preeminent position would be more secure than ever.

The 1977 elections were a landslide victory for the monarchy. The National Independent Rally (RNI), a loosely organized front of independent candidates whose only platform was "unconditional loyalty" to the king, won eighty-one of the 176 seats contested for the Majlis. Thirty-three additional seats were won by right-wing parties, which declared their intention of working with the RNI. Thus the monarchy was assured a large and comfortable majority. The Istiqlal made a respectable showing, winning forty-five seats, but the same could not be said of the leftist USFP, which gained only sixteen seats. Even the party's popular leader, Abderrahim Bouabid, lost in his bid for a seat in the Majlis.

Despite the success of candidates loyal to the king, most observers believed the elections were relatively free from government interference and saw them as an important step in the opening up of the political process. The Istiqlal, in opposition since the early 1960s, thus agreed to enter the ruling coalition. Even the USFP acknowledged that its losses were in substantial measure due to the popularity of the king, particularly in the wake of the Green March, and the party accordingly agreed to participate in parliamentary life as a "loyal and constructive" opposition.

Political tranquility did not last long, however. An insurgency by the Polisario Front, claiming the right to an independent Sahara, had broken out in 1976, shortly after Morocco gained sovereignty over the northern part. By the early 1980s, the war had become a major burden to the Moroccan economy, consuming 40–45 percent of the annual state budget. Despite numerous efforts to negotiate a settlement by the United Nations and the Organization of African Unity (OAU), Morocco was able to forestall a resolution of the dispute until 2001. One reason for the government's tenacity is the loss of "national honor" it would risk at home by making humiliating concessions. Moreover, there is the fear that a full accounting of the territory's population would confirm Saharawi assertions of self-determination, thereby undermining the territory's "Moroccaneity."

A severe drought ravaged the economy on a regular basis as well. Between 1980 and the late 1990s, according to the journal *Sécheresse: Science et changements planétaires*, Morocco experienced sharp rainfall deficits an astonishing six times. The drought not only devastated the agricultural sector, but it also encouraged the urban migration of hundreds of thousands of peasants. Coupled with the progressive loss of access to European markets, the drought caused severe dislocations for the agricultural sector.

World phosphate prices also began their steep decline during this period. After placing very strong emphasis on phosphate exports to earn foreign exchange, the state grew increasingly indebted to foreign lenders and was forced to reduce public investment in development projects.

In the face of such sharp economic difficulties, public discontent reemerged in 1978 and 1979. Unemployment reached as high as 35 to 40 percent of the workforce and was particularly pronounced among the young. Corruption also became an issue of discontent. With access to wealth determined largely by family or political connections, the elite continued to prosper, despite the economic crisis. Labor unrest increased; militant Islamist groups opposed to the established political order also emerged.

In response to these challenges, the king began to retreat from the political reforms of the mid-1970s. In 1981, he "asked" the nation to postpone for two years elections scheduled for that year. Although he claimed to be awaiting a resolution of the Saharan conflict, Hassan's decision was heavily influenced by the declining popularity of his government.

Major riots broke out in Casablanca in June 1981: Roving bands from the city's slums attacked banks, car dealerships, and other symbols of authority and privilege. Security forces were barely able to regain order in some areas; they fired into the crowds and killed at least 200 protesters, possibly many more. The rioting was followed by numerous arrests, including those of trade union leaders and even some members of the Majlis belonging to the USFP.

In January 1983, there were reports of another military plot against the king. Senior officers were arrested, and General Ahmed Dlimi, commander of Morocco's forces in the Sahara, was killed in a bizarre car accident. It is widely believed that Hassan's supporters arranged the crash, presumably for fear that the general was planning a military action against the king. The armed forces had grown to over 200,000 as a result of the war, and the regime was becoming increasingly concerned about political consciousness and discontent within the military ranks, especially among younger officers. Following Dlimi's death, Hassan fragmented the military command structure.

In 1983, Hassan again postponed the elections to the Majlis as well as elections for provincial and prefectural assemblies. Elections for municipal and rural councils took place, but they were accompanied by serious irregularities, rendering meaningless the victory of Hassan's supporters. In fact, the elections deepened public alienation and cynicism. Widespread intimidation and fraud accompanied the balloting, and many complained about interference in candidate registration and campaign procedures.

January 1984 brought new and more widespread riots. They began with strikes by students in Marrakech and spread throughout the country. The security forces killed at least 150 people by the time order was restored. Arrests followed. The International League of Human Rights put the arrest figure at 1,500–2,000, which is consistent with the government's own reports. The league also monitored the detention and trial of prisoners, reporting that it found no instances of torture but considered many sentences exorbitant. The courts condemned some individuals to life in prison. Verdicts handed to Islamists were especially harsh, including thirteen death sentences, the first for political crimes since 1972.

Fall 1984 brought even more tension. Legislative elections were scheduled for September, but there were fears that these would be either delayed again or, like the local elections of 1983, blatantly rigged. Concern was also fueled by the announcement in early summer of major cuts in the educational budget. The proposed austerity measures would eliminate up to 40,000 secondary-school places—a situation that most assumed would spark new protests when the school year began.

Events unfolded in an unexpected way, however. The biggest surprise was the conclusion of a union between Morocco and Libya on August 13, 1984. The union secured Qaddafi's agreement to withdraw support from the Polisario Front, a major source of economic distress. Moreover, it set in motion a series of economic cooperation efforts, including employment opportunities in oil-rich Libya for Moroccan migrant labor, purchase of Libyan oil at preferential prices, and several agreements on trade and investment ties. The Moroccan electorate overwhelmingly endorsed the union in a referendum later in August; and although such plebiscites do not necessarily constitute a true indication of popular sentiment, preliminary reaction did appear to be highly favorable. All Morocco's political parties, including the opposition, endorsed the union. Indeed, they organized hundreds of public meetings on its behalf during the two-week campaign preceding the referendum. Moreover, the palace claimed to have received thousands of messages endorsing the treaty.

The union with Libya was a tactical move on both sides. For Morocco, it diverted attention from immediate problems, raised hopes of economic benefits, and boosted the popularity of the king. Seeking to exploit the situation, Hassan finally allowed the twice-postponed parliamentary elections to be held in September 1984. The elections seem to have been reasonably fair. Although there were some complaints, they were not excessive, and Hassan had released 354 political prisoners shortly before the balloting to forestall criticism. The union was not bound to last, however. After Qaddafi denounced Morocco for its pro-Western orientation—and support for Reagan Administration policies—and after Qaddafi's overtures to Algeria, Hassan abrogated the treaty on August 29, 1986.

The 1984 elections produced some surprises. The leftist USFP became the third-largest party, with 17 percent of the direct vote (one-third of the seats were selected indirectly by regional assemblies, thus ensuring a conservative majority), indicating a certain tolerance of dissent during the election. Conversely, the Istiqlal dropped to fifth place, with only 12 percent of the popular vote (although its position improved in the indirect balloting). The biggest winner was the Constitutional Union (UC), formed in 1983 and closely allied with the king. It received 27 percent of the vote in both the popular and the indirect balloting. Since the party is not highly institutionalized and has no secure constituent base, it is particularly dependent on ties to the palace. Nevertheless, it is a party of the moderate center, with many young technocrats in its ranks. It achieved success largely at the expense of electoral fronts controlled by feudal barons who had years of participation in patrimonial politics. Despite these developments, the Majlis remained at the margins of power. It was allowed to debate but not to determine government policy, and the king, in his speech on March 3, 1986, the twenty-fifth anniversary of his accession to the throne, reaffirmed the chamber's subordinate position.

With the continuing war in the Sahara, the cycle of unrest motivated by economic privation followed by harsh security measures continued throughout the 1980s. Unrest was led by both leftists and Islamists. For example, in 1986 the government charged that the Polisario was backing leftist efforts to conduct subversive activities among Moroccan students and labor. In February, the criminal court of Casablanca sentenced twenty-six activists from the banned Marxist-Leninist association *Ila al-Amam* to prison. The legal defense charged the security forces with using torture to extract confessions; one defendant had died after his arrest, and the cause, according to official statements, was an "asthma attack."

Some of these detainees began hunger strikes. The strikes began among a group of prisoners known as the Marrakech group, arrested for their participation in the 1984 riots. Prisoners on strike were bound, sedated, and kept alive by gastric drip. In June 1989, four hunger strikers demanded that they be given the status of political prisoner and that their conditions be improved. Hassan invariably disregarded specific demands, but maintained his long-established practice of pardons and amnesties, especially on national or religious holidays or on anniversaries of his accession to throne. In January 1987, Hassan amnestied 353 detainees, and in July he amnestied prominent political exile Mohamed "Fkih" Basri, a founder of the nationalist Moroccan Resistance Movement. Fkih is a term of reverence ascribed to a religious leader. In 1989, Hassan released 400 detainees to mark the Id al-Adha celebration. (Id al-Adha, the Festival of Sacrifice that marks the end of the Hajj, is celebrated in Islam as a commemoration of Abraham's willingness to sacrifice his son.)

The government has been relatively lenient on press freedoms. It suspended the communist daily *Al Bayane* briefly in 1986 for disparaging Hassan and his advisers, but other papers have been permitted to criticize the government so long as they do not mention the king personally. For example, the USFP's *Al Ittihad Al Ichtiraki* and the Istiqlal's *L'Opinion* reproached the government for its heavy-handed "attack on freedom of the press." On the other hand, in 1988, the government banned the Moroccan Human Rights Organization (OMDH) because of its plans to hold a constitutive assembly in Rabat-Agdal in May. The OMDH was the initiative of Fatima Mernissi, a feminist sociologist; Mehdi El-Mandjra, a member of the Royal Academy; and Mohamed Bouzoubaa, a socialist lawyer. Other Moroccan human rights organizations are the Moroccan Association of Human Rights, linked to the USFP; Istiqlal's Moroccan League of Human Rights; and the Ila al-Amam-led Association for the Defense of Human Rights in Morocco, which is based in Paris. After international and domestic pressure, however, Hassan finally approved the establishment of the OMDH, which held its assembly in December 1988. As Morocco struggled throughout the 1990s to improve its international image on its human rights record, the OMDH remained a key player on the scene.

In a measure aimed at Islamic sentiment, the king also began to secure "contributions" for the construction in Casablanca of the huge Hassan II Mosque. Completed in the early 1990s, the mosque has a minaret over 500 feet tall and an internal capacity of 25,000. Many Moroccans take great pride in the mosque's grandeur and beauty, but there have been complaints about a cost estimated at $800 million U.S. Some charge that it would have been much better to devote these resources to development projects than to an edifice intended to be a regal reflection of a self-indulgent Moroccan monarchy.

Throughout the stormy 1980s, the king was able to maintain his hold on popular attitudes. When he held a referendum in December 1989 authorizing the postponement of parliamentary elections until 1992 in order to give the United Nations time to organize a self-determination referendum in the Western Sahara, both the participation rate and the "yes vote" were exceptionally high (though not so high as the government claimed).

Despite riots in December 1990 and the Gulf crisis in 1990–1991, Morocco's situation generally stabilized in the early 1990s, due largely to international economic assistance. The riots began with a general strike protesting rises in the price of basic commodities and an insufficient minimum wage. In quelling the protests, security forces opened fire, and in Fez alone, thirty-three were reportedly killed. The underlying reasons for the riots were the high levels of poverty and structural unemployment, and with continued austerity planned, the situation looked bleak. The situation remained tense during Desert Storm in early 1991. Hassan sent a contingent of soldiers to the Gulf to join the anti-Iraq coalition, prompting much domestic criticism from a population that generally sided with Saddam Hussein. The king adroitly navigated the criticism, however, allowing carefully controlled public protests to take place. The protests were immense, with as many as 300,000 people filling the streets in Rabat during one demonstration. Nonetheless, the king's stance was rewarded with debt relief and enhanced aid from the European Union, the United States, Saudi Arabia, and international financial institutions, which have substantially improved his financial situation.

Yet disturbances continued in 1991. Student riots in April and November included active participation by Justice and Charity (*al-Adl wal-Ihsan*), a banned Islamist group. Islamist opposition does not enjoy mass support, but its presence is growing.

In 1992, the king announced that the deferred elections would be held by the end of the year, in part to respond to ongoing criticism from the international community about Morocco's human rights record. In September, a referendum approved a revised constitution that allowed the prime minister rather than the king to distribute portfolios, although the monarch maintained final approval. After several delays, the legislative elections finally took place in June 1993, the first vote for the Majlis since 1984. Although Hassan sharply limited the authority of the chamber—and, as noted, is not obligated by the constitution to approve a cabinet that reflects electoral outcomes—the government touted the election to both foreign observers and the domestic population as an important display of democratic reform. Turnout was relatively low, with only about 62.75 percent of the nearly 12 million eligible voters participating. This figure undoubtedly reflected an increase in official candor, however, especially after the implausible 97.2 percent turnout claimed for the 1992 constitutional referendum. There were comparatively few reports of corruption and electoral interference.

In the election itself, the USFP and the Istiqlal agreed not to compete against each other; the USFP thus fielded only 104 candidates, while the Istiqlal fielded candidates in only 118 different constituencies. On the other hand, despite these efforts, the opposition was hindered by its inability to forge a common economic platform to challenge the government's vigorous promarket approach. As a result, the election turned on more ambiguous concerns, such as calls for greater attention to issues of human rights. With characteristic savvy, Hassan undermined the potency of these issues by inviting Amnesty International to visit the country, by promoting the efforts of the Consultative Council for Human Rights (CCDH), by ratifying international conventions against torture, and by granting yet another amnesty to prisoners in June 1993 during the Id al-Adha celebration.

The 1993 elections provided a clear example of the electoral system's structural bias toward the palace, similar to the experience in 1977 and 1984. Of the 333 seats in the Majlis, only two-thirds (222) were elected by popular vote. Local councils, chambers of commerce, and official unions elected the remaining third of the members. This system consistently resulted in a propalace body because of the conservative interests of the local bodies. The 1993 elections took place in two stages, a direct election on June 25 followed by an electoral college vote on September 17. As Table 15.1 shows, 54 percent of the seats went to loyalist parties in the summer's direct election, a slight majority of the seats. In the electoral college vote three months later, however, 79 percent of the seats went to progovernment representatives, cementing their control of the Majlis. Cries of fraud and manipulation of the 1993 election remained a central component of the political scene until the 1997 election. Finally, in a noteworthy development, women were elected to the chamber for the first time in 1993: One was a USFP candidate elected from Casablanca, while the other was an Istiqlal candidate from Fez.

The period from 1993 to 1997 was characterized by a certain "waiting"—an *attentisme*—that led to a paralysis of the political system. Still, observers noted a gradual glasnost in the system, with increasing discussions about human rights issues and the inevitable succession of the monarchy. Hassan was visibly unwell on several occasions and traveled to New York City to receive medical treatment in 1996. To be sure, assessments of the degree of glasnost depended on one's perspective. In July 1994, during a royal discourse to mark his sixty-fifth birthday, Hassan announced that 424 prisoners would be released. Shortly thereafter, he abrogated the French protectorate *dahir* of June 29, 1935, a decree that had permitted the incarceration of political prisoners by colonial authorities, a power maintained by postindependence Morocco to suppress opposition. In lifting the decree, Hassan emphasized that he, too, was taken prisoner under the same *dahir* in 1954 when he and his father were exiled in Madagascar. This step, along with the establishment of a Ministry of Human Rights in November 1993, demonstrated Hassan's willingness to make public overtures to change. To be sure, many questioned the independence of the new ministry from the palace, but the steps were warmly received by international observers.

In July 1995, Hassan permitted the USFP's former leader, Mohamed "Fkih" Basri, to return to Morocco after thirty years of exile. Basri had been condemned to death for plotting against the state in the 1960s, and later linked to the 1972 coup attempt, but Hassan dropped the charges in 1988. The return of the elderly Fkih shook the political landscape not only in the USFP, but in other parties of the Kutla as well. For example, the Progress and Socialism Party's (PPS) Congress in July 1995 was affected positively by the Fkih's return as it was galvanized by his attendance.

In September 1996, a new referendum changed the constitution and created a bicameral Majlis, with a directly elected Chamber of Representatives and an upper house, the Chamber of Councilors. In turn, in November 1997, the first election resulting in a directly elected chamber in the Majlis was held, inaugurating an *alternance*, or accountable, competitive government. The opposition had argued for years that, if given the opportunity, they would do well in an election, and they did. Table 15.2 shows the results of the 1997 election. In March 1998, Hassan appointed the USFP's Abderrahman Youssoufi to the post of prime minister, a move that granted significant power, albeit hardly omnipotence, in the Moroccan political landscape. Perhaps most deftly, by co-opting the opposition into power, Hassan put himself in a position to deflect criticism of the state of the economy.

In the end, a full assessment of Hassan's ability to rule under *alternance* was rendered impossible by his death in July 23, 1999, and the accession to the throne of his son, Muhammad VI, on July 30, 1999. Upon his accession, Muhammad VI claimed to aspire to the model of the Spanish monarch, King Juan Carlos I, with a

TABLE 15.1   Outcome of the 1993 Elections by Suffrage

Party and Year of Formation	Direct Votes	Indirect Votes
Loyalist		
Constitutional Union (UC), 1983	27	27
Popular Movement (MP), 1958	33	18
National Independent Rally (RNI), 1977	28	13
Popular National Movement (MPN), 1991	14	11
National Democratic Party (PND), 1982	14	10
Democratic Independence Party (PDI), 1946	3	6
_ _ _ _ _		
Moroccan Workers Union (UMT)	− −	3
Subtotal:	119	88
	54%	79%
Opposition		
Istiqlal Party (PI), 1943	43	7
Popular Democratic Action Organization (OADP), 1983	2	− −
Socialist Union of Popular Forces (USFP), 1974	48	4
Progress and Socialism Party (PPS), 1974	6	5
Action Party (PA), 1974	2	− −
_ _ _ _ _		
General Union of Moroccan Workers (UGTM)	− −	2
Democratic Workers Confederation (CDT)	− −	4
Subtotal:	101	22
	46%	20%
Independents	2	1
Total	222	111

TABLE 15.2   Outcome of the November 1997 Elections

Party and Leader	Chamber of Counselors	Chamber of Representatives
Wifaq		
Constitutional Union (UC)—Semlali	28	50
Popular Movement (MP)—Laenser	27	40
National Democratic Party (PND)—El Jadidi	21	10
Center		
National Independent Rally (RNI)—Osman	42	46
Popular National Movement (MNP)—Ahardane	15	19
Democratic and Social Movement (MDS)—Archane	33	32
Democratic Independence Party (PCI)—Bouachrine	4	1
Action Party (PA)—Abaakil	13	2
Popular Democratic Constitutional Movement		
(MPDC)—Benkirane	boycott	9*
Opposition		
Democratic Kutla		
Istiqlal Party (PI)—Boucetta	21	32
Popular Democratic Action Organization (OADP)—Ben Said	0	4
Socialist Union of Popular Forces (USFP)—Youssoufi	16	57
Progress and Socialism Party (PPS)—Alaoui	7	9
Social Democratic Party (PSD)—el-Ouardighi	4	5
Democratic Forces Front (FFD)—collective	12	9
Democratic Movement (MD)—collective	0	0
Party of the Socialist & Democratic	boycott	boycott
Avant-Garde (PADS)—collective		
Labor Unions		
Democratic Workers Confederation (CDT)**—el Amaoui	11	
Moroccan Workers Union (UMT)—Ben Seddik	8	
General Union of Moroccan Workers (UGTM)***—Afilal	3	
Other Unions	5	
Total	270	325

 * The MPDC (in its electoral pact with Reform and Renewal, al-Islah wal-Tajdid) won 9 seats, but
   gained a seat when a USFP member was found to have won his post by fraud.
  ** Linked to the USFP
 *** Linked to the Istiqlal.

devotion to a constitutional, limited role for the monarchy. In his first years, he distinguished himself as presiding in a less-engaged reign than his father. Moreover, Muhammad—along with the system of *alternance*—has also nurtured vibrant discussions of human rights. The new king has been dubbed the "king of the poor" because of his constant trips throughout the country and his willingness to wade into crowds. Some have even called Muhammad "*Al Jawal*"—the Moroccan word for the cellular phones that are increasingly ubiquitous throughout Moroccan cities—because of his high mobility. As Morocco moves into the next decade, Muhammad's position seems secure: He has the benefit of strong support from the international community, as well as significant political capital within the domestic political system. At the same time, however, he may have further to fall if the high expectations are not met with performance.

Political Structure and State-Society Relations

A primary feature of Moroccan political culture is distrust. This is visible both in the attitude of the people toward their leaders and in relations among political elites. For decades, Moroccans viewed the political structure as a coercive instrument rather than as a basis for cooperative action, and the extent to which the inauguration of *alternance* and the accession of Muhammad VI might change that circumstance is unclear. Colonial repression reinforced distrust of authority and made cooperative sharing of power difficult to achieve. The forced imposition of a bureaucratic and impersonal administration further reinforced this tendency.

A second, related feature of postindependence Morocco is conspiratorial politics. Political authority is derived only secondarily from formal political roles and offices, and the system thus lacks accepted rules by which decisions are cooperatively reached. Instead, patterns of patrimonialism and clientelism dominate political life, as do personal associations and political connections. What keeps the system intact is the overriding desire of its elite members to preserve their stake in it, containing but not destroying their rivals and resisting change that might overwhelm the system. Such attitudes often lead to political stalemate, or *attentisme*, a third feature of Moroccan political life.

An emphasis on patron-client relationships produces a group orientation that has always existed and that continues to play an important role in Morocco's political culture and behavior. It is within this group framework that one can best understand the almost continuous process of alliance building and maintenance. A political culture dominated by norms of clientelism and patrimonialism encourages others to defend themselves through the formation of alliances; a politician must always be alert to rivals who might outmaneuver and isolate him by offering more to his clients or rendering superior service to his patrons. Non-elites in this system defend themselves and obtain resources by acquiring the protection of more powerful individuals, who in turn share in the authority and resources of their own patrons to the extent that they have the loyalty of many clients to deliver.

A peculiar irony of this system of cleavages, with its high degree of tension and conflict, is that it inhibits the creation of nationwide consensus. Primary loyalty is to smaller political groupings. Except for political beliefs predicated upon Islamic principles, beliefs that have meaning for many, it seems doubtful that a broad-based nationalist ideology could be established in such a fluid milieu. The various political groupings display no commitment to a comprehensive political or economic program, focusing almost entirely on short-term tactical objectives. Thus it is almost meaningless to talk about a coherent political ideology in present-day Morocco, despite the extensive use of ideological slogans by alienated intellectuals, dissident university students, and disaffected opposition politicians.

This political culture facilitates the maintenance of the monarch's power, wherein lèse-majesté, or criticism of the monarch, is entirely forbidden. The security apparatus, housed in the powerful Ministry of the Interior and Information, controls domestic affairs tightly. For years, the Ministry of the Interior was headed by Driss Basri, a confident of Hassan's from Settat. Basri was viewed as the most powerful man in Morocco, after Hassan, because he controlled such a wide array of governmental powers: police, security, human rights, media and information, electoral mechanisms, even foreign affairs. In a celebrated move in September 1999, however, Muhammad VI dismissed Basri, satisfying the opposition's long-standing demand for his removal.

According to the provisions of the constitution, Morocco is a constitutional, democratic, and social monarchy, and Islam is the official state religion. The constitution provides for equality under the law and guarantees freedom of movement, speech, opinion, and assembly. Amendments to the constitution may be initiated by either the king or the legislature, but such initiatives require approval by popular referendum.

Judicial and administrative institutions reflect both French and Spanish influences. The country is administratively divided into nineteen provinces and two urban prefectures, Casablanca and Rabat. The provinces are further divided into seventy-two administrative areas and communes. Each of the administrative regions is headed by a governor, who is appointed by the king and responsible to him.

There is a supreme court composed of four chambers: civil, criminal, administrative, and social. In 1965, the government also established a special court to deal with corruption among public officials. The king appoints all judges, with the advice of the Supreme Judicial Council. Moroccan courts administer a system that is based on Islamic law but strongly influenced by the French and Spanish legal systems. A separate system of courts administers the religious law of Morocco's Jewish citizens, although there is today only a small remnant of the country's once large and prosperous Jewish community.

The king is the center of the political system. He is the supreme civil and religious authority—the *amir al-mu'minin,* or "commander of the faithful"—as well as commander in chief of the armed forces. The eldest son inherits the crown, although the king may designate another son, should he so desire. The king appoints the important officials, including the prime minister, and approves the cabinet. He promulgates legislation passed by the legislature and has the authority to dissolve the legislature, to submit legislation for popular referendum, to declare a state of emergency, during which he may rule by decree, and to sign and ratify treaties. He presides over the cabinet, the Council for National Development and Planning, and the Supreme Judicial Council.

The sources of the monarchy's power and prestige are diverse and interdependent. The king's moral authority is based on his role as imam, or spiritual leader, of the Islamic community. He is concurrently a member of the Alawite dynasty, formally accepted as legitimate ruler by the Islamic community in Morocco for over 300 years. Because of his noble religious ancestry and the attendant powers ascribed to him, the Moroccan king satisfies the aspirations of rural Muslims who seek the miraculous qualities inherent in the monarch's *baraka.* Muhammad, like his father and grandfather, is thus deeply venerated by the rural population, who view him as a *sharif* (descendant of the Prophet) and a dispenser of God's blessing. His legitimacy as an Islamic leader is said to successfully defuse Islamist opposition efforts.

The monarchy also represents the symbolic leadership of the nationalist struggle. In the minds of many Moroccans, national independence and political unification are intimately associated with the monarchy—however limited may have been Muhammad V's actual involvement in the preindependence nationalist movement. The irony is that after independence the king suppressed the nationalist movement that had elevated the monarchy as a symbol of opposition to French rule.

The monarchy's ability to manipulate competing groups and rival factions for decades and, when necessary, to eliminate them altogether is an additional source of power. Another source is the fact that the monarch is the nation's most prominent dispenser of patronage and the ultimate source of spoils in the system. The palace commands Morocco's economy and distributes patronage, which sustains the king's clientele and builds alliances. Indeed, these commercial and patronage resources are probably the king's most effective levers of political control. Using royal patronage, Muhammad balances and dominates the political elite.

Although systems of consultation and advice exist within the broader structures of power, including those mandated by constitutional provisions, there are no formal systemic procedures that require the king to accept advice. If all else fails, the king can maintain his power and control by coercion through the intelligence and security services and the armed forces, all controlled by loyal lieutenants.

Beyond the king, Moroccan political life is dominated by a small group of men who constitute the country's political elite. As leaders of the various political parties, labor unions, agricultural interests, business associations, and other formal and informal groups, they speak for and control most of those who are politically active.

As long as the elite remains small, homogeneous, and politically fragmented, the current political arrangements—with monarchical dominance—are likely to remain substantially unchanged. Nonetheless, the equilibrium of the elite cannot be guaranteed in the future. Moreover, rapid population and educational challenges will inevitably threaten the equilibrium at all levels of society, including the elite.

The present system continues to receive pressure from non-elite sectors of society. Economic and political grievances, which are growing among the population, may ultimately erode the legitimacy accorded to the monarchy and become the most salient dimension of public attitudes toward authority. Such pressures have already made themselves felt on some occasions, particularly during the rioting of 1981, 1984, 1990, and 1991, as well as riots in 1998 and 2000 by Islamist opponents of the regime. These disturbances are a strong indication that the population is beginning to demand greater accountability from the king and his government and that the people may no longer respond to symbolic appeals based on historic or religious criteria.

Important differences exist among the parties in both structure and influence. On the loyalist, right-wing side of the political spectrum are three parties, known as the Wifaq, or Covenant: the Popular Movement (MP), the Constitutional Union (UC), and the National Democratic Party (PND). The MP is a Berber movement, founded by resistance leaders in 1958 to counter the preponderance of the Istiqlal. The UC was created in 1983, with a decidedly technocratic orientation, while the PND is a party of rural notables.

Center-right parties include the National Independent Rally (RNI), the National Popular Movement (MNP), and the new Democratic and Social Movement (MDS). The RNI was formed in 1977 and soon splintered off from the PND. Like the PND, the RNI is comprised of rural notables. Its leader, Ahmed Osman, is the brother-in-law of Hassan. The MNP was created in 1991, after a 1986 break with the MP, and espouses a more Berber, or Tamazigh, authenticity. The MDS was created in 1996, after a break with the MNP, and seems very similar to its MNP parent, except for a greater emphasis on participatory democracy.

On the opposition side, the venerable Istiqlal and the Socialist Union of Popular Forces (USFP) dominate the Kutla. The Istiqlal's secretary general is Mohammed Boucetta, and it draws its strength from the bourgeoisie and petty bourgeoisie. The USFP, for its part, continues to derive its support from labor and intellectuals and is currently the dominant faction in the lower chamber. The Progress and Socialism Party (PPS) was formed in 1974 and grew out of the former Communist Party. Since the late 1970s, it had evolved toward a "modern socialism" under the tutelage of its leader of forty years, Ali Yata. Yata was killed in an auto accident in August

1997, a few months before the 1997 elections. Finally, the left-wing Popular Democratic Action Organization (OADP) was formed in 1983. After boycotting the 1993 election and the 1996 constitutional referendum, it participated in the 1997 election.

Other parties of the opposition that are rather new on the scene include the Social Democratic Party (PSD), which broke from the OADP in 1996 over the OADP's decision to boycott the referendum; its platform is very similar to its parent party. The Democratic Forces Front formed in July 1997 after breaking off from the PPS. The Democratic Movement (MD) formed in 1997 also and consists of former political prisoners; its ideological base is also very similar to the OADP. Finally, the Party of the Socialist and Democratic Avant-Garde (PADS) consistently boycotts elections and referendums.

Finally, three small groups participated in the 1997 election. The centrist Democratic Independence Party (known as the *Hezb al-choura wa istiqlâl*, or PCI by its French acronym), has been on the scene since the nationalist struggle. It presented itself at the time as more modernist than the Istiqlal, and has only returned in recent years. The Action Party (PA) is also a centrist formation, perhaps a bit to the left, with an emphasis on supporting its membership of professionals and artisans. The Popular Democratic Constitutional Movement (MPDC), which had been rather inactive since its formation in 1967, was revitalized in 1996 when it paired up with a moderate Islamist movement, Reform and Renewal (*al-Islah wa al-Tajdid*).

Finally, the Islamist organization, Justice and Charity (*al-Adl wal-Ihsan*), remains outside the Moroccan political process. Its leader, the septuagenarian 'Abd al-Salam Yassin, was placed in and out of house arrest throughout the 1990s for his harsh condemnations of the monarchy as insufficiently Islamist and beholden to Western interest. In May 2000, Muhammad VI released him from house arrest.

The Moroccan military, once viewed as a staunch pillar of the monarchy, has on occasion been a serious threat to the king; the 1971 and 1972 coup attempts and the alleged discovery of a plot in January 1983 are sharp examples. Although Muhammad is the head of the Royal Armed Forces and served in that capacity for years as crown prince, the prospect that the military will remain indifferent to the profound social and economic dislocations occurring in Moroccan society can never be certain. Shortly after assuming the throne in 1999, Muhammad launched an inquiry into corruption within the armed forces, only to back off when it became apparent that the military would not countenance such examination. The changing social background and educational levels of new army recruits and younger officers are likely to make them less committed to patrimonial attachments and the power of local and national patrons, including the king. The greatly expanded size and combat experience of the army in fighting the Polisario Front add to the potential military threat to the king. Although resolution of the Western Sahara—discussed below—seems a long way off, the military's role is likely to be reduced as the diplomatic process continues to unfold. Contending with demobilized military units may be a difficult source of pressure on the economy.

Despite these developments, the military will most likely remain supportive of the regime, not only because of the monarch, but also because of close ties with NATO. Since the early 1980s, the FAR has established and maintained close collaboration with NATO, conducting joint, bilateral exercises with, among others, the United States, France, and Spain and also securing much-needed military assistance. In turn, the civil war in neighboring Algeria has prompted the West to devote greater attention to Moroccan security.

Other important political institutions include the National Union of Moroccan Students (UNEM) and the various labor unions. Since the 1960s, the UNEM has been extensively involved in radical activities directed against the government and its leaders, most of whom are viewed with hostility, contempt, or indifference. In recent years, student activism has taken on a decidedly Islamist cast, with supporters of Yassin's Justice and Charity frequently active in protests. In 1998 in Casablanca and, again, in 2000 in Marrakech, students rioted protesting government policies.

The Moroccan trade union movement has acquired extensive organizational conviction and solidarity as a result of its struggles against colonialism. The Moroccan Workers Union (UMT) was the sole labor and trade union confederation until 1960, when the Istiqlal organized a rival union, the General Union of Moroccan Workers (UGTM). The UGTM, however, was unable to compete with the UMT for political influence. In the late 1970s, the Democratic Workers Confederation (CDT), a socialist-oriented union with ties to the USFP, overtook the UMT in prominence and militancy.

Despite the UMT's historic role and the CDT's occasional success in opposing the government, the political and economic climate in Morocco remains hostile to the development of a vigorous and independent labor movement. There are several reasons for this. First, the high level of unemployment makes unions insecure and vulnerable to sudden, unplanned changes in membership recruitment, financial support, and organizational solidarity. Second, the government subjects the unions to harsh pressure, blandishments, and manipulation, especially in its efforts to attract foreign investment. Finally, very serious differences exist between trade union interests and those of the politicians. As Morocco seeks to implement a Free Trade Agreement with the European Union by 2012, its ability to maintain a calm labor environment will be of paramount importance.

Domestic and Foreign Economic Policy

Agriculture remains Morocco's largest sector in terms of the number of persons employed. Over 40 percent of the population is engaged in agricultural activity. Its economic importance, however, has declined since independence, contributing only 16 percent of gross domestic product in 1998.

The decline has to do in part with land tenure and exports. Wealthy landlords own the best 10–15 percent of the land. Although the productivity of that sector exceeds that of the subsistence farming on much of the rest of the land and the government provides subsidies to the landlords, their exports dropped significantly throughout the 1990s. Traditional markets in Europe were denied to Morocco because of trade restrictions levied by the European Union as a part of its Common Agricultural Policy. Moreover, with the entrance of Greece to the European Community in 1981 and, more important, of Spain and Portugal in 1986, the EU became self-sufficient in the citrus, olive oil, and wine that Morocco had long exported. Moroccan intellectuals have been heard to remark ruefully that the country enjoyed better agricultural trade ties with Europe during colonialism.

A second factor is drought. As noted above, Morocco experienced some of its worst droughts in recent memory in the 1980s and 1990s, including 1999–2000. Drought most affects the subsistence farmers, particularly those cultivating more marginal lands in the south and southeast.

Principal crops grown by peasant smallholders are wheat, barley, maize, beans, and chickpeas. In addition, there is a large government sugar beet sector to satisfy the domestic market's insatiable appetite for sweets and reduce the import bill for expensive sugarcane. Livestock productivity and crop yields remain low, and the government imports relatively inexpensive food regularly from the EU and the United States to meet domestic requirements.

For its part, the fishing sector offers substantial promise, although export markets for the main product, sardines, remain limited by competition from Spain, Portugal, France, and West African countries such as Senegal, Ivory Coast, and Mauritania. Since the 1970s, the government has sought to develop the deep-sea fishing fleet that plies the abundant Atlantic waters. In so doing, however, it has come up against the interests of Spain and, to a lesser extent, Portugal. European boats wish to fish in Morocco's territorial waters, and sharp diplomatic disputes have occurred, most recently in 1995 and again 2001. In 1995, Morocco and the EU signed a fishing accord, but only after protracted dispute. The accord permitted Spanish boats to fish Moroccan waters, but only to a limited extent and in exchange for enhanced financial aid. After the accord expired in 2000, negotiations resumed, only to fall apart in 2001.

For its part, manufacturing and industry accounted for 47 percent of GDP in 1998. Processing of phosphates into phosphoric acid and fertilizers and oil refining are Morocco's main industries, although light manufactures, such as textiles and leather, are growing rapidly. Most industry is concentrated in the Rabat-Casablanca region along the western seaboard.

The mining sector plays an essential economic role. Morocco possesses three-quarters of the world's known phosphate reserves. Since 1981, the parastatal Office Cherifien des Phosphates (OCP) has reduced the production of phosphate rock because of low prices on the international market and instead emphasized the production and processing of phosphate derivatives.

Finally, tourism remains an extremely important economic sector. The government aggressively markets Morocco to high-end European travelers, and luxurious world-class hotels and top-notch golf courses can be found in the midst of severe economic deprivation and drought in such popular tourist destinations as Fez and Marrakech. As the economy moves into the 2000s, the government is aggressively promoting tourism, seeking to grow the sector dramatically by 2010. Specifically, the government wishes to increase the number of annual visitors from 2.5 million in 2001 to 10 million in 2010, a goal that will necessitate the rapid construction of new resorts at Larache, Taghazout, Saïda, Essaouira, Plage Blanche, and El Jadida. Such moves will require working closely with French investors (Accord, Club Med, and Fram), as well as Spanish (Sol Melia) and German (Neckerman) concerns.

The government has placed primary emphasis on the manufacturing sector since the 1983 adoption of a structural adjustment program (SAP). The SAP was adopted with heavy conditionality by the World Bank and the IMF to alleviate the economic strain caused by the war in the Sahara. The policies combined austerity with the liberalization of the economy. To attract foreign investors, for example, the government lifted barriers on foreign investment and loosened exchange controls. It also reformed the tax system and began a program to privatize state land and industries. The overall intention is to move away from the import substitution policies of the 1960s and 1970s and toward export-oriented industries. Officially, the SAP lasted ten years, until 1993, but the policies put in place in the 1980s remained in force throughout the 1990s. In recent years, the government has projected Morocco as a new newly industrialized country (NIC), on the order of, say, Thailand, Turkey, or Argentina. Morocco has even touted itself as "the Mexico of Europe." In pursuit of these efforts, Hassan authorized the creation of a new Ministry of Privatization in 1989 and a Ministry of Foreign Trade in 1990, with constant efforts throughout the 1990s to energize the state. It appears that Mohammed VI will continue these efforts into the 2000s.

Since the 1980s, the economy has performed reasonably well, at least in terms of economic growth. In the late 1980s, the economy expanded at an impressive rate of 5.1 percent per year. With the world recession of the early 1990s, however, growth shrank to 2.3 percent in 1992. By the end of 1990s, the IMF resumed its overall positive reports regarding the Moroccan economy, projecting 6 percent growth in the early 2000s. The World Bank and IMF have also applauded gradual privatization of state-owned industries, such as the 2001 privatization of the state-run telecommunications company, Itissalat Al Maghreb, or Morocco Telecom. In terms of meeting basic human needs, however, in 1999 Morocco ranked number 127 on the United Nations Development Program's Human Development index.

Much of the population remains impoverished and locked outside of an economic system designed to benefit a very few.

The palace has long made clear its intention to obtain closer trading relations with the European Union. As early as July 1987, Morocco applied for full membership in the European Community. Although the European Commission rejected the request, Hassan's message was clear: The future for Morocco's political economy rested on improving its position within an economic space dominated by Europe. In 1995, after years of thorny negotiations, Morocco secured a partnership agreement with the EU for a free trade zone. Implementation of the accord began in 2000, and it is to be gradually phased in over a twelve-year period, with more vulnerable sectors being opened to European competition and investment later than the stronger sectors are. Morocco's ability to upgrade its economy in the face of European firms remains an uncertain issue.

Finally, immigration remains an economic issue that transcends the domestic-international divide. Europe's demand for low-wage labor seems hypocritical given the degree of xenophobia that Moroccan and other immigrants frequently experience. Nonetheless, Moroccan migrants will remain in demand in European service and agricultural sectors for years to come. This provides a valuable opportunity for Morocco's domestic economy to obtain crucial remittances from overseas workers, especially those who are more affluent and can directly invest in and contribute to the home economy. On the other hand, the impact of the FTA with Europe may have uncertain implications for the politics of Moroccan migration. Indeed, Morocco wants the free movement of labor to be added to the FTA agreement, a step that Europe is unlikely to take.

Western Sahara

Western Sahara, a territory rich in deposits of phosphates, oil, and uranium, was occupied by Spain in the 1880s. However, its nomadic population was not brought under control until General Francisco Franco suppressed resistance in 1936 (with French assistance). Despite the rise of Saharawi nationalism in the 1950s and 1960s, Spain did not relinquish control until the Madrid Accord of November 14, 1975. With the accord, Spain ceded the colony to Mauritania and Morocco, setting the stage for Hassan's *massira,* or Green March, in the same month.

Spain withdrew its last remaining troops on February 26, 1976, and the next day, the Polisario Front (its full name is the Popular Front for the Liberation of Saguit al-Hamra and Rio de Oro) declared that the area was the Saharan Arab Democratic Republic (SADR). It also initiated a guerrilla war against Morocco and Mauritania, which it charged with thwarting the Saharawi people's desire for independence.

Initially, Hassan devoted his energies to crushing the Polisario, sending in troops and authorizing a massive defensive sand wall to inhibit Polisario guerrilla operations. By the mid-1980s, he had deployed over 80,000 men in the Sahara.

Nevertheless, victory eluded Morocco. Algeria and Libya supported the Polisario, the former with safe haven across the Algerian frontier. Libyan support ceased in 1984 with its "union" with Morocco.

In 1984 the SADR won a diplomatic victory by becoming a member of the OAU, and in April 1986 the United Nations and the OAU together hosted indirect talks between Morocco and the Polisario Front, with Mauritania (which renounced its claim in 1978) and Algeria invited as observers. The goal of the talks was to establish the terms of agreement for a referendum on self-determination for the Saharawi people.

Although the SADR was initially successful in diplomatic terms—sixty-three countries had recognized its legitimacy by the mid-1980s—Morocco continued to dominate militarily. This position enabled Hassan to balk at accepting U.N. Resolution 40/50 advocating direct negotiations between the SADR and Morocco. In addition, Hassan began to receive crucial support from allies. For example, the United States and Morocco conducted joint military exercises off the coast of the Western Sahara in November 1986, and U.S. Defense Secretary Caspar Weinberger visited the following month to thank Hassan for his efforts in the Arab-Israeli peace process and in seeking to mediate the United States's clash with Muammar Qaddafi of Libya. In September 1987, the United States approved the sale to Rabat of 100 M-48A5 tanks, suitable for desert terrain.

In February 1987, fighting resumed after a two-year lull during which diplomatic efforts to find a solution to the conflict had been pursued. The Polisario Front attacked Moroccan forces in Mahbes, near the Algerian and Moroccan borders, and claimed victory. For his part, Hassan continued to work to repair relations with OAU heads of state. Still, fierce fighting continued as the Saharawis sought to breach the Moroccan defensive wall. The Moroccans responded with the construction of a new defensive fortification that extended to the Mauritanian border in the south of the territory. The Mauritanian president, Maaouiya Ould Sid Ahmad Taya, protested, expressing concern that his country would be brought back into the conflict, but his protests were ignored.

By August 1988, both sides had accepted a U.N. plan for a cease-fire and a referendum in which the Saharawis would choose between independence and union with Morocco. Although the cease-fire suffered intermittent interruptions, both parties agreed that all Saharawis over the age of eighteen would be eligible to vote. The plan was delayed, primarily because the Polisario Front wanted Morocco to withdraw its troops before the vote, which Rabat refused to do. In June 1990, however, the Security Council approved the secretary general's plan in Resolution 658, and in April 1991, in Resolution 690, the council also authorized establishment of the U.N. Mission for the Referendum in Western Sahara, MINURSO, to monitor the cease-fire and balloting. Since 1991, the cease-fire has held.

Problems had reemerged by summer 1991, however. Most significant was a dispute over voting eligibility for the referendum on self-determination. The Polisario

Gregory W. White, Mark A. Tessler, and John P. Entelis

Front wanted to restrict the voting list to the 74,000 names on the Spanish census of 1974. But Rabat wanted to include those of Saharan birth or parentage, which would have added another 120,000 names to the register—votes that would have ensured Morocco's claims. In September 1991, in violation of U.N. guidelines, Morocco began to relocate tens of thousands of people from southern Morocco who were purportedly Saharawis and who carried what appeared to be old Spanish documents.

Since 1991, the United Nations has tried to get both sides to agree to arrangements for a referendum. Beginning in 1997, former U.S. Secretary of State James Baker has served as negotiator. Rabat, for its part, devoted its efforts to the delay of a vote while consolidating its superior position on the ground. To be sure, such dawdling has not met with consistent criticism from the international community. Indeed, the European Parliament routinely criticizes Moroccan handling of the Sahara conflict, even as the European Commission attempts to ensure access to Moroccan waters off the coast of the territory. The United States has remained largely silent, preferring to back Morocco, a close ally in the region. The Polisario, for its part, has lost much of its diplomatic capital, suffering particularly from the progressive loss of support from its most important backer, Algeria.

Despite efforts by U.N. Secretary Generals Boutros Boutros-Ghali and Kofi Annan in the 1990s to resolve the dispute over voting eligibility, the referendum issue was not settled as of 2002 and was not likely to be settled in the years to come. If the referendum is conducted without the Polisario Front's acquiescence and Morocco wins, then the Saharawis would be effectively marginalized and their credibility diminished. Of course, if Morocco loses, then Rabat would not be able to retreat from the referendum's results.

In 2001, the U.N. secretary general advanced an "autonomy plan," an arrangement that would give Morocco control over defense and security, with the Saharawis gaining some control over phosphates and the fishing sector. While such economic sectors are significant, the Saharawis and Algeria have denounced the autonomy plan. Most importantly, in their view, is the plan to conduct a referendum in five years that would include all residents of the territory, a strategy that would surely result in Moroccan victory.

Foreign Diplomacy

For decades, foreign policy decisions in Morocco were made by Hassan and a small group of personal advisers. Morocco's foreign policy objectives were to enhance Hassan's domestic prestige and to protect the status and position of the country's elites; to generate international support for (and to counter criticism against) Morocco's efforts in the Western Sahara; and to maintain strong diplomatic ties with the Afro-Arab world. Muhammad appears likely to maintain strong control of the country's decisionmaking apparatus, although the commencement of *alternance* has broadened the involvement of key leaders from the opposition. Muhammad is most likely to continue his father's efforts to develop and maintain the country's long-established ties with the European Union and the United States. Morocco's interests in the European Union stem from geopolitical and economic realities as well as historical conditioning. Not surprisingly, France is a particularly important focus of these efforts, given the Moroccan elite's close affinity with French culture, language, and civilization.

From 1990 to 1992, Franco-Moroccan relations were strained. Difficulties emerged with the publication in 1990 of a book by Gilles Perrault, *Notre Ami le Roi* (Our Friend the King), in which Hassan received harsh criticism for his human rights record (and France for its long-term support of the monarch). Interior Minister Basri had asked his French counterpart, Pierre Joxe, to ban the book, but Paris refused. In turn, Hassan castigated Danièlle Mitterrand, the wife of the French president and leader of a human rights group, France-Libertés, for her support of the Polisario and her visit to refugee camps in southern Algeria. The severing of ties was threatened, and Morocco banned French newspapers and television broadcasts. Since resolution of the issue in 1993, however, Morocco has enjoyed warmer relations with the right-wing governments of Edouard Balladur and Jacques Chirac. Chirac and Hassan were reportedly close friends and frequently held consultations, and France views Morocco as a lynchpin in its policies of supporting its Francophone policies in Africa.

Despite some ongoing tension over competition with Spanish agriculture and fisheries in the EU, Moroccan-Spanish relations improved steadily after the 1975 death of Franco. Spain is Morocco's second-largest trading partner after France and, according to recent estimates, will overtake France during the next decade. Private-sector investment in Morocco coming from Spain surpassed that of France in 1992. Spanish-Moroccan relations were cemented by Hassan's visit to Spain in September 1989 and by the signing of a friendship treaty in July 1991 during the visit to Rabat of Spanish King Juan Carlos. In addition, Spanish and Moroccan government officials and businessmen have been collaborating comprehensively on such projects as underwater electricity links, the completed trans-Maghribi gas line, and financial-sector ties. The trans-Maghribi gas line runs from Algeria, through Morocco, across the Strait of Gibraltar, and to Spain and Portugal. In addition, joint Spanish and Moroccan air force exercises, code named "Atlas92," were conducted in June 1992. Finally, as part of the ever expanding collaboration between Maghribi and Southern European security apparatuses, interior ministers from Spain, Portugal, and Morocco frequently meet to sign agreements on immigration, drugs, and security cooperation.

The Gulf crisis highlighted clearly the stark discontinuity that exists between elite and popular attitudes about the government's approach to development, including its pro-Western orientation. As noted earlier, mass demonstrations in support of Iraq were held in major cities. Nonetheless, the United States and Europe rewarded Morocco's contribution of a contingent of 6,000 soldiers to the anti-Iraq coalition with military aid and economic assistance. In September 1991, Hassan traveled to Washington and signed a $250 million agreement securing twenty F-16A and F-16B planes. Shortly after the Algerian military crackdown in January 1992 nullifying the election victory of Algeria's Islamic Salvation Front, a team of U.S. military experts visited Rabat. In February, the United States delivered twelve F-16 fighters to Morocco ahead of schedule. Throughout the 1990s, Morocco deftly played the "security card," requesting support for its economy and society in order to preclude the emergence of an Islamist threat. Morocco has also bought commercial aircraft from the United States. In 1993, Royal Air Maroc ordered twelve Boeing aircraft worth $525 million, despite heavy pressure from France to buy its Airbus. In 2001, Morocco agreed to purchase four Airbus aircraft, but this was only after it had purchased twenty-two Boeing planes in 2000.

In regional affairs, Hassan long sought to play a mediating role in Arab politics, hosting a number of important Arab summits. Hassan's July 1986 meeting with Israeli Prime Minister Shimon Peres in the Moroccan resort town of Ifrane was the first public meeting between an Israeli and an Arab leader since the 1981 assassination of Egyptian president Anwar Sadat. Despite harsh criticism from Libya, Algeria, Syria, and several other states, however, the PLO and moderate Arab states, including Jordan and Egypt, backed the move. In January 1989, Syria resumed ties broken off after the Peres-Hassan meeting, and relations with Egypt were also accelerated after Egypt's readmission into Arab League affairs in 1989. Hassan proudly hosted the 1989 Arab League summit in Casablanca.

In the 1990s, Hassan sought to persuade Arab countries, particularly Saudi Arabia, to develop ties with Israel in the context of the peace process. In a striking illustration, Hassan welcomed the Israeli leadership to Rabat the day after the signing in Washington of the September 1993 PLO-Israeli accord. Morocco was keen throughout the 1990s to encourage Israeli investment in the Moroccan economy, particularly from the large population of Israeli citizens of Moroccan descent. After the collapse of Palestinian-Israeli peace negotiations in the fall of 2000, however, diplomatic and economic relations between Morocco and Israel stagnated.

Morocco has also devoted much effort to relations with its North African and Middle Eastern neighbors. Saudi Arabia, for example, has been a firm ally, providing aid to Morocco in recent years in order to help with the high cost of the Western Sahara conflict. Not surprisingly, this support continued after Morocco's efforts during the Gulf crisis.

Since 1989, some of Morocco's greatest efforts in the region were for the establishment of the Arab Maghrib Union (UMA), and the agreement setting up the UMA was signed in February 1989 in Marrakech. Morocco's energies in the early years of the UMA were devoted to improving relations with Algeria (and to a lesser extent Mauritania) in connection with the conflict in the Western Sahara. Morocco and Algeria announced in May 1988 that they would resume full diplomatic relations, severed since 1976. In June 1988, the border was reopened and

Hassan visited Algiers for an Arab League summit. Because their regional goals have been mainly met, however, Morocco and Tunisia have been less than full participants in UMA endeavors, preferring to set their sights on partnership with the European Union.

On the plus side, Moroccan foreign diplomacy seems to be working in favor of its carefully cultivated role as a mediator and as an alternative to the Islamist chaos currently engulfing Algeria. The fact that Morocco is "not Algeria" has led the European Union to champion economic growth and employment generation there, and Morocco's previous receptivity to contact with Israel has provided an additional incentive for U.S. support.

Bibliography

Pre-independence Morocco is systematically analyzed in Allal al-Fasi, *The Independence Movement in Arab North Africa* (New York: Octagon, 1970); Stephane Bernard, *The Franco-Moroccan Conflict, 1943–1956* (New Haven: Yale University Press, 1968); Robin Bidwell, *Morocco Under Colonial Rule: French Administration of Tribal Areas, 1912–1956* (London: Frank Cass, 1973); Edmund Burke, *Prelude to Protectorate in Morocco: Precolonial Protest and Resistance, 1860–1912* (Chicago: University of Chicago Press, 1976); Alan Scham, *Lyautey in Morocco: Protectorate Administration, 1912–1925* (Berkeley: University of California Press, 1970); and Janet Abu-Lughod, *Rabat: Urban Apartheid in Morocco* (Princeton: Princeton University Press, 1980). French language works include Abdallah Laroui, *Les origins sociales et culturelles du nationalisme marocain (1830–1912)* (Casablanca: Centre Culturel Arabe, 1993).

For analyses of Morocco's political system, see Douglas E. Ashford, *Political Change in Morocco* (Princeton: Princeton University Press, 1961); Mark Tessler, "Morocco: Institutional Pluralism and Monarchical Dominance," in I. William Zartman et. al., *Political Elites in Arab North Africa* (New York: Longman, 1982); John P. Entelis, *Culture and Counterculture in Moroccan Politics*, 2nd ed., (Boulder: Westview Press, 1996); Azzedine Layachi, *State, Society and Democracy in Morocco* (Washington, D.C.: Georgetown University CCAS, 1998); and Abdellah Hammoudi, *Master and Disciple: The Cultural Foundations of Moroccan Authoritarianism* (Chicago: University of Chicago Press, 1997). John Waterbury, *The Commander of the Faithful: The Moroccan Political Elite—A Study in Segmented Politics* (New York: Columbia University Press, 1970), provides probably the finest work on the nature of elite politics in Morocco. French language works include Remy Levau, *Le fellah marocain: Défenseur du trône.* 2nd ed. (Paris: Presses de la Fondation nationale des sciences politiques, 1985); and Ali Benhaddou, *Maroc: Les Élites du Royaume: Essai sur l'organisation du pouvoir au Maroc* (Paris: L'Harmattan, 1997).

For treatments of King Hassan II, Rom Landau's *Hassan II: King of Morocco* (London: George Allen and Unwin, 1962) offers a sympathetic account. For more critical (and controversial) accounts, see Gilles Perrault, *Notre Ami le Roi* (Paris: Gallimard, 1992), and Malika Oufkir and Michelle Fitoussi, *Stolen Lives: Twenty Years in a Desert Jail* (New York: Talk Miramax Books/Hyperion, 2001). The king's own perspective, as well as much additional information about Moroccan political life, is presented in *The Challenge: The Memoirs of King Hassan II of Morocco* (London: Macmillan, 1978), and also in the more recent *Hassan II: La Mémoire d'un Roi, Entretiens avec Eric Laurent* (Paris: Plon, 1993).

For analyses of Islam in Moroccan politics, see Henry Munson, *Religion and Power in Morocco* (New Haven: Yale University Press, 1993); François Burgat, *The Islamic Movement in North Africa*, trans. William Dowell, (Austin: University of Texas Press, 1993); John Entelis, ed., *Islam, Democracy and the State in North Africa* (Bloomington, Ind.: Indiana University Press, 1997); Dale Eickelman, *Moroccan and Islam: Tradition and Society in a Pilgrimage Center* (Austin: University of Texas Press, 1976) and *Knowledge and Power in Morocco: The Education of a Twentieth-Century Notable* (Princeton: Princeton University Press, 1985); and M. E. Combs-Schilling, *Sacred Performances in Morocco: Precolonial Protest and Resistance (1860–1912)* (Chicago: University of Chicago Press, 1989). Accounts of Morocco's Jewish community are provided in Norman A. Stillman, "The Moroccan Jewish Experience: A Revisionist View," *Jerusalem Quarterly* 9 (fall 1978): 111–123; and Mark A. Tessler, "The Identity of Religious Minorities in Non-Secular States: Jews in Tunisia and Morocco and Arabs in Israel," *Comparative Studies in Society and History* 20, no. 3 (July 1978); and "Israel and Morocco: The Political Calculus of a 'Moderate Arab State,'" in G. Mahler, ed., *Israel After Begin* (Albany: State University of New York Press, 1990).

Studies on the role of women include Fatima Mernissi, *Doing Daily Battle: Interviews with Moroccan Women* (New Brunswick, N.J.: Rutgers University Press, 1989); Deborah Kapchen, *Gender on the Market: Moroccan Women and the Revoicing of Tradition* (Philadelphia: University of Pennsylvania Press, 1998); Alison Baker, *Voices of Resistance: Oral Histories of Moroccan Women* (Albany: State University of New York Press, 1998); Laurie Brand, *Women, the State, and Political Liberalization: Middle Eastern and North African Experiences* (New York: Columbia University Press, 1998).

Analyses of Morocco's economic situation are available in Will Swearingen, *Moroccan Mirages: Agrarian Dreams and Deceptions, 1912–1986* (Princeton: Princeton University Press, 1986); Serge Leymarie and Jean Tripier, *Maroc: Le Prochain Dragon? De nouvelles idées pour le développement* (Casablanca: Eddif, 1992); Richard Pomfret, "Morocco's International Economic Relations," in I. William Zartman, ed., *The Political Economy of Morocco*, and *Mediterranean Policy of the European Community: A Study of Discrimination in Trade* (New York: St. Martin's Press, 1986); Gregory White, *A Comparative Political Economy of Tunisia and Morocco: On the Outside of Europe Looking In* (Albany: State University of New York Press, 2001) and "Too Many Boats and Not Enough Fish: The Political Economy of Morocco's 1995 Fishing Accord with the European Union," *The Journal of Developing Areas* 31 (Spring 1997): 313–336. An intriguing book is Muhammad VI's published doctoral dissertation, Mohamed Ben El-Hassan Alaoui, *La cooperation entre l'Union Européenne et les pays du Maghreb* (Paris: Éditions Nathan, 1994).

The war with the Polisario Front is carefully documented and discussed by John Damis, *Conflict in Northwest Africa: The Western Sahara Dispute* (Stanford: Hoover Institute Press, 1983), and I. William Zartman, *Ripe for Resolution: Conflict and Intervention in Africa* (New York: Oxford University Press, 1987). Other dimensions of Morocco's foreign relations are treated in Jerome B. Bookin-Weiner and Mohamed El Mansour, eds., *The Atlantic Connection: 200 Years of Moroccan-American Relations, 1886–1986* (Rabat: Edino, 1991); Mark A. Tessler, "Libya in the Maghreb: The Union with Morocco and Related Developments," in Rene Lemarchand, ed., *The Green and the Black: Qadhafi's Policies in Africa* (Bloomington, Ind.: Indiana University Press, 1988), and "Morocco and Israel: The Political Calculus of a 'Moderate' Arab State," in Gregory Mahler, ed., *Israel in the Post-Begin Era* (Albany: State University of New York Press, 1990).

16

Democratic and Popular Republic of Algeria

Azzedine Layachi
John P. Entelis

Historical Background

Algeria's political history is as much a reflection as a product of its struggle for nationality and a national identity, a struggle made difficult by the pervasive nature of the influence of its foreign conquerors. Invaded in the early seventh century by the Arabs, the nation today reflects both the Arab tradition and the culture of the indigenous Berber (*Amazigh*) tribes. Its central location on the Mediterranean, making it an outpost for piracy until well into the eighteenth century, has resulted in the absorption of many other cultural traditions. People of Greek, Italian, Spanish, and French descent also constituted a substantial part of the Algerian population throughout its history. Ruled under the Ottoman regency until the nineteenth century and subsequently conquered by the French, under whose reign it remained until independence in 1962, Algeria has struggled to assert its autonomy and nationality. The Arabo-Islamic tradition has served as a powerful unifying tool in the struggle against foreign domination, most notably in the war for independence against the French in 1954–1962. Nonetheless, the integrationist policy pursued by the French heavily infiltrated French values and culture into the Algerian tradition and is partially responsible for the nature of contemporary Algerian politics, which is split between Western-oriented elites and the masses, who identify more with their Arab, Berber, and Islamic cultures. Algerian political culture and tradition today reflect the impact of these diverse traditions and the divisive role they played in shaping the historical experience of the country.

Until the sixteenth century the Maghrib region of North Africa consisted of a large number of autonomous and independent tribes. United in a loose configuration under the Ottoman regency from 1518 to 1830, the tribes continued to play a highly autonomous role in the politics of the region. The French are often credited with the definition and consolidation of the Algerian political state (though it may also be argued that the elements of statehood already existed during the era of allegiance to the Ottoman empire). The French occupation was certainly far more intensive than the Ottoman regency. The conquest of Algiers was completed in three weeks, and in 1834 the region was made a colony of France. However, it took France more than forty years to conquer and subdue the rest of the country. Lands were sequestered, colonists were quickly settled, and political and economic links were firmly established to secure France's interests. By the end of the first fifty years of French occupation, the indigenous Muslim population of Algeria had lost its land, its independence, and its freedom.

The administration of the Algeria colony was placed under the office of a governor-general, a military officer who was authorized to rule by decree. The majority of European settlers were peasant or working class, on the one hand, or army officers or bureaucrats, on the other, the latter two groups interested in speculation and profiting from the potentially prosperous arable land along the coast. Within fifteen years, there were more than 150,000 European settlers in Algeria. By 1900 more than 3 million native inhabitants had died, from mass repression and diseases. The entire political and economic structure of the region was dramatically transformed under the "civilizing" program of the French government, which included the seizure and expropriation of land and the revision of property laws and regulations, all in the interest of the Europeans.

Concerned that British interest in bolstering the Ottoman Empire might challenge French control of the Algerian territory, France quickly devised an extensive plan to assert and reinforce its control over the autonomous regions vacated by the Turkish rulers following the French conquest. This attempt to assert authority over the relatively independent and autonomous tribes and regions of the hinterland and the intensive "total colonialism" policy drew the antagonism of the inhabitants, and a nationalist movement began to appear.

The Nationalist Struggle

The Algerian nationalist movement can be divided into four distinct historical periods: early resistance, pacification, the rise of nationalism, and the liberation period. From 1830 to about 1870 traditional Algerian nationalists resisted colonial rule. The most prominent leader of this era was Amir Abd al-Qadir, called *amir al-mu'minin,* or "commander of the faithful." Abd al-Qadir set about establishing a Muslim state that would lay claim to all land in the interior not occupied by the French. However, Abd al-Qadir was suppressed by 1847 (imprisoned, and sent into exile in Syria), and shortly thereafter virtually all Algerian territory was firmly secured under French control. The French government established Arab offices (*bureaux arabes*) that were to serve as a liaison between the military government and the tribal leaders. In fact, these offices became a means of subverting tribal authority and undermining the limited self-government that was officially tolerated. By 1870, the Algerian society was so dislocated that an indigenous Algerian political identity all but ceased to exist.

In the 1850s the French government rescinded Algeria's colonial status and declared the territory part of France. Algerians were officially recognized as French nationals, though not citizens. Three "civil territories" were established. The territories were organized as *départements,* or local administrative units, under civilian (indigenous) administration, though highly supervised by French military officers. Civilian government was again revoked under Napoleon III, and Algeria fell again under military rule. New laws in 1870 allowed for a token Algerian representation in the French National Assembly but also strengthened the colonial control.

French extension of authority triggered additional nationalist revolts in the 1870s, but all were quickly suppressed. French officials strengthened their control of the region and placed much of the territory under "exceptional rule," which allowed for virtually unlimited French authority and suspended most civil freedoms. Gradually the indigenous Muslim population resigned itself to the French presence, at least until it was able to reject it forcibly. A new nationalist fervor surfaced in 1920.

The period from 1920 to 1954 witnessed the rise of a new, urban-based nationalism and the gradual shift from resignation to the French domination to a radical opposition that would lead to the struggle for independence. The strength of this movement owes much to the highly integrationist policy pursued by the French. The "civilizing" policy undertaken by the French government included the education in, and infusion of, French values. By the early 1900s, this policy had created a small social group of well-educated and well-informed indigenous Algerians. During World War I, with the high number of Algerians serving in the French army in Europe, this group of francophone Algerians resented even more Algeria's subordinate status as a nation and their inferior standard of living. They decried the contradictory policy pursued by a country that prided itself on its democratic features at home while colonizing other people and their territory. Algerian activists initially called for equality with the Europeans in Algeria, but their peaceful demands, which remained unanswered, soon turned into calls for independence.

In response the French government attempted to appease the Algerian nationalists by allowing for the direct representation of Muslims in the local governments through advisory councils, but even this was circumscribed by other legislative restrictions that created a two-college system and preserved the near hegemony of the European minority. Restrictions governing acquisition of full

French citizenship were similarly reduced but were limited in application to certain classes of Algerians.

Early resistance movements (for example, Jeunesse Algérienne and Féderation des Elus Musulmans) aimed for full assimilation and integration of Algerians into the French community without the surrender of their Muslim identity (existing laws required the Muslims to renounce Islamic law in favor of the French civil code). A number of parties formulated demands for independence in the 1920s; the most ardent among them were leftist and Islamist groups. World War II and a number of failed compromise proposals soon demonstrated the polarization between the native Algerians and the French colonists.

On November 1, 1954, the Algerian Revolution erupted after all hope for an evolutionary settlement had dissipated. France had failed to make any sizable concessions to Algerian nationalist aspirations. For the angry young nationalists, who formed the backbone of the revolution, the various reformist efforts had become irrelevant. In early 1954 the Comité Révolutionnaire d'Unité et d'Action (CRUA) was created by dissidents from the earlier movements, ex-soldiers in the French army, and miscellaneous groups of dedicated men disillusioned with the French administration and unafraid of violence and dangerous risks. The nine historic chiefs who formed the CRUA—Hocine Aït Ahmed, Ahmed Ben Bella, Rabah Bitat, Mohamed Boudiaf, Moustafa Ben Boulaïd, Mourad Didouch, Mohammed Khider, Belkacem Krim, and Larbi Ben M'Hidi—shared four basic experiences. All were radical militants of peasant or working-class backgrounds. All had served in the French army. All had served time in French prisons. And finally, all were members of the Organisation Spéciale (OS), a clandestine nationalist organization, formed in the 1940s by Aït Ahmed and Ben Bella, which engaged in a number of violent operations and demonstrations.

The CRUA set up a military administration for Algeria during the early part of 1954 that divided the territory into six *wilayate* (provinces) under the direction of military officers. In October, the CRUA was transformed into a political organization, the Front de Libération Nationale (FLN), and its military arm, the Armée de Libération Nationale (ALN). On November 1, 1954, the FLN issued a proclamation calling on all Algerians to rise and fight for their freedom. The revolution had begun.

A provisional government was formed in 1958, but fighting continued until a final accord with France on a cease-fire was reached at Evian, France, on March 19, 1962. Serious divisions within the revolutionary leadership and its rank and file had threatened the success of the revolution and left a weak organization to inherit the postindependence government. The Evian Accords stipulated a national referendum on the question of Algerian independence that was to include both European colonists and indigenous Algerians. The referendum took place on July 1. Formal independence was declared on July 5, 1962.

Independence

The absence of a unifying revolutionary ideology, the lack of an incontestable leader, and the factional fighting that had characterized the revolutionary years carried over into the postindependence period. The superficial tactical unity that had marked the FLN's military and diplomatic efforts broke down immediately after independence, and a vicious struggle for power began. The three major contestants for power were the Algerian provisional government, the *wilayate* command councils, and the external army (ALN). The fighting quickly involved factional rivalries and loyalties, competing visions for the emerging Algerian state, and conflicting ideologies. At stake was the political control of the new Algerian state.

The first round of the political contest took place in May 1962 at the first congress of the FLN national council, which was to choose a political bureau to assume the leadership of the party and to devise the political and economic agenda for the country. The meeting closed with Ahmed Ben Bella—in a tentative alliance with Colonel Houari Boumediene—assuming control of the party and what would become independent Algeria.

On September 20, 1962, the first postindependence elections were held for the newly created Algerian National Assembly, which on September 26 elected Ben Bella premier and issued a formal declaration of the Democratic Republic of Algeria. Ben Bella's government was formed from the ranks of the military and close personal and political allies, including Boumediene; this indicated that the factional rivalries were destined to remain an intrinsic feature of Algeria's postindependence politics.

The first and most pressing task of the new government was to restore some normality to the war-torn Algerian economy and polity. The mass exodus of Europeans had caused Algeria a severe shortage in highly skilled workers, technicians, educators, and property-owning entrepreneurs, which meant huge unemployment for the remaining population whose employers had left. The national government quickly assumed ownership of the abandoned industrial and agricultural properties and commenced a program of "autogestion," a socialist form of workers' management. Workers were responsible for overseeing their own administration through a hierarchy of elected officials and under the supervision of a national system of directors and agencies that was responsible for ensuring that the workers conformed to a national plan of development.

The next most urgent task was the consolidation of the government. Ben Bella was not a charismatic leader and had failed to gain the confidence of the Algerian population. Formal changes were necessary to secure his political dominance. A new constitution was drafted that established a strong presidential system with the president serving as military commander in chief, head of state, and head of government. The new constitution also preserved the hegemonic role of the FLN as the single political party. Ben Bella assumed control of the FLN as general secretary in April 1963. In September, he was elected president for a five-year term. The government was increasingly tending toward a dictatorship, and the concentration of power in the hands of Ben Bella caused the factionalism within the leadership to resurface.

Ben Bella owed his political position to his legacy as "historic chief of the revolution," not to his leadership abilities. He was a key figure in the struggle against French colonialism and had served several years in French prisons. But in independent Algeria, his inability to manage the various rivalries and controversies facing his regime, his ouster of the traditional leaders, his repeated political attacks on the labor union, Union Générale des Travailleurs Algériens (UGTA), and his failure to transform the FLN into an effective mass party eventually led to his defeat. Despite his mass appeal as a revolutionary leader, his support continued to decline as the public (and the military) lost confidence in his political acumen. Desperate efforts to thwart the rival military factions by appealing to leftist groups failed, and Ben Bella was eventually undone by the very ally who had helped put him into office in 1962, Colonel Houari Boumediene. In June 1965 Ben Bella was overthrown in a bloodless coup and Boumediene assumed the leadership of the country.

Boumediene Regime, 1965–1978

The political transformation was smooth and efficient. All political power was transferred to Boumediene and his military-dominated Council of the Revolution. The constitution and National Assembly were suspended, and Boumediene was named president, head of government, and minister of defense. Twenty close personal associates filled the remaining cabinet positions. The Council of the Revolution—designated the "supreme" political institution—was also the only national political institution. Virtually all public political participation was suspended for the duration of the council's incumbency.

For his support Boumediene relied on the mujahidin, or veterans of the war of independence, and a technocratic elite drawn partially from the military. His initial program was cautious. Boumediene was wary of radical change and timid about drastic political upheavals that could threaten the precarious political base on which he relied. He himself described the coup as a "historic rectification" of the Algerian Revolution. The objectives of the regime were to reestablish the principles of the revolution, to remedy the corruption and personal abuses associated with Ben Bella, to eliminate the internal divisions, and to build a solid socialist economy. Support for Boumediene's program was high but not universal. There were several aborted or failed coup attempts in the first few years of his regime; the most significant of these was the one led by Colonel Tahar Zbiri on December 14,

1967, which stimulated uprisings in the countryside and on the city streets. By the early 1970s, however, Boumediene had consolidated his regime and could focus on the more pressing economic problems. He had sacrificed political change for regime stability and state consolidation. From a strategic perspective, Boumediene's "bargain" had paid off. By 1975 the factional infighting had ceased and he was secure enough to allow for the resurrection of public political institutions and a constitutional government.

In June 1976 a new national charter was approved by a national referendum. The charter was essentially an ideological proclamation that reaffirmed the socialist tradition and implicitly maintained the authoritarian nature of the regime and state. The FLN again received explicit recognition as a "unique" national front representing the revolutionary heritage and ideological identity of Algeria. The drafting of a new constitution, which was put to a popular referendum in November 1976, quickly followed the adoption of the national charter.

The new constitution reestablished a national legislature, the Assemblée Populaire Nationale (APN), but maintained the monopoly of the FLN as the single legitimate and legal political party. Effective power remained concentrated in the executive. Boumediene was again named head of state and head of government, commander in chief, and minister of defense, as well as secretary general of the FLN. His presidency was reaffirmed a month later when he was elected through a single-candidate ballot with the support of well over 95 percent of the electorate.

Elections for the new national assembly were finally held in February 1977. All candidates on the ballot were members of the FLN, but there was considerable variation in their occupations and qualifications. The diverse membership of the new assembly and the high proportion of industrial and agricultural workers were lauded as the final step in the creation of a socialist state, a process that had begun in earnest with the creation of workers' self-management assemblies at the local level in the late 1960s.[1]

Boumediene died suddenly in late 1978 of a rare kidney ailment. His legacy included a consolidated national government, a stable political system, a rapidly industrializing economy, a well-secured and extensive state-centered socialist program, and an expanding petroleum and gas export industry. He also left a political vacuum. His charismatic leadership and his political acumen were very much responsible for Algeria's political development during the 1970s. At his death, Algeria was without a designated successor. As stipulated in the constitution, the National Assembly president was named interim head of state until a special congress of the FLN met to select a successor. Following the army's recommendation, the congress named Colonel Chadli Bendjedid secretary general of the party and candidate for president in January 1979. His selection was confirmed one week later in a national election.

Bendjedid Regime, 1979–1992

President Bendjedid was initially very cautious in his policy proposals. Despite his strong electoral mandate, he did not command the same respect as Boumediene. His policy of "change within continuity" allowed for some continuity in the course pursued by Boumediene while enabling him to consolidate his power and take full control of the state, party, and military apparatus. By the end of his first term in office in 1984, he had completed this process of "de-Boumedienization," his position and power were firmly secured, and state authority was consolidated. Bendjedid was reelected in 1985 with more than 95 percent of the vote. With this second popular mandate and some significant changes in government personnel, Bendjedid seemed more confident in his ability to make sweeping reforms, which eventually radically altered the nature of the Algerian economy and polity.

Boumediene's socialist policy had focused exclusively on the development of the industrial sector financed through energy exports. Bendjedid's program sought to reverse that. The decline of energy prices in the 1980s, the inefficiency of over-sized industrial complexes, and the neglect of the agricultural sector, as well as a sweltering population growth rate and increasing unemployment, left the Algerian economy in dire straits. Bendjedid's initial reforms concentrated on structural changes and economic liberalization. These measures included a shift in domestic investment away from heavy industry and toward agriculture, light industry, and consumer goods. State enterprises were broken up into smaller, more manageable units, and several small state-owned firms were privatized. Also important was the anticorruption campaign taken on by the new regime. The effects of this campaign, aside from the obvious benefits of adding to the legitimacy of the regime, allowed Bendjedid to eliminate much of the old-guard opposition still loyal to Boumediene's legacy, thus firming up his control of the political realm. Other changes included the opening up of the Algerian economy to certain limited foreign investment, the expansion and revitalization of the country's private sector, a shift away from the Soviet Union and toward the West in strategic considerations, and the lowering of Algeria's once highly visible profile in global and Third World affairs.

By 1988 political liberalization was added to the agenda and a commitment was made to free-market principles. New legislation allowed for independent associations to "recruit, organize, and propagate"—this right was even extended to some of the regime's most strident opponents, including a very active human rights league that had condemned the regime's coercive tactics and suppression of public political activity. State enterprises were entirely freed from the socialist central planning. Subsidies were reduced, price controls were lifted, and all firms became responsible to the laws of supply and demand. The fiscal deficit was attacked through a cut in government spending.

However, Bendjedid's reforms exacerbated an already dismal economic situation. The dismantlement and privatization of some state enterprises only augmented the rapidly growing unemployment and produced a drop in industrial output. Trade liberalization and the removal of price controls and subsidies resulted in a drastic increase in prices. The purchasing power of the majority of Algerian citizens plummeted. At the same time, the bourgeoisie and upper class were profiting from the economic liberalization. Economic reforms legalized the private accumulation of wealth, and privileged access to foreign currency and goods and the relative economic security at the top of recently privatized state enterprises ensured that the burden of reform was carried, not by the upper class, but by the masses. A wide generation gap was increasing between the masses, 70 percent of which were under the age of thirty and had no memory of the national revolution, and the elites, who relied on their revolutionary credentials for their political legitimacy. By the late 1980s Algeria was a very polarized society.

In October 1988, this economic crisis exploded in the most violent and extensive public demonstrations since Algeria's independence. Weeks of strikes and work stoppages were followed by six days of violent street rioting in several cities. Thousands of Algerians attacked city halls, police stations, post offices, state-owned cars and supermarkets—anything that was seen to represent the regime or the FLN. It was a demonstration of lack of confidence in the public leadership—a product of corruption and inefficiency, of declining living standards, rapidly increasing unemployment, and frequent food shortages, and a revolt against the persistent inequality and alienation.

The military was quickly called in to suppress the riots, a state of siege was declared, and tanks rolled in, but the demonstrations continued to spread. Hundreds of young rioters—who made up the bulk of demonstrators—were killed. Then on October 10 President Bendjedid, in a speech on national television, accepted blame for the suppression and promised new economic and political reforms. The state of siege was lifted and the tanks were called back, and days later a national referendum on constitutional reform was announced. Bendjedid may simply have found himself in a political bind and saw political liberalization as the only way to quell the discontent. Whatever his motivations, the changes that followed were substantial. With the military severely discredited by its brutal role in the quashing of the demonstrations, the president seemed to have more autonomy and independence. In the weeks that followed, he tried to distance himself from the party and the old-guard forces. He dismissed the prime minister, the head of the military security, and a number of other officials associated with the most conservative faction of the FLN and the military. The new government he put in place was made up almost entirely of young technocrats and was marked by the absence of FLN party cadres. President Bendjedid resigned from the FLN party leadership in July 1989. The reforms included the separation of party and state and free representation in local and national elections. Some restructuring of executive and legislative authority was proposed in late autumn and approved in a national referendum on November 3, 1988. A revision of the constitution followed.

The new constitution, accepted by national referendum in February 1989, marked a radical departure from the socialist manifestos that preceded it. It eliminated the ideological commitment to socialism, formalized the political separation of the FLN and the state apparatus, allowed for the creation and participation of independent parties and associations, strengthened—again—the powers of the president, but diminished the role of the military in the political sphere, and only briefly alluded to the historical role of the National Liberation Front.

Laws establishing a new system of proportional representation were passed in preparation for the country's first multiparty elections. The Law Relative to Political Associations (July 4, 1989), which was to formally encode the constitutional provisions, was fairly broad in its extension of legal status to political parties. The law allowed for the recognition of all political parties committed to the principles of national sovereignty, unity, and independence. Only those political parties of purely religious or regional orientation that might threaten the "interests of the revolution of national liberation" were prohibited (Article 8, National Constitution, 1989). The new electoral code, however, was less promising. Designed undoubtedly to preserve the rapidly diminishing hegemony of the FLN, the electoral changes ensured that, in the absence of a clear majority, the party winning even a slim plurality of votes would receive an absolute majority, 51 percent, of the seats. This was expected to benefit the FLN, which was faced with a narrow mandate and a plethora of newly formed and legalized rival political parties.

On June 12, 1990, Algeria held its first multiparty elections for local and regional offices, involving more than twelve political parties. Their results delivered a decisive blow to the FLN, in spite of the new electoral code. In fact, the changes favored the FLN's greatest rival, a new popular party, the Front of Islamic Salvation (FIS). With 65 percent of the electorate participating, the FIS received nearly 5 million votes, securing 853 of the 1,520 local councils (55 percent) and thirty-two of the forty-eight provincial assemblies (67 percent). The FLN won only 487 local and fourteen provincial constituencies. The mass appeal of the FIS was due more to its ideological view and its challenge of the ruling regime than to a clear economic and social program. The elections were officially boycotted by Aït Ahmed's Front of Socialist Forces (FFS), Ben Bella's Movement for Democracy in Algeria (MDA), and a number of smaller opposition parties.

Following the FLN's massive electoral defeat, it was anticipated that the government would annul the results. Instead, the commitment to political liberalization was reinforced as the election results were allowed to stand, council members assumed their new positions, and the date for national legislative elections was moved up. At that time, Algeria appeared to be moving forward with the region's boldest experiment in political liberalization. Yet it was not an unimpeded course. On June 5, 1991, as campaigning opened for what was to be the first national multiparty elections, the whole process came to a rapid halt when public demonstrations erupted in reaction to yet another round of electoral changes that again appeared to favor the FLN.

Attempts to undermine the FIS also included new restrictions on proxy voting and a prohibition of the use of mosques for political purposes. However, nothing drew more partisan criticism than the electoral changes of March 1991, which increased the number of parliamentary seats and altered their distribution to achieve rural overrepresentation. More than 20 percent of the seats were designated for the rural regions of the south, whose population represented less than 5 percent of the total. This gerrymandering overrepresented traditional FLN strongholds while undervaluing the heavily populated urban districts where the FIS had made strong inroads. The new rules also established a two-round voting system by which, if no party secured an absolute majority, the vote would go to a second round, in which only the top two parties would be paired off. This may have been intended to result in a runoff between the FIS and FLN, a contest that the FLN expected to win by appealing to the public trepidation about an Islamist regime. This new voting system marginalized the remaining parties, which were expected to win no more than 10 percent of the vote each. The FFS and other secular opposition parties argued that reforms ensured that the elections would be nothing more than a runoff between the FLN and FIS. By minimizing the impact of the other parties, the elections would present the Algerian public with an awkward choice between a "police state" and a "fundamentalist state."

The FIS called for a general strike on May 25 to protest the electoral reforms and to ask for an early presidential election. The strike was not particularly successful, largely because the bulk of the FIS support was drawn from the ranks of unemployed. In spite of this, the Islamist protest, which joined that of other political parties, drew unprecedented support. On June 1, hundreds of people rallied in the streets and organized sit-ins in main squares of Algiers. On June 5, the army intervened to restore order, and the president declared a four-month state of siege, dismissed the government, and indefinitely postponed the parliamentary elections.

The military, once hailed as the "protector of the revolution," had been severely discredited by its role in the brutal suppression of the October 1988 riots, and subsequently retreated into a much less obtrusive and less visible role in the political process of the country. But, in June 1991, with the political leadership in crisis, the military saw a means of reasserting its historically predominant role in the political configuration of the state. The military had as little faith in the government as it had taste for the Islamists. The state of siege was taken as authorization for a severe military crackdown. On June 13, 1991, the army issued a warning against political gatherings on the streets. After Abassi Madani called on June 15 for another general strike and a mutiny within the army, troops and tanks were deployed outside mosques, where weekly meetings often spilled over into the streets, and in city squares. The showdown culminated in more Islamist-led demonstrations and the arrests of thousands of Islamist protesters, among them the leaders of the FIS, Abassi Madani and Ali Belhadj. They were accused of "conspiracy against the state" and "plotting against national security" and were later tried by a military tribunal, which sentenced both to twelve years in prison.

The Islamists were not the only targets, however. The government was also targeted because of its "accommodationist" tactics toward the opposition and because of its liberal political and economic program. Prime Minister Mouloud Hamrouche and his cabinet were replaced. Sid Ahmed Ghozali, a former executive of Sonatrach, the state-owned gas and oil company, was named prime minister on June 5; he was more closely linked to the politics of the Boumediene era and the FLN old guard than to the reformist views of his predecessor. This transitional government was to restore order and stability until the democratic process could be resumed. It was largely made up of conservative technocrats, many of whom had served in the top ranks of the civil service or headed the huge state-owned enterprises. It was a technocratic rather than a party government, and it was immediately hailed for its distance from the FLN party cadres. Unfortunately the new leadership was subservient to the military and the old-guard elites that dominated the military's ranks; it curtailed political freedoms and continued the crackdown on the Islamists.

In September 1991, the state of emergency was lifted several days ahead of schedule, as the government maintained that it was committed to resuming the democratic process. New elections were set for December 1991. With the FIS leadership in jail, there seemed to be little threat to the FLN at the polls. Despite the proliferation of political parties since 1989, only the FIS had managed to evolve into a national party of a sizable influence.

Not leaving anything to chance, however, new efforts were made in October 1991 at electoral manipulation. The FIS threatened to boycott the elections, and the weeks leading up to the elections were tense. Remarkably, however, the campaign period proceeded relatively smoothly, and nearly fifty political parties participated in the first round of the elections on December 26, 1991. To the surprise of many people, the result was another resounding victory for the FIS and a brutal blow to the remnants of the FLN legacy. The Islamists had triumphed in a democratic game, which many had doubted they would respect. The FIS won 188 of the 198 seats contested in the first round of elections for the 430-member parliament and was only 99 seats short of achieving a two-thirds majority in the new assembly. Leading in 140 of the 232 remaining districts, the FIS appeared certain of achieving a controlling position in government. In second place was the FFS, which took twenty-five seats, while the FLN came in a distant third, with only sixteen seats. No other political party won any seats in this first round, but independent candidates won three seats. The runoff was scheduled for January 16, 1992.

These electoral results were certainly unexpected, but in the weeks that followed, President Bendjedid actually initiated talks with the FIS, apparently with a plan to establish some sort of cohabitation agreement. The military, however, quickly showed that it was not inclined to accept a transfer of power to a political party it regarded as a threat to security and stability. President Bendjedid's move toward cohabitation with the Islamists was perceived as an intolerable concession. The president was asked to resign and the second round of elections was suspended. On January 11, President Bendjedid delivered his resignation to the seven-man Constitutional Council; the country was to be temporarily ruled by a High State Committee, headed by Defense Minister General Khaled Nezzar.

Failed Democratization and the Rule of Political Violence

For two years following Bendjedid's forced resignation, the state pursued a strategy of crackdown, control, and containment of the Islamists and all other opposition groups. Besides suspending the constitution, annulling the first-round electoral results of December 1991, disbanding parliament, and banning the FIS, the army initiated a hard-line policy toward the Islamists and their supporters. Thousands of alleged militants were imprisoned in makeshift camps in the Sahara, scores killed, and a virtual situation of war set in. A newly radicalized Islamist opposition emerged to contest by force and terror the authority of the state and to claim power in the name of electoral victory. In actions reminiscent of the most brutal days of the colonial war against the French, the Armed Islamic Group (known by its French acronym as the GIA), the Armed Islamic Movement (MIA), and the Islamic Salvation Army (AIS) engaged in an almost daily terror campaign of killing not only security personnel, but also civilians (journalists, professors, poets, doctors, union officials, opposition party leaders, simple citizens suspected of cooperating with the state, women not abiding by the commandment of the Islamists, and foreigners). They also engaged in the destruction of infrastructure (telephone centers, food stocks, public utility vehicles, and schools) and merchandise stocks. State countermeasures also left scores of people dead, thousands jailed, and hundreds unaccounted for. This situation of sheer terror led to the flight of most foreigners living and working in Algeria, along with hundreds of frightened intellectuals, artists, and others who feared being direct targets of either the Islamist rage or government forces. Within a few years, Algeria had quickly descended in a vicious spiral of political violence with no immediate end in sight. By January 1995, around 50,000 people had been killed, and the number was 200,000 by 2001.

On the political front, the governing regime was unable to assemble a civilian government that commanded confidence and respect of all Algerians. President Mohamed Boudiaf—who was invited to return from exile and lead the country in January 1992—was assassinated six months after his appointment. He was followed by Ali Kafi, whose one-year presidency was virtually symbolic. The appointment on January 31, 1994, of retired general Lamine Zeroual as the country's new president stimulated some hope that the situation would stabilize, after previous presidents and prime ministers had failed to solve the worsening economic and security conditions. To help him rule during a three-year transition period, a 180-member Transitional National Council (TNC) was established in replacement of the National Consultative Council (NCC) that was created immediately after the 1992 military intervention. The eight-member Higher Security Committee (HSC), which formally selected Zeroual as president, remained in place.

President Lamine Zeroual was a career military man who rose in the military hierarchy to become general and to be appointed, in 1989, as the commander of the land forces and deputy chief of staff. But, after a disagreement with President Chadli Bendjedid, he resigned from the military. He was appointed ambassador to Romania from 1990 to 1991. In July 1993, he was called from retirement to head the Ministry of Defense, in replacement of Khaled Nezzar, the ailing strong man of the regime. Just like his two predecessors, (Mohamed Boudiaf and Ali Kafi), Zeroual rose to power in the midst of a serious crisis and leadership vacuum.

He was, in theory, appointed to lead for a transitional period that was to be followed by new elections for the president and National Assembly. But the plan was changed. On November 16, 1995, Algeria held its first free presidential elections, in which Zeroual won a six-year term by 61 percent of the vote. The vote was a historic moment for most Algerians, since it was the first multiparty presidential election ever held in independent Algeria. It was hoped that the new electoral legitimacy obtained by Zeroual would lead to a solution of the crisis. However, violence against civilians increased even more, notably by way of car bombs and decapitation and mutilation of civilians. To many, Zeroual's appointment in 1994 and his subsequent election reflected a continuing attempt to put a civilian front on the political leadership, while the high army officers ruled.

Zeroual, who kept the defense portfolio, was considered a hard-liner but had repeatedly given assurances that he was committed to dialogue with all social forces (including the Islamists who renounced using violence). He also had to convince, if not win over, elements in the government and the army who opposed any compromise with the Islamists. But first he needed to quell the disruptive Islamist violence. On the economic front, he needed to move quickly with economic stabilization and adjustment through an IMF-approved plan. Such a plan was needed to help reschedule the stifling debt-servicing burden and to attract more foreign capital to help Algeria meet its immediate needs and long-term economic growth requirements.

In April 1994, a formal letter of intent was sent to the IMF, committing Algeria to a restructuring program in exchange for a debt rescheduling. After a structural adjustment program was approved, Algeria devaluated its currency by 40 percent and drastically cut the remaining subsidies on primary consumption items. On April 11, a fifty-four-year-old technocrat, Mokdad Sifi, was appointed prime minister, in replacement of Redha Malek. Sifi declared his commitment to restarting the economy and to achieving a national concord. Under Zeroual, the state created a Social and Economic Council (CNES) and a National Council of Transition (CNT), which would serve as a temporary legislative body of two hundred representatives of parties, trade unions, managers' associations, professional organizations, and other civil associations.

After attempts at dialogue with the jailed FIS leaders had failed, the state turned to a firmer repression of radical Islamists and an overture toward moderate opposition parties, both Islamist and secular. In January 1995, most opposition parties (including the banned FIS) met in Rome, Italy, at a meeting facilitated by the religious Sant'Egidio Community, and agreed on a national platform for resolving the crisis, but the government rejected the document.[2]

In 1996, a constitutional amendment reconfirmed Islam as the state's religion, prohibited parties based on a "religious, linguistic, racial, gender, corporatist or regional" grounds, reinforced the powers of the president, and created a second parliamentary chamber, "the Council of the Nation," with one third of the members appointed by the president and the rest elected by indirect suffrage. New parliamentary elections held in June 1997 produced Algeria's first multiparty parliament. The main winners were the National Democratic Rally (RND—a party created to support the incumbent president); the Movement of Society for Peace (MSP), a moderate Islamist party formerly known as HAMAS; Nahda, also moderate Islamist; and the FLN. The RND and the FLN constituted a progovernment coalition that controlled an absolute majority and seven ministerial posts each. The Islamists were also awarded seven posts.

Bouteflika and National Concorde

In spite of the political and economic changes initiated, the general conditions of the country continued to deteriorate and scores of people were being killed every year by armed groups and government forces. Lamine Zeroual, who attempted a discreet dialogue with the jailed FIS leaders, faced strong resistance from the regime's hard-liners and decided in fall 1998 to resign from the presidency, well before the end of his term. There were many contending candidates to replace him, but the former foreign minister during Boumediene's era, Abdelaziz Bouteflika, quickly became the candidate favored by the military and many elements in society. Two days before the vote of April 15, 1999, six other candidates on the ballot withdrew, angered that the state refused to act on their complaints against electoral irregularities. By default, Bouteflika became the only candidate. This situation hurt the credibility of both the election and the winner. According to official results, Bouteflika won by 73.79 percent of the vote cast. He had secured the support of the military and that of the FLN, the RND, and MSP parties. It was for him a triumphant return from a twenty-year self-exile abroad after the military objected to his accession to the presidency when Boumediene died in 1978.

After Bouteflika came to power, violence and terror, which had started to sub-
side during Zeroual's tenure, continued to diminish. Security improved markedly
after an amnesty program called "National Concord"—approved by referendum
in September 1999—invited armed Islamists to give up the fight and avoid persecution. The first to take advantage of this was the Army of Islamic Salvation (a
military wing of FIS), which had been observing a unilateral cease-fire since October 1, 1997.

In spite of this relative improvement, the country has remained engulfed in the
same crisis that began with the riots of 1988 challenging the existing political and
economic systems. The factors that caused the crisis are still unresolved. They include: a forgotten youth that suffers from deprivation, unemployment, and lack of
hope for the future; a politically managed economy, which lacks diversification, ra-
tionality, and efficiency; a large public sector that is paralyzed by red tape and corruption; a heavy reliance on oil-rent, which maintains the country's vulnerability
to external shocks; a political regime that remains authoritarian and exclusionary
in spite of recent institutional changes; and a military institution that dominates
the political sphere. The crisis that began in the late 1980s created additional problems, which must also be addressed. They include: a sudden and massive impover-
ishment of the population; an increased rate of unemployment, mainly among the
young; political violence, which, in spite of its recent reduction, remains a major
concern; a dangerous mobilization by the state of armed civilians in the fight
against radical Islamist groups; the unknown fate of thousands of people who have
disappeared in the last ten years for political reasons; a political deadlock on major
and urgent economic, social, and political decisions; and rising Berberist demands
for the recognition of the Berber language, *Tamazight*, as a national language and
of the inherent *Amazigh* essence of Algeria's identity. Clashes in the Kabylie region—stronghold of the Berberist sentiment—that began on June 14, 2001, led to
more than fifty deaths. Since the beginning of the crisis, Berber-based movements
have seen themselves as caught between a totalitarian Islamist movement, which,
through its inherent Arabism, negated the Amazigh aspect of Algeria's identity, and
a regime that has always ignored their cultural demands. The bulk of the Berberist
movement has positioned itself in opposition to both and has been trying to extract as many concessions as possible from a weakened regime.

The National Concord enacted by Bouteflika did not bring about genuine
peace and stability, mainly because it was wrapped in total secrecy as to the deals
made with the armed groups that surrendered; it was not part of a comprehensive
political solution—it was merely a judicial action; it allowed alleged "terrorists" to
be free with impunity, which caused the resentment of their victims and of international human rights organizations; and it did not help dissipate existing tensions.
As a result of this, and also because political violence rebounded at the end of
2000 and continued throughout most of 2001, President Bouteflika's image was

tarnished. He lost popularity among the public,[3] and the army seemed unhappy with him for various reasons, including his acquiescence to visits by international human rights associations that suspect the Algerian military of sharing responsibility in the violent atrocities committed against civilians in the last few years.

The first two years of Bouteflika's presidency were characterized by political deadlock and stalled economic reforms. Many people lost hope in the ability of the National Concord to put an effective end to the rebellion of the Islamists who rejected the amnesty offer—mainly the GIA of Antar Zouabri,[4] the Salafist Group for Predilection and Jihad (GSPC) of Hassan Hattab, and the League for Preaching and Jihad (LIDD).

People's disapproval extended also to the political parties, which, in most part, lost much of their appeal because of internal dissensions and because of their marginalization in the political process. Many former adamant opposition leaders were coopted by way of election to parliament or appointment to government offices. Political needs often led some of these parties into unnatural political affinities with each other, such as those between the communist Labor Party (PT) and the Islamist MSP.

The main parties can be divided into those that oppose the government (FFS and MDA), or support it (FLN, and RND, MSP), or into those that favor an all-inclusive political compromise among all nonviolent forces (FFS and PT) and those that want to keep the Islamists at bay (RCD and Ettahadi). They are also divided on their attitudes toward the army and its anti-Islamist campaign. A new party with a moderate Islamist tendency, WAFA, led by the highly respected Ahmed Taled Brahimi (foreign minister from 1982 to 1988), was refused legalization by the government because it was suspected of being the FIS under a new name.

Algeria appears to be finally coming out its long, nightmarish era of vicious and unrelenting political violence in the hands of both the Islamist rebellion and the state. Even though badly needed economic reforms have yet to start, aggregate economic indicators have finally improved, and the country was blessed by a $20 billion income from oil in 2000, up from $12 billion just a year earlier. Also, the general environment has slowly started to attract domestic and foreign interest in investment. This was partly due to Bouteflika's efforts to improve the external image of Algeria, not only by creating a more secure environment at home, but also by making (too) many trips around the world and stimulating an intense international media campaign.

The government's most pressing tasks undoubtedly lie in resolving the country's disastrous economic problems and quelling political violence. With regard to the economy, the fear of the negative consequences that severe economic reform might have on an already discontented population have led to hesitation and contradictory policies. Concerning security, the leadership maintains its resolve to thwart radical Islamism, at a time when the most radical elements in Islamic ranks have vowed to continue the fight until the regime falls.

The Military

The relative political opening that the military allowed after the late 1980s was required by the critical circumstances of that time, but such opening is now so tightly controlled that it does not constitute a menace to the military's central role and views. In the summer of 2001, a new law restricting the freedom of the press was adopted, and many journalists spent more time in courts defending their rights than at their desk. The opposition parties and movements that are tolerated are only those that do not threaten the regime and the army's role, views, or interests. Members of the opposition who are allowed to enter political institutions serve to give the country a semblance of democracy, while their power, just like that of the institutions in which they serve, remains subordinate to that of the military establishment. Also, they serve the political purpose of forming progovernmental coalitions for resisting or countering public attacks against the regime.

The management of domestic security issues has always been in the hands of the military. The army has led both military and political counteroffensives against the Islamist rebellion. Even the truce signed by the major armed wing of the FIS, the AIS, and the amnesty laws are credited to the military, not the civilians. Of course, along with this credit also comes the liability of allegations that the army may have been involved in some of the horrible massacres that occurred in the 1990s. New publications and eyewitness accounts point to high officers of the army who stand accused of crimes against humanity that may have been committed by their troops and then attributed to the Islamists.[5] Inquiries by international human rights organizations and grassroots movements into the massacres and torture in Algeria since 1992 have also irritated some military officials who believe that the civilian authorities are not doing enough to defend them.

Being under strong domestic and international pressure to retreat from the political sphere and to allow elected civilians to run the country, some army officers have began to contemplate the possibility and to speak about it in terms of "professionalization" of the army. This may not be an easy or immediate task in the current context, where the armed rebellion is still active and challenging. The professionalization of the army would mean a return to the barracks, a major cut in the number of conscripts, and a modernization of training and education for the professional soldiers. It would also entail reducing the politicization of the military ranks to curtail the temptation to intervene in politics in the future. Of course this major undertaking may become possible only when the legitimacy of power comes to rest in the ballot box and the constitution, rather than in historical credentials alone. Unfortunately for Algeria, the military has manifested a strong resistance to relinquishing any of its control.

Whatever measures the army may seek to impose on Algeria in the near future, the fundamental structural problems that first led to the massive uprising against the state in October 1988 and that forced Bendjedid's reformers to push for ever greater political and economic reforms remain unchanged and unsolved. Despite the revival of authoritarian politics, the Algerian state will inevitably have to be decentralized, deconcentrated, and democratized if it is to overcome its myriad socioeconomic problems. Political stability will hinge on the tolerance and degree of freedom the population is willing to extend to the new leadership. This tolerance will undoubtedly be a product of the degree to which President Bouteflika can revive the economy and satisfy the streets.

Political Environment and Political Culture

Algeria remains a country severely divided between the elites and the masses. Extensive mass-level "Arabization" programs and an intrinsic identification with Islam and an Arab identity conflict with elite-level secular outlooks and ideology. One cause for the hostility clearly emanates from the leftovers of the colonial era, when secularization was utilized by the French as a means to "divide and conquer." The extensive European presence in colonial Algeria ensured that the minuscule domestic elite controlled the bulk of the Algerian population. The elite-mass divide remains a constant source of hostility and mistrust that reflects historical experience and cultural and ideological values.

One consequence of this is the political and military leaders' pervasive lack of trust in the masses. There is distrust of any form of political opposition, which has led to years of authoritarian rule. That distrust reappeared in response to the emergence of opposition parties in the late 1980s and early 1990s. Political differences among the leaders themselves have been limited by the degree of "personalization." Personal rivalries and clashes have long substituted for legitimate political discourse. Political ambitions are served better by personal loyalties than by purely political objectives and opinions.

Despite the persistence of these attitudes at the elite level, tolerance for limited "legitimate" dissent and discourse has gradually evolved. Since the late 1980s, there has been a significant leap of faith on the leadership's part in the validity of popular participation and political discussion. In the 1980s and early 1990s, remarkably open and candid debates over the national charter and the restitution of local and national representative legislatures evolved into a radical liberalization program that allowed for the existence of competitive political parties. Even the current situation demonstrates that although tolerance for opposition may be only superficial at best, achieving "legitimacy" has become a sought-after end, even if it includes the troublesome matter of incorporating the opposition.

An even more paradoxical feature of the Algerian political culture lies in an innate distrust for those in power. A willing tolerance for rebellion and sporadic violence, however, sometimes conflicts with more conformist social mores of appropriate behavior. The revolutionary experience and the authoritarian leadership of Ben Bella, and more notably Boumediene in the years that followed, resulted in a strange dichotomy between populism and centralized leadership. On the one hand, the colonial and war experiences have exerted a particularly profound impact on perceptions of the "proper" role of government—of the need for a strong, centralized state with respect to economic and political development and organization. On the other hand, Algerian political culture remains strongly committed to the populism that fueled the revolution. Algerian populism is a belief in the will of the people, a belief that in part subsumes the purely political. It places justice and morality above all other norms and emphasizes the importance of a direct relationship between the leadership and the people. This relationship, which is not dependent on intermediary political structures, accounts for the phenomenal success of the charismatic leadership of Boumediene.

Nationalism and socialism have long been an intrinsic part of the Algerian political culture. Although there appears to be more commitment to the rhetoric and symbolic content of these two concepts than to their substance, most statist policies appeal heavily to the notion of nationalism to justify heavily interventionist policies and government actions. The entire revolutionary period looms large in the minds of the Algerians and reinforces the nationalist cause. The preservation of national unity and the Algerian nation supersedes all other commitments and affiliations. In fact, it is this commitment to national unity that has been used by the military leadership since 1992 to screen certain political opposition groups from legalization. The 1989 constitution legalized all political parties on the condition that they never "violate national unity, the integrity of the territory, the independence of the country or the sovereignty of the people" (Article 40).

Algeria is a Muslim country with a primarily secular state. Islam in Algeria is part of the cultural and political tradition dating back at least as far as the independence war, when the revolutionary rhetoric of the FLN drew upon the unifying force of Islam to strengthen national cohesion and opposition to colonial rule. Islam directly contributed to a uniquely Algerian form of socialism under Boumediene ("Islamic socialism") and a conservative political outlook throughout Algeria's independent history. Conservative policies in respect to personal, family, religious, and moral affairs have predominated despite sweeping secular and modernizing policies in the economic and financial sectors. The populist Islam that arose in the 1980s and 1990s and that has infiltrated virtually every segment and class of Algerian society finds its roots in the nation's conservative and traditional mass political culture.

Economic Conditions

Exploitation by France during the colonial period and the subsequent loss of assets, with the mass exodus of French human and physical capital meant that Algeria's survival in the postindependence period depended on rapid and extensive modernization. In the years following independence, Algeria nationalized all major foreign business interests and most of the private domestic sector. Socialism and heavy industrialization marked the next fifteen years.

Ben Bella's *autogestion* program was envisioned as a socialist economic system based on workers' self-management. Workers elected representatives, who cooperated with the state through an extensive system of national agencies and directors. The state agencies were to "guide, counsel, and coordinate" worker activities within the framework of an evolving national plan that would give Algeria a socialist economy. This program never really took off, and Boumediene, upon assuming office in 1965, quickly centralized command and coordinated an extensive industrialization program that involved government control of most, if not all, of the foreign trade, major industries, retail, agriculture, public utilities, and the entire banking and credit system. By the early 1970s, almost 90 percent of the industrial sector and more than 70 percent of the industrial workforce were under state control.

The 1970–1973 four-year plan marked Algeria's first effort at a comprehensive economic policy, which was entirely financed by petroleum revenues. Nearly 50 percent of the total capital investment was allotted to the capital-intensive industrial sector; about 40 percent went to social and economic infrastructure, and only 15 percent to agriculture. The "agrarian revolution" called for the transformation of the agricultural sector into a system of cooperatives; however, with insufficient funding and infrastructure, that policy actually led to agriculture's decline in terms of percentage of gross national product.

The second four-year plan (1974–1977) tried to remedy some of the earlier oversights by focusing on job creation and attacking regional economic disparities. The agricultural sector and small to mid-sized industries were encouraged, but the emphasis on heavy industry was left unchallenged. Many of the large-scale industrialization projects were poorly designed and, instead of providing the impetus for national development, eventually became a source of economic drain. Large-scale industries were driven by nationalist sentiments rather than the ambition of economic efficiency. The fall of energy prices in the mid-1980s left Algeria with a substantial national deficit and an underdeveloped agricultural sector. Production was underdeveloped, poorly organized, and collectivized according to the socialist tenets of the national constitution. The consequence of this was a heavy dependency on food imports, frequent food shortages, rapidly rising agricultural prices, and urban migration.

By the mid-1980s, Algeria's economic crisis was threatening its political stability. High unemployment, which was growing at a rate of 3.5 percent a year, uneven (hyper) urbanization, the unbalanced industrial sector (concentrated almost entirely on heavy industries), highly polarized and dualistic economic conditions, and rapidly declining export revenues eroded the state's welfare capacities and its ability to maintain security and stability. The massive foreign debt had also become cause for concern. Unpredictable global prices and a high level of external dependence (on both food imports and petroleum-product export prices) left the country dangerously vulnerable.

Economic policy under Chadli Bendjedid attempted to undo some of the inefficiency and centralization of the Boumediene years but did so gradually and with little success. In 1980, outlining a new economic program, the regime emphasized that, despite a dramatic redirection of funds away from heavy industry and toward agriculture, light industry, and public services, maintaining a high level of industrial development was vital to the economy. It is notable that this early period of reform was motivated more by pragmatism and administrative concerns than by any abrupt change in economic orientation or commitment to liberalization.

Economic policy focused on increasing decentralization, land reform, the institution of private-sector incentives, industrial restructuring, regional development, reprioritizing of investment options, and privatization. As early as 1986, economic reformers began to recognize the need to consider a post-petroleum economy and to include the foreign sector in Algeria's economic revitalization. Formerly considered a threat to the country's national integrity, foreign investment was up to then strongly circumscribed or prohibited outright.

The changes aimed first at breaking down the massive state enterprises into more manageable and more efficient entities, with the hope that the gradual removal of restrictions would allow for the growth of the private sector. Restrictions on both foreign and domestic capital were loosened, and the private sector came to be seen as a potentially powerful asset in the plan for modernization, as Algeria gradually moved away from the ardent socialism that had characterized the Boumediene years. With nearly 95 percent of all investment having come from the state, the regime hoped to tap into private resources to help bolster the economy.

The restructuring of the money and credit laws opened the way for foreign involvement and investment, which came to be seen as a potential asset rather than a threat. In addition, contract laws were revised, the central bank was given full independence, and a system of banks specializing in trade finance and capital investment were established, all in an effort to encourage private investment. The state has been disengaging from the economy, making significant progress toward a market-driven economy. Hydrocarbons, which still dominate the economy and are likely to continue to do so, account for more than 95 percent of Algeria's export earnings. Their sale increased by 4.3 percent in 1997, but that of nonhydrocarbon products dropped by 43.8 percent. The Algerian economy will remain largely dependent on hydrocarbon exports for the foreseeable future.

The neglect of the agricultural sector was a costly mistake for Algeria. In theory, Algeria should have no need for foreign food imports. In practice, however, it imports half its grain, it is the world's largest importer of eggs, and it relies on imports for meat and dairy products. Its import bill reached $2.2 billion in 1997.[6]

Agricultural programs have gradually taken on more importance in economic policy, as state collectives were privatized, a new agricultural bank was established, and funds were allotted for irrigation development. However, even though its productivity has drastically increased since the mid-1990s, agriculture's growth rate continues to suffer because of drought, and in fact was −24 percent in 1997. Overall, agriculture contributes nowadays 12 per cent of the GDP and employs 25 percent of labor.

In the end, the transition to market rule did not take hold and the ad hoc reforms worsened the overall situation. By 1988, the industrial output had dramatically declined and most public enterprises were in deficit; the state was almost bankrupt, and social inequality had increased to a point where 5 percent of the population earned 45 percent of the national income and 50 percent earned less than 22 percent.[7] Unemployment reached 22 percent of the workforce—mostly among the youth, 70 percent of whom remained unemployed.[8]

The failed reforms and important drop in oil and gas export earnings in the late 1980s worsened the economic situation and further discredited the state, which was no longer able to support the generous services and subsidies it used to provide. After 1988, the state in fact retreated from many areas. A growing black market made up for the empty shelves of the state distribution networks; corruption and private appropriations of state funds by some officials multiplied; and political and social challenges remained unchecked.

Structural Adjustment

The adoption of a structural adjustment program in 1994 improved some of the aggregate indices. The reforms enacted between 1994 and 2000 stabilized macroeconomic indicators, and foreign investors began showing interest in nonhydrocarbon areas. The inflation rate was brought down from 30 percent in 1995 to less than 6 percent in 2000. The state budget experienced in 1997 a surplus of 2.6 percent of GDP.[9] The trade balance also recorded a surplus—mostly due to increased hydrocarbon revenues and exchange rate fluctuations—and the oil and natural gas industry grew by 4 percent. The hard currency reserves increased from $1.5 billion in 1993 to $7.5 billion in 2000.[10] The country's ability to reimburse its external debt also improved. After years of poor performance, the GDP growth rate improved substantially in 1998 and fluctuated between 3 percent and 5 percent between 1999 and 2001.

In spite of their overly positive aggregate results, the reforms carried a heavy social cost. Since 1994, around 500,000 workers were laid off as a result of the restructuring or closing of public enterprises (815 public enterprises were dissolved and the economic units that survived had to lay off 60 percent of their workers).[11] Unemployment reached 30 percent, mostly among the young,[12] including some 100,000 unemployed school graduates. As a result of this, employment in the informal sector increased significantly. The number of people living below the poverty line has also substantially increased within the last ten years, reaching a high of 12 million in 2000.

The "shock therapy" sponsored by the IMF and the World Bank did not fulfill its promises for a variety of reasons. Fears of social cost, as well as the very important vested interests, stimulated a strong resistance to the reforms from many forces, including: the largest labor union, the UGTA; civil and professional associations; public enterprises managers; small private entrepreneurs who have been particularly hurt by high interest rates and by the currency devaluation; and the few big private import/export businesses for whom the reforms constitute a threat to their monopolies.

Since the late 1980s, Algeria's economic problems have been compounded by the grave political crisis that destabilized the country. For this reason, recovery will depend heavily on restoring social peace. To begin and sustain economic growth and weather the tide of social discontent, Algeria also needs to reexamine its economic policies and to dampen their most negative effect.

The economic plight of the country is far from resolved and remains the most pressing problem facing the current regime. The leadership is caught between pressure for reform and fear of instituting sudden and drastic reforms, with the likely consequences that further cost-of-living increases will have on an already discontent population. Unfortunately the frequent change of leadership has proven costly in and of itself, as consistent economic policy proves as elusive as political stability.

Long considered a high point in Algeria's economic policy history, the dispersion and decentralization of regional administration (including the expansion of the provincial government from thirty-one *wilayate* to forty-eight), which was heralded as a major factor in propelling local economic development, has been reversed. In addition, the regime has repeatedly turned to previous leaders, often those linked to the socialist policies of the Boumediene era, in its search for a viable leadership. Algeria's state capitalism created a bifurcated society, a polar economy characterized by stagnant and declining growth at the same time that it has fostered and fed a sizable elite. Artificially sustained long past its viability by centralized control and fortuitous energy exports, the economy is now trying to rechannel its energies and focus.

Political Structure and Dynamics

Algeria's war of national liberation left a political legacy in the form of a competitive authoritarian political structure. Those that have controlled the Algerian polity since independence have been the main actors in the national liberation war. This tradition evolved into a triangular system of government in which the army, party, and state apparatus share, but continually compete for, power. Political reforms in the 1980s effectively eliminated the FLN from the political configuration while strengthening the hand of the president through constitutional reforms. The coup of January 1992 reasserted the military's presence and dominance, as the officers called for the resignation of the president and assumed the leadership of the country. The appointment of yet another military general as president in early 1994 (Zeroual) and the election in 1999 of the candidate favored by the army (Bouteflika) indicate that the military held and continues to hold the upper hand in the political triangle. The lasting legacy of Algerian authoritarianism has greatly impeded pluralistic political development despite a substantial amount of political liberalization. Opposition parties, though increasingly potent, remain on the outside of the political configuration, vying for participation but not penetrating the political configuration that governs the country.

Algeria's political structure has evolved from a strongly centralized regime with virtually all political institutions suspended to the near realization of a competitive pluralistic multiparty democracy, and reverted back to a political authoritarianism controlled by a centralized command of military leaders. As of late 2001, Algeria was governed by a civilian president whose power was subordinate to that of the military, and all other political institutions have yet to enjoy power of their own.

Historically, constitutional provisions have concentrated virtually all important powers of the Algerian state in the executive branch, which has both formally and effectively remained the supreme institution. Designed as a means of legitimating and consolidating Ahmed Ben Bella's precarious regime, Algeria's first constitution (August 1963) explicitly declared Algeria to be a presidential regime and gave more powers to the party apparatus (headed by the president, who served as the party secretary) than to the formal structure of the national legislature. However, that constitution lasted only two years; it was suspended with Colonel Boumediene's military coup on June 19, 1965. For the following ten years, Algeria was ruled without a constitution and under the highly centralized command of the Council of the Revolution and the Council of Ministers, both headed by Boumediene. The Council of Ministers assumed all legislative, executive, and administrative responsibilities. All other political institutions were allowed to atrophy so that Boumediene's vision of a strong, secure, and centralized government could evolve without the challenge that such organizations could present. Institutional development was to be a process of political education from the bottom up and included the creation of local and provincial representative institutions. The local and regional institutions had very little effective authority and remained more administrative bodies than legislative or representative institutions. Though elected, all representatives were drawn from a well-supervised list of FLN nominations and all candidates had to be party members. There was also no party competition nor did candidates engage in an electoral contest. These new assemblies had effectively concentrated, not diffused, political control at the center.

448   *Azzedine Layachi and John P. Entelis*

Gradually, Boumediene began to call for greater mass political participation and politicization. National referenda and public debates were held to discuss and approve a new national charter and constitution in 1976. The new constitution reestablished the legislature, but the system maintained a highly presidential distribution of effective power. The president was even authorized to rule by decree during legislative recess. Parliament was a unicameral legislature with representatives elected by secret ballot, but coming solely from the FLN. The new constitution signaled the return to constitutional government, but the president's serving as head of state, head of government, commander in chief of the armed forces, head of national defense, and head of the FLN ensured that he had virtually unlimited rule. The republican nature of the state was reaffirmed, as were the Islamic character and the socialist commitment of the country. The FLN was recognized as the nation's "only authentic representative of the people's will." Envisioned as a "true" national front, the FLN, it was believed, would allow for a truly participatory role for Algerian citizens. From 1968 until 1989 all mass associations were incorporated under the direct administration of the FLN. From the party's perspective, integrating the independent organizations enabled it to serve as a unique representative body of the Algerian people.

Constitutional Amendments and Political Liberalization

In 1985, President Chadli Bendjedid announced his intention to modify the national charter to bring it in line with the "practical realities" and the political ideals of the contemporary regime. The new national charter strayed little from the conservative nature of the previous constitutions, though the socialist commitment was largely relinquished. Following the riots of October 1988, President Bendjedid promised a constitutional revision, which took place and was approved by national referendum on February 23, 1989. The revision significantly altered the configuration of the state and allowed for the competition of political parties, opening the way for political liberalization. The new constitution promised a "state of law" and removed all references to the socialist commitment and to the historically unique role of the FLN and the military in "guarding the revolution." The provisions for a unicameral legislature remained.

Despite sweeping mass-level support for the constitutional changes, not everyone was in favor. Much of the discontent centered on symbolic issues, such as the removal of explicit references to the role of Islam and the abandonment of the national commitment to socialism; but also at issue was the political livelihood of the party institution. By allowing for the legal recognition of other political parties, the constitution deprived the FLN of its single-party status and made it accountable to popular approval. Also, no longer constitutionally recognized as the "guardian of the revolution," the army's role was limited to defense and external security responsibilities. The presidential authority, by contrast, was even further enhanced. As head of state, head of the Higher Judicial Council, commander in chief of the military, and presiding officer of all legislative meetings, the president was given effective control over all institutions of the state. He has power to appoint and dismiss the prime minister and all other nonelected civilian and military officials. Officially, all presidential appointments must meet the approval of the APN; however, if the nominations are rejected twice, the assembly is dissolved. Only the president is authorized to initiate constitutional amendments, and he may bypass the assembly by submitting legislation of "national importance" directly to a national referendum. President Bendjedid's term was characterized by this "rule by decree."

Formal constitutional provisions, which were expanded in the Law Relative to Political Associations of July 1989, extended the right to form political parties to all organizations that remained committed to national unity and integrity, and explicitly prohibited all parties of a specifically religious, ethnic, or regional character. This last preclusion was laxly enforced: Two of the most important parties to emerge in the months that followed were the FIS and the Berberist FFS, from the Kabylie region. The legislative structure was left intact, and Algeria's first test of its new multiparty system came in the June 1990 local and regional elections. However, this pluralist experience was short-lived. Competitive elections were tolerated at the local level but aborted when national elections threatened to overturn the historical hegemony of the FLN and the army. An unchallenged and bloodless military coup in January 1992 removed President Bendjedid from office, suspended the constitution and all political institutions in favor of a new collective presidency with unlimited political authority, and reasserted the military in the political configuration of the state.

The High Security Council, which assumed power immediately after the coup, was soon replaced by a more "legitimate" transitional institution—the High State Council (HCE, Haut Conseil d'État). Despite being a thinly guised military group, the HCE was officially a civilian body, and its mandate expired at the end of 1993 when it was to hand over power to a transition government that would directly lead the country to new elections. The National Consultative Council that was established by President Zeroual was to fill the legislative vacuum and validate HCE legislation. It served as an advisory board that would research and analyze policy initiatives and, in the absence of a working parliament, provide "an institutional framework for passing legislation."

Over time, the High State Council came to be more and more visibly dominated by military officials. Due to disband on December 23, 1993, the HCE extended its mandate for another month in the hope that it could obtain at least tacit approval from the major opposition parties for a new transitional government. The boycott by all the major parties of a national conference organized to this effect led the regime to abandon all pretenses of popular approval. The HCE was replaced by a singular presidency held by retired general Lamine Zeroual. The newly appointed president was to rule by decree, and the country remained essentially under martial law.

The Algerian armed forces (Armée Nationale Populaire, ANP) has remained a constant, if not consistent, force in Algerian politics, at times quite visible, at others more discreet. In Algeria's early postindependence years, the military, endowed with organizational capacity and technical competency, quickly occupied the power vacuum left by traditional and religious forces whose bases of power were almost completely undermined by the revolution. The armed forces, by way of their "national, professional, and technical attributes," managed to capitalize on this situation to secure a unique position in Algeria's political structure.

The military clearly has a monopoly on the coercive instruments of force, but it also has a valuable asset in its symbolic role as "guardian of the revolution" and guarantor of the country's integrity and stability. Historically, the army has maintained a discretionary role in state politics, interfering only when conditions "necessitated" military intervention to ensure the stability and security of the state. Following the brutal military suppression of the October 1988 riots, however, the military found its image severely discredited and quickly retreated from the political forum. Further constitutional changes and political maneuverings under President Bendjedid helped keep the army away from the political stage, while the country was moving toward full-scale political liberalization. However, in January 1992, the military resurfaced in a very visible role, overturning the elections, the constitutional framework, and the president's authority. The military remained the ultimate guarantor of the Algerian state if only because it alone decides the country's fate.

Until the 1989 constitutional revisions, the National Liberation Front similarly enjoyed explicit constitutional recognition of its historic role in the fight for independence and its unique role in guaranteeing the revolution. However, despite its key position in the revolution, the party was reduced to a minor role in the years immediately following independence. Boumediene's military "oligarchy," in an effort to concentrate and centralize all political authority and to prevent the emergence of any significant opposition while the regime was being consolidated, allowed the FLN and other political institutions to atrophy.

As Boumediene became more secure in his command, he gradually began to call for renewed political institutionalization and mass politicization, and the party came to be seen as a valuable instrument. The elimination of the Council of the Revolution and the subsequent absorption of its remaining members into the party congress after Boumediene's death further improved the FLN's national status.

The party relied heavily on its revolutionary image, an image that soon came to be outdated: In the late 1980s more than 70 percent of the population was too young to remember the war of independence. A low level of technical competence and a high level of corruption within the party further undermined its credibility. By mid-1988, both the president and the military leadership had begun to distance themselves from the party in an attempt to escape the political legitimacy crisis undermining the FLN leadership. The 1989 constitutional revisions helped undermine further its position in the system, and when it became just one of many political parties, the FLN immediately lost its cohesiveness, breaking into a number of factions and falling into a politically inferior position in the national hierarchy of parties. In 1995, the FLN faced a new challenger that emerged from within its own ranks, the National Democratic Rally, which was created to lend support to the presidential candidate Lamine Zeroual.

A constitutional amendment approved by referendum on November 26, 1996, declared Islam the state religion, prohibited the creation of parties on a "religious, linguistic, racial, gender, corporatist or regional" basis, and prohibited the use of partisan propaganda based on these elements. Besides creating a second parliamentary chamber, "the Council of the Nation," whose third is appointed by the president and the rest elected by indirect suffrage, it reinforced the powers of the president over those of parliament and the prime minister and officially recognized the Berber culture—along with the Arabic heritage and Islam—as a fundamental characteristic of the Algerian identity.

Many people supported the 1996 constitutional reform, which, however, was also the object of a strong opposition. First among those that opposed it were two Berberist parties (RCD and FFS) and the Berber Cultural Movement (MCB). They were particularly upset that the revision almost totally ignored the claims and grievances of the Berber-speaking segment of the Algerian society. For them, the constitution failed to recognize the Berber language (*Tamazight*) as a national language and did not respect the secular nature of the republic. They argued that the constitution reaffirmed the predominance of the Islamic religion and its corollary, the Arabic language. For the RCD leader, Said Saadi, the amended constitution was a "legal consecration of the alliance of FLN conservatives and the Islamists." For the FFS, it was an "institutionalization of dictatorship" and a negation of democracy. The former communist party, Ettahadi (Challenge, led by Hachemi Cherif) perceived the new constitution as a compromise with radical Islamism. The new constitution was also opposed by the former prime minister Mould Hamrouch, former FLN boss, Abdelhamid Mehri, and former president Ahmed Ben Bella.

The Islamist Movement

The Islamist movement in Algeria has been a constant source of agitation for the political leadership. Recognizing the powerful message and capabilities of the movement, the regime has alternated between attempts to suppress and efforts to befriend the Islamist movement's leadership. A Ministry of Religious Affairs was established to control the mosques and oversee the appointment of *imams* (religious leaders). Urban growth led to a rapid proliferation of mosques and neighborhood associations, which the government could not contain, and opened up the opportunity for an independent Islamist movement to emerge. The Islamist message was accompanied with extensive voluntary social works and charitable actions, in areas such as education, garbage pickup, and aiding the poor, the sick, and the elderly. These actions were warmly welcomed at a time of diminishing government services, as the government faced increasing economic constraints. The Islamists' social actions fostered a loyal and extensive mass political base that the Islamists could draw on once legislation allowed for the creation of independent political parties.

Although more than thirty independent parties and more than one Islamist organization emerged in the months following the legalization of parties, the Front of Islamic Salvation became the only *national* contender to the political hegemony of the FLN. The FIS, which was officially recognized as a political party on September 16, 1989, was led by Abassi Madani, a moderate and Western-educated university professor, and Ali Belhadj, a high school teacher from a poor urban neighborhood, who was known for his "fiery militant rhetoric" and radical notions on the role of political Islam. The contrast in their styles was a clear testimony to the pluralistic nature of their party.

Despite its electoral victories in 1990 and 1991 and its impressive skills at political mobilization, the FIS was disqualified, dismissed, and discredited by many who have argued that its successes at the polls misrepresented true support for its programs. According to many of its critics, the FIS has profited from the discontent of the masses of unemployed youths in the urban slums. Some have argued that, apart from its dubious sociological roots, the FIS lacked the organizational and technical capabilities to lead an effective government. Most directly, many have questioned the FIS's commitment to the principles of democracy should it be elected to national office.

The FIS presented a possible alternative to the existing regime at a time when there were few alternatives. Its electoral success constituted a large protest vote against the existing regime from those who were less than confident in the party's governing capabilities. To the extent that people were willing to risk the outcome of an FIS electoral victory, even only as an alternative to the FLN, however, it seems it had a "legitimate" sweep at the polls.

As history has repeatedly demonstrated, repression leads to radicalization. As the political crackdown by the state continued, the Islamist movement became increasingly radical. Splits in the FIS leadership and membership divided the more moderate "pragmatists" from the hard-liners, who criticized the party's leadership for cooperating with the government. This division led to the emergence of a number of radical, armed Islamist groups composed of people who had grown impatient not only with the government, but also with what they consider to be the accommodationist tactics of the FIS. After the FIS was banned in 1992, most of the FIS leaders were in jail or in exile, and many others and their followers either defected to the more radical Islamist groups or retreated from political activity altogether.

Civic Associations

Following political legalization in 1989, the FIS was but one of many political parties. By the time campaigning opened for the country's first multiparty elections, sixty-two had come into existence, some of which were led by such noted exiled political leaders and historic independence war figures as Ahmed Ben Bella (MDA) and Hocine Aït Ahmed (FFS).

Algerian civil society has largely been inhibited and far from having an autonomous existence. However, hundreds of associations have become in recent years a vibrant part of Algerian political life. Many organizations—mainly those of journalists, women, and human rights advocates—played a significant role in Algeria's brief democratic experiment and continue to constitute a source of serious challenge to the governing regime.

Following political independence and throughout most of Algeria's recent history, civil associations and mass organizations were subordinate to the state-party apparatus and relegated to functions of recruitment and propaganda. Officially incorporated under the direct administration of the FLN, the civil associations were constrained, though not entirely circumscribed. Strikes were not uncommon, and students' associations proved to be a volatile source of government opposition, with demonstrations frequently breaking out on university campuses. But what is most important is that these organizations, however limited in autonomy or independence they were, provided a vital resource for pressuring the government for political liberalization and the freedom to create the political associations that proliferated in the late 1980s and throughout the 1990s. Many of these independent associations have become an imposing element of the political dynamics of Algeria.

In the spring and summer of 2001, a series of persistent protests against the regime and its policies began in the Kabylie region and quickly spread to many parts of the country. This movement was unique in the sense that no political party initiated it. It was rather started by a grassroots movement led by traditional village and tribal leadership structures called the *aarch*, following the killing of a young man in late April while in the custody of the paramilitary force, the Gendarmerie. The riots that erupted as a consequence of this event quickly spread across the five provinces of the Kabylie region in northeastern Algeria, including Tizi Ouzou, Bejaia and Bouria, and resulted in the death of more than fifty protesters. The unrest continued and spread to other parts of the country. Rather than focusing on Berber cultural demands, it was primarily directed against the entire regime, which was criticized as being repressive and not responsive to the pressing demands of the people, and to the grave social and economic problems faced by the youth, such as mass unemployment and housing shortages.

President Boutefika responded to the unrest with the creation of an independent commission of investigation, which later found the Gendarmerie guilty of misconduct, and with a major economic revival program. Of course, the protesters were not satisfied by yet another set of promises and continued their protest, which turned violent at times, such as in Algiers on June 14, 2001.

Political and Economic Prospects

While the debates and struggles rage on Algeria's multitude of problems, the overall social and economic conditions in the country continue to deteriorate; they constitute today a fertile ground for yet another major social explosion, which may be far more difficult to control than the one the country experienced in 2001. The will to enact serious reforms—albeit stringent and painful—is shared by a great number of technocrats and members of the political elite, but there is no consensus on the form, depth, and timing of such reforms.

A resolution of the current crisis in Algeria would have to include, in addition to sound and urgent economic reforms, important political changes not only in the institutional set-up but also in the informal practices. Many facilitating factors, which could help thrust Algeria in the right direction, are already in place. They include: important economic assets—hydrocarbons, an industrial base, and a large pool of skilled workers and technocrats; a good windfall of oil income that could help re-start the non-oil economy and respond to the most pressing needs of the population; an already existing multiparty political scene that can be rendered more meaningful and more helpful in nurturing tolerance of divergent views in the context of peaceful policy compromises; and a thriving independent press, the freest in North Africa, which should be allowed to push for the accountability of office holders and the disclosure of gross corruption and to serve as an outlet in public policy debates.

Moreover, some crucial elements must also be revamped fundamentally, including the army's political role, which must be reduced and controlled by an elected civilian president. The powers of the various state institutions need be revised so as to avoid the overwhelming and unproductive dominance of the presidential office over those of the prime minister and parliament. The judicial system must also be enhanced and made to guarantee basic freedoms and protection against power abuse and retribution for political reasons. Notwithstanding the power of conservative forces—both secular and religious—a united core reformist elite, backed by constitutional and popular legitimacy, is needed to get Algeria out of its current predicament.

Foreign Policy

Algeria's revolutionary tradition has strongly influenced its foreign policy. Its revolution against colonial France was extended to encompass a challenge to the domination of imperialist powers worldwide. This lent Algeria a prominent position in the Maghrib, the Arab and Middle East region, and the Third World. Pursuing an independent, if often abrasive, course in its foreign policy, Algeria has profited from its strategic geopolitical location and its nonalignment in acquiring an influential role in world politics, a role which, in the eyes of many, far exceeded its resources and capabilities.

Gradually however, Algeria's own economic and political problems and the changed global situation and international economy have restricted Algerian foreign policy. Algeria's strategic, economic, and political interests in its region began to take precedence over a greater ideological commitment to the Third World and Africa, as economic constraints severely circumscribed its capabilities. Political liberalization further increased the constraints, and Algerian foreign policy came to reflect the actions of a nation accountable to, rather than superior to, its citizens and their perspectives (as evidenced by the dramatic reversal of the government's position on the Iraqi invasion of Kuwait in 1990).

Despite significant assistance from the other Maghribi countries (Morocco, Tunisia, Mauritania, and Libya) during the revolutionary period, Algeria's relations with its neighbors after independence were strained and remained so throughout the 1970s, especially with Morocco, whose conservative ideological orientations conflicted with Algeria's stringently socialist directions. In the 1980s, however, political and economic liberalization in Algeria drew the two countries closer together and relations improved dramatically, but only to deteriorate again in 1994 after Morocco accused Algeria of being behind an armed Islamist attack in a Marrakech tourist hotel and required a visa from all Algerian visitors. Algeria responded by closing the common border.

Efforts toward building a Greater Maghrib, including an economic union, have provided a unifying objective to which all Maghribi leaders have subscribed. Following a historic diplomatic rapprochement between Algeria and Morocco (over the issue of the Western Sahara, which had plagued Algerian-Moroccan relations for years), an accord was finally reached, establishing an economic and political Arab Maghrib Union (UMA). The treaty—signed in February 1989 in Marrakech, by Algeria, Libya, Mauritania, Morocco, and Tunisia—provides a loose framework for regional cooperation. The objectives for the union are fairly limited. Plans for a common economic market, which were to go into effect in 2000, remain elusive and remote as Algeria and Morocco continue to be opposed on a host of issues, the most important being the resolution of the Western Sahara problem. Political negotiations in the Maghrib have been dominated by bilateral agreements rather than universal arrangements. The union, however, has the potential of presenting a distinctly North African response to the European Union, whose consolidation undermines Maghribi exports and migrant workers.

Having resolved its border disputes with Mali, Niger, and Mauritania, Algeria generally maintains harmonious relations with its southern counterparts. Yet, despite its membership and founding role in the OAU, Algeria is still a society that is much more closely affiliated with its Arab neighbors and southern Europe than with the African countries to the south. It remains committed to the OAU out of tactical considerations more than genuine commitment and has often utilized the organization to its own benefit in furthering distinctly self-informed views. An OAU resolution pledging respect for existing national borders and the constrained foreign policy resources have severely circumscribed Algerian activism in the realm of its African foreign policy, as elsewhere.

Upon assuming power, President Bouteflika attempted to reverse Algeria's aloofness of the 1980s and 1990s by making the country play again an active role in the African organization. Algeria hosted the OAU's 1999 summit; Bouteflika assumed the presidency of the organization for one year and committed himself an active role in conflict resolution in Africa—he successfully mediated a peace agreement between Ethiopia and Eritrea—and in negotiations with the industrialized countries over the African debt.

Algeria joined the League of Arab States immediately after independence in 1962 and has remained an active member, though its involvement in Middle Eastern and Arab affairs has largely been limited to its support for the Palestinian cause. Its historical and ideological commitment to self-determination fostered a strong affinity for the Palestinians in the occupied territories and Israel, one of the Arab League's most compelling causes. Consequentially, Algeria's strident pursuit of the Palestinian cause has often complicated its relations with other Arab countries (for example, Jordan, Lebanon, Syria, and Egypt). Algerian-Egyptian relations have frequently been marred by differences over matters related to Israel, though more recently relations have improved, as both countries have tended toward more moderate policies. Algeria found itself in diplomatic difficulty with Iraq over its involvement in the peace talks concluding the eight-year war between Iran and Iraq. Algerian efforts to end the conflict and the construction of a peace proposal deemed to be in favor of Iran are alleged to have provoked Iraqi fighters to shoot down an Algerian aircraft carrying prominent Algerian officials involved in the peace talks. In a rather uncharacteristic development in Algeria, the Iraqi invasion of Kuwait in August 1990 and the subsequent retaliation by the Western coalition forces drew substantial popular mobilization. Iraqi calls to the Arab community resonated with the Algerian people and led to a dramatic reversal of the government stance, as the regime quickly backpedaled from its neutral position.

Pursuing a much more moderate foreign policy in recent years than in its early postindependence years, Algeria has witnessed significantly improved relations with the Western countries. A decisive change of course in domestic orientation toward political and economic liberalization, and the downplaying of its activist revolutionary role, have facilitated relations with Europe and the United States. In January 1981, Algeria played a predominant role in mediating the release of the fifty-two U.S. hostages from Iran. Western foreign policies have likewise shown an increasing tolerance for the resolute authoritarian nature of the Algerian state, which has moved toward the West in its economic orientation and affiliation. Algeria's energy resources and the West's growing need for energy have led to increased interaction and diplomatic improvement.

Undoubtedly Algeria's most significant foreign partner is its former colonial master. More than 20 percent of all Algerian exports and imports head to or originate from France. There are more than one million Algerians living in France, and many people in Algeria speak French, creating thereby a tremendous cultural overlap. This is not to say, however, that French-Algerian relations have always been cordial. Throughout Algerian history, a high level of dependence on France and a competing desire to be free of that dependency have complicated diplomatic relations between the countries. Despite a sizable exodus of colonial settlers following Algeria's independence, a significant number remained in the country. Nationalization policies of confiscating many French-owned assets in the immediate post-independence years, French intervention in the Western Sahara against the Sahrawi nationalist movement, Polisario, and "exploitative" French trade and economic initiatives, have repeatedly strained relations. As with many countries, however, diplomatic relations are largely determined by economic ones, in this case by gas and oil exports. Despite problematic political relations, economic ties have persisted since Algeria's independence, though they have not been problem-free. Undoubtedly the most damaging issue in French-Algerian relations is that of Algerian emigration to France. French policies toward Algerian immigrants have been less than consistent, and mass sentiment in France has generally been unfavorable toward the North African population in France. French government policies have vacillated; bureaucratic obstacles pose sizable challenges for Algerians trying to attain housing, education, and employment in France. Racially motivated flare-ups between migrant workers and French ethnocentrists are common. The Algerian government has also criticized France's relaxed policy toward Islamist networks in France, which have channeled money and arms to their brethren in Algeria. It has also been very unhappy with the decision of France to halt all civilian flights into Algeria after the highjacking of a French Airbus at the Algiers airport in December 1994. All other European airlines followed suit and imposed a de facto air embargo on Algeria; by 2001, only Alitalia had resumed its flights to Algeria. Furthermore, in the wake of the Kabylie riots of spring 2001, the Algerian government accused France of supporting the Berberist movement and encouraging an independence ambition in the Kabylie region.

A paradoxical feature of Algerian foreign policy is its unwaveringly independent posture, despite its frequently radical, often austere, and always highly visible role in international politics. Algeria's wide range of contacts qualifies it as one of the few countries in the world to advocate and maintain a truly independent position in the international arena. Throughout the most difficult years of the cold war, Algeria remained actively involved with both the Soviet Union and the

United States. Even during times of antagonism between the United States and France, Algeria has similarly pursued an extensive economic relationship with both countries. Despite conflicting and often contradictory sentiments toward its former colonial power, Algeria remains closely linked to France economically, politically, and culturally. Economic relations continue to be strong, if distinct, from political and diplomatic maneuverings. Since Bouteflika came to power, Algeria has been actively trying to balance its relations with Europe with an increased interaction with the United States.

Notes

1. For a discussion of the new legislature of 1977, see John P. Entelis, *Algeria: The Revolution Institutionalized* (Boulder: Westview Press, 1986).

2. Through the Rome Platform, the participants pledged to help end the crisis and proposed a plan for a return to the multiparty system and the resumption of the democratic process started in 1989. According to the document, the FIS was to be rehabilitated as a legal political party.

3. This feeling was reflected in a public opinion poll conducted by ACOM for *El-Watan* newspaper between March 30 and April 8, 2001. The results show that in the security area, 51.9 percent were satisfied with him against 34.1 percent that were not. 30.8 percent approved his amnesty while 36.9 percent did not. Only 22.2 percent were satisfied with his reforms while 43.2 percent disapproved. For more details see "Algérie: forte érosion de la cote de Bouteflika, selon un bondage," Associated Press news dispatch, April 14, 2001.

4. The GIA activities have focused on the regions of Blida, Médéa, Aïn-Defla, and their western extensions, while the GSPC has been active in the regions of Grande Kabylie.

5. Habib Souaidia, *La Sale Guerre* (Paris: Découverte, 2001), prefaced by Italian judge Ferdinando Imposimato; Nesroulah Yous, *Qui a tué à Bentalha* (Paris: Découverte, 2000). Souaidia's book, which may suffer from some factual errors, is perceived as a strong indictment of the Algerian military in particular and the regime in general for crimes against civilians. It accuses the military of using the same violent methods used by the Islamists for political purposes. According to Judge Imposimato, the book's accounts of crimes may serve in criminal suits by the victims of their families in European tribunals.

6. Some economic figures can be found in the special insert on Algeria published by the *Washington Times*, July 2, 1999.

7. *El Moudjahid* (Algeria), January 29, 1990.

8. Zakya Daoud, "L'Economie du Maghreb en Difficulté," *Le Monde Diplomatique*, June 1991, p. 26.

9. Arezki Daoud, "Algeria Outlook, " *North Africa Journal*, September 1997. URL: http//www.north-africa.com.

10. *Liberté*, "Balance Commerciale: Un excédent de plus de 5 milliards de dollars," (Algeria) July 17, 2000, p. 24.

11. CNES, *Rapport Préliminaire sur Les Effets Economiques et Sociaux du Programme d'Ajustement Structurel* (Algiers: CNES, November 1998).

12. Liberté, "La Mauvaise Note du CNES," (Algeria) April 13, 1998, p. 3.

Bibliography

A good analysis of contemporary Algerian history is found in John Ruedy, *Modern Algeria: The Origins and Development of a Nation* (Bloomington, Ind.: Indiana University Press, 1992). A more polemical account sympathetic to the Boumediene regime and its socialist policies is found in Mahfoud Bennoune, *The Making of Contemporary Algeria, 1830–1987* (Cambridge: Cambridge University Press, 1988).

Algeria's war of national liberation has been treated extensively in both the French- and English-language literature. The best account remains that of Alistair Horne, *A Savage War of Peace: Algeria, 1954–1962* (London: Penguin Books, 1979). Competent interpretations can be found in David Gordon, *The Passing of French Algeria* (New York: Oxford University Press, 1966), and Alf Andrew Heggoy, *Insurgency and Counterinsurgency in Algeria* (Bloomington, Ind.: Indiana University Press, 1972). The war's psychocultural consequences are evocatively treated in Frantz Fanon, *The Wretched of the Earth* (New York: Grove Press, 1963), and *A Dying Colonialism* (New York: Grove Press, 1967). The impact of the war on France is the concern of Tony Smith, *The French Stake in Algeria, 1945–1962* (Ithaca: Cornell University Press, 1978).

A good sociological analysis of colonial and postcolonial Algeria is that of Pierre Bourdieu, *The Algerians* (Boston: Beacon Press, 1962). A Marxist interpretation of colonialism's impact on Algerian society is found in Marnia Lazreg, *The Emergence of Classes in Algeria* (Boulder: Westview Press, 1976). Socialist experiments at workers' self-management are the subject of Thomas L. Blair, *The Land to Those Who Work It* (Garden City, N.Y.: Anchor Books, 1970), and Ian Clegg, *Workers' Self-Management in Algeria* (New York: Monthly Review Press, 1971). Questions of culture, women, and society are treated in Ali El Kenz, *Algerian Reflections on Arab Crises* (Austin: University of Texas Press, 1991), Peter Knauss, *The Persistence of Patriarchy* (New York: Praeger, 1987), and I. William Zartman and William Mark Habeeb, eds., *Polity and Society in Contemporary North Africa* (Boulder: Westview Press, 1993).

Treatments of Algeria's modern political history from elite perspectives are found in William B. Quandt, *Revolution and Political Leadership* (Cambridge, Mass.: MIT Press, 1969), David and Marina Ottaway, *Algeria: The Politics of a Socialist Revolution* (Berkeley: University of California Press, 1970), and John P. Entelis, *Algeria: The Revolution Institutionalized* (Boulder: Westview Press, 1986). The role of the military is treated in I. William Zartman, "The Algerian Army in Politics," in Claude E. Welch, ed., *Soldier and State in Africa* (Evanston, Ill.: Northwestern University Press, 1970), and John P. Entelis, "Algeria: Technocratic Rule, Military Power," in I. William Zartman et. al., *Political Elites in Arab North Africa* (New York: Longman, 1982). A leftist interpretation of Algeria's political development is found in Rachid Tlemcani, *State and Revolution in Algeria* (Boulder: Westview Press, 1986). A moderate socialist perspective is provided by Hugh Roberts, "The Politics of Algerian Socialism," in Richard Lawless and Allan Findlay, eds., *North Africa* (London: Croom Helm, 1984).

Analyses of Algerian political economy developments from the late 1980s to 2001, including the role of Islamism, can be found in Azzedine Layachi, "Domestic and International Constraints of Economic Adjustment in Algeria," in Dirk Vandewalle, ed., *The New Global Economy: North African Responses*, (New York: St. Martin's Press, 1996), "The Private Sector in the Algerian Economy," *Mediterranean Politics*, summer 2001, pp. 29–50; "Reinstating the

State or Instating Civil Society: The Dilemma of Algeria's Transition," in I. W. Zartman, *Collapsed States: The Disintegration and Restoration of Legitimate Authority* (Boulder: Lynne Rienner, 1995), "Reform and the Politics of Inclusion in the Maghrib," *Journal of North African Studies*, Autumn 2001, "The Algerian Economy After Structural Adjustment," *Middle East Insight*, November–December 1999; John P. Entelis and Phillip C. Naylor, eds., *State and Society in Algeria* (Boulder: Westview Press, 1992); François Burgat and William Dowell, *The Islamic Movement in North Africa* (Austin: University of Texas Press, 1993); Hugh Roberts, "A Trial of Strength: Algerian Islamism," in James Piscatori, ed., *Fundamentalisms and the Gulf Crisis* (Chicago: Fundamentalism Project, 1991), and John P. Entelis and Lisa Arone, "Algeria in Turmoil: Islam, Democracy, and the State," *Middle East Policy* 1, 2 (1992), pp. 23–25.

The best work on Algerian foreign policy is found in French: Nicole Grimaud, *La Politique Extérieure de l'Algérie* (Paris: Karthala, 1984). In English, the articles of Robert Mortimer in *African Studies*, March 1984, *Orbis*, Fall 1977, and *Current History*, 1991, 1993, 1994, are sound and reliable. The chapter on foreign policy in Helen C. Metz, ed., *Algeria: A Country Study* (Washington, D.C.: Library of Congress, 1995), is straightforward and comprehensive.

Comprehensive English and French-language bibliographies can be found in Azzedine Layachi, *Economic Crisis and Political Change in North Africa*, (Westport, Conn.: Praeger, 1998), Helen C. Metz, ed., *Algeria: A Country Study* (Washington, D.C.: Library of Congress, 1995), also mentioned above, and John P. Entelis and Phillip C. Naylor, eds., *State and Society in Algeria* (Boulder: Westview Press, 1992).

17

Republic of Tunisia

Gregory W. White
John P. Entelis
Mark A. Tessler

Historical Background

The French colonial experience in Tunisia, although not benign, brought less social disruption than occurred in neighboring Algeria. It formally began on May 12, 1881, when the French forced the king, or bey, of Tunis (under penalty of death) to sign the Treaty of Ksar Said. Also known as the Treaty of Bardo, the document granted France control over defense and foreign affairs for a "temporary but indefinite period." In 1883, the French gained control over Tunisia's domestic affairs as well in the Treaty of Marsa. Resistance to colonial rule in the countryside was substantial, yet did not approach the intensity of Abd al-Krim al-Khattabi's Rifian Berber resistance in Morocco, nor the Emir Abd al-Qadir's protracted, fierce resistance in Algeria. Although the traditional hierarchy of the Tunisian government was preserved, the bey himself was in fact reduced to a figurehead. The French established a separate parallel "protectorate" administration under a resident-general and quickly acquired all effective control in the state. Administrative offices were in theory open to both Tunisian and European civil servants, but in practice the French occupied all major government posts until after World War I.

Although no large-scale colonization occurred, as it had in Algeria, the French administration placed the European settlers' interests first and subjected Tunisia to reforms that were clearly not in the interest of the Muslim population. As Italian and French settlers bought land, the dispossessed rural Muslim population sank into destitution. Nonetheless, the settler population remained relatively small, never exceeding 7 percent of the total Tunisian population. The colonists also penetrated the country's economic and commercial life with far less intensity. For example, the French left the fertile and commercially prosperous area of the Sahel—the central-eastern coast of the country—in Tunisian hands.

The French colonial experience in Tunisia also featured some relatively positive reforms, many building on efforts that had been under way for several decades. Because local government was already relatively ordered and effective, the French were able to rule by discreet and indirect means, and the French military presence, so pronounced in Algeria and eventually in Morocco, was virtually absent in Tunisia.

France's contribution to Tunisia's development was perhaps greatest in the field of education. Despite qualitative limitations, the French instituted a bilingual system of Arabic- and French-language instruction—discouraged in Algeria and never really developed during the brief protectorate period in Morocco—which enabled Tunisia's educated elite to acquire bilingual cultural and language skills. University training for Tunisians in France reinforced these skills, which were used to great advantage in the nationalist struggle for independence and in the subsequent formation of a modern state.

Tunisia was the first Maghribi country to be influenced by modern nationalism. In 1905 the Young Tunisian movement was established by members of the European-educated, professional middle class of Tunis, emulating the Young Turk movement of the decaying Ottoman Empire. The Young Tunisians demanded better education, a combination of French and Arab cultures, and Tunisian access to government. They also sought to modify but not to overthrow French colonial rule. Some even welcomed the French as allies in their struggle to modernize and reform traditional institutions and practices. Primarily an intellectual movement, the Young Tunisians never commanded mass support.

The Liberal Constitutional Party, or Destour Party (*destour* means "constitution" in Arabic), was organized in February 1920 by Shaykh Abdelaziz al-Thaalibi, also one of the founders of the prewar Young Tunisian movement. The emergence of the Destour Party marked a new moment in Tunisian nationalism—that is, that of traditionalistic anticolonialism. In contrast to the bicultural orientation of the Young Tunisians, the Destour called for greater emphasis on Arab culture and Islam and criticized the French for introducing an alien cultural order, one they declared to be "superfluous" in Tunisia. Composed primarily of middle-class urbanites, the Destour also functioned as an essentially bourgeois pressure group. Nevertheless, the party provided an ideological foundation for opposition to French colonialism and, over the next decade, recruited many well-educated young men who were eventually to take control of the nationalist movement.

In March 1934 these young men broke away to form the Neo-Destour Party. The principal force behind the new party's creation was a thirty-one-year-old French-educated lawyer, Habib Bourguiba, who eventually led Tunisia to independence and, in the process, earned the label "father of his country." Bourguiba was born of middle-class parents in 1903 at Monastir in the Sahel and was educated at the Sorbonne. Like many of his generation who were trained in French universities in the 1920s, he adopted a populist brand of nationalist consciousness. Bourguiba and his contemporaries inherited from the Young Tunisians a strong faith in French liberalism. They also admired the Young Tunisians' economic and cultural innovations. From the old Destour they took the banner of anticolonialism. What they reacted against was not the actual French presence but rather the relationship of subordination it implied.

The Neo-Destourians were the first Tunisian secular nationalists (although they used Islamic symbols as instruments of political mobilization when seeking mass public support). The party was committed to both national independence and economic development via extensive grassroots organization and political education. Unchallenged by rival nationalist groups, it was able to create a mass movement despite occasional French attempts to suppress it.

The movement did not resort to violence until 1954, with the onset of the Algerian war for independence in November of that year. Groups of Tunisian and Algerian guerrillas began to operate in the countryside, thereby paralyzing nearly 70,000 French troops. Preoccupied with insurgencies in Algeria and Morocco—and recovering from the catastrophic defeat at Dien Bien Phu in Indochina—the French government under Premier Pierre Mendès-France granted full internal autonomy to Tunisia on June 3, 1955. Less than a year later, on March 20, 1956, the French formally granted Tunisia independence.

Independent Tunisia

The first three decades of postindependence Tunisian politics were dominated by Bourguiba and the Neo-Destour, renamed the Destourian Socialist Party in 1964 and the Democratic Constitutional Rally in 1988. Bourguiba's charisma and popular appeal proved durable. He was the country's only president until his peaceful removal from office on November 7, 1987. At the same time, the party maintained political supremacy over all other national organizations and governmental institutions, and the use of repression against opponents was certainly not unheard of. Despite Bourguiba's increasingly authoritarian character, especially in the latter years of his regime, the "Supreme Combatant," provided crucial national unity and political stability in the years following independence. Indeed, it is not an exaggeration to credit Bourguiba's authoritarian presence and manipulative skills with the evolution of Tunisia into a relatively stable polity.

There are nine historical phases in postindependence Tunisia. In the first period, 1955–1959, Bourguiba overcame internal challenges and consolidated power. When Bourguiba signed the internal autonomy convention with France in 1955, the secretary general of the Neo-Destour, Salah Ben Youssef, denounced it as a "step backward" and openly attacked Bourguiba as a "moderating collaborationist." Ben Youssef, who called for immediate Tunisian independence within the framework of pan-Arabism, had the support of strongly religious and conservative groups, as well as of urban elements that sympathized with his espousal of a radical Arab nationalism drawing inspiration from Nasserism in Egypt. In contrast, Bourguiba, who represented moderation and an attachment to specifically Tunisian (as opposed to broader pan-Arab and pan-Islamic) national identity, had the support of educated, Western-trained elites from the Sahel and Tunis.

Bourguiba prevailed in the bitter and personal confrontation that followed, largely because of the overwhelming support of the international arena, the party, and the crucial backing of the trade union movement. The union movement was headed by Bourguiba's ally, Ahmed Ben Salah. Ben Youssef organized a guerrilla insurrection in the south after independence, but this was quashed with the assistance of French troops. He then fled to Libya in 1956 and was later assassinated in 1961 in Frankfurt, Germany. Although Ben Youssef's uprising failed, it constituted the greatest challenge to Bourguiba and the Neo-Destour during this formative period. It helped to crystallize the authoritarian manner in which the regime continued to exercise power, and it marked the political ascendancy of a Sahelian, pro-Western, and secular elite over a conservative, Islamist opposition, a schism that persists to this day.

The defeat of Ben Youssef did not completely eliminate challenges to Bourguiba's leadership. Following independence in 1956, trade union leader Ben Salah broke with his old ally, at least for a while. Ben Salah was a socialist who espoused nationalization of the country's resources, state economic planning, and the transformation of the General Union of Tunisian Workers (UGTT) into the primary instrument for social and economic development. Bourguiba, on the other hand, although he sought to secure a virtual monopoly of power for the party, wanted to create within it the widest possible political base. A believer in the market economy, he wished to avoid risking national unity or foreign investment by radical economic change. Bourguiba prevailed and replaced Ben Salah with Ahmed Tlili, who shared Bourguiba's liberal and reformist political philosophy.

Thus, in the first years of autonomy and independence, Bourguiba was able to establish his supremacy not only in the party but also in the formal machinery of the state. In April 1956 he became prime minister, leading a government in which sixteen of the seventeen ministers belonged to the Neo-Destour. In July 1957, he became head of state as well when his government abolished the powerless and unpopular monarchy and proclaimed Tunisia a republic.

A new constitution, promulgated in June 1959, established Tunisia as an Islamic republic within the greater Maghrib, with Arabic as its official language and a presidential form of government. The government was responsible to the president rather than to the legislature. On November 8, 1959, Tunisia held its first elections under the new constitution. President Bourguiba ran unopposed, and all ninety candidates in the unicameral *Majlis al-Nuwaab*, or Chamber of Deputies, were backed by the Neo-Destour. Thus, by 1959 Bourguiba and his Neo-Destour Party had placed their indelible imprint on the Tunisian political system.

The second period, 1960–1964, was highlighted by a series of internal and external crises and by the regime's shift to socialist economic policies dominated by the state. In July 1961, fighting broke out between Tunisian and French troops over the Tunisian demand for France's evacuation of the large naval base at Bizerte, on Tunisia's northern coast. The French finally departed in March 1963, but relations with France remained strained until the early 1970s. Relations were also strained with Algeria over charges that Algeria—which had received independence in 1962—had supported Ben Youssef in the late 1950s.

Although the confrontation with France enhanced Bourguiba's prestige and popularity at home and in the Third World, an assassination plot against him was discovered in December 1962. Several military officers were tried and executed. In January 1963, Bourguiba also took action against the Communist Party of Tunisia (PCT) and banned it, under the pretext that it was attempting to expand its membership among students and workers.

The shift from private enterprise to state socialism began in 1961. To emphasize its commitment to the new policy, the Neo-Destour Party officially changed its name to the Destourian Socialist Party (PSD) in October 1964. Relatively mild ideologically, "Destourian socialism" included a rejection of class struggle and embraced notions such as "cooperation," "freedom," and the "promotion of man." It also sustained a rather consistent effort to suppress and control opposition from organized labor. To implement the new economic policies, Bourguiba appointed his former rival, Ben Salah, as the minister of planning and national economy. Ben Salah to this day is inextricably associated with the 1960s.

In May 1964, the Tunisian Majlis enacted legislation authorizing the expropriation of all foreign-owned land, a move that exacerbated the already strained relations with the French. The nationalization legislation also signaled a new political commitment to socialism. A month later there were new elections. Bourguiba again ran unopposed, and the PSD, which was the only party to present candidates, won all the seats in the Majlis.

The third period, 1964–1969, was dominated by Ben Salah's efforts to collectivize agriculture, with the full backing of Bourguiba and the PSD. The core of his strategy was a system of agricultural cooperatives. It was to be developed primarily on the large nationalized French estates in the north of the country but was also to involve the small landholdings of many Tunisian farmers. Many peasants opposed incorporation into the new cooperatives, but more important, larger Tunisian landowners also saw the policy as a threat; and since many of them wielded influence in government circles, opposition soon became more directly political. Mismanagement also became an issue, as productivity levels remained low, despite large subsidies.

In January 1969, Ben Salah attempted to extend the cooperative structure further, resulting in riots by small private landowners in the Sahelian town of Ouardanine. Opposition from a key constituency of the PSD—especially so close

to Monastir—led Bourguiba to withdraw his support of Ben Salah's socialist economic policies and to dismiss him in September 1969. That same month an Agrarian Reform Law was pushed through; it affirmed the importance of three sectors:
the state, the cooperative sector, and, most importantly, the private sector. Ben
Salah was later arrested and in May 1970 was sentenced to ten years of hard labor
on assorted charges of financial mismanagement and other irregularities. In February 1973 he escaped to Europe, where he became a vocal critic of the regime.

Bourguiba was chronically ill during this period and frequently out of the
country for treatment. His illness doubtless exacerbated the political crisis, as Ben
Salah and other political leaders positioned themselves to succeed him. Moreover,
Bourguiba's early support of the unpopular socialist policies had become a liability. Nevertheless, the president's control of the party and the government remained secure, as reflected in the 1969 presidential and Majlis elections. Within a
few years Bourguiba had regained his health sufficiently to return to active participation in political life.

The fourth period, 1970–1974, witnessed a brief reemergence of political liberalism, as Bourguiba sought to reestablish his popularity and prestige and to stabilize the country's economic and political systems. Bourguiba reappointed several
former high officials to important positions in the party and the government.
These included Ahmed Mestiri, the leader of a Tunis-based liberal and social democratic faction; Habib Achour, who returned as head of the UGTT; Muhammad
Masmoudi, who became minister of foreign affairs; and Bahi Ladgham, who
served briefly as prime minister before being replaced in November 1970 by
Bourguiba's close ally, former Central Bank governor Hedi Nouira. Nouira was
from Bourguiba's hometown of Monastir and had been serving as the secretary
general of the PSD since 1969. As prime minister he portrayed himself to the Majlis as a serious technocrat and an impersonal arbiter interested in solving the economic and financial problems of the country.

The government's sensitivity to charges of authoritarianism was clearly demonstrated at the 1971 PSD congress, where the regime's characteristic balance between authority and liberalism tipped toward liberalism and reconciliation. Discussion was free, open, and democratic in spirit and practice. Bourguiba, however,
chose his own men for key positions in the PSD's political bureau, ignoring the
general sentiment at the congress that was in favor of movement toward competitive politics. In the years that followed, the experiment in political liberalism lost
momentum. It came to an end entirely at the 1974 PSD congress, where the dele-
gates unanimously acclaimed Bourguiba party president for life and called for a
constitutional amendment to make him president of the country for life as well. In
December 1974, the Majlis voted by acclamation to permit Bourguiba to remain
president for life "as an exceptional measure and in recognition of services rendered." The measure made the prime minister–at this time Nouira—the automatic
successor in the event of the president's death or incapacity. Although basic political

order had been maintained and popular support for the regime continued, the regime exercised power in an increasingly authoritarian manner, especially against students and other outspoken leftist critics of the regime.

At the same time, within the economic sphere, Nouira and his technocrats engineered a dramatic economic policy reorientation, known in Arabic as *infitah,* or economic opening. The state dismantled barriers to external investment and trade, pursued export-oriented industrialization, and espoused the "hard law" of the market. Nouira's new economic strategy emphasized developing a private industrial-export sector while seeking to expand Tunisia's tourism industry. The state remained intensely involved in the economy, but its aim was to encourage the private sector. The *infitah* continues to this day, and Tunisia once again proved to be one of the innovators in the region.

During the fifth period, 1975–1979, the PSD continued to become more politically and ideologically monolithic while losing much of its early effectiveness as a vehicle of mass mobilization. At the same time, important new political actors emerged, some who operated within the established political system and some who challenged the dominant political order from without. The overall result was a weakened PSD and an increasingly heterogeneous and conflict-ridden political environment. Bourguiba and Prime Minister Nouira showed little interest in the policies of social and cultural reform that had been a hallmark of Ben Salah. With concern for social mobilization diminished, they placed much less emphasis on popular participation in the grassroots activities of the PSD. Proclaiming that they were *évolutionnistes,* not revolutionaries, Bourguiba and Nouira continued to devote themselves to expanding the private sector of the economy, dismantling most of the nation's remaining cooperatives, and aggressively encouraging foreign investment.

Under those conditions, the machinery of the PSD was permitted to atrophy. Mass political activity diminished sharply, and the party lost much of its dynamism at the local level. As efforts to foster popular awareness and participation virtually ceased, most local PSD committees did little more than dispense patronage in order to retain the support of area notables. Moreover, the new regime was increasingly less tolerant of dissent and more narrowly tied to a single ideological tendency.

A particular target was the socialist-oriented Popular Unity Movement (MUP), established by Ben Salah from his European exile. He accused Bourguiba and Nouira of favoring the foreign and domestic privileged classes and of ceasing to work for the Tunisian people. The MUP was banned in Tunisia, however, and in 1975 and 1976 many leftists sympathetic to Ben Salah were arrested. In summer 1977, thirty-three members of the MUP were tried for threatening state security and defaming the president.

The liberals, who had helped to oust Ben Salah and had been a major force within the PSD in the early 1970s, fared somewhat better. Nonetheless, their fate also reflected the regime's continued opposition to political pluralism. Led by Interior Minister Mestiri, the liberals formed the Democratic Socialist Movement

(MDS) in 1976, declaring that a single-party regime was "no longer adapted to the needs and aspirations of the people." Nevertheless, the June 1978 request by Mestiri and the liberals for authorization to establish an independent social democratic party was denied. The MDS was permitted to publish newspapers in Arabic and French, although these papers were sometimes temporarily shut down for criticizing the government.

During the late 1970s, two new societal forces emerged to challenge the regime: the labor movement and the nascent Islamist movement. Habib Achour now led the UGTT. Although the UGTT had been an ally of the PSD, it began to defy the government. Following labor strikes in 1976, the government and the UGTT negotiated a "social contract" in 1977 that gave industrial workers pay raises linked to inflation. Even so, labor unrest continued, and the government was especially disturbed by the presence at demonstrations of many unemployed young people, most of whom were not UGTT members. Although some government officials argued that disturbances were an understandable response to economic and social dislocations, Nouira took a hard line and Bourguiba supported him, leading to a major cabinet reshuffle.

The UGTT's response came in January 1978. First, Achour resigned his position on the PSD political bureau and central committee. Then the union challenged the government directly by calling a general strike for January 26. Extensive rioting in Tunis and several other cities accompanied the strike, demonstrating the anger of the urban poor. The army killed at least one hundred people in its efforts to restore order. Security forces arrested hundreds more, including Achour and thirty other UGTT leaders, all of who were charged with subversion. Thereafter, January 26, 1978, became known as Black Thursday. Achour was sentenced to prison and, after Bourguiba pardoned him in 1979, remained under house arrest until 1981. The UGTT, for its part, moderated opposition to the government and appointed a new secretary general.

The second major source of opposition was militant Islamism. Vastly different from the supporters of Ben Youssef, the Islamists of the late 1970s were more explicitly political, calling themselves Movement of the Islamic Way—or *Harakat al-Ittajah al-Islami*—known by its French acronym MTI. It was denied legal status by the government.

One manifestation of MTI's opposition to the government was its attack during Ramadan 1977 on a union-supported cafe in Sfax. Although most militant Islamist leaders repudiated such violence, they nonetheless spoke out forcefully in opposition to the regime and its policies. For example, Hassan Ghodbani, the young imam of an important Tunis mosque, stated in 1979, "We stand against Bourguiba's pretension of being the Supreme Combatant. No one is greater than another unless he is God." The government was visibly concerned about growing popular support for antiestablishment Islamist groups, and by the early 1980s it had arrested many MTI leaders.

The sixth period, 1980–1986, saw some halting movement toward the creation of a multiparty political system. More important, however, was the continuation and intensification of political trends that had emerged in the middle and late 1970s. Although the PSD remained dominant, its vitality continued to erode. At the same time, the emergence of rival groups challenging the regime contributed to the complexity of the political scene. Finally, deepening public anger over political and economic grievances brought new violence, of a scope and intensity unprecedented in Tunisia.

Early in 1980 Prime Minister Nouira suffered a stroke. Bourguiba replaced him with Mohammed Mzali, a former minister of education, and Mzali's government moved tentatively in the direction of political liberalization. Indeed, such movement had begun in 1979. Even though Nouira and the PSD had formally rejected the idea of a multiparty system, the Majlis in that year amended the electoral code to permit two candidates to compete for each seat in parliamentary elections. In 1980, Mzali released most political prisoners. He also brought into his cabinet a member of the MDS and several former ministers who had lost their positions in 1977 for opposing Nouira's hard line against labor. Early in 1981, amnesty was granted to all members of the MUP except Ben Salah, who remained in exile.

At a special PSD congress in April 1981, Bourguiba declared that non-PSD candidates would be permitted to participate in November legislative elections and that any group receiving 5 percent of the vote would be recognized as a political party. Furthermore, in July the PCT was officially recognized and exempted from the 5 percent rule. The PCT and the MDS both presented candidates in the 1981 elections, as did a Tunis-based faction of the MUP. Sometimes known as MUP-2, the new faction distanced itself from Ben Salah's group in Europe and was headed by Mohammed Bel Hadj Amour. Only the MTI was excluded from the limited opening given to groups seeking to challenge the PSD. None of these factions, however, won a seat in the Majlis. The PSD, operating with the UGTT in an electoral front, won 95 percent of the popular vote and took all the seats in the chamber.

The possibility of increased political pluralism continued when the government recognized the MDS and Amour's faction of the MUP in November 1983. Yet some within the PSD opposed this move. In any event, many observers saw relatively little substance in what had been accomplished. Noting the weakness of groups outside the PSD, as well as claims of irregularities in the 1981 balloting, some concluded that Mzali was more interested in outmaneuvering PSD rivals than in encouraging multiparty politics.

Among his major rivals were Driss Guiga, minister of the interior and an opponent of multiparty politics, and Mohammed Sayah, a former PSD secretary general who had supported Nouira's hard line in 1978. Mzali's position as heir apparent was also challenged by Bourguiba's wife, Wassila, who used her influence on behalf of several of the prime minister's rivals during this period. Adding to the confusion, Bourguiba turned eighty in 1983, and although he remained politically active, his advancing age added to concern about the country's political future.

The resulting political drift and frustration of this period were manifested dramatically in widespread public rioting in late 1983 and early 1984. The disturbances were sparked by the government's announcement on December 29 of a rise in the price of bread and flour. By the time the disturbances were put down on January 5, they had spread throughout the country. About 150 people were killed and hundreds more wounded by security forces seeking to restore order. The immediate cause of the "bread riots" was removed on January 6, when Bourguiba went on television to announce that price rises would be rescinded. The price rollback brought spontaneous popular celebrations, and the country gradually returned to normal. Nevertheless, the scope and intensity of the rioting showed that public anger was based on much more than the price of bread. Indeed, the most intense anger appeared to be directed not only at the government but also at the consumption-oriented middle and upper classes, population categories perceived to be prospering from the government's economic policies at a time when the economic situation of the poor was steadily deteriorating and the government was asking the poor to tighten their belts even more.

The riots of January 1984 intensified the power struggle within the PSD, forcing a showdown between Mzali and Interior Minister Guiga. Supported by Wassila Bourguiba, Guiga was Mzali's most important rival for PSD leadership. Nevertheless, Mzali succeeded in laying much of the responsibility for the rioting on the interior minister. Guiga was forced to resign. He later fled the country and was tried in absentia for high treason. Mzali's position remained insecure, however, due to other challengers such as Bourguiba's protégé, Sayah.

The first military officer to hold high political office in post-independence Tunisia, General Zine al-Abidine Ben Ali, was brought into the government in October 1984 as secretary of state for national security. In summer 1986, Bourguiba dismissed Prime Minister Mzali, who was perceived to have been unable to resolve the country's economic and social problems. His successor, Rached Sfar, an economic and financial technocrat, endeavored to resolve Tunisia's economic crises. Having only mixed success, however, he was replaced in summer 1987 by Ben Ali, by then minister of national security. That set the stage for the Supreme Combatant's own removal.

The seventh period, 1987–1990, was marked by spectacular changes: The most significant was the effective end of Bourguiba's domination of Tunisian politics. There were also economic and political dislocations prompted by Iraq's invasion of Kuwait in August 1990 and the onset of Desert Storm in January 1991.

Bourguiba's removal from office on November 7, 1987, was, in large part, the culmination of an increasingly intractable relationship with MTI and its leadership, most notably Rachid Ghannouchi. Ghannouchi had studied in Damascus in the 1960s. There he had become disillusioned with Arab nationalism and turned to the normative study of Islamic unity. In the late 1970s, Ghannouchi founded MTI; along with Abdelfatah Mourou, he circulated an Islamist paper, *al-Ma'arifa*, until it was banned in 1979.

The crux of the Islamist criticism in Tunisia—as with their counterparts elsewhere in the Muslim world—is that the regime is too pro-Western and too willing to compromise the country's integrity by allowing non-Islamic foreign influences into the country. For example, a key component of Tunisia's *infitah* economic strategy has been an emphasis on "mass tourism"—that is, the opening of the tourism sector to enormous numbers of middle-class vacationers from northern Europe. Such a strategy is in contrast to Morocco's high-end tourism. In 2000, Tunisia received two times the number of tourists as Morocco, but earned less foreign exchange. Islamists perceive European tourists in Tunisia as arrogant, insensitive, and decadent.

Bourguiba had authorized Ghannouchi's imprisonment from 1981 until 1984, and the government accused MTI of inciting riots during the bread riots of 1984. In 1987, a high court, with Bourguiba's authorization, condemned Ghannouchi to life with hard labor. Ben Ali, realizing that Bourguiba's actions would make martyrs of the MTI leaders, decided the time had come for him to replace the aging president. The ostensible reason for Bourguiba's stepping down was medical; he was eighty-four years old at the time and in failing health. Under Article 57 of the Constitution, and with a medical report signed by seven doctors purportedly treating Bourguiba, Ben Ali proclaimed himself president on November 7, 1987. Ben Ali released Ghannouchi in 1988 and, despite his stated hostility to Islamism, met with the Islamist leader in November. Ghannouchi then went to live in exile in London, where he continued to write and be active. For its part, the MTI remains politically engaged as well. To comply with new electoral laws, it changed its name to the Renaissance Party, or Hizb Ennahdha.

In 1988, Ben Ali and the party leadership also approved the PSD's name change to the Democratic Constitutional Rally (RCD) and legalized a wide array of political parties. Throughout 1988, statues of Bourguiba came down across the country. Ben Ali emphasized technical competence in his cabinet appointments and exhibited a willingness to incorporate outspoken opposition figures from the latter years of Bourguiba's rule. Moreover, he pushed through constitutional amendments in July 1988 designed to limit the president's term of office to a maximum of three five-year terms, abolishing the lifetime presidency (created in 1975 for Bourguiba) and its succession predicament. Such a limitation should result in Ben Ali leaving office in 2004, unless his supporters are successful in crafting a new revision.

A year after the removal of Bourguiba from office, on November 7, 1988, Ben Ali promulgated a national pact, a "code of honor" for the government and legal opposition entities. During the year, presidential clemency was extended to former opponents. Ghannouchi, Mourou, and other Islamists sentenced in absentia, as well as Ben Salah, were pardoned.

Despite these openings, however, with the national elections of April 1989, troubles began to brew. Because of new electoral laws instituting a single-ballot-majority formula, small parties found it difficult to compete. Indeed, Ben Ali won 99 percent of the votes, and the RCD won all the seats in the Majlis. The ruling party denied all allegations of widespread irregularities. For their part, Islamists running on independent slates in seventeen districts gathered 14 percent of the overall vote and, by some estimates, as much as 30 percent of the vote in urban areas. Islamist sources put the figures even higher.

The eighth period, 1990–1999, was marked by the Gulf War and the civil war in neighboring Algeria. Opposition to the government in the early 1990s continued to smolder. In January 1990, three legal opposition parties and the unrecognized Ennahdha Party boycotted the first meeting of the "higher council" of the national pact. In May, three opposition parties—the liberal MDS, the Communist Party, and the unrecognized Popular Unity Movement of Ben Salah (who had returned to Tunisia from exile in 1989)—formed a coalition to criticize the RCD's power monopoly. Meanwhile, unrest continued at several universities in early 1990, caused by students from all sides of the political spectrum. Most of the country's 72,000 students called for the abolition of police stations within the confines of university campuses, and Ennahdha and the General Union of Tunisian Students (UGTE) called for the government to remove the minister of education, Mohamed Charfi.

The opposition boycotted the municipal elections in the summer 1990, although the RCD pointed to the large turnout (80 percent) as evidence that the boycott was ineffective. Moreover, the elections coincided with the June 13 success of the Islamic Salvation Front (FIS) in the Algerian municipal election, a cause of tremendous and continuing concern for the Tunisian leadership.

The Iraqi invasion of Kuwait in August 1990 and the Gulf War of 1991 wrenched Tunisia. Few were enamored of Saddam Hussein and the invasion of Kuwait, but many were equally critical of the U.S.-led coalition's buildup of force. Tunisian elites, for example, were quick to point out that a prominent member of the anti-Iraq coalition, Saudi Arabia, had provided support to Islamist movements. The Tunisian government sided with the popular anti-Western feelings, and foreigners left the country before and during the war. For a development policy based upon encouraging European (and Middle Eastern) trade and investment, the exodus of the foreign community placed a sharp strain on diplomacy and commerce. Nonetheless, the strategy of the government appeared to work; the largest demonstrations gathered fewer than 10,000 people, and foreign nationals slowly returned.

In spring 1991, during the turmoil in the aftermath of the Gulf War, Islamist militants allegedly bombed the RCD party headquarters. At the same time, unrest broke out in the universities, culminating in the death of two students. The government claimed an "Islamic plot" and suspended the Islamist-dominated UGTE.

The following autumn, the government claimed that it had discovered another plot: Ennahdha planned to assassinate Ben Ali and other leaders "to create a constitutional vacuum." Ghannouchi vehemently denied the charges from exile.

The early 1990s, then, were marked by the emergence of two trends, which obtain to this day: the consolidation of power by Ben Ali and attempts by the government to balance security imperatives in the face of a continuing Islamist challenge with the need to maintain an image, for both domestic and foreign consumption, of a liberal, democratizing state, one suitable for foreign investment.

On the electoral side of the ledger, elections have occurred with sharp irregularities. In October 1991, by-elections were held in nine vacant constituencies. The six legal opposition parties boycotted them, arguing that the electoral law gave an unfair advantage to the RCD, and as a result, the RCD won all the seats.

In March 1994, Ben Ali was reelected to a second term by an overwhelming majority. Ennahdha was barely a force, as the cancellation of Algeria's election in January 1992 and the subsequent civil war gave the Tunisian government the pretext for a sharp crackdown on Islamists. Moreover, reforms in the electoral code gave the government the confidence that it would win in the Majlis, even as it appeared that the system was opening. The reforms included the introduction of a hybrid electoral code combining first-past-the-post with proportional representation. The system resulted in the opposition parties competing among themselves and being co-opted into the process. For the presidency, the only candidate who attempted to challenge Ben Ali, Moncef Marzouki, former president of the Tunisian League of Human Rights (LTDH), could not obtain sufficient signatures from MPs. He was ultimately arrested for his activities. The result was that the RCD won 97.73 percent of the vote and gained 144 seats in the 163-seat Majlis. The other parties won fractions of 1 percent, but were able to gain seats under the new electoral code. The MDS achieved ten seats; the former Communist Party, El Ettajdid, or Renewal, gained four seats; the Democratic Unionist Union (UDU) obtained three seats; and the Popular Unity Party (PUP) won two seats.

For the presidency, Ben Ali won 99.91 percent of the vote.

In 1995, Tunisia sealed an association agreement with the European Union to create a free trade area over a twelve-year period. The agreement entered into force in 1998. As part of the Barcelona process begun by Europe that same year, the agreement is designed to open the Tunisian economy further to European exports and investment. Tunisia was the first country to sign an agreement in the Mediterranean, followed by Israel and Morocco. Egypt and Lebanon are also in negotiation. The Association Agreement was a clear demonstration of the importance of the European economy to Tunisia, and it illustrated Europe's interest in supporting the economy of a neighboring nonmember, one dealing with issues of stability.

The ninth period of Tunisia's post-independence history began in 1999. In October 1999, Ben Ali won election to a third term by an extraordinary margin, and the RCD dominated the Majlis. In contrast to previous elections, however, Ben Ali had distinct opposition from two other candidates: the PUP's Mohamed Belhaj Amor and the UDU's Abderrahmane Tlili. Thus, the election was touted as the first multi-party election in Tunisia's history. Nonetheless, with 89 percent turnout, Ben Ali's margin was a whopping 99.4 percent. According to press reports, even Amor and Tlili supported Ben Ali in the end. As for the Majlis, with the electoral code guaranteeing thirty-four of the 182 seats to the opposition, the RCD won 91.6 percent of the vote and gained 148 seats. The MDS gained thirteen seats; the UDU and PUP each won seven; El Ettajdid won five; and the Social Liberal Party (PSL) won two seats.

Throughout the electoral experience of the 1990s and into the present period, the government has sought to display a process of a gradual opening, taking reform steps to satisfy critics without challenging the RCD position of prominence. In November 1999, shortly after the election, a new reshuffling of the government created a ministerial portfolio, the minister delegate to the prime minister in charge of human rights, headed by Dali Jazi. In May 2000, in turn, in the run-up to municipal elections, the RCD stipulated that 20 percent of its candidates would be women. Taking a cue from Hassan in Morocco, the government also periodically grants amnesty to political prisoners.

Despite these efforts, Tunisia remains the target of sharp criticism from human rights observers. Since the early 1990s, the internal security services have increased censorship, detained suspected Ennahdha members, and harassed men with beards or women with veils. Foreign researchers are sharply limited in their access to the country, the Internet is monitored closely, undercover cops abound, and an independent, vibrant press is nonexistent. The government closed down the venerable LTDH—created in 1977 and the oldest league in the region—in June 1992. The LTDH was reopened in late 1993 but has been subject to periodic banning and chronic harassment. Similarly, the Tunisian National Council for Liberties (CNLT) and the Tunisian section of Amnesty International are banned. The press is not allowed to publish releases from Ennahdha or reports by the LTDH. In seeking to crack down on the Islamists, however, the government must contend with the damage to its public image from charges of human rights abuses. Amnesty International and the LTDH have both claimed that Tunisia has violated the human rights of detainees, many of whom were held illegally. Ghannouchi, from exile, further denounced the government for the use of torture to extract confessions from detainees. In 2001, detainees included the CNLT's Sihem Bensedrine, who was released after six weeks in jail to await trial. Similarly, the MDS's Mohamed Mouadda was rearrested in 2001, after serving jail time in 1995 and 1996. Finally, former LTDH president Marzouki, now affiliated with the CNLT, appealed his 2000 conviction on spreading false information.

The government has consistently responded to the charges by arguing that it must maintain public order, and that moreover, without public order, government efforts to attract foreign capital to expand the economy for the good of all Tunisians would fail. Interior Minister Abdallah Kallel famously stated in 1992: "We don't have oil. We have sun. And the sun needs security."

Moreover, Ben Ali has tried to lay the groundwork for a fourth term, contrary to the three-term limit of the constitution he revised in 1988. He has modified the constitution to permit the president unilateral prerogative to revise the constitution in national emergency and to permit the holding of office for an indefinite period. The president's supporters embrace the prospect of a fourth term, while opposition critics view it as an attempt to maintain a Mediterranean "crony capitalism" for Ben Ali's family and his followers. At any rate, Ben Ali now seems to have consolidated sufficient power to withstand any major challenges from within the party itself.

Thus, the main problem of the regime as it looks to the future is how to contend with Ben Ali's succession, if it does, and how to meet the challenge of the opposition from the left and from the Islamists. If the economic success of growth turns down—or if investors turn away because of the human rights situation—then the support for the regime could also be drastically cut.

Political Structure and State-Society Relations

Tunisia's political culture has been influenced by a distinct and historically legitimized tradition of national unity, which gave the country an important advantage in the early years of post-independence. There are both geopolitical and demographic dimensions to this unity. The geographical basis of modern Tunisia appeared in rough outlines in Roman times, and with few exceptions, the area has been ruled as a unified polity since that time. The various dynasties that governed the country possessed centralized and cohesive administrative networks that, for the most part, extended to the whole of the territory. Thus, even though such dynasties were often nominally subservient to the authority of a foreign power, such as the Ottoman sultan, Tunisia's borders remained constant and the state gained legitimacy in the eyes of those living within it.

Demographically, Tunisia has no significant ethnic and cultural cleavages, in contrast to Algeria and Morocco. Virtually all Tunisians are Arabs and Sunni Muslims. The Berber-speaking population makes up no more than 2 to 3 percent of the population, and even when there was a flourishing Jewish community, it never exceeded 3 percent. Tunisia thus has a degree of homogeneity that is rare in today's world.

Bourguiba and the Neo-Destours instituted a specific set of beliefs about modernity and development. These included a commitment to balancing Tunisia's Arab and Islamic legacy with what they called its Mediterranean personality. Drawing inspiration from Tunisian history as far back as the Carthaginian and Roman Empires, this balancing act, after 1956, involved the regime in both increased Arabization and the construction of a multicultural (Arabo-Islamic and Franco-European) normative order. The emphasis on Tunisia's diversity and unity has continued with Ben Ali. In his Declaration of November 7, 1987, broadcast on state radio and television, Ben Ali stressed the Islamic, Arabic, African, Maghrebi, and Mediterranean character of Tunisia.

The regime also placed great emphasis on the role and responsibilities of the individual citizen in promoting national development, reflected in the importance given to education and social mobilization. The goal was to carry out a "psychological revolution" that would restructure social and human relationships in a way that would make modernity possible. As defined by Bourguiba himself, the objective was to make each Tunisian "a good citizen, capable of initiative, eager to learn and cooperate, so the battle against underdevelopment will be won."

At the same time, the concept of guided democracy was another component of Bourguiba's political philosophy. He believed that until a psychological revolution took place and the nation possessed an enlightened and politically mature citizenry, a dedicated, competent, and progressive-minded elite must assume leadership and exercise control of the state.

The policies and programs that characterized Tunisia during the first decade and a half of independence reflected these values and objectives. They gave the country a reputation for innovation, bold reform, and progressive social engineering that has not entirely faded, despite the fact that the ideological character of Tunisian political life narrowed sharply and became more conservative after the early 1970s. Moreover, these policies and programs helped to shape a postindependence generation of educated Tunisians whose political weight is only beginning to be felt and whose contribution to the nation's political culture will become visible in the years ahead.

The reforms introduced by the regime touched on many areas. For example, a personal status code, adopted in 1956, was designed in part to promote women's emancipation. It abolished polygamy, established a minimum age of fifteen for women to marry, provided women with the right to sign their own marriage certificates, and permitted them to demand divorce, to vote, and to hold office. Bourguiba believed in a more liberal interpretation of the Quran; he repeatedly denounced in public the veil as a "dishrag" and viewed traditional Muslim customs for women as "servility, decadence, and bondage." Such an orientation vis-à-vis the status of women has earned Tunisia the reputation as one of the most liberal countries in the Middle East and North Africa. Although Islamist criticism of the personal status code in the early 1990s pulled Ben Ali and the RCD in more conservative directions, reforms in the 1990s have included extending additional rights to divorced women, especially concerning child support and alimony. Most notably, in the event of divorce, support is extended to a child's maternal grandparents, a service previously devoted only to the paternal grandparents. In 1996, the government also extended the right for women to obtain loans independent of their husbands.

In other realms, the government nationalized Muslim landed estates (*habous*) in 1956 and 1957, arguing that the religious leaders in control of the land failed to encourage their rational exploration. The Neo-Destour later redistributed these lands as political patronage. In 1958 the government established a new bilingual educational system. Attention was given to the increased use of Arabic, but from the third grade on, French was the language of instruction for many subjects. The newly established University of Tunis taught most of its courses in French, although plans were laid for increased Arabization in higher education. In 1960, Bourguiba began a campaign against the traditional observance of Ramadan, the Muslim holy month of fasting, arguing that it decreased economic productivity. Moreover, Muslims were excused from fasting during war. According to Bourguiba and Ben Salah, Tunisia was fighting a war against underdevelopment. Bowing to a storm of public protest, however, Bourguiba had to retreat.

The Neo-Destour was an effective organization for social change during these years. Members of the party's approximately 1,250 territorial and professional units met often to discuss national problems and raise public awareness. The party performed important regulatory and distribution functions at the local level, too, helping citizens to solve personal problems and dispensing patronage. All these activities built loyalty to the political system and helped to foster popular support for the party's reforms. The party claimed to have 400,000 active members in 1965, and auxiliary organizations, such as the Union of Tunisian Women and the UGTE, were also active in mobilizing and politicizing the populace.

A major effort was made to expand education, which regularly absorbed 25 to 30 percent of the state budget. In the decade following independence, literacy climbed from 15 percent to 35–40 percent, the percentage of primary-school-age children attending classes grew from 25 to 60–70, and the percentage completing high school rose from 3 to almost 30. In 1960, Tunisia was third among Arab countries in the percentage of children attending school. By 1965 it had moved into second place, behind Lebanon. The regime also took care to see that women as well as men shared in the expansion of education. The proportion of girls in the student population rose steadily during this period, climbing from less than 30 percent at independence to over 40 percent a decade later. Vocational training was also offered to students who terminated their education without completing high school.

Although serious opposition was not tolerated in this dynamic but centralized political environment, Bourguiba's exercise of power during the early years was not totalitarian and was directed primarily at national, not personal, advancement. He consulted widely on important policy matters and permitted senior officials to exchange ideas vigorously. He also addressed the people in countless speeches and rehabilitated former opponents willing to work with him in the party. Meaningful competition sometimes existed at non-elite levels too, as local officials struggled with one another and with the party hierarchy. Thus, despite some abuses of power, the government was genuinely committed to far-reaching social change and was highly popular with the masses.

By the mid-1970s, however, the major structures of government—the Majlis, the cabinet, and the PSD—had all become little more than appendages to Bourguiba's system of personal rule. Under him was a ruling elite composed of an old guard, longtime associates dating from the preindependence struggle, and younger technocrats, men brought into government by Bourguiba because of their specialized education, technical skills, and modernist outlook. Nonetheless, Bourguiba did not allow any of these groups to achieve an independent base of power strong enough to challenge the president's rule.

Bourguiba acquired his preeminent role in the political process by deftly manipulating and controlling his political subordinates, maintaining an atmosphere of insecurity as they struggled for presidential favor. He was particularly effective in removing dissidents from office, even forcing them into exile, and "recycling" them later to positions of responsibility. His success can be explained only in terms of his own enormous charisma, his prestige as the father of his nation, his deftly developed skills as a political tactician, and the availability of talented individuals to manage the affairs of state and party in effective style.

A political counterculture began to emerge in the 1970s, accompanying and reinforced by changes in the ideological orientation of the top elite and the increasing authoritarianism of the government. These new trends, including a reinvigorated labor movement and growing public support for militant Islamism, reflected the unfulfilled expectations of an increasingly mobilized populace and the intensification of economic problems and inequities. Many Tunisians lost faith in the vision and development strategy articulated by the government—a loss of faith that continues to this day. This is particularly true of the growing ranks of young people whose social origins are modest and whose education does not go much beyond primary school. Tunisia's bicultural orientation also limits opportunities for advancement among persons from traditional backgrounds, whose familiarity with the French language and culture is limited. Moreover, rapid industrialization intensifies competition for jobs and status and increases the relative deprivation of those who are unable to seize the new opportunities being created.

Internal government operations have changed considerably under Ben Ali, although the effect of that change on the general population is still limited. In contrast to Bourguiba, who had an aloof style and played "musical chairs" with his cabinet ministers, Ben Ali is much more of a "hands-on" person, surrounding himself with experienced professionals who have served him for many years: Minister of Foreign Affairs Habib Ben Yahia, Prime Minister Mohamed Ghannouchi, National Defense Minister Dali Jazi, and Interior Minister Abdallah Kaâbi. At the same time, Ben Ali is very much in charge. In the view of some observers, he exercises power with an "iron fist in a velvet glove," conducting exhaustive and multiple consultations before reaching a final decision.

Conscious of the declining popularity of Western-inspired images and symbols in some quarters, since the late 1980s the regime has sought to invoke Arab and Islamic symbols as a means of buttressing its rule and undercutting the appeal of opposition groups, particularly Ennahdha. Nevertheless, secular Western values are still an integral part of Tunisian national identity, exemplified by the country's deep ties with the European Union. Numerous diplomatic agreements and aid protocols in the 1970s, 1980s, and 1990s—as well as the infusion of French and Italian television broadcasts—have brought Tunisia increasingly into an economic and cultural sphere dominated by Europe.

The Iraqi invasion of Kuwait complicated the government's balancing act, the attempt to incorporate both Arab-Islamic and Western influences. Opposition movements—particularly the Islamists—capitalized on the Gulf War to criticize the pro-Western orientation of the Tunisian government and economy. As a precaution against disturbances, the government lined the streets of major cities with tanks, barbed wire, and troops. In the aftermath of Desert Storm, European tour groups canceled their trips to North Africa, a move that devastated the Tunisian economy in 1991. Nonetheless, the economy recovered robustly in 1992 and 1993. Tunisia's repression of Islamists continued to raise questions about the prospects for internal stability.

Domestic and Foreign Economic Policy

From 1956 to 1961, Tunisia pursued a liberal, laissez-faire economic policy. However, the results of private investment and initiatives were disappointing, largely owing to the exodus of capital and human resources when the French and Italian colonial communities departed. The departure of the highly skilled indigenous Jewish population in the 1950s also had a negative impact.

Faced with a deteriorating economic situation, Bourguiba turned to Ben Salah in 1961 to develop a planned economy, with strict import substitution industrialization (ISI) controls ensuring protected internal markets and a fixed exchange rate and currency regulation. Under Ben Salah, the Ministry of Planning and National Economy drafted a ten-year economic development strategy, *Perspectives décennales de développement (1962–1971)*. The first two plans, 1962–1965 and 1966–1971, set goals in four broad categories: (1) decolonization; (2) reform of economic structures, including industrialization; (3) human development, including education, anti-illiteracy, and unemployment campaigns; and (4) the generation of internal investment, designed to lessen the dependence on foreign assistance. Most of Ben Salah's objectives were unrealistic, however, since they required expenditures and investment disproportionate to the economic capabilities of a small country without a large domestic market.

The most distinctive feature of Tunisian economic policy in the 1960s was the promotion and imposition of a system of agricultural and commercial cooperatives. The intention was that cooperatives not only play an important political and social role in the development of the country but also contribute to the solution of economic problems.

By 1969, the state-led economic experiment had proved a failure. State-run enterprises were rife with waste, mismanagement, and low productivity; collectivization met with widespread opposition from the rural middle classes; and the public-sector capital and operating costs were greater than the economy could bear. In addition, state socialism had lost its popularity with the discrediting of Egyptian President Nasser's Arab socialism following his humiliating loss in the 1967 Arab-Israeli war.

In 1969, Tunisia moved back toward a free-market economy. Prime Minister Nouria formalized the shift with the *infitah*. The strategy of economic openness emphasized encouraging foreign investment in export-oriented industries—for example, shoes and textiles—directed to European markets. A major aim was to create more jobs. A 1972 law gave financial incentives to foreign investors producing primarily for export to Europe, and a 1974 law provided for similar incentives based on the number of jobs created.

In its effort to attract foreign investors, a key component of its fourth development plan (1973–1976), the government emphasized the availability of cheap labor and the relative absence of social conflict. The government moved to repair its estranged relations with France and signed an association accord with the European Community (EC) in 1969 and a more comprehensive cooperation accord in 1976. The agreements allowed for the duty-free export to the EC of industrial products from the country's growing light-manufacturing sectors. Traditional agricultural exports did not fare so well, however. Although the agreements allowed for some exceptions, EC import barriers sharply restricted European markets for Tunisia's traditional agricultural products—olives, citrus, and wine. These trade barriers have continued to grow, deeply affecting Tunisia's rural population as the agricultural sector has struggled. Economic problems in the sector have prompted migration to the cities, increasing unemployment and unrest in sprawling suburbs.

In the early years of the new strategy, the economy expanded dramatically. Between 1973 and 1976, the gross domestic product increased about 7 percent annually, and it climbed even higher between 1977 and 1980. Not all the credit goes to the new policy, however. The economy also benefited from earlier investments in social and economic infrastructure, including education, as well as the import-reduction policies of Ben Salah. The high oil prices of the 1970s were also a major factor. By 1980, Tunisia's fledgling oil industry was accounting for over half the country's exports.

Tunisia paid a price for the new prosperity. As new industrialists became wealthy and the agricultural sector more impoverished, the gap between rich and poor increased; the rapid expansion of the export sector made the economy far more vulnerable to international economic cycles; and concentration of exports to Europe was a mixed blessing. EC member states began putting up tariff walls against cheap Tunisian industrial imports.

The EC's inclusion of Greece in 1981, followed by Spain and Portugal in 1986, caused further drastic reductions in agricultural exports. About 46,000 tons of Tunisia's high-quality olive oil continues to be admitted to the European Union (EU, formerly the European Community) annually because of the lobbying efforts of powerful Italian interests. Tunisian olive oil—celebrated for its superiority by connoisseurs—is admixed in Italy with cheaper Italian oils, bottled, packaged, and marketed vigorously in the United States. Packages in U.S. supermarkets honestly label the commodity as "Mediterranean olive oil" or "Made in Italy." According to the government National Olive Office (ONH), in 1996 the EU combined was responsible for 55 percent of the world's olive oil exports, with Tunisia by itself in second place at an enormous 33 percent of the total. (Turkey accounts for 6 percent, and Morocco 2 percent.) At the same time, the ONH acknowledges that the bulk of Tunisia's exports go to the EU.

The other major emphasis of the *infitah,* tourism, has also been a mixed blessing. There was a boom in hotel construction, and although tourism brought needed foreign exchange, most Tunisians lacked the skills (including language fluency) to get any but the most menial jobs. Environmental problems have emerged as well, with a "concretization" of the Mediterranean coast line occurring as hotels and swimming pools are built. Sewage processing and water service remains a challenge for a drought-plagued part of the world. Finally, seminude, sun-worshiping Europeans have become a symbol of decadence to the Islamists.

The economic boom diminished in the 1980s. In addition to European tariff barriers, oil prices plummeted and a serious drought and overcultivation drastically reduced agricultural productivity. Moreover, the migration of labor was no longer able to counteract runaway population growth, over 3.5 percent a year, causing the shortage of jobs to become even more acute.

Tunisia's economic problems reached crisis proportions in the mid-1980s. Foreign debt skyrocketed, reaching nearly $5 billion; and foreign exchange reserves plummeted to almost zero in June 1986. In August, the Sfar government implemented a series of drastic austerity measures, a structural adjustment plan (SAP) encouraged by the IMF and World Bank. The government devalued the dinar by 10 percent to make exports more competitive, reduced import tariffs, and decreased national budget expenditures for social services. Moreover, the government announced plans to privatize nonstrategic sectors of the state-led economy, reduce costly food subsidies, and liberalize prices. Finally, the government eased restrictions on foreign oil exploration in southern Tunisia. To ease the foreign exchange crisis, Tunisia took out two World Bank loans, and the IMF granted a standby credit and compensatory financing facility of $250 million.

At the end of the decade, during the period of the seventh development plan (1987–1991), the economy was still ailing. Production in nonagricultural sectors was up, but the agricultural sector remained devastated, owing to a continuation of the worst drought in the century and an infestation of desert locusts. As a result, the food import bill continued to rise. In addition, the international oil glut continued to depress oil revenues, down from 45 percent of the GNP in 1980 to 16 percent in 1988. Privatization of inefficient state enterprises continued, but slowly, and the country's rapidly expanding population continued to exceed the availability of employment.

There are nonetheless a few economic bright spots, including the expanding light manufactures and, increasingly, service sectors. For example, by 1995 textile companies provided 50 percent of the jobs in the manufacturing sector and accounted for 30 percent of the value of Tunisia's exports. Not surprisingly, the countries of Europe are the main customers, buying 90 percent of the products.

Above all, tourism enjoyed the benefits of a cheap dinar after 1986, attracting European and Maghribi visitors to Tunisia's beaches and ancient ruins. Tourism had surpassed crude petroleum as the main foreign exchange earner in 1986, and in the words of the Ministry of National Economy's monthly publication, *Conjoncture,* tourism has become "an essential pawn in the economic chessboard."

Tunisia's criticism of the coalition in the Gulf War strained relations with its major trading partners, and after the war, Ben Ali sought to repair external diplomatic and economic relations. Once again, he focused conspicuously on the Islamist challenge. Political instability created by the Islamists, according to the government and its western supporters, is a threat to foreign investment and tourism. Ben Ali has thus linked his efforts to improve economic relations with efforts to get European governments to crack down on Islamist exile groups in their countries.

The years leading into the twenty-first century have been reasonably good to Tunisia economically, especially in comparison to its neighbors. Ben Ali has been adept at managing concerns that the benefits of economic growth are not equitably shared. In the visit to rural areas in December 1992, he created the National Solidarity Fund, better known as "2626," after the number of its current account in the national budget. Tunisians were asked to contribute to the fund, and monies are used in poorer regions to support development projects. In addition, the Tunisian Solidarity Bank was created in 1997 to provide micro-credit for small development projects. The size of the funds deployed is not clear, but the Ministry of Women and Family Affairs has received monies for its projects.

Three solid years of good rainfall in 1991–1993 and repaired relations with the European Union have helped Ben Ali continue his efforts to portray Tunisia's small, extroverted economy as stable and healthy and, therefore, suitable for foreign investment. The government also continued its efforts to attract business concerns seeking access to the EU market. For example, in June 1992 it created a Ministry of International Cooperation and Investment, in which Mohammed Ghannouchi, the current prime minister, served as minister. In addition, the same year, Tunis and Brussels opened tentative negotiations toward the establishment of a new "partnership," finalizing the association agreement that in 1995 created a NAFTA-style free-trade agreement (FTA). Tunisia was the first in the region to sign, followed closely by Morocco and other countries in the Machrek. The implementation of the partnership accords is to take place over twelve years, and the government is keen on pursuing a *mise à niveau*, or upgrading, strategy in order to position the economy against future European competition. Many of Tunisia's family-owned enterprises, especially the small and medium-sized enterprises, are ill-equipped to contend with European firms.

In the late 1990s, the ninth plan (1996–2001) was devoted to growth and to a considerable extent the economy was successful in that regard. According to the government, the economy grew at an annual rate of 5.4 percent at constant prices, and inflation was drawn down to 2.7 percent by 1999. In 1999, according to the World Bank, the economy grew at a rate of 6.2 percent. The state has streamlined procedures for foreign investors, with parastatals such as the Industrial Promotion Agency (API) and the Center for Export Promotion (CEPEX) offering a wide array of services and "one-stop" investment incentives. Other indicators were also positive: the 1987 poverty rate of 12 percent had shrunk to 6 percent in 2001; 99 percent of school-age children attended school, including girls, up from 90 percent in 1988; and life expectancy grew from sixty-six years in 1988 to seventy-three years in 2000.

The government has also devoted considerable effort to supporting the mineral sector, including oil production, phosphate rock processing, and base-metal mining. Again, Europe dominates Tunisian trade in such commodities, accounting for 73 percent of total trade in 1996. Special attention has been given to the development of the natural gas sector, with the Miskar natural gas field coming onstream in 1995. Key players include Italy's Agip, British Gas, and France's Elf-Aquitaine. State-owned industry maintains control of refining operations, with operations at Bizerte producing one-half of the country's petroleum product requirements.

On the other hand, the economy remains severely indebted because of borrowing from foreign lenders. In 1999, Tunisia owed $11 billion, and debt servicing is a chronic burden on the national budget. The ratio of debt service to the overall GDP hovers between 45–50 percent annually, and in 2000, debt servicing consumed nearly 20 percent of export earnings. Although the Tunisian government is proud that it has never rescheduled its debt, the national budget devotes more to debt service than it does to education or to health care.

Looking to the future, Tunisia still faces severe economic challenges. First, on the domestic front, the agricultural sector continues to struggle, for a wide array of reasons. A pivotal sector in terms of the number of Tunisians employed, agriculture's overall contribution to GDP has declined dramatically since independence. In 1990, 16 percent of the GDP was derived from agriculture, with the figure declining to an even lower 13 percent in 1999. One might argue that such a figure is a result of robust economic growth in other sectors, yet slow growth in the sector—on average, 2.1 percent during the 1990s—prompts dislocation within the country's rural regions. In addition, because of the relative decline in domestic production of foodstuffs, the government must spend valuable foreign exchange for imports from Europe and the United States.

In addition, the distribution of available resources is highly skewed. The gap between rich and poor, though not as large as in some developing countries, has increased appreciably in recent years. On the one hand, luxurious villas and apartment complexes are multiplying in some areas, particularly along the coast, as are other visible signs of wealth and consumption. On the other hand, poverty is growing, too, with an increasing divide between regularly employed workers who are protected by trade unions and social legislation and those who work on an intermittent or seasonal basis, in the informal sector, or perhaps not at all. Members of the latter group, whose material conditions are deteriorating, feel powerless and resent the fact that the nation's economic burden is not distributed equitably. Overall, the country's young, growing population continues to outpace the economy's ability to generate employment opportunities.

Internationally, the dependence on the European Union as well as an overreliance on export industries will continue to expose Tunisia's small, open economy to external economic shocks, especially when the EU goes into periods of recession. This may be unavoidable in the near term, but in the long term the government will have to explore the possibility of diversifying trade partners. It will also have to deepen industrialization, preferably without concomitant environmental degradation.

Foreign Diplomacy

Tunisian postindependence foreign policy was the creation of Habib Bourguiba, with clear continuities subsequently maintained by Ben Ali. Deeply influenced by Western liberal thinking, Bourguiba shunned radical and extremist policies. He consistently assumed a moderate, pro-Western stance on East-West issues, generally remaining suspicious of the Communist bloc and of African and Middle Eastern leaders who sought Soviet friendship in the form of military aid agreements and tacit military-political alliances.

During the cold war, therefore, it was natural for Tunisia to turn to the United States as a countervailing force in order to balance the power of the Soviet bloc.

When decolonization disputes during the 1960s undermined Franco-Tunisian cooperation, the United States also became Tunisia's principal supplier of economic assistance.

Tunisia has nevertheless consistently demonstrated a close affinity to France, with which it maintains extensive cultural, educational, and commercial ties. The country's ties to the European Union have also assumed significant proportions. Close relations have been cultivated with Germany, Belgium, and Italy. Italy, in particular, is the focus of close cooperation because of the colonial legacy and because of the large number of Tunisians who work in Italy's agricultural and service sectors on a seasonal basis. For its part, the European Commission in Brussels has sought to support Tunisia's economic development because of the impact that economic instability and political unrest in the Maghrib has on Europe.

Despite the importance of close ties to the United States, France, and the European Union, Bourguiba diligently sought to avoid compromising the country's nonaligned status during the cold war era. Tunisia maintained proper diplomatic and economic relations with all the major states of the communist world and was a member in good standing of Third World international groupings. The country's receipt of significant economic and technical aid from numerous international organizations, petroleum-exporting Arab states, Soviet bloc countries, and China, as well as Western industrialized states, reflected its general acceptance by the world community. Since the end of the cold war, Tunisia has focused its diplomatic efforts on the twin goals of attracting foreign investment for its economy and of containing the Islamist opposition.

Tunisia's major foreign policy problems have arisen from ideological, political, territorial, and economic disputes with its neighbors. Tunisia's pro-Western orientation for a time brought it into conflict with both Algeria and Libya. Its failure to implement the hastily announced January 1974 merger with Libya strained relations between the two countries and led to Libyan economic retaliation, political subversion, and military threats.

The U.S. bombing of Tripoli and Bengazi in April 1986 complicated Tunisia's relations with Libya and greatly embarrassed Tunis. By not publicly condemning the raid, Tunisia left itself open to charges by Libya of kowtowing to the Americans. Privately, the government had no love for the mercurial Qaddafi, and moreover, the United States had been a major contributor to Tunisia's military ever since Libyan-backed riots in the southern Tunisian town of Gafsa in 1980. In retaliation for Tunisia's not condemning the raid, Qaddafi expelled 30,000 Tunisians working in Libya's oilfields, eliminating a valuable source of employment and remittances to Tunisia.

Relations with Algeria, historically cool but correct, warmed in the early 1980s, in part as a result of Tunisia's desire to find a regional counterweight to Libyan pressure and in part owing to the increased moderation of Algeria's leadership. Thus, Tunisia and Algeria, along with Mauritania, signed a Treaty of Fraternity and

Concord in 1983. Tunisia has long regarded Morocco as its closest ally in the Maghrib, but its own improved relations with Algeria and its neutral position on the conflict in the Sahara somewhat diminished the importance of this relationship.

The creation of the Arab Maghrib Union (UMA) in 1989 by the five Maghribi states—a response to the EU's accelerated efforts to integrate in the late 1980s—calmed regional tensions. Yet divergent responses to the Gulf War, the Algerian civil war, the economic sanctions imposed by the United Nations on Libya, and each country's half-hearted participation in the UMA do not augur well for future cooperation. Indeed, given the bilateral, vertical relationships that Morocco and Tunisia have crafted with the EU, horizontal, south-south integration may continue to remain elusive.

Despite its European focus, Tunisia has also maintained its credentials as a loyal member of the Arab community. During the 1960s, Bourguiba alienated most of Tunisia's Arab allies by advocating the then-unthinkable recognition of (and negotiations with) Israel. Aware of the strong emotional identification of Tunisia's population with the Palestinian cause, the Tunisian leadership has since been careful to maintain its solidarity with the Arab world. In 1979, for example, Tunisia deepened its involvement in inter-Arab politics by becoming host to the League of Arab States, which left its Cairo base in protest of Egypt's signing of the Camp David Accords and a peace treaty with Israel. In 1991, however, the Arab League returned to Cairo. In addition, after the expulsion of the PLO leadership from Beirut in 1982, Tunis became the PLO's headquarters. Although over the years there have been numerous instances of strain between the PLO leadership and the Tunisian government, throughout the 1980s, especially under the Mzali government, Tunisia turned toward a more explicitly pro-Palestinian perspective. The PLO presence enhanced Tunisia's diplomatic prestige. Later, when the Palestinian Authority was established in the Gaza Strip and West Bank in the wake of an accommodationist period in Israeli-Palestinian relations, Tunisia was among the handful of Arab states to establish consular, commercial, and tourist ties with the Jewish state. Indeed, a concerted effort has been undertaken by the Ben Ali regime to attract back from overseas locations its native Tunisian Jewish population. Outside observers, however, question the sincerity of such efforts, viewing them as little more than a public relations campaign to demonstrate the country's "Western-style" credentials.

Bibliography

A useful historical overview is found in Kenneth J. Perkins, *Tunisia: Crossroads of the Islamic and European Worlds* (Boulder: Westview Press, 1986). A Jewish "native son," Albert Memmi, writes about Tunisia's colonial experience in *The Colonizer and the Colonized* (Boston: Beacon Press, 1967). Tunisia's political history from the precolonial period through independence is found in L. Carl Brown, *The Tunisia of Ahmad Bey: 1837–1855* (Princeton: Princeton University Press, 1974); Lisa Anderson, *State and Social Transformation in Tunisia and Libya, 1830–1980* (Princeton: Princeton University Press, 1986); and Julia A. Clancy-Smith, *Rebel and Saint: Muslim Notables, Populist Protest, Colonial Encounters (Algeria and Tunisia, 1800–1904)*, (Berkeley: University of California Press, 1994).

The early years of independence are treated in Charles A. Micaud, Leon Carl Brown, and Clement Henry Moore, *Tunisia: The Politics of Modernization* (New York: Praeger, 1964); and Clement Henry Moore, *Tunisia Since Independence: The Dynamics of One-Party Government* (Berkeley: University of California Press, 1965). The cooperative era under Ben Salah is analyzed in Lars Rudebeck, "Development Pressure and Political Limits: A Tunisian Example," *Journal of Modern African Studies* 8, no. 2 (1970): 173–198; and John Simmons, "Agricultural Cooperatives and Tunisian Development: Part I and II," *Middle East Journal* 24, no.4 (1970): 455–465 and 25, no.1 (1971): 45–75.

Bourguiba's death at the age of ninety-eight on April 6, 2000, has brought a renewed interest in his political legacy as reflected in L. Carl Brown, "Bourguiba and Bourguibism Revisited: Reflections and Interpretation," *Middle East Journal* 55, no. 1 (Winter 2001): 43–57. The ideological underpinnings of "Bourguibism" are captured in John P. Entelis, "Reformist Ideology in the Arab World: The Cases of Tunisia and Lebanon," *The Review of Politics* 37, no. 4 (October 1975): 513–546.

Political institutions are analyzed in Derek Hopwood's *Habib Bourguiba of Tunisia: The Tragedy of Longevity* (New York: St. Martin's Press, 1992). The declining popular legitimacy of the Tunisian government in the early and mid-1970s and the shift in the country's ideological orientation and economic development strategy are treated by John P. Entelis, "Ideological Change and an Emerging Counter-culture in Tunisian Politics," *Journal of Modern African Studies* 12, no. 4 (1974): 543–568; Mark Tessler, "Tunisia at the Crossroads," *Current History,* May 1985; and Ahmed Ben Salah, "Tunisia: Endogenous Development and Structural Transformation," in *Another Development: Approaches and Strategies* (Uppsala, Netherlands: Dag Hammarskjöld, 1977). A valuable compendium of social science analyses from this period is Russell Stone and John Simmons, eds., *Change in Tunisia* (Albany: State University of New York Press, 1976).

Tunisia in the 1980s is treated in I. William Zartman, ed., *Tunisia: The Political Economy of Reform* (Boulder: Lynne Rienner, 1991); and Michel Camau, ed., *Tunisie au Present: Une Modernité au-dessous de tout soupcon?* (Paris: CNRS, 1987). Other accounts include L. B. Ware, "Ben Ali's Constitutional Coup in Tunisia," *Middle East Journal* 42, no. 3 (1988); Mark Tessler, "Tunisia's New Beginning," *Current History,* April 1990; Dirk Vandewalle, "From the New State to the New Era: Toward a Second Republic in Tunisia." *Middle East Journal* 42 (1988): 602–620; and Rémy Leveau, "La Tunisie du président Ben Ali: Equilibre interne et environnement Arabe," *Maghreb-Machrek* 124 (1989): 4–17.

Politics in the 1990s is treated by Iliya Harik, "Privatization and Development in Tunisia." In *Privatization and Liberalization in the Middle East,* ed., Iliya Harik and Denis J. Sullivan. (Bloomington, Ind.: Indiana University Press, 1992); and Gilles Denoeux, "Tunisie: les élections présidentielles et legislatives, 20 mars 1994," *Maghreb-Machrek* 145 (1994): 49–72. Political economy concerns are treated by Gregory White, *A Comparative Political Economy of Tunisia and Morocco: On the Outside of Europe Looking In* (Albany: State University of New York Press, 2001); Emma Murphy, *Economic and Political Change in Tunisia: From Bourguiba to Ben Ali* (New York: St. Martin's Press, 1999); and Nicole Grimaud, "Tunisia: Between Control and Liberalization." *Mediterranean Politics* 1, no. 1 (summer 1996): 95–106.

The status of women in Tunisia is treated by Barbara Larson, "The Status of Women in a Tunisian Village: Limits to Autonomy, Influence, and Power," *Signs: Journal of Women in Culture and Society* 9, no. 3 (1984); Laurie Brand, *Women, the State, and Political Liberalization: Middle Eastern and North African Experiences* (New York: Columbia University Press, 1998); and Sophie Ferchiou, *Les femmes dans l'agriculture tunisienne.* (Marseilles: Edisud, 1985). Susan Marshall and Randall Stokes, "Tradition and the Veil: Female Status in Tunisia and Algeria." *The Journal of Modern African Studies* 19, no. 44 (1981): 625–46, offer a comparison to Algeria.

The political role of Islam in Tunisia is examined by Susan Waltz, "Islamicist Appeal in Tunisia," *Middle East Journal* 40, no. 4 (1986): 651–670; Mark Tessler, "Political Change and the Islamic Revival in Tunisia," *Maghreb Review* 5, no. 1 (1980); Elbaki Hermassi, "La société tunisienne au miroir islamiste," *Maghreb-Machrek* 103 (1984); John Entelis, ed., *Islam, Democracy and the State in North Africa* (Bloomington, Ind.: Indiana University Press, 1997); and Azzam S. Tamimi, *Rachid Ghannouchi: A Democrat within Islamism* (New York: Oxford University Press, 2001). Extensive excerpts of interviews with Ghannouchi are available in François Burgat, *The Islamic Movement in North Africa.* William Dowell, trans. (Austin: University of Texas, 1993). Mohamed Elhachmi Hamdi, *The Politicisation of Islam: A Case Study of Tunisia* (Boulder: Westview, 1998) offers a view of the Ennahda from an insider's perspective. Tunisia's Jewish population two decades after independence is treated by Mark Tessler and Linda Hawkins, "The Political Culture of Jews in Tunisia and Morocco," *International Journal of Middle East Studies* 11, no. 1 (1980).

Tunisia's controversial human rights record is treated in Ahmed Manaï, *Supplice Tunisien: Le Jardin secret du général Ben Ali* (Paris: La Découverte, 1995). Nicolas Beau and Jean-Pierre Turquoi, *Notre ami Ben Ali* (Paris: La découverte, 1999) evokes Gilles Perrault's scathing critique of Morocco's King Hassan II. Andrew Borowiec, *Modern Tunisia* (New York: Praeger, 1998), offers a defense of Ben Ali.

For analyses of the UMA, see Ahmed Aghrout and Keith Sutton, "Regional Economic Union in the Maghreb." *Journal of Modern African Studies* 28, no. 1(1990): 115–139; Claire Spencer, *The Maghreb in the 1990s: Political and Economic Developments in Algeria, Morocco, and Tunisia* (London: International Institute for Strategic Studies, 1993); and I. William Zartman, "The Ups and Downs of Maghrib Unity," *Middle East Dilemma: The Politics and Economics of Arab Integration*, Michael Hudson, ed., (New York: Columbia University Press, 1999).

Tunisia's experience with immigration to Europe is treated by Gildas Simon, *L'Éspace des travailleurs Tunisiens en Structures et fonctionnement d'un champ migratoire international* (Aix-en-Provence/Marseille, France: Edisud, 1979); Jean-Pierre Cassarino, *Tunisian New Entrepreneurs and Their Past Experiences* (London: Ashgate, 2000); and Sarah Collinson, *Shore to Shore: The Politics of Migration in Euro-Maghreb Relations* (Washington, D.C.: Brookings, 1996).

About the Book and Editors

Rapid social, economic, and political change is endemic to the Middle East and is often more revolutionary than evolutionary in nature. In many ways, the entire political landscape of the Middle East has been transformed in the past decade in the realm of both international relations and domestic politics: The collapse of the Soviet Union, the end of the cold war, and the Iraqi invasion of Kuwait have all had a profound effect on relations among states within the region and between those states and countries outside the region.

In this revised edition, Long and Reich provide comprehensive and up-to-date analyses of many critical contemporary events and issues. The contributors explain how Desert Storm isolated Iraq and brought Syria back into the mainstream of Arab politics, contributing to the revival of the Arab-Israeli peace process. They also show how the peace process has evolved over the decade after the Madrid conference. Evaluating the economic costs of the Kuwait war and the continuing oil glut, the authors find that resulting changes in the domestic economies of the oil-producing states have created additional pressures for social and political change. The most profound change in government and politics, however, is the rise of Islam as the idiom of political discourse among moderates as well as extremists. And, they consider the effects of September 11, 2001, and the interrelationship with regional politics.

David E. Long is a consultant on the Middle East and counterterrorism. He is retired from the U.S. Foreign Service and has taught and lectured extensively on Middle Eastern subjects. He is the author of *The United States and Saudi Arabia: Ambivalent Allies* and *The Anatomy of Terrorism*. **Bernard Reich** is professor of political science and international affairs at George Washington University in Washington, D.C. He is a member of the board of advisory editors of the *Middle East Journal* and of the international editorial board of *Israel Affairs*. He is the author of *Quest for Peace: United States-Israel Relations and the Arab-Israeli Conflict, The United States and Israel: Influence in the Special Relationship, Israel: Land of Tradition and Conflict, Historical Dictionary of Israel, Securing the Covenant: United States-Israel Relations After the Cold War, Arab-Israeli Conflict and Conciliation: A Documentary History*, and of *Political Dictionary of Israel* as well as the author of numerous articles, book chapters, and monographs on Middle East politics, international politics, and United States foreign policy.

About the Contributors

M. Graeme Bannerman is president of Bannerman and Associates, a foreign policy consulting firm. Previously he served on the staff (and later as staff director) of the Senate Foreign Relations Committee. Before that he served in the Department of State. He holds a Ph.D. in modern Middle East history from the University of Wisconsin. He has taught at Georgetown University, George Washington University, and the American University of Beirut.

Sally Ann Baynard holds a Ph.D. in political science from George Washington University. She is a professorial lecturer in the School of Foreign Service at Georgetown University and has written and lectured widely on Middle Eastern politics.

Louis J. Cantori is professor of political science, University of Maryland, Baltimore County, and adviser to the president, Graduate School of Islamic and Social Sciences, Leesburg, Virginia. He studied in the Faculty of Theology, al-Azhar University in Cairo, and also taught at the American University in Cairo. He is author of over fifty articles on the Middle East and on political science and the author or editor of four books, including *Local Politics and Development in the Middle East*.

Mary-Jane Deeb is the Arab world specialist at the Library of Congress. She was the editor of *The Middle East Journal* and a professor of international relations and Middle East politics at The American University. Deeb is the author of *Libya's Foreign Policy in North Africa* and coauthor with Marius K. Deeb of *Libya Since the Revolution: Aspects of Social and Political Development*. She is the co-editor with Mary E. King of *Hasib Sabbagh: From Palestinian Refugee to Citizen of the World* and is co-editing a book on *Gender and Politics in the Middle East* with Dr. Mary Ann Tetreault. She has also written over seventy articles, book chapters and book reviews for numerous publications.

John P. Entelis is professor of political science and director of the Middle East Studies Program at Fordham University. He is the author, coauthor, and editor of numerous books and articles on the comparative and international politics of the Middle East and North Africa. His most recent edited book is *Islam, Democracy and the State in North Africa*. Entelis is the editor of *The Journal of North African Studies* and secretary of the American Institute for Maghrib Studies (AIMS).

Mark J. Gasiorowski is a professor in the Department of Political Science, Louisiana State University. He is the author of *U.S. Foreign Policy and the Shah* and co-editor, with Nikki Keddie, of *Neither East Nor West*. He is currently writing a book about Iranian politics since the 1978–1979 revolution.

F. Gregory Gause III is associate professor of political science at Columbia University and was a fellow for Arab and Islamic studies at the Council on Foreign Relations (1993–1994). He is the author of *Saudi-Yemeni Relations: Domestic Structures and Foreign Influence* and *Oil Monarchies: Domestic and Security Challenges in the Arab Gulf States*.

George S. Harris is former director of the Office of Analysis for Near East and South Asia in the Bureau of Intelligence and Research of the Department of State. He has taught at the School of Advanced International Studies of Johns Hopkins University and at George Washington University. Among his publications are *The Origins of Communism in Turkey, Troubled Alliance: Turkish-American Problems in Historical Perspective, 1945–1971*, and *Turkey: Coping with Crisis* .

Azzedine Layachi is associate professor of politics and associate director of the Center for Global Studies at St. John's University. He received a Ph.D. and M.A. in politics from New York University and a B.A. from the Institut des Etudes Politiques of the University of Algiers, Algeria. He is the author of numerous books, book chapters, and articles on North Africa, including *Economic Crisis and Political Change in North Africa*; *State, Society and Liberalization in Morocco*; and *The United States and North Arica: A Cognitive Approach to Foreign Policy*.

Ann Mosely Lesch is professor of political science at Villanova University. She worked for the Foreign Policy Research Institute in Philadelphia (1972–1974), the American Friends Service Committee in Jerusalem (1974–1977), the Ford Foundation in New York and Cairo (1977–1984), and Universities Field Staff International in Cairo (1984–1987). She wrote *The Politics of Palestinian Nationalism*, with William Quandt and Fuad Jabber; *Arab Politics in Palestine, 1917–1939*; *Political Perceptions of the Palestinians on the West Bank and the Gaza Strip*; *Transition to Palestinian Self-Government*; and *Origins and Development of the Arab-Israeli Conflict*, with Dan Tschirgi. She has published numerous articles on Palestinian issues and is U.S. director of the Palestinian American Research Center. She was president of the Middle East Studies Association in 1994–1995 and serves on the advisory committee of Human Rights Watch/Middle East.

John W. Limbert has been a U.S. Foreign Service officer since 1973 and is currently serving at the U.S. Embassy in Conakry, Guinea. He earned a Ph.D. in history and Middle Eastern studies from Harvard University and has taught in Iran and at the U.S. Naval Academy. His most recent sojourn in Iran included fourteen months as a prisoner at the U.S. Embassy in Tehran. He is the author of *Iran: At War with History* and has contributed articles on Iran to the *Christian Science Monitor*, the *Foreign Service Journal*, and the *Washington Quarterly*.

Phebe Marr is senior fellow, Institute for National Strategic Studies, National Defense University. She is the author of *The Modern History of Iraq* and co-editor and contributor to *Riding the Tiger: The Middle East Challenge After the Cold War*. She received her Ph.D. in Middle Eastern history from Harvard University.

Malcolm C. Peck is senior program officer in the Programming Division of Meridian International Center in Washington, D.C., where he designs and implements professional study tours for international visitors sponsored by the U.S. Department of State. Previously, he was director of programs at the Middle East Institute in Washington and Arabian peninsula affairs analyst at the State Department. He is the author of *The United Arab Emirates: A Venture in Unity* and *Historical Dictionary of the Gulf Arab States*. He has contributed chapters on Middle East subjects to several books and has contributed entries to *Encyclopedia of the Modern Middle East, Microsoft Encarta Encyclopedia*, and the *World Book Encyclopedia*. Peck holds A.B. and A.M. degrees from Harvard University, the latter in Middle Eastern studies, and M.A., M.A.L.D., and Ph.D. degrees in international affairs from the Fletcher School of Law and Diplomacy.

Curtis R. Ryan is an associate professor of political science at Mary Washington College in Fredericksburg, Virginia. He holds a Ph.D. from the University of North Carolina at Chapel Hill. He was a Fulbright scholar at the Center for Strategic Studies, University of Jordan (1992–1993) and was twice named a Peace Scholar by the United States Institute of Peace (1992–1994). His articles on politics have appeared in *Middle East Insight, Middle East Policy, Middle East Report,* and the *Southeastern Political Review*. He is finishing a book on political transitions in Jordan.

Mark A. Tessler is professor of political science at the University of Michigan. His recent books include *Area Studies and Social Science: Strategies for Understanding Middle East Politics* and *Democracy and Its Limits: Lessons from Latin America, The Middle East and Asia*. He is also president of the American Institute for Maghrib Studies.

Gregory W. White is an associate professor of government and director of international relations at Smith College, Northampton, Massachusetts. His research focuses on the comparative politics and international political economy of the Maghreb and sub-Saharan Africa. He is the author of *A Comparative Political Economy of Tunisia and Morocco: On the Outside of Europe Looking In* and co-editor of a forthcoming volume on African development in the twenty-first century. He is also the author of articles in the *Middle East Journal*, the *Journal of Developing Areas, Third World Quarterly*, and *Policy Studies Journal*.

Index